THE
MAKING
OF MODERN
ECONOMICS

THE MAKING OF MODERN ECONOMICS

The Lives and Ideas of the Great Thinkers

SECOND EDITION

MARK SKOUSEN

M.E.Sharpe
Armonk, New York
London, England

Library of Congress Cataloging-in-Publication Data

Skousen, Mark.
  The making of modern economics : the lives and ideas of the great thinkers
/ Mark Skousen. — 2nd ed.
    p. cm.
  ISBN 978-0-7656-2226-6 (alk. paper) — ISBN is 978-0-7656-2227-3 (pbk. : alk. paper)
  1. Economics—History. 2. Economics—Philosophy. 3.
Economists—Biography. I. Title.
  HB75.S545 2009

  330.09—dc22   2008061114

Printed in the United States of America

The paper used in this publication meets the minimum requirements of
American National Standard for Information Sciences
Permanence of Paper for Printed Library Materials,
ANSI Z 39.48-1984.

BM (c)   10   9   8   7   6   5   4   3   2
BM (p)   10   9   8   7   6   5   4   3   2

Dedicated to my uncle, W. Cleon Skousen

The pursuit of wealth . . . is, to the mass of mankind, the greatest source of moral improvement.

—Nassau Senior

[T]he ideas of economists and political philosophers, both when they are right and when they are wrong, are more powerful than is commonly understood. Indeed the world is ruled by little else.

—John Maynard Keynes

Economics concerns itself with the greatest of all human dramas, the struggle of humanity to escape from want.

—John M. Ferguson

CONTENTS

LIST OF FIGURES, ILLUSTRATIONS, PHOTOGRAPHS, AND TABLES

Figures

Illustrations

Photographs

Tables

ACKNOWLEDGMENTS

No one's work is entirely his own and in the case of this work, I want to especially thank two writers for their influence on my writing: first, John Chamberlain for his pioneering book *The Roots of Capitalism*, an inspiring account of economic ideas; and second, my uncle, W. Cleon Skousen, who transformed my thinking about Adam Smith and his profound doctrines of the invisible hand and natural liberty. I wish I could achieve the felicity of expression of these two authors.

In writing a history of ideas, it is always vital to seek the counsel of wise authorities. In addition to the above, I wish to thank the following, who helped with the first edition: Gary Becker (University of Chicago), Mark Blaug (University of Amsterdam), Don Boudreaux (George Mason University), William Breit (Trinity University), Eamonn Butler (Adam Smith Institute), Bruce Caldwell (University of North Carolina), David Colander (Middlebury College), Peter Drucker (Claremont College), Richard Ebeling (Trinity College), Ken Elzinga (University of Virginia), Milton Friedman (Hoover Institution), Roger Garrison (Auburn University), Robert Heilbroner (New School for Social Research), Robert Higgs (Independent Institute), Jesús Huerta de Soto (Complutense University), Steven Kates (Australian Chamber of Commerce), Greg Mankiw (Harvard University), Murray Rothbard (University of Nevada at Las Vegas), Paul A. Samuelson (Massachusetts Institute of Technology), Robert Skidelsky, Erich Streissler (University of Vienna), Richard Swedberg (University of Stockholm), Ken Taylor (Rollins College), and Larry Wimmer (Brigham Young University). I also appreciate the extra efforts of the staff at the Olin Library at Rollins College, especially Pat, Patti, and Patricia.

For the second edition, I thank especially Jeremy Siegel (Wharton School), Roger Garrison (Auburn University), the late Milton Friedman, and Rob Bradley. Lynn Taylor, Mike Sharpe, and Elizabeth Granda at M.E. Sharpe have shown unwavering support in publishing a new edition. Thanks also to the meticulous efforts of the production group, including managing editor Angela Piliouras and copyeditor Debra E. Soled.

Finally, I wish to thank an editor and English professor who wields a ubiquitous mind and a mighty pen—my wife, Jo Ann. She reviewed the entire new edition for corrections and style and improved all aspects of the second edition.

INTRODUCTION

I will tell you a secret. Economists are supposed to be dry as dust, dismal fellows. This is quite wrong, the reverse of the truth.

—Paul Samuelson (1966: 1408)

The history of modern economics is a cunning plot that can match the best of historical novels. The running story line is man's search for wealth and prosperity and the economic model that best serves the needs of the common man.

The main character is Adam Smith, a child of the Scottish Enlightenment, and the philosophy he represents, the self regulating system of natural liberty and competition. Our hero has gone through untold triumphs and tragedies in the unfolding of over 200 years of economic history. Sometimes he appears lifeless following the blows of his opponents. But he always recovers.

A QUICK OVERVIEW

The plot begins in dramatic fashion in 1776, when a London publisher printed Adam Smith's monumental work, *The Wealth of Nations*, the intellectual shot heard around the world. Smith's captivating philosophy of natural liberty and the invisible hand rapidly became the central character of modern economics as the industrial revolution and political liberty exploded on the scene, and created a new era of wealth and economic growth over the next two centuries. The enlightened Scottish model of prosperity quickly spread to France (via J.-B. Say and Bastiat), America (via Thomas Jefferson), and the rest of the Western world.

Yet the optimistic world of Adam Smith was almost immediately challenged by Robert Malthus and David Ricardo, two serious scholars who propound the gloomy doctrine of the iron law of subsistence wages and the permanent misery of the working class. These pessimistic forecasts were followed by the appearance of John Stuart Mill, who vacillated between liberty and socialism as utopian communitarianism reached its zenith of popularity. Then, in the middle of the nineteenth-century industrial revolution, Karl Marx suddenly strode onto the scene with talk of exploitation and alienation among the industrial workers, and plunged economics into a new dark age. The rise of socialism would be the biggest challenge Smithian capitalism would face over the next century.

THE MARGINAL REVOLUTION

Fortunately, a new light appeared to counter the dark forces of social engineering. This "marginal" revolution gave new life to our main character, the invisible-hand model of Adam Smith. It came from three sources in the early 1870s—from Carl Menger in Austria, Léon Walras in Switzerland, and William Stanley Jevons in England. Eugen Böhm-Bawerk, a colleague of Menger, was the first economist to take on Marx with a devastating critique of his labor theory of value and exploitation. Through the textbooks of Alfred Marshall in England, and Frank Taussig and Irving Fisher in the United States, the Smithian model of modern economics was rebuilt. Thus resuscitated, it made an effective counterattack on the growing socialist movement. Scientific economics had come of age.

Nevertheless, the late nineteenth century was the era of big business and the giant trusts of Carnegie and Rockefeller. Institutionalists like Thorstein Veblen swayed the crowds of cynics with their warnings of conspicuous consumption and monopoly power, while German sociologist Max Weber wrote of the religious underpinnings and the "iron cage" of capitalism.

KEYNES AND THE GREAT DEPRESSION

But the biggest blow to Adam Smith's world of free-market capitalism came with the 1929 crash and the Great Depression of the 1930s. Neoclassical economists comprehended the nuances of supply and demand, but failed to grasp the mysteries of the "money nexus," the vital connection between the micro economy and the macro economy. The great Yale professor Irving Fisher made bold attempts at solving the missing link between micro and macro in the early twentieth century, and the Austrian Ludwig von Mises, relying on the profound work of the Swede Knut Wicksell, finally bridged the gap in his *Theory of Money and Credit*. But the Mises-Wicksell theories didn't take hold in academia or the halls of government, and by the early 1930s, banks collapsed, businesses failed, and millions of workers begged for a living wage as governments around the globe struggled to overcome the decade-long financial nightmare.

Who would save capitalism? The battle lines were drawn between the classical economists who defended the policies of laissez faire, and the Marxists and socialists who demanded a revolutionary overthrow of the old order. Amid the global intellectual conflict appeared John Maynard Keynes, the economist as savior. This Cambridge don proposed a new, sophisticated model based on a "financial instability hypothesis" inherent to the capitalist system. This "new economics" required government intervention in the monetary and fiscal arena to stabilize the market economy. Yet, unlike its chief rival, Marxism, the Keynesian model did not require nationalization or micro control of supply and demand. The classical model of thrift, balanced budgets, low taxes, and the gold standard was relegated to periods of full employment, while the Keynesian prescription of consumer demand, deficit financing, progressive taxation, and fiat money played out during periods of economic recession and unemployment. It was viewed as the ideal compromise and soon college instructors, their heads buried in a popular new textbook by MIT wunderkind Paul Samuelson, were teaching students strange new tools—the multiplier, the marginal propensity to consume, the paradox of thrift, aggregate demand, and $C + I + G$. Keynesian economics reflected the high tide of macroeconomic theorizing and mathematical modeling.

THE RETURN TO MARKET ECONOMICS

The final chapter in our story begins after World War II. Through the monetarist counterrevolution, led by Chicago's Milton Friedman, economists began to focus more on the instability of government macro policies. Friedman, relying on empirical work more than abstract model building, demonstrated how the Federal Reserve, a government creation, was the principal culprit in causing the Great Depression. By adopting a stable monetary policy, the self-regulating market economy of Adam Smith could once again flourish. The Chicago School became the driving force behind the return to classical economics and the need for empirical evidence to support theory. Soon other schools of free-market economics—supply side, rational expectations, and Austrian—challenged the Keynesian monolith.

The triumph of the market reached its zenith of success with the collapse of the Soviet economic system in the early 1990s. The Austrian economists Ludwig von Mises and Friedrich Hayek had predicted the demise of socialistic central planning for years, and now their prediction was finally fulfilled. The failure of the socialist paradigm ushered in a new era of free trade, denationalization, and privatization throughout the developing world.

Our story of modern economics ends here on an optimistic note, even as battles are still being fought over the right kind of economic policies to pursue in the face of financial crises, war, uncertainty, and globalization. In many ways, this final chapter of modern economics foreshadows the continuing battle between two paradigms, laissez faire versus socialist interventionism, and Adam Smith's world of imperfect capitalism appears to be challenged again.

STRANGE AND TORRID LIVES

Yet our story is not just an account of conflicting ideas. It is also an amazing tale of idle dreamers, academic scribblers, occasional quacks, and madmen in authority. The lives of economists are often just as exciting and unusual (even bizarre) as those of most famous people. In these pages, you will find the story of:

- A professor of moral philosophy who burned his clothes, then burned his papers before dying;
- A Cambridge economist who may have been a secret agent for the Soviet Union during World War II;
- A revolutionary who, though his income was in the top 5 percent in Europe, constantly begged for money and speculated wildly in the stock market;
- A government advisor who was so fascinated with people's palms that he had casts made of his friends' hands;
- A multimillionaire who lost everything during the stock market crash of 1929;
- A wealthy economist who was murdered by his housekeeper;
- A utilitarian thinker who demanded that his preserved body remain on display at the University College of London;
- A free-market advocate who invented income tax withholding to help finance World War II;
- A multimillionaire broker who gave all his wealth to his three sons;
- An economist who spent two months in jail, charged with blasphemy against the Virgin Mary;
- A philosopher who learned Greek at age three and suffered a mental breakdown at age twenty;
- An economist who fancied himself as an informal consultant to Italian dictator Benito Mussolini;

- A famous minister of finance who paraded around the streets of Vienna with two prostitutes and later became president of the American Economic Association;

- An American economist who refused to use a telephone, make his bed, do the dishes, or clean his clothes, and gave all his students the same grade, regardless of their work;

- A European professor who was determined not to use charts or graphs of any kind in his voluminous writings, and who was a confirmed bachelor until age fifty-seven.

Welcome to the bizarre world of academic economists!

Why study the lives of the economists, and not just their ideas? It would be unfair to dismiss a philosopher's theories simply because he may have been a bad husband or a drunk. We may find Karl Marx's life reproachful, but does that mean his theories of alienation and exploitation are wrong? Ideas must stand on their own merit, not on the basis of who invented them. Yet we study and judge the actions of our heroes and villains, not just to prove or disprove their philosophies, but to better understand them, and why they said what they said.

The history of economic thought is not normally taught this way, but then this book is not a normal history. It is, candidly, an irreverent, passionate, sometimes humorous, and often highly opinionated account of the lives and theories of famous economists, from Adam Smith and Karl Marx to John Maynard Keynes and Milton Friedman.

To enhance the readers' interest in the book, I've added a variety of sidelights, including photographs, diagrams, boxed commentaries, and even classical music selections appropriate to the different chapters.

THE NEED FOR A NEW HISTORY

But this book is more than a collection of biographical sketches and radical ideas. I wrote this book, in part, out of frustration. One of the most disappointing classes I took as an undergraduate was in the history of economic ideas. The course was convoluted, the textbook was dry, the lives of economists seemed uninteresting, and even the A students came away from the class wondering whether economists made any sense at all. It wasn't at all what Paul Samuelson promised in the quotation at the beginning of this chapter. Certainly, there appeared no consensus about how the economy functions and what policies the government should pursue to ensure prosperity. Typically, students in economics are exposed to a wide number of schools of thought—neoclassical, Keynesian, monetarist, Austrian, supply side, institutionalist, Marxist—without any effort to determine the veracity of their theories, and how they are linked together. In short, we the students were left in a state of bewilderment.

Most students would probably agree with Adam Smith, the founder of modern economics, who derided the "sham-lecture" professors who have only a slight knowledge of the subject and end up saying things that are "foolish, absurd, or ridiculous." Smith noted in *The Wealth of Nations,* "It must too be unpleasant to [the professor] to observe that the greater part of his students desert his lectures; or perhaps attend upon them with plain enough marks of neglect, contempt, and derision" (1965 [1776]: 720).

Why does the economics profession suffer from such a propensity to confuse?

The fundamental reason is that the story of economics is traditionally told in a haphazard, disjointed manner. In a sense, it's not a story at all. There is no running plot, no engaging drama, and no single heroic figure. Economists are presented on the pages of history, one after another, with an account of their lives and their contributions, and that's it. Each stands alone, isolated. Today's histories of economics lack a running thread of truth, a consistent point of view that allows the student to realize when an academic scribbler is heading off the strait and narrow path.

My approach is distinct. It is to tell how this new science called modern economics was built—hence the title *The Making of Modern Economics.* It focuses on the architects and the building they constructed. The leading architect of this building is Adam Smith. His working model, "the system of natural liberty," is found in *The Wealth of Nations.* The work he began wasn't perfect by any means and required extensive remodeling from time to time. But its foundation is sound.

In each subsequent chapter, I try to demonstrate how each major subject added to or subtracted from Smith's edifice of modern economics. Many, such as Menger, Marshall, and Friedman, strengthened the foundation, remodeled where necessary, and added wings. Some, like Veblen and Galbraith, were cynics who stood back and pointed their fingers in scorn at the building being built. Others, like Keynes, tried to reconstruct the building after it was halfway complete. Finally, there were radicals like Marx who wanted to tear down the building and start over. The critics of the work did not attack in vain. Their assaults forced the builders of modern neoclassical economics to reexamine their fundamentals and work out new plans. The result was a newer, better, more resilient economics.

Ultimately, the building is near completion as we enter the twenty-first century. It's not a perfect structure, there's more work to be done, but what has been created is worth admiring. Millions around the world have felt the power of neoclassical economic analysis, the house that Adam Smith built. In fact, economics has impacted so many other disciplines—history, law, politics, and finance, to name a few—that critics no longer label it a "dismal" science, but an "imperial" science (see chapter 17).

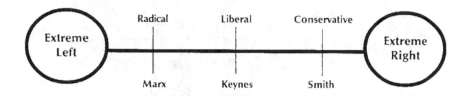

Figure A
The Pendulum Approach to Competing Economic Theories
Source: Maier and White (1998: 42). Reprinted by permission of McGraw-Hill.

PENDULUM VERSUS TOTEM POLE HISTORY: WHICH IS BETTER?

Historically, there have been two approaches to writing about the lives and ideas of economists: the *pendulum* and the *totem pole*.

In the pendulum formula, the historian categorizes each economist along a political spectrum, from extreme left to extreme right. The history of economics may swing from one extreme to another, or may land in the middle, depending on the economist and the time. The diagram in Figure A, reproduced from a current history of economic thought, illustrates the pendulum type.

The problem with this pendulum approach is that Karl Marx and Adam Smith are treated as coequals; in this case, both economists are viewed as "extreme" in their positions. By implication, neither position is sensible. The "moderate," middle-of-the-road position held by John Maynard Keynes appears to be more balanced and ideal. A pendulum that experiences friction will eventually come to rest in the middle, between the extremes. But is that the best way to go?

I prefer a bolder alternative, what I would call the top-down or "totem pole" approach. In Indian folklore, the most favored chiefs are placed at the top of the totem pole, with less favored, though important, chiefs below. If the goal is to discover which economist maximizes economic freedom and the most rapid economic growth (rising standard of living), that economist should be placed at the top of the totem pole. Others, who advocate less freedom and whose policies generate slower growth, should be placed below the man on the top. Instead of comparing economists horizontally on a pendulum or spectrum, one should rank them from top to bottom according to this measure of liberty and growth.

Using this totem pole structure, I would reformulate the diagram (see Figure B, page 8).

Adam Smith advocated maximum economic freedom, in the microeconomic behavior of individuals and the firm, and minimal macroeconomic

Figure B
The Totem Pole Approach:
The Ranking of Three Economists (Smith, Keynes, and Marx)
According to Economic Freedom and Growth

intervention by the state. The countries that have come the closest to adopting Smith's vision of laissez-faire capitalism have achieved the highest standards of living. Next on the list is John Maynard Keynes. He supported individual freedom, but frequently endorsed macroeconomic intervention and nationalization of investment. His big-government formula has resulted in slower, albeit more stable, economic growth. The low man on the totem pole is Karl Marx, who advocated command economies at both the micro and the macro level. Historically, centrally planned socialist regimes have vastly underperformed the market economies.

Few readers will be agnostic about my views in this book. You may not agree with me as far as my rankings of economists are concerned, but I have tried to be consistent in my totem pole approach.

RECENT BIOGRAPHIES ENHANCE THE STORY OF ECONOMICS

The story of economics has been greatly enhanced by some excellent biographies published lately. Until recently, the only subject about whom numerous biographies had been written was Karl Marx. In fact, the amount of material on Marx's life is challenging if not overwhelming. There are even full-scale biographies of his daughter, Eleanor. Meanwhile, there was little written detail available on the lives of Adam Smith, Alfred Marshall, Irving Fisher, and other important economists. Now that is all changing, slowly but surely. The new biographers are digging deeply, studying private correspondence and unpublished manuscripts, and interviewing contemporaries if they are alive. The following works represent the future of biography: Robert Skidelsky's *John Maynard Keynes* (1992), Richard Swedberg's *Schumpeter* (1991), Robert Loring Allen's *Irving Fisher* (1993), Peter Groenewegen's *A Soaring Eagle* (1995), and William Stafford's *John Stuart Mill* (1998). It is to be hoped that additional in-depth biographies will be published in the future.

WESTERN ECONOMICS ONLY?

After taking my course on the history of economics, one of my Rollins students asked, "Are there any famous economists outside the West?" He had correctly noted that Westerners have traditionally dominated, even monopolized, the history of economic thought. This bias is justified on two grounds: First, significant economic progress began in the West with the industrial revolution. Second, Western-style economics has directed much of the economic thinking in Asia, Africa, and Latin America during the twentieth century. Pick up any book on the history of modern economics in Japan, India, or Argentina, and you will see the dominating influence of Smith, Keynes, and Marx.

Non-Western economics has flourished over the ages, but has seldom been associated with material progress in any meaningful way. Max Weber observed this fact in his worldwide study of economics and religion. E.F. Schumacher (1973) has a famous chapter entitled "Buddhist Economics" in his ever-popular *Small Is Beautiful*. In many ways, Schumacher's glorification of Buddhist economics explains this failure to achieve material prosperity. According to Schumacher, traditional Buddhism rejects labor-saving machinery, assembly-line production, large-scale multinational corporations, foreign trade, and the consumer society (Schumacher 1973: 44–51).

There are, of course, many bright non-Western economists, and their prestige is growing as Asia expands. Amartya Sen (India) and Michio Morishima (Japan) are two prime examples. In 2006, Muhammad Yunus, an economics professor from Bangladesh, won the Nobel Peace Prize. Robert Ozaki's *Human Capitalism* (1991) explains how the West can learn better business–labor management relations from the East; but in a one-volume work, one must focus primarily on the principal movers and shakers in the making of modern economics.

HOW I CAME TO WRITE THIS BOOK

Before we begin our adventures, let me tell you a story relevant to this book. In 1980, I asked libertarian economist Murray N. Rothbard to write an alternative to Robert Heilbroner's *The Worldly Philosophers* (1999).

Heilbroner's little history was immensely popular (over 4 million sold) and well written, but the content and context left much to be desired. Heilbroner, reflecting his bias, focused heavily on the economics of socialists, Marxists, and Keynesians, and spent less space on free-market schools, the followers of Adam Smith. Heilbroner essentially ignored, for example, the French laissez-faire school of Say and Bastiat, the monetarist school of Irving Fisher and Milton Friedman, and the Austrian school of Mises and Hayek. Free-market advocates cried out for a more balanced approach to the history of economics.

Rothbard heartily agreed to my proposal, which included an enticing advance of $20,000. I made several specific requirements in our contract: the book should address the general public (economists and laymen). Like Heilbroner's book, it should be around a dozen chapters, starting with Adam Smith and ending with modern times. It should not exceed 300 pages in published form. And the manuscript must be finished in a year.

Rothbard and I signed the contract.

One year passed. Two years. Three years. No completed manuscript. No 300 pages. No layman's discourse. No Adam Smith. Oh, Rothbard was writing all right, but he wasn't writing a 300-page book for the general public. He was writing what we in the economics profession call a Schumpeterian tome: a several-volume, dense history of economic thought for professionals and advanced students of economics. In the 1940s, Joseph Schumpeter, the iconoclast Harvard professor, wrote his voluminous *History of Economic Analysis,* which reached 1,260 pages by the time it was published. Rothbard's laborious work began with the Greeks and the tenuous writings of Aristotle, moved slowly along to the Catholic Fathers and the Enlightenment, and finally, by chapter 16, reached the celebrated Adam Smith. I was a great admirer of Murray Rothbard as an iconoclastic economist and radical historian, but I could see this was not what I had contracted for. Years later, after tiring of asking the question, "Have you reached Marx yet?" I sent Rothbard a copy of a statement made by Joseph Schumpeter in an interview with the *Harvard Crimson* in 1944: "My research program grows longer and my life shorter. My *History of Economic Analysis* drags, and I am always hunting other hares" (Swedberg 1991: 167). It reminded me of Rothbard's dragging history.

Fifteen years later (!)—1995—Edward Elgar (the publisher, not the composer) published the first two volumes of Rothbard's history, *Economic Thought Before Adam Smith* (556 pages) and *Classical Economics* (528 pages). Rothbard's second volume ends with his chapters on Marx. I have enjoyed studying Rothbard's stimulating and often critical remarks, and agree with most of what he wrote (with the strong exception of his negative assessment of Adam Smith). But he never finished the job.

I frequently commented to friends that Rothbard was writing a Schumpeterian tome, which also meant that he would probably die before completing the book, it was taking so long. After Schumpeter's death in

1950, Schumpeter's devoted wife, Elizabeth, tried to get the almost finished manuscript ready for publication, but also passed away before completing the task, and the manuscript was prepared for publication by Harvard colleagues.

Sadly, my concern became prophetic. Rothbard died suddenly of a heart attack in New York City in January 1995, at the age of sixty-nine, only a few weeks before the first copies of his two-volume work appeared. He never got to the next two planned volumes.

One of my motives in writing *The Making of Modern Economics* was to publish something along the lines of what I asked Murray Rothbard to write. Now, here it is, twenty years later.

REFERENCES

Allen, Robert Loring. 1993. *Irving Fisher: A Biography*. Cambridge: Blackwell.

Groenewegan, Peter. 1995. *A Soaring Eagle: Alfred Marshall 1842–1924*. Cheltenham: Edward Elgar.

Heilbroner, Robert L. 1999 [1953]. *The Worldly Philosophers,* 7th ed. New York: Simon & Schuster.

Ozaki, Robert. 1991. *Human Capitalism*. New York: Kodansha International.

Maier, Mark and White, Steven. 1998. *The First Chapter: Foundations of Economic History and the History of Economic Thought,* 3d ed. New York: McGraw-Hill.

Samuelson, Paul A. 1966. *Collected Scientific Papers of Paul A. Samuelson,* vol. 2. Cambridge, MA: MIT Press.

Schumacher, E.F. 1973. *Small Is Beautiful.* London: Penguin.

Skidelsky, Robert. 1992. *John Maynard Keynes: Economist as Savior, 1920–1937.* London: Macmillan.

Smith, Adam. 1965 [1776]. *The Wealth of Nations.* New York: Modern Library.

Stafford, William. 1998. *John Stuart Mill.* London: Macmillan.

Swedberg, Richard. 1991. *Schumpeter: A Biography.* Princeton, NJ: Princeton University Press.

1

IT ALL STARTED WITH ADAM

*Adam Smith was a radical and a revolutionary in his time—
just as those of us who preach laissez faire are in our time.*

—Milton Friedman (Glahe 1978: 7)

The story of modern economics began in 1776.

Prior to this famous date, six thousand years of recorded history had passed without a seminal work being published on the subject that dominated every waking hour of practically every human being: making a living.

For millennia, from Roman times through the Dark Ages and the Renaissance, humans struggled to survive by the sweat of their brow, often only eking out a bare existence. They were constantly guarding against premature death, disease, famine, war, and subsistence wages. Only a fortunate few—primarily rulers and aristocrats—lived leisurely lives, and even those were crude by modern standards. For the common man, little changed over the centuries. Real per capita wages were virtually the same, year after year, decade after decade. During this age, when the average life span was a mere forty years, the English writer Thomas Hobbes rightly called the life of man "solitary, poor, nasty, brutish and short" (1996 [1651]: 84).

1776, A PROPHETIC YEAR

Then came 1776, when hope and rising expectations were extended to the common workingman for the first time. It was a period known as the Enlightenment, what the French called *l'Âge des lumières*. For the first time in history, workers looked forward to obtaining a basic minimum of food, shelter, and clothing. Even tea, previously a luxury, had become a common beverage.

♪ **Music selection for this chapter: Aaron Copland, "Fanfare for the Common Man"**

The celebration of America's Declaration of Independence on July 4 was one of several significant events of 1776. Imitating John Locke, Thomas Jefferson's proclamation of "life, liberty, and the pursuit of happiness" to be inalienable rights, thus establishing the legal framework for a struggling nation that would eventually become the greatest economic powerhouse on earth, and provided the constitutional foundation of liberty which was to be imitated around the world.

A MONUMENTAL BOOK APPEARS

Four months earlier, an equally monumental work had been published across the Atlantic in Mother England. On March 9, 1776, the London printers William Strahan and Thomas Cadell released a 1,000-page, two-volume work entitled *An Inquiry into the Nature and Causes of the Wealth*

Illustration 1.1
Memorial Print of Adam Smith, 1790
"I am a beau in nothing but my books."
Reprinted by permission of Glasgow University Library.

of Nations. It was a fat book with a long title destined to have gargantuan global impact. The author was Dr. Adam Smith, a quiet absent-minded professor who taught "moral philosophy" at the University of Glasgow.

The Wealth of Nations was the intellectual shot heard around the world. Adam Smith, a leader in the Scottish Enlightenment, had put on paper a universal formula for prosperity and financial independence that would, over the course of the next century, revolutionize the way citizens and leaders thought about and practiced economics and trade. Its publication promised a new world—a world of abundant wealth, riches beyond the mere accumulation of gold and silver. He promised that new world to everyone—not just the rich and the rulers, but the common man, too. *The Wealth of Nations* offered a formula for emancipating the workingman from the drudgery of a Hobbesian world. In sum, *The Wealth of Nations* was a declaration of economic independence.

Certain dates are turning points in the history of mankind. The year 1776

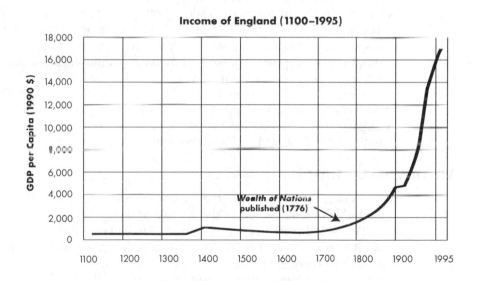

Figure 1.1
The Rise in Real Per Capita Income, United Kingdom, 1100–1995
Courtesy of Larry Wimmer, Brigham Young University.

is one of them. In that prophetic year, two vital freedoms were proclaimed, political liberty and free enterprise, and the two worked together to set in motion the industrial revolution. It was no accident that the modern economy began in earnest shortly after 1776 (see Figure 1.1).

THE IMPORTANCE OF THE ENLIGHTENMENT

The year 1776 was significant for other reasons as well. For example, it was the year the first volume of Edward Gibbon's classic work, *History of the Decline and Fall of the Roman Empire* (1776–88), appeared. Gibbon was a principal advocate of eighteenth-century Enlightenment, which embodied unbounded faith in science, reason, and economic individualism in place of religious fanaticism, superstition, and aristocratic power.

To Smith, 1776 was also an important year for personal reasons. His closest friend, David Hume, died. Hume, a profound philosopher, was a great influence on Adam Smith. (See "Pre-Adamites" in the appendix to this chapter.) Like Smith, he was a leader of the Scottish Enlightenment and an advocate of commercial civilization and economic liberty.

THE RUMBLINGS OF ECONOMIC PROGRESS

For centuries, the average real wage and standard of living had stagnated, while almost a billion people struggled against the harsh realities of daily life. Suddenly, in the early 1800s, just a few years after the American Revolution and the publication of *The Wealth of Nations*, the Western world began to flourish as never before. The spinning jenny, power looms, and the steam engine were the first of many inventions that saved time and money for enterprising businessmen and the average citizen. The industrial revolution was beginning to unfold, real wages started climbing, and everyone's standard of living, rich and poor, began rising to unforeseen heights. It was indeed the Enlightenment, the dawning of modern times, and people of all walks of life took notice.

ADVOCATE FOR THE COMMON MAN

As George Washington was the father of a new nation, so Adam Smith was the father of a new science, the science of wealth.

The great British economist Alfred Marshall called economics the study of "the ordinary business of life." Appropriately, Adam Smith would have an ordinary name. He was named after the first man in the Bible, Adam, which means "out of many," and his last name, Smith, signifies "one who works." Smith is the most common surname in Great Britain. In fact, Adam Smith's father was also named Adam Smith, as were his guardian and his cousin.

The man with the pedestrian name wrote a book for the welfare of the average working man. In his magnum opus, he assured the reader that his model for economic success would result in "universal opulence which extends itself to the lowest ranks of the people" (1965 [1776]: 11).[1]

---

1. All quotes from *The Wealth of Nations* are from the Modern Library edition (Random House, 1937, 1965, 1994, 2000). In this book I refer to the 1965 edition, which has an introduction by Max Lerner. There have been many editions of *The Wealth of Nations,* but this edition is the most popular. (See the box on page 21 for more information about the various editions.)

It was not a book for aristocrats and kings. In fact, Adam Smith had little regard for the men of vested interests and commercial power. His sympathies lay with the average citizens who had been abused and taken advantage of over the centuries. Now they would be liberated from sixteen-hour-a-day jobs, subsistence wages, and a forty-year life span.

ADAM SMITH FACES A MAJOR OBSTACLE

After taking twelve long years to write his big book, Smith was convinced he had discovered the right kind of economics to create "universal opulence." He called his model the "system of natural liberty." Today economists call it the "classical model." Smith's model was inspired by Sir Isaac Newton, whose model of natural science Smith greatly admired as universal and harmonious.

His biggest hurdle would be convincing others of his system, especially legislators. His purpose in writing *The Wealth of Nations* was not simply to educate, but to persuade. Very little progress had been achieved over the centuries in England and Europe because of the entrenched system known as *mercantilism*. One of Adam Smith's main objectives in writing *The Wealth of Nations* was to smash the conventional view held by the mercantilists, who controlled the commercial interests and political powers of the day, and to replace it with the real source of wealth and economic growth, thus leading England and the rest of the world toward the "greatest improvement" of the common man's lot.

THE APPEAL OF MERCANTILISM

The mercantilists believed that the world's economy was stagnant and its wealth fixed, so that one nation grew only at the expense of another. The economies of all ancient and Middle Age civilizations were based either on slavery or different forms of serfdom. Under either system, wealth was acquired largely at the expense of others or through the exploitation of man by man. As Bertrand de Jouvenel observes, "Wealth was therefore based on seizure and exploitation" (1999: 100). Consequently, they established government-authorized monopolies at home and supported colonialism abroad, sending agents and troops into poorer countries to seize gold and other precious commodities.

According to the established mercantilist system, wealth consisted entirely of money per se, which at the time meant gold and silver. The primary goal of every nation was always to aggressively accumulate gold and silver, and to use whatever means necessary to do so. "The great affair, we always find, is to get money," Smith declared in *The Wealth of Nations* (1965: 398).

How to get more money? First, nations such as Spain and Portugal sent their emissaries to faraway lands to discover gold mines, and to pile up as much as of the precious metal as they could. No expedition or foreign war was too expensive when it came to their thirst for bullion. Other European countries, imitating the gold seekers, frequently imposed exchange controls, forbidding, under the threat of heavy penalties, the export of gold and silver.

Second, mercantilists sought a favorable balance of trade, which meant that gold and silver would constantly fill their coffers. How? "The encouragement of exportation, and the discouragement of importation, are the two great engines by which the mercantilist system proposes to enrich every country," reported Smith (page 607). Smith carefully delineated the host of high tariffs, duties, quotas, and regulations that aimed at restraining trade, production, and ultimately a higher standard of living. Such commercial interferences naturally led to conflict and war between nations.

SMITH DENOUNCES TRADE BARRIERS

In a direct assault on the mercantile system, the Scottish philosopher denounced high tariffs and other restrictions on trade. Efforts to promote a favorable balance of trade were "absurd," he declared (page 456). He talked of the "natural advantages" one country has over another in producing goods. "By means of glasses, hotbeds, and hotwalls, very good grapes can be raised in Scotland," Smith said, but it would cost thirty times more to produce Scottish wine than to import wine from France. "Would it be a reasonable law to prohibit the importation of all foreign wines, merely to encourage the making of claret and burgundy in Scotland?" (page 425).

According to Smith, mercantilist policies only imitate real prosperity and benefit only the producers and the monopolists. Because it did not benefit the consumer, mercantilism was antigrowth and shortsighted. "But in the mercantile system, the interest of the consumer is almost always constantly sacrificed to that of the producer" (page 625).

Smith argued that trade barriers hurt the ability of both countries to produce and thus must be torn down. By expanding trade between Britain and France, for example, both nations would gain. "What is prudence in the conduct of every private family, can scarce be folly in that of a great kingdom," declared Smith. "If a foreign country can supply us with a commodity cheaper than we ourselves can make it, better buy it of them" (page 424).

REAL SOURCE OF WEALTH REVEALED

The accumulation of gold and silver might have filled the pockets of the rich and the powerful, but what would be the origin of wealth for the whole nation and the average citizen? That was Adam Smith's paramount question. *The Wealth of Nations* was not just a tract on free trade, but a world view of prosperity.

The Scottish professor forcefully argued that the keys to the "wealth of nations" were *production* and *exchange*, not the artificial acquisition of gold and silver at the expense of other nations. He stated, "the wealth of a country consists, not of its gold and silver only, but in its lands, houses, and consumable goods of all different kinds" (page 418). Wealth should be measured according to how well people are lodged, clothed and fed. In 1763, he said, "the wealth of a state consists in the cheapness of provisions and all other necessaries and conveniences of life" (1982 [1763]: 83).

Smith began his *Wealth of Nations* with a discussion of wealth. He asked, what could bring about the "greatest improvement in the productive powers of labour"? A favorable balance of trade? More gold and silver?

No, it was a superior management technique, "the division of labor." In a well-known example, Smith described in detail the workings of a pin factory, where workers were assigned eighteen distinct operations in order to maximize the output of pins (1965: 3–5). This stages-of-production approach, in which management works with labor to produce goods and fulfill consumer desires, forms the basis of a harmonious and growing economy. A few pages later, Smith used another example, the woolen coat, that required "the assistance and co-operation of many thousands" of laborers and various machinery from around the world to produce this basic product used by the "day-laborer" (1965: 11–12).[2] Furthermore, expanding the market through worldwide trade meant that specialization and division of labor could expand. Through increased productivity, thrift, and hard work, the world's output could increase. Hence, wealth was not a fixed quantity after all, and countries could grow richer without harming others.

SMITH DISCOVERS THE KEY TO PROSPERITY

How can production and exchange be maximized and thereby encourage the "universal opulence" and the "improvement of the productive power of labor"?

Adam Smith had a clear answer: Give people their economic freedom! Throughout *The Wealth of Nations*, Smith advocated the principle of "natural liberty," the freedom to do what one wishes without interference from the state. It encouraged the free movement of labor, capital, money, and goods. Moreover, said Smith, economic freedom not only leads to a better material life, but is a fundamental human right. To quote Smith: "To prohibit a great people . . . from making all that they can of every part of their own produce, or from employing their stock and industry in the way that they judge most advantageous to themselves, is a manifest violation of the most sacred rights of mankind" (page 549).

Under Adam Smith's model of natural liberty, wealth creation was no longer a zero-sum game. No longer was there a conflict of interests, but a harmony of interests. According to Jouvenel, this came as an "enormous

---

2. This passage in the first chapter of *The Wealth of Nations* is remarkably similar to the theme developed by Leonard Read in his classic essay "I, Pencil," which describes how a simple product like a pencil involves cooperative production processes from around the world (1999 [1958]).

innovation" that greatly surprised European reformers: "The great new idea is that it is possible to enrich all the members of society, collectively and individually, by gradual progress in the organization of labor" (1999: 102). This development could be rapid and unlimited.

Here was something that could capture the imagination and hope of not only the English worker but the French peasant, the German laborer, the Chinese dayworker, and the American immigrant, for Smith was advocating a worldwide principle of abundance. The freedom to work could liberate everyone from the chains of daily chores.

What constitutes this new economic freedom? Natural liberty includes, according to Smith, the right to buy goods from any source, including foreign products, without the restraints of tariffs or import quotas. It includes the right to be employed in whatever occupation a person wants and wherever desired. Smith trenchantly criticized European policy in the eighteenth century wherein laborers had to obtain government permission (via certificates) to move from one town to another, even within a country (pages 118–43).

Natural liberty also includes the right to charge whatever wage the market may bear. Smith strongly opposed the state's efforts to regulate and artificially raise wages. He wrote, "Whenever the law has attempted to regulate the wages of workmen, it has always been rather to lower them than to raise them" (page 131). Like every worker, Smith desired high wages, but he thought they should come about through the natural workings of the labor market, not government edict.

Finally, natural liberty includes the right to save, invest, and accumulate capital without government restraint—important keys to economic growth. Adam Smith endorsed the virtues of thrift, capital investment, and labor-saving machinery as essential ingredients to promote rising living standards (page 326). In his chapter on the accumulation of capital (chapter 3, book II) in *The Wealth of Nations,* Smith emphasized the need for saving and frugality as keys to economic growth, in addition to stable government policies, a competitive business environment, and sound business management.

ADAM SMITH'S CROWN JEWEL

George Stigler called Smith's model of competitive free enterprise the "crown jewel" of *The Wealth of Nations* and "the most important substantive proposition in all of economics." He stated, "Smith had one overwhelmingly important triumph: he put into the center of economics the systematic analysis of the behavior of individuals pursuing their self-interests under conditions of competition" (Stigler 1976: 1201). In sum, an economic system that allows men and women to pursue their own self-interest under conditions of "natural liberty" and competition would be a self-regulating and highly prosperous economy. Eliminating restrictions on imports, labor, and prices meant that universal prosperity could be maximized through lower prices, higher wages, and better products.

Would You Pay $100,000 for a First Edition of *The Wealth of Nations*?

A collector paid over $100,000 in March 2008 for a first edition of Adam Smith's *Wealth of Nations*. The original price in 1776 was thirty-six shillings. The collector paid a premium because this particular copy was unopened and distinguished by the auctioneer as "a superlative set." Prices have moved up steadily since the famed work was published in London over 200 years ago, and lately have skyrocketed, according to rare book collector Robert Rubin.

There is no question that copies of the 1776 edition of Smith's magnum opus are scarce. Only a thousand copies were published and a handful sell each year at auction. The original publisher was Strahan and Cadell, who had published Gibbon's *History of the Decline and Fall of the Roman Empire* a month earlier. *An Inquiry into the Nature and Causes of the Wealth of Nations*—the full title—was published in two sumptuous leather-bound volumes (called "quartos") on March 9, 1776. Strahan paid Smith £500 for the first edition.

The work became an immediate bestseller, especially after Smith's friend David Hume spread the word. ("Euge! Belle! I am much pleased with your performance," he wrote Smith.) It sold out in six months, but was not reprinted until 1778. Editions in German, French, Italian, and other languages were published. The first American edition was published in Philadelphia in 1789. None of these editions has commanded the premium prices of the first, nor have the four subsequent editions (printed in three volumes or "octavos") published during Smith's lifetime.

Is the first edition still a good buy? The large sum of money needed to purchase a first edition is obviously not within the budget of the average collector, let alone the average economist. Rumor among antiquarian booksellers has it that one or two speculators (undoubtedly noneconomists who have little appreciation for the book itself) have tried to corner the market from time to time. In the past, the Japanese have been heavy buyers of first editions. Given the limited number of first editions, the price is likely to remain beyond the reach of most aficionados.

No economists worth their salt should go through their career without reading this magnificent classic. Which edition should you read? Since the copyright expired, many publishers have put out their own editions, including the University of Glasgow, University of Chicago, Everyman's Library, and Liberty Press. Even Bantam has released a paperback edition—unabridged! My preference is the 1937 (latest reprint, 2000) Modern Library edition, edited by Edwin Cannan.

The Wealth of Nations has reached such biblical proportions that a complete concordance was done by Fred R. Glahe (1993), economics professor at the University of Colorado. Did you know that the word "a" appears 6,691 times in *The Wealth of Nations*? Oh, the wonders of computers! A concordance is undoubtedly valuable, especially for scholars. For example, "demand" appears 269 times while "supply" appears only 144 times. Keynes would be pleased.

In order to use *The Wealth of Nations* concordance, you will need a University of Glasgow edition, available at most college libraries.

SMITH'S CLASSIC WORK RECEIVES UNIVERSAL ACCLAIM

Adam Smith's eloquent advocacy of natural liberty fired the minds of a rising generation. His words literally changed the course of politics, dismantling the old mercantilist doctrines of protectionism and human bondage. Much of the worldwide move toward free trade can be attributed to Adam Smith's work. *The Wealth of Nations* was the ideal document to usher in the industrial revolution and the political rights of man.

Smith's magnum opus has received almost universal acclaim. H.L. Mencken stated, "There is no more engrossing book in the English language" (Powell 2000: 251). Historian Arnold Toynbee asserted that *"The Wealth of Nations* and the steam engine destroyed the old world and built a new one" (Rashid 1998: 212). The English historian Henry Thomas Buckle stretched the hyperbole even further to claim that, in terms of its ultimate influence, Smith's tome "is probably the most important book that has ever been written," including the Bible (Rogge 1976: 9). Paul A. Samuelson placed Smith "on a pinnacle" among economists (Samuelson 1962: 7).[3] Even Marxists sometimes extol the virtues of Adam Smith.

SMITH IDENTIFIES THREE INGREDIENTS

Smith began his book with a discussion of how wealth and prosperity are created through a democratic free-market order. He highlighted three characteristics of this self-regulating system or classical model:

1. Freedom: individuals have the right to produce and exchange products, labor, and capital as they see fit (self-interest).
2. Competition: individuals have the right to compete in the production and exchange of goods and services.
3. Justice: the actions of individuals must be just and honest, according to the rules of society.

Note that the following statement by Adam Smith incorporates these three principles: "Every man, as long as he does not violate the laws of justice, is left perfectly *free* to pursue his own interest his own way, and to bring both his industry and capital into *competition* with those of any other man, or order of men" (1965 [1776]: 651; emphasis added).

---

3. This was Samuelson's presidential address before the American Economic Association. A year later, Samuelson declared, "The first human was Adam. The first economist . . . was Adam Smith" (Samuelson 1966: 1408).

THE BENEFITS OF THE INVISIBLE HAND

Smith argued that these three ingredients would lead to a "natural harmony" of interests between workers, landlords and capitalists.

The voluntary self-interest of millions of individuals would create a stable, prosperous society without the need for central direction by the state. His doctrine of enlightened self-interest is often called "the invisible hand." To quote two famous passages from *The Wealth of Nations*:

> It is not from the benevolence of the butcher, the brewer, or the baker, that we expect our dinner, but from their regard to their own interest. We address ourselves, not to their humanity, but to their self-love. . . . Every individual . . . [who] . . . employs capital . . . and . . . labours . . . neither intends to promote the public interest, nor knows how much he is promoting it . . . he is . . . led by an invisible hand to promote an end which was no part of his intention. . . . By pursuing his own interest he frequently promotes that of the society. (1965: 14, 423)[4]

Although Smith uses the term only once in *The Wealth of Nations* and sparingly elsewhere, the phrase "invisible hand" has come to symbolize the workings of the market economy. Defenders of market economics use it in a positive way, describing the market hand as "gentle . . . wise . . . and far reaching," one that "improves the lives of people," while contrasting it with the "visible and . . . the hidden hand . . . the grabbing hand . . . the dead hand . . . and the iron fist of government whose invisible foot tramples on people's hopes and destroys their dreams" (Skousen 2007: 19–20). Critics use contrasting comparisons to express their hostility toward capitalism. To them, the invisible hand of the market may be a "backhand . . . trembling . . . amputated . . . palsied . . . bloody . . . and an iron fist of competition" (Rothschild 2001: 119; Roemer 1988: 2–3).

The invisible hand concept has received surprising praise from economists across the political spectrum. One would expect high praise from free-market advocates, of course. Milton Friedman refers to Adam Smith's symbol as a "key insight" into the cooperative, self-regulating "power of the market [to] produce our food, our clothing, our housing" (1980: 1). "His vision of the way in which the voluntary actions of millions of individuals can be coordinated through a price system without central direction . . . is a highly sophisticated and subtle insight" (Friedman 1978:17).

Not to be outdone are Keynesian economists. Despite its imperfections, "the invisible hand has an astonishing capacity to handle a coordination problem of truly enormous proportions," declare William Baumol and Alan Blinder (2001: 214). Frank Hahn honors the invisible hand theory as

---

4. Some economists have observed that the "invisible hand" symbolism may be religious, meaning the "invisible hand" of the Creator: "perhaps the 'Invisible Hand' can be thought of as the directing hand of the Deity" (Rashid 1998: 219).

"astonishing" and an appropriate metaphor: "Whatever criticisms I shall level at the theory later, I should like to record that it is a major intellectual achievement. . . . The invisible hand works in harmony [that] leads to the growth in the output of goods which people desire" (1982: 1, 4, 8). In a broader perspective, Kenneth Arrow and Frank Hahn declare that Smith's vision "is surely the most important intellectual contribution that economic thought has made to the general understanding of social processes" (1971: v, vii, 1).

DOES ADAM SMITH CONDONE EGOTISM AND GREED?

Critics worry that the Scottish blueprint for freedom would also give license to avarice and fraud, even "social strife, ecological damage, and the abuse of power" (Lux 1990). Is not *The Wealth of Nations* an unabashed endorsement of selfish greed and vanity? How could Adam Smith ignore everyday cases of rapacious capitalists deceiving, defrauding, and taking advantage of customers, thus pursuing their own self-interests at the expense of the public?

Contrary to popular belief, Smith did not condone greed, egotism, and Western-style decadence, nor did he want economic efficiency to replace morality. Self-interest does not mean ignoring the needs of others; in fact, it means just the opposite; his system assures that both buyer and seller benefit from every voluntary transaction. Most readers have misjudged Smith's famous quotation, "It is not from the benevolence of the butcher, the brewer, or the baker, that we expect our dinner, but from their regard to their own interest." Here is the context of this statement:

> But man has almost constant occasion for the help of his brethren, and it is in vain for him to expect it from their benevolence only. He will be more likely to prevail if he can interest their self-love in his favour, and shew them that it is for their own advantage to do for him what he requires of them. . . . Give me that which I want, and you shall have this which you want, is the meaning of every such offer. It is not from the benevolence of the butcher, the brewer, or the baker, that we expect our dinner, but from their regard to their own interest. We address ourselves, not to their humanity but to their self-love, and never talk to them of our own necessities but of their advantages. (1965: 14)

What Adam Smith is saying is that you can only help yourself by helping others—the Golden Rule. Businesses that focus on fulfilling the needs and desires of their customers will be the most profitable. Although capitalists are motivated by the desire for personal gain, the way that they maximize their profits is by focusing their everyday attention on meeting the needs of the public. Thus, the successful capitalist inevitably orients his everyday conduct toward the task of helping and serving others. Self-interest leads to empathy.

UPDATE 1: FREE ECONOMIES ARE RICHER

Has economic freedom led to higher living standards? If Adam Smith were alive today, he would undoubtedly credit a free and democratic capitalism with the widespread increase in the standard of living. An exhaustive study by James Gwartney, Robert A. Lawson, and Walter Block (1996) and updated subsequently each year by Gwartney and Lawson (2007) appears to confirm this Smithian view that economic freedom and prosperity are closely related. They painstakingly constructed an index measuring the level of economic freedom for more than a hundred countries, based on five criteria (size of government, property rights and legal structure, sound money, trade, and regulations). Then they compared the level of economic freedom with their growth rates, based on per capita income in purchasing power parity terms. Their conclusion is documented in the remarkable graph in Figure 1.2.

According to this study, the greater the degree of freedom, the higher the standard of living, as measured by real per capita gross domestic product (GDP) in purchasing power parity terms.

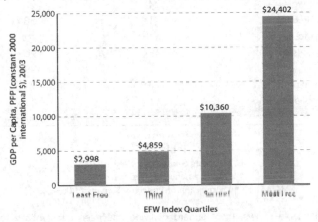

Figure 1.2
Relationship Between Economic Freedom and Per Capita GDP, 2005
Source: Gwartney and Lawson (2007). Courtesy of the Fraser Institute, Vancouver, B.C.

Countries with the highest level of freedom (e.g., United States, New Zealand, Hong Kong) grew faster than those with moderate degrees of freedom (e.g., United Kingdom, Canada, Germany) and substantially more rapidly than those with little economic freedom (e.g., Venezuela, Iran, Congo). The authors conclude, "Countries with more economic freedom attract more investment and achieve grater productivity from their resources. As a result, they grow more rapidly and achieve higher income levels" (2004: 38).

What about countries that change policies? The authors state, "Countries stagnate when their institutions stifle trade and erode the incentives to engage in productive activities. . . . Countries with low initial levels of income, in particular, are able to grow rapidly and move up the income ladder when their policies are supportive of economic freedom" (2004: 38).

UPDATE 2: THE POOR BENEFIT FROM CAPITALISM

Adam Smith also argued that both rich and poor benefit from a liberal economic system. He declared, "universal opulence . . . extends itself to the lowest ranks of the people" (1965: 11).

(continued)

The modern-day statistical work of Stanley Lebergott and Michael Cox confirms this Smithian view and disputes the commonly held criticism that under a free market the rich get richer and the poor get poorer. The poor also get rich, according to recent studies by Lebergott (1976) and Cox (1999).

Stanley Lebergott, professor emeritus at Wesleyan University, has studied individual consumer markets in food, clothing, housing, fuel, housework, transportation, health, recreation, and religion.

For example, he developed the statistics shown in Table 1.1 to show improvements in living standards from 1900 to 1970.

Percentage of Households With	Among All Families in 1900	Among Poor Families in 1970
Flush toilets	15%	99%
Running water	24	92
Central heating	1	58
One (or fewer) occupants per room	48	96
Electricity	3	99
Refrigeration	18	99
Automobiles	1	41

Table 1.1
U. S. Living Standards, 1900–1970
Source: Lebergott (1976: 8).
Reprinted by permission of Princeton University Press.

As Lebergott's table shows, the standard of living has risen substantially for all classes, including the lowest, in the twentieth century. He confirms the statement once made by Andrew Carnegie, "Capitalism is about turning luxuries into necessities." Through the competitive efforts of entrepreneurs, workers and capitalists, virtually all American consumers have been able to change an uncertain and often cruel world into a more pleasant and convenient place to live and work. A typical homestead in 1900 had no central heating, electricity, refrigeration, flush toilets, or even running water. Today even a large majority of poor people benefit from these goods and services.

Another recent study by Michael Cox, an economist at the Federal Reserve Bank of Dallas, and Richard Alm, a business writer for the *Dallas Morning News,* concludes that the real prices of housing, food, gasoline, electricity, telephone service, home appliances, clothing, and other everyday necessities fell significantly during the twentieth century. The researchers also demonstrate that the poor in America have also seen gradual improvements in their economic lives. More poor people own homes, automobiles, and other consumer products than ever before, and televisions are found in even the poorest households (Cox and Alm 1999).

Finally, Gwartney and Lawson have done studies showing that the poorest 10 percent of the world's population earn more income when they adopt institutions favoring economic freedom (2004: 23). Economic freedom also reduces infant mortality, the incidence of child labor, black markets, and corruption by public officials, while increasing adult literacy, life expectancy, and civil liberties (2004: 22–26).

UPDATE 3: RELIGIOUS COMPETITION IS GOOD

Adam Smith was a firm believer in competition in all walks of life, not just business. He favored competition in education, medicine, and even religion. He was opposed to any state-established religion, which encouraged intolerance and fanaticism. Natural liberty, on the other hand, favored numerous small sects which, in turn, would generate more interest among followers. "In little religious sects, the morals of common people have been almost remarkably regular and orderly: generally much more so than in the established church" (1965: 747–48).

Smith disagreed with his friend David Hume on this issue. Hume was hostile to all religions and therefore favored a noncompetitive state religion precisely because it would sap the zeal of religious followers and maintain political order. Smith, on the other hand, thought religion was beneficial if religious beliefs and organizations were free and open. He favored "a great multitude of religious sects," which would reduce zeal and fanaticism and promote toleration, moderation and rational religion (1965: 744–45). Smith himself secretly made many charitable contributions in his lifetime, and once helped a blind young man to prepare for an intellectual career (Sowell 1993: 220; Fitzgibbons 1995: 138).

Laurence Iannaccone (George Mason University) tested Smith's hypothesis on religious freedom, comparing attendance at church and the degree of religious monopoly in various Protestant and Catholic countries between 1968 and 1976 (Iannaccone 1991: 156–77; West 1990: 151–64). The graph in Figure 1.3 shows an interesting phenomenon.

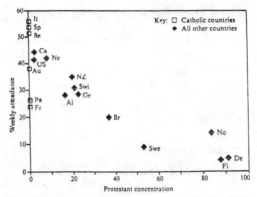

Notes: Al = Australia, Au = Austria, Be = Belgium, Br = Britain, Ca = Canada, De = Denmark, Fi = Finland, Fr = France, Ge = West Germany, It = Italy, Ne = Netherlands, NZ = New Zealand, No = Norway, Po = Portugal, Sp = Spain, Swe = Sweden, Swi = Switzerland, US = United States.

Figure 1.3
Church Attendance and Religious Concentration in Selected Countries
Sources: Iannaccone (1991: 157); West (1990: 161). Reprinted by permission of Sage Ltd.

Iannaccone's test produced a striking result: church attendance rate varied inversely with church concentration in Protestant nations. Church attendance among Protestants was high in freely competitive nations and low in countries monopolized by a single Protestant denomination. (However, it should be noted that there was no significant effect of monopoly on church attendance in Catholic countries.)

Smith favored self-restraint. Indeed, he firmly asserted that a free commercial society functioning within the legal restraints that he outlined would moderate the passions and prevent a descent into a Hobbesian jungle, a theme that he inherits from Montesquieu (see the appendix at the end of this chapter, page 40) and, later, Nassau Senior.[5] He taught that commerce encourages people to become educated, industrious, and self-disciplined and to defer gratification. It is the fear of losing customers "which restrains his frauds and corrects his negligence" (1965: 129).

All legitimate exchanges must benefit both the buyer and the seller, not one at the expense of the other. Smith's "invisible hand" works only if businesspeople have an enlightened long-term view of competition, and they recognize the value of reputation and repeat business. In short, self-interest promotes the interests of society only when the producer responds to the needs of the customer. When the customer is defrauded or deceived—an event that occurs all too frequently in the marketplace—self-interest succeeds at the expense of society's welfare.

Smith recognized that people are motivated by self-interest. It is natural to look out for one's self and one's family above all interests, and to reject self-interest would be to deny human nature. Yet, at the same time, Smith did not condone greed or selfishness. For Adam Smith, greed and selfishness are vices. He would be uncomfortable with Ayn Rand's calling "selfishness" a virtue (1964) or Walter Williams' labeling "greed" a good thing. He accepted them as human frailties. However, Smith contended that these base motives cannot be outlawed or prohibited, only that they could be discouraged and moderated in a commercial society with the right incentives. As Dinesh D'Souza interprets Smith, "Capitalism civilizes greed in much the same way that marriage civilizes lust. Greed, like lust, is part of our human nature; it would be futile to try to root it out. What capitalism does is to channel greed in such a way that it works to meet the wants and needs of society" (2005).

In fact, Smith's ideal society would be infused with virtue, mutual benevolence, and civic laws prohibiting unjust and fraudulent business practices. Smith's "impartial spectator" reflected the moral standards and judgment of the community (1982 [1759]: 215 passim). His economic man is cooperative and fair without harming others. A good moral climate and legal system would benefit economic growth. Smith supported social institutions—the market, religious communities, and the law—to foster self-control, self-discipline, and benevolence (Muller 1993: 2). After all, Adam Smith was not just an economist, but a professor of moral philosophy.

Smith's model reflects this essential attribute: "Every man, *as long as he does not violate the laws of justice*, is left perfectly free to pursue his own

---

5. In his inaugural address as the first Drummond Professor of Political Economy at Oxford, Nassau Senior predicted that the new science "will rank in public estimation among the first of moral sciences" and claimed that "the pursuit of wealth . . . is, to the mass of mankind, the great source of moral improvement" (in Schumacher 1973: 33–34).

PROFESSOR STIGLER WARNS STUDENTS NOT TO READ THIS PASSAGE FROM *THE WEALTH OF NATIONS*

I earnestly recommend that all of this book except page 720 be read!
—Professor George Stigler (1966: 168n)

Chicago economist and Nobel-winning economist George J. Stigler (1911–91) was famous for his dry humor. He was a big fan of Adam Smith's *Wealth of Nations* and recommended all of it—except for page 728.

What's on page 728? Check out the 1965 Modern Library edition of *The Wealth of Nations*. (For other editions, look under Book V, Part III, Article 2.)

What did Professor Stigler find annoying in *The Wealth of Nations*? It was Adam Smith's denunciation of college professors!

Here are the highlights of Smith's condemnation of the "education of youth" and the "sham-lecture":

> If the teacher happens to be a man of sense, it must be an unpleasant thing to him to be conscious, while he is lecturing his students, that he is either speaking or reading nonsense, or what is very little better than non-sense. It must too be unpleasant to him to observe that the greater part of his students desert his lectures; or perhaps attend upon them with plain enough marks of neglect, contempt, and derision. . . .
>
> The discipline of colleges and universities is in general contrived, not for the benefit of the students, but for the interest, or more properly speaking, for the ease of the masters.

Photograph 1.1
Portrait of George Stigler
Holding His Favorite Book,
Adam Smith's *Wealth of Nations*
Courtesy of George J. Stigler
Center, Graduate School of
Business, University of Chicago.
Photograph by Lesley Skousen.

Clearly, Adam Smith's observation is just as relevant today!

BEWARE OF THIS "ABSURD" ENGLISH CUSTOM

But if you ask me, the above citation is nothing compared to what Adam Smith says a few pages later, where he condemns a certain "English custom" that will cause a young person to become "more conceited, more unprincipled, more dissipated, and more incapable of any serious application either to study or to business. . . ." A father who allows his son to engage in this "absurd practice" will soon see his son "unemployed, neglected and going to ruin before his eyes."

Find out what this terrible practice is on page 728 of Smith's book. (Okay, if you can't wait—see the footnote.)[6]

---

6.   Youth (ages seventeen to twenty-one) traveling abroad! Smith criticized the practice of sending teenage children abroad, contending that it weakens character by removing them from the control of parents.

ADAM SMITH BURNS HIS CLOTHES . . . AND THEN BURNS HIS PAPERS!

Ugly Hell, gape not!
Come not, Lucifer!
I'll burn my books.
—Christopher Marlowe, *Doctor Faustus*

What! Adam Smith, a pyromaniac?

The first incident is full of irony. In *The Wealth of Nations,* the Scottish professor argued in favor of free trade. He endorsed the elimination of most tariffs and even wrote in sympathy of smuggling. Two years later, in 1778, Smith actively sought a high-level government appointment, possibly to enhance his financial condition. Smith succeeded and was named Commissioner of Customs in Scotland! Never mind his previous writings on free trade, or the words of his friend Dr. Samuel Johnson, who said that "one of the lowest of all human beings is a Commissioner of Excise" (Viner 1965: 64). The job was a prestigious position that paid a handsome £600 a year, and, in a strange paradox, the champion of free trade and laissez faire spent the last twelve years of his life enforcing Scotland's mercantilist import laws and cracking down on smugglers.

Once in office, Smith acquainted himself with all the rules and regulations of customs law, and suddenly discovered that for some time he had personally violated it. Most of the clothes he was wearing had been illegally smuggled into the country. Writing to Lord Auckland, he exclaimed, "I found, to my great astonishment, that I had scarce a stock [neck cloth], a cravat, a pair of ruffles, or a pocket handkerchief which was not prohibited to be worn or used in Great Britain. I wished to set an example and burnt them all."[7] He urged Lord Auckland and his wife to examine their clothing and do the same.

It's sad to think of such a bright mind spending a dozen fruitless years enforcing arcane customs laws when he could have pursued much more profound interests. He intended to write a third philosophical work on politics and jurisprudence, a sequel to his *Theory of Moral Sentiments* and *The Wealth of Nations.* Yet such perhaps is the lure of government office and job security to all, including the strongest advocates of the free market.

ANOTHER BURNING AFFAIR

The second burning incident occurred at the end of Smith's life in 1790. He dined every Sunday with his two closest friends, Joseph Black the chemist and James Hutton the geologist, at a tavern in Edinburgh. Several months before his demise, he begged his friends to destroy all his unpublished papers except for a few he deemed nearly ready for publication. This was not a new request. Seventeen years earlier, when he traveled to London with the manuscript of *The Wealth of Nations,* he instructed David Hume, his executor, to destroy all his loose papers and eighteen thin, paper folio books "without any examination," and to spare nothing but his fragment on the history of astronomy.

(continued)

7. Letter to William Eden (Lord Auckland), Edinburgh, January 3, 1780, in Smith 1987: 245–46. In his letter, Smith advocated the complete abolition of all import prohibitions, to be replaced by reasonable duties.

Smith had apparently read about a contemporary figure whose private papers had been exposed to the public in a "tell-all" biography, and he feared the same might happen to him. He may have also been concerned about letters or essays written in defense of his friend Hume, who was a religious heretic during a period of intolerance. But Hume died before Smith, and a new executor of his estate was needed.

Approaching the end of his life, Smith became extremely anxious about his personal papers, and repeatedly demanded that his friends Black and Hutton destroy them. Black and Hutton always put off complying with his request, hoping that Smith would come to his senses and change his mind. But a week before he died, he expressly sent for them and insisted that they burn all his manuscripts, without knowing or asking what they contained, except for a few items ready for publication. Finally, the two acquiesced and burned virtually everything—sixteen volumes of manuscript! Thrown into the fire was his manuscript on law. Fortunately, extensive student notes on these lectures were discovered in 1958 and published later as *Lectures on Jurisprudence.*

After the conflagration, the old professor seemed greatly relieved. When his visitors called upon him on the following Sunday evening for their regular supper, he declined. "I love your company, gentlemen, but I believe I must leave you to go to another world." It was his last sentence to them. He died the following Saturday, July 17, 1790.

Photograph 1.2
Eamonn Butler, president of the Adam Smith Institute; Vernon Smith, Nobel laureate; and Mark Skousen in front of the Adam Smith statue on Mile High Street in Edinburgh on July 4, 2008.
Courtesy of Sue Easton.

interest his own way, and to bring both his industry and capital into competition with those of any other man, or order of men" (1965: 651, italics added).

DAS ADAM SMITH PROBLEM: SYMPATHY VERSUS SELF-INTEREST

In his 1759 work, *The Theory of Moral Sentiments*, Adam Smith wrote that "sympathy" was the driving force behind a benevolent, prosperous society. In his later work, *The Wealth of Nations*, "self-interest" became the primary motive. German philosophers called this apparent contradiction *Das Adam Smith Problem*, but Smith himself saw no conflict between the two. He took a historical perspective. In a precapitalist community described in *The Theory of Moral Sentiments,* benevolence, or love, was probably the most dominant factor in a village where everyone knew each other. However, in the capitalist industrialist world, cities such as London and Paris attract thousands of strangers and the motivation changes from sympathy to self-interest in economic activity, for "it is in vain to expect it from their benevolence only" (1965: 14).

Smith combined both motives in *The Wealth of Nations,* in which both sympathy and self-interest were the driving motivators in a modern capitalist society. Smith believed that every man has a basic desire to be accepted by others. To obtain this sympathy, people act in a manner so as to gain respect and admiration. In economic life, this means enlightened self-interest, wherein both seller and buyer mutually benefit in their transactions. Moreover, Smith contended that economic progress and surplus wealth are a prerequisite for sympathy and charity. In short, Smith desired to integrate economics and moral behavior (Fitzgibbons 1995: 3–4; Tvede 1997: 29).

The Scottish philosopher believed man to be motivated by both self-interest and benevolence, but in a complex market economy, where individuals move away from their closest friends and family, self-interest becomes a more powerful force. In Ronald Coase's interpretation, "The great advantage of the market is that it is able to use the strength of self-interest to offset the weakness and partiality of benevolence, so that those who are unknown, unattractive, and unimportant will have their wants served" (Coase 1976: 544).

HOW MONOPOLY HURTS THE MARKET SYSTEM

Smith said that competition was absolutely essential to turning self-interest into benevolence in a self-regulating society. He preferred the cheaper "natural price, or the price of free competition" to the high price of monopoly power and "exclusive privileges" granted certain corporations and trading companies (such as the East India Company). Smith vehemently opposed the "mean rapacity" and "wretched spirit of monopoly"

(1965: 428) that privileged businessmen were accustomed to. Competition means lower prices and more money to buy other goods, which in turn means more jobs and a higher standard of living.

According to Smith, monopoly power creates a *political* society, characterized by flattery, fawning, and deceit (Muller 1993: 135). Monopoly fosters quick and easy profits and wasteful consumption (Smith 1965: 578).

While believing in the marketplace, Smith was no apologist for merchants and special interests. In one of his more famous passages, he complained, "People of the same trade seldom meet together, even for merriment and diversion, but the conversation ends in a conspiracy against the public, or in some contrivance to raise prices" (1965: 128). His goal was to convince legislators to resist supporting the vested interests of merchants and instead to act in favor of the common good.

WHO WAS ADAM SMITH?

Who was Adam Smith? And how did he come to write his revolutionary work on modern economics?

Seaports and commerce were an integral part of Adam Smith's life. Born in Kirkcaldy, on the east coast of Scotland near Edinburgh, in June 1723, he had the unfortunate distinction of being born in the same year that his father died. It appeared that the newborn Adam Smith was destined to be a student of trade and a customs agent. His father, also named Adam Smith, was a comptroller of customs at Kirkcaldy. His guardian, again named Adam Smith, was a customs collector at the same town. And a cousin served as customs inspector at Alloa. His name was—you guessed it—Adam Smith.

The last occupation of our Adam Smith (the famous one) was, not surprisingly, customs commissioner of Scotland. But we're getting ahead of our story.

In his early days in Kirkcaldy, Adam was regarded as a "delicate child." At age four, he was kidnapped by gypsies but was soon returned to his mother. "He would have made a poor gypsy," commented biographer John Rae (1895: 5). His focus of affection was always his mother, whom he cherished.

Although the Scottish professor had many female acquaintances, he never married. "He speaks harshly, with big teeth, and he's ugly as the devil," wrote Madame Riccoboni, a French novelist, upon meeting Adam Smith for the first time in Paris in May 1766. "He's a most absent-minded creature," she later wrote, "but one of the most lovable" (Muller 1993: 16). We know pitifully little about his love interests. We know from his biographers that as a young man Smith was in love with a beautiful and accomplished young lady, but unknown circumstances prevented their marriage (Ross 1995: 402). Several French ladies pursued this unhandsome savant, but nothing came of it. (His private life remains a bit of a mystery because of an event at the end of his life. See box, pages 30–31, for details.)

Smith occupied his spare time attending numerous clubs, such as the Poker Club, the Club of Edinburgh, the London "literati," and Johnson's Club, although David Hume frequently scolded Smith for being too reclusive. "His mother, his friends, his books—these were Smith's three great joys," declared John Rae (1895: 327).

At the youthful age of fourteen, Smith attended Glasgow University, then won a scholarship to Oxford, where he spent half a dozen years studying Greek and Latin classics, French and English literature, and science and philosophy. Later he wrote in *The Wealth of Nations*, referring to Oxford University, "the greater part of the public professors have, for these many years, given up altogether even the pretence of teaching" (Smith 1965: 718).

In terms of physical appearance, Smith was of average height and slightly overweight. He never sat for a picture, but several sketches show "rather handsome features, full forehead, prominent eyeballs, well curved eyebrows, slightly aquiline nose, and firm mouth and chin" (Rae 1895: 438). He himself exclaimed, "I am a beau in nothing but my books" (page 329).

After graduation, he held the position of Professor of Moral Philosophy at the University of Glasgow between 1751 and 1763. His first major work, *Theory of Moral Sentiments*, was published in 1759 and established Adam Smith as an influential Scottish thinker.

THE ABSENT-MINDED PROFESSOR

As to his personality quirks, the famous Professor of Moral Philosophy had a harsh, thick voice and often stuttered. He was the quintessential absent-minded professor. His life was one of ubiquitous disorganization and ambiguity. Books and papers were stacked everywhere in his study. From his childhood, he had the habit of speaking to himself, "smiling in rapt conversation with invisible companions" (Rae 1895: 329). Stories abound of his bumbling nature: the time he fell into a tanning pit while discoursing with a friend; the morning he put bread and butter into a teapot, and after tasting it, declared it to be the worst cup of tea he had ever had; and the time he went out walking and daydreaming in his old nightgown and ended up several miles outside town. "He was the most absent man I ever knew," declared one acquaintance (West 1976: 176).

HOW HE WROTE HIS MAGNUM OPUS

In 1764, Charles Townsend, a leading British member of Parliament, offered Smith a handsome fee and lifetime pension to tutor his stepson, Henry Scott, the Duke of Buccleuch. They traveled to France, where Smith met with Voltaire, Turgot, Quesnay, and other great French thinkers. "This Smith is an excellent man!" exclaimed Voltaire. "We have nothing to compare with him" (Muller 1993: 15).

It was in France that Smith indicated he had lost interest in his tutoring duties and began researching and writing *The Wealth of Nations*. An instant bestseller, it sold out in six months. David Hume and Thomas Jefferson, among others, praised the book, which went through several editions and foreign translations during Smith's lifetime.

HIS FINAL YEARS

Following the publication of his classic book, Smith was appointed customs commissioner in Edinburgh, as noted earlier. He also spent time revising his published books, lived a modest life despite his pension, and over the years gave away most of his income in private acts of charity, which he took care to conceal (Rae 1895: 437). He lived in Edinburgh for the remainder of his life and died in 1790 at the age of sixty-seven.

ADAM SMITH FAVORS A STRONG BUT LIMITED GOVERNMENT

As a proponent of the Scottish Enlightenment and the virtues of natural liberty, Adam Smith was a firm believer in a parsimonious but strong government. He wrote of three purposes of government: "Little else is required to carry a state to the highest degree of opulence from the lowest barbarism, but peace, easy taxes, and a tolerable administration of justice" (Danhert 1974: 218). More specifically, Smith endorsed (1) the need for a well-financed militia for national defense, (2) a legal system to protect liberty, property rights, and to enforce contracts and payment of debts, (3) public works—roads, canals, bridges, harbors, and other infrastructure projects, and (4) universal public education to counter the alienating and mentally degrading effects of specialization (division of labor) under capitalism (Smith 1965: 734–35).

In general, the Scottish professor favored a maximum degree of personal liberty in society, including a diversity of entertainment—as long as it was "without scandal or indecency" (page 748). Smith was no pure libertarian!

SMITH WARNS ABOUT THE DANGERS OF BIG GOVERNMENT

At the same time, he was a sharp critic of state power. Politicians are usually spendthrift hypocrites, according to Smith. Some of the following quotes from *The Wealth of Nations* could be used in political debates today:

> There is no art which one government sooner learns of another, than that of draining money from the pockets of the people. (page 813)

> It is the highest impertinence and presumption, therefore, in kings and ministers, to pretend to watch over the economy of private people, and to

restrain their expense, either by sumptuary laws, or by prohibiting the importation of foreign luxuries. They are themselves always, and without exception, the greatest spendthrifts in the society. Let them look well after their own expense, and they may safely trust private people with theirs. If their own extravagance does not ruin the state, that of their subjects never will. (page 329)

Great nations are never impoverished by private, though they sometimes are by public prodigality and misconduct. The whole, or almost the whole public revenue, is in most countries employed in maintaining unproductive hands. Such are the people who compose a numerous and splendid court, a great ecclesiastical establishment, great fleets and armies, who in time of peace produce nothing, and in time of war acquire nothing which can compensate the expense of maintaining them, even while the war lasts. Such people, as they themselves produce nothing, are all maintained by the produce of other men's labour. (page 325)

Smith pleaded for balanced budgets and opposed a large public debt. He advocated privatization, the sale of "crown lands" as a way to raise revenues and cultivate property. He favored minimal government interference in citizens' personal lives and economic activity. Smith argued that war is unnecessary and is ill advised in most cases, and that ending a war will not result in massive unemployment (pages 436–37).

He sounded as if he had just been audited by revenue agents when he expressed sympathy to taxpayers "continually exposed to the mortifying and vexatious visits of the tax-collectors" (page 880). After lambasting the complexity and inequality of the tax system, he prescribed tax cuts across the board, although he favored rigid usury laws and progressive taxation.

SMITH ENDORSES SOUND MONEY AND THE GOLD STANDARD

Smith also worried about governments' manipulation of the monetary system. While rejecting the idea that gold and silver alone constitute a country's wealth, he favored a stable monetary system based on gold and silver, and supported the doctrine of free banking. He also rejected the prevalent "quantity theory of money" (see the discussion of Irving Fisher in chapter 11), which holds that the price level rises or falls in proportion to changes in the money supply. In his "Digression on Silver," Smith showed that prices have varied considerably when the supply of silver (money) increased (page 240).

THE ESSENCE OF THE CLASSICAL MODEL OF ECONOMICS

In sum, the classical model developed by Adam Smith, and endorsed by his disciples in generations to come, consisted of four general principles:

1. Thrift, hard work, enlightened self-interest, and benevolence toward fellow citizens are virtues and should be encouraged.
2. Government should limit its activities to administer justice, enforcing private property rights, and defending the nation against aggression.
3. The state should adopt a general policy of laissez-faire noninterventionism in economic affairs (free trade, low taxes, minimal bureaucracy, etc.).
4. The classical gold/silver standard restrains the state from depreciating the currency and provides a stable monetary environment in which the economy may flourish.

As we shall see, the classical model of Adam Smith would repeatedly come under attack over the next 200 years by friends and foes alike.

ADAM SMITH AND THE AGE OF ECONOMISTS

Adam Smith was not perfect by any means. In future chapters, we will comment on and amend his crude labor theory of value, his critique of landlords, his strange distinction between "productive" and "unproductive" labor, and his failure to recognize the fundamental principle of subjective marginal utility in price theory. But these are parenthetical deviations from an overwhelmingly positive contribution to economic science.

Adam Smith is to be congratulated for his fierce defense of free trade and free markets, his central theme of "natural liberty" and a self-regulating system of competitive free enterprise and limited government. His eloquent expression of economic liberty helped free the world from provincial mercantilism and heavy-handed intervention by the state. Without his leadership, the industrial revolution might have stalled for another century or more.

THE GREAT OPTIMIST

Adam Smith, a child of the Scottish Enlightenment, was above all an optimist about the future of the world. His principal focus throughout his economic magnum opus was the "improvement" of the individual through "frugality and good conduct," saving and investing, exchange and the division of labor, education and capital formation, and new technology. He was more interested in increasing wealth than dividing it (in sharp contrast to his disciple David Ricardo, as we shall see in chapter 4).

According to Adam Smith, even a powerful, sinister government cannot stop progress: "The uniform, constant, and uninterrupted effort of every man to better his condition . . . is frequently powerful enough to maintain the natural progress of things toward improvement, in spite both of the extravagance of government, and of the greatest errors of administration" (1965: 326; cf. 508).

ADAM SMITH MAKES A FAMOUS REMARK

During the American Revolution, Adam Smith was approached by a citizen who was alarmed by the defeat of the British at Saratoga in 1777. "The nation must be ruined," the man exclaimed with panic in his voice. Smith, then in his fifties, replied calmly, "Be assured, my young friend, that there is a great deal of ruin in a nation" (Rae 1895: 343; Ross 1995: 327). Smith's dictum is frequently cited by Milton Friedman, Gary Becker, and other economists in response to "economic doomsdayers." It suggests that when a nation has built up tremendous wealth, institutions, and goodwill over the centuries, it would take more than a major war or natural disaster to destroy a country.

His life complete, Adam Smith may well have entertained the words of the Psalmist, "Return unto thy rest, O my soul: for the Lord hath dealt bountifully with thee" (Psalm 116: 7).

While he rested in the grave, his classical model of economics would spread throughout Europe and America. Surprisingly, his most passionate disciples came from a country that had for centuries been England's fiercest enemy—the subject of our next chapter.

APPENDIX
The Pre-Adamites

Adam Smith didn't create modern economics out of a vacuum, the way Athena sprang full grown and fully armed from the brow of Zeus. Instead, Smith was influenced by a wide number of economic thinkers, going all the way back to the ancient Greek philosophers.

PLATO AND ARISTOTLE

A child of the Scottish Enlightenment, Smith would find little appeal in reading Plato's *Republic*, which advocated an ideal city-state ruled by collectivist philosopher-kings. He considered Aristotle better, because of his defense of private property and his critique of Plato's communism. Private property, according to Aristotle, would give people the opportunity to practice the virtues of benevolence and philanthropy, all part of the Aristotelian "golden mean" and "good life." But Adam Smith would have no part of Aristotle's scorn of money-making and his denunciation of monetary trade and retail commerce as immoral and "unnatural," a philosophy that was later sanctioned by many Christian writers in the Middle Ages.

PROTESTANTS, CATHOLICS, AND THE SPANISH SCHOLASTICS

Adam Smith was greatly influenced by Calvinist doctrines favoring thrift and hard work while condemning excessive luxury, usury, and "unproductive" labor (see chapter 7, pages 175–76, footnote 2). Catholics and Protestants alike debated what constituted "just price" in a market economy. The Spanish scholastics in the sixteenth century determined that the "just price" was nothing more than the common market price, and they generally supported a laissez-faire philosophy (Rothbard 1995: 97–133). As Montesquieu later wrote, "It is competition that puts a just price on goods and establishes the true relations between them" (Montesquieu 1989 [1748]: 344).

In many ways, Adam Smith aimed to replace the antimaterialist Greco-Christian doctrines of Western Europe, which were a hindrance to liberty and economic growth, with a system that combined moral living and the reasonable pursuit of material desires (Fitzgibbons 1995: v, 16).

BERNARD MANDEVILLE AND *THE FABLE OF THE BEES*

Some economists contend that Adam Smith developed his "invisible hand" concept from the scandalous work *The Fable of the Bees* (1997 [1714]), by **Bernard Mandeville (1670–1733)**, a Dutch psychiatrist and pamphleteer. In the first version, Mandeville told the story of a thriving "grumbling hive" of bees that was swiftly reduced to poverty and destruction after converting to a moral community. In the second popular edition, Mandeville described a prosperous community in which all the citizens decided to abandon their luxurious spending habits and military armaments. The result was a depression and collapse in trade and housing.

His conclusion: private vices of greed, avarice and luxury lead to public benefits of abundant wealth, "and that the Moment Evil ceases, the Society must be spoiled, if not totally dissolved." Clearly, under Mandeville's infamous paradox, self-interest results in social benefit.

Both Friedrich Hayek and John Maynard Keynes have written approvingly of Mandeville's fable. According to Hayek, Adam Smith gained insights into the division of labor, self-interest, economic liberty, and the idea of unintended consequences from Mandeville (Hayek 1984: 184–85). Keynes approved of Mandeville's anti-saving sentiments and statist pressures to assure full employment in society (Keynes 1973: 358–61).

However, it is clear in *The Theory of Moral Sentiments* that Smith did not approve of Mandeville. Calling his book "wholly pernicious" and his thesis "erroneous," Smith disagreed that economic progress is achieved through greed, vanity, and unrestrained self-love, complaining that Mandeville seems to make no distinction between vice and virtue (Smith 1976 [1759]: 308–10).

MONTESQUIEU AND *DOUX COMMERCE*

Smith's attitude toward self-interest was more positively affected by the great French jurist and philosopher **Charles de Secondat Montesquieu (1689–1755)**. His book *The Spirit of the Laws*, first published in 1748, encouraged James Madison and Alexander Hamilton to push for constitutional separation of powers, a concept endorsed by Adam Smith. Montesquieu, who wrote before the industrial revolution, saw many virtues in *doux commerce* (gentle commerce). He expressed the novel view that the pursuit of profit making and commercial interests serve as a countervailing bridle against the violent passions of war and abusive political power. "Commerce cures destructive prejudices," Montesquieu declared, "it polishes and softens barbarous mores. . . . The natural effect of commerce is to lead to peace" (1989: 338). According to Montesquieu, Sir James Steuart, and other *philosophes* of the era, the image of the merchant and moneymaker as a peaceful, dispassionate, innocent fellow was in sharp contrast with "the looting armies and murderous pirates of the time" (Hirschman 1997: 63). Commerce improves the political order: "The spirit of commerce brings with it the spirit of frugality, of economy, of moderation, of work, of wisdom, of tranquility, of order, and of regularity" (Hirschman 1997: 71).[8] As we pointed out in chapter 1, Smith endorsed this progressive view of commercial society.

DR. FRANÇOIS QUESNAY AND HIS *TABLEAU ÉCONOMIQUE*

The most prominent physiocrat encountered by Adam Smith in France was the eminent surgeon **François Quesnay (1694–1774)**, who at one time was the personal physician of King Louis XV's favorite mistress. His famous diagram, the *tableau économique*, was considered by contemporaries as one of the three greatest economics inventions of mankind, after writing and money (Smith 1965: 643).

Quesnay's zigzag diagram, first published in 1758, has created considerable interest and controversy over the years (see Table 1.2). It has been hailed as a forerunner of many developments in modern economics: econometrics, Keynes's multiplier, input-output analysis, the circular flow diagram, and a Walrasian general equilibrium model. It is certainly a "macro" view of the economy, without any reference to prices, but no one is sure of its real meaning. As the principal spokesman for the physiocrats, Quesnay endorsed the fallacy of agriculture as the only "productive" expenditure and industry as "sterile."

8. Montesquieu's propitious image of capitalism reflects the famous line by Dr. Samuel Johnson, "There are few ways in which a man can be more innocently employed than in getting money" (Boswell 1933, I: 657). It was John Maynard Keynes who wrote, "It is better that a man should tyrannise over his bank balance than over his fellow-citizens" (Keynes 1973 [1936]: 374). Today we might say, "Better that a person tyrannizes over his favorite sports team (or his favorite stock) than over his fellowman."

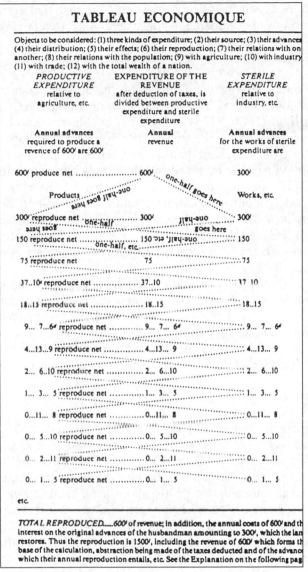

Table 1.2
Quesnay's *Tableau économique*
Source: Vaggi (1987: 23). Reprinted by permission of W.W. Norton.

As to Quesnay's influence, *The Wealth of Nations* proclaimed Dr. Quesnay a "very ingenious and profound author" who promoted the popular slogan "Laissez faire, laissez passer," a phrase Smith would endorse wholeheartedly, although he himself never referred to his system as *laissez-faire* economics. (He preferred "natural liberty" or "perfect liberty.") As a leading physiocrat, Quesnay opposed French mercantilism, protectionism and state interventionist policies. However, *The Wealth of*

Nations denied the basic physiocratic premise that agriculture, not manufacturing and commerce, is the source of all wealth (1965: 637–52).

RICHARD CANTILLON

The other prominent influences on the Scottish economist were Richard Cantillon, Jacques Turgot, and Etienne Bonnot de Condillac. **Richard Cantillon (1680–1734)** is regarded by Murray Rothbard and other economic historians as the true "father of modern economics."

An Irish merchant banker and adventurer who emigrated to Paris, Cantillon became involved in John Law's infamous Mississippi bubble in 1717–20, but shrewdly sold all of his shares before the financial storm hit. His independent status allowed him to write a short book on economics, *Essay on the Nature of Commerce in General* (published posthumously in 1755). He died mysteriously in London in 1734, apparently murdered by an irate servant who subsequently burned down his house to cover up the crime.

Cantillon's *Essay* is really quite impressive and undoubtedly influenced Adam Smith. It focuses on the automatic market mechanism of supply and demand, the vital role of entrepreneurship (downplayed in *The Wealth of Nations*) and a sophisticated "pre-Austrian" analysis of monetary inflation that shows how inflation not only raises prices, but changes the pattern of spending (see chapter 12 on the Austrian economists Mises and Hayek).

JACQUES TURGOT

Jacques Turgot (1727–81) was a leading French physiocrat whose profound work, *Reflections on the Formation and Distribution of Wealth* (1766), also inspired Adam Smith. As a devoted free trader and advocate of laissez faire, Turgot, an able minister of finance under Louis XVI, dissolved all the medieval guilds, abolished all restrictions on the grain trade, and maintained a balanced budget. He was so effective that he earned the King's ire, who fired him in 1776.

As a physiocrat, Turgot defended agriculture as the most productive sector of the economy, but beyond that, his *Reflections* exhibited a profound understanding of economics, even surpassing Smith in many areas. His lucid work offers a brilliant understanding of time preference, capital and interest rates, and the role of the capitalist-entrepreneur in a competitive economy. He even described the law of diminishing returns, later popularized by Malthus and Ricardo.

CONDILLAC

Another influential French economist and philosopher was **Etienne Bonnot de Condillac (1714–80)**. He lived the life of a Paris intellectual in the mid-1770s and in 1775 came to the defense of Turgot, who faced difficulties as finance minister during the grain riots. Like Turgot and Montesquieu, Condillac supported free trade. His important work, *Commerce and Government*, was published in 1776, only one month before *The Wealth of Nations*. Condillac's economics was amazingly advanced. He recognized manufacturing as productive, exchange as representing unequal values, that both sides gain from commerce, and that prices are determined by utility value, not labor value (Macleod 1896).

DAVID HUME

The great philosopher **David Hume (1711–76)** was a close friend of Adam Smith's and was highly influential in his limited writings on trade and money. Smith identified his Scottish friend as "by far the most illustrious philosopher and historian" of his age (Fitzgibbons 1995: 9) and "nearly to the ideal of a perfectly wise and virtuous man, as perhaps the nature of human frailty will permit" (Smith 1947: 248). Hume opposed ascetic self-denial and endorsed luxury and the materialistic good life.

Like Smith, Hume condemned the mercantilist restraints on international trade. Using his famous "specie-flow" mechanism, Hume proved that attempts to restrict imports and increase specie inflow would backfire. Import restrictions would raise domestic prices, which in turn would reduce exports, increase imports, and generate a return outflow of specie.

Hume also debunked mercantilist claims that acquiring more specie (precious metals) would lower interest rates and promote prosperity. Hume made the classical argument that real interest rates are determined by the supply of saving and capital, not the money supply. An adherent to the quantity theory of money, Hume felt that an artificial expansion of the money supply would simply raise prices.

Smith's close friendship caused many observers to conclude that Smith endorsed Hume's antireligious rebellion and his purely secular commercial society. They point to the fact that God is not mentioned in *The Wealth of Nations*. However, Smith did not abandon his religious beliefs. His *Theory of Moral Sentiments*, which Smith edited again after the publication of *The Wealth of Nations*, makes numerous references to God and religion. He was admittedly no longer a practicing Presbyterian, rebelling against austere Calvinist behavior, but he was a believer, a Deist who adopted the Stoic belief that God works through nature. As an optimist, Smith believed in the goodness of the world and envisioned a heaven on earth.

BENJAMIN FRANKLIN

Biographers John Rae and Ian Simpson Ross give credence to the tradition that the American founding father **Benjamin Franklin (1706–90)** developed a friendship with Adam Smith and had some influence on his writing

The Wealth of Nations. John Rae recounted how Franklin visited with Smith in Scotland and London and, according to a friend of Franklin's, "Adam Smith when writing his *Wealth of Nations* was in the habit of bringing chapter after chapter as he composed it to himself [Franklin], Dr. Price, and others of the literati; then patiently hear their observations and profit by their discussions and criticisms, sometimes submitting to write whole chapters anew, and even to reverse some of his propositions" (Rae 1895: 264–65; see also Ross 1995: 255–56).

In his economic writings, Franklin wrote about the advantages of thrift, free trade, and a growing population, themes readily apparent in *The Wealth of Nations.* (However, I'm not sure Smith would agree with Franklin's case, published in 1728, for expanding the paper currency in Pennsylvania.) Smith's favorable remarks toward American independence may have been due to Franklin (Smith 1965: 557–606).

REFERENCES

Arrow, Kenneth J., and F.H. Hahn. 1971. *General Competitive Analysis.* San Francisco: Holden-Day.

Baumol, William J., and Alan S. Blinder. 1988. *Economics: Principles and Policy,* 4th ed. New York: Harcourt Brace Jovanovich.

Boswell, James. 1933. *Boswell's Life of Johnson.* 2 vols. New York: Oxford University Press.

Coase, Ronald H. 1976. "Adam Smith's View of Man." *Journal of Law and Economics* 19, 529–46.

Cox, Michael, and Richard Alm. 1997. "Time Well Spent: The Declining Cost of Living in America." Annual Report of the Federal Reserve Bank of Dallas.

———. 1999. *The Myths of Rich and Poor.* New York: Free Press.

Danhert, Clyde E., ed. 1974. *Adam Smith, Man of Letters and Economist.* New York: Exposition.

D'Souza, Dinesh. 2005. "How Capitalism Civilizes Greed." www.dineshdsouza.com/articles/civilizinggreed.html.

Fitzgibbons, Athol. 1995. *Adam Smith's System of Liberty, Wealth, and Virtue.* New York: Clarendon.

Friedman, Milton. 1978. "Adam Smith's Relevance for 1976." In *Adam Smith and the Wealth of Nations: 1776–1976 Bicentennial Essays,* ed. Fred R. Glahe, 7–20. Boulder: Colorado Associated University Press.

Friedman, Milton, and Rose Friedman. 1980. *Free to Choose: A Personal Statement.* New York: Harcourt Brace Jovanovich.

Glahe, Fred R., ed. 1978. *Adam Smith and the Wealth of Nations: 1776–1976 Bicentennial Essays.* Boulder: Colorado Associated University Press.

———. 1993. *Adam Smith's An Inquiry into the Nature and Causes of the Wealth of Nations: A Concordance.* Lanham, MD: Rowman and Littlefield.

Gwartney, James D., Robert A. Lawson, and Walter E. Block. 1996. *Economic Freedom of the World: 1975–1995.* Vancouver, BC: Fraser Institute.

Hahn, Frank. 1982. "Reflections on the Invisible Hand." *Lloyds Bank Review* (April), 1–21.

Hayek, Friedrich. 1984. *The Essence of Hayek,* ed. Chiaki Nishiyama and Kurt R. Leube. Stanford, CA: Stanford University Press.

Hirschman, Albert O. 1997. *The Passions and the Interests,* 2d ed. Princeton, NJ: Princeton University Press.

Hobbes, Thomas. 1996 [1651]. *Leviathan.* New York: Oxford University Press.

Iannaccone, Laurence. 1991. "The Consequences of Religious Market Structure." *Rationality and Society* 3: 2 (April), 156–77.

Jouvenal, Bertrand de. 1999. *Economics and the Good Life: Essays on Political Economy,* ed. Dennis Hale and Marc Landy. New Brunswick, NJ: Transaction.

Keynes, John Maynard. 1973 [1936]. *The General Theory of Employment, Interest and Money.* London: Macmillan.

Lebergott, Stanley. 1976. *The American Economy.* Princeton, NJ: Princeton University Press.

———. 1993. *Pursuing Happiness: American Consumers in the Twentieth Century.* Princeton, NJ: Princeton University Press.

Lux, Kenneth. 1990. *Adam Smith's Mistake.* Boston: Shambhala.

Macleod, H.D. 1896. *The History of Economics.* London: Bliss, Sands.

Mandeville, Bernard. 1997 [1714]. *The Fable of the Bees, and Other Writings.* New York: Hackett.

Montesquieu, Charles. 1989 [1748]. *The Spirit of the Laws,* ed. Anne Cohler, Basia Miller, and Harold Stone. Cambridge, UK: Cambridge University Press.

Muller, Jerry Z. 1993. *Adam Smith in His Time and Ours.* Princeton, NJ: Princeton University Press.

Powell, Jim. 2000. *The Triumph of Liberty.* New York: Free Press.

Rae, John. 1895. *Life of Adam Smith.* London: Macmillan.

Rand, Ayn. 1964. *The Virtue of Selfishness.* New York: Signet.

Rashid, Salim. 1998. *The Myth of Adam Smith.* Cheltenham, UK: Edward Elgar.

Roemer, John E. 1988. *Free to Lose.* Cambridge: Harvard University Press.

Rogge, Benjamin A., ed. 1976. *The Wisdom of Adam Smith.* Indianapolis: Liberty Press.

Ross, Ian Simpson. 1995. *The Life of Adam Smith.* Oxford: Clarendon.

Rothbard, Murray N. 1995. *Economic Thought Before Adam Smith.* Hants, UK: Edward Elgar.

Rothschild, Emma. 2001. *Economic Sentiments: Adam Smith, Condorcet, and the Enlightenment.* Cambridge: Harvard University Press.

Samuelson, Paul A. 1962. "Economists and the History of Ideas." *American Economic Review* 52: 1 (March), 1–18.

———. 1966. *Collected Scientific Papers of Paul A. Samuelson,* vol. 2. Cambridge, MA: MIT Press.

Schumacher, E.F. 1973. *Small Is Beautiful.* London: Penguin.

Schumpeter, Joseph A. 1954. *History of Economic Analysis.* New York: Oxford University Press.

Skousen, Mark. 2007. *The Big Three in Economics: Adam Smith, Karl Marx, and John Maynard Keynes.* Armonk, NY: M.E. Sharpe.

Smith, Adam. 1947. Letter from Adam Smith to William Strahan. In Supplement to David Hume, *Dialogues Concerning Natural Religion,* ed. Norman Kemp Smith, 248. Indianapolis: Bobbs-Merrill.

———. 1965 [1776]. *An Inquiry into the Nature and Causes of the Wealth of Nations.* New York: Modern Library.

———. 1976 [1759]. *The Theory of Moral Sentiments,* ed. D.D. Raphael and A.L. Macfie. Indianapolis: Liberty Fund.

———. 1982 [1763]. *Lectures on Jurisprudence,* ed. R.L. Meek, D.D. Raphael, and P.G. Stein. Indianapolis: Liberty Classics.

———. 1987. *Correspondence of Adam Smith,* ed. E.G. Mossner and I.S. Ross. Indianapolis: Liberty Classics.

Sowell, Thomas. 1993. "Adam Smith." *Forbes* (December 20), 220.

Stigler, George J. 1966. *The Theory of Price,* 3d ed. New York: Macmillan.

———. 1976. "The Successes and Failures of Professor Smith." *Journal of Political Economy* 84:6 (December), 1199–213.

Tvede, Lars. 1997. *Business Cycles: From John Law to Chaos Theory.* Amsterdam: Harwood.

Vaggi, G. 1987. "François Quesnay." In *The New Palgrave: A Dictionary of Economics*, vol. 4, 22–29. London: Macmillan.

Viner, Jacob. 1965. "Guide to John Rae's Life of Adam Smith." In John Rae, *Life of Adam Smith*. New York: Augustus M. Kelley.

West, Edwin G. 1976. *Adam Smith, The Man and His Works*. Indianapolis, IN: Liberty Press.

———. 1990. "Adam Smith's Hypotheses on Religion: Some New Empirical Tests." In *Adam Smith and Modern Economics*, 151–64. Hants, UK: Edward Elgar.

2

THE FRENCH CONNECTION:
LAISSEZ FAIRE AVANCE!

*The celebrated work of Dr. Adam Smith can only be considered
as an assemblage of the soundest principles of political economy,
supported by luminous illustrations.*

—Jean-Baptiste Say (1970 [1880]: xix)

It fell upon the shoulders of the eminent French economists Jean-Baptiste
Say and Frédéric Bastiat to improve upon the classical model of Adam
Smith and promote it as a universal model of prosperity. Say and Bastiat
championed the boundless possibilities of a free industrial economy, led by
creative entrepreneurs. Say's law of markets, in particular, became the fundamental principle of classical macroeconomics, and its veracity was so
sweeping throughout the profession that it remained virtually unchallenged
until the Keynesian revolution of the next century. And there has never
been a better, more lucid proponent of free trade than Frédéric Bastiat.

In addition, the French economists clarified and advanced upon many
of the concepts expounded in *The Wealth of Nations* and built upon the
sound economic principles developed by Cantillon, Montesquieu, Turgot,
and Condillac. Furthermore, Say and Bastiat rejected the notions of a
labor theory of value and the exploitation of workers under free-enterprise
capitalism.

♪ **Music selection for this chapter: Hector Berlioz,** *Symphonie Fantastique*

WHAT DO YOU MEAN, PRAY TELL, BY LAISSEZ FAIRE?

Laissez faire ought to be the motto of every public authority.
—Marquis d'Argenson

*I abandon laissez faire, —not enthusiastically . . . but because,
whether we like it or not, the conditions of its success have disappeared.*
—John Maynard Keynes (Skidelsky 1992: 186)

In the late seventeenth century, the famous French mercantilist minister, Jean-Baptiste Colbert, once asked a group of businessmen what he could do for them. One of the men, Legendre, is supposed to have replied, "Laissez nous faire"—leave us alone. Several French authors in the earlier part of the eighteenth century, including the Marquis d'Argenson, used the slogan "Laissez faire." The great economist Turgot attributed the rule *Laissez faire, laissez passer*—leave things alone, let goods pass through—to Gournay. Other French sayings with similar meaning became popular: *Le monde va de lui même* (the world goes by itself), and *Pour gouverner mieux, il faudrait gouverner moins* (in order to govern better, we ought to govern less).

"Laissez faire" has come to represent the hands-off policies advocated by Adam Smith, although he never used the phrase. In the twentieth century, John Maynard Keynes gave laissez faire a bad name; it represented the "do-nothing" policies prevalent during the Depression years. "For good or evil, in present day conditions laissez-faire can no longer be relied upon to furnish economic projects with the capital they need," he wrote (Skidelsky 1992: 185). According to Keynes, government was needed to rescue laissez-faire capitalism.

In fact, laissez faire was never meant to be a heartless "do-nothing" government policy. Adam Smith and the classical laissez-faire economists actually aimed at dismantling the old system of regulations and special privilege, and thus improving the general welfare.

The French economists were very much involved in Smith's magnum opus, starting when he spent time in France preparing his book and discussing ideas with Quesnay, Turgot, and Voltaire. Once *The Wealth of Nations* was published, the French were highly successful in publicizing Smith's model of free enterprise and liberalized trade throughout the Western world. They translated Smith's book into French, published the first encyclopedia of economics and the first history of economic thought, and wrote the first major textbook in economics, Say's *Treatise on Political Economy,* which was the principal textbook in the United States and Europe during the first half of the nineteenth century. Many of the Smithian principles were adopted by Alexis de Tocqueville in his profound study of *Democracy in America* (see box, pages 59–61). In short, the French laissez-faire school dominated Western economic thought for nearly half a century and, in the case of Say's law, well into the twentieth century.

WHO WAS THE GREATEST FRENCH ECONOMIST?

Of the four greatest economists in the world, three were French.
—Joseph Schumpeter

When Paul Samuelson began graduate study at Harvard in 1935, Joseph Schumpeter, considered the most influential historian in economics, shocked his students by announcing that three out of the four greatest economists were French (Samuelson 1962: 3). Whom did Schumpeter have in mind?

First was **Léon Walras (1834–1910)**, whom Schumpeter curiously but unhesitantly ranked as the greatest economist of all time, due to his development of general equilibrium theory (Schumpeter 1954: 827; see chapter 8). This choice seems incongruous since Schumpeter is famous for his theories of "creative destruction" and general dynamic disequilibrium, and for his deft criticism of perfect competition and static equilibrium analysis.

His second choice was even more cryptic: **Antoine Cournot (1801–77)**, a French mathematician who was the first to draw a demand curve and demonstrate how monopolists maximize profits at the point where marginal cost equals marginal revenue. Cournot's work was eventually picked up by Alfred Marshall and incorporated into standard price theory.

Third was **François Quesnay (1694–1774)**, famous for his mysterious *Tableau,* the circular flow diagram in economics. Samuelson thought Schumpeter's third pick was even more bizarre, calling it "far fetched."

Who was Schumpeter's favorite non-French economist? At first Samuelson thought Schumpeter meant Adam Smith, but later he discovered it to be Alfred Marshall. Schumpeter is understandably referred to as the *enfant terrible* of the Austrian school. You could never predict what he was going to say or believe.

KEYNES'S FAVORITE FRENCHMAN

John Maynard Keynes also had an unexpected preference. In the French edition of his *General Theory,* written in early 1939, Keynes labeled this French writer as "the real French equivalent of Adam Smith, the greatest of your economists, head and shoulders above the physiocrats in penetration, clearheadedness and good sense (which are the qualities an economist should have)" (1973: xxxiv). No, it was not Say or Bastiat.

It was Montesquieu!

This, too, seems an odd choice, for several reasons. Few historians would regard Montesquieu (1689–1755) as a pure economist, since he wrote primarily as a political philosopher, historian, and sociologist. Only 15 percent of his book, *The Spirit of the Laws* (1748), is devoted to economic issues. Moreover, unlike Keynes, Montesquieu was a "passionate supporter of the doctrine of laissez faire" (Devletoglou 1963: 42). He detested authoritarian regimes and rejected all forms of central planning, which, he said, robbed society of its natural dynamics. He defended free trade as a civilizing, educating, and cooperative force between nations. Like Adam Smith, he recognized

(continued)

that goods and services rather than precious metals represented the real wealth of a nation. He opposed excessive monetary inflation as ruinous, using Spain as an example. Before the Physiocrats popularized the erroneous doctrine that agriculture was the sole source of wealth, Montesquieu taught that industry and commerce were equally significant as fountains of prosperity. Entrepreneurship and frugality were essential ingredients to economic growth. And, unlike Malthus, Montesquieu regarded a large, growing population as highly desirable.

Thus Keynes was right to honor Montesquieu, but he did not do it for these reasons. Keynes was attracted to Montesquieu's embryonic liquidity-preference theory of interest (Montesquieu 1989: 420–21 [Part 4, Book 22, chapter 19]), his opposition to hoarding and his advocacy of a high level of money expenditure to maintain and promote economic welfare (Devletoglou 1963: 37).

Oddly enough, there are no references to the French philosopher in Keynes's books, other than in the French introduction to *The General Theory,* and none of Keynes's closest friends recalled his mentioning Montesquieu as the greatest French economist (Devletoglou 1963: 44).

Illustration 2.1
Charles Louis de Montesquieu
(1689–1755)
Courtesy of Hulton-Getty Archives.

J.-B. SAY: BORN AT THE RIGHT TIME

The most important character in this French drama is an economist born nine years before *The Wealth of Nations* was printed. In his sixty-five years, **Jean-Baptiste Say (1767–1832)** lived as "an economist in troubled times," to quote the title of a recent biography (Palmer 1997). He witnessed the American and French revolutions, bore the brunt of Napoleon's political power, and lived through the beginning of the industrial revolution. He invented the term "entrepreneur," now a household word of modern economics and business, and became an entrepreneur himself (a cotton manufacturer). He was appointed the first professor of political economy in France, wrote a popular textbook, and today is best known for his "law of markets," the classical macroeconomic theory that focuses on production, trade, and saving as the keys to economic growth and higher consumption.

J.-B. Say was born in Lyon, France. He came from an old Protestant family in southern France, which moved to Geneva and finally to Paris. At the age of fifteen, during the height of the French Revolution, he, like many French citizens, was greatly influenced by the *Autobiography* of

Benjamin Franklin, and he wrote in praise of Franklin as a model citizen and applauded his principles of thrift, education, and moral living.

"THE FRENCH ADAM SMITH"

Illustration 2.2
Jean-Baptiste Say (1767–1832)
"Shorter, clearer and sounder"
than the *Wealth of Nations*.
Courtesy of British Library of
Political and Economic Science.

Jean-Baptiste also spent two years in London, where he learned English and read *The Wealth of Nations*. It was a propitious opportunity which affected Say's entire career. He would become known as "the French Adam Smith."

Say's influence was felt at the age of thirty-two when in 1799 he became a member of Napoleon's Tribunat. However, Napoleon was a power-hungry dictator who opposed Say's laissez-faire policies and ousted Say from the Tribunat in 1806 following the publication of Say's *Treatise on Political Economy*. In fact, Napoleon banned Say's textbook for criticizing his policies.

The first edition of *A Treatise on Political Economy, or the Production, Distribution, and Consumption of Wealth* was published in 1803 and, despite Napoleon's ban, went through four editions in Say's lifetime.

Thomas Jefferson was so impressed with Say that he had the first English edition translated in 1821, telling his friends that Say's book was "shorter, clearer and sounder" than *The Wealth of Nations*. Jefferson wanted to bring him to the University of Virginia, but Say declined, preferring to live in Paris. Say's English edition was the most popular textbook in the United States until it was superseded by John Stuart Mill's textbook following the Civil War.

In 1815, after the fall of Napoleon, J.-B. Say became France's first professor of industrial economics at the Conservatoire des Arts et Metiers, and in 1830 was appointed chair of political economy at the College de France in Paris. He corresponded regularly with Thomas Malthus and David Ricardo, whom he regarded as close friends, though he disagreed with them on many issues. He died in 1832 in France at the age of sixty-five, only two short years after being appointed a professor, thus ending an illustrious career.

SAY MAKES SEVERAL IMPORTANT CONTRIBUTIONS

J.-B. Say was a major supporter of Adam Smith's self-directing economic system of competition, natural liberty, and limited government. He was an uncompromising defender of laissez-faire capitalism.

In addition, his analysis went further than Smith's and Ricardo's by breaking new ground in classical economics in four areas.

These four contributions are: first, a firm belief in testing theories with facts and observations; second, a subjective utility theory rather than a labor theory of value; third, an appreciation of the vital role of the entrepreneur; and fourth, Say's law of markets, which forms the foundation of the classical macro model of business fluctuations and economic growth.

Let's examine each one of these contributions.

LOOK WHO'S BURIED NEXT TO JIM MORRISON

Thousands of adoring American fans flock to Paris each year to pay homage to Jim Morrison, leader of the rock-and-roll band the Doors in the 1970s. Morrison died of a drug overdose in Paris and was unceremoniously buried at the Père Lachaise Cemetery.

Morrison is one of many famous people buried in this romantic graveyard, including many foreigners: playwright Oscar Wilde, composer Frédéric Chopin, singer Maria Callas, dancer Isadora Duncan, writer Honoré de Balzac, and feminist Gertrude Stein. Many of the grave markers in this vast cemetery full of shady trees, flowers, and sculptures are unique creations. Especially noteworthy is the sculptured body of murdered journalist Victor Noir, dressed in a tuxedo. The superstition among local women is that if they rub a certain part of his statue they will conceive a child.

RESURRECTING SAY

When I visited the Père Lachaise Cemetery with my son Tim in 1999, we were surprised that the great French economist Jean-Baptiste Say was not officially listed among the notables. After obtaining directions to the location of his gravesite, we spent half an hour searching. When we finally located his large tomb, we saw that it was painfully neglected. As I cut away the heavy moss covering his name, I felt I was resurrecting his notable contribution to economics, Say's law of markets. (See Photograph 2.1.)

Photograph 2.1
J.-B. Say Resurrected!

SAY CRITICIZES ABSTRACT THEORIZING

J.-B. Say was deeply concerned about economists engaging in ivory-tower theorizing far beyond the real economy. Model building is not necessarily wrong, Say reasoned, and in fact, he favored a model not unlike geometry, starting with "the rigorous deductions of undeniable general facts . . . a few fundamental principles, and of a great number of corollaries or conclusions, drawn from these principles" (Say 1971 [1880]: xx, xxvi). But this model, he insisted, must always be tested by observation lest it become unrealistic and misleading. According to Say, all theories and models need to be constantly tested against contemporary facts and observations.

He was especially worried about the influence of his friend David Ricardo—one of the fountainheads of classical economics—because of the incessant abstract reasoning and ethereal model building in his book *On the Principles of Political Economy and Taxation* (1817). Without mentioning him by name, Say accused Ricardo of creating a model full of "gratuitous assertions" and "systems [having] been formed before facts have been established" (page xvii). As a result, economics was being drawn down a dangerous road, including a labor theory of value. (This abstract model-building methodology is often called the "Ricardian vice"—see chapter 4.)

Say proclaimed, "Nothing can be more idle than the opposition of theory to practice!" Writing to Robert Malthus, he stated, "It is better to stick to facts and their consequences than to syllogisms." He lauded Adam Smith for assembling "the soundest principles of political economy, supported by luminous illustrations," but added that economists like Ricardo who don't support their theories with facts are "but idle dreamers, whose theories, at best only gratifying literary curiosity, were wholly inapplicable in practice" (pages xxi, xxxv).

THE FLAW IN MATHEMATICAL ECONOMICS

By the same token, Say had misgivings about mathematical and statistical economics. He expressed fear of "our always being misled in political economy, whenever we have subjected its phenomena to mathematical calculation" (Sowell 1987: 249).

Say demonstrated the subjective nature of supply and demand, and how price and elasticity of demand can never be precisely predicted. In other words, economics is a qualitative, not a quantitative, science, and therefore not subject to "mathematical calculation." He used the example of next year's price of French wine, where supply and demand inevitably varies from year to year. New supplies are dependent on the "vicissitudes of the wealth," its quality, the quantity of remaining supplies, the capital markets, interest rates, the export market, and "the stability of the laws and the government." On the demand side, the quantity demanded depends on the changing "tastes and means of the consumers," general economic conditions, substitute drinks, and so on. In short, the prices of next year's wines can "never [be] calculated with exactness" (Say 1971: xxvi–xxvii).

He was also wary of blind empiricism and the gathering of statistical facts without relating them to theory: "But a knowledge of facts, without a knowledge of their mutual relations, without being able to show why one is the cause, and the other a consequence, is really no better than the crude information of an office-clerk" (Say 1971: xxi).

SAY INTRODUCES AN ALTERNATIVE THEORY OF VALUE

Say broke with his friend David Ricardo, leader of the British classical school, on another major issue—the labor theory of value. Ricardo, under the influence of Adam Smith, searched for an invariable standard of value and found it in labor. But Say wrote in his translated copy of Ricardo's *Principles,* "an invariable measure of value is pure chimera" (Rothbard 1995: 19).

Instead, Say took a more positive approach by favoring a subjective utility theory of value. Utility, or the way consumers value a good or service, determines its production. Producers create value or utility by transforming inputs into outputs, sold at prices sufficient to cover costs.

Unfortunately, the French economist did not discover the marginal theory of utility, but he did come close by recognizing that utility, not cost, determined the ultimate price or value of a good or service.

THE ROLE OF THE ENTREPRENEUR

Say invented the term *entrepreneur.* Literally, it means "undertaker," but given the ambivalence of the word, entrepreneur was translated "adventurer." It suggests the image of a commercial adventurer or a venture capitalist, one who combines the inputs of capital, knowledge, and labor to launch and manage a business for profit. Adam Smith was a teacher and never ran a business. Not having any experience as an entrepreneur, Smith underplayed this vital subject in his *Wealth of Nations.* But J.-B. Say was an entrepreneur, a cotton manufacturer, and included the concept as an essential part of his economic model.

In chapter 7 of book II, "on distribution," Say introduced the entrepreneur, the "master-agent" or "adventurer," as an economic agent separate from the landlord, worker, and even capitalist. "Not that he [the entrepreneur] must be already rich; for he may work upon borrowed capital." To succeed, the entrepreneur must have "judgment, perseverance, and a knowledge of the world," Say noted. "He is called upon to estimate, with tolerable accuracy, the importance of the specific product, the probable amount of the demand, and the means of production: at one time he must employ a great number of hands; at another, buy or order the raw material, collect laborers, find consumers, and give at all times a rigid attention to order and the economy; in a word, he must possess the art of superintendence and administration." He must be willing to take on "a degree of risk" and there is always a "chance of failure," but when successful, "this class of producers . . . accumulates the largest fortunes" (Say 1971: 329–32).

Say noted that the entrepreneur "shifts economic resources out of an area of lower and into an area of higher productivity and greater yield" (Drucker 1985: 21). He is a risk-taking profit maximizer who looks for above-average opportunities.

OH, SAY, CAN YOU SEE?
ENTREPRENEURSHIP MAKES A COMEBACK IN THE TEXTBOOKS

Only in recent textbooks has Say's "entrepreneur" come back into vogue. For years, it was almost completely lost in modern economics textbooks, especially under the omnipresent "perfect competition" model, which was adopted almost universally by the economics profession in the twentieth century (especially under the influence of the general equilibrium model of French economist Léon Walras).

Under the perfect competition model of general equilibrium, there are no differentiated products and no variation in price. All products are generic. There are so many buyers and sellers that no one can influence price.

Obviously, under such a general equilibrium model, there is little need for entrepreneurs to create new products or to advertise. Innovation, vision, creativity, and risk taking are unnecessary. According to textbook authors Edwin Dolan and David Lindsey, "There is no way to capture entrepreneurial behavior precisely in terms of equations or graphs, because the notion of entrepreneurship is itself one of change, uncertainty, and innovation" (1988: 603). Dolan was one of the first textbook writers to attempt to include the role of the entrepreneur in economic analysis.

As economic historian Mark Blaug writes, "it is a scandal that nowadays students of economics spend years in the study before hearing the term entrepreneur" (1986: 229).

Blaug's *Economic History* was published in 1986, and a great deal has changed since then in the textbooks. Today entrepreneurship is regularly listed as one of the factors of production, in addition to land, labor, and capital. It is the responsibility of the entrepreneur to combine the right amounts of land, labor, and capital to create a product or service that customers can use. In their popular textbook, William Baumol and Alan Blinder devote an entire chapter to "Innovation and Growth: The Free-Market's Greatest Triumph," illustrating the positive impact of cost-cutting technological breakthroughs, research and development, and entrepreneurship with numerous charts and theoretical graphs (2008, chap. 16).

THE AUSTRIAN SCHOOL TO THE RESCUE

It has been principally through the Austrian School that Say's entrepreneur has been rescued and is now prominently displayed in the textbooks. Joseph Schumpeter,

(continued)

Austrian-born Harvard professor, is famous for focusing on the entrepreneur as the central figure in advancing the wealth of nations and creating dynamic disequilibrium in the global economy. Through the process of "creative destruction," entrepreneurs are constantly changing the economic landscape for the better. Schumpeter rejects the "imaginary golden age of perfect competition," saying that it "is not only impossible but inferior, and has no title to being set up as a model of ideal efficiency" (Schumpeter 1950: 106). Leaving out the entrepreneur from the competitive process is like leaving out the Danish prince from Shakespeare's *Hamlet* (1950: 86).

Israel Kirzner, a London-born Austrian economist at New York University (now retired), has devoted most of his career to studying entrepreneurship and its essential role in the economy. Like Schumpeter, Kirzner criticizes modern theory of the firm, saying that "the model of perfect competition fails to help us understand the market process" (Kirzner 1973: 8). While Schumpeter emphasizes how entrepreneurs move away from equilibrium, Kirzner focuses on the "discovery process" by which entrepreneurs discover error and new profitable opportunities, and thus move the market toward equilibrium (1973: 72–75).

Finally, Peter F. Drucker, the Austrian-born management guru, wrote extensively on entrepreneurship in the business world. Drucker extended Schumpeter's view of the entrepreneur as a disrupter in the firm and the economy, one who tries new products and new processes, makes mistakes, and learns from those mistakes. Like Say, Drucker sees the entrepreneur as an investor in sectors of the economy showing above-average potential. The entrepreneur is above all an "opportunity seeker" (Drucker 1985).

Yet, despite all the talk about entrepreneurship, most textbooks still use the general equilibrium models of the economy, which view innovative firms that seek to monopolize the markets as inefficient.

SAY'S BREAKTHROUGH: THE LAW OF MARKETS

In addition to introducing entrepreneurship as the critical factor of production, Say is most famous for developing the classical model of macroeconomics, known as Say's law of markets.

Say's law is often quoted as "Supply creates its own demand," a phrase that many students of economics—steeped in Keynesian thinking—find paradoxical and even counterintuitive. "Isn't it the other way around?" they ask. "Doesn't demand create supply?"

Actually, it was John Maynard Keynes, not Say, who defined Say's law as "Supply creates its own demand" in *The General Theory* (1973: 18). Today most economists agree that Keynes gravely distorted the true meaning and deep implications of Say's law. As Australian economist Steven Kates, who has devoted an entire book to the subject, declared, "Keynes . . . misunderstood and misrepresented Say's Law. . . . This is Keynes's most enduring legacy and it is a legacy which has disfigured economic theory to this day" (Kates 1998: 1). (See box in chapter 13, page 348, "What Does Keynes Say About Say?")

SAY EXPOSES AN ERROR AND DISCOVERS A NEW LAW

Say's law is much more profound than the misleading inscription "Supply creates its own demand."

To understand the broad meaning of Say's law, one must first examine the origin of the principle. One of the major issues in the eighteenth century (as discussed in chapter 1) was the mercantilist doctrine that money, especially the discovery of gold and silver and a favorable balance of trade, created wealth and economic growth. During periodic economic crises and depressions, people constantly complained about the scarcity of money. The solution to their economic troubles seemed simple enough—find more money and spend it, and that would lead to recovery.

In chapter 15 of his textbook, Say attacked this scarcity-of-money doctrine by pointing out that it is not money that creates demand but the production of goods and services. Money is only a mechanism of exchange, and the real cause of economic depression isn't a shortage of money, but the lack of sales by farmers, manufacturers, and other producers of goods and services. As Say stated, "Sales cannot be said to be dull because money is scarce, but because other products are so. . . . To use a more hackneyed phrase, people have bought less, because they have made less profit" (Say 1971: 134). In an earlier edition, Say declared, "It is not the abundance of money but the abundance of other products in general that facilitates sales. . . . Money performs no more than the role of a conduit in this double exchange. When the exchanges have been completed, it will be found that one has paid for products with products" (Kates 1998: 23).

Say denied that there is any general "overproduction" or "glut" in an economic downturn, but claimed that production is merely "misdirected." Too much of some products are produced for which there is insufficient demand. Once prices and costs readjust themselves to the new demand structure, the economy will start growing again. Consumers will not start spending again, according to Say, until laborers go back to work and producers begin making a profit.

This analysis led Say to make a remarkable discovery: *Production is the cause of consumption, or in other words, increased output leads to higher consumer spending.* In the words of Say, "a product is no sooner created, than it, from that instant, affords a market for other products to the full extent of its own value" (Say 1971: 134). When a seller produces and sells a product, the seller instantly becomes a buyer who has spendable income. To buy, one must first sell.

In short, Say's law is this: Supply of X creates demand for Y. Say illustrated his law with the case of a good harvest by a farmer: "The greater the crop, the larger are the purchases of the growers. A bad harvest, on the contrary, hurts the sale of commodities at large" (1971: 135). Another example: When a profitable business moves into the area, it creates jobs and demand for goods and services. The increased consumption is ulti-mately derived from the new supply—a new business moving into the area.

Say has a point. According to business-cycle statistics, when a downturn starts, production is the first to decline, ahead of consumption. And, when the economy begins to recover, it's because production starts up, followed by consumption. Economic growth begins with an increase in produc-tivity, an increase in new products and new markets. Hence, production spending is always ahead of consumption spending and is therefore a leading indicator.

SAY EXTENDS HIS ARGUMENT TO ECONOMIC GROWTH

Say extended his argument to economic growth. Encouraging production of new and better products rather than simply increasing consumption is the key to economic performance.

We can see why this is the case on an individual basis. The key to a higher standard of living is first to increase your income (i.e., your pro-ductivity) by getting a raise, changing jobs, going back to school, or starting a money-making business. It would be foolish for you to go out and spend more money on a bigger house or new automobile, by either spending your savings or going into debt, as a way to achieve a higher stan-dard of living, before you increase your income. You may be able to live the Champagne life for a while, but eventually you will have to pay the piper—or the credit card bill.

According to Say, the same principle applies on a national basis. The creation of new and better products opens up new markets and increases consumption. Hence, "the encouragement of mere consumption is no ben-efit to commerce; for the difficulty lies in supplying the means, not in stimulating the desire of consumption; and we have seen that production alone, furnishes those means." Then Say added, "Thus, it is the aim of good government to stimulate production, of bad government to encourage consumption" (1971: 139).

SAVING IS A BLESSING, NOT A CURSE

A corollary of Say's law is that savings is beneficial to economic growth. He denied that "frugality" might lead to a decline in expenditures and output. Since consumption is, by its very definition, the using up of utility, saving is a better form of spending because it is used in the production of capital goods in fur-therance of production. No doubt Say was influenced by his reading of Benjamin Franklin's defense of thrift as a virtue, in adages such as "A penny saved is a penny earned" and "Money begets money."

An expanding economy is always producing more wealth than it is con-suming. Production therefore exceeds consumption. The rest is saving, which goes toward the production of investment goods. Remember, there are two kinds of production—production of consumer goods (consumption) and production of investment goods (saving).

SAY'S LAW SUMMARIZED

Kates summarizes the conclusions of Say's law of markets (1998: 29):

1. A country cannot have too much capital.

2. Investment is the basis for economic growth.

3. Consumption not only provides no stimulus to wealth creation but is actually contrary to it.

4. Demand is constituted by production.

5. Demand deficiency (i.e., over-production) is never the cause of economic disturbance. Economic disturbance arises only if goods are not produced in the correct proportions to each other.

WHERE DID TOCQUEVILLE LEARN HIS ECONOMICS?

Men in democratic times always need to be free in order easily to provide themselves with the physical pleasures for which they ever hanker.
—Alexis de Tocqueville (1988 [1848]: 539)

Alexis de Tocqueville (1805–59), the eminent French statesman and author of the masterpiece *Democracy in America,* wrote primarily about the social and political aspects of American society. His aim was to discuss statecraft more than economics. Although he did not focus much of his research on the industrialization and the building of cities in the United States, he made several significant observations about economic conditions.

Illustration 2.3
Alexis de Tocqueville (1805–59)
Courtesy of Brown Brothers.

SUPPORTER OF DEMOCRATIC CAPITALISM

Based on his travels in the United States in the 1830s, Tocqueville recognized that America represented a "great democratic revolution," one that has become the "most prosperous but also the most stable of all the peoples in the world" (Tocqueville 1988 [1848]: xiv). He predicted that the United States would "become one of the greatest nations in the world" (1988: 383). According to the French observer, America was a nation that embodied the Smithian model of natural liberty more than any other, where Americans enjoyed "true liberty," "sovereignty," an

(continued)

"equality of conditions," and "guaranteed private property" (1988: xiv). By 1848, a year of revolution throughout Europe, Tocqueville observed, "America has not even suffered from riots." Americans were educated, patriotic, religious, and law-abiding. In order to preserve stable democracy, Tocqueville favored decentralization of government power and widespread individual ownership of small parcels of land. Tocqueville favored individualism, not the state or a utopian community.

Tocqueville observed that Americans were always trying to advance their financial condition. Each man was entrepreneurial who had "a passion for prosperity . . . [who was] a man of burning desires, enterprising, adventurous, and, above all, an innovator" (1988: 404, 538). As a result, "commoners were growing rich by trade" (1988: 10). "In America," noted Tocqueville, "I never met a citizen too poor to cast a glance of hope and envy toward the pleasures of the rich" (1988: 531).

Tocqueville lauded the "decent materialism" of Americans. "But love of physical pleasures never leads democratic peoples to such excesses." Most Americans were not seeking to build vast palaces. "It is more a question of adding a few acres to one's fields, planting an orchard, enlarging a house, making life easier and more comfortable" (1988: 533).

SMITHIAN THEMES IN *DEMOCRACY IN AMERICA*

Tocqueville wrote that individual "enlightened self-love . . . coincides with the general interest" in America, clearly a Smithian theme (1988: 525–26).

Like Smith, Tocqueville recognized a "close link . . . between . . . freedom and industry. . . . Men in democratic times always need to be free in order easily to provide themselves with the physical pleasures for which they ever hanker" (1988: 539). In the United States, citizens were never too busy to neglect their civic duties.

Similarly, Tocqueville favored religious and moral persuasion while opposing a state religion. "In the United States," he wrote, "when the seventh day comes, trade and industry seem suspended throughout the nation. All noise stops" (1988: 542).

PRE-MARXIST CRITIQUE?

However, Tocqueville warned that too much mindless assembly work can "degrade" workers and make them "brutes." It could lead to greater inequality between worker and master and create a "commercial aristocracy." Thus "at the same time that industrial science constantly lowers the standing of the working class, it raises that of the masters" (1988: 555–56). Tocqueville specifically referred to Adam Smith's classic example of "making heads for pins" in his criticism of the effect of the division of labor.

Even Tocqueville's concept of alienation imitates the chapter in *The Wealth of Nations* entitled "Education of Youth." Smith warned that the "man whose whole life is spent in performing a few simple operations . . . generally becomes stupid and ignorant" (Smith 1965 [1776]: 734). Both Smith and Tocqueville endorsed moral and intellectual education as a solution.

(continued)

SAY'S INFLUENCE

Where did Tocqueville learn his economics? We do not know whether he read *The Wealth of Nations,* but he did study Say's *Treatise on Political Economy.* In fact, Alexis de Tocqueville and his traveling companion Gustave de Beaumont took a copy on their trip to the United States in 1831 and studied it daily on the ship. Beaumont wrote in his diary while on their trip to America, "Now with all our energies we are doing political economy with the work of J.-B. Say. This study has an extreme attraction" (Pierson 1938: 46).

FRÉDÉRIC BASTIAT, LAISSEZ-FAIRE ADVOCATE

Frederic Bastiat [was] the most brilliant
economic journalist who ever lived.
—Joseph Schumpeter (1954: 500)

Illustration 2.4
Frédéric Bastiat (1801–50)
"Unrivaled in exposing fallacies."
Courtesy of the Foundation for
Economic Education.

Charles Darwin had his bulldog, Thomas Huxley, and J.-B. Say had his patron, **Frédéric Bastiat (1801–50)**. Bastiat was an indefatigable advocate of free trade and laissez-faire policies, a passionate opponent of socialism, and an unrelenting debater and statesman. He has been compared to Voltaire and Franklin in his integrity and purity, and in the elegance of his message.

Using entertaining fables, the French essayist attacked statism of all kinds— socialism, communism, utopianism, and mercantilism. His two most famous essays, "Petition of the Candlemakers" and "The Broken Window," are still reprinted and referred to today (Bastiat 1995: 1–50; Roche 1971: 51–53).

The New Palgrave considers Bastiat "unrivaled in exposing fallacies" (Hébert 1987: 205).

A FRAIL ORPHAN CHALLENGES THE WORLD

Yet Frédéric Bastiat's personal life was tragic. He lived a life of poor health, somehow managing to survive for forty-nine years. He suffered from weak lungs throughout his life. Born in 1801 in Bayonne, the south of France, Frédéric was the son of a landowner and merchant in the

Spanish trade. His mother died when he was seven, his father when he was nine. He was raised by his aunt, and worked for an uncle in Bayonne at age seventeen. Later he tried his hand at farming, but was not successful in that occupation, either. Finally, he turned to something he could love—books and ideas. The country scholar, who married in the late 1820s, was a strong believer in the Catholic faith.

Like Adam Smith, Bastiat grew up in a port city, which had a major effect on his beliefs. Hard times followed the Napoleonic wars, and Bastiat witnessed firsthand the effect of government controls and tariffs in Bayonne. Under the influence of Say and Smith, the evil of tariffs became a main focal point for Bastiat. Despite the persuasive writings of these free-market economists, the French government continued to raise import duties throughout the first half of the nineteenth century. Bastiat supported the Revolution of 1830 against Charles X and the abuses of the Bourbons. Somewhat quixotically, the eccentric philosopher led a group of 600 youths to storm a royalist citadel, but was greeted without protest and invited in for a feast.

BASTIAT FIGHTS AGAINST THE TIDE

The fight for economic and political freedom was still an uphill battle for Bastiat and the followers of Say. To help Say's legacy, Bastiat started writing on free trade. In 1846, he moved to Paris and began a nationwide free-trade association, imitating English trade reformists. He published *Le libre échange,* a free-trade journal.

That same year he wrote his most famous fable, "The Petition of the Candlemakers," a satire of protectionists. (See the box on page 63.)

THE REVOLUTION OF 1848 AND THE SECOND FRENCH REPUBLIC

A major turning point came in 1848, when peasants in France rebelled against the French monarchy, raised the red flag in defiance, and fought bloody battles against the National Guardsmen. The rally cry was socialism, but Bastiat, still going against the grain, complained, "We have tried so many things; when shall we try the simplest of all: freedom?" (Roche 1971: 79).

BASTIAT SITS ON THE LEFT IN THE NATIONAL ASSEMBLY

The result of the Revolution of 1848 was the second French republic and democratic general elections. Bastiat was elected to the National Assembly and became vice president of the assembly's finance committee. He was most remembered as a stooped, thin figure sitting on the left, where the liberals and radicals sat, opposite the conservatives on the right (hence, the origin of right and left in politics). While he vehemently opposed the

THE PETITION OF THE CANDLEMAKERS

Frédéric Bastiat

The following satire appeared in Le libre échange, *the free-trade newspaper published in Paris by Bastiat starting in 1846. "The Petition of the Candlemakers" was his most famous example—it is genuinely funny to read. Using this ridiculous case, Bastiat never tired of attacking the notion that the French could enrich themselves by retarding production through tariffs and other trade restrictions* (Roche 1971: 51–53).

From the Manufacturers of Candles, Tapers, Lanterns, Candlesticks, Street Lamps, Snuffers, and Extinguishers, and from the Producers of Tallow, Oil, Resin, Alcohol, and Generally of Everything Connected with Lighting.

To the Honorable Members of the Chamber of Deputies.

Gentlemen:

We are suffering from the ruinous competition of a foreign rival who apparently works under conditions so far superior to our own for the production of light that he is flooding the domestic market with it at an incredibly low price; for the moment he appears, our sales cease, all the consumers turn to him, and a branch of French industry whose ramifications are innumerable is all at once reduced to complete stagnation. This rival . . . is none other than the sun. . . .

We ask you to be so good as to pass a law requiring the closing of all windows, dormers, skylights, inside and outside shutters, curtains, casements, bull's-eyes, deadlights, and blinds—in short, all openings, holes, chinks, and fissures. . . .

Be good enough, honorable deputies, to take our request seriously, and do not reject it without at least hearing the reasons that we have to advance in its support.

First, if you shut off as much as possible all access to natural light, and thereby create a need for artificial light, what industry in France will not ultimately be encouraged?

If France consumes more tallow, there will have to be more cattle and sheep, and, consequently, we shall see an increase in cleared fields, meat, wool, leather, and especially manure, the basis of all agricultural wealth.

If France consumes more oil, we shall see an expansion in the cultivation of the poppy, the olive and rapeseed. These rich yet soil-exhausting plants will come at just the right time to enable us to put to profitable use the increased fertility that the breeding of cattle will impart to the land. . . .

It needs but little reflection, gentlemen, to be convinced that there is perhaps not one Frenchman, from the wealthy stockholder of the Anzin Company to the humblest vendor of matches, whose condition would not be improved by the success of our petition.

socialists' and communists' policies, he felt more comfortable on the left side of the aisle, arguing against jailing socialists, outlawing peaceful trade unionism, or declarations of martial law.

Bastiat died in 1850, at the age of forty-nine, of tuberculosis, but not until he published two major works, *Economic Harmonies* and *The Law*.

Bastiat Update: *Economics in One Lesson*

One of Bastiat's famous parables is "The Broken Window," found in a pamphlet, "What Is Seen and What Is Not Seen," written in 1850, the last year of his life. (He lost the manuscript during a move and had to rewrite it, finishing it only months before he died.) It tells the story of Jacques Bonhomme, a solid citizen of the community whose incorrigible son breaks a pane of glass. At first the onlookers feel sympathy for Jacques, who now has to spend six francs to replace the glass window.

But then they start reasoning that perhaps the broken window is good for business. After all, "what would become of the glaziers if no one ever broke a window?" Indeed, the public begins to wonder whether breaking windows "helps to circulate money, [and] results in encouraging industry in general" (Bastiat 1995: 2).

Bastiat noted, "That is what is seen." The destruction encourages new spending by the glass business.

But then Bastiat asked, "What is not seen?" In this third level of analysis, Bastiat pointed out that Jacques Bonhomme no longer has six francs to spend on his worn-out shoes or another book for his library.

Bastiat concluded: "Let us next consider industry *in general*. The window having been broken, the glass industry gets six francs' worth of encouragement; *that is what is seen*. If the window had not been broken, the shoe industry (or some other) would have received six francs' worth of encouragement; *that is what is not seen*."

The moral of the story: "Destruction is not profitable" (Bastiat 1995: 2–3).

In general, Bastiat made the following generalization about the role of economists in exposing fallacies: "There is only one difference between a bad economist and a good one: the bad economist confines himself to the visible effect; the good economist takes into account both the effect that can be seen and those effects that *must be foreseen*" (Bastiat 1995: 1; italics in original).

Henry Hazlitt: A Modern-Day Bastiat

Henry Hazlitt (1894–1993) was a modern-day, twentieth-century follower of Frédéric Bastiat who wrote a classic book based on the parable of the broken window, *Economics in One Lesson*. Hazlitt, like Bastiat, was an unrelenting journalist who wrote for a broad audience, attacking collectivism in all its forms. He penned editorials for *The Wall Street Journal, The New York Times,* and *The Nation;* wrote a *Newsweek* column for two decades; and succeeded H.L. Mencken as editor of *The American Mercury.* Mencken, a literary critic who seldom praised anyone, called Hazlitt "one of the few economists who could really write" (Hazlitt 1979: cover).

(continued)

Though he could write, his books and columns were not always well received, especially by the economics profession. After he published *The Failure of the "New Economics,"* a scathing point-by-point refutation of John Maynard Keynes's *General Theory,* the bad reviews poured in. Apparently, journalists without degrees in economics were not welcomed into the club.

Of the eighteen books he authored, only one remains a best-seller. First published in 1946, *Economics in One Lesson* has sold nearly a million copies and been translated into eight languages.

Hazlitt began his book by retelling Bastiat's story of the broken window. He reduced the lesson of the broken window to a single lesson: "The art of economics consists in looking not merely at the immediate but at the longer effects of any act or policy; it consists in tracing the consequences of that policy not merely for one group but for all groups" (Hazlitt 1979 [1946]: 5). Hazlitt then skillfully applied the lesson to a wide variety of economic problems: rent controls, minimum wage laws, the alleged benefits of war, public works and deficit spending, monetary inflation, tariffs, and the assault on savings. When we read in the newspapers or hear on the television news that earthquakes are good for the economy, that imports impoverish us, or that deficit spending is the key to lasting prosperity, we are seeing the results of a society ignorant of Henry Hazlitt—and Frédéric Bastiat.

Hazlitt may be eschewed by the profession as a "non-economist," yet few economists can better his skill at attacking today's plethora of economic fallacies.

Photograph 2.2
Henry Hazlitt (1894–1993)
A Modern-Day Bastiat
"But he's not an economist!"
Courtesy of the Foundation for
Economic Education.

BASTIAT EXTENDS THE CASE FOR LIBERTY

Bastiat was more than an economic journalist. He was also a legal philosopher who wrote extensively on the social organization best suited for a free people and free market. His main work is *The Law*, a pamphlet published in June 1850 (1996). He was astonishingly prolific in the final year of his life, knowing that the end was near.

For Bastiat, the proper role of government is to defend the "God-given right" to life, liberty and property," and "to prevent injustice from reigning" (Bastiat 1996: 2). Mankind's freedom should be as broad as possible, the right "of every person to make full use of his faculties, so long as he does not harm other persons while doing so" (1996: 51). Freedom includes the liberty of conscience, education, labor, trade, and association (page 62).

If these rights are defended properly, there is no limit to a society's prosperity and happiness. "This is the principle of justice, peace, order, stability, harmony, and logic. . . . And if everyone enjoyed the unrestricted use of his faculties and the free disposition of the fruits of his labor, social progress would be ceaseless, uninterrupted, and unfailing" (pages 20, 5). Moreover, "every person will attain his real worth and the true dignity of his being," declared Bastiat (page 73). He asked, "Which countries contain the most peaceful, the most moral, and the happiest people?" The ones that least interfere with citizens' private affairs, that minimize taxes, tariffs and regulations, and maximize freedom to speak, travel, and assemble (page 74).

BASTIAT WARNS OF THE DANGER OF LEGAL PLUNDER

Unfortunately, Bastiat declared, the law has been perverted by two causes, "stupid greed" and "false philanthropy." Greed causes the public to plunder the fruits of others: "the law takes property from one person and gives it to another; the law takes the wealth of all and gives it to a few" (page 13). In short, the law violates property instead of protecting it. Bastiat specifically referred to slavery and tariffs in the United States as examples of legal plunder. "The law has come to be an instrument of injustice" (page 15).

Legal plunder, the "seductive lure of socialism," comes in many forms, according to Bastiat: "Tariffs, protection, benefits, subsidies, encouragements, progressive taxation, public schools, guaranteed jobs, guaranteed profits, minimum wages, a right to relief, a right to the tools of labor, free credit, and so on" (page 18).

Bastiat also warned against "false philanthropy," that is, charitable causes that are not voluntary. He opposed all forms of forced welfare, education, or religion. "We repudiate the forms of association that are forced upon us, not free association." Bastiat made a distinction between "government," a forced system, and "society," a voluntary network. In polemical style, Bastiat responded to his critics: "We disapprove of state education. Then the socialists say that we are opposed to any education. We object to a state religion. Then the socialists say that we want no religion at all. We object to a state-enforced equality. Then they say that we are against equality. . . . It is as if the socialists were to accuse us of not wanting persons to eat because we do not want the state to raise grain" (page 29).

Bastiat objected to the ever-growing arrogance of social "do-gooders" to make everyone conform to myriad rules and regulation, undermining individual liberty. Worried that citizens will inevitably degrade themselves if left free, "the legislators must make plans for the people in order to save them from themselves" (page 63). To overzealous legislators who want to regiment all citizens, Bastiat wrote: "Please remember sometimes that this clay, this sand, and this manure which you so arbitrarily dispose of, are men! They are your equals! They are intelligent and free human beings like yourselves! As you have, they too have received from God the faculty to observe, to plan ahead, to think, and to judge for themselves!" (page 48).

Bastiat ended his pamphlet with a call for freedom: "May they reject all systems, and try liberty; for liberty is an acknowledgement of faith in God and His works" (page 76).

ECONOMICS REACHES A PINNACLE, THEN HEADS DOWNHILL

Adam Smith's vision was never in more capable hands than those of the French devotees Turgot, Condillac, Condorcet, Say, Bastiat, and Tocqueville—and even Montesquieu before Smith. They carried the doctrine of the invisible hand and the natural harmony of the market system to its zenith. But as we shall see in the next few chapters, the story of economics was about to shift unexpectedly from the upbeat world of Adam Smith and plunge down a dark road from which it would not recover for another generation. Remarkably, the falling away from Smith's masterpiece began with the writings of two of his own disciples in his own country.

REFERENCES

Bastiat, Frédéric. 1995. *Selected Essays on Political Economy*. Introduction by F.A. Hayek. New York: Foundation for Economic Education.

———. 1996 [1850]. *The Law*. Translated by Dean Russell. New York: Foundation for Economic Education.

Baumol, William J., and Alan S. Blinder. 2008. *Economics: Principles and Policy*, 10th ed. New York: Southwestern.

Blaug, Mark. 1986. *Economic History and the History of Economics*. New York: New York University Press.

Devletoglou, Nicos E. 1963. *Montesquieu and the Wealth of Nations*. Athens: Center of Economic Research.

Dolan, Edwin G., and David E. Lindsey. 1988. *Economics*, 5th ed. Hinsdale, IL: Dryden.

Drucker, Peter F. 1985. *Innovation and Entrepreneurship*. New York: Harper and Row.

Hazlitt, Henry. 1979 [1946]. *Economics in One Lesson*, 2d ed. New York: Crown.

Hébert, R.F. 1987. "Claude Frédéric Bastiat." *The New Palgrave: A Dictionary of Economics*, vol. 1, 204–5. London: Macmillan.

Kates, Steven, 1998. *Say's Law and the Keynesian Revolution*. Cheltenham, UK: Edward Elgar.

Keynes, John Maynard. 1973 [1936]. *The General Theory of Employment, Interest and Money*. London: Macmillan.

Kirzner, Israel M. 1973. *Competition and Entrepreneurship*. Chicago: University of Chicago Press.

Montesquieu, Charles. 1989 [1748]. *The Spirit of the Laws*. Cambridge, UK: Cambridge University Press.

Palmer, R.R. 1997. *J.-B. Say, An Economist in Troubled Times*. Princeton, NJ: Princeton University Press.

Pierson, George Wilson. 1938. *Tocqueville in America*. Baltimore: Johns Hopkins University Press.

Ricardo, David. 1951 [1817]. *On the Principles of Political Economy and Taxation.* Cambridge, UK: Cambridge University Press.

Roche, George Charles III. 1971. *Frederic Bastiat: A Man Alone.* New York: Arlington House.

Rothbard, Murray N. 1995. *Classical Economics.* Hants, UK: Edward Elgar.

Samuelson, Paul A. 1962. "Economists and the History of Ideas." *American Economic Review* 52: 1 (March): 1–18.

Say, Jean-Baptiste. 1971 [1880]. *A Treatise on Political Economy.* Transl. from the 4th ed. by C.R. Prinsep. New York: Augustus M. Kelley.

Schumpeter, Joseph A. 1950 [1942]. *Capitalism, Socialism and Democracy,* 3d ed. New York: Harper and Row.

———. 1954. *History of Economic Analysis.* New York: Oxford University Press.

Skidelsky, Robert. 1992. *John Maynard Keynes: Economist as Saviour, 1920–1937.* London: Macmillan.

Smith, Adam. 1965 [1776]. *The Wealth of Nations.* New York: Modern Library.

Sowell, Thomas 1987. "J.-B. Say." *The New Palgrave: A Dictionary of Economics,* vol. 4, 249. London: Macmillan.

Tocqueville, Alexis de. 1988 [1848]. *Democracy in America,* 12th ed. Ed. J.P. Mayer, transl. by George Lawrence. New York: Harper Perennial.

3

THE IRREVERENT MALTHUS CHALLENGES THE NEW MODEL OF PROSPERITY

*The human race [is] emancipated from its shackles, released
from the empire of fate . . . advancing with a firm and sure step
along the path of truth, virtue and happiness!*

—Marquis de Condorcet (Kramnick 1995: 38)

*[T]he superior power of population cannot be checked without
producing misery or vice.*

—Robert Malthus (1985 [1798]: 79)

The publication of Adam Smith's *Wealth of Nations* in 1776 accompanied a new era of optimism in Europe. Social reformers were hopeful following an American Revolution that promised "life, liberty, and the pursuit of happiness," and a French Revolution that promised *liberté, egalité, fraternité*. William Wordsworth described the early idealism of the French Revolution when he wrote in *The Prelude* (1986 [1850] Book 11, lines 108–109):

> Bliss was it in that dawn to be alive,
> But to be young was very Heaven!

Ever since Sir Thomas More wrote *Utopia*, philosophers have dreamed of a world of universal happiness with no wars, no crimes, and no poverty. The genius of Adam Smith, and his French counterparts Montesquieu, Say,

---

♪ **Music selection for this chapter: Edvard Grieg, "In the Hall of the Mountain King" from *Peer Gynt***

Bastiat, and Tocqueville, was their development of an economic system of "natural liberty" that could bring about a peaceful, equitable, and universal opulence.

Now that model faced its most difficult challenge, ironically from two of Adam Smith's disciples, Thomas Robert Malthus and David Ricardo. Malthus in particular raised an issue that plagues us even to this day: Will an overcrowded planet and exhausted resources cut short Adam Smith's vision of democratic prosperity?

THE UTOPIAN VISION OF CONDORCET AND GODWIN

Malthus's theory of population developed in reaction to the ideas of two popular philosophers of the Enlightenment in the late eighteenth century: distinguished French philosopher **Marquis de Condorcet (1743–94)** and radical English minister **William Godwin (1756–1836)**.

The eighteenth-century Enlightenment was led by a group of scientists, philosophers, and writers who favored science over superstition, reason over faith, tolerance over fanaticism, individualism over collectivism, and materialism over austerity. These men of the Enlightenment—Locke, Voltaire, Montesquieu, Jefferson, Paine, Franklin—had an unbounded faith in economic progress and egalitarianism. Most of them agreed that population growth was beneficial and a major source of political and economic strength and innovation.

One of the optimists in *l'age des lumières* was Marie-Jean-Antoine-Nicholas de Caritate (1743–94), known as the Marquis de Condorcet. Condorcet was a mathematician and libertarian who had an amazing gift of prophecy. In a profound look into the next 200 years, Condorcet envisioned a future of greater productivity in manufacturing and agriculture, improvements in housing and food, a substantial increase in world population and life expectancy, rapid advancement in medical technology and a diminuation of disease and illnesses (Kramnick 1995: 26–38). He wrote this final work entitled "The Future Progress of the Human Mind," while in hiding under a sentence of death. He supported equal rights for all but ran afoul of the Jacobin extremists when he opposed the execution of Louis XVI. A few weeks after completing his book he was arrested and then mysteriously died in prison.

The younger William Godwin was equally optimistic, but rather eccentric. The English minister was an idealistic anarcho-communitarian who was inspired by the French Revolution. He debunked the Hobbesian vision of a "nasty, brutish and short" life, and sided with Adam Smith in envisioning a wonderful new world of opulence. But Godwin was far more of a social engineer than Smith. He firmly believed that if only law and property were abolished, crime would disappear, human relations would be perfectly harmonious, and man might even become immortal. Godwin voiced supreme optimism in his work, *Political Justice* (1793), about a new day characterized by health, longevity, justice, and the goodness of mankind. "There will be neither disease, anguish, melancholy nor resentment," he predicted, and government would be unnecessary since "every man will seek with ineffable ardour the good of all" (Downs 1983: 244). The anarchist Godwin also opposed marriage, calling it "evil, odious, selfish, and the worst of monopolies" (Kramnick 1995: 478–79), although he married the feminist Mary Wollstonecraft. He even envisioned a time when sleep, "one of the most conspicuous infirmities of the human frame," might be eliminated, and overpopulation would not be a problem because powerful sexual passions would be subdued or even extinguished.

Voltaire satirized this naive spirit of utopia in his novel *Candide,* whose character Dr. Pangloss blindly accepts all events, both good and bad, as a necessary and beneficial part of life. As Dr. Pangloss proclaims repeatedly, "all is for the best in this best of all possible worlds" (Voltaire 1947 [1758]: 20). Even Mary Shelley, daughter of Godwin and wife of the famous poet Percy Shelley, took a more somber view of human nature in her novel, *Frankenstein.* And, following the destructive extremes of the French Revolution, Edmund Burke (1963: 591) replaced the optimism of Wordsworth with:

. . . troublous storms that toss
The private state, and render life unsweet.

Malthus Challenges the Optimists

But the greatest challenge to this new era of philosophy came from an irreverent young parson, **Thomas Robert Malthus (1766–1834)**. In 1798, at the age of thirty-two, Malthus published an anonymous work, entitled *Essay on Population,* which in essence argued that earth's resources could not keep up with the demands of an ever-growing population. His brooding tract has forever changed the landscape of economics and politics, and quickly cut short the positive outlook of Smith, Condorcet, Godwin, and other Enlightenment advocates. Malthus, along with his best friend and fellow economist, David Ricardo, asserted that pressures on limited resources would always keep the overwhelming majority of human beings close to the edge of subsistence. Accordingly, Malthus and Ricardo reversed the course of cheerful Smithian economics, even though they were stringent followers of Smith's laissez-faire policies.

Malthus's Remarkable Impact

Malthus has had a powerful impact on modern-day thinking:

1. He is considered the founder of demography and population studies. (In fact, England took its first census of population in 1801, a demonstration of Malthus's influence.)

2. He is considered the mentor of social engineers who advocate strict population control and limits to economic growth (see Update 1, page 81).

3. His essay on population underlines the gloomy and fatalistic outlook of many scientists and social reformers who forecast poverty, death, misery, war, and environmental degradation due to population pressures on resources (see Update 2 on page 88).

4. He inspired Charles Darwin's theory of evolution (see the box on page 73).

5. His principles textbook influenced John Maynard Keynes's theory of macroeconomics based on the idea that business cycles were caused by changes in total "effective demand" by consumers and investors (see chapter 13).

6. The fatalistic pessimism of Malthus and Ricardo has given economics its reputation as a "dismal science" (see the box on page 82).

Over the years, Malthus's thesis of overpopulation was accepted by many notable economists, including David Ricardo, John Stuart Mill, Knut Wicksell, and William Stanley Jevons. A number of prominent social critics and modern-day ecologists have also endorsed Malthus's views, blaming overpopulation for famines, shortages, war, and pollution (see Update 2). Even some political conservatives such as Russell Kirk have defended Malthus (Nickerson 1975: 3–7).

However, not everyone bought Malthus's arguments of a pessimistic future. Marxists rejected the despair of Malthus's population theory, which Friedrich Engels labeled "the crudest, most barbaric theory" imaginable (Malthus 1985: 51–52). And most mainstream economists since the late 1900s have also abandoned Malthus's thesis in view of the tremendous rise in food production and economic output (see Update 2 on page 88).

Nevertheless, during the rest of the nineteenth century, Malthus's conundrum of overpopulation and limited resources haunted the modern world.

WHO IS ROBERT MALTHUS?

Who was this young minister and why did he have such a powerful influence in derailing Adam Smith's new world of universal opulence?

Born into a wealthy family in Surrey in 1766, Malthus was christened Thomas Robert, but was always known as Robert or Bob by his family and friends. (He is commonly referred to as "Thomas Malthus" today by historians, however.) As the last son in a family of eight, he was well familiar with the issue of overpopulation. A large family was encouraged by his Christian faith (in Genesis 1:28, God told Adam and Eve to "multiply and replenish the earth") and the common wisdom of the time that more children increased the parents' chances of being taken care of in old age.

WHERE DID DARWIN GET HIS THEORY OF EVOLUTION? FROM MALTHUS!

The influence of Malthus's essay on population has been immense, and not just among social scientists. The founder of modern evolutionary theory, Charles Darwin, credited Malthus for his theory of natural selection and survival of the fittest. In his *Autobiography,* Darwin freely expressed this indebtedness:

> In October 1838, that is, fifteen months after I had begun my systematic inquiry, I happened to read for amusement Malthus on Population, and being well prepared to appreciate the struggle for existence which everywhere goes on, from long-continued observation of the habits of animals and plants, it at once struck me that under these circumstances favourable variations would tend to be preserved, and unfavourable ones to be destroyed. The result of this would be the formation of a new species. (Darwin 1958: 120)

Photograph 3.1
Charles Darwin (1809–82)
read Malthus for amusement.
Courtesy of Hulton-Getty Archives.

Remarkably, Alfred Russell Wallace, who independently discovered the theory of organic evolution, also credited Malthus's book. In his autobiography, *My Life,* Wallace recounted how he read Malthus at about the same time as Darwin had his inspiration: "Perhaps the most important book I read was Malthus's *Essay on Population*. . . . It was the first work I had yet read treating of any of the problems of philosophical biology, and its main principles remained with me as a permanent possession, and twenty years later gave me the long-sought clue to the effective agent in the evolution of organic species" (Wallace 1905: 232).

Malthus's *Essay* implies an evolutionary process in human development. In chapter 18, he expressed the idea that it took "a certain process . . . a certain time" for God the creator to form human creatures (Malthus 1985: 201).

In 1784, at the age of eighteen, Malthus went to Cambridge University, where he excelled in mathematics and languages (he learned five). He liked to play cricket and enjoyed a lively social life, joining numerous clubs throughout his life. Upon graduation in 1788, he took Holy Orders and became a cleric for the Church of England. He dropped his clerical role after six years when he decided to marry in 1804. Only later in life did he use the designation "Reverend" in an effort to defend his controversial views regarding population.

WHY MALTHUS REFUSED TO HAVE HIS PORTRAIT DONE UNTIL AGE 67!

Until the last year of his life, Malthus refused to have his portrait done. Why? He suffered from a birth defect that ran in the family. He was born with a cleft palate, which affected his speech and haunted him throughout his life. A woman referred to his "uncouth mouth and horrid voice," but others were not bothered by his disfigured face, and noted that he was otherwise handsome. However, Malthus was so embarrassed by his disfigurement that he only had one portrait in his life, and that was done in 1833, one year before his death (James 1979: 2–4). The artist made the mouth defect virtually undetectable, as you can see in the reproduction below.

Illustration 3.1
Thomas Robert Malthus (1766–1834)
"The most abused man of the age." (Downs 1983: 249)
Courtesy of Hulton-Getty Archives.

REVEREND MALTHUS WRITES A CONTROVERSIAL TRACT

Malthus's classic work came about because of an argument he had with "a friend" over William Godwin's utopian theories. The friend turned out to be his father, Daniel Malthus, a lovable old crank and a disciple of the scandalous French philosopher Jean-Jacques Rousseau. Rousseau's most famous line, "Man was born free and is everywhere in chains," reflected the conflict between idealism and reality of the age.

The contention over Godwin's new vision of life was so strong that the youthful Malthus wrote a powerful polemical tract to refute it. Following the tradition at the time, Malthus's work had a lengthy title, *An Essay on the Principle of Population as It Affects the Future Improvement of Society, with Remarks on the Speculations of Mr Godwin, M. Condorcet, and other Writers* (1798). Concerned about embarrassing his father in public, he used a pseudonym and referred to his father as a "friend." Yet it wasn't long before everyone knew who the author was.

"THE MOST ABUSED MAN OF THE AGE"

Malthus's doomsday thesis is that "the power of population is indefinitely greater than the power of the earth to produce subsistence for man," and therefore the majority of humans were doomed to live a Hobbesian existence (1985 [1798]: 71).

It created a sensation from the moment the essay was published, and Malthus was attacked repeatedly. His essay created a storm of criticism and vituperation from theological conservatives, market liberals, and utopian radicals. Clergy considered it an irreligious book that questioned the benevolence of the Creator, and social reformers accused Malthus of being uncharitable toward the poor.

Malthus disapproved of England's Poor Laws, a modest welfare system administered locally. According to Malthus, any effort to better society and alleviate want had to be counterproductive. A welfare system would inevitably increase population without increasing food production, leading to more misery of the masses. (Later, in 1815, Malthus also came out in favor of the English Corn Laws, import duties on grain that raised the price of bread for the working poor.)

As a pious Anglican, Malthus was strictly opposed to any form of birth control. In the second edition of his *Essay on Population*, he discussed the possibility of delayed marriage, continence in marriage, and other forms of "moral restraint" on population growth, but he did not mean contraception, which he regarded as repugnant. Ironically, birth control advocates frequently cite Malthus to support "family planning" in Third World countries and in China's one-child policy (see Update 1 on page 81). Malthus was not an advocate of zero population growth and, in truth, his religious convictions favored population growth in fulfillment of God's commandment to multiply. He was opposed to population growth only when it surpassed the means of subsistence and resulted in misery and vice (Pullen 1981: 46).

MALTHUS OPPOSES POVERTY PROGRAMS, BIRTH CONTROL, EVEN VACCINES?

William Cobbett, who dubbed him "Parson Malthus," wrote the following critique: "How can Malthus and his nasty and silly disciples, how can those who want to abolish the Poor Rates, to prevent the poor from marrying;

how can this at once stupid and conceited tribe look the labouring man in the face, while they call on him to take up arms, to risk his life in defense of the land?" (Downs 1983: 249–50).

Thus, Malthus was put down as antisocial, "a man who defended smallpox, slavery and child murder, who denounced soup kitchens, early marriage and parish allowances; who had the impudence to marry after preaching against the evils of a family; who thought the world so badly governed that the best actions do the most harm; who, in short, took all romance out of life" (Downs 1983: 249).

Only a small printing was made of the first edition of *An Essay on Population* in 1798, so that today it is a rare and expensive collector's item, valued at considerably more than a first edition of *The Wealth of Nations,* when you can find a copy. (According to rare book dealer Robert Rubin, a first edition *Essay on Population* can fetch $100,000 or more.) During Malthus's lifetime, six editions were published. The book became ever larger with added appendixes and data, but only the first edition—devoid of statistics and empirical facts—is considered a classic.

Malthus spent the rest of his life defending and revising his overpopulation thesis, even though he went on to write numerous other pamphlets and books, including *The Principles of Political Economy* in 1820. He traveled extensively in Europe, assessing population problems.

MARRIAGE, TEACHING, AND DEATH

In April 1804, at the age of thirty-eight, Malthus married Hariett Eckersall. They had their first child in December, only eight months after marriage. This fact elicited ribald comments from friends and relatives, even though the birth of their son was probably premature. Malthus and his wife went on to have three children, and were happily married.

In 1805, he was appointed professor of modern history and political economy at the newly established East India Company's college at Haileybury, for the general education of civil servants of the East India Company. Thus Malthus held the first chair in economics. He stayed in this position until his death in 1834. His closest friend was fellow economist David Ricardo, who corresponded with him regularly until Ricardo's death in 1824 (more on their relationship in the next chapter).

Malthus died of a heart attack in December 1834. He was buried in Bath Abbey.

MALTHUS'S FAMOUS TWO LAWS OF NATURE

Now that we have reviewed Malthus's life, let us look more carefully at his theories. What was he trying to prove?

His *Essay on Population* contained two basic "laws of nature" which he regarded as "incontrovertible truths":

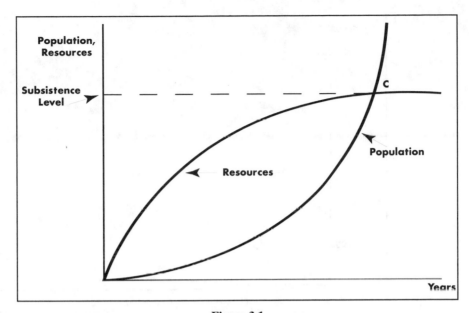

Figure 3.1
Growth of Population, Resources, and Subsistence

First, population tends to increase geometrically (1, 2, 4, 8, 16, 32 . . .).

Second, food production (resources) tends to increase only arithmetically (1, 2, 3, 4, 5, 6 . . .).

The result would be an inevitable crisis of "misery and vice" whereby the earth's resources would not satisfy the demands of a growing population (Malthus 1985: 67–80). Malthus's thesis can be illustrated by Figure 3.1. In this figure, we see that the supply of resources is growing under diminishing returns, while the demands of a growing population are increasing more rapidly at a geometric rate. Point *C* represents the subsistence level, at which the vast majority of human beings barely survive. If the world exceeds point *C*, starvation, death, and vice bring the world's population back to the subsistence level. Thus, according to Malthus, the world is doomed to a life of "unconquerable difficulties," including misery, famine, and crime (Malthus 1985: 69, 250).

ISSUE 1: THE GROWTH OF POPULATION

Is Malthus right about his first "law of nature," that human population grows geometrically? Figure 3.2 tends to confirm Malthus's first proposition. The world's population has been indeed growing geometrically, until recently anyway. Fewer than 1 billion people existed on earth in Malthus's time. Today human population exceeds 6 billion.

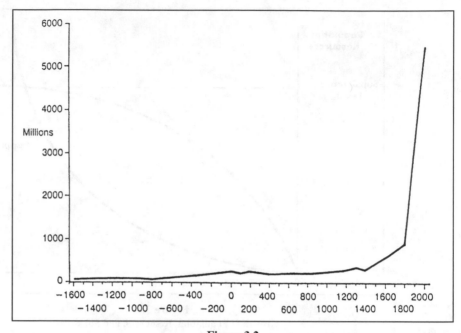

Figure 3.2
Estimated World Population, 1600 B.C. to A.D. 2000
Source: Simon (1995: 35). Reprinted by permission of Blackwell Publishers.

However, in looking more deeply into the sharp rise in world population since 1800, we see that the cause is not Malthusian in nature. The rise in population has been due to two factors unforeseen by Malthus. First, there has been a sharp drop in the infant mortality rate due to the elimination of many life-threatening diseases and illnesses through medical technology. Second, there has been a steady rise in the average life span of individuals, due to higher living standards; medical breakthroughs; improvements in sanitation, health care, and nutrition; and a decline in the accident rate. As a result, more people are living into adulthood, and more adults are living longer. Both factors stand in opposition to Malthusian fears of misery and death. Figure 3.3 demonstrates the dramatic shift in the infant mortality rates around the world.

ISSUE 2: THE DECLINING BIRTHRATE

Another flaw in the doomsday vision of Malthus and his followers is the slowing down of the birthrate in the second half of the twentieth century, both in the industrial world and in developing countries. Over the past fifty years, the birthrate in developed countries has fallen from 2.8 to 1.9, and

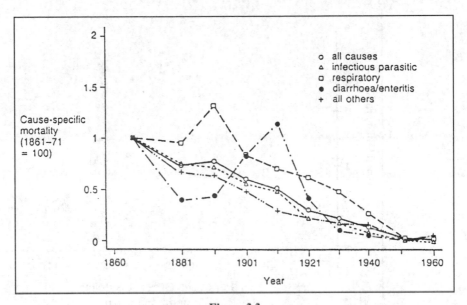

Figure 3.3
Falling Mortality Rates in Various Countries, 1860–1960
Source: Simon (1995: 43). Reprinted by permission of Blackwell Publishers.

in developing countries from 6.2 to 3.9. The trend is unmistakable: women are having fewer children and in some more developed countries, the birthrate is far below replacement. In sum, the geometric rate of population growth may be slowing down to an arithmetic rate.

The long-run decline in the fertility rate is due to two factors: medical breakthroughs and rising income. Because of better medical technology, better nutrition, better sanitation, and better health care, couples see that they don't need to produce more children to make up for children who die.

Malthus argued that a higher income level would only encourage having more children. As per capita income rose, he said, the population would grow faster, which in turn would suppress per capita income down to the subsistence level.

However, recent historical evidence indicates just the opposite. Wealthier people tend to have fewer children (see Figure 3.4). There are several reasons why wealthier families have fewer children in general. In many cultures, having as many children as possible increases the chance that the parents will be taken care of in old age. Thus, children are viewed as a powerful financial asset that can provide future income. With higher incomes, the need for more children declines, and, in fact, children are now often seen as expensive to raise. Moreover, increased income usually means higher levels of education and better understanding of birth control methods.

The impact of higher income on birthrates has sent a clear message to developing nations concerned about population control: a better method of

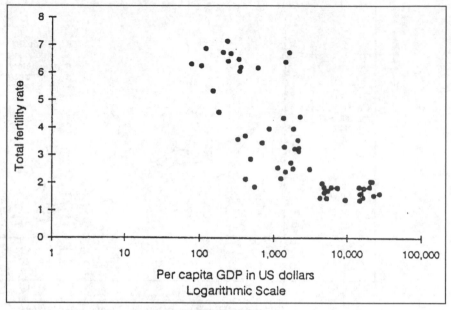

Figure 3.4
Per Capita Income and Birthrates for Selected Nations
Source: Simon (1996: 353). Reprinted by permission of Princeton University Press.

reducing the fertility rate is to encourage economic growth and "universal opulence," as Adam Smith put it. A higher standard of living may be far superior to government invasion of personal privacy in family matters.

In his second and subsequent editions, Malthus revised his simplistic theory and determined that human beings do not necessarily breed like flies, but are more likely than animals or plants to alter their behavior. Malthus called this human ability the "preventive check" on population growth. In the first edition, he identified several checks on population growth, including the scarcity of food, diseases, plagues, famines, and crime, but concluded that these checks would ultimately fail to slow down the innate powerful forces of sexual reproduction. In the second edition, Malthus felt that the preventive checks, such as later marriages and sexual abstinence in marriage, could reduce the growth rate. Yet Malthus had his doubts and repeated his earlier conviction that the population would tend to double every twenty-five years (Malthus 1985: 24, 238). Clearly, Malthus underestimated the ability of humans to alter their child-bearing behavior.

TESTING MALTHUS'S SECOND LAW: ARE RESOURCES LIMITED?

Malthus's second "law of nature" was "subsistence increases only in an arithmetical ratio" (Malthus 1985: 71). This contention seems rather curious, if not patently false. Both plants and animals are far more fertile

UPDATE 1: MALTHUS AND CHINA'S ONE-CHILD POLICY

No country has adopted a more stringent policy of population control than Communist China. This may seem odd, considering Marx and Engel's assault on Malthusian economics. Marxist doctrine emphasizes the strength of the industrial work force as a key ingredient of progress. Yet, various birth control measures, such as encouraging later marriages, had not worked, and by the early 1970s, China's 750 million people were increasing at a 3 percent rate. The Chinese communists made two changes in an effort to balance resources and a growing Chinese population. They freed the economy and imposed a strict one-child policy.

The new free economy has done wonders to stimulate economic growth, and the one-child policy has sharply curtailed population growth. Today China has over a billion people, but the growth rate has slowed to 1 percent a year. Nevertheless, China has paid a high price for this deep intrusion into the personal lives of the Chinese:

1. Abortions, especially of females, have skyrocketed in China. (The Chinese have a strong preference for male children.)

2. China has a serious aging problem, with a huge and growing senior population and relatively fewer young workers to support them.

3. China has a growing imbalance of male and female adults. Today 55 percent of Chinese are male, creating a serious shortage of female mates. Chinese men have resorted to female abduction and slavery from other countries.

4. The traditional Chinese extended family has gradually disintegrated.

Here's what the one-child policy ultimately means to the Chinese (I thank my wife, Jo Ann, for pointing this out):

No brothers
No sisters
No nieces
No nephews
No uncles
No aunts
No cousins
And four grandparents and two parents doting on one child!

The most tragic aspect of this one-child policy is that it is unnecessary. As Julian Simon and other economists have pointed out, higher per capita income causes lower birthrates. Therefore, China could accomplish the same goal without resorting to extreme population control measures, simply by encouraging strong economic growth through economic liberation.

than humans. Women take nine months to deliver a child, and seldom give birth to twins or triplets, while many animals—especially cows, chickens, pigs, fish, and other animals that people use as food—are vastly more productive. Plants such as wheat, corn, and other crops are even more fertile than animals. As economist Julian Simon states, "Humans and wheat are both biological species, and the growth of each is constrained by various forces. There is no a priori reason why the two species should follow different growth patterns" (Simon 1996: 333).

DEARTH OF RESOURCES

But Malthus did offer a reason to support his view that plant and animal life may not be as productive as human population. He readily acknowledged that "nature has scattered the seeds of life abroad with the most

---

WHAT DISMAL CRITIC LABELED ECONOMICS THE "DISMAL SCIENCE"?

Question: Who was the person responsible for naming economics the "dismal science"?

A. Benjamin Franklin, who wrote in *Poor Richard's Almanac,* "Experience keeps a dear school, yet fools will learn in no other" (1986: 225).

B. J.-B. Say, who described economists in *A Treatise on Political Economy* as "idle dreamers, whose theories, at best only gratifying literary curiosity, were wholly inapplicable in practice" (1880: xxxv).

C. Edmund Burke, who wrote in his *Reflections on the French Revolution,* "The age of chivalry is gone. That of sophisters, economists and calculators has succeeded; and the glory of Europe is extinguished for ever" (1955: 86).

D. Walter Bagehot, editor of *The Economist,* who wrote, "No real Englishman in his secret soul was ever sorry for the death of a political economist" (Reynolds 1989: xiii).

E. Thomas Carlyle, the English essayist who wrote in "The Negro Question" that economics is "not a 'gay science,' [but] a dreary, desolate, and indeed quite abject and distressing one" (1904: 354).

All five of the above statements are quoted accurately, and were made by well-known economists, but only Thomas Carlyle is responsible for the term "dismal science."

WHO WAS THIS CRITIC?

Thomas Carlyle (1795–1881) was a prominent biographer; historian; and social, literary, and political critic. A Scotsman who lived most of his adult life in a London suburb, he held strong views on a variety of subjects. Near the end of his life, he was known as the Victorian Sage of Chelsea.

(continued)

WHAT DOES "DISMAL SCIENCE" MEAN?

Next question: What did Carlyle mean when he used the phrase "dismal science"?

A. Malthus, Ricardo, and other classical economists were deeply pessimistic about overpopulation, the miserly nature of the earth's resources, and the iron law of wages.

B. Economists are always counting the costs of policies and remedies that could improve the economy, and warning politicians anxious to spend money on a new pet project, "It costs too much!"

C. Economists do a lousy job of forecasting inflation, interest rates, and the next recession.

The correct answer: None of the above! All three answers, while plausible and frequently used to explain Carlyle's meaning, are inaccurate or misleading. Carlyle, a Victorian romantic, was actually complaining about the decline of the *ancien régime* of benevolent monarchy and the rise of utilitarian individualism and democracy. He collided with the classical economists who favored laissez faire, free competition, the "cash nexus" of supply and demand, and "superficial speculations . . . to persuade ourselves . . . to dispense with governing" (Milgate 1987: 371). Much of Carlyle's language seems to imitate Marx and Engels's *Communist Manifesto*. In short, Carlyle was lashing out against free-market capitalism, which he defined as "anarchy plus the constable."

Photograph 3.2
Thomas Carlyle (1795–1881)
The Victorian Sage of Chelsea
"A dreary, desolate,
distressing . . . dismal science!"
Courtesy of Hulton-Getty Archives.

He first labeled economics the dismal science in a racist speech he made in 1848, which was entitled "The Nigger Question." Today's audiences may be shocked by the N word, but at the time, it was commonly used. Recent reprintings of Carlyle's pamphlet have renamed it "Occasional Discourse on the Negro Question," but Carlyle definitely meant it as a racial slur. Interestingly, in the quote cited above, Carlyle refers to the "gay science," using an adjective that has also changed meaning significantly in the past century.

In this speech, Carlyle dealt with the controversial issue of slavery. The British Empire had outlawed slavery in the 1830s, but still debated the issue of labor unrest between ex-slaves and commercial interests in the West Indies. Carlyle, his Calvinist heritage deeply ingrained, was sympathetic to the plight of workers, but was also a firm believer in the gospel of work. He couldn't understand why ex-slaves in the West Indies lay idle, unwilling to labor. Idleness is a "perpetual blinder on the skin of the State," Carlyle declared, and therefore all citizens, black or white,

(continued)

should "be compelled" to work if they can't be persuaded. "But if your Nigger will not be induced? In that case, it is full certain, he must be compelled; should and must" (Carlyle 1904 [1849]: 355–56).

Carlyle, the Victorian moralist, was heavily criticized for this fascist tendency. The pamphlet reported several citizens walking out on his speech in protest. Carlyle, always the "antiliberal" reactionary, made other controversial judgments. He opposed the universal right to vote, was anti-Semitic, and regarded the Irish as feckless and lazy. Because of his bigoted views, Carlyle lost many friends, including John Stuart Mill, who called his speech "a true work of the devil" (Stafford 1998: 113).

It was during his controversial speech on West Indies blacks that Carlyle attacked economists who substituted "supply and demand" over "command and obedience" in analyzing labor unrest in the West Indies. He shouted, "And the Social Science— not a 'gay science,' but a rueful—which finds the secret of this Universe in 'supply and demand,' and reduces the duty of human governors to that of letting men alone, is also wonderful. Not a 'gay science,' I should say, like some we have heard of; no, a dreary, desolate, and indeed quite abject and distressing one; what we might call, by way of eminence, the dismal science" (Carlyle 1904: 353–54).

On another occasion, Carlyle remarked, "Of all the quacks that ever quacked, the political economists are the loudest. Instead of telling us what is meant by one's country, by what causes men are happy, moral, religious, or the contrary, they tell us how flannel jackets are exchanged for pork hams" (Viner 1963: 8–9).

Ever since 1849, the designation has stuck, especially given the proclivity of many social scientists to assail the dynamics of global capitalism.

profuse and liberal hand," but "she has been comparatively sparing in the room and the nourishment necessary to rear them" (1985: 71–72, 224–25). In other words, there is not sufficient fertile ground, not enough natural resources to sustain life.

THE LAW OF DIMINISHING RETURNS

Malthus developed this scarcity concept further in later editions. The means of supporting human life are "limited by the scarcity of land—by the great natural barrenness of a very large part of the surface of the earth—and by the decreasing proportion of produce which must necessarily be obtained from the continual additions of capital applied to land already in cultivation" (1985: 225). This "constant tendency to diminish" the use of resources is known today as the law of diminishing returns. Malthus is considered the first economist to develop this vital concept in economics. It refers to the fact that as one adds more labor or capital to a fixed amount of land, the production or output increases at a slower and slower rate. That is why the production function in Figure 3.1 is slightly bowed.

WHY WAS MALTHUS SUCH A PESSIMIST?
WAS IT BECAUSE OF HIS RELIGION?

Cursed is the ground for thy sake.

—Genesis 3:17

Malthus the demographer cannot be separated from Malthus the theologian.

—J.M. Pullen (1981: 54)

Malthus was convinced that although Mother Earth "has scattered the seeds of life abroad with the most profuse and liberal hand . . . she has been comparatively sparing in the room and the nourishment necessary to rear them" (1985 [1798]: 71–72, 224–25). What caused him to think so? Perhaps it was his religious convictions. As a devout Anglican minister, Malthus had been taught that animal and plant life "may breed abundantly in the earth" (Genesis 8:17), but after the fall, God cast Adam and Eve out of the Garden of Eden and "cursed the ground" (Genesis 3:17).

Would a benevolent God create an earth unable to support his creations? Malthus's religious critics responded that if this were true, how then could humans fulfill their mandate to "be fruitful, multiply and replenish the earth" (Genesis 1: 26–31)? Did not the Psalmist write, "O Lord, how manifold are thy works! In wisdom hast thou made them all: the earth is full of thy riches" (Psalms 104:24)? Yet Malthus, who often held unorthodox views, took God's statement "cursed be the land" quite literally. Malthus confirmed this immutable "law of nature" near the end of his essay: "The Supreme Being has ordained that . . . population should increase much faster than food" (1985: 204–5).

The Book of Genesis also raises the first discussion of the possibility of overpopulation, an event that Malthus may have noted. The Bible tells of a shortage of land among Abraham's and Lot's people and animals: "And the land was not able to carry them . . . and Abraham said to Lot: . . . Is not the whole land before thee?. . . If thou will take the left hand, then I will take the right; or if thou take the right hand, I will go to the left" (Genesis 13:6–9).

MALTHUS OPPOSES "UNIVERSAL OPULENCE"

Malthus also appeared to have adopted an antiwealth attitude common among Christians at the time, a view expressly opposite to Adam Smith's optimistic vision. Malthus wrote that prosperity tends to "degrade [rather] than exalt the character" (1985: 209), leisure "will produce evil rather than good" (208), and, "Had population and food increased in the same ratio, it is probable that man might never have emerged from the savage state" (206). According to Malthus, overpopulation and subsistence living have benefits, forcing humans to work, develop skills, "soften and humanize the heart," and "to generate all the Christian virtues" (205–6, 209).

Malthus omitted these comments (and the entire final two chapters) from all subsequent editions "in deference to the opinions of some distinguished persons in our church" (Pullen 1981: 48).

Interestingly, he added to the second edition the following harsh statement regarding the unworthy poor:

(continued)

> A man who is born into a world already possessed, if he cannot get subsistence from his parents on whom he has a just demand, and if the society does not want his labour, has no claim of right to the smallest portion of food, and, in fact, has no business to be where he is. At nature's mighty feast there is no vacant cover for him. She tells him to be gone. (Ross 1998: 22)
>
> Perhaps Malthus was pondering the words of St. Paul: "If any would not work, neither should he eat" (2 Thessalonians 3:10).

Malthus warned that the most fertile land and resources are used up first, and that we are faced with a gradual decline in the quality of land and resources as time goes along. But the law of diminishing returns only works if we assume "all other things equal," that technology and the quantity of other resources is fixed. But no input is fixed in the long run—neither land, labor, nor capital. The economic importance of land has in fact dwindled in the modern world, due to intensive farming techniques. Unfortunately Malthus and his disciples ignored this critical fact.

MALTHUS OMITS A VITAL INGREDIENT

What Malthus ignored were technological advances in agriculture, the constant discovery of new minerals and other natural resources in the earth, and the role of prices in determining how fast or slow resources are used up. In short, he failed to recognize human ingenuity.

Malthus proved to be spectacularly wrong about food production. With the advent of the McCormick combine and the tractor, the use of fertilizers, the vast expansion of irrigation, and other scientific and management breakthroughs, the amounts of cultivated land and food production have risen dramatically. Figure 3.5 illustrates U.S. farm labor productivity in corn, wheat, and cotton.

The rise in food production has supported a much larger world population and has reduced the problem of famine around the globe. Moreover, most famines that still occur are due to ill-advised government policies that deny farmers the fruits of their labors, restrict foreign imports, and discourage the use of the new agricultural production processes (Simon 1996: 92). According to Nobel laureate in economics Amartya Sen, liberal democracies avoid famines: "In the terrible history of famines around the world, no substantial famine has ever occurred in any independent and democratic country with a relatively free press" (1999).

"THE TRAGEDY OF THE COMMONS"

Although the extreme predictions of the environmentalists have not come true, overuse of resources can still be a problem. Various parts of the world face serious concerns over air and water pollution, deforestation in some areas, depletion of fisheries, land erosion, extinction or near extinction of some animals, and possible disruptions in the earth's atmosphere.

In a 1968 article in *Science,* Garrett Hardin, professor of human ecology at the University of California at Santa Barbara, wrote a seminal essay in environmental literature on this subject. Titled "The Tragedy of the Commons," it has been reprinted in over 100 anthologies. Hardin noted that there is a tendency for a resource to be overused when it is owned by the public. He used the example of public grazing land. Because no one individual owns the land, each herdsman has an incentive to add another animal to the herd on the grazing land. As a result the land is overgrazed and, in the words of Hardin, "Freedom in a common brings ruin to all" (Hardin and Baden 1977: 20).

The lack of property rights and market prices creates a "tragedy of the commons"—causing unnecessary pollution, extinction of animals, destruction of forests, and environmental degradation. Many environmentalists stress government regulation of the commons, while economists favor privatization of the commons area, if possible, and full pricing of resources as the best way to reestablish the proper management of a scarce resource.

SUMMARY: MALTHUS ABANDONS SMITH'S VISION

The story of Robert Malthus is instructive in developing an understanding of the dynamics of a growing economy and a rising population. Granted,

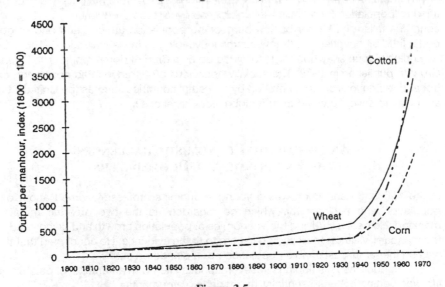

Figure 3.5
U.S. Farm Labor Productivity in Corn, Wheat, and Cotton, 1800–1967
Source: Simon (1995: 375). Reprinted by permission of Blackwell Publishers.

Update 2: The Ultimate Malthusian Debate: Erhlich Versus Simon

Overpopulation is the most serious threat to human happiness and progress in this very critical period in the history of the world.
—Julian Huxley, "Too Many People" (Osborn 1962: 223)

Ultimately the only solution to the food problem will be the curbing of world population growth.
—Lester Brown (Ross 1998: 138)

Malthusian theory tends to attribute any deadly famine, extreme poverty, or environmental damage to excess population and economic growth, rather than to underdevelopment or government policy. Fears of overpopulation and environmental degradation reached their zenith in the 1970s. In 1968, the Sierra Club published an alarmist book, *The Population Bomb,* by a young Stanford biologist, Paul R. Ehrlich. Ehrlich wrote a scary scenario, warning that "at this late date nothing can prevent a substantial increase in the world death rate. . . . In the 1970's the world will undergo famines—hundreds of millions of people are going to starve to death." What could bring about this disaster? Ehrlich spoke in Malthusian tones: "We must take action to reverse the deterioration of our environment before population pressure permanently ruins our planet. The birth rate must be brought into balance with the death rate or mankind will breed itself into oblivion" (Ehrlich 1968: Prologue).

Ehrlich and the Sierra Club argued that uncontrolled population was a menace, using up too many precious resources, destroying the wilderness and polluting the environment. In developing countries, Ehrlich took a page from Malthus when he identified a "population-food crisis," in which "each year food production in undeveloped countries falls a bit further behind burgeoning population growth, and people go to bed a little bit hungrier. . . . It now seems inevitable . . . mass starvation" (1968: 17).

Ehrlich's doomsday book was followed up by a Club of Rome report, *The Limits to Growth,* published in 1972. The socially conscious group advocated population control and restrictions on consumption by industrial countries such as the United States as a way to save the world from a global ecological crisis.

An Optimistic Economist Challenges the Environmental Doomsdayers

In the 1960s, Julian Simon was a young economics professor worried about overpopulation and nuclear war, which he regarded as the two greatest threats to mankind. He began studying the economics of population growth and discovered that the standard Malthusian view didn't seem to fit the evidence. He concluded that there was neither an unsustainable population nor a plundered earth.

Simon published his findings in several books filled with an arsenal of data on how life was getting better. Essentially, he made two arguments:

(continued)

First, on the supply side, natural resources are virtually unlimited in the long run. If a nonrenewable resource such as coal is used up, higher prices will encourage the discovery and use of substitutes, such as crude oil. In addition, entrepreneurs are making new discoveries all the time, increasing substantially the level of known reserves of natural resources, or new cost-cutting techniques allowing more resources to be constantly developed. The law of diminishing returns can be postponed indefinitely because land, labor, capital, and technology are not fixed in the long run. Accordingly, we are not running out of food, water, oil, trees, clean air, or any other natural resource because throughout human history the quantities of usable commodities are constantly increasing.

In sum, "every forecast of the doomsdayers [including Malthus] has turned out flat wrong. Metals, foods, and other natural resources have become more available rather than more scarce throughout the centuries" (Simon 1996: 12–15).

Second, on the demand side, a large and growing population is beneficial and leads to a higher standard of living because it increases the stock of useful knowledge and trained workers. According to Simon, "Human beings are not just more mouths to feed, but are productive and inventive minds that help find creative solutions to man's problems, thus leaving us better off over the long run." Moreover, he said, "population growth spurs the adoption of existing technology as well as the invention of new technology" (Simon 1996: 376). Figure 3.6 is a reproduction of a rather fascinating figure illustrating a close relationship between scientific activity and population size.

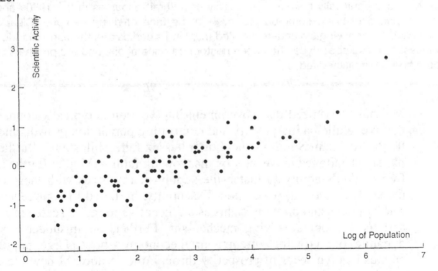

This diagram illustrates the close relationship between the total amount of scientific activity and the population of countries, after per capita income is allowed for in the 1970's. This fits with the idea that more people imply faster increases in technology and economic growth. Technically, this is a plot of log population versus the residuals of the model log (authors in country) = a + b log (per capita income).

Figure 3.6
Relationship of Scientific Activity to Population Size, After Per Capita Income Is Allowed, 1970s
Source: Simon (1996: 381). Reprinted by permission of Princeton University Press.

(continued)

Simon added that excessive population growth is not inevitable. The birthrate has been declining in most countries around the world as a result of higher wealth and use of birth control devices.

THE $1,000 BET BETWEEN EHRLICH AND SIMON

Simon was so sure of his findings that he offered a $1,000 bet that the price of five commodities would be lower in ten years. Ehrlich agreed to the bet in October 1980. The five commodities were industrial metals—chrome, copper, nickel, tin, and tungsten. If the combined prices of acquiring the metals in 1990 turned out to be higher than $1,000 (inflation-adjusted), Simon would pay the difference in cash. If prices fell, the Ehrlich group would pay him.

During the decade, the world's population grew by more than 800 million, the greatest increase in history, yet in the fall of 1990, with the prices of metals down sharply, Ehrlich mailed Simon a check for $576.07. Simon sent a thank you note, along with another challenge to raise the wager to $20,000, tied to any other resource at a future date. Ehrlich declined the offer.

Simon had a bit of luck going for him, since he would have lost the bet in the inflationary 1970s. In 1995, Simon bet David South, professor at the Auburn University School of Forestry, that timber prices would be lower in five years. When he died in 1998, Simon was losing the bet, and timber prices have continued to increase ever since. Still, Simon was correct in his judgment that new technology and new discoveries would dramatically increase the supply of natural resources in the 1980s and reduced prices of basic commodities, even in the face of rising demand. Clearly, Ehrlich and other ecologists underestimated mankind's genius and the earth's hidden bounties. A global apocalypse had been postponed once again, and the prophets of gloom had been discredited.

Malthus recognized that government intervention is typically counterproductive in alleviating poverty and controlling population growth, and thus he joined Adam Smith in adopting a laissez-faire philosophy. But he ultimately abandoned his mentor by disavowing faith in Mother Earth and the free market's ability to match the supply of resources with the growing demands of a rising population. Essentially, he failed to comprehend the role of prices and property rights as an incentive to ration scarce resources and as a problem-solving mechanism. Further, he misunderstood the dynamics of a growing entrepreneurial economy—how a larger population creates its own seeds of prosperity through the creation of new ideas and new technology.

Although Adam Smith did raise the issue of a subsistence wage, he firmly believed that wage earners could rise above subsistence through the adoption of machinery, tools, and equipment. Free-market capitalism was the escape mechanism from poverty. Malthus, on the other hand, was gloomy and even fatalistic about man's ability to escape misery and vice. Mankind was destined to be chained to the iron law of wages. David

Ricardo, Malthus's best friend, fell into the same trap. In the next chapter, we explore how Ricardo joined forces with Malthus in taking another step down the road of the dismal science.

REFERENCES

Burke, Edmund. 1955. *Reflections on the Revolution in France.* New York: Bobbs-Merrill.
———. 1963. *The Best of Burke*, ed. Peter J. Stanlis. Washington, DC: Regnery.
Carlyle, Thomas. 1904 [1849]. "The Nigger Question." In *Critical and Miscellaneous Essays,* vol. 4, 348–83. London: Charles Scribner's Sons.
Club of Rome. 1972. *The Limits to Growth.* New York: University Books.
Darwin, Charles. 1958. *Autobiography of Charles Darwin.* New York: Norton.
Downs, Robert B. 1983. *Books That Changed the World.* New York: Penguin.
Ehrlich, Paul R. 1968. *The Population Bomb.* New York: Sierra Club.
Franklin, Benjamin. 1986. *The Autobiography and Other Writings.* New York: Penguin.
Hardin, Garrett, and John Baden, ed. 1977. *Managing the Commons.* San Francisco: W.H. Freeman.
James, Patricia. 1979. *Population Malthus: His Life and Times.* London: Routledge and Kegan Paul.
Keynes, John Maynard. 1973 [1936]. *The General Theory of Employment, Interest and Money.* London: Macmillan.
Kramnick, Isaac, ed. 1995. *The Portable Enlightenment Reader.* New York: Penguin.
Malthus, Thomas Robert. 1985 [1798]. *An Essay on the Principle of Population.* New York: Penguin. (This edition contains the original 1798 first edition and *A Summary View of the Principle of Population,* published in 1830.)
———. 1989 [1820]. *Principles of Political Economy.* New York: Cambridge University Press.
Marx, Karl, and Friedrich Engels. 1964 [1848]. *The Communist Manifesto.* New York: Monthly Review Press.
Milgate, Murray. 1987. "Thomas Carlyle." In *The New Palgrave: A Dictionary of Economics,* vol. 1, 371. London: Macmillan.
Montesquieu. 1989 [1848]. *The Spirit of the Laws.* Cambridge: Cambridge University Press.
Nickerson, Jane Soames. 1975. *Homage to Malthus.* New York: Kennikat.
Osborn, Fairfield, ed. 1962. *Our Crowded Planet: Essays on the Pressures of Population.* New York: Doubleday.
Pullen, J.M. 1981. "Malthus' Theological Ideas and Their Influence on His Principle of Population." *History of Political Economy* 13: 1, 39–54.
Ross, Eric B. 1998. *The Malthus Factor.* London: Zed.
Reynolds, Morgan O. 1989. "A Tribute to W.H. Hutt." *Review of Austrian Economics* 3: xi–xii.
Rousseau, Jean-Jacques. 1968. *The Social Contract.* New York: Penguin.
Say, J.-B. 1880. *A Treatise on Political Economy,* 6th ed. New York: Augustus M. Kelley.
Sen, Amartya. 1999. "Democracy as a Universal Value." *Journal of Democracy* 10, 3: 3–17.
Skidelsky, Robert. 1992. *John Maynard Keynes: The Economist as Saviour.* London: Macmillan.
Simon, Julian L., ed. 1995. *The State of Humanity.* Cambridge, UK: Blackwell.
———. 1996. *The Ultimate Resource 2.* Princeton: Princeton University Press.
Stafford, William. 1998. *John Stuart Mill.* London: Macmillan.
Viner, Jacob. 1963. "The Economist in History." Richard T. Ely Lecture. *American Economic Review* 53: 2 (May), 1–22.

Voltaire. 1947 [1758]. *Candide*. New York: Penguin.
Wallace, Alfred Russell. 1905. *My Life*. London: Chapman and Hall.
Woodsworth, William. 1986 [1850]. *The Prelude*. London: Penguin.

4

TRICKY RICARDO
TAKES ECONOMICS DOWN
A DANGEROUS ROAD

David Ricardo is par excellence an economist's economist.
—Paul A. Samuelson (1962: 8)

That able but wrong-headed man, David Ricardo, shunted the car of economic science on to a wrong line—a line, however, on which it was further urged toward confusion by his equally able and wrong-headed admirer, John Stuart Mill.
—William Stanley Jevons (1965: li)

The eminent British economist **David Ricardo (1772–1823)** is known for many things: He was the wealthiest economist ever. He was Malthus's dearest friend. He promoted free trade, hard money, the law of comparative advantage, and other sound principles of classical economics. His laissez-faire policies were in strict accordance with those of Adam Smith.

HIS INFLUENCE FOR GOOD . . .

Ricardo had his moment in history, and it was pivotal. His persuasive case for sound money eventually led the British Parliament to pass the Peel Act of 1844, which established a strict anti-inflation monetary standard, and his devastating and convincing attack against trade restrictions undoubtedly helped to repeal the Corn Laws, England's notorious high tariff on agricultural goods in 1846.

♪ **Music selection for this chapter: Johann Sebastian Bach, Toccata and Fugue in D Minor, BWV 565**

Following these two historic policy changes, Britain rapidly became the "workshop of the world," importing most of its food and exporting clothing and manufacturing goods, and thus harnessing the industrial revolution. As a result, we can see that there is much to laud about Ricardo, whose policies were in line with the principles of Adam Smith and with market-driven prosperity.

Moreover, Ricardo is considered by many as the founder of economics as a rigorous science involving mathematical precision. The financial economist had a remarkable gift of abstract reasoning, developing a simple analytical model involving only a few variables that yielded, after a series of manipulations, powerful conclusions. This model-building approach has been adopted by many prominent economists, including John Maynard Keynes, Paul Samuelson, and Milton Friedman in the twentieth century, and has led to the popularity of econometrics.

Illustration 4.1
David Ricardo (1772–1823)
"He literally invented the technique of economics."
Courtesy of Hulton-Getty Archives.

. . . AND FOR BAD

Yet David Ricardo had a dark side. His analytical modeling is a two-edged sword. It gave us the quantity theory of money and the law of comparative advantage, but it also gave us the labor theory of value, the iron law of subsistence wages, and something economists call the "Ricardian vice," defined as either the excessive use of abstract model building or the use of false and misleading assumptions to "prove" the results one desires (such as his labor theory of value). Some of the worst ideas picked up by Karl Marx and the socialists came directly from reading Ricardo's *Principles* (1951). In fact, Marx hailed Ricardo as his intellectual mentor. A school of "neo-Ricardian" socialists has developed under the influence of Piero Sraffa, Ricardo's official biographer.

Essentially, Ricardo, for all his love of Smith, took economics down a very different road, apart from his policy recommendations. He created a new economic way of thinking, away from the harmonious "growth" model of Adam Smith and toward an antagonistic "distribution" model, where workers, landlords, and capitalists fought over the economy's desserts. Marx and the socialists exploited Ricardo's hostile system to the fullest. Smith's model focuses on how to make the economy grow, while Ricardo's model stresses how the economy is divided up among various groups or classes. Ricardo emphasized class conflict rather than Smith's "natural harmony" of interests.

THE RICARDIAN VICE

Finally, there is the "Ricardian vice." Economists are particularly vulnerable to it. Mill, Walras, Pareto, Fisher, Samuelson, Mises, yes, even Keynes, suffered from it. Today's graduate students are "perversely" enamored of it (Colander and Brenner 1992: 2).

What is it? Paul Samuelson calls it "abstract methodology" (Samuelson 1962: 8). Ronald Coase names it "blackboard economics" (Coase 1992: 714). Simply put, it is the chronic divorcing of theory and history. It is stripping economics of the past, present, and future. It is pure deductive reasoning and high mathematical formulas without reference to history, sociology, philosophy, or the institutional framework. It is abstract thinking and model building using unrealistic and even false assumptions. Take a look at Samuelson's *Foundations of Economic Analysis* (1947) or neo-Ricardian Piero Sraffa's *Production of Commodities by Means of Commodities* (1960). Samuelson's book is practically nothing but differential equations and assumptions far removed from reality. Sraffa's work has hardly a single sentence that refers to the real world (see the box on Sraffa, page 110). They are both very much in the tradition of Ricardo.

"The origin of the misapprehension upon which the whole of economic theory is based must be traced to David Ricardo," wrote Elton Mayo, a business professor at Harvard (1945: 38). Mayo blamed Ricardo's unrealistic theorizing on his background as a stockbroker, far removed from the realities of the producing economy (1945: 39).

RICARDO CARRIES HIS TECHNIQUE TOO FAR

Abstract theorizing began in earnest with British economist David Ricardo. Adam Smith's *Wealth of Nations* abounds with theoretical propositions, but his theories are followed by numerous historical illustrations. Not so with Ricardo. "His ingenious mind," one historian wrote, "essentially that of a brilliant theoretician, never displayed any significant interest in the past" (Snooks 1993: 23).

It was this kind of abstract theorizing that caused Jean-Baptiste Say to declare economists to be "idle dreamers." Even Paul Samuelson (himself an abstract thinker) confessed once, "It has sometimes been suggested that our most advanced students know everything except common sense" (Samuelson 1960: 1652). In the 1980s, Robert Kuttner said, "Departments of economics are graduating a generation of idiot savants, brilliant at esoteric mathematics but innocent of actual economic life" (Colander 2007: 9). Indeed, studies by Arjo Klamer and David Colander suggest a certain disillusionment with the highly abstract mathematical modeling that pervades Ph.D. programs in economics. After surveying the graduate programs at six Ivy League schools, Klamer and Colander concluded that "economic research was becoming separated from the real world" (1990: xv). Formalism has an iron grip on the discipline.[1] David Colander updated their book in 2007 and suggested that the profession has changed for the better: "The commitments to theorems and proofs have declined, and there is a much stronger empirical branch of economics" (2007: 15).

Heuristic model building can be extremely useful in generating best estimates and decent results, but modeling can also easily distort reality and lead to damaging results. Ricardo carried his theorizing to extreme levels, whereby he made all kinds of limiting and dubious assumptions in order to get the results he was looking for—in this case, his assertion that prices are determined by labor costs.

Let us review now the life and ideas—for both good and bad—of this famous financial economist.

RICARDO IS BORN INTO A JEWISH HOUSEHOLD

David Ricardo was third in a family of at least seventeen and perhaps as many as twenty-three children (Sraffa 1955: 24). His prolific father had a very Jewish name, Abraham Israel Ricardo. Abraham Ricardo was a

---

1. For a cynical look at the Ricardian vice in modern economics, see Axel Leijonhufvud's delightful "Life Among the Econ" (1981: 347–59). In Leijonhufvud's fable, the Econ are a backward and poverty-stricken tribe whose caste system is built on abstract "modls." The fable concludes, "Having lost their past, the Econ are without confidence in the present and without purpose and direction for the future" (1981: 359).

RICARDO: LOVE HIM OR HATE HIM

Few economists are indifferent to David Ricardo. He is either loved or hated, and sometimes loved *and* hated by the same person. John Maynard Keynes could say that "Ricardo's mind was the greatest that ever addressed itself to economics," and then complain that "the complete domination of Ricardo's [economics] for a period of a hundred years has been a disaster to the progress of economics" (Keynes 1951: 117).

Paul Samuelson could laud the British economist as profound, a speculator par excellence, and an economist's economist, and then declare him "the most overrated of economists" (Samuelson 1962: 9).

Early on in his career, Mark Blaug, today's annointed historian of economic thought, was so impressed that he did his Ph.D. dissertation on Ricardo, named his first son David Ricardo, and had Ricardo's picture on the wall in his office. He praised Ricardo's methodology: "If economics is essentially an engine of analysis, a method of thinking rather than a body of substantial results, Ricardo literally invented the technique of economics" (Blaug 1978: 140). Blaug once wrote an article in which he cited every article and book written about Ricardo in one footnote. The footnote is four pages long, perhaps the longest in academic history (Blaug 1997: 46–49).

Then, years later, the mature Blaug changed his mind, blaming Ricardo for taking economics down a dangerous road of "pessimistic" models and criticizing him for his "lugubrious and obscure" attempt to find an invariable measure of value (1997: 45, 24, n. 1). In the fifth edition of his *Economic Theory in Retrospect*, Blaug quoted Archilochus, the Greek poet: "The fox knows many things but the hedgehog knows one big thing." According to Blaug, Adam Smith was a fox who knew many things, but Ricardo "was a hedgehog through and through." He added, "I used to love hedgehogs, but those were 'my salad days when I was green in judgement.' Now I prefer foxes—Smith over Ricardo" (Blaug 1996: xviii).

devout Sephardic Jew of Spanish-Portuguese ancestry who settled in Holland after being expelled from Spain at the end of the fifteenth century. A successful stockbroker looking to build a family dynasty, he moved his family to London in 1760. David was born there twelve years later. By age fourteen, after spending two years at a Hebrew school in Amsterdam, David was employed by his father on the London Stock Exchange.

RICARDO MARRIES AND IS IMMEDIATELY DISINHERITED

However, everything changed in 1793, when, at the age of twenty-one, David married a Quaker. (He later became a Unitarian, and most of his brothers and sisters eventually followed his example and left the Jewish community.) His mother was so offended that she compelled Abraham to kick David out of the house and disinherit him, although his father even-

HOW RICARDO BECAME THE RICHEST ECONOMIST IN HISTORY

When Ricardo started out in business at the age of twenty-one, his property base amounted to £800. By the time he died in 1823, a mere thirty years later, his estate was worth an unimaginable £675,000 to £775,000, from which he enjoyed a yearly income of £28,000 (Sraffa 1955: 103). No other economist, not even John Maynard Keynes, has reached this level of affluence.

Ricardo has the distinction of writing erudite theoretical works and making a fortune. Few economists can boast doing both. Keynes would be one of the few to join Ricardo in this distinction, amassing an estate worth £650,000 during the Great Depression while writing *The General Theory* (see chapter 13).

How did Ricardo do it? If he had written a book on investment, what secrets would he tender?

THE ARBITRAGE KING

Ricardo made his money primarily as a stockjobber, handling his own accounts, rather than as a broker. A stockjobber might be compared to a specialist on the floor of the New York Stock Exchange who handles large sums of stock and constantly makes a market in specific issues. During the early nineteenth century, most transactions involved government bonds, known as consols, although great chartered companies such as the Bank of England and the East India Company issued shares. Otherwise, there were no corporations or corporate stock at this time.

Ricardo made most of his money early on as an arbitrager of government debt. He played the forward market, which was ten times bigger than the cash market. A contemporary wrote of Ricardo: "He is said to have possessed an extraordinary quickness in perceiving in the turns of the market any accidental difference which might arise between the relative price of different stocks [government bonds]." His transactions would tend to be short-term and he would "realise a small percentage upon a large sum," typically £200 to £300 a day. He wrote a friend, "I play for small stakes, and therefore if I'm a loser I have little to regret" (Sraffa 1955: 73, 81).

Historians have debated the extent to which Ricardo profited from insider dealings and stock manipulations. According to Professor Norman J. Silberling (1924), Ricardo often played the villain, a leader of an "inner clique of exchange professionals" known as "bear-jobbers" who would attempt "bear raids" on the government loan market. By panicking the public and pushing consol prices sharply lower, Ricardo and his band could pick up consols on the cheap and profit from high interest rates. Silberling accused Ricardo of writing his pamphlet, *The High Price of Bullion*, in early 1810, in order to bring about a fall in bond prices. Indeed, the price of bonds fell abruptly in late 1810 and one of the Goldsmids, a primary financier of government loans, committed suicide. However, Piero Sraffa, Ricardo's biographer, disputes this claim, noting that Ricardo had made a firm bid on a government loan in 1810 and it would have been to his disadvantage if consol prices had fallen. It should also be noted that Ricardo failed in his bid (Sraffa 1955: 91–92).

(continued)

Ricardo's Golden Rules of Investing

Ricardo never wrote down his trading techniques, but business associates said that he held scrupulously to his two "golden rules": "Cut short your losses" and "Let your profits run on." He also took advantage of undervalued and overvalued situations, based on the observation that the investing public often exaggerates events, and he may at times have engineered these overbought and oversold conditions, as noted above.

Ricardo was no miser, however. As quickly as he profited, he moved his wife and family into larger and more expensive housing, and frequently vacationed in Brighton. He became a country gentleman, buying Gatcomb Park, a large estate, and investing in land, mortgages, and French stocks after retiring around 1815.

Ricardo, the Financier

Ricardo's budding financial career took a gigantic leap forward when he began bidding as a loan contractor for the government. During the Napoleonic wars in the early 1800s, the government relied on the Stock Exchange to finance its burgeoning expenditures. Ricardo and his partners were soon competing against some of the biggest names in high finance, such as the Goldsmids, the Barings, and the Rothschilds. The successful bidders received a special bonus from the chancellor of the exchequer. Ricardo and company were so successful in their bidding that they obtained every government loan during the war years of 1811 through 1815.

The Day Ricardo Made £1 Million Sterling

The last and biggest loan of the war (worth £36 million) was raised on June 14, 1815, just four days before the Battle of Waterloo. The price of the bonds was extremely depressed because of the size of the loan and the uncertainty of the outcome of the war. There were four bidders for the loan contract, but Ricardo's firm won.

Ricardo bravely held onto his position in the deeply depressed bonds, his biggest gamble ever. Other more timid investors sold early, before the Battle of Waterloo (see Malthus's story below), but not Ricardo. He held on after the shocking news arrived that Wellington had won the battle against Napoleon. The government consols skyrocketed and Ricardo became an instant millionaire. The *Sunday Times* reported in Ricardo's obituary (September 14, 1823) a popular rumor that during the Battle of Waterloo Ricardo had "netted upwards of a million sterling" (Sraffa 1955: 84).

Ricardo Helps His Friend Malthus

Ricardo frequently helped his friends, such as Robert Malthus, with stock market tips. Prior to the issuance of the Waterloo bonds, Malthus asked his close friend to reserve for him £5,000 of the new loan. As the Battle of Waterloo approached, Malthus got scared and begged Ricardo to sell his position early at a small profit, provided this was not "either wrong, or inconvenient for you." Ricardo promptly sold Malthus out, and consequently Malthus never participated in the bonanza enjoyed by Ricardo (Sraffa 1955: 84).

tually reconciled with him. In any case, David was forced to strike out on his own with only a few hundred pounds.

Relying on his experience as his father's apprentice and his connections at the Stock Exchange Coffee House on Threadneedle Street, Ricardo amassed a huge fortune over the years as a stockjobber and government loan contractor. (See the box on page 98, "How Ricardo Became the Richest Economist in History.")

Although pleasantly well-proportioned, Ricardo was slender and diminutive in stature. He had an extremely high-pitched voice, which benefited him in speaking in the House of Commons. Late in life, he complained of losing the use of one ear and losing his teeth.

RETIREMENT, POLITICS, AND EARLY DEATH

In 1814, at the age of forty-two, Ricardo became a country gentleman and purchased a large estate called Gatcomb Park in Gloucestershire (now occupied by Princess Anne). Having a wide interest in mathematics, chemistry, geology, and mineralogy, he frequently had intellectual meetings at his Gatcomb estate. Later he took an active part in the Geological Society of London. His interest in economics began as early as 1799, when during a stay at Bath, he picked up a copy of Adam Smith's *Wealth of Nations* (1776).

Once he had gained his fortune in the mid-1810s, he lost interest in the Stock Exchange and began writing regularly about economic issues. In 1817, he published his dense magnum opus, *On the Principles of Political Economy and Taxation*, and in 1819, he purchased a seat in the House of Commons.

In 1823, at the relatively youthful age of fifty-one, he died suddenly of an ear infection. He was survived by his wife Priscilla and seven of their eight children. His estate was divided quite unequally in favor of his three sons (see the box "Were Ricardo and Malthus Anti-Female?" on page 113), and he bequeathed a sum to his friend Malthus and another to James Mill, father of John Stuart Mill.

RICARDO MAKES SEVERAL POSITIVE CONTRIBUTIONS

As I mentioned at the beginning of this chapter, David Ricardo made several important contributions, despite having never gone to college. Let us begin by reviewing his positive additions to economic science.

RICARDO: A HARD-MONEY MONETARIST

First, as an early mentor of the Currency School, Ricardo endorsed a stringent anti-inflation monetary policy. In the 1809–10 period, England was suffering from a raging inflationary price spiral due to the costs of war, and the Bank of England suspended the gold standard. Ricardo entered the bullion controversy by writing his first major economic study, *The High Price of Bullion* (1811), in which he argued that his country's inflation was caused by the Bank of England issuing excess bank notes. Ricardo was a believer in a rigid quantity theory of money, a view held by David Hume and others that the general price level was closely related to changes in the quantity of money and credit.

To restore sound money in England, Ricardo argued for the resumption of specie payments by the Bank of England. His solution was stated as follows: "The remedy which I propose for all the evils in our currency, is that the Bank should gradually decrease the amount of their notes in circulation until they shall have rendered the remainder of equal value with the coins which they represent, or, in other words, till the prices of gold and silver bullion should be brought down to their Mint price" (Ricardo 1876: 287). Ricardo recognized the "most disastrous consequences to the trade and commerce of the country" as a result of this deflationary measure, but argued that this was the "only means of restoring our currency to its just and equitable value." If this policy were enforced gradually, there would be "little inconvenience," contended Ricardo. In short, he was a hard-money man who favored a gold exchange standard, simple convertibility with an objective that the price of bullion remain the same value as the banknotes. The central bank should have no discretionary power: "The issuers of paper money should regulate their issues solely by the price of bullion, and never by the quantity of their paper in circulation" (1876: 403).

Following Ricardo's death, a group of influential bankers known as the Currency School led a fight to safeguard the value of the British pound. They favored a resumption of a specie standard, holding up gold and silver as ideal. They opposed discretionary management of the currency by a central bank and endorsed the principle that all future issues of money and currency could increase or decrease solely according to changes in the country's bullion reserves, without deviation. In 1844, under the influence of David Ricardo, Parliament passed the Peel's Bank Charter Act in support of the currency principle. Unfortunately, the Peel Act failed to preserve a sound monetary system in England, as it did not regulate money substitutes, especially the rapidly expanding checking account deposits in the banking system.

THE LAW OF DIMINISHING RETURNS

Second, Ricardo (along with Malthus) developed the famous law of diminishing returns. Ricardo developed the law in 1815 in his *Essay on the Influence of a Low Price of Corn on the Profits of Stock*. His approach in this work was a precursor to his abstract theorizing in the 1817 *Principles*. Ricardo's main thesis was that the scarcity of land leads to lower economic growth.

In developing his "corn model," the British economist made a number of simplifying assumptions to make his case. First, since the British economy was dominated by agriculture, Ricardo assumed one giant farm producing corn. (In Britain, "corn" referred to wheat, barley, and other agricultural crops.) Second, he assumed a constant real (after inflation) fixed wage at the subsistence level, based on the "iron law of wages" held by Malthus and himself.

Third, he assumed fixed capital, one spade per worker to produce the corn crop.

Therefore, in Ricardo's corn model, land had no alternative use and all inputs (land, labor, and capital) were linked to the price of corn. As the labor force increases, the extra corn to feed the workers requires additional land—land that of necessity is less fertile or productive. Even if more capital and labor are applied to the same quantity of land, the effect is the same. Net output falls, and economic growth declines.

In his major work *On the Principles of Political Economy and Taxation*, published in 1817, Ricardo replaced his simple one-sector "corn model" with a three-sector model, but the arguments and the results are the same: a declining yield per acre of land.

To postpone or even reverse this dismal result, Ricardo vigorously attacked the Corn Laws, the British restrictions and tariffs on wheat and other agricultural products. By importing more corn and lowering corn prices, farmers could lower money wages, enjoy higher profits, promote more investment, and thereby create higher economic growth. Consequently, Ricardo became a major advocate of free trade and of repealing the Corn Laws.

Ricardo Reveals a Law That Revolutionizes World Trade

Third, Ricardo annunciated one of the greatest laws in economics, comparative advantage, which dealt a theoretical death blow to protectionism.

As indicated above, Ricardo came out strongly in favor of free trade during the debates over the Corn Laws in 1813–15, but his most important contribution to the free-trade issue came a few years later when he developed the law of comparative advantage in chapter VII of *Principles* (1817).

This law argues that free trade benefits both nations, and most surprisingly that it pays for each nation to specialize even when one nation has an absolute advantage in certain products.

A Subtle Doctrine

His celebrated doctrine came about through lengthy discussions with his friend and fellow economist, James Mill, father of John Stuart Mill. In fact, some scholars consider James Mill, and Robert Torrens before him, to be the real founders of this law (Rothbard 1995: 96–98). (Historians are always learning of an antecedent who discovered this or that famous principle. Perhaps there is nothing new under the sun after all. Nevertheless, Ricardo popularized the concept.)

RICARDO USES A FAMOUS EXAMPLE TO PROVE HIS CASE

Ricardo illustrated the law of comparative advantage with a celebrated example of English cloth and Portuguese wine (Ricardo 1951: 133–42). Again, to demonstrate his point, he used highly simplifying examples. Suppose it takes 50 workers to produce one unit of cloth in England, and 25 workers in Portugal. On the other hand, it takes the same number of laborers—25—to produce a unit of wine in Portugal, but 200 in England. (We are slightly altering Ricardo's numbers to make it easier to understand—see de Vivo 1987: 194.)

The following chart summarizes the two countries' two-good situation:

Number of Laborers per Unit

	England	Portugal
1 unit of cloth	50	25
1 unit of wine	200	25

As we can see from the chart, Portugal has a clear absolute advantage in the production of both goods. Therefore, Portugal should produce both cloth and wine, and should export them to England. The casual observer might conclude that, under the circumstances, it might not appear beneficial for Portugal to specialize in only one commodity and trade with England, since it has an absolute advantage in both cloth and wine. But Ricardo brilliantly demonstrated that specialization and trade do indeed make sense.

Here's why: Suppose Portugal took 25 workers from the production of cloth and employed them in the production of wine. The result would be an increase of one more unit of wine, and one less unit of cloth in Portugal. If at the same time England took 100 workers from the wine industry, and employed them making cloth, England would gain two more units of cloth, and lose half a unit of wine.

If we add up the total output of both countries after this act of specialization, we come to a remarkable conclusion: there would be one more unit of cloth and one-half more unit of wine produced in the aggregate as a result of trade!

Ricardo made an amazing discovery: Trade between two countries increases total output, even when one country has a natural advantage over the other.

Moreover, Ricardo's law of comparative advantage can be applied within a nation's boundaries, not just between nations. A medical doctor might have an absolute advantage in both medicine and secretarial work, but it pays for the doctor to specialize in medicine and hire a secretary if he wants to maximize his income. The law of comparative advantage is at work in every exchange and every production process.

The classical argument for free trade, led by Adam Smith, David Ricardo, and others, has been so powerful and persuasive that trade barriers have gradually declined since the 1830s (see Update 1 on page 105). James Wilson, a passionate free-trader, was so impressed by Ricardo's and Smith's arguments that in 1843 he began publishing *The Economist,* a weekly magazine devoted to "free trade and free markets." Wilson even went so far as to declare, "We seriously believe that FREE TRADE, free intercourse, will do more than any other visible agent to extend civilization and morality throughout the world—yes, to extinguish slavery itself." (Edwards 1993: 21). With the help of Wilson's son-in-law, Walter Bagehot, and writers such as Herbert Spencer, *The Economist* gradually became an influential magazine of international politics, economics, and finance. Today it has over a million subscribers.

A few years later—in 1846—the Corn Laws were repealed and Britain soon became an industrial powerhouse by importing its food requirements and exporting manufactured goods. The rest of the world followed suit by reducing their trade barriers.

THE CORN MODEL: RICARDO'S "BOOK OF HEADACHES"

Fourth, Ricardo's obtuse "corn model" created a major stumbling block in economics.

Ricardo was a paradox, an economist who profoundly influenced the world in both good ways and bad: good in his theoretical support for sound money and free trade, bad in his macromodel of antagonistic class interests.

Ricardo's approach was radically distinct from Adam Smith's. Smith's *Wealth of Nations* was vibrant and full of life, peppered with colorful examples. Ricardo's *Principles* was tedious and abstract, full of Euclidian-like deductions with no historical case studies. Students often called it "Ricardo's Book of Headaches" (St. Clair 1965: xxiii).

Smith developed an upbeat economic science focusing on the "invisible hand" of wealth creation and how working capital combined intelligently with labor and land could create more wealth to everyone's benefit. Smith only parenthetically commented on the role of landlords, workers, and capitalists in creating value. Granted, he often did so in a critical way, but the overriding theme was growth, not distribution of income.

On the other hand, Ricardo's book dragged out Smith's parenthetical clauses and footnotes and made them the main text, "a wild tangle of antagonisms and fated oppositions" (Chamberlain 1965: 75).

UPDATE 1: FREE TRADE AND THE DEMISE OF MERCANTILISM

Ideas have consequences! There is no better example of this refrain than the gradual decline in trade restrictions between nations. Adam Smith and his disciple, David Ricardo, were tremendously influential in gradually breaking down the barriers of trade between nations.

The chart in Figure 4.1 shows the history of duties in the United States since 1820:

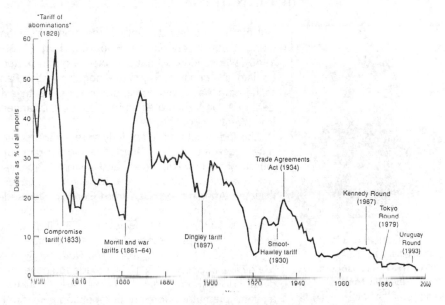

Duties were high for most of our nation's history, but trade negotiations since the 1930s have lowered tariffs significantly.

Figure 4.1
The Gradual Decline in U.S. Tariffs, 1820–2000:
Duties Calculated as a Percentage of Dutiable Imports
Source: Samuelson (1998: 708). Reprinted by permission of McGraw-Hill.

Despite temporary setbacks, such as the "Tariff of Abominations" in 1828 and the Smoot-Hawley Tariff in 1930, the downward trend in trade duties is clear.

At the beginning of U.S. history, tariffs represented nearly 100 percent of the new government's revenues. By 1910, they brought in only 50 percent of revenues, and today they are less than 2 percent of the government's budget.

Free trade has won the day, not only in the United States but in Great Britain and around the world. The creation of the European Union during the postwar period has now achieved a remarkable situation where capital, labor, and money flow between a dozen European nations without restriction or regulation. Free-trade agreements flourish between nations in North America, South America, Asia, and Europe. In addition, many economists are convinced that Japan, Hong Kong, and the rest of Asia were able to grow rapidly in the postwar period because the United States opened its doors to cheap products from abroad.

(continued)

Among economists, there is no greater conformity to principle than free trade. Several surveys of professional economists show that over 95 percent support free trade, the highest percentage of agreement in any category. Such universal support is due largely to the pathbreaking work of David Ricardo and Adam Smith, the founder of modern economics.

FRIEDRICH LIST DEFENDS THE ECONOMIC SOVEREIGNTY OF THE NATION-STATE

Illustration 4.2
Friedrich List (1789–1846)
"The tree is more important than the fruit."
Courtesy of the British Library of Political and Economic Science.

But there are a few dissenters, the most prominent being German economist **Friedrich List (1789–1846)**, whose ideas of national planning and protectionism are considerably more popular in the East than in the West. His books are as prominently evident in Asian bookstores as they are equally absent from Western bookstores.

List led a colorful, disorderly career as a sometime accountant, professor, farmer, politician, journalist, author, diplomat, and railroad capitalist, but committed suicide due to chronic financial trouble. After being exiled from Germany for sedition, he emigrated with his family to the United States in 1825, where he was especially impressed with the American system of protective tariffs.

In his most significant work, *The National System of Political Economy* (1841), List made the case for a state-led economy that protected key industries against premature foreign competition. He firmly believed in a tariff-free zone within the nation but protectionism of infant industries from outside competition. He contrasted his vision of a paternalistic "national economy" with Adam Smith's laissez-faire "individual economy." His books extol the benefits of economic sovereignty of the nation-state, and paint a grim picture of unrestrained markets. According to List, Great Britain achieved dominance by encouraging her trades. (List apologists point to the United States and Japan as similar cases.) In List's system, promoting the producers is more important than protecting the consumers from high prices, a popular mercantilistic approach in Japan and other Asian nations that promote exports and discourage imports. "The tree which bears the fruit is of greater value than the fruit itself," List argued (Fallows 1993: 67). In the long run, List agreed that free trade is the best global system once nations are fairly equal in development, but as Keynes noted, the long run can be a long way off. Today the List model is under attack, as more nations have reduced their tariffs and trade restrictions. Certainly Hong Kong has not suffered from being a free-trade zone.[2]

2. The ongoing debate over trade can be seen in contrasting *Economics and World History*, by Paul Bairoch (1993), which analyzes the historical evidence against free trade, and *Free Trade Today* (2003), a series of provocative essays by Columbia professor Jagdish Bhagwati doggedly defending free trade.

RICARDO FOCUSES ON DISTRIBUTION, NOT GROWTH

In a letter to Malthus, Ricardo explained: "Political economy, you think, is an enquiry into the nature and causes of wealth [Adam Smith's view]; I think it should rather be called an enquiry into the laws which determine the division of the produce of industry among the classes who concur in its formulation" (Rothbard 1995: 82).

The difference between the Adam Smith approach and the Ricardo model is best visualized as shown in Figure 4.2.

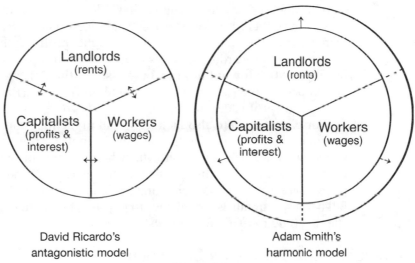

David Ricardo's
antagonistic model

Adam Smith's
harmonic model

Figure 4.2
Two Models of the Economy

For Ricardo's "class conflict" model, the focal point is how the fruits of the economy (the pie) should be divided among workers, landlords, and capitalists. Clearly, if landlords and capitalists get more of the pie, workers get less, and vice versa. For Adam Smith's "harmony of interests" model, the focal point is on making the economy grow—to make the pie bigger. In Smith's model, capitalists work together with the workers and landlords to produce goods and services throughout the production process. In this way, there need not be a conflict of interests. If the pie gets bigger, everyone—the workers, landlords, and capitalists—gets more.

RICARDO'S LAW OF IRON WAGES AND DECLINING PROFITS

Ricardo developed his "corn model" as a way of predicting the movement of the output and the factors of production—wages, profits, interest, and rents. His system was tragic for everyone except the landlords. Ricardo's workers were machinelike units earning only subsistence wages over the long run. If wages rose, workers would have more children, which would in turn increase the supply of workers and force wages back down. Thus, Ricardo's "iron law of wages" presented a tragic outlook for workers.

The outlook for profits and interest were not much better. Capitalists were not animated merchants with a "propensity to truck, barter, and exchange," as noted by Adam Smith, but a uniform, boring lot mechanically saving and accumulating capital. Moreover, profits could increase only at the expense of lower wages, and vice versa. In Ricardo's system, there was no room for higher wages and higher profits at the same time. In his *Principles*, Ricardo called this inverse relationship between wages and profits the **"fundamental theorem of distribution."** He repeatedly stated, "In proportion then as wages rose, would profits fall" (Ricardo 1951, vol. I: 111) and "profits depend on wages" (1951, vol. I: 143, 35).

Worse, profits were also inclined to fall in the long run due to the "law of diminishing returns." Under Ricardo's myopic worldview, higher wages would stimulate population growth, which in turn meant farming more land to feed more mouths, and that meant using less productive land. The price of grain would rise, benefiting the landlords' rents, but profits would fall because capitalists would have to pay workers more to keep them from starving (due to rising food prices).

RICARDO'S FATAL ATTACK ON LANDLORDS

The only beneficiaries in Ricardo's bleak picture were the landlords. They earned higher rents as grain prices rose. The tenant farmers did not benefit from higher grain prices because they had to pay higher rents. Ricardo vindicated the words of Adam Smith: "landlords love to reap where they never sowed" (Smith 1965 [1776]: 49).

According to Ricardo's fatalistic system, wages tend toward subsistence levels, profits decline long term, and landlords keep adding to their share of unjust returns. As Oswald St. Clair comments, landlords "though contributing nothing in the way of work or personal sacrifice, will nevertheless receive an ever-increasing portion of the wealth annually created by the community" (St. Clair 1965:3).

What was the flaw in Ricardo's thinking? His corn model ignored the benefits that workers accrue from technological advances that made workers more productive. Their wages would tend to rise as companies became more profitable. (Empirical studies demonstrate that industries with high profit margins tend to pay workers more.) He failed to see land-lord rents as price signals determining the highest value or opportunity cost of land. Yet most economists would not recognize these insights for another generation.

Meanwhile, Marx and the socialists picked up on Ricardo's attack on the idle landlords. Ricardo's critique also encouraged Henry George's land nationalization and single tax movement (see chapter 9).

RICARDO SEARCHES IN VAIN FOR INSTRINSIC VALUE

Finally, Ricardo was determined to find an "invariable measure of value." Instead of gold, the ultimate unit of account, he focused on quantity of labor units (not wages!) as the *numeraire*. In classical tradition, Ricardo fixed upon a cost-of-production theory of value, arguing that price was generally determined by costs (supply) rather than utility (demand). He was aware of exceptions to this cost theory, such as "rare statues and pictures, scarce books and coins, wines of a peculiar quality" (Ricardo 1951: 12), and the impact of machinery. But machinery and capital were nothing

---

THE NEW PALGRAVE: A MARXIST/SRAFFIAN PLOT?

Marx and Sraffa are quoted more frequently, indeed, much more frequently than Adam Smith, Alfred Marshall, Léon Walras, Maynard Keynes, Kenneth Arrow, Milton Friedman, Paul Samuelson or whoever you care to name.
—Mark Blaug (1988: 15)

Neo-Ricardian socialists made a major coup in 1987 when they published the prestigious *New Palgrave Dictionary of Economics*. So accuses Mark Blaug, historian extraordinaire, who took on the daunting task of reading all four volumes cover to cover, over 4,000 oversized pages. The *New Palgrave* replaced the old *Dictionary of Political Economy*, compiled by R.H. Palgrave in 1894, and can be found as a standard reference in virtually every university library in the world. It was a huge undertaking by John Eatwell and Murray Milgate of Cambridge University, and Peter Newman from Johns Hopkins. Over 900 economists around the world agreed to contribute, including many free-market advocates.

But while the editors promised an "unbiased" approach, in reality they gave us "a hopelessly distorted picture" (Blaug 1988: 46). "Literally every article on Marxian economics in the four volumes is written by an avowed Marxist" (Blaug 1988: 30). And the entry on "capitalism" is not written by Milton Friedman or Friedrich Hayek, but by socialist Robert Heilbroner, whose bibliography excludes Friedman, Hayek, and other free-market advocates.

(continued)

WHAT IS SRAFFIAN ECONOMICS?

With over fifty expositions on the obscure subject of Sraffian economics, *The New Palgrave* is, according to Blaug, "designed to promote Sraffian economics."

What is Sraffian economics? **Piero Sraffa (1898–1983)** was an Italian who spent most of his career at Cambridge University under the influence of John Maynard Keynes. He wrote little, but served for over twenty years as the editor of David Ricardo's 10-volume work (1951–73). As he studied Ricardo, Sraffa came to believe he had discovered a defect in the standard neoclassical model that dominated the profession since the marginal revolution of the 1870s.

In 1960, Cambridge University Press published Sraffa's oddly titled work, *Production of Commodities by Means of Commodities.* This slim book established Sraffa as the leader of a "neo-Ricardian" school. Sraffa's thesis, like Ricardo's, is very abstract, with no empirical studies and no marginal analysis. Sraffa used a Ricardian "corn" model, with severely limited assumptions of homogeneous labor, a single commodity, and a single production technique. There are no references to demand, prices, or human action. Everything is mechanical. Blaug concluded elsewhere, "Sraffa's book is after all a perfect example of what some economists have come to believe is wrong with economics: there is hardly a sentence in the book which refers to the real world" (Blaug 1975: 28).

Sraffa concluded that national output is virtually independent of wages and prices. In his model, relative product demand has no effect on prices. Monopolistic businesses can pass along their costs in higher prices without hurting profits. Only inputs determine prices. The implications of this "neo-Ricardian" (also known as "Post-Keynesian") model are strong: the state can engage in massive and radical wealth and income distribution schemes—through taxation, regulation, and confiscation—without doing undue harm to the productive capability of the nation.

Sraffian economics is a strange mixture of Ricardo, Marx, and Keynes, in the end rejecting orthodox neoclassical economics, the theory of consumer demand, and marginal utility. It is an ideal document for wholesale government interventionism and totalitarian central planning. Needless to say, Sraffian economists represent a very small percentage of the economics profession.

UPDATE: SECOND EDITION OF THE NEW PALGRAVE DOWNPLAYS RADICAL ECONOMICS

In 2008, Palgrave Macmillan published a second edition of *The New Palgrave Dictionary of Economics,* including an online edition. This time it was edited by two more mainstream economists, Steven N. Durlauf (University of Wisconsin) and Lawrence E. Blume (Cornell University), who sharply curtailed the Sraffian/Marxist contributions. "Around 80 percent of the text was either entirely new or substantially rewritten to reflect the depth of change within the discipline between the editions," the editors state. The print version is twice as long as the 1987 edition, increasing from four to eight volumes (7,344 pages). The cost is around $3,000, although there is a cheaper version online at www.dictionaryofeconomics.com.

more than "accumulated labour" (1951: 410). He later wrote, "my proposition that with few exceptions the quantity of labour employed on commodities determines the rate at which they will exchange for each other . . . is not rigidly true, but I say that it is the nearest approximation to truth, as a rule for measuring relative value, of any I have ever heard" (de Vivo 1987: 193).

He struggled with the labor theory of value until the very last days of his life. About a month before his death he wrote a fellow economist, "I cannot get over the difficulty of the wine which is kept in a cellar for 3 or 4 years, or that of the oak tree, which perhaps had not 2/- expended on it in the way of labour, and yet comes to be worth £100" (de Vivo 1987: 193).

Even Robert Malthus disagreed with his friend, writing, "neither labour nor any other commodity can be an accurate measure of real value in exchange" (Ricardo 1951: 416).

ECONOMISTS RESPOND TO RICARDO'S MODEL

Economists over the years have had difficulty understanding Ricardo's "corn model" and his *Principles* textbook, especially the twisted assump-

---

UPDATE 2: "RENT SEEKING"

Comparative advantage. Increasing costs. Quantity theory of money. Labor theory of value.

Ricardo has made a huge contribution to the body of economics. Years later, economists have devised two additional laws from Ricardo's writings: the concept of rent seeking and Ricardo's equivalence theorem.

"Rent seeking" is a term invented by Gordon Tullock, one of the creators of the public-choice school. It refers to monopolistic gains (excessive rents or profits above the competitive price) obtained by a firm or industry through the use of political influence (lobbying). Examples include farm programs, taxi licensing, central banks, and radio and television licenses. David Henderson, editor of *The Concise Dictionary of Economics,* prefers to call it "privilege seeking."

Rent seeking originates from Ricardo's theory of rent. In his corn model, as more land is cultivated to feed more people, farmers must lease less productive land. However, a bushel of corn sells for the same price, whether the land is less or more productive. Hence, only the landowners, not the tenant farmers, gain from higher land prices. Applying Ricardian analysis today, economists note that agricultural price supports tend to favor owners of farmland rather than the farmers who lease land. Or, in the case of the New York taxicab industry, taxi medallions benefit the owners of the medallions, not the taxi drivers.

(continued)

UPDATE 3: RICARDO'S EQUIVALENCE THEOREM

Modern economists, notably Harvard's Robert J. Barro, have also popularized the "Ricardian equivalence theorem," the argument that hidden trade-offs abound in policy changes. For example, according to Barro, it doesn't matter how the government funds new expenditures, whether it borrows, taxes, or prints new money. The effect is all the same in the end—high costs, more inflation. Even then, argues Barro, a budget deficit has "no effect" on investment or real interest rates. A budget deficit will be offset by an increase in private saving in order to pay for future taxes (to pay for the deficit). Therefore, he argues, a deficit causes no change in national saving or investment. In effect, federal deficit spending is not a problem (Barro 1996: 93–98).

Barro and other economists point to the fact that household saving in the United States declined in the 1990s even as the federal deficit began to shrink. In other words, a decline in private savings offset an increase in public savings (federal surpluses), and the national saving rate remained the same. Similar behavior occurred in Europe, Australia, and Canada in the 1990s. Many Western countries showed sharp declines in their personal-savings rates in the 1990s and improvements in their government budget balances. According to *BusinessWeek*, "This suggests that people's savings behavior is highly responsive to government borrowing—an idea first proposed by David Ricardo in 1817" (Koretz 2000: 40).

Herbert Stein, former chairman of the Council of Economic Advisors, made a similar Ricardian argument when he said that privatizing Social Security would have no positive effect on the economy. It can be "easily seen," he wrote, that "privatizing social security funds does not add to national saving, private investment, or the national income" (Stein 1998: 202–3). To prove his case, he applied the "crowding-out" principle, the idea that increased private savings will merely offset public savings.

Barro, Stein, and others credit Ricardo with the equivalence theorem. In his discussion of public debt in chapter 17 of *Principles of Political Economy and Taxation*, Ricardo argued that a "country will neither be richer nor poorer" whether a government spending program is paid by taxes or borrowing (Ricardo 1951: 244).

Critics call the Ricardian equivalence theorem a classic example of fairy tale theorizing, devoid of relevance and perhaps even nutty (Barro 1996: 98). Most trade-offs are not a zero-sum game. Reducing tariffs hurts some domestic businesses and helps others, but the net result is positive. Economies that don't tax investment grow faster than those that do, other things being equal. In the case of privatizing Social Security, nations such as Chile have grown faster and have a higher rate of national investment after switching to a private pension system. Private savings tends to be more efficient than public savings. Moreover, the saving ratio did not rise in the 2000s as deficits rose. In sum, trade-offs do exist in economics, but benefits can exceed costs by establishing the right *structure* of taxation and financing.

Ricardo himself wrote that deficit spending would "tend to make us less thrifty" (Ricardo 1951: 247), so even he is not consistent on the matter.

WERE RICARDO AND MALTHUS ANTI-FEMALE?

Female land . . . plays the role of the devil in the Ricardian system.
—Walter A. Weisskopf (1955: 127)

Freudian pyschology has reached the halls of economics. In his provocative work *The Psychology of Economics*, Walter A. Weisskopf blames the pessimistic ideas of Ricardo and Malthus on their distinctly "anti-female" biases. Weisskopf notes that "land . . . is the source of all evil" in both Ricardian and Malthusian thought, and the earth is traditionally a female symbol in religion and mythology (1955: 126).

Malthus's thesis in *An Essay on Population* is that earth's ability to produce is "comparatively sparing" in contrast to the population of humans. "The earth, the soil, and the land—all primeval female symbols—are niggardly in producing food," interprets Weisskopf (1955: 126).

In similar fashion, Ricardo's gloomy views are all due to the scarcity of fertile land. Ricardo's system depends on three assumptions: (1) the law of diminishing returns, (2) the principle of population, and (3) the subsistence theory of wages. Weisskopf declares, "All three of these assumptions have to do with the scarcity of fertile lands" (1955: 127).

Ricardo and Malthus may have subconsciously harbored an anti-female disposition, but were they misogynists?

MALTHUS AND THE BIBLE

Being a Christian minister, Malthus may have had anti-female sentiments in early life. We noted in chapter 9 that Malthus was a firm believer in the Bible, which teaches that Mother Earth was "cursed" when Adam and Eve were cast out of the Garden of Eden. Malthus may also have sympathized with St. Paul's strong anti-women doctrines in the New Testament, such as his admonition "I do not permit a woman to teach or to have authority over a man; she must be silent" (1 Timothy 2:12) or "women should remain silent in the churches" (1 Corinthians 14: 34). However, all this is circumstantial evidence in support of Weisskopf's controversial thesis. After all, Malthus was happily married.

RICARDO'S BIASED WILL

There is better evidence that Ricardo was, to a degree, anti-female. While his father, Abraham, took pains to divide his fortune equally among his fifteen surviving sons and daughters (£3,000 pounds apiece), David was not so egalitarian. He rejected the equal provision of property among children by heavily discriminating against his four daughters, with his will specifically insisting upon the "portion of a son being no less than eight times the value of that of a daughter" (Sraffa 1955: 104). He left his three sons huge estates, including the Gatcomb residence. His reason for making these provisions in his will is not known.

tions he required to prove his theories. Ricardo himself once remarked that probably only twenty-five people in the entire country could understand his *Principles* textbook (1951). A century later, bright Chicago economist Frank H. Knight remarked, "there is much [here] I cannot follow" (1959: 365). Schumpeter lambasted Ricardo for making most of the economic players "frozen and given," piling "one simplifying assumption upon another," and developing a theory "that can never be refuted and lacks nothing save sense" (Schumpeter 1954: 472–73).

Perhaps Keynes had Ricardo in mind when he wrote, "It is astonishing what foolish things one can temporarily believe if one thinks too long alone, particularly in economics" (Keynes 1973 [1936]: Preface).

SUMMARY OF RICARDO'S IMPACT

David Ricardo was able to convince practically all his contemporaries of his labor theory of value and his laissez-faire doctrines. "Ricardo conquered England as completely as the Holy Inquisition conquered Spain," said Keynes (1973: 32). Only now do we see the defects of his arguments. In the next chapter, we shall see how far Ricardian thinking carried economics down the wrong road, further and further away from the sound principles enunciated by Adam Smith.

REFERENCES

Bairoch, Paul. 1993. *Economics and World History*. Chicago: University of Chicago Press.
Barro, Robert J. 1996. *Getting It Right*. Cambridge, MA: MIT Press.
Bhagwati, Jagdish. 2003. *Free Trade Today.* Princeton: Princeton University Press..
Blaug, Mark. 1975. *The Cambridge Revolution: Success or Failure?* 2d ed. Cambridge: Cambridge University Press.
———. 1978. *Economic Theory in Retrospect,* 3d ed. Cambridge: Cambridge University Press.
———. 1988. *Economics Through the Looking Glass: The Distorted Perspective of the New Palgrave Dictionary of Economics.* London: Institute of Economic Affairs.
———. 1996. *Economic Theory in Retrospect,* 5th ed. Cambridge: Cambridge Univerity Press.
———. 1997. *Not Only an Economist.* Cheltenham, UK: Edward Elgar.
Chamberlain, John. 1965. *The Roots of Capitalism.* Princeton: D. Van Nostrand.
Coase, Ronald. 1992. "The Institutional Structure of Production." *American Economic Review* 82: 4 (September), 713–19.
Colander, David. 2007. *The Making of an Economist, Redux.* Princeton: Princeton University Press.
Colander, David, and Reuven Brenner. 1992. *Educating Economists.* Ann Arbor: University of Michigan Press.
Durlauf, Steven N., and Lawrence E. Blume. 2008. *The New Palgrave Dictionary of Economics,* 2d ed. London: Palgrave Macmillan.
Eatwell, John, Murray Milgate, and Peter Newman, eds. 1987. *The New Palgrave: A Dictionary of Economics.* London: Macmillan.
Edwards, Ruth Dudley. 1993. *The Pursuit of Reason: The Economist, 1843–1993.* Boston: Harvard Business School Press.

Fallows, James. 1993. "How the World Works." *Atlantic Monthly* (December), 61–87.

Jevons, W. Stanley. 1965 [1871]. *The Theory of Political Economy,* 5th ed. New York: Augustus M. Kelley.

Keynes, John Maynard. 1951. *Essays in Biography*. New York: W.W. Norton.

———. 1973 [1936]. *The General Theory of Employment, Interest and Money*. London: Macmillan.

Klamer, Arjo, and David Colander. 1990. *The Making of an Economist*. Boulder, CO: Westview.

Knight, Frank H. 1959. "Review of Ricardian Economics." *Southern Journal of Economics* 25:3 (January), 363–65.

Koretz, Gene. 2000. "Are Surpluses Hurting Savings?" *BusinessWeek* (October 2), 40.

Leijonhufvud, Axel. 1981. *Information and Coordination*. New York: Oxford University Press.

List, Friedrich. 1885 [1841]. *The National System of Political Economy*. New York: Augustus M. Kelley.

Mayo, Elton. 1945. *The Social Problems of an Industrial Civilization*. Cambridge, MA: Harvard University Press.

Palgrave, R.H. Inglis, ed. 1926 [1894]. *Palgrave's Dictionary of Political Economy*. London: Macmillan.

Ricardo, David. 1876. *Works of David Ricardo*. London: John Murray.

———. 1951. *On the Principles of Political Economy and Taxation,* ed. Piero Sraffa. Cambridge: Cambridge University Press.

———. 1951–73. *The Works and Correspondence of David Ricardo*, vols. I–XI, ed. Piero Sraffa. Cambridge: Cambridge University Press.

———. 1811. *The High Price of Bullion, a Proof of the Depreciation of Bank Notes*. London: J. Murray.

Rothbard, Murray N. 1995. *Classical Economics*. Hants, UK: Edward Elgar.

Samuelson, Paul A. 1960. "American Economics." In *Postwar Economic Trends in the U.S.*, ed. Ralph E. Freeman. New York: Harper.

———. 1962. "Economists and the History of Ideas," AEA Presidential Address. *American Economic Review* 52: 1 (March), 1–18.

Schumpeter, Joseph A. 1954. *History of Economic Analysis*. New York: Oxford University Press.

Silberling, Norman J. 1924. "Ricardo and the Bullion Report." *Quarterly Journal of Economics* (May), 397–439.

Smith, Adam. 1965 [1776]. *The Wealth of Nations*. New York: Modern Library.

Snooks, Graeme Donald. 1993. *Economics Without Time*. Ann Arbor: University of Michigan Press.

Sraffa, Piero. 1955. *The Works and Correspondence of David Ricardo: Biographical Miscellany,* vol. X. Cambridge: Cambridge University Press.

———. 1960. *Production of Commodities by Means of Commodities*. Cambridge: Cambridge University Press.

St. Clair, Oswald. 1965. *A Key to Ricardo*. New York: A.M. Kelley.

Stein, Herbert. 1998. *What I Think*. Washington, DC: American Enterprise Institute.

Vivo, G. de. 1987. "David Ricardo." In *The New Palgrave: A Dictionary of Economics*, vol. 4, 183–98. London: Macmillan.

Weisskopf, Walter A. 1955. *The Psychology of Economics*. London: Routledge.

5

MILLING AROUND:
JOHN STUART MILL AND THE
SOCIALISTS SEARCH FOR UTOPIA

> *I am personally convinced that the reason which led the intellec-*
> *tuals to socialism was a man who is regarded as a great hero of*
> *classical liberalism, John Stuart Mill.*
>
> —Friedrich Hayek (Boaz 1997: 50)

The year was 1848, a time of rebellion and mass protest in continental Europe. It was the year Karl Marx and Friedrich Engels wrote their revolutionary tract, *The Communist Manifesto*. A specter was indeed haunting Europe—not just communism, but a whole string of isms—Fourierism, Owenism, Saint-Simonism, and transcendentalism. They all fell under the new expression "socialism." There was utopian socialism, revolutionary socialism, and national socialism. They all grew out of a reaction to the rapid transformation from a rural economy to an industrialized world.

The first half of the nineteenth century was an era of discontent—the industrial revolution, the Napoleonic wars, and democratic revolts throughout Europe. The growth model of Adam Smith was not a straight line of advance, but a line that took a number of sharp turns and corrections. Smith's idealistic model was already undermined by the discouraging works of Malthus and Ricardo. The revolt of the masses culminated in 1848, another one of those critical times, such as 1776. In 1848 popular revolts occurred in France, Germany, Austria, and Italy.

♪ **Music selection for this chapter: Camille Saint-Saëns, "Dans Macabre"**

The Importance of the Year 1848

The year 1848 was also significant for John Stuart Mill and his influence in the world: the publication of Mill's textbook, *Principles of Political Economy*, which would dominate the Western world for half a century, going through thirty-two editions, until Alfred Marshall's textbook took over in 1890.

It was this textbook that declared that the laws of production were objectively determined but the laws of distribution were variable. "[T]he Distribution of Wealth is a matter of human institution solely. They can place them at the disposal of whomsoever they please, and on whatever terms" (Mill 1884: 155). He added, "If the choice were to be made between Communism with all its chances and the present state of society with all its sufferings and injustices, all the difficulties, great or small, of Communism, would be but as dust in the balance" (1884: 159). His book also questioned the veracity of private property.

Mill's textbook was Ricardian through and through, focusing on the inequality of income, not growth.

The Enigmatic Mill Loses a Great Opportunity

John Stuart Mill (1806–73) was a reflection of his times—enigmatic and lost in an age of turmoil. In many ways, Mill was the embodiment of a Greek tragic hero, a dashing protagonist who ended his career in bewildered misfortune. Here was a great intellect, a classical liberal, and the last major proponent of the classical school of economics. Like Ricardo, Mill espoused personal liberty and vigorously defended Say's law of markets, the foundation of classical macroeconomics, and he opposed irredeemable paper money. He objected to coercive morality, intolerance, and a state religion. And he was an abolitionist who supported a woman's right to vote.

Yet he was famous for his inconsistencies and contradictions. He defended free enterprise but insisted he was a socialist. He flirted with socialism throughout his career, favored revolutionary change in Victorian culture, railed against overpopulation, and advocated Ricardo's distribution theory, separating production entirely from distribution. His love of Benthamite utilitarianism blinded him to frequent government intervention in the economy. He saw nothing wrong with heavy taxation of inheritances and nationalization of land, and questioned the justice of private property. This latter action is why Hayek made the statement that the influential Mill encouraged the cause of socialism.

Mill Grows Up in a Home Without Love

Mill's home life had a great deal to do with his career. Born in 1806 near London, he grew up in the clutches of a brilliant but overbearing father, **James Mill (1773–1836)**. The elder Mill was a close friend of David Ricardo and Jeremy Bentham, and was a radical utilitarian, energetic but

Photograph 5.1
John Stuart Mill (1806–1873)
"A chilly, bloodless man, overintellectual, undersexed, uxorious, priggish and humourless."
Courtesy of Hulton-Getty Archives.

unfeeling and hard-nosed. Writing of his father, John indicated that "he professed the greatest contempt for passion or emotion, a form of madness." In an earlier draft of his autobiography, he reported, "I thus grew up in the absence of love and in the presence of fear" (Mill 1961: 184). Mill's mother was uneducated and without strong opinions. He blamed her for his father's coldness and irritability. He despised and disliked her, and never mentioned her in his autobiography.

GREEK AT THREE, LATIN AT EIGHT, ECONOMICS AT FOURTEEN, AND A NERVOUS BREAKDOWN AT TWENTY

John Stuart Mill was a precocious child educated by his omnipresent father, who was determined to perform an experiment on his eldest son. (His three younger brothers and five sisters were treated differently.) His was the most famous education of the nineteenth century. John had no formal schooling, no college graduation. He was entirely home schooled by James Mill, his taskmaster. He learned Greek at three, and by age eight was reading Plato. By then he was also speaking and writing in Latin, and went quickly on to learning calculus, geometry, and philosophy. He read Newton's *Principia Mathematica* when he was eleven. Instead of religion, he was taught the utilitarianism of his father's friend Bentham, whose writings converted him into a "philosophic radical."

As a teenager, he read the classical economists. Following Malthus, he wrote anonymous articles advocating artificial contraception and was arrested for distributing birth control literature to servant girls (Stafford 1998: 5). At age fourteen, he read and reread Ricardo. For hours on end, he and his father would walk in the woods discussing the classical economist. His father sent him to France, where he acquired a lifelong love for French literature and political radicalism. As a young man, he had few friends and never participated in sports. "I was never a boy," he wrote (Courtney 1889: 40). Contemporaries characterized Mill as "a chilly, bloodless man, over-intellectual, undersexed, uxorious, priggish and humourless" (Stafford 1998: 23). But it would be wrong to say he had no hobbies or friends, as some commentaries have alleged. He played the piano, loved botany, enjoyed travel to foreign countries, and, except for a period of withdrawal in the 1840s and 1850s, frequently socialized.

His upbringing was often cruel and dehumanizing—an observer wrote of cuffs, deprivation of dinner, and long hours of work (Stafford 1998: 44–45)—and, not surprisingly, Mill suffered a nervous breakdown at twenty years of age. Losing all sense of meaning to life, he contemplated suicide. Consoled by reading Wordsworth, he eventually recovered from this black despair, although he suffered numerous relapses, including one following his father's death in 1836.

His father and he were close throughout their lives. John worked with his father in the East India Company in a position that would be comparable to the Secretary of State, given the status of the East India Company in British-controlled India. As biographer William Stafford noted, "they played a major role in ruling India though neither ever went there, neither spoke an Indian language and neither, in all probability, ever met an Indian" (1998: 4). John Stuart practiced a disciplined lifestyle; he would breakfast on a boiled egg and tea, taking nothing else till the end of the working day.

James Mill died in 1836 of tuberculosis; his death so affected his son that he developed a permanent nervous facial twitch.

MILL MEETS THE MOST INFLUENTIAL WOMAN IN HIS LIFE

The year 1830 was a turning point in Mill's private life. He met Harriet Taylor, a radical Unitarian full of intellectual passion and dogmatism, and fell deeply in love with her. Unfortunately, Harriet Taylor was married, and having an intense friendship with another man's wife was not respectable in Victorian society. Her husband was astonishingly liberal-minded in this regard and clandestinely opened his home to the philosopher. He even bought a country cottage where she and Mill could spend weekends together, and paid for her long trips abroad with Mill. According to Taylor's correspondence, the twenty-year friendship did not involve sex and was purely platonic until her husband died and they finally married in

Illustration 5.1
Harriet Taylor (1807–58)
Led Mill into socialism.
Portrait courtesy of F.A. Hayek.

1851. Their marriage created a stink at home, however. When Mill's siblings objected to the marriage, Mill broke off all relations with them and visited his mother only once before she died of cancer in 1854. It would be years before he reconciled with his family.

The Mills were inseparable, and John Stuart acknowledged Harriet's deep influence on him, especially in turning him toward socialism. Of course, not everyone agreed with Mill's high assessment of his wife. Carlyle thought she was "full of unwise intellect, asking and re-asking stupid questions" with her "great dark eyes, that were flashing unutterable things while he was discoursin' the utterable concerning all sorts o' high topics" (Stafford 1998: 21).

She took care of him when he contracted tuberculosis in the early 1850s. Harriet fell ill also, and thinking they would die within a year, they toured together in 1854–55 to Italy, Sicily, and Greece. Miraculously, they recuperated.

Following their recovery, Mill and his wife acquired an increasing streak of elitism and snobbery. When traveling abroad, Mill regularly graded the people he met, for intelligence, language, and political views. He found no one to be his (or his wife's) match.

"The Spring of My Life Is Broken"

Mill's ultimate achievement was the writing of *On Liberty*, which he and his wife worked on together. *On Liberty* was "so carefully composed," wrote Mill, that "I have made no alteration or addition to it, nor shall I ever" (1989 [1859]: xi). He *consecrated* the book to Harriet, who tragically died—of tuberculosis!—in 1858, a year before its publication. He wrote an extravagant eulogy, addressing her as "unparalleled in any human being that I have known or read of" (Stafford 1998: 10). He erected a costly marble tomb for her at Avignon, which he visited daily.

Mill's stepdaughter, Helen Taylor, became his constant companion, and greatly comforted him. Mill had published little for ten years, but after Harriet's passing, he wrote constantly, and had his books published in cheap People's Editions; in order to keep the price low, he agreed to forgo his royalties. He was elected a Liberal member of Parliament for Westminster from 1865 to 1868, opposing slavery in America and campaigning for women's suffrage. He received death threats after advocating the death penalty for Governor Edward Eyre, who had brutally put down a Negro rebellion in Jamaica. (For more on Mill's views of racism, see the

UTILITARIANISM AND THE STRANGE CASE OF JEREMY BENTHAM

How disappointing are the fruits, now that we have them,
of the bright idea of reducing Economics to a mathematical application
of the hedonistic calculus of Bentham!

—John Maynard Keynes (1951:155)

The Mills (father and son) were great admirers and followers of their elder friend and mentor, **Jeremy Bentham (1748–1832)**, the author of social utilitarianism. The younger Mill was so enamored that he founded the Utilitarian Society in London. He said utilitarianism gave him purpose in life.

Who was Bentham and why was his philosophy so enticing?

Jeremy Bentham was a generation ahead of James Mill. The son of a lawyer, he was born in London in 1748. His inherited wealth allowed him to be a self-proclaimed philosopher, with a lifetime focus on law and legislation, and penal reform.

Bentham was old enough to know Adam Smith and in fact sent a long letter to Smith in March 1787 castigating him for advocating usury laws in *The Wealth of Nations*. "Usury, if it must be an offence, is an offence committed with consent," Bentham argued. He later published the letter in the second edition of *Defence of Usury* (1790). This is surely one

Illustration 5.2
Jeremy Bentham (1748–1832)
A legacy to totalitarian regimes?
Courtesy of Hulton-Getty Archives.

of the most remarkable ironies in economics, the utilitarian interventionist lecturing the guru of market economics on the virtues of the free market (Adam Smith 1987: 386–404).

Bentham introduced the concept of utilitarianism in *Introduction to the Principles of Morals and Legislation* in 1789, stating, "Nature has placed mankind under the governance of two sovereign masters, *pain* and *pleasure*. . . . His only object is to seek pleasure and to shun pain" (1789: 11). In Bentham's mind, the battle in life is not between good and evil, or between reason and passion, but between pleasure and pain. He may have discovered this form of psychological hedonism from his travels to Europe.

Furthermore, Bentham felt that the pleasure-pain nexus needed to be quantified, what he called "felicific calculus." He went to great lengths to measure the degrees of pleasure and pain, called "utils," so that utils of pleasure can be measured against utils of pain. Today we can liken Bentham's method to cost-benefit analysis. A project is not worth doing unless the benefit exceeds the cost.

Benthamite utilitarianism has been identified as the "turning point" in modern economic thought in support of extreme individualism. According to this view, the community is a "fictitious body" that does not exist behind "the sum of the interests

(continued)

of the several members who compose it" (Bell 1996 [1976]: xii). However, as we shall see below, Bentham abandoned this individualistic methodology.

FIRST CAME DEMOCRATIC REFORM

In addition to his development of the pleasure-pain dychotomy, Bentham wrote about the need for legislative reform. The goal of society, he maintained, should be the "greatest happiness principle"—"the greatest happiness of the greatest number." He identified the social total of utility equal to the sum of all actions. The common good could be maximized.

Bentham's "greatest happiness" principle was immediately viewed as a cry for democratic reform and universal suffrage. Every person's utility was measured equally. Aristocrats had no right to superiority in Bentham's system. Bentham advocated that Britain give up its colonies and grant them independence. (Mill made an exception for India.)

Bentham's democratic leanings also encouraged more humanitarian treatment of criminals, the reduction of capital offenses, and the creation of the first metropolitan police force. He favored laws against mistreating animals, even to the point of prohibiting sports fishing.

THEN CAME UTILITARIAN FASCISM

In Bentham's system, there was little talk of individual rights. The national demand was to abandon laissez faire if it meant maximizing pleasure for the majority of citizens. Bentham's radicals worshipped the god of utility, not the invisible hand.

Moreover, Bentham applied the law of diminishing returns to utility, claiming that an extra shilling of income brings less utility to a wealthy man than it does to a poor man. Bentham's theory of declining marginal utility of income formed the underlining assumption of the progressive income tax and other redistribution schemes.

Without a bill defending individual rights to income, property, and life itself, Bentham's world could easily transform itself into a tyranny of the majority or, worse, totalitarian statism, in which dictators determine what is best for the majority. If the majority favors high taxes on the rich, so be it. If the majority hates Jews, blacks, or Christians, that's the way it is. It is the will of the people! If a minority group's interests and rights are trampled upon, it doesn't matter—as long as the majority's interests are met. Contemporaries such as Carlyle and Dickens regarded Benthamite utilitarianism as "hard, heartless, mechanical, philistine, godless and base" (Stafford 1998: 13).

Richard Posner adds, "Many of Bentham's radical proposals . . . prefigured the totalitarian assault on language by Newspeak, Hitler, and the Soviet Press" (1983: 40).

INSPECTION HOUSES

In fact, Bentham created a totalitarian monster upon advocating the building of a series of *Panopticons*, a name taken from the Greek word for "all seeing." Also called "Inspection Houses," they would serve as an ideal society. Panopticons would be set

(continued)

up as "houses of industry, work houses, poorhouses, manufactories, mad-houses, lazrettos, hospitals, and schools" (Rothbard 1995: 63). Bentham expected this ideal society to eventually control up to three-fifths of the British population.

Under this arrangement, an "all-seeing" inspector would oversee the prisons, schools, and factories, constantly spying on everyone—and Bentham hoped to be the Great Inspector (Rothbard 1995: 62–64)!

So, ultimately, Jeremy Bentham turned full circle, from his defense of laissez faire to his advocacy of Big Brother. Mill, the author of *On Liberty*, should have known better than to have hitched his star to this character.

THE IMMORTAL BENTHAM—ON PERMANENT DISPLAY!

Bentham not only sought to be the Great Inspector, but also to be never forgotten. His will contained an unusual demand: Upon his death, he was to become the great benefactor of the University College in London, on condition that his corpse be preserved and wheeled into the annual meetings of his disciples.

Today his movable mausoleum is free for anyone to see at the London University.

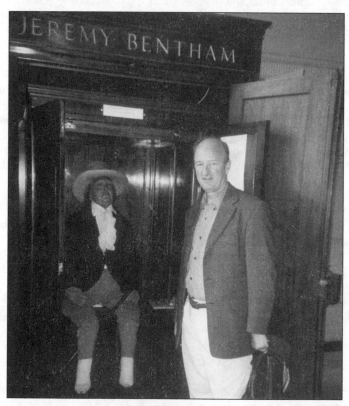

Photograph 5.2
Author Next to the Preserved Body of Jeremy Bentham
"Hard, heartless, mechanical, philistine, godless, and base."

discussion of Thomas Carlyle in chapter 3.) In 1869, he published *The Subjection of Women* and in 1873, he died of a fever with skin inflammation at the age of sixty-seven, and was buried next to Harriet. Immediately following his death, Helen Taylor published his *Autobiography* and a few years later, in 1879, his *Chapters on Socialism* came out. His *Collected Works* (containing thirty-three volumes) was published between 1963 and 1994 and edited by J.M. Robson.

MILL WRITES A LIBERTARIAN CLASSIC

Mill made three major contributions. His first was in the area of personal liberty and individuality. His short book *On Liberty* is considered a classic in philosophy, "the single most eloquent, most significant, and most influential statement of human individuality" (Collini in Mill 1989 [1859]: vii).

However, free-market advocates will be disappointed if they expect to read an attack on state interventionism. *On Liberty* is a protest more against coercive moralism than against government. Heavily influenced by his long "unrespectable" relationship with the married Harriet Taylor, his principal theme is a rejection of Victorian attitudes—intolerance, self-righteousness, the bland uniformity of Calvinism, Puritanism, and rigid Christianity. Mill denounced prejudice, custom, and uniformity of thought.

On the other hand, Mill favored tolerance, skepticism, and free thinking. He spoke out in favor of a woman's right to vote, and her right to hold public offices and participate in all careers. He defended freedom of thought and individualism, even to the point of condoning eccentric behavior. Contemporaries were largely hostile to Mill's message, considering it an attack on Christianity and an apology for divorce, but today's civil libertarians would find much to like.

Mill's classic work did not dwell on government policy, although he opposed Sunday blue laws, and various forms of prohibition. In general, his personal philosophy was laissez faire: Individuals are free to act as long as they do not harm others.

MILL, A THOROUGH RICARDIAN WHO SUPPORTED SAY'S LAW

Mill was thoroughly steeped in Ricardian economics, which, as we have seen, is both good and bad. It's good in the sense that he usually supported Adam Smith's system of natural liberty, and Say's law of markets. In 1829–30, he wrote *Essays on Some Unsettled Questions of Political Economy* (published in 1844). Among the essays in this volume was one entitled "Of the Influence of Consumption on Production" (1874: 47–74). He called the proto-Keynesian consumer society—that demand creates supply—a "pernicious" doctrine and a "palpable absurdity." He declared, "consumption need never be encouraged" (pages 47–48). Furthermore:

The person who saves his income is no less a consumer than he who spends it: he consumes it in a different way; it supplies food and clothing to be consumed, tools and materials to be used, by productive laborers. Consumption, therefore, already takes place to the greatest extent which the amount of production admits of; but, of the two kinds of production, reproductive and unproductive, the former alone adds to the national wealth, the latter impairs it. What is consumed for mere enjoyment is gone; what is consumed for reproduction leaves commodities of equal value, commonly with the addition of a profit. (Mill 1874: 48)

Regarding government's efforts to artificially stimulate consumption, Mill wrote,

The usual effect of the attempts of government to encourage consumption is merely to prevent saving; that is, to promote unproductive consumption at the expense of reproductive, and diminish the national wealth by the very means which were intended to increase it. (1874: 48–49)

It was Say through and through. Not surprisingly, when Mill wrote his textbook in 1848, he excluded any discussion of consumption and focused entirely on production and distribution.

Like Ricardo, Mill also opposed irredeemable paper money.

However, on the bad side, Mill's economics strictly correlated with the Ricardian theory of distribution: wages and profits varied inversely, prices were determined by labor costs, and long-run wages would fall to subsistence levels. Mill adopted the Ricardian rent theory, which was highly antilandlord. Mill accordingly advocated the nationalization of land in India when he worked for the East India Company. Moreover, in terms of property in general, Mill favored complete confiscation of land and property in the case of individuals who died with no heirs. In addition, according to Mill, there was no justification for the speculative holding of unused land, a theme enjoined by Henry George. "When land is not intended to be cultivated, no good reason can in general be given for its being private property at all" (Mill 1884 [1848]: 173).

MILL FAVORS REDISTRIBUTION OF WEALTH AND INCOME

Finally, Mill followed Ricardo in totally divorcing the principles of distribution from the laws of production, as we noted in the beginning of this chapter. The most famous quotation comes from the first paragraph in book II under "Distribution." Mill stated:

The laws and conditions of the production of Wealth partake of the character of physical truths. There is nothing optional or arbitrary in them. It is not so with the Distribution of Wealth. That is a matter of human institution solely. The things once there, mankind, individually or collectively, can do with them as they like. They can place them at the disposal of whomsoever they please, and on whatever terms. The Distribution of Wealth depends on the laws and customs of society. (Mill 1884: 155)

According to Hayek, it was this kind of thinking that has led intellectuals to support all kinds of attacks on property and wealth, and grandiose tax and confiscation schemes aimed at redistributing wealth and income, thinking that such radical schemes can be accomplished without hurting economic growth. "I am personally convinced that the reason which led the intellectuals to socialism, was John Stuart Mill" (Boaz 1997: 50).

Mill influenced intellectuals from H.G. Wells to the Webbs toward socialist thinking, so much so that Sir William Harcourt, chancellor of the exchequer, could say in 1894, "we are all socialists now" (Stafford 1998: 18). It would be years later before economists, educated in marginal analysis, would counter the redistributionists, arguing that the theory of distribution cannot be separated from the theory of production. According to the marginalist revolution, the producers of goods and services are paid according to the fruits of their labor, based on their discounted marginal product.

DID FRIEDRICH HAYEK SEE HIMSELF AS MILL REINCARNATE?

Friedrich von Hayek, the Nobel Prize–winning economist, showed an intense interest in John Stuart Mill in the late 1940s and 1950s. In 1951, Hayek published a book, *John Stuart Mill and Harriet Taylor: Their Friendship and Subsequent Marriage.* He was intrigued by the intense love affair between Mill and Taylor, and by how Mill's beloved wife influenced his thinking, especially in the writing of *Principles* (1848).

Hayek himself went through a rearrangement of his own love life in the 1940s. He was married to his wife Helen in the 1920s, and they had two children. They fought frequently when Hayek was teaching at the London School of Economics. Hayek returned to Vienna after World War II and fell in love with Helene Bitterlich, a cousin and former sweetheart. Helene had been previously married but was now available. Hayek immediately decided to get a divorce. His first wife objected and he lost all his friends at the London School of Economics. Lionel Robbins, chairman of the economics department, did not reconcile with Hayek for decades because of the bitter divorce. Hayek spent a year teaching in Arkansas in 1950 because of its liberal divorce laws. He married Helene and lived in the United States, Germany, and the Austrian Alps until he died in 1992.

That's not the end of the story. In 1954, Hayek applied for a grant from the Guggenheim Foundation to retrace the journey Mill and his wife had taken through Italy and Greece exactly a hundred years earlier. On January 15, 1855, Mill was on the steps of the Roman Forum and "thought that the best thing to write and publish at present would be a volume on Liberty" (Hayek 1994: 130). Hayek was in Rome on the same date a hundred years later and felt inspired by Mill to write *The Constitution of Liberty.* It was published in 1960 (a hundred years after Mill's *On Liberty*).

Despite all these events, including helping Michael St. John Packe write a full-length biography of John Stuart Mill, Hayek would write years later, oddly, that Mill "in fact never particularly appealed to me" (1994: 128).

Socialist measures to redistribute wealth and income do indeed affect economic activity. As Hayek stated, "if we did do with that product whatever we pleased, people would never produce those things again" (Boaz 1997: 50).

MILL'S FLIRTATION WITH SOCIALISM

In introducing the theory of distribution, Mill immediately began with a discussion of the virtues of socialism. He had serious reservations about capitalism and felt that private property is not always justly or properly owned. He described three types of socialism:

1. **Utopian socialism:** cooperative communities, such as those developed by Robert Owen, Saint-Simon, and Fourier (see the box on page 129).

2. **Revolutionary socialism:** radical groups, including communists, who seek to seize power by force, nationalize industry, and abolish private property (see chapter 6 on Marx).

3. **Fascist socialism:** bureaucratic regulation and control of industry and the means of production, distribution and exchange, as advocated later by the Fabian Society and the British Labour Party.

CHRISTIAN REFORMERS AND UTOPIAN SOCIALISTS

But if you'd been with me in Utopia, and seen it all for yourself, as I did . . .
you'd be the first to admit that you'd never seen a country so well organized.
—Rafael in Sir Thomas More, *Utopia* (1965 [1516]: 67)

Mill and other social reformers have often dreamed of a "utopia," such as Sir Thomas More's ideal community, where there were no poor, no beggars, no lawyers, and no war—and where a citizen could obtain anything "without any sort of payment"; work six hours a day and spend the evening hours talking, reading, or listening to music. Children received a top education for free, and hospitals were "so well run" that "practically everyone would rather be ill in hospitals than at home" (More 1965: 81).

The first half of the nineteenth century was full of reformers seeking such an idyllic life. Utopian socialists (the term "socialist" was first used in the late 1820s in England and the early 1830s in France) rose up throughout Europe and America, creating optimistic communities like New Harmony, Modern Times, and Brook Farm.

They shared some common objectives:

1. Abolition of private property and competition.
2. Treating everyone as equals.
3. Communal living.

All members of the community were expected to work hard in the job they were assigned, and to share equally the fruits of labor. "From each according to his ability, to each according to his needs" was a popular phrase. Other social reformers went to greater extremes, for instance, abolishing marriage and money. Following are some prominent examples.

(continued)

THE FRENCH PHALANXES

Utopian thinking was paramount in the mind of many Frenchmen prior to and following the French Revolution of 1789. But the French were strongly divided between the laissez-faire school (Montesquieu, Quesnay, Condorcet, Say, Bastiat) and the utopian socialists (Saint-Simon, Charles Fourier, Simonde de Sismondi, and Pierre-Joseph Proudhon). In fact, socialism was in many ways a French idea. Just as Malthus and Ricardo undermined their mentor, Adam Smith, so the French socialists countered the French laissez-faire advocates, Say and Bastiat.

Prominent among the French socialists were **Count Henri de Rouvroy de Saint-Simon (1760–1825)** and **François Marie Charles Fourier (1772–1837)**. Saint-Simon, who fought in the Revolutionary War in America, warned that the industrial society is gravely unjust, because the idle rich take a disproportionate share of the wealth. His followers demanded an end to private property.

Fourier, though eccentric, was more organized than Saint-Simon. He favored centralized communities, which he called *phalanstères*, or phalanxes. Everyone would live in a large central building. The Fourierist idea took hold in hundreds of places around the world, even in the United States: Trumbull Phalanx in Ohio, Modern Times in New York, and Brook Farm in Massachusetts. But none of these dream communities took root.

ROBERT OWEN AND NEW HARMONY

Illustration 5.3
Robert Owen (1771–1858)
Courtesy of Hulton-Getty Archives.

Robert Owen (1771–1858) was a Welsh boy wonder who became an entrepreneur in the cotton business. He became famous after buying the textile mills in the squalid village of New Lanark, near Glasgow, Scotland, and converting it into paradise—with nice homes for workers, a ten-hour workday, no child labor, a schoolhouse for children, and no corporal punishment. His objective was to make the poor productive with proper incentives. He used his profits to improve working and living conditions.

His new form of "compassionate capitalism" paid off handsomely, and hundreds of observers came from all around the world to admire his success. He was a resolute champion of social change, advocating "villages of cooperation" throughout Britain, child labor laws, and a ten-hour workday. He was a big supporter of labor unions and producer and consumer cooperatives.

His success in New Lanark was based largely on sound economic and social principles, but like so many reformers, he went off the deep end when he established a utopian society called New Harmony in Indiana. The old capitalist had become a new socialist. New Harmony was officially dedicated on July 4, 1826, when Owen pronounced his own

(continued)

declaration of independence "From Private Property, Irrational Religion, and Marriage!" Within two years, the experiment was a miserable failure, suffering from fraud, a lack of planning, and money. Owen lost four-fifths of his fortune in the scheme and spent the last years of his life writing pamphlets and pursuing spiritualism.

GEORGE RIPLEY AND BROOK FARM

George Ripley (1802–80), literary critic and transcendentalist, headed Brook Farm near Boston starting in 1841. The village consisted of twenty shareholders forming a joint stock company, with each one having a vote. Nathaniel Hawthorne and other famous writers came and visited. Members all enjoyed the same wages, the same hours, and the same room and board. Teachers and students were to be "free and equal." Brook Farm was discontinued in 1847, due to its rising debts.

THE PILGRIMS EXPERIMENT WITH COMMUNISM

Many Christian groups practiced Christian communism, including the Pilgrims when they landed at Plymouth in 1620. They were determined to create a communal society based on the New Testament Christians who had "all things in common" (Acts 2: 44–45). However, Governor William Bradford reported that the plan failed miserably, and "was found to breed much confusion and discontent and retard much employment." Bradford abandoned the practice and assigned each family a plot of land, which proved highly successful, "for it made all hands very industrious, so that much more corn was planted than otherwise would have been" (Bradford 1948: 160–62).

MORMONS AND THE UNITED ORDER

When Joseph Smith established the Mormon Church in the 1830s, Protestant groups in the area, failing to heed the lessons of the Pilgrim Fathers, created utopian "common stock" societies. But Joseph Smith opposed such practices, "as it opens such a dreadful field for the avaricious, the indolent, and the corrupt hearted to prey upon the innocent and virtuous, and honest" (1972: 144). Instead, the Mormons created the "United Order," which asked members to voluntarily consecrate their properties and wealth to the Church and receive in return a "stewardship," or property sufficient for their family and business needs. This stewardship became the private property of the member, who could develop it or sell it as his own. Thus private property was maintained among the Mormon utopian villages.

However, when the Mormons fled to the Rocky Mountains in the late 1840s, following the martyrdom of Joseph Smith, their new leader, Brigham Young, established highly communal United Orders without private property. Most of them lasted only a few years, and all were eventually disbanded.

UTOPIAN UPDATE: THE KIBBUTZ

Today few communal societies exist, and those that do tend to be small, close-knit groups. The longest-lasting communal organizations are the kibbutzim in Israel, which have been in existence since the early twentieth century. By the late 1980s, over 250 kibbutzim were in existence, but the number has been in sharp decline recently. A typical kibbutz has fewer than 300 members, who live and share property together. All property belongs to the kibbutz. Members have regular daily jobs, and receive goods and services for their labor instead of wages. In most kibbutzim, the adults and children live apart.

Some kibbutzim have been highly profitable by selling their products outside the collective community. But in the 1990s, kibbutzim fell into decline and suffered serious problems, including heavy debts, internal labor turmoil, and young people leaving for better opportunities in the outside world. Ezra Dalomi, member of the Kibbutz Rosh Hanikra, wrote in 1999, "The end is near. Next year the kibbutz movement will celebrate its ninetieth birthday, but it probably won't get up to a hundred. . . . There is no energy left. Fifteen years of crisis, of stalling, have had their effect. . . . There is no more gas, we've run out of fuel. The car will continue to run aimlessly, slow down until it stops altogether" (Dalomi 1999: 25).

Today kibbutzim have changed dramatically. Only 38 percent of kibbutz employees are kibbutz members, and many now hire Palestinians. Many people who live on kibbutzim have to work outside the kibbutz. They are expected to return a percentage of their earnings to the collective.

WHY DO UTOPIAN COMMUNES FAIL?

The history of utopian societies has been long on promise and short on success. Economics explains why: In an environment where resources are scarce and needs are unlimited, competition is inevitable. Institutions must provide incentives to encourage an expansion of resources and discourage unlimited demands. Property rights and the market price system provide the proper incentives to accomplish this goal; socialist systems that abolish property and prices do not. Socialist societies that adopt the well-meaning but uneconomic "From each according to his abilities, to each according to his needs" have in essence adopted a 100 percent marginal tax system. It's hard to maintain a successful, upbeat utopian society under this kind of burden.

In *Utopia*, even Thomas More warned of the drawbacks: "I don't believe you'd ever have a reasonable standard of living under a communist system. There'd always tend to be shortages, because nobody would work hard enough. In the absence of a profit motive, everyone would become lazy, and rely on everyone else to do the work for him. Then, when things really got short, the inevitable result would be a series of murders and riots, since nobody would have any legal method of protecting the products of his own labour—especially as there wouldn't be any respect for authority, or I don't see how there could be, in a classless society" (More 1965: 67).

Mill was critical of revolutionary and fascist forms of socialism, but expressed considerable sympathy with utopian communitarianism, which operated with a high degree of individual liberty and without violence. It was this kind of socialism that he identified with. Thus, Mill set the stage "on a downward slope leading from the eighteenth-century sanity and conservativism of David Hume to the Fabian socialism and collectivism of Beatrice Webb" (Stafford 1998: 19).

SUMMARY

John Stuart Mill longed for the bliss of a voluntary communitarian village, but all such communities have suffered from one defect: They never lasted. New Harmony, Modern Times, United Order—they all had high-minded names, yet they all eventually disintegrated as a result of laziness, debt, or fraud.

Not long after Mill's time, a new form of socialism appeared on the horizon, the violent revolutionary kind. If fellow citizens couldn't be persuaded to cooperate, then they must be forced to obey through the iron fist and the bayonet. Gradually, the eyes of reformers all turned toward one authority, the subject of chapter 6.

REFERENCES

Bell, Daniel. 1996 [1976]. *The Cultural Contradictions of Capitalism*, 2d ed. New York: Basic Books.

Bentham, Jeremy. 1789. *Introduction to the Principles of Morals and Legislation*. London: T. Payne and Son.

Boaz, David. 1997. *Libertarianism: A Primer.* New York: Free Press.

Bradford, William. 1948. *History of Plymouth.* New York: Walter J. Black.

Courtney, W.L. 1889. *Life of John Stuart Mill.* London: Walter Scott.

Dalomi, Ezra. 1999. "It's a Waste of Time, Chaverim." *Kibbutz Trends* 33 (Spring), 25–29.

Hayek, Friedrich A. 1951. *John Stuart Mill and Harriet Taylor*. Chicago: University of Chicago Press.

———. 1960. *The Constitution of Liberty*. Chicago: University of Chicago Press.

———. 1994. *Hayek on Hayek*. Chicago: University of Chicago Press.

Keynes, John Maynard. 1951. *Essays in Persuasion.* New York: W.W. Norton.

Marx, Karl, and Friedrich Engels. 1964 [1848]. *The Communist Manifesto*. New York: Monthly Review Press.

Mill, John Stuart. 1874 [1844]. *Essays on Some Unsettled Questions of Political Economy,* 2d ed. New York: Augustus M. Kelley.

———. 1884 [1848]. *Principles of Political Economy,* ed. J. Laurence Laughlin. New York: D. Appleton.

———. 1989 [1859]. *On Liberty and Other Writings.* Introduction by Stefan Collini. Cambridge: Cambridge University Press.

———. 1989 [1873] *Autobiography.* New York: Penguin.

———. 1989. *Selections: On Liberty, the Subjection of Women, and Chapters on Socialism,* ed. Stefan Collini. Cambridge: Cambridge University Press.

———. 1961. *The Early Draft of John Stuart Mill's Autobiography*, ed. J. Stillinger. Champaign: University of Illinois Press.

More, Sir Thomas. 1965 [1516]. *Utopia.* London: Penguin.

Posner, Richard A. 1983. *The Economics of Justice*. Cambridge, MA: Harvard University Press.

Rothbard, Murray N. 1995. *Classical Economics*. Hants, UK: Edward Elgar.

Smith, Adam. 1987. *Correspondence of Adam Smith*. Oxford: Oxford University Press.

Smith, Joseph. 1972. *Teachings of the Prophet Joseph Smith*. Salt Lake City: Deseret.

Stafford, William. 1998. *John Stuart Mill*. London: Macmillan.

6

MARX MADNESS
PLUNGES ECONOMICS
INTO A NEW DARK AGE

*Jenny! If we can but weld our souls together, then with contempt
shall I fling my glove in the world's face, then shall I stride
through the wreckage a creator!*

—Karl Marx to his fiancée (Wilson 1940: 116)

*Karl [Marx] was possessed of demonic genius that was to
transform the modern world.*

—Saul K. Padover (1978:1)

If the work of Adam Smith is the Genesis of modern economics—that of
Karl Marx is its Exodus. If the Scottish philosopher is the great creator
of a system of natural liberty, the German revolutionary is its great
destroyer.[1]

For all the horrors committed in Marx's name, the German philosopher
has for more than a century struck an inspirational chord among workers
and intellectuals disenfranchised by market capitalism. Malthus and

---

1. After writing this opening sentence, I discovered that Marxist John E. Roemer said practically the
same thing. According to him, the "main difference" between Smith and Marx is as follows: "Smith
argued that the individual's pursuit of self-interest would lead to an outcome beneficial to all,
whereas Marx argued that the pursuit of self-interest would lead to anarchy, crisis, and the dissolu-
tion of the private property-based system itself. . . . Smith spoke of the invisible hand guiding
individual, self-interested agents to perform those actions that would be, despite their lack of concern for such an outcome, socially optimal; for Marxism the simile is the iron fist of competition,
pulverizing the workers and making them worse off than they would be in another feasible system,
namely, one based on the social or public ownership of property" (Roemer 1988: 2–3).

♪ **Music selection for this chapter: Gustav Holst, "Mars, the Bringer of War," from *The Planets***

Ricardo may have sown the seeds of dissention, but **Karl Marx (1818–83)** reaped the harvest by breaking bonds of capitalism and tearing asunder the foundations of Adam Smith's system of natural liberty. No longer could the commercial system be viewed as "innocent" (Montesquieu), "mutually beneficial" (Smith), or "naturally harmonious" (Say and Bastiat). Now, under Marx, it was pictured as alien, exploitative, and self-destructive.

His mark on the world is indelible and the evidence of a brilliant if not disturbed mind. That Marx was a genius is not in dispute—he had a genuine doctorate in Greek philosophy, spoke French, German, and English fluently, could talk intelligently about science, literature, art, and philosophy, and wrote a classic book that created a powerful new model of economic thinking. Never mind that he couldn't balance a checkbook or keep a job. A non-Marxist biographer called him a "towering, learned, and extraordinarily gifted man" (Padover 1978: xvi). Martin Bronfenbrenner deemed Marx "the greatest social scientist of all times"[2] (1967: 624).

Photograph 6.1
Karl Marx as Chief Editor (1818–83)
"Who comes rushing in, impetuous and wild."
Courtesy of Hulton-Getty Archives.

2. Personally, I think German sociologist Max Weber deserves this honor. See chapter 10.

MARX AND COMMUNISM

Yet, like Cain in the Bible, Marx is cursed with a black mark in history. His name will forever be associated with the dark side of communism. A specter is haunting Karl Marx—the history of Lenin, Stalin, Mao, and Pol Pot, and the millions who died and suffered under their regimes. Apologists say Marx can't be held accountable for his communist followers' atrocities and even assert that Marx would have been one of the first to be executed or sent to the Gulag. Perhaps. For one thing, he vehemently opposed press censorship throughout his career. Yet, without Marx, could there have been such a violent revolution and repression? Did not Marx support a "reign of terror" on the bourgeoisie? As one bitter critic put it, "In the name of human progress, Marx has probably caused more death, misery, degradation and despair than any man who ever lived" (Downs 1983: 299).

MARX ENGENDERS YOUTHFUL FANATICISM

Among schools of thought, no other economist (or should I say philosopher) engenders so much passion and religious fervor as Marx. Above all, Marx was a visionary and a revolutionary idol, not just an economist. In reading *The Communist Manifesto*, written over 160 years ago, one can't help feeling the passionate power, the pungent style, and the astonishing simplicity of Marx and Engels's words (1964 [1848]).

Youthful followers become true believers, and it usually takes them years to grow out of their Marxist addiction. It happened to Robert Heilbroner, Mark Blaug, Whittaker Chambers, and David Horowitz. I even saw it among my students at Rollins College, a decade after Soviet communism had collapsed and Marxism was supposedly dead. In my class, "Survey of Great Economists," I require students to read a book authored by an economist. One student chose *The Communist Manifesto*. After reading it, he came to me and exclaimed with some emotion, "This is *incredible!* I *must* do my book report on *this!*" pointing to his well-marked copy. It was eerie. Despite my lectures countering Marxian doctrine, he was hooked.

I can easily see how a young revolutionary could be swayed by these unforgettable lines from the polemical *Communist Manifesto*: "A specter is haunting Europe—the specter of Communism. . . . The history of all hitherto existing society is the history of class struggles. . . . The bourgeoisie has pitilessly torn asunder the motley feudal ties that bound man to his 'natural superiors,' and has left remaining no other nexus between man and man than naked self-interest, than callous 'cash payment.' . . . Veiled by political and religious illusions, it has substituted naked, shameless, direct, brutal exploitation. . . . Let the ruling classes tremble at the communistic revolution. The proletarians have nothing to lose but their chains. They have a world to win. WORKING MEN OF ALL COUNTRIES, UNITE!" (1964 [1848] passim).

Marshall Berman, a longtime Marxist living in New York City, recounts how he, as a youth, encountered another book by Marx, *Economic and Philosophical Manuscripts of 1844*. This book generated the same kind of fanatic enthusiasm. "Suddenly I was in a sweat, melting, shedding clothes and tears, flashing hot and cold"—not from staring at *Playboy* magazine or trading a penny stock for the first time, but from reading Marx! (Berman 1999: 7).

In many ways, Marxism has become a quasi-religion, with its slogans, symbols, red banners, hymns, party fellowship, apostles, martyrs, bible, and definitive truth. "Marx had the self-assurance of a prophet who had talked to God. . . . He was a poet, prophet, and moralist speaking as a philosopher and economist; his doctrine is not to be tested against mere facts but to be received as ethical-religious truth. . . . Marx was to lead the Chosen People out of slavery to the New Jerusalem. . . . Becoming a Marxist or a Communist is like falling in love, an essentially emotional commitment" (Wesson 1976: 29–30, 158).

Marx's Contributions to Economics

Few economists venture into other disciplines as did Karl Marx. We find Marx the philosopher, Marx the historian, Marx the political scientist, Marx the sociologist, and Marx the literary critic. He was prolific and wrote unendingly about nearly everything. Even today a compilation of the complete works of Marx and his colleague Friedrich Engels has not been finished. The commentaries on Marx and related subjects are so vast that it would take volumes to tell it all. (On the Internet, Amazon.com lists over 4,000 entries on Marx and communism, second only to Jesus and Christianity.) Thus, our chapter on Marx must of necessity be limited largely to his economic contributions. Even then, Marx the economist is not an easy subject.

Marx was probably the first major economist to establish his own school of thought, with its own methodology and specialized language. In creating his own school in his classic work, *Capital* (1976 [1867]), he contrasted his system with the proponents of laissez faire—Adam Smith, J.-B. Say, and David Ricardo, among others. It was Marx who dubbed laissez faire the "classical school." In developing a Marxist approach to economics, he created his own vocabulary: surplus value, reproduction, bourgeoisie and proletarians, historical materialism, vulgar economy, monopoly capitalism, and so on. He invented the term "capitalism." Since Marx, economics has never been the same. Today, there is no universally acceptable macro model of the economy as there is in physics or mathematics—there are only warring schools of economics.

EARLY TRAINING: MARX'S INTERNAL CONTRADICTIONS

Who was this German philosopher? Who could have brought about such passion, such devotion, such a powerful new model in economics that would challenge the classical model of Adam Smith?

Karl Heinrich Marx was born on May 5, 1818, in an elegant townhouse in Trier in the Rhine province of Prussia. Trier is the oldest town in Germany.

From crib to coffin, Marx was full of contradictions. He railed against the petty bourgeoisie, yet grew up in a bourgeois family. He lived years of his adult life in desperate poverty, yet was born in a relatively well-to-do household. He exalted capitalism's technology and material advances, yet damned the capitalist society. He felt deeply for the working man, yet never held a steady job or visited a factory during his adult life. His mother complained, "If only Karl had made capital instead of writing about it!" (Padover 1978: 344).

Marx shouted anti-Semitic epithets at his opponents, yet was Jewish from both sides of his family (see the box on page 138, "Marx: An Anti-Semitic Jew?"). He cherished his children, yet saw them die prematurely from malnutrition and illness or drove them to suicide. Marx protested the evils of exploitation in the capitalist system, and yet, according to one biographer, he "exploited everyone around him—his wife, his children, his mistress and his friends—with a ruthlessness which was all the more terrible because it was deliberate and calculating" (Payne 1968: 12). Paul Samuelson adds, "Marx was a gentle father and husband; he was also a prickly, brusque, egotistical boor" (Samuelson 1967: 616). In sum, Marx ranted about the inner contradictions of capitalism, yet he himself was constantly beset by inner dissension.

MARX'S CHRISTIAN FAITH

The most surprising irony is that Karl Marx—considered one of the most vicious opponents of religion—was brought up a Christian though many of his ancestors were rabbis.

His father, Heinrich Marx, overcame insuperable obstacles to become a well-to-do Jewish lawyer. When he was faced with a new Prussian law in 1816, prohibiting Jews from practicing law, he switched from Judaism to the Lutheran faith. His mother, Henrietta Pressborch, was the daughter of a rabbi, yet she also saw the social value of converting to Christianity.

Karl, the oldest surviving son in a family of nine children, was baptized a Christian and wrote several essays on Christian living while attending gymnasium (high school). As a senior in high school, Karl wrote an essay, "The Union of the Faithful with Christ," which spoke of alienation, a fear of rejection by God. He was mesmerized by the story of a peaceful paradise in Genesis and the coming of a dreadful Apocalypse in The Revelation of St. John. Later these first and last books of the Bible would help formulate Marx's doctrines of alienation, class struggle, a revolutionary overthrow of bourgeois society, and the glories of a stateless, classless millennial-type era of peace and prosperity. His vision of a proletariat victory may have come from this early training in Christian Messianism. He was first and foremost a millennial communist.

Many of Marx's dogmas were not original. They came from the Bible, which he twisted and changed to suit his purposes. As biographer Robert Payne notes, "when he [Marx] turned against Christianity he brought to his ideas of social justice the same passion for atonement and the same horror of alienation" (1968: 42).

MARX BECOMES A COLLEGE RADICAL

Marx's faith was challenged almost immediately upon attending the University of Bonn, where he, like many college freshmen, spent more

---

MARX: AN ANTI-SEMITIC JEW?

The Jew becomes impossible.
—Karl Marx, "On the Jewish Question"

Marx has been accused of being a self-hating Jew: born of Jewish parents, but anti-Semitic throughout life. In an essay published in 1843, "On the Jewish Question," Marx expressed anti-Jewish sentiments that were common in Europe at the time. His language was vindictive: "What is the worldly cult of the Jew? *Schacher.* What is his worldly God? Money! . . . Money is the jealous god of Israel before whom no other god may exist. Money degrades all the gods of mankind—and converts them into commodities. . . . What is contained abstractly in the Jewish religion—contempt for theory, for art, for history" (Padover 1978: 169).

Marx's racial slander never let up. He never retracted his 1843 defamation of the Jews. "On the contrary," wrote biographer Saul Padover, "he harbored a lifelong hostility toward them. . . . His letters are replete with anti-Semitic remarks, caricatures, and crude epithets: 'Levy's Jewish nose,' 'usurers,' 'Jew-boy,' 'nigger-Jew,' etc. For reasons perhaps explainable by the German concept *Selbsthass* [self-hate], Marx's hatred of Jews was a canker which neither time nor experience ever eradicated from his soul" (Padover 1978: 171).

DEFENDING MARX

Prominent Marxists have denied Marx's anti-Semitism, however. *A Dictionary of Marxian Thought* states, "Although we know that Marx was not averse to using offensive vulgarisms about some Jews, there is no basis for regarding him as having been anti-Semitic" (Bottomore 1991: 275). Gareth Stedman Jones writes, "Marx's alleged anti-Semiticism . . . cannot be understood except in the context of his hatred of all forms of national and ethnic particularism" (Blumenberg 1998 [1962]: x).

time drinking and carousing than studying. He piled up bills, joined a secret revolutionary group, and was wounded in a duel. Later he was arrested for carrying a pistol, and jailed for rowdiness.

His father hoped to reform this eldest son by transferring him to the renowned University of Berlin, where he spent the next five years. But his undisciplined lifestyle continued. He read voraciously and lived the life of a bohemian. He fancied himself a poet, translated Greek plays, and filled his notebooks with dark tragedies and romantic poetry. He joined the Doctor's Club (*Doktorklub*), a small society of radical Young Hegelians.

Students described him as having a brilliant mind and being ruthlessly opinionated, his dark excitable eyes staring in defiance. His black beard and thick mane of hair, his shrill voice and violent temper, stood out. He was so exceptionally swarthy that his family and friends called him "Mohr" or "Moor." During his college years, he was described colorfully in a short poem (Payne 1968: 81; Padover 1978: 116):

> Who comes rushing in, impetuous and wild—
> Dark fellow from Trier, in fury raging?
> Nor walks nor skips, but leaps upon his prey
> In tearing rage, as one who leaps to grasp
> Broad spaces in the sky and drags them down to earth,
> Stretching his arms wide open to the heavens.
> His evil fist is clenched, he roars interminably
> As though ten thousand devils had him by the hair.

Illustration 6.1
G.W.F. Hegel (1770-1831):
A recurring rhythm of
destruction and re-creation.
Courtesy of Hulton-Getty Archives.

THE INFLUENCE OF RADICAL GERMAN PHILOSOPHERS

Two radical philosophers greatly influenced Marx during these college years and soon after: **G.W.F. Hegel (1770–1831)** and a contemporary, **Ludwig Feuerbach (1804–72)**. From Hegel, Marx developed the driving force of his "dialectical materialism"—that all progress was achieved through conflict. From Feuerbach's *Essence of Christianity* (1841), Marx rationalized his mythical view of religion and his rejection of Christianity. God did not create man; man created God! Engels described the liberating impact of Feuerbach's book: "In one blow it . . . placed materialism back upon the throne. . . . The spell was broken. . . .

The enthusiasm was universal: We were all for the moment Feuerbachians" (Padover 1978: 136).

His parents were worried sick about their prodigal son who wanted to become a writer and a critic instead of a lawyer. One of the saddest things recorded in the history of economics is the often harsh correspondence between Marx and his parents. His father, Heinrich, was a classical liberal and a defender of bourgeois culture, so one can imagine his despair over his son. His letters charged Karl with being "a slovenly barbarian, an anti-social person, a wretched son, an indifferent brother, a selfish lover, an irresponsible student, and a reckless spendthrift," all accurate accusations that haunted Marx throughout his adult life. Heinrich Marx railed, "God help us! Disorderliness, stupefying dabbling in all the sciences, stupefying brooding at the gloomy oil lamp; barbarism in a scholar's dressing-gown and unkempt hair" (Padover 1978: 106–7). In another letter, he accused Karl of being possessed by a "demonic spirit" that "estranges your heart from finer feelings" (Berman 1999: 25). This letter of Karl's father would not be the only time Marx would be accused of devilish behavior, however. (See the box below.)

KARL MARX'S SATANIC VERSES

Everything in existence is worth destroying.
—Mephistopheles, in Goethe's *Faust*

One of the nightmarish aspects of Marx's life was his fascination with Goethe's *Faust*, the story of a young man who is at war with himself between good and evil and makes a pact with Satan. Faust exchanges his soul (through his intermediary Mephistopheles) for a life of pleasure and ultimately for the right to control the world through massive organized labor. Goethe's *Faust* was Marx's bible throughout his life. He memorized whole speeches of Mephistopheles, and could recite long passages to his children. (He equally loved Shakespeare, whom he also quoted regularly.)

While he was a student at Berlin University in 1837, Marx wrote romantic verses dedicated to his fiancée, Jenny von Westphalen. One of these poems, "The Player," was published in a German literary magazine, *Athenaeum*, in 1841 (reprinted in Payne 1971: 59). It describes a violinist who summons up the powers of darkness. The player, either Lucifer or Mephistopheles, boldly declares,

> Look now, my blood-dark sword shall stab
> Unerringly within thy soul.
> God neither knows nor honors art.
> The hellish vapors rise and fill the brain.
>
> Til I go mad and my heart is utterly changed.
> See this sword—the Prince of Darkness sold it to me.
> For me he beats the time and gives the signs.
> Ever more boldly I play the dance of death.

(continued)

MARX WRITES A GREEK TRAGEDY

A pact with the devil was the central theme of *Oulanem*, a poetic play Marx wrote in 1839. He completed only the first act, but it reveals a number of violent and eccentric characters. The main character, Oulanem, is an anagram for Manuelo, meaning Immanuel or God (Payne 1971: 57–97). In a Hamlet-like soliloquy, Oulanem asks himself if he must destroy the world. Oulanem begins,

> Ruined! Ruined! My time has clean run out!
> The clock has stopped, the pygmy house has crumbled,
> Soon I shall embrace eternity to my breast, and soon
> I shall howl gigantic curses at mankind.

And ends,

> And we are chained, shattered, empty, frightened,
> Eternally chained to this marble block of Being,
> Chained, eternally chained, eternally.
> And the worlds drag us with them on their rounds,
> Howling their songs of death, and we—
> We are the apes of a cold God.

MARX AND SUICIDE

Marx's fixation with self-destructive behavior was prevalent through most of his life. He even composed and published an entire book on suicide while living in exile in Belgium in 1835. Marx translated the work of Jacques Peuchet, detailing the accounts of four suicides, three by young women. The focus is on the industrial system that would encourage suicidal behavior (Plaut and Anderson 1999).

MARX MARRIES AND MOVES TO PARIS

Finally, Marx left Berlin on grounds that the university administration had been taken over by anti-Hegelians. Fearing his Ph.D. dissertation on Greek philosophy might be rejected, he submitted it to the University of Jena, which accepted it without any attendance requirements. In 1842, he worked briefly as editor of a German newspaper, fearlessly defending free speech. He resigned when the censors made it impossible for him to continue.

In 1843, Marx married his teenage sweetheart and neighbor, Jenny von Westphalen, over objections from both families. Jenny, four years older than Marx, was the daughter of Baron Johann Ludwig von Westphalen, a wealthy aristocrat who represented the Prussian government in the city council. After the baron died, the Marxes lived off the baroness's largess. Jenny was deeply devoted to Karl and his revolutionary ideas. For the rest of their lives, Jenny and Karl were inseparable through poverty, illness, and failure. Their love was deep and lasting, though not without heartache and trouble. They exchanged numerous love letters. They had six children, although only two daughters survived them.

In less than a year, Karl and his new wife moved to Paris, where he became editor of a monthly German magazine. Karl and Jenny Marx loved Paris and French culture. Here Marx had little interest in associating with Bastiat and the French laissez-faire school—he later labeled Bastiat the most "superficial" apologist of the "vulgar economy" (Padover 1978: 369)—but fell in among the radical French socialists, including Pierre Proudhon and Louis Blanc. He plunged into oceans of books and would often go three to four days without sleep (Padover 1978: 189). Seeing the class struggle firsthand, he wrote eloquently of alienation and labor suffering under capitalism in *The Economic and Philosophical Manuscripts of 1844*, a compilation of articles not published until 1932.

MARX MEETS ENGELS AND CHANGES HISTORY

Illustration 6.2
Friedrich Engels (1820–95):
"À la guerre comme à la guerre;
we do not promise any freedom,
nor any democracy"
(Lenin 1970, vol. ix: 242).
Courtesy of Hulton-Getty Archives.

It was there in Paris that Marx met his lifelong colleague-in-arms, **Friedrich Engels (1820–95)**. Considered "tall" (though his height was only five feet, six inches), blond, Teutonic-looking with cold blue eyes, Engels had a critical eye for detail. Together Marx and Engels started working on a book attacking their socialist rivals. It would be a close collaboration that would last another forty years, until Marx died in 1883.

Engels, the son of a wealthy German industrialist, hated his tyrannical father and his "boring, dirty, and abominable" business, even as Engels himself achieved financial success running a textile operation in Manchester (though there is no evidence he improved the condition of his workers). Engels was as fascinating as Marx: a gifted cartoonist, an expert on military history, and a master of nearly two dozen languages. When excited, he could "stutter in twenty languages"! He was also a notorious womanizer.

Engels' influence on Marx was twofold: His vast financial resources allowed him to subsidize Marx for decades, and he played a critical role in directing Marx's thinking toward political economy. Engels's own work, *The Condition of the Working Class in England in 1844*, had a profound impact on Marx, and it was Engels who converted Marx into being a revolutionary communist, not the other way around. He coauthored *The Communist Manifesto* but, in every other way, lived in the shadow of the great philosopher Marx.

Engels outlived Marx by a decade, corresponding with revolutionaries, editing and publishing Marx's books, and keeping the Marxist flame ablaze.

THE WORLD'S GREATEST CRITIC

The spiteful nature of Marx and Engels's style was clear in the title of their first collaboration: *Critique of Critical Critique*! (A more palatable title, *The Holy Family,* was superimposed on the cover while the book was being printed.) This emphasis on fault-finding reflected Marx's harsh hostility and his hot-blooded anger against his enemies. "He denounced everyone who dared to oppose his opinions" (Barzun 1958 [1941]: 173). He initiated the practice of "party purges," which would be perfected a generation later by Lenin and Stalin (Wesson 1976: 34). In 1847, responding to fellow socialist Proudhon's *Philosophy of Poverty*, Marx wrote a caustic rejoinder, *The Poverty of Philosophy*. If the Guinness Book of World Records listed the World's Most Critical Man, Marx would have easily won the award. Almost every one of his book titles contained the word "critique." He wrote sparingly about the happy world of utopian communism, prodigiously about the flaws of capitalism.

MARX WRITES A POWERFUL POLEMIC

Marx's life in Paris didn't last long. He was expelled from Paris for inciting revolution in Germany. He left for Brussels, the first stage of a life of permanent exile. It was in Belgium that Marx and Engels were commissioned by the League of the Just, later renamed the Communist League, in London, to write their famous pamphlet, *The Communist Manifesto*.

The Communist Manifesto, the final version written by Marx, was a forceful call to arms, a powerful reflection of the new machine age and new hardships as men, women, and children moved to enormous chaotic cities, worked sixteen hours a day in factories, and often lived in desperate squalor. "The bourgeoisie, wherever it has got the upper hand, has put an end to all feudal, patriarchal, idyllic relations. . . . It has left remaining no other bond between man and man than naked self-interest, than callous 'cash-payment.'" Consequently, "the bourgeoisie has stripped of its halo every occupation hitherto honored and looked up to with reverent awe. It has converted the physician, the lawyer, the priest, the poet, the man of science into its paid wage-laborers." Further, "all that is solid melts into air, all that is holy is profane." Capitalism "has substituted naked, shameless, direct, brutal exploitation" (Marx and Engels 1964 [1848]: 5–7).

When the *Manifesto* was published in German in February 1848, the timing couldn't have been better. By the summer, worker revolts spread throughout Europe—in France, Germany, Austria, and Italy. Images of the French Revolution a generation earlier dominated the spirit of the times. However, the European revolts were quickly quelled and Marx was arrested by Belgian police for spending his inheritance from his father (6,000 gold francs) on arming Belgian workers with rifles. He was released from jail in 1849, and moved to Cologne, Germany, where he edited another journal. The last issue was printed in red ink, the revolutionary color.

HUNGRY YEARS IN LONDON

Marx was constantly getting into trouble and continually on the run. After being expelled from Germany in August 1849, and deeply depressed by the failure of worker revolutions, he moved to London with his wife and their three children. This would turn out to be his final move. For the next thirty years, he would live, research, and write in the largest bourgeois city in the world.

The first six years in London were trying times for the Marx family, which suffered from serious illness, premature death, and desperate poverty. Marx pawned everything to keep his family alive—the family silver, linens, even the children's clothing (Padover 1978: 56). While the family was living in a small apartment in Soho, a Prussian police spy came by in 1853, and made a detailed report:

> Marx is of medium height, 34 years old; despite his relative youth, his hair is already turning gray; his figure is powerful. . . . His large, piercing fiery eyes have something uncannily demonic about them. At first glance one sees in him a man of genius and energy. . . .
>
> In private life he is a highly disorganized, cynical person, a poor host; he leads a real gypsy existence. Washing, grooming, and changing underwear are rarities with him; he gets drunk readily. Often he loafs all day long, but if he has work to do, he works day and night . . . very often he stays up all night. . . .
>
> Marx lives in one of the worst, and thus cheapest, quarters in London. . . . Everything is broken, ragged and tattered; everything is covered with finger-thick dust; everywhere the greatest disorder. When one enters Marx's room, the eyes get so dimmed by coal smoke and tobacco fumes that for the first moments one gropes. . . . Everything is dirty, everything full of dust. . . . But all this causes no embarrassment to Marx and his wife. (Padover 1978: 291–93)

Marx, living in squalor and sorrow, was constantly broke and took few work opportunities, mainly as a part-time journalist for the *New York Daily*

Tribune and other newspapers. He stubbornly refused to be "practical." At times Engels had to ghostwrite his articles. Three of Marx's young children died of malnutrition and illness. Such was the life of this demonic genius and his long-suffering wife.

COVER-UP: MARX FATHERS AN ILLEGITIMATE SON

In 1850–51, Marx had an affair with his wife's unpaid but devoted maid-servant Helene Demuth, known as Lenchen, and fathered an illegitimate son. The affair was hushed up by Marx, who begged Engels to pretend to be the father. Engels agreed, even though the boy, named Freddy, looked like Marx. "If Jenny had known the truth, it might have killed her, or at the very least destroyed her marriage" (Padover 1978: 507). Jenny may in fact have known; she and Karl allegedly did not sleep together for years.

Marx completely disowned this son. Finally, Engels declared the child to be Marx's on his deathbed in 1895. He was speaking to Marx's daughter Eleanor, who took the news hard (she later committed suicide). The facts became public only in the next century in Werner Blumenberg's 1962 biography of Marx (Blumenberg 1998: 111–13). They proved to be an embarrassment to Marxist apologists who had always maintained that Marx was a good family man, despite the premature deaths of three children and the suicides of two daughters in adulthood. For decades, Robert Heilbroner declared Marx a "devoted husband and father" in his best-seller, *The Worldly Philosophers* (1961:124), only later to admit knowledge of Marx's indiscretion. Yet Heilbroner defended Marx, arguing that the infidelity "could not undo a relationship of great passion" (1999: 149).

MARX: RICH OR POOR?

Things finally started looking up in 1856. Money from Engels and a legacy from Jenny's mother's estate allowed the Marx family to move from Soho to a nice home in fashionable Hampstead. Suddenly Marx started living the life of a bourgeois gentleman, wearing a frock coat, top hat, and monocle. The Marxes gave parties and balls, and traveled to seaside resorts. Marx even played the stock market. He speculated in American shares and English joint-stock shares, realizing sufficient gains to write Engels in 1864, "The time has now come when with wit and very little money one can really make a killing in London." Details of his speculations are lost, however (Payne 1968: 354; North 1993: 91–103).[3]

Sympathetic historians have always noted the poor conditions under which Marx lived, but during most of his life it was not for lack of money. Historian Gary North investigated Marx's income and spending habits, and

---

3. Marx's stock market speculations are all the more ironic given that one of the first acts in a communist takeover is to abolish the stock exchange as a case of "vulgar economy."

concluded that except for his self-imposed poverty of 1848–63, Marx begged, borrowed, inherited, and spent lavishly. In 1868, Engels offered to pay off all the Marxes' debts and provide him with an annuity of £350 a year, a remarkable sum at the time. North concludes: "He was poor during only fifteen years of his sixty-five-year career, in large part due to his unwillingness to use his doctorate and go out to get a job. . . . The philosopher-economist of class revolution—the 'Red Doctor of Soho' who spent only six years in that run-down neighborhood—was one of England's wealthier citizens during the last two decades of his life. But he could not make ends meet. . . . After 1869, Marx's regular annual pension placed him in the *upper two percent* of the British population in terms of income" (North 1993: 103).

MARX SHOULD HAVE HIS HEAD EXAMINED!

Keynes was fascinated by people's hands, Marx by people's skulls. Wilhelm Liebknecht, one of Marx's disciples, wrote that when he met his leader for the first time at a summer picnic for communist workers near London in the 1850s, Marx "began at once to subject me to a rigid examination, looked straight into my eyes and inspected my head rather minutely." Liebknecht was relieved to have passed the examination (Liebknecht 1968 [1901]: 52-53).

Not everyone survived Marx's skull-duggery. Ferdinand Lassalle, a German social democrat and labor organizer, was viciously attacked by Marx, who called him "the Jewish Nigger" and a "greasy Jew." "It is now perfectly clear to me," Marx wrote Engels in 1862, "that, as the shape of his head and the growth of his hair indicates, he is descended from the Negroes who joined in Moses' flight from Egypt (unless his mother or grandmother on the father's side was crossed with a nigger [sic]). This union of Jew and German on a Negro base was bound to produce an extraordinary hybrid" (Marx and Engels 41: 388–90).

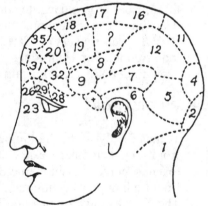

Figure 6.1
A Phrenological Chart Shows the
Supposed Relation of Personal Abilities, Talents,
and Emotions to the Shape of the Head

PHRENOLOGICAL CRAZE OF THE NINETEENTH CENTURY

Marx was apparently taken in by the pseudoscience of phrenology, the practice of examining a person's skull to determine his or her character, developed during the early 1800s by two German physicians (see the diagram in Figure 6.1). Marx wasn't the only person who believed in phrenology. Queen Victoria in Great Britain and American poets Walt Whitman and Edgar Allan Poe also believed in it.

MARX WRITES *DAS BUCH* AND CHANGES THE COURSE OF HISTORY

Basically, Marx didn't want to waste his time doing routine work to support his young family. He preferred to spend long hours, months, and years at the British Library in London researching and writing. He would come home and tell Jenny he had made the colossal discovery of economic determinism, that all society's actions were determined by economic forces. His work culminated in his classic *Das Kapital*, published in German in 1867. *Capital* (the English title) introduced economic determinism and a new "exploitation" theory of capitalism based on universal "scientific" laws discovered by Marx.

Marx considered his work the "bible of the working class," and even expected laborers to read his heavy, pedantic tome. He saw himself as "engaged in the most bitter conflict in the world," and hoped his book would "deliver the bourgeoisie a theoretical blow from which it will never recover" (Padover 1978: 346). Marx viewed himself as the "Darwin of society," and in 1880 he sent Charles Darwin a copy of *Capital*. Darwin courteously replied, begging ignorance of the subject.

Only a thousand copies were printed and it sold slowly, primarily because "Das Buch" was theoretically abstract and scholastically dense, with over 1,500 sources cited. The reviews of *Capital* were almost universally poor, but through the efforts of Engels and other die-hard supporters, the work was translated into Russian in 1872 and French in 1875. The Russian edition was a momentous publishing event, luckily passing czarist censors as "nonthreatening" high theory. It was studied heavily by Russian intellectuals, and eventually a copy fell into the hands of Vladimir Ilyich Ulyanov—V.I. Lenin. It was Lenin, Marx's most powerful disciple, who brought Marx to light. "Without Marx there would have been no Lenin, without Lenin no communist Russia" (Schwartzchild 1947: vii).

The English edition didn't appear until 1887. In 1890, an American edition became a bestseller and the print run of 5,000 sold out quickly because *Capital* was promoted as a book informing readers "how to accumulate capital"—a course on making money (Padover 1978: 375)!

Most economists wonder how such a "long, verbose, abstract, tedious, badly written, difficult labyrinth of a book [could] become the Talmud and Koran for half the world" (Gordon 1967: 641). Marxists respond, "That's the beauty of it!" *Capital* has survived and blossomed as a classic in part because of its intellectual appeal. According to an eminent socialist, the prestige of *Capital* owes much to "its indigestible length, its hermetic style, its ostentatious erudition, and its algebraical mysticism" (Wesson 1976: 27).

WHY DID MARX GROW SUCH A LONG BEARD?

Zeus spoke, and nodded with his darkish brows,
and immortal locks fell forward from the lord's deathless head,
and he made great Olympus tremble.

—Homer, *Iliad* (Book I, line 528)

Revolutionary followers often played on Marx's vanity by comparing him to the Greek gods. He was much pleased by an 1843 political cartoon of Marx as Prometheus when his newspaper, *Rheinische Zeitung*, was banned. Marx is chained to his printing press, while an eagle representing the King of Prussia tears at his liver. The editor looks defiant, hoping someday to free himself and pursue his revolutionary causes.

While working on *Das Kapital* in the 1860s, Marx received a larger-than-life statue of Zeus as a Christmas present. It became one of his prized possessions, which he kept in his London study. From then on, Marx sought to imitate the statue of Zeus. He stopped cutting his hair and let his beard grow out until it assumed the shape and size of Zeus's head. He pictured himself as the god of the universe, casting his thunderbolts upon the earth. One of the last photographs of Marx shows his white hair flowing everywhere in magnificent splendor (see Photograph 6.2).

Illustration 6.3
Marx's Statue of Zeus
"He made great Olympus tremble."

Photograph 6.2
Karl Marx
"With contempt shall I fling my
glove in the world's face."

Courtesy of Brown Brothers.

Marx established the bearded trend that has distinguished the appearance of many revolutionaries ever since. Yet, "Everything must come to an end, and so did the rule of Zeus and the other Olympian gods. All that is left of their glory on earth are broken temples and noble statues" (D'Aulaire 1962: 189).

MARX DIES IN OBSCURITY

Marx was only forty-nine years old when he published *Capital*, but he refused to finish any more full-length books and instead read, researched, and took notes on huge quantities of books and articles on such wide topics as mathematics, chemistry, and foreign languages. "He delved into such problems as the chemistry of nitrogen fertilizers, agriculture, physics, and mathematics. . . . Marx immediately wrote a treatise on differential calculus and various other mathematical manuscripts; he learned Danish; he learned Russian" (Raddatz 1978: 236).

Marx had a hard time completing anything in his later years, especially with regard to economics. He never finished the next two volumes of *Capital*, which exasperated Engels, who finally edited and published them himself.

Marx was a sick man most of his life, constantly beset with chronic illnesses—asthma attacks, prolonged headaches, strep throat, influenza, rheumatism, bronchitis, toothaches, liver pains, eye inflammations, laryngitis, and insomnia. His boils and carbuncles were so severe that by the end of his life, his entire body was covered with scars. His "eternally beloved" Jenny died of cancer in 1881; Marx was so ill he couldn't attend her funeral. His daughter, also named Jenny, died of the same disease two years later. That same year, on March 17, 1883, Marx passed away, sitting in his easy chair. Not surprisingly, there was no will or estate.

Photograph 6.3
Author Views Karl Marx's Tomb in Highgate Cemetery, London

Marx was buried at Highgate Cemetery in London, along with his wife Jenny, his housemaid Lenchen (in 1890), and other family members. The twelve-foot monument with a bust of Marx was erected in the 1950s by the Communist Party. The famous phrase "Workers of all lands, unite!" is emblazoned on the monument in gold. At the bottom are printed the words of Marx, "The philosophers have only interpreted the world in various ways; the point, however, is to change it" (see Photograph 6.3 on page 149).

Engels conducted the service at Marx's burial. He spoke eloquently of Marx's position in history, proclaiming him the Darwin of the social sciences.[4] "His name will live on through the centuries, and so will his work."

Indeed. In *The 100 Most Influential Books Ever Written*, by Martin Seymour-Smith (1998), seven economists are listed: Adam Smith, Thomas Robert Malthus, John Stuart Mill, Herbert Spencer, John Maynard Keynes, Friedrich von Hayek, . . . and Karl Marx.

THE LIVING MARX: A DISMAL FAILURE

But Engels would have to wait until the twentieth century before Marx's influence would be felt. In 1883, it was merely a delusion of grandeur. At the time of his death Marx was practically a forgotten man. Fewer than twenty people showed up for his funeral. He was not mourned by his fellow workers in the Siberian mines, as Engels had suggested, and few remembered even *The Communist Manifesto*, let alone *Capital*. John Stuart Mill never heard of him. At the end of his life, Marx could recall with agreement the words of the Bible, "For a testament is of force after men are dead: otherwise it is of no strength at all while the testator liveth" (Hebrews 9: 17).

The fate of his family is sad to contemplate. It was a nightmare. Marx was survived by only two daughters and his illegitimate son. In 1898, his daughter Eleanor Marx, known as Tussy and a strong-willed revolutionary like her father, committed suicide after learning that Freddy was the illegitimate son of her father and that her cynical Irish revolutionary husband was a bigamist. In 1911, his surviving daughter, Laura, an eloquent speaker and a striking beauty, consummated a suicide pact with her husband, another French socialist. In sum, there was little joy in the last years of Karl and Jenny Marx and their descendants. Engels, known as "the General," died of cancer in 1895.

MARX'S EXPLOITATION MODEL OF CAPITALISM

Let us now review Marx's major contributions to economics and determine what has had a lasting impact and what has been discarded.

---

4. There is a long-persistent myth that Marx wrote Darwin to ask if he could dedicate a volume of *Capital* to Darwin. In fact, no such letter was written. See Colb (1982: 461–81).

In *Capital*, published in 1867, Karl Marx attempted to introduce an alternative model to the classical economics of Adam Smith. This system aimed to demonstrate through immutable "scientific" laws that the capitalist system was fatally flawed, that it inherently benefited capitalists and big business, that it exploited workers, and that it was so crisis-prone that it would inevitably destroy itself. In many ways, the Marxist model rationalized his belief that the capitalist system must be overthrown and replaced by communism.

The Labor Theory of Value

Marx found the Ricardian system well suited for his exploitation model. In many ways, David Ricardo was his mentor in economics. As noted in chapter 4, Ricardo focused on production and how it is distributed among large classes—landlords, workers, and capitalists. Ricardo and his successor, John Stuart Mill (chapter 5), attempted to analyze the economy in terms of classes rather than the actions of individuals.

Say and the French laissez-faire school (chapter 2) did focus on the subjective utility of individuals, but Marx rejected Say and followed Ricardo by concentrating on the production of a single homogeneous "commodity," and the distribution of income from commodity production into classes.

In Ricardo's class system, labor played a critical role in determining value. First Ricardo and then Marx claimed that labor is the sole producer of value. The value of a "commodity" should be equal to the average quantity of labor-hours used in creating the commodity.

The Theory of Surplus Value

If indeed labor is the sole determinant of value, then where does that leave profits and interest? Marx labeled profits and interest "surplus value."

It was only a short logical step to conclude, therefore, that capitalists and landlords are exploiters of labor. If indeed all value was the product of labor, then all profit obtained by capitalists and interest by landlords must be "surplus value," unjustly extracted from the true earnings of the working class.

Marx developed a mathematical formula for his theory of surplus value. The rate of profit (p) or exploitation is equal to the surplus value (s) divided by the value of the final product (r).

Thus,

$$p = s / r$$

For example, suppose a clothing manufacturer hires workers to make dresses. The capitalist sells the dresses for $100 apiece, but labor costs are $70 per dress. Therefore the rate of profit or exploitation is

$$p = \$30 \ / \ \$100 = 0.3, \text{ or } 30\%$$

Marx divided the value of the final product into two forms of capital, *constant capital* (*C*) and *variable capital* (*V*). Constant capital represents factories and equipment. Variable capital is the cost of labor.

Thus, the equation for the rate of profit becomes

$$p = s \ / \ [v + c]$$

Marx contended that profits and exploitation are increased by extending the workday for employees, and by hiring women and children at lower wages than men. Moreover, machinery and technological advances benefit the capitalist, but not the worker, Marx declared. Machinery, for example, allows capitalists to hire women and children to run the machines. The result can only be more exploitation.

Critics countered that capital is productive and deserves a reasonable return, but Marx offered the rebuttal that capital was nothing more than "frozen" labor and that consequently, wages should absorb the entire proceeds from production. The classical economists had no answer to Marx, at least initially. And thus Marx won the day by "proving" through impeccable logic that capitalism inherently created a monstrous "class struggle" between workers, capitalists, and landlords—and the capitalists and landlords had an unfair advantage. Murray Rothbard observed, "As the nineteenth century passed its mid-mark, the deficiencies of Ricardian economics became ever more glaring. Economics itself had come to a dead end" (Rothbard 1980: 237). It was not until the work of Philip Wicksteed, the British clergyman, and Eugen von Böhm-Bawerk, the influential Austrian economist, that Marx was answered effectively, with a focus on the risk-taking and the entrepreneurial benefits the capitalists provide. But this topic must wait until chapter 7.

FALLING PROFITS AND THE ACCUMULATION OF CAPITAL

Marx had a perverse view of machinery and technology. The accumulation of capital was constantly growing in order to meet competition and keep the costs of labor down. "Accumulate, accumulate! That is Moses and the prophets! . . . Therefore, save, save, i.e., reconvert the greatest possible portion of surplus-value, or surplus-product into capital!" pronounced Marx in *Capital* (1976 [1867]: 742).

Yet this leads to trouble, a crisis in capitalism. For according to Marx's formula for the profit rate, $s/[v + c]$, we can see that adding machinery increases c and therefore drives down profits. Big business becomes more concentrated as the larger firms produce more cheaply, which "always ends in the ruin of many small capitalists." Meanwhile, workers become all the more miserable, having less and less with which to buy consumer goods.

More and more workers are thrown out of work, becoming increasingly unemployed in an "industrial reserve army."

THE CRISIS OF CAPITALISM

Lowering costs, falling profits, monopolistic power, underconsumption, massive unemployment of the proletariat class—all these conditions lead to "more extensive and more destructive crises" and depressions for the capitalistic system (Marx and Engels 1964 [1848]: 13). And all this is derived from the labor theory of value!

Marx rejected Say's law of markets, which he labeled "childish babble . . . claptrap . . . humbug" (Buchholz 1999: 133). There was no stability in capitalism. Marx emphasized both the boom and the bust nature of the capitalist system, and that its ultimate demise was inevitable.

THE IMPERIALISM OF MONOPOLY CAPITALISM

Marx was greatly impressed with the ability of capitalists to accumulate more capital and create new markets, both domestically and abroad. *The Communist Manifesto* described this phenomenon in a famous passage: "The bourgeoisie, during its rule of scarce one hundred years, has created more massive and more colossal productive forces than have all preceding generations together." The capitalists are engaged pell-mell "by the conquest of new markets, and by the more thorough exploitation of the old ones" (Marx and Engels 1964: 12–13).

Marxists ever after have characterized capitalism and big business as inherently "imperialistic," exploiting foreign workers and foreign resources. The theory of imperialism and colonialism was developed largely by J.A. Hobson and V.I. Lenin. Much of the developing world's anti-American and antiforeign attitudes during the twentieth century came from Marxist origins, and the results of this anticapitalist attitude have been devastating, resulting in retarded and even negative growth in many parts of Asia, Africa, and Latin America.

HISTORICAL MATERIALISM

So where was capitalism headed? Marx was heavily influenced by **George Wilhelm Hegel (1770–1831)** in developing his process of economic determinism. Hegel's basic thesis was "Contradiction (in nature) is the root of all motion and of all life." Hegel described this contradiction in terms of the dialectic, opposing forces that would eventually bring about a new force. An established "thesis" would cause an "antithesis" to develop in opposition, which in turn would eventually create a new "synthesis." This new synthesis becomes the "thesis" and the process starts all over again as civilization progresses.

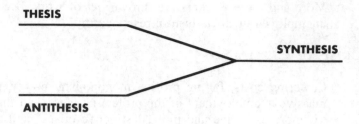

The Hegelian Dialectic

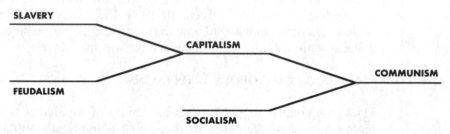

Figure 6.2
The Hegelian Dialectic Used to Describe the Course of History

The diagram in Figure 6.2 reflects this Hegelian dialectic. Marx applied Hegel's dialectic to his deterministic view of history. Thus, the course of history could be described by using Hegelian concepts.

According to this theory, slavery was viewed as the principal means of production or thesis during Greco-Roman times. Feudalism became its main antithesis in the middle ages. The synthesis became capitalism, which became the new thesis after the Enlightenment. But capitalism faced its own antithesis—the growing threat of socialism. Eventually, this struggle would result in the ultimate system of production, communism. In this way, Marx was an eternal optimist. He firmly believed that all history pointed to higher forms of society, culminating in communism.

MARX'S SOLUTION: REVOLUTIONARY SOCIALISM

But while communism was supposedly inevitable, Marx felt that revolution was necessary to bring it about. First and foremost, Marx was a leading proponent of the violent ("forceful") overthrow of government and the establishment of revolutionary socialism. He delighted in violence. Marx declared revolutionary causes in *The Communist Manifesto* in 1848, the First International in 1860, and the Paris Commune in 1871.

Although the German revolutionary failed to reveal his plans in detail, *The Communist Manifesto* did include a ten-point program (Marx and Engels 1964: 40):

1. Abolition of property in land and applications of all rents of land to public purposes.

2. A heavy progressive or graduated income tax.

3. Abolition of all right of inheritance.

4. Confiscation of the property of all emigrants and rebels.

5. Centralization of credit in the hands of the state by means of a national bank with state capital and an exclusive monopoly.

6. Centralization of the means of communication and transport in the hands of the state.

7. Extension of factories and instruments of production owned by the state; the bringing into cultivation of waste lands, and the improvement of the soil generally in accordance with a common plan.

8. Equal obligation of all to work. Establishment of industrial armies, especially for agriculture.

9. Combination of agriculture with manufacturing industries; gradual abolition of the distinction between town and country, by a more equitable distribution of the population over the country.

10. Free education for all children in public schools. Abolition of child factory labor in its present form. Combination of education with industrial production, and so on.

It's difficult to imagine instigating some of these measures without violence. But this was not all. Marx also advocated an authoritarian "dictatorship of the proletariat." He favored a complete abolition of private property, based on his theory that private property was the cause of strife, class struggle, and a form of slavery (1964: 27). He agreed with Proudhon, "property is theft." Without private property, there would be no need for exchange, no buying and selling, and therefore Marx and Engels advocated the elimination of money (page 30). Production and consumption could continue and even thrive through central planning without exchange or money.

Marx and Engels also demanded the abolition of the traditional family in an effort to "stop the exploitation of children by their parents" and to "introduce a community of women." The founders of communism supported a program of youth education that would "destroy the most hallowed of relations," and "replace home education by social" (pages 33–35).

What about religion? Marx noted that "religion is the opium of the people." "Communism abolishes eternal truths, it abolishes all religion, and all morality, instead of constituting them on a new basis; it therefore acts in contradiction to all past historical experience" (page 38).

WHY KEYNES DESPISED MARXISM AND SOVIET RUSSIA

We have everything to lose by the methods of violent change.
In Western industrial conditions the tactics of Red Revolution
would throw the whole population into a pit of poverty and death.
—John Maynard Keynes (1931: 306)

John Maynard Keynes, the most influential economist of the twentieth century, was an interventionist and a supporter of Britain's Liberal Party. Like Marx, he was no friend of laissez faire. He argued that capitalism was inherently unstable and required government intervention.

But that was as far as it went. Keynes couldn't stand Karl Marx or the communist experiment, which he regarded as "an insult to our intelligence" (Moggridge 1992: 470; Skidelsky 1992: 519). Following a trip to Russia in 1925, Keynes wrote three articles for *The Nation*, debunking the Soviet "religion" as "unscrupulous," "ruthless," and "contrary to human nature." There was none of that naive "I've seen the future" optimism for Keynes. Individual freedom meant too much to him. "For me, brought up in a free air undarkened by the horrors of religion, with nothing to be afraid of, Red Russia holds too much which is detestable." He added, "How can I adopt a creed which, preferring the mud to the fish, exalts the boorish proletariat above the bourgeois and the intelligentsia who, with whatever faults, are the quality in life and surely carry the seeds of all human achievement?" He lambasted Marx's magnum opus, *Capital*, as "an obsolete economic textbook" which was "scientifically erroneous" and "without interest or application for the modern world" (Keynes 1931: 298–300).

In the middle of the Great Depression, the best and the brightest intellectuals embraced Marxism, but not Keynes. At a dinner among friends in 1934, Keynes said that, of all the "isms," Marxism was "the worst of all & founded on a silly mistake of old Mr Ricardo's [labor theory of value]" (Skidelsky 1992: 517). In a letter to playwright Bernard Shaw, Keynes labeled *Das Kapital* "dreary, out-of-date, academic controversialising." He compared it to the Koran. "How could either of these books carry fire and sword round half the world? It beats me." In a second letter to Shaw dated January 1, 1935, he complained of Marx's "vile manner of writing." Then he added a postscript that proved prescient: "I believe myself to be writing a book on economic theory, which will largely revolutionise—not, I suppose, at once but in the course of the next ten years—the way the world thinks about economic problems" (Skidelsky 1992: 520).

The book would become *The General Theory of Employment, Interest and Money*, and it would indeed revolutionize the world of economics, eclipsing Marx's *Capital* among academics.

MARXISTS TURN ON KEYNES

Keynes, a thoroughgoing member of the bourgeoisie, disliked Marx, and undoubtedly the feeling would have been mutual if they had known each other. Marxists, in turn, have disdained Keynes and Keynesian economics. "Such a theory is a serious danger to the working class," wrote Marxist John Eaton in his little book, *Marx Against Keynes* (1951: 12). According to Eaton, Keynesianism defends "wage slavery" and "policies of imperialism" (page 75). Eaton accused Keynes of not having "ever read and understood Marx's profoundly scientific analysis" in *Capital* (page 33). In short, Keynesian economics is the "vulgar economy of monopoly capitalism in crisis and decay" (page 85), according to Eaton, and thus is doomed to fail.

Marx anticipated that revolutionary socialism would for the first time allow the full expression of human existence and happiness. The goal of "universal opulence" that Adam Smith sought would finally be achieved under true communism. Marx was a millennialist at heart. Heaven could be achieved on earth. Eventually the dictatorship of the proletariat would be replaced by a classless, stateless society. *Homo Marxist* would be a new man!

MARX'S PREDICTIONS FAIL TO MATERIALIZE

But all this was not to be. Marx's predictions have gone awry, though not all right away. As late as 1937, Wassily Leontief, the Russian émigré who later won the Nobel Prize for his input-output analysis, proclaimed that Marx's record was "impressive" and "correct" (Leontief 1938: 5, 8). But Leontief's praise was premature. Since then, as Leszek Kolakowski, former leading Polish Marxist philosopher, declared, "All of Marx's important prophecies turned out to be false" (Denby 1996: 339). To review:

1. Under capitalism, the rate of profit has failed to decline, even while more and more capital has been accumulated over the centuries.

2. The working class has not fallen into greater and greater misery. Wages have risen substantially above the subsistence level. The industrial nations have seen a dramatic rise in the standard of living of the average worker. The middle class has not disappeared, but has expanded. As Paul Samuelson concludes, "The immiserization of the working class . . . simply never took place. As a prophet Marx was colossally unlucky and his system colossally useless" (1967: 622).

3. There is little evidence of increased concentration of industries in advanced capitalist societies, especially during the growing trend toward globalization.

4. Socialist utopian societies have not flourished, nor has the proletarian revolution inevitably occurred.

5. Despite business cycles and even an occasional great depression, capitalism appears to be flourishing as never before (see "Update: Marxists as Modern-Day Doomsdayers" in the box on page 158).

CRITICISMS OF MARX

Why was Marx so terribly wrong after establishing what he insisted were "scientific" laws of economics?

First and foremost, his labor theory of value was defective. In rejecting Say's law of markets, he also denied Say's sound theory of value. Say correctly noted that the value of goods and services is ultimately determined by utility. If individuals do not demand or need a product, it doesn't matter

RUSSIAN ECONOMIST DEFIES MARXISTS AND IS BANISHED TO SIBERIA!

This theory is wrong and reactionary.
—*Soviet Russian Encyclopedia* (Solomou 1987: 60)

Russian economist **Nikolai Kondratieff (1892–1938)** contradicted the Marxist prediction of capitalism's inevitable demise when he delivered a paper before the prestigious Economic Institute in Moscow in 1926, making the case for a fifty- to sixty-year business cycle. Based on price and output trends since the 1780s, Kondratieff described two-and-a-half upswing and downswing "long-wave" cycles of prosperity and depression. Kondratieff found no evidence of an irreversible collapse in capitalism; rather a strong recovery always succeeded depression.

In 1928, Kondratieff was removed from his position as head of Moscow's Business Conditions Institute and his thesis was denounced in the official Soviet encyclopedia (Solomou 1987: 60). In 1930, he was arrested for being a member of the illegal Peasants Labor Party and sentenced to eight years in a prison near Moscow. In 1938, during Stalin's Great Purge, Kondratieff was subjected to a second trial and executed by firing squad at the age of forty-six.

KONDRATIEFF CYCLE DISCREDITED

Yet the so-called Kondratieff long-wave cycle still lives on among some economists, historians, and financial analysts who regularly predict another depression and economic crisis. However, it has now been over seventy years since the last worldwide depression. As Victor Zarnowitz concluded, "There is much disagreement about the very existence of some of the long waves even among the supporters of the concept, and more disagreement yet about the timing of the waves and their phases" (Zarnowitz 1992: 238).

UPDATE 1: MARXISTS AS MODERN-DAY DOOMSDAYERS

It is enough to mention the commercial crises that by their periodical return put on its trial, each time more threatening, the existence of the entire bourgeois society.
—Marx and Engels (1964: 11–12)

Following their leader's footsteps, modern-day Marxists are constantly predicting the collapse of capitalism, only to be rebuffed time and again. Since the end of World War II, Marxists have frequently written of the "twilight of capitalism," a favorite book title (William Z. Foster in 1949, Michael Harrington in 1977, and Boris Kagarlitsky in 2000). Paul M. Sweezy, the Marxist professor, was a longtime pessimist. Since the 1930s, he forecast that capitalism was on the decline and that socialism, promoting higher standards of living, would advance "by leaps and bounds" (1942: 362). In 1977 he coauthored a book called *The End of Prosperity.*

Thirty years later, despite robust global capitalism, the Marxists continued to preach doom and gloom and that the next great depression is just around the corner. For example, Michael Perelman, a neo-Marxist who teaches at the University of California at Chico, wrote a book in 2007 called *The Confiscation of American Prosperity*, in which he argued that American-style capitalism has created deepening inequality of wealth and income that will lead inevitably to an "economic catastrophe" (2007).

(continued)

Yet, as it began a new century, capitalism is even more dynamic than ever before. The modern-day Marxists, always the pessimists, have been proved wrong again.

Interestingly, Lord Meghnad Desai, an economist at the London School of Economics, recently proposed a startling thesis: that Marx would have supported the resurgence of capitalism around the world. *The Communist Manifesto* spoke eloquently about the "ever growing . . . constantly expanding . . . rapid" advance of vigorous and vital capitalist forces, reading beyond natural borders to a world market (Marx and Engels 1964 [1848]). According to Desai, the old Marxists were premature in their dire predictions.

But what happens after global capitalism runs its course? Desai asks, "Will there ever be Socialism Beyond Capitalism?" (2004: 315). Some Marxists, such as David Schweickart, suggest that some form of "economic democracy" will develop after the "current late decadent" stage of capitalism plays itself out (2002).

how much labor or effort is put into producing it; it won't command value. As historian Jacques Barzun noted, "Pearls are not valuable because men dive for them; men dive for them because pearls are valuable" (Barzun 1958: 152.) And Philip Wicksteed, writing the first scientific criticism of Marx's labor theory in 1884, noted, "A coat is not worth eight times as much as a hat to the community because it takes eight times as long to make it. . . . The community is willing to devote eight times as long to the making of a coat because it will be worth eight times as much to it" (Wicksteed 1933: vii).[5]

And what about all those valuable things that keep increasing in value even though they require little or no labor, such as art or land? Marx recognized these were exceptions to his theory, but considered them of minor importance to the fundamental issue of labor power.

THE TRANSFORMATION PROBLEM

Marx also faced a dilemma which became known as the "transformation problem," also known as the profit rate and value problem. A conflict arises under Marx's system because some industries are labor intensive and others are capital intensive. (In Marxist language, they have a higher organic composition of capital.) In volume 1 of *Capital*, Marx insisted that prices varied directly with labor time, concluding therefore that capital-intensive industries should be *less* profitable than labor-intensive industries. Yet the evidence seemed to indicate similar profitability across all industries over the long run, since capital and investment could migrate from less to more profitable industries. Marx never could resolve this thorny issue, which Rothbard called "the most glaring single hole in the Marxian model" (1995: 413).

5. It was precisely this article, appearing in the socialist monthly *Today* in October 1884, that convinced George Bernard Shaw and Sidney Webb that the labor theory of value was untenable and thereby brought the whole Marxist edifice down in ruins (Lichtheim 1970: 192–93).

Marx wrestled with this transformation problem his entire life, promising to have an answer in future volumes of *Capital*. In the introduction to volume 2 of *Capital*, Engels sponsored an essay contest on how Marx would solve it. For the next nine years, a large number of economists tried to solve it, but upon the publication of volume 3 of *Capital*, Engels announced that no one had succeeded[6] (Rothbard 1995: 413). Böhm-Bawerk jumped on this singular failure in Marxian economics and, in the words of Paul Samuelson, "make no mistake about it, Böhm-Bawerk is perfectly right in insisting that volume III of *Capital* never does make good the promise to reconcile the fabricated contradictions" (Samuelson 1967: 620).

THE VITAL ROLE OF CAPITALISTS AND ENTREPRENEURS

Second, Marx blundered in failing to value the knowledge and work of capitalists and entrepreneurs. As we shall see in the next chapter, Böhm-Bawerk, as well as Alfred Marshall and other great economists, recognized the huge contribution capitalists and entrepreneurs make in taking on risk and providing the necessary capital (saving) and management skills necessary to operate a profitable enterprise.

THE WORKER-CAPITALIST PHENOMENON

One of the biggest problems facing Marxism today is the gradual disintegration of economic classes. No longer is there a clear division between capitalist and worker. Fewer and fewer workers are simply employees or wage earners. They are often shareholders and part owners of the companies they work for—through profit-sharing and pension plans, where they own shares in the companies they work for. Many workers are self-employed, and are part-time capitalists. Today over half of American families own stock in publicly traded companies. Main Street has linked with Wall Street to create a new mass of worker-capitalists, which has greatly diminished revolutionary zeal within the labor markets.

Finally, Marx's view of machinery and capital goods is perverse and one-sided. Time-saving and labor-saving machinery does not simply lay off workers or reduce wages. It frequently makes the job easier to perform, and allows workers to engage in other productive tasks. Machinery and technology have done an amazing job in reducing or eliminating the "worker alienation" Marx complained about so bitterly. By cutting costs, machinery and technological advances create new demands and new opportunities to produce other products. They create other jobs, often at better pay, for workers who are displaced. As Ludwig von Mises stated a generation later, "there is only one means to raise wage rates permanently and for the benefit of all those eager to earn wages—namely, to accelerate

---

6. A complete summary of the transformation debate among Marxists can be found in Howard and King (1989: 21–59).

the increase in capital available as against population" (Mises 1972: 89). The evidence is overwhelming that increasing labor productivity (output per man hour) leads to higher wages.

To sum up Marxist economics, Paul Samuelson concluded (way back in 1957) that almost nothing in the economics of classical Marxism survives analysis. And Jonathan Wolff, a British professor sympathetic to Marxist

---

UPDATE 2: PAUL SWEEZY KEEPS MARXISM ALIVE AND KICKING

At least a tenth of U.S. economists fall into the radical category.
—Paul Samuelson (1976: 849)

Marxism has never made much of an inroad into economics. The few Marxists on campus included Maurice Dobb at Cambridge, Paul Baran at Stanford, and Paul Sweezy at Harvard. Sweezy was the most fascinating, being the only economist I know who went from laissez faire to Marxism. (Whitaker Chambers, Mark Blaug, and Thomas Sowell all went in the opposite direction.) Born in New York City in 1910 to a Morgan banker, Paul Sweezy graduated with honors from the best private schools, Exeter and Harvard. Brilliant, handsome, and witty, Sweezy left Harvard in 1932 as a classical economist, went to the London School of Economics for graduate work, became an ardent Hayekian, then briefly fell under the spell of Harold Laski and John Maynard Keynes, and finally converted to Marxism. From then on, the debonair Sweezy made every effort to make Marxism respectable on college campuses.

Photograph 6.4
Paul Sweezy (1910–2004)
Brilliant, debonair, witty Marxist.
Courtesy of Monthly Review Press.

Returning to Harvard as an instructor during the golden era of the Keynesian revolution, he befriended John Kenneth Galbraith, tutored Robert Heilbroner, and collaborated with Joseph Schumpeter on his forthcoming *Capitalism, Socialism and Democracy*. Sweezy wrote his most famous article on the "kinked" demand curve, helped organize the Harvard Teachers' Union, and published *The Theory of Capitalist Development* (1942), an extremely coherent and compelling exposition of Marxism (although the author overly committed himself to citing Stalin). Like Schumpeter, Sweezy predicted at the end of his book that capitalism would inevitably collapse and socialism would "demonstrate its superiority on a large scale" (1942: 352–63).

His teaching at Harvard was interrupted when he joined the Office of Strategic Services (the predecessor of the Central Intelligence Agency) in 1942. After the war, Sweezy came up for tenure at Harvard, but despite vigorous backing by Schumpeter, was rejected, never to have a permanent academic position again. In 1949, he

(continued)

cofounded *Monthly Review,* "an independent socialist magazine," whose first issue made a major splash by publishing "Why Socialism?" by Albert Einstein. (Einstein's essay is remarkably Marxist in tone.) Sweezy has been associated with *Monthly Review* ever since, in addition to collaborating with Paul Baran on writing *Monopoly Capital* (1966). Yet throughout his career, Sweezy was known for taking "far-fetched and unreal" positions (his words), such as his arch defense of Fidel Castro's Cuba (a nation currently ranked by the UN as the world's worst human rights violator) and his constant anticipation of capitalism's imminent collapse (1942: 363). In 1954, during the McCarthy era, he was jailed for refusing on principle to answer questions about "subversive activities" in New Hampshire; in 1957 the Supreme Court overturned the verdict.

OTHER RADICAL TRENDS

Other radical journals and organizations emerged during the Vietnam War: the journals *Dissent* and *New Left Review,* and the Union of Radical Political Economists, or URPE for short. They all reached their heyday in the protest days of the 1960s and the crisis-prone 1970s. It was 1968 when several Marxists met at the University of Michigan to establish the Union of Radical Political Economists and chose the acerbic-sounding URPE. The purpose of URPE is to develop a "critique of the capitalist system and all forms of exploitation and oppression while helping to construct a progressive social policy and create socialist alternatives" (URPE Website).

By 1976, Paul Samuelson reported that at least 10 percent of the profession consisted of Marxist-style economists. Although Marxism has had a far greater influence in sociology, political science, and literary theory, some economics departments are known for their radicalism, including the University of Massachusetts at Amherst, the New School of Social Research in New York City, the University of California at Riverside, and the University of Utah.

Since the collapse of the Soviet Union and the central-planning socialist paradigm, the lure of Marxism has fallen, at least in economics. Attendance at URPE sessions at the annual American Economic Association meetings is down, and URPE membership has fallen to around 800.

ideas, recently concluded that while "Marx remains the most profound and acute critic of capitalism, even as it exists today, we may have no confidence in his solutions. . . . Marx's grandest theories are not substantiated" (2002: 125–26).

MARX, THE ANTI-ECONOMIST?

Michael Harrington claimed that Marx was the ultimate anti-economist (1976: 104–48). Indeed, he may be right. Marx was a naive idealist who failed profoundly to comprehend the role of capital, markets, prices, and money in advancing the material abundance of mankind.

The irony is that it is capitalism, not socialism or Marxism, that has liberated the worker from the chains of poverty, monopoly, war, and oppression, and has better achieved Marx's vision of a millennium of hope, peace, abundance, leisure, and aesthetic expression for the "full" human being.

Could Marxist socialism create the abundance and variety of goods and services, breakthrough technologies, new job opportunities, and leisure time of today? Hardly. Marx was incredibly gullible in thinking that his brand of utopian socialism could achieve a rapid rise in the workers' living standards. He wrote in the 1840s, "in communist society . . . nobody has one exclusive sphere of activity but each can become accomplished in any branch he wishes, . . . thus making it possible for me to do one thing today and another tomorrow, to hunt in the morning, fish in the afternoon, rear cattle in the evening, criticize after dinner, in accordance with my inclination, without becoming hunter, fisherman, shepherd or critic" (Wesson 1976: 15). This is sheer ivory-tower naiveté, a characteristic of the early Marx. Marx's idealism would take us back to a primitive, if not barbaric, age of barter and tribal living, without the benefit of exchange and division of labor.

Thus, as we enter the twenty-first century, Adam Smith—the father of capitalism—is moving back in front of Karl Marx—the father of socialism. In the first edition of *The 100: The 100 Most Influential People in the World* (1978), author Michael Hart placed Marx ahead of Smith. But in the second edition, written in 1992 after the collapse of Soviet communism, Smith leads Marx.

WHAT'S LEFT OF MARXISM?

If Marx's economic theories and predictions have proved to be inaccurate, is there anything salvageable from *Capital* and the rest of Marx's economic writings? Indeed, there is.

First, the issue of economic determinism. Are they ideas or vested interests that move society? In his "law" of historical materialism, Marx countered the traditional view that religion or other institutional philosophy determined the culture of a community. Instead, Marx contended the opposite, that the material or economic forces of society determined the legal, political, religious, and commercial "superstructure" of national culture. In *Poverty of Philosophy*, Marx explained, "the handmill gives you society with the feudal lord, the steam-mill gives you society with the industrial capitalist" (2000: 219–20). Today most sociologists recognize the important role that economic forces play in society.

Second, the issue of classes in society. Marx's theory of class consciousness and class conflict has engaged historians and sociologists. To what extent are behavior and thought a reflection of bourgeois or proletarian values; to what point does the ruling class protect and advance its interests through the political process? Does the group that owns or controls property and the means of production dominate? Is it true that "law and politics are in the service of industrial capital"? If so, asks Jonathan Wolff, "why are trade unions allowed? Why do universities have Arts Faculties as well as Engineering (indeed, why allow the teaching of Marxism)? What don't the multinationals win every one of their court cases?" (2002: 59). If the state is under the thumb of the capitalist interests, why did the Great Depression occur, since it severely harmed them? Karl Popper ridiculed the all-knowing Marxist position: "A Marxist could not open a newspaper without finding on every page confirming evidence for his interpretation of history; not only in the news, but also in its presentation—which revealed the class bias of the paper—and especially of course in what the paper did not say" (1972: 35).

Third, Marxists stress several contemporary issues that Marx raised:

- The problem of alienation and monotonous work in the workplace.

- The issue of greed, fraud, and materialism under a money-seeking capitalist society.

- The concerns over inequality of wealth, income, and opportunity.

- Issues over race, feminism, discrimination, and environment.

David Denby, an essayist who read Marx as an adult in a college classic literature course, discussed several modern-day issues frequently raised by today's Marxists.

He began with the issue of alienation. Denby states: "Alienation is a loss of self: We work for others, to fulfill other people's goals, and often we confront what we produce with an indifference bordering on disgust" (1996: 349). How do we deal with boredom and meaninglessness in today's business world? Yet what is the alternative? Is a communal or socialist society any less boring or meaningless? A capitalist society that gradually improves the quantity, quality, and variety of goods and services offers less boredom and a greater chance of fulfillment, often by providing shorter work days that allow workers to find fulfillment in avocations outside their work.

What about greed? Denby writes, "Capitalism created envy and the desire to define oneself through goods. Capitalism itself, in its American version, bears part of the responsibility for low morals" (1996: 349). This argument is popular, but is countered by the thesis of Adam Smith and Montesquieu, among others, that the business culture gradually restrains fraud and greed (see chapter 1). Capitalism also produces wealthy individuals who spend much time and effort on spiritual, artistic, nonmaterial, nongreedy initiatives, providing many benefits to society.

Denby's college professor posed another Marxist criticism: "In bourgeois society the relations between human beings imitate the relations between commodities. . . . If cash is the only thing connecting us, what keeps society together?" The yearning for community in a highly individ-

---

DID MARX RECANT?

All I know is that I am no Marxist.

—Karl Marx

Marx is said to have made the above remark in the late 1870s, but apparently it has been taken out of context. At times he was so despairing over his son-in-law Lafargue's socialist "theoretical gibberish," that Marx declared, "If that is Marxist, I am no Marxist." Biographer Fritz J. Raddatz concludes, "It is certainly not to be taken as a recantation or deviation from his own doctrine but, on the contrary, as a defense of that doctrine against those who would distort it" (1978: 130).

But while Marx may not have relinquished his taste for violent revolution and his own theories, Engels appears to have revised his views in latter years. He conceded that workers may earn more than subsistence wages, that other noneconomic factors may play a role in society, and that legal political means may achieve reform. "The one-time would-be dashing general of revolution had almost become a Social-Democratic reformer," writes Robert Wesson (1976: 37–38).

---

ualistic market economy is a major concern. Does the chasing of the almighty dollar cause the tearing down of historic homes and the building of high-rise apartments? Does capitalism pressure us to work so long and hard that we don't have time to develop relationships outside the office? Denby warns, "In America, there seemed less and less holding us together" (1996: 344–51).

There is no question that the fast-paced market economy makes us live more independently from the community. The exchange of goods and services often becomes anonymous and unfriendly. Undoubtedly in a communitarian society, we would all know our neighbors and local business people better. But what would we be giving up?

THE MONEY NEXUS

Beyond the issues of alienation, inequality, and materialism, Marx's commentary on the evolutionary role of money can be most useful. Chapter 3 of *Capital* begins with a discussion of barter between two commodities, C and C'. The exchange takes place as follows:

$$C - C'.$$

When money is introduced, the relationship changes to

$$C - M - C'.$$

Here money represents the medium of exchange between two commodities. Normally in the production process from raw commodities to the final product, money is exchanged several times. The focus of the capitalist system is on the production of useful goods and services, and money simply serves as a medium of exchange—a means to an end.

However, Marx pointed out that it is very easy for the money capitalist to start viewing the world differently and more narrowly in terms of "making money" rather than "making useful goods and services." Marx represents this new business way of thinking as follows:

$$M - C - M'.$$

In other words, the businessman uses his money (capital) to produce a commodity, C, which in turn is sold for more money, M'. By focusing on money as the beginning and end of their activities, it is very easy to lose sight of the ultimate purpose of economic activity—to produce and exchange goods. The goal is no longer C, but M.

Finally, the market system advances one step further to the point where commodities (goods and services) do not enter the picture at all. The exchange process becomes

$$M - M'.$$

THE RISE AND FALL OF LIBERATION THEOLOGY

In the late 1960s and early 1970s, a Marxist-driven ideology known as "liberation theology" developed in Latin America, especially among Catholic priests who worked in the barrios and favelas. While rejecting the Marxist extremes of atheism and materialism, these political activists sought to liberate the poor by combining Marxist doctrines of exploitation, class struggle, and imperialism with the Christian theology of compassion for the poor and underprivileged. Popular books carried the titles *Communism and the Bible* and *Theology of Liberation,* published in English by Orbis Books, a subsidiary of the Catholic missionary order of the Maryknoll Fathers and Sisters. "Christ led me to Marx," declared Ernesto Cardenal, the Nicaraguan priest, to Pope John Paul II in 1983. "I'm a Marxist who believes in God, follows Christ and is a revolutionary for the sake of his kingdom" (Novak 1991: 13).

The father of liberation theology, Gustavo Gutiérrez, is a short-statured, mild-mannered professor of theology who wrote about his work with the poor in his native city of Lima, Peru, in *Theology of Liberation* (1973). Gutiérrez explained his "liberation theology" in Marxist terms.

> I discovered three things. I discovered that poverty was a destructive thing, something to be fought against and destroyed, not merely something which was the object of our charity. Secondly, I discovered that poverty was not accidental. The fact that these

This final stage reflects the capital or financial markets, such as money markets and securities (stocks and bonds). By now, it is easier for commodity capitalism to become pure financial capitalism, further removed from its roots of commodity production. In this environment, businesspeople often forget the whole purpose of the economic system—to produce useful goods and services—and concentrate just on "making money," whether through gambling, short-term trading techniques, or simply earning money in a bank account or from T-bills. Ultimately the goal of making money is best achieved by providing useful goods and services, but it is a lesson that must be learned over and over again in the commercial world.

---

people are poor and not rich is not just a matter of chance, but the result of a structure. It was a structural question. Third, I discovered that poverty was something to be fought against. . . . It became critically clear that in order to serve the poor, one had to move into political action. (McGovern 1980: 181–82)

Marxist theologists blamed this oppressive atmosphere in Latin America on capitalism and especially the "imperialistic" United States and its multinational corporations. They expressed a radical hostility to private property, markets, and profits as an "exploitive" process in favor of the rich at the expense of the poor. And if the choice was between revolution and democracy, revolution, even violent revolt, was preferable. Their policies included nationalization, an aversion to foreign investment, and the imposition of price controls and trade barriers.

Critics of liberation theology contend that these statist policies have only made poverty and inequality worse in Latin America. Michael Novak criticizes the Latin American system: "The present order is not free but statist, not mind-centered by privilege-centered, not open to the poor but protective of the rich. Large majorities of the poor are propertyless. The poor are prevented by law from founding and incorporating their own enterprises. They are denied access to credit. They are held back by an ancient legal structure, designed to protect the ancient privileges of a pre-capitalist elite" (1991: 5).

What is the Adam Smith solution to poverty and inequality in Latin America? The challenge, according to Novak, is to create genuine private-sector jobs, the real solution to poverty. "Revolutionaries," he states, "seem mostly to create huge armies. Economic activists create jobs." To truly liberate Latin America, he and other disciples of Adam Smith advocate open markets, foreign investment, low taxes, opportunities for business creation and ownership of property by all citizens, and political stability under the rule of law—"liberal, pluralistic, communitarian, public-spirited, dynamic, inventive" countries not unlike the Asian tigers, which adopted such policies in the recent past (1991: 32).[7]

Since the fall of Soviet communism and the socialist central-planning model, enthusiasm for liberation theology has waned, and most Latin American countries have adopted a more open economy. Consequently, Latin American economies have grown rapidly and the percentage of poor there has declined. Orbis Books and the Maryknoll Fathers and Sisters no longer publish books on liberation theology.

---

7. Peruvian economist Hernando de Soto has written several popular books on the need for legal and economic reforms in Latin America and developing countries in general (2002, 2003).

Thus, we can see how a capitalistic culture can lead to the loss of ultimate purpose and a sense of community. This tendency to move away from the true purpose of economic activity constantly challenges business leaders, investors, and citizens to get back to basics.

SUMMARY: MARX LEAVES HIS MARK

In sum, Karl Marx cannot be entirely dismissed. His economic theory may have been defective, his revolutionary socialism may have been destructive, and Marx himself may have been irascible, but his philosophical analysis of market capitalism has elements of merit and deserves our attention.

Only a few years after Marx's masterpiece, *Capital*, was published, a new breed of European economists would come on the scene. These economists would correct the errors of Marx and the classical economists, and bring about a permanent revolution. As noted earlier, the cost-of-production approach to price theory had put economics in a box, a box containing a bombshell that could annihilate the classical system of natural liberty. It would take a revolutionary breakthrough in economic theory to rejuvenate the dismal science and restore the foundations of Adam Smith's model. That is the subject of chapter 7.

REFERENCES

Barzun, Jacques. 1958 [1941]. *Darwin, Marx, Wagner,* 2d ed. New York: Doubleday.

Berman, Marshall. 1999. *Adventures in Marxism.* New York: Verso.

Blaug, Mark. 1986. *Great Economists Before Keynes.* Atlantic Heights, NJ: Humanities Press International.

Blumenberg, Werner. 1998 [1962]. *Karl Marx: An Illustrated Biography.* London: Verso.

Bottomore, Tom, ed. 1991. *A Dictionary of Marxist Thought,* 2d ed. Oxford: Blackwell.

Bronfenbrenner, Martin. 1967. "Marxian Influences in 'Bourgeois' Economics." *American Economic Review* 57: 2 (May), 624–35.

Buchholz, Todd G. 1999. *New Ideas from Dead Economists,* 2d ed. New York: Penguin.

Colb, Ralph, Jr. 1982. "The Myth of the Marx-Darwin Letter." *History of Political Economy* 14: 4, 461–82.

D'Aulaire, Ingri, and Edgar D'Aulaire. 1962. *D'Aulaire's Book of Greek Myths.* New York: Doubleday.

Denby, David. 1996. *Great Books.* New York: Simon & Schuster.

Downs, Robert B. 1983. *Books That Changed the World,* 2d ed. New York: Penguin.

Eaton, John. 1951. *Marx Against Keynes.* London: Lawrence and Wishart.

Engels, Friedrich. 2000 [1844] *The Condition of the Working Class in England.* New York: Pathfinder.

Feuerbach, Ludwig. 1957 [1841]. *The Essence of Christianity.* New York: Harper Torchbooks.

Gordon, H. Scott. 1967. "Discussion on *Das Capital*: A Centenary Appreciation." *American Economic Review* 52: 2 (May), 640–41.

Harrington, Michael. 1976. *The Twilight of Capitalism.* New York: Macmillan.

Hart, Michael H. 1978. *The 100: A Ranking of the Most Influential Persons in History.* New York: Hart.

————. 1992. *The 100: A Ranking of the Most Influential Persons in History,* 2d ed. New York: Citadel.

Heilbroner, Robert. 1961. *The Worldly Philosophers*, 2d ed. New York: Simon & Schuster.

————. 1999. *The Worldly Philosophers*, 7th ed. New York: Simon and Schuster.

Howard, M.C., and J.E. King. 1989. *A History of Marxian Economics, 1823–1929.* Princeton: Princeton University Press.

Keynes, John Maynard. 1931. *Essays in Persuasion.* New York: W.W. Norton.

————. 1936. *The General Theory of Employment, Interest and Money.* London: Macmillan.

Lenin, V.I. 1970. *Selected Works.* 12 vols. Moscow: Progress.

Lichtheim, George. 1970. *A Short History of Socialism.* New York: Praeger.

Liebknecht, Wilhelm. 1968 [1901]. *Karl Marx Biographical Memoirs.* New York: Greenwood.

Leontief, Wassily. 1938. "The Significance of Marxian Economics for Present-Day Economic Theory." *American Economic Review* 28: 2 (March supplement), 1–9.

McGovern, Arthur F. 1980. *Marxism: An American Christian Perspective.* Maryknoll, NY: Orbis Books.

Marx, Karl. 1976 [1867]. *Capital*, vol. 1. New York: Penguin.

————. 1980. *The Holy Family, or Critique of Critical Criticism.* New York: Firebird.

————. 1988. *The Economic and Philosophic Manuscripts of 1844.* New York: Prometheus.

————. 1995. *The Poverty of Philosophy.* New York: Prometheus.

Marx, Karl, and Friedrich Engels. 1964 [1848]. *The Communist Manifesto.* New York: Monthly Review Press.

————. *Collected Works (Letters 1860–64)*, vol. 41. New York: International Publishers.

Mises, Ludwig von. 1972. *The Anti-Capitalist Mentality.* Spring Mills, PA: Libertarian Press.

Moggridge, D.E. 1992. *Maynard Keynes.* London: Routledge.

North, Gary. 1993. "The Marx Nobody Knows." In *Requiem for Marx,* ed. Uri N. Maltsev. Auburn, AL: Ludwig von Mises Institute.

Novak, Michael. 1991. *Will It Liberate?* New York: Madison Books.

Padover, Saul K. 1978. *Karl Marx: An Intimate Biography.* New York: McGraw-Hill.

Payne, Robert. 1968. *Marx.* New York: Simon & Schuster.

————. 1971. *The Unknown Marx.* New York: New York University Press.

Perelman, Michael. 2007. *The Confiscation of American Prosperity: From Right-Wing Extremism and Economic Ideology to the Next Great Depression.* New York: Palgrave Macmillan.

Plaut, Eric A., and Kevin Anderson. 1999. *Marx on Suicide.* Evanston, IL: Northwestern University Press.

Raddatz, Fritz J. 1978. *Karl Marx: A Political Biography.* Boston: Little, Brown.

Roemer, John E. 1988. *Free to Lose.* Cambridge, MA: Harvard University Press.

Rothbard, Murray N. 1980. "The Essential Von Mises." In Ludwig von Mises, *Planning for Freedom*, 4th ed., 234–70. Spring Mills, PA: Libertarian Press.

————. 1995. *Classical Economics.* Hants, UK: Edward Elgar.

Samuelson, Paul A. 1957. "Wages and Interest: A Modern Dissection of Marxian Economic Models." *American Economic Review* 47: 6 (May), 884–910.

————. 1967. "Marxian Economics as Economics." *American Economic Review* 57: 2 (May), 616–23.

————. 1976. *Economics.* New York: McGraw Hill.

Schumpeter, Joseph. 1942. *Capitalism, Socialism and Democracy.* New York: Harper.

Schwartzchild, Leopold. 1947. *Karl Marx, the Red Prussian.* New York: Grosset and Dunlap.

Seymour-Smith, Martin. 1998. *The 100 Most Influential Books Ever Written.* Toronto: Citadel.

Skidelsky, Robert. 1992. *John Maynard Keynes: The Economist as Saviour, 1920–1937.* London: Macmillan.

Solomou, S.N. 1987. "Nikolai Kondratieff." In *The New Palgrave: A Dictionary of Economics,* vol. 3, 60. London: Macmillan.

Soto, Hernando de. 2002. *The Other Path,* 2d ed. New York: Perseus Books.

———. 2003. *The Mystery of Capital.* New York: Basic Books.

Sweezy, Paul M. 1942. *The Theory of Capitalist Development.* New York: Modern Reader.

Sweezy, Paul M., and Paul Baran. 1966. *Monopoly Capitalism.* New York: Monthly Review.

Sweezy, Paul M., and Harry Magdoff. 1977. *The End of Prosperity.* New York: Monthly Review.

Wesson, Robert G. 1976. *Why Marxism? The Continuing Success of a Failed Theory.* New York: Basic Books.

Wicksteed, Philip H. 1933. *The Common Sense of Political Economy,* rev. ed. London: Routledge and Kegan Paul.

Wilson, Edmund. 1940. *To the Finland Station.* New York: Harcourt, Brace.

Zarnowitz, Victor. 1992. *Business Cycles.* Chicago: University of Chicago Press.

7

OUT OF THE BLUE DANUBE: MENGER AND THE AUSTRIANS REVERSE THE TIDE

No book since Ricardo's Principles *has had such a great*
influence on the development of economics as
Menger's Grundsätze.

—Knut Wicksell (1958: 191)

Menger is the vanquisher of the Ricardian theory. . . .
Menger's theory of value, price, and distribution is the
best we have up to now.

—Joseph Schumpeter (1951: 86)

Karl Marx was right about one thing: the colossal forces of the industrial revolution catapulted the Western world into a new age of prosperity never before witnessed in history. Living in London, the center of the "first industrial nation," the German philosopher could not help but notice the massive power of capitalism as industrial might spread from Britain to Germany to the United States during the nineteenth century. However, Marx overlooked a significant event: all economic classes—capitalists, landlords, and workers—experienced improvement in their material conditions. The average real wage rose only an estimated 1 percent a year, but over Marx's lifetime that was a significant gain. Economic historian Rondo Cameron concludes that "the per capita real income of Britons increased by roughly 2.5 times between 1850 and 1914, income

---

♪ **Music selection for this chapter: Johann Strauss, Jr., "The Emperor's Waltz"**

distribution became *slightly* more equal, the proportion of the population in dire poverty fell, and the average Briton in 1914 enjoyed the highest standard of living in Europe" (Cameron 1997: 228).

The United States witnessed even more rapid economic growth in the nineteenth century. According to Cameron, the average per capita income at least doubled between 1776 and the Civil War, even though population increased nearly tenfold. By the 1870s, the United States was the richest nation on earth (Cameron 1997: 228).

By the time Karl Marx died in 1883, evidence was mounting that the Malthus-Ricardo-Marx "subsistence wage" thesis was terribly wrong. Adam Smith's upbeat system of universal prosperity was gaining credence.

ECONOMICS FACES A MAJOR STUMBLING BLOCK

Yet, while the industrial economy was making progress, economic theory was at a dead end. Adam Smith recognized that economic freedom and limited government would create wealth and ubiquitous prosperity, but he had no sound theoretical framework (other than the division of labor) with which to explain how consumers and producers worked through the price system to achieve a higher standard of living. Ricardo, Mill, and the classical school developed a cost-of-production rationale for prices of goods, commodities, and labor, but in doing so, they became hostage to Marxian economics. If profits or rents increased, they did so only at the expense of workers' wages. As class struggle appeared inevitable, the Smithian world of universal prosperity and harmony of interests disintegrated. The classical economists tragically separated the questions of "production" and "distribution," which, as we have noted, gave ammunition to the socialist cause of redistribution, nationalization, and state central planning.

Economics as a science stagnated in England. John Stuart Mill had arrogantly declared in his *Principles*, "Happily, there is nothing in the laws of value which remains for the present or any future writer to clear up; the theory of the subject is complete" (Black et al. 1973: 181). Classical economics was out of favor in France. The profession had reached such a low point that professors in Germany, Marx's homeland, rejected the idea that there was any such thing as economic theory. "Under the onslaughts of the Historical School," Friedrich Hayek wrote, "not only were the classical doctrines completely abandoned—but any attempt at theoretical analysis came to be regarded with deep distrust" (1976: 13).

If capitalism was to survive and prosper, it would require a new epistemology, a breakthrough in economic theory. Economics desperately needed a new impetus, a general theory that could explain how all classes gain—landlords, capitalists and workers—and all consumers benefit. But where would it come from?

THREE ECONOMISTS MAKE A REMARKABLE DISCOVERY ALMOST SIMULTANEOUSLY

We have noted how certain years stand out in the history of economics, how major events occur at the same time, such as 1776, the year of the Declaration of Independence and *The Wealth of Nations*, and 1848, the year of European revolution and *The Communist Manifesto*. The early 1870s—and especially the year 1871—was a similar time, marking the period that three economists independently discovered the principle of marginal utility and ushered in the "neoclassical" marginalist revolution. The idea that prices and costs were determined by final consumer demand and their relative marginal utility was the last major piece missing from the evolution of modern economics. Its discovery resolved the paradox of value that had frustrated the classical economists from Adam Smith to John Stuart Mill. It was also the undoing of Marxian economics.

The marginal utility revolution reignited a moribund science. It was an exciting time to be an economist.

Who were these economists? From Britain came **William Stanley Jevons (1835–82)**, from France, **Léon Walras (1834–1910)**, and from Austria, **Carl Menger (1840–1921)**. While it is true that a few forerunners, such as Hermann Gossen, Samuel Longfield, Antoine Cournot, and Jules Dupuit, had earlier employed the principles of marginal utility, it was not until these three came together that the marginality principle became widely recognized and adopted in the profession.[1] Swedish economist Knut Wicksell, who lived through the marginalist revolution, described it as a "bolt from the blue" (1958: 186).

WHAT THE MARGINALIST REVOLUTION MEANT

Both Menger and Jevons published their new theories in 1871, although Jevons gave a lecture on his fundamental ideas in 1862. Menger published his *Grundsätze der Volkswirtschaftslehre,* later translated as *Principles of Economics* (1976 [1871]), and Jevons issued *The Theory of Political Economy.* A few years later, in 1874 and 1877, Walras published his two-part *Elements of Pure Economics.* Together, they developed what is called the "neoclassical" school of economics. It combined Adam Smith's laissez-faire model of prosperity with the marginal theory of value. Within the next generation, the marginalist revolution swept through the economics profession and replaced, to a large extent, the Ricardian framework with a new orthodoxy. Though not as rapid as the Keynesian revolution in the 1930s, the marginalist revolution of the 1870s conquered the profession with equal unanimity and force over the next generation.

---

1. Auburn economists Robert Ekelund, Jr., and Robert Hébert contend that French engineer Jules Dupuit (1804–1866) was the ultimate forerunner of modern microeconomics, including marginal utility theory. See Ekelund and Hébert (2000). The authors point out that Dupuit's contributions were largely ignored because he wrote primarily for engineers.

The triumvirate of the marginalist revolution—Jevons, Walras, and Menger—rejected the objective cost-of-production theories of value and focused instead upon the subjective principle of utility and consumer demand as the keystone of a new approach to economics. They noted that individuals make choices on the basis of preferences and values in the real world. Like J.-B. Say, they recognized that no amount of labor or production confers value on a product. Value consists of the subjective valuations of individual users. In short, demand had to be high enough before producers would employ productive resources to produce a product. Demand must always supersede supply.

The marginalists even went a step further and argued that in the long run there is no such thing as an independent supply curve; supply is ultimately determined by final demand. For example, if the demand curve shifts forward, eventually a new supply (cost) schedule develops as new resources enter the industry. As Philip Wicksteed, one of the strongest proponents of the marginalist revolution in the early twentieth century, stated, "cost of production is coordinate with the schedule of demands" (1933: 812). The Austrians indicated that cost is nothing more than forgone alternatives.

PRODUCTION AND DISTRIBUTION ONCE AGAIN LINKED

A new generation of economists found that production and distribution could once again be linked together. The demands of consumers ultimately determine the final prices of consumer goods, which in turn sets the direction for productive activity. Final demand establishes the prices of the cooperative factors of production—wages, rents, and profits—according to the value they add to the production process. In short, income was not distributed, it was produced, according to the value added by each participant in the production process. In the case of labor, the idea that wages are determined by the marginal productivity of labor evolved out of this marginal principle of value and was more fully perfected by John Bates Clark, an American economist at Columbia University, at the turn of the century (see chapter 9).

THE MARGINALIST PRINCIPLE RESOLVES THE PARADOX OF VALUE

The neoclassical economists took the principle of utility one step further. They realized that the greater the quantity of a good that individuals possess, the less they will value any given unit. If there is a large amount of water available everywhere, an additional glass of water will be relatively cheap. On the other hand, if a community lives in the Arabian desert, where water is fairly scarce, the community will highly prize each additional unit of water. The same principle applies to diamonds. If diamonds are abundant, the price of diamonds falls. If diamonds are scarce, the price goes up.

Thus, the neoclassical economists discovered the principle of diminishing marginal utility. In short, prices were determined by *marginal* buying and selling, fulfilling the demands of consumers based on the relative abundance or scarcity of a product. They had solved once and for all the so-called paradox of value that had frustrated Adam Smith and other classical economists.

Why is an essential commodity like water so cheap while a nonessential, impractical commodity like diamonds so expensive? In *The Wealth of Nations*, Adam Smith separated utility from price and created an artificial dichotomy between "goods in use" and "goods in exchange," as if nothing connects price and utility. Smith noted that water had great "use," but very little "value." A diamond had scarcely any practical use (this was before diamonds were used in industry), but great "exchange" value. Thus, the classical economists were unable to resolve the famous diamond-water paradox, resulting in confusion about the micro foundations of economics for an entire generation.

Moreover, the impact of Smith's artificial dichotomy between value in "use" and in "exchange" was not harmless. It gave ammunition to socialists, Marxists, and other critics of capitalism who complain about the difference in the marketplace between "production for profit" and "production for use." They blame capitalists for being more interested in "making profits" than in "providing a useful service," as if profitable exchange is unrelated to consumer use.

Now the marginalist revolution resolved the paradox of value and, in doing so, undercut the socialists' argument. Under the new microeconomics, profits and use are directly connected. Prices reflect consumer demands, and profit-driven production seeks to meet those needs.

Resolving the diamond-water paradox, the marginalists demonstrated that the difference in value between water and diamonds is due to the relative abundance of water and the relative scarcity of diamonds (given the demands). Since the supply of water is abundant, the demand for each additional unit is low. Since the supply of diamonds is extremely limited, the demand for each additional diamond is high. Hence, there was no longer a contradiction between value in use and value in exchange.[2]

---

2. Here's a strange twist in the history of economics: Adam Smith actually had the correct answer to the diamond-water paradox a decade prior to writing *The Wealth of Nations*. Smith's lectures on jurisprudence, delivered in 1763, reveal that he recognized that price was determined by scarcity. Smith said, "It is only on account of the plenty of water that it is so cheap as to be got for the lifting, and on account of the scarcity of diamonds . . . that they are so dear." The Scottish professor added that when supply conditions change, the value of a product changes also. Smith noted that a rich merchant lost in the Arabian desert would value water very highly. If the quantity of diamonds could "by industry . . . be multiplied," the price of diamonds would drop (Smith 1978: 33, 3, 358). Oddly, his cogent explanation of the diamond-water paradox disappeared when he was writing chapter 4, book 1, of *The Wealth of Nations*. Was Smith suffering from absent-mindedness? Economist Roger Garrison doesn't think so. He blames the change on Smith's Calvinist background, which emphasized the goodness of hard work, useful production, and frugality. In his

(continued)

Both Jevons and Walras compared the marginalist revolution to the discovery of calculus by Newton and Leibniz, especially since both calculus and price theory involve marginal changes.

MENGER'S CRITICAL ROLE IN THE MARGINALIST REVOLUTION

In this chapter, we start with the pioneering contributions of Carl Menger and the Austrian school he founded. Of the three "neoclassical" economists, Menger was the first to systematically develop a new approach to value and price theory and successfully challenge the Ricardian paradigm. Jevons's book was read but not well received in England; his influence was stunted by the overwhelming acceptance of the Ricardian orthodoxy. (We will discuss Jevons's and Marshall's critical roles in transforming economics in the next chapter on the British neoclassical school.) Walras's system of general equilibrium and marginal analysis was highly mathematical and scared off most of his contemporaries. It was ignored for several decades and then gradually gained prominence in the twentieth century. In short, it was Menger and his Austrian school who got the ball rolling and had the greatest impact on changing the course of economic thinking in the latter half of the nineteenth century. To cite a contemporary, Knut Wicksell, on the influence of the three inventors, "one can safely say that no book since Ricardo's *Principles* has had such a great influence on the development of economic theory as Menger's *Grundsätze*—not even excluding the ingenious, but too aphoristic work of Jevons, nor that of Walras, which is unfortunately extremely difficult to read" (Wicksell 1958: 191).

Surprisingly, Menger's influence was largely indirect. His subjective utility theory and marginal analysis were popularized primarily through his two disciples, Eugen Böhm-Bawerk and Friedrich Wieser. Moreover, Böhm-Bawerk was the first "neoclassical" economist to take on Karl Marx in a serious way and debunk Marxian economics.

THE ACHIEVEMENTS OF THE AUSTRIAN SCHOOL

The Austrian school rescued Adam Smith and his model of natural liberty in three ways (in this sense, it was really a multiple revolution):

---

mind, diamonds and jewels were vain luxury items and relatively "useless" compared to water and other "useful" products. Garrison points to Smith's odd dichotomy between "productive" and "unproductive" labor; see the third chapter of book II in *The Wealth of Nations*, where Smith referred to ministers, physicians, musicians, orators, actors, and other producers of services as working in "frivolous" occupations. Farmers and manufacturers, on the other hand, are "productive." Why? Because Smith's preference for Presbyterian conscience argues against consumption in favor of saving and work. As Garrison states, "The basis for the distinction is not Physiocratic fallacies but Presbyterian values. Productive labor is future oriented; unproductive labor is present oriented" (Garrison 1985: 290; Rothbard 1995: 444–50).

1. *The consumer origin of value:* Menger and the Austrians established the supreme role of the consumer in determining productive activity—that final demand, not labor time or the costs of production, determines the structure and pricing of the production process. The Austrians called this their "theory of imputation." Utility imputed (determined) the value of inputs. By demonstrating this relationship, the Austrians established a new model no longer held hostage by the Marxian-socialist heterodoxy.

2. *Marginal utility/cost:* The Austrians demonstrated that prices and costs are determined at the margin—by the marginal benefit-cost to buyers and sellers. Marginal analysis forms the basis of modern-day microeconomics.

3. *Subjective value:* The Austrians demonstrated that Ricardo's search for an "invariable measure of value" was, like Ponce de Leon's search for the fountain of youth, all in vain. Menger and his followers revealed that value is entirely dependent on the desires of consumers and producers; that wages, rents, interest, and profits are determined by the subjective valuations of the customers and users. Thus, costs are never really fixed in the long run.

On a broader level, the Austrian contribution was the most radical. Menger and the Austrians replaced the objective mechanistic determinism of Ricardian economics with a subjective reality of human action and valuations.

The Austrian economists made many other contributions in the theory of capital and interest, money, and public finance. Primarily through the work of Eugen Böhm-Bawerk, the Austrians created a non-Marxist theory of capitalism that incorporated the importance of saving and capital formation as the keys to growth and universal prosperity.

In short, Menger and his followers enhanced Smith's positive vision of economics and the capitalist system. As such, Menger founded a new school of thought that has had a deep impact on both macroeconomics (how the economy works as a whole) and microeconomics (the theory of individual prices, costs, and production). In many ways, he was a revolutionary discoverer of both macroeconomics (through his time structure of production model) and microeconomics (subjective demand and marginal analysis). Carl Menger is without peer the greatest *theoretical* economist in support of Adam Smith's system of natural liberty.

VIENNA: THE SETTING FOR A REVOLUTION

In the 1870s, the University of Vienna was considered one of the largest and most prestigious schools of learning in Europe. Over the centuries, the Austro-Hungarian Empire under the rule of the Habsburgs established

Vienna as the political, cultural, and intellectual center of Eastern Europe. Located on the beautiful Danube River, Vienna became the third largest city in Europe, behind London and Paris. During the nineteenth century, it was famous for its magnificent museums, palaces, parks, opera houses, and cafes. For a century and a half, from the late 1700s until the early 1900s, there occurred an extraordinary intellectual flowering within the Austro-Hungarian Empire. Vienna attracted some of the world's most creative musicians, scientists, philosophers, and economists. The world's greatest musicians lived there—Mozart, Beethoven, Haydn, Schubert, Brahms, Mahler, and Strauss. Sigmund Freud, the famed psychologist, and Ludwig Wittgenstein, the philosopher, also lived and worked in Vienna.

Another revolution took place at the University of Vienna. Menger founded the Austrian school of economics, a school focusing on individual behavior, entrepreneurship, subjective values, and the roles of time and capital in the market process. Many Austrian concepts, such as marginal utility, opportunity cost, and time preference, have been incorporated into standard economic analysis. In the late nineteenth century, under Menger's direction, the Austrian school challenged its two principal rivals, the British classical school and the German historical school, and imposed a broadside attack on the emerging Marxist school.

THE AUSTRIANS GENERATE A NEW EPOCH IN ECONOMICS

The Austrian-led "neoclassical" revolution was a dramatic moment in economic history, but most historians don't do justice to the excitement this revolution generated among economists throughout the Western world at the time. The utility/marginalist/subjectivist revolution in Austria spawned numerous articles in the economics journals. Economics historian James Bonar wrote in the October 1888 issue of the *Quarterly Journal of Economics* that, because of Menger and his followers, Austria had become "more prominent in economical discussion than she has been for at least a century" (1888: 1). H.R. Seager wrote a report for the March 1893 issue of the *Journal of Political Economy*, saying that the University of Vienna was attracting students from all countries (1893). In 1891, Eugen Böhm-Bawerk was asked to submit an article on the Austrian-led revolution in neoclassical economics to the *Annals* of the American Academy of Political and Social Sciences. According to Böhm-Bawerk, the new Austrian theory of value had the following impact: "The most important and most famous doctrines of the classical economists are either no longer tenable at all, or are tenable only after essential alterations and additions" (Böhm-Bawerk 1962: 5).

The Austrian vision was also promoted by the **Reverend Philip Wicksteed (1844–1927)**, a British unitarian minister and a medieval scholar who translated the works of Dante and Aristotle. He turned to economics when he was middle-aged, upon reading Henry George's *Progress* *and Poverty.* A member of the Fabian Society and sympathetic to socialist causes all his life (including land nationalization), he nevertheless became a purist in marginalist theory and was one of the foremost advocates of Jevons and the Austrians through his influential work, *The Common Sense of Political Economy* (1933). In fact, he is credited with introducing the term "marginal utility" as a translation of the Austrian word *Grenznutzen*.

MENGER'S MYSTERIOUS BACKGROUND

How did this revolution come about? We begin with the story of its founder.

Carl Menger's personal life is shrouded in mystery. No full-length biography exists. His son, Karl, worked on a history of his father, but never finished it. There may be reasons why, as explained below.

Photograph 7.1
Carl Menger (1840–1921)
"A man of extraordinarily impressive appearance."
Courtesy of Adam Smith Archiv.

The early life and education of Carl Menger is not well known. Carl, one of three sons, was born in 1840 in Neu-Sandez, a city in Austria that later became part of southern Poland. Menger's father was a lawyer, and his mother was the daughter of a wealthy Bohemian merchant. Carl studied law and political science at the University of Vienna (1859–60). For a few years, he wrote a number of short novels and comedies serialized in the local newspapers, but he had more serious goals. In 1867, he earned his doctorate at the University of Krakow, and began his career as a reporter in the press section of the Prime Minister's office in Vienna, where he was responsible for reporting on economic conditions and the stock market, often writing for the official newspaper *Wiener Zeitung*. According to Friedrich Wieser, it was here as an economic journalist that Menger came to recognize the importance of subjective demand in determining prices and set out to reshape economic theory.

There are few impressions of him physically. He was considered tall and had a wealth of hair and a full beard. "In his prime Menger must have been a man of extraordinarily impressive appearance" (Hayek 1976: 33).

While an economic journalist, Menger began writing his revolutionary magnum opus. He was young, in his late twenties. He felt inspired with his breakthrough findings, wrote furiously in a state of "morbid excitement," and published his *Grundsätze* in 1871 at the youthful age of thirty-one.

The year 1871 was significant for Menger. He gained employment with the Austrian Civil Service, but upon presenting his book to the faculty at the University of Vienna, he quickly resigned to become a *privatdozent*, an unsalaried lecturer. By 1873, his academic colleagues were so impressed with Menger that they appointed him "extraordinary" professor of law and political science at the university.[3] (Note: In Europe, "extraordinary" professor is similar to "associate" or "assistant" professor; the next higher rank is "ordinary" or full professor!) No other economist achieved such rapid success as Menger. Most innovators have to wait a generation or until old age before their theories are accepted. Jevons died before his theories were accepted, and Walras spent a considerable fortune promoting his ideas before they were recognized a generation later. But Menger's new value theory was so well received in his own country that he attained a professorship at the young age of thirty-three.

Menger Tutors the Heir to the Throne

It wasn't long before Menger built a reputation as a popular lecturer who could explain economics clearly and simply, while still challenging the brightest students. His renown apparently reached the highest levels of government, because in 1876, Menger fell into a remarkable opportunity that had the potential for making him famous. Following in Adam Smith's footsteps, Menger was asked to tutor an aristocrat. Not just any aristocrat, but the eighteen-year-old Archduke Rudolf, crown prince of Austria and heir to the throne! The emperor was the authoritarian Franz Joseph, famous for his mutton-chop whiskers.

During the first three months of 1876, Menger gave the archduke a crash course in economics. As his primary text he used Adam Smith's 100-year-old *Wealth of Nations*.

After each lecture, Rudolf was required to submit copious notes on the lecture entirely from memory, after which they were reviewed and edited by Menger. The crown prince's notebooks, which have recently been published in both German and English, demonstrate the archduke's amazing ability of near-perfect recall. Rudolf, though high strung, was extremely intelligent and spoke seven languages fluently.

The notebooks are important because they demonstrate Menger's biases regarding economic policy. His previous works scrupulously avoided any references to government policy. Although he hid behind his authorities, it is clear from the notebooks that Menger was a classic liberal in the Adam Smith tradition. "Menger's Rudolf Lectures are, in fact, probably one of the most extreme statements of the principles of laissez faire ever put to paper in the academic literature of economics" (Streissler 1994: 17).

---

3. Before his appointment to the university, Carl Menger was investigated by the security police because of his "notorious" older brother Max's pro-union activities as a member of the Austrian parliament (Hennings 1997: 52, n. 133). Later, Carl had to worry about his younger brother, Anton, a lawyer who wrote the influential socialist tract *The Right to the Whole Produce of Labour* (1886).

Photograph 7.2
Archduke Rudolf and Princess Stephanie
Menger tutors the heir to the throne.
Courtesy of AKG London.

Menger's laissez-faire philosophy was dangerous, because it went counter to the interventionist policies of the Austro-Hungarian Empire under Franz Joseph. But he avoided the appearance that he was expressing his own ideas by citing Adam Smith and other older economists. Perhaps that's why he did not use his own treatise.

The oddest revelation about the notebooks is that Menger said nothing about marginal utility, his theory of imputation, or subjective value, the three breakthrough concepts developed in the *Grundsätze* published five years earlier. Menger's primary reason for the lectures was to help the archduke understand economic *policy*, so perhaps he thought new theories outside the principles of Adam Smith were unnecessary.

After the lectures, Menger stayed on and served for nearly two years as Archduke Rudoph's traveling companion through Germany, France, Switzerland, and Britain.

Emperor Franz Joseph was apparently so impressed with Menger's abilities that in 1879 he approved Menger's appointment as chair of law and political economy at the University of Vienna, a prestigious and highly rewarding position. Some have suggested that Menger was being groomed to become the prime minister.

Menger's lectures must have made a deep impression on Rudolf, because the archduke frequently wrote articles critical of his father's conservative policies, though always under an assumed name. Apparently the emperor failed to connect these anonymous heretical ideas with Menger, who remained largely silent on policy matters.

MENGER'S HOPES DASHED AFTER THE CROWN PRINCE'S MURDER-SUICIDE SCANDAL

Menger's high expectations came crashing down a decade later when Archduke Rudolf unexpectedly committed suicide. Rudolf was emotionally unstable, notorious for his womanizing, and politically unpredictable. In late January 1889, at a hunting lodge in the Vienna Woods, Rudolf shot his mistress and then himself. He was only thirty years old.[4]

MENGER BECOMES A WEALTHY PROFESSOR

Menger was undoubtedly distressed by the shocking news of the murder-suicide scandal. He maintained his position as full professor of political economy at the University of Vienna, but gone forever was his potential as a government leader. Fortunately, his lucrative professorship gave him the means to complete his other goals. Apart from their salaries, professors received substantial lecture fees and an extremely high examination fee for each student. Given that Menger had at least 400 students a year, by 1903—the year he retired—he was earning around $4,000 a year. In today's purchasing power, his income would amount to around half a million dollars! As Erich Streissler concludes, "Professorial chairs thus were not only among the very highly honored but also among the best-paid positions of the establishment in the German-speaking world" (1990: 63).

His high compensation allowed Menger to create an outstanding library of over 20,000 volumes (now housed at the Hitotsubashi University Library in Tokyo, along with Adam Smith's library). He wrote numerous articles on economics and methodology, and attracted a devoted group of followers. But for reasons we shall see, it was largely the second generation of Austrian economists, especially Eugen Böhm-Bawerk and Friedrich Wieser, who would carry the banner of Austrian principles throughout the Western world. By the turn of the century, Böhm-Bawerk—not Menger—was the best-known economist on continental Europe.

WHY HIS MOST FAMOUS WORK IS NEVER REPRINTED

After retiring from university life in 1903 (see the box on page 183 to find out why he left early), Menger became somewhat of a recluse, devoting

4. In 1936 the murder-suicide tragedy of Prince Rudolf was the subject of a popular French film, *Mayerling*, starring Charles Boyer.

A DARK SECRET REVEALED!
A SEXUAL SCANDAL FORCES MENGER TO RESIGN

In 1903, at the age of sixty-three, Menger suddenly retired from his prestigious chair at the university. Normally, university professors retire at around age seventy. Why the early retirement? The official cause was "illness," but that was a cover-up. Only recently has evidence surfaced that Carl Menger had a long-term unmarried relationship with a woman named Hermine Andermann. She may have been his housekeeper. Menger ceased to teach at Vienna University from the moment their son, Karl, was born, and a year and a half later, he retired early. Carl Menger died unmarried but sought and eventually received from the Emperor Franz Joseph an act of legitimacy for his son, who became a famous mathematician.

According to Erich Streissler, professor of economics at the University of Vienna and highly regarded in his knowledge of the history of the Austrian school, Menger probably could not marry Hermine, either because she was divorced or because she was Jewish. Menger was Catholic, and a Catholic could not marry a Jew, as all marriages then were religious ceremonies. Apparently, the birth of their son was not the result of a short-term affair and their relationship could be best thought of as a "common-law" marriage due to the circumstances.

Hermine Andermann inherited Menger's substantial and highly valued library, nearly all he possessed. The Japanese professor who bought Menger's library for Tokyo addressed her in the negotiations as "Mrs. Menger."

In 1987, Menger's granddaughter, Eve, donated the papers of Carl Menger to Duke University.

himself to a complete revision of his *Grundsätze*. He was honored as a life member of the upper chamber of the Austrian parliament, but was not very active. His hobbies were fishing and book collecting. It was traditional for students at Vienna University to undertake a pilgrimage to his home to pay homage to the grand old man of the Austrian school.

In many ways, Menger's life ended somewhat tragically. His first love was economics and his long-term goal throughout his career was a thorough systematic updating of his *Grundsätze*. Unfortunately, Menger had a habit of chasing other hares; especially, he conducted a never-ending and fruitless battle over methodology with his German rivals. His interests and the scope of his reading material continued to expand. He studied philosophy, psychology, sociology, enthnography, and other disciplines. A perfectionist, he was never satisfied with his revisions, which were voluminous and fragmentary, and the publication of his "second edition" was postponed over and over again (shades of Marx and, later, Schumpeter).

While the never-ending revised version was still pending, Menger's magnum opus went out of print and became extremely scarce. The author never permitted another printing during his lifetime, nor any translations, because he felt his first book was incomplete. *Grandsätze* was not published in English until 1950. Hayek concludes, "It is difficult to think of a parallel case where a work such as the *Grundsätze* has exercised a lasting and persistent influence but has yet, as a result of purely accidental circumstances, had so extremely restricted a circulation" (1976: 12).

Fortunately, the principal works of his followers, Wieser's *Natural Value* and Böhm-Bawerk's *Positive Theory of Capital*, were translated into English in the late nineteenth century and thereby advanced the theories of Menger. Menger is like Marx, in that if it weren't for his enthusiastic and gifted followers, he would be unknown today.

MENGER OUTLIVES HIS MOST FAMOUS STUDENT

Menger outlived his most famous student, Eugen Böhm-Bawerk, who died in 1914. Menger went on to live through the horrors of World War I, and died within three days of his eighty-first birthday in 1921, at the depths of the Austrian hyperinflation and "Red Vienna," the socialist takeover of Vienna. His younger brother, Anton, who died in 1906, might have been pleased, having authored the famous socialist tract *The Right to the Whole Produce of Labour*, but Carl, who was generally opposed to radical reform, was not at all happy. Not surprisingly, Menger died a pessimistic man. He had never completed his updated version of *Grundsätze*, and the signs of the times worked against him. Many of his theories had been incorporated into contemporary economic thinking, but he constantly worried about petty arguments with his colleagues.

MENGER SEEKS TO CONVERT THE GERMAN HISTORICAL SCHOOL

What was Menger trying to accomplish when he wrote *Grundsätze* in 1871? As mentioned earlier, the German historical school, founded by Wilhelm Roscher, Bruno Hildebrand, and Karl Knies, reacted negatively to the English Enlightenment and classical economics. They disliked both the deductive method and the laissez-faire conclusions of Smith, Malthus, and Ricardo. According to the Germans, there could be no scientific economic "laws" separate from politics, custom, and the legal system. Only through the study of history could scholars come to any conclusions about economic issues and policies. Gustav Schmoller, an extreme member of the German historical school, went so far as to declare publicly that members of the "abstract" classical school were unfit to teach in a German university, and for years followers of Menger were excluded from academic positions in Germany. It was Germany's loss. It would be decades before German institutions hired competent theoreticians in economics.

In what has become known as *Methodenstreit* (the battle of methods), Menger's goal was to demonstrate that economic truth should not be rejected simply because the classical economists had the wrong theory (the labor theory of value). The whole purpose of Menger's first book was to convince the Germans that universal scientific laws of economics do exist, and that he had developed the principles to prove it. He even dedicated his book to Dr. Wilhelm Roscher, founder of the German historical school.

During the nineteenth century, German universities were regarded as the best in Europe, and Carl Menger was convinced that if a new economic science was to flourish, the leaders of the German historical school had to be converted.

MENGER USES A PATHBREAKING METHOD

Like Adam Smith, Menger's grand interest was economic growth, "The causes of progress in human welfare" (Menger 1976 [1871]: 71). But as Menger's son pointed out in the second edition of the *Grundsätze*, published posthumously, his father's aim was to replace the classical model with an entirely new theoretical approach.[5]

The classical method of Smith and Ricardo focused on how land, labor, and capital—the factors of production—produced and distributed consumer goods and wealth. Menger took a different road. Instead of focusing on the division of labor, as Adam Smith did, the Austrian thinker began with a discussion of the character of goods. According to Menger, it was not so much the division of labor that created a higher living standard, but the constant and gradual increase in the range of goods and services, and the improvement in their quality. As Erich Streissler notes, "Mengerian goods are three-dimensional: they have *quantity*, *quality*, and *variety* as separate dimensions of dynamic change" (Black et al. 1973: 165).

THE STRUCTURE OF PRODUCTION

In his first chapter, "The General Theory of the Good," Menger noted that all goods and services undergo a series of production processes, from raw commodities to final consumer goods. Menger started with final consumer goods, those that "satisfy human needs directly"—and defined them as "goods of the first order." Examples might be bread, shoes, or a dress. The ultimate purpose of production, noted Menger, was to satisfy human needs through the creation of better and cheaper goods and services.

After final consumer goods, there are "goods of a second order," producer goods-in-process, such as flour, leather, or cloth. Moving another step back, there are "goods of a third order," such as wheat, cowhide, and wool.

---

5. There is an undated quotation from the notes of Menger maintaining that he had "set himself the task of countering the theories of Adam Smith which he saw to be erroneous." See the introduction by Menger's son, Karl, to the second edition of the *Grundsätze* (1923), pp. vii–viii.

The Law of Imputation: Inputs Depend on Outputs

Menger labeled final consumer goods "lower order" and an array of producer goods "higher order." He then attempted to demonstrate a universal principle, that the demand for higher-order producer goods "is derived from that of the corresponding goods of lower order" (Menger 1976 [1871]: 63).

In an example that sounds all too modern, Menger used tobacco to prove his theory. "Suppose that the need for direct human consumption of tobacco should disappear" (page 64). What would happen?

First, the price for all tobacco products would fall to zero, even those already produced at considerable cost.

Second, "But what would happen to the corresponding goods of higher order?" asked Menger. What of the demand for "raw tobacco leaves, the tools and appliances used for the production of the various kinds of tobacco, the specialized labor services employed in the industry" (page 64)?

They, too, would lose part or all of their value. In other words, the demand for the factors of production are dependent on final consumer demand. The value of inputs is clearly linked to the value of outputs. By using a dynamic example, where the demand for tobacco products fell, Menger was able to show that the value of the inputs—the tobacco leaves, the tobacco machinery, the tobacco farmers, and the farmland—were entirely dependent on individual consumers who desire their product.

Menger's discovery was labeled the "law of imputation." The law of imputation was a direct assault on the Ricardo-Marx labor theory of value. Menger wrote, "The determining factor in the value of a good, then, is neither the quantity of labor or other goods necessary for its production nor the quantity necessary for its reproduction, but rather the magnitude of importance of those satisfactions with respect to which we are conscious of being dependent on command of the good" (page 147).

In short, Menger had reversed the direction of causation between value and cost. A consumer good is not valued because of the labor and other means of production used. Rather, the means of production are valued because of the prospective value of the consumption goods. The values of all producer and capital goods are ultimately consumer driven.

Menger wanted the German antitheoretical economists to know that the law of imputation was valid in all circumstances. "This principle of value determination is universally valid, and no exception to it can be found in human economy" (page 147).

Menger's Theory Leads to the Marginality Principle

After promulgating the law of imputation, Menger went on to discover the marginality principle. Again, using the tobacco example, he pointed out that many of the tobacco-related inputs did not lose all their value when the demand for human consumption ended. "The land and agricultural implements used in the cultivation of tobacco," he wrote, "would retain their goods-character with respect to other human needs" (page 66).

In other words, land and capital goods that had multiple uses could be employed in other industries. For example, tools and machinery previously used to grow tobacco could now be used to produce cotton. Land used to produce tobacco leaves could now be used to grow wheat or soybeans. Their value would fall, but not to zero. Rather, they would fall to the value of their *next best alternative use.*

Indirectly, Menger had discovered the principle of marginal utility, that the price or value of a particular good is based on its next best or marginal use. Inherent in his analysis is also the principle of "opportunity cost," the idea that every activity or product in the economy has an alternative use. Both principles would become staples in every economist's toolbox.

DOES INTRINSIC VALUE EXIST?

Finally, Menger demonstrated that the desperate search for an "invariable measure of value" by Ricardo and the classical economists was over—it didn't exist. Intrinsic value is a chimera; only subjective value exists. Labor hours, or more generally, the cost of production, could not establish an objective standard by which to determine prices. In the long run, costs and prices are not fixed, but are subject to the variations of supply and demand.

A recent example is the energy crisis during the late 1970s and early 1980s. Increasing demand and curtailed supply led to sharply higher oil prices in the late 1970s. Higher retail prices for petroleum and gasoline products dramatically increased the demand for means of production in the oil industry. The cost of oil rigs, workers, capital goods and supplies, and oil and natural gas properties all rose significantly. Then, when the oil boom turned into a bust in the early 1980s, the reverse happened. Costs associated with the oil industry were not set in stone. When the price of oil and gasoline declined, so did the demand for oil inputs. Workers were laid off, rigs became unused, and oil and gas properties declined in value. In short, costs did not constitute an invariable measure of value. In Menger's language, all values were subjective.

THE GERMANS RESPOND

Menger's message was almost immediately accepted in his home country, but fell on deaf ears in Germany. Schmoller rejected his "universal" laws as "useless." Menger responded in kind: Schmoller was like someone who came to a building site, dumped some materials on the ground, and declared himself an architect. The insults continued for years.

Fortunately, however, the Austrian banner of marginalism and neoclassical analysis was picked up in England and the rest of Europe, as well as in the United States. Within twenty years, it was adopted in principle in the major economics textbooks, including the works of Alfred Marshall, Philip Wicksteed, and Frank Fetter. As Sherwin Rosen stated, "The Austrian approach dominated American economics at the turn of the century" (1997: 151).

MENGER'S FOLLOWERS PROMOTE THE AUSTRIAN CAUSE

Menger's analysis was original and clear. But his refusal to reprint or translate his work kept his laws of imputation, marginal analysis, and subjective theory from becoming well known right away. It fell upon the shoulders of his intellectual descendants, Eugen Böhm-Bawerk and Friedrich Wieser, to spread the Austrian gospel.

WIESER: INFLUENTIAL TEACHER AND INVENTOR OF TERMS

Friedrich von Wieser (1851–1926) never achieved the stature that his colleague **Eugen Böhm-Bawerk (1851–1914)** did, but they must be forever linked together. They were the same age, went to high school together, became public servants, wrote books, and taught at the University of Vienna. They even had the same hobby—mountain climbing. Then they became brothers-in-law. Böhm-Bawerk married Wieser's sister in 1880. Only death could separate them—Wieser outlived both his friend Böhm-Bawerk and his mentor Carl Menger.

Wieser, born in Vienna, was the son of a general in the Austrian army and a baron (hence the designation "von"). After studying economics in Germany, he was appointed associate ("extraordinary") professor at the University of Vienna in 1884, and he succeeded Menger as chair of economic theory in 1903. Many students considered Wieser the best teacher at the university as well as the "unquestioned authority in general economic theory in Vienna," including monetary theory (Hülsmann 2007: 467, 471). His most influential book, *Social Economics* (1927 [1914]), continued Menger's subjectivist approach and was the standard textbook at the university for many years.

Wieser prided himself on inventing new terms in economics. For example, he is credited with inventing "marginal utility" (*Grenznutzen*), "opportunity cost," and "economic planning."

Wieser also placed special emphasis on the creative individual in the economic process—inventors, pioneers, capitalists, and entrepreneurs. His constant hero worship probably stemmed from his aristocratic, elitist background. In fact, "Führer" (leader or commander) was Wieser's pet word, and in later life he flirted with German national fascism, although he died in 1926, too early to see the devastating effects of this hero worship. He also wrote about the benefits of a centrally planned economy, an unpopular approach among the normally laissez-faire Austrians (especially Ludwig von Mises).

BÖHM-BAWERK'S ILLUSTRIOUS CAREER

Böhm-Bawerk was able to advance the Austrian theory in new directions, especially in the area of economic growth and capital theory. His influence was so huge that he was considered the best-known economist on the continent at the turn of the century (Samuelson 1967: 662).

Böhm, as he was affectionately known, was born in Bruno, Austria, in 1851, the youngest son of an Austrian civil servant and deputy governor. He received his doctorate of law at the University of Vienna in 1875.

The year 1880 was highly significant in his life. Not only was he appointed to a professorship at the University of Innsbruck but also he married the sister of his best friend, Friedrich Wieser. It was a fruitful decade, highlighted in 1884 with the publication of his *Capital and Interest*. A few years later, his second most important work, *The Positive Theory of Capital*, was translated into English and published by Macmillan in 1891, considered a high honor as already mentioned. His reputation as a forceful new leader in the "neoclassical" school rose rapidly. He was then immediately appointed to the Ministry of Finance, where he helped Austria clean

Photograph 7.3
Eugen Böhm-Bawerk (1851–1914)
"An untiring polemicist and . . . a tedious hairsplitter."
Courtesy of Adam Smith Archive.

up its finances and return to the gold standard. In 1896, his full-scale critique of Marx was published. It was translated two years later as *Karl Marx and the Close of His System* (1984 [1898]).

In 1904, Böhm-Bawerk left government service and became a full professor at the University of Vienna, along with Wieser and Philippovich. A special chair in economics was created in his honor. His lectures on capital theory and his private seminar attracted many students, including Ludwig von Mises, Friedrich Hayek, and Joseph Schumpeter, all of whom would lead major careers in economics.

Not much is known about Böhm-Bawerk's personal life. He was considered a typical Austrian—"quiet, modest and affectionate" (Hennings 1997: 19). He was a gifted cellist, a keen mountaineer, and a cross-country bicyclist. He and his wife had no children. If he had one vice, it was his love of controversy and his meticulous, overarching criticisms of other men's theories. Biographer Klaus Hennings condemned his "long-winded, over-critical, and ungenerous" style (1997: 81), and Paul Samuelson caricatured him as "a forceful writer, an untiring polemicist, and, it must be confessed, a tedious hairsplitter" (1967: 663).

Politically, Böhm-Bawerk was a liberal and independent member of the upper house of the Austrian parliament. He believed in top-down reform

WHAT ECONOMIST IS PICTURED ON AN OFFICIAL CURRENCY?

Adam Smith was recently pictured on an official Bank of Scotland £20 note. And, before him, Eugen Böhm-Bawerk had his photograph on the Austrian 100 schilling note, before Austria adopted the euro in 2002.

Because of his supreme economic skills, Böhm-Bawerk was appointed minister of finance three times—in 1893, 1896–97, and 1900–1904—and was instrumental in bringing order to Austria's financial condition.

Illustration 7.1
Austrian 100 Schilling Note
Do Austrians know who this man was?

from the aristocrats, favoring mostly free trade, social security, and welfare schemes for the working class.

Unfortunately, Böhm-Bawerk's life was cut short at the age of sixty-three. Most Austrian economists were renowned for living into their eighties, but not Böhm-Bawerk. He considered himself an old man in poor health in 1914 and died right before World War I began. Thus he avoided witnessing the collapse of the great Austro-Hungarian Empire.

THE MAN WHO ANSWERED MARX

Böhm-Bawerk made several major advances in economics. He was the first economist to take Marx seriously, and launched a blistering attack on his economic theories. His critiques were so devastating that Marxism has never really taken hold in the economics profession as it has in other disciplines (sociology, anthropology, history, and literary theory).

But Böhm-Bawerk was not simply a bitter critic of Marx. After scrutinizing Marxian and socialist doctrines, he built upon the work of Menger and made original contributions in the areas of saving and investing, capital and interest, and economic growth. Even today no work on economic growth theory is complete without a discussion of Böhm-Bawerk's contributions.

Böhm-Bawerk introduced his critique of Karl Marx in his classic work, *Capital and Interest* (1959a [1884]), in which he first fully reviewed the history of interest theories from ancient times. The last half of this section deals with the exploitation theories of Rodbertus, Proudhon, Marx, and other socialists.

BÖHM-BAWERK MAKES TWO DEVASTATING ARGUMENTS AGAINST MARX

Recall from chapter 6 that Marx's theory of surplus value argued that workers deserve the full value of the products they produce. Landlords who earn rent and capitalists who earn profits and interest exploit the workers and take from them the fruits of their labors. In response, Böhm-Bawerk made two points of rebuttal:

First, Böhm-Bawerk's "waiting" argument. Here, he relied on the abstinence theory of interest, a concept developed earlier by Nassau Senior. Capitalists abstain from current consumption and use their savings to invest in capital goods and higher-order production goods, all in an effort to expand and improve goods and services. Interest income reflects this waiting factor in all economic life, and is therefore justified as a legitimate compensation to capitalists and investors. Capital-goods producers must wait for their goods to be manufactured and sold to their customers (further down the road toward consumption) before they can be paid. Investors in bonds and real estate must wait before they are paid. Landlords who develop land must wait years before they earn back the money they originally invested.

In short, business people, capitalists, investors, and landlords all have to wait to be paid. But what about hired workers? They do not have to wait. They agree to perform a certain amount of labor for a wage or salary, and they are paid every month or every two weeks, regardless of whether the products they produce are sold or not. They do not have to worry about accounts receivable or accounts payable, about investment debt or changing markets. They do not have to wait until the products are sold before being paid. They get paid like clockwork, assuming their employers are honest and solvent. In fact, the capitalist-owner is constantly *advancing* the funds to pay the workers' wages, prior to receipt of payment for the products to be sold, which may mean waiting months and sometimes years, depending on how quickly the products can be sold and the money received. As Böhm-Bawerk concluded, "the workers cannot wait. . . . They continue to be dependent on those who already possess a finished store of the so-called intermediate products, in a word, on the capitalists" (1959b: 83).

Therefore, argued Böhm-Bawerk, hired workers are rightly paid their *discounted* product or value, and interest income as well as profits are justifiably returned to capitalists.

CAPITALISTS AS RISK-TAKERS

Böhm-Bawerk made another important point. Business capitalists take risks that workers don't. They combine land, labor, and capital, and they create a product that competes in the marketplace, a product on which they may or may not make a profit. The capitalist-entrepreneur takes that risk but hired workers do not. They get paid regularly and, if the business goes bankrupt, the most they will lose is a paycheck; they only need to search for another job. But the business entrepreneur may face financial ruin, heavy debts, and bankruptcy. In short, the workers' risk level is substantially less than that of the capitalist-entrepreneurs.

How does the market reward this additional risk? By compensating the capitalist-entrepreneur with a significant portion of the product's value, via profits and interest.

In sum, the hired workers are justifiably not paid the full product of their labor, but only that part commensurate with their immediate satisfaction in wages and the lower degree of risk involved in running the business.

After Böhm-Bawerk's attack on Marxist doctrines of surplus value, few mainstream economists accepted the labor theory of value, Marx's exploitation theory, or his theory of surplus value. Marxists ever after have been on the defensive when it comes to theoretical rigor. Interestingly, while the rest of the economics profession has moved on beyond Marx, the Marxists are still fighting old battles with Böhm-Bawerk and other critics. Today Böhm-Bawerk's *Karl Marx and the Close of His System* is published by Marxists, with an introduction by Paul M. Sweezy and a response by Rudolph Hilferding (Böhm-Bawerk 1984 [1898]).

BÖHM-BAWERK INTRODUCES A NON-MARXIST CAPITALIST THEORY

One thing Böhm-Bawerk would agree with Marx about was that the true focus of capitalism should be on *capital*. Capital in all its many forms—saving, investing, technology, capital goods, productivity, knowledge, education—is the key to fulfilling Adam Smith's world view of universal prosperity. The difference is that while Marx usually viewed capital in a highly negative way, Böhm-Bawerk and the Austrians recognized that capital is the savior of the worker and all classes of people. It is the key to a higher standard of living.

After demolishing the socialist arguments against the capitalist system, Böhm-Bawerk created a whole new chapter in economic theory by focusing on his "positive" theory of capital development. In fact, his 1884 book was aptly titled in English, *The Positive Theory of Capital*. And unlike Menger's *Grundsätze*, Böhm-Bawerk's magnum opus was translated almost immediately into English. In 1890, *The Positive Theory of Capital* was translated and published in London (by Macmillan) and in New York (by G.E. Stechart), and it quickly became a popular introduction to a non-Marxist theory of capitalism.

THE KEY TO ECONOMIC GROWTH

Böhm-Bawerk's objective was to demonstrate how economic growth can take place, how individuals can improve their living standards and achieve Adam Smith's goal of universal prosperity. Böhm-Bawerk was out to prove that the workingman can surpass a subsistence wage, contrary to the dismal forecasts of Ricardo, Malthus, and Marx.

Böhm-Bawerk first pointed out that simple labor or hard work was not enough to achieve a higher standard of living. "It is simply not true that the man is 'merely industrious.' He is both industrious and thrifty" (1959b: 116).

Adam Smith focused on the division of labor as the principal driving force behind economic growth. The Austrians emphasized the critical role of saving and investment in technically advancing economic growth, as measured by the quantity, quality, and variety of goods and services.

The Austrians, like Adam Smith, have always been strident defenders of saving and investment as a critical element in economic growth. Throughout the history of modern economics, the virtue of thrift has come under attack—from Hobson and the underconsumptionists, John Maynard Keynes and the demand deficit school, and Paul Samuelson and the paradox-of-thrift theorists.[6]

---

6. See my article "Keynes and the Anti-Saving Mentality," in Skousen (1992: 89–102).

In justifying the need for saving and investment, Böhm-Bawerk began his theory with a discussion of the function of capital as a tool of production. Using Menger's terminology in the *Grundsätze*, Böhm-Bawerk stated, "The ultimate goal of all production is to provide things with which to satisfy wants, that is to say, consumers' goods or 'goods of the first order'" (1959b: 10).

BÖHM-BAWERK USES A SIMPLE BUT POWERFUL EXAMPLE

Böhm-Bawerk used this simple example: Suppose a farmer desires drinking water. The most direct way to satisfy his thirst is to go to the spring and drink from cupped hands. But the spring is far away; thus, fulfilling his need for water day after day is inconvenient and inadequate. Is there a way that the farmer can satisfy his thirst more quickly? Yes. He can build a pipeline from the spring to his house. Böhm-Bawerk called it an "indirect" or "roundabout" method of production. But there is a cost—it takes tools, time, labor, and technology to accomplish the task. He must give up other farming tasks in order to build the pipeline. Once accomplished, the pipeline will be highly productive. The farmer "has at all times a copious supply of absolutely fresh water right in the house" (Böhm-Bawerk 1959b: 11).

The point is irresistible: investing in capital goods results in greater productivity and a higher standard of living. By its very nature, capitalism—the application of capital investment to the production process—leads to economic growth.

Böhm-Bawerk examined three cases to support his thesis. First, suppose the individuals in a nation have no net savings, that is, savings beyond the payment for depreciation or upkeep of its buildings, tools, and equipment. As a result, the nation would "do no more than preserve its capital" (page 112).

Second, suppose individuals began saving 25 percent of their income. Such an event would dramatically alter the production process. Demand for consumer goods would decline initially, but this decline would be offset by an increase in the demand for capital goods. "For an economically advanced nation does not engage in hoarding, but invests its savings. It buys securities, it deposits its money at interest in savings banks or commercial banks, puts it out on loan, etc. . . . In other words, there is an increase in capital, which rebounds to the benefit of an enhanced enjoyment of consumption goods in the future" (page 113).

But there is a third possibility: the citizens of the nation could consume more than their income; instead of saving, they could use up their stock of wealth, and thus diminish their nation's capital. The result of this "squander" of capital? A lower standard of living.

BÖHM-BAWERK DEFENDS SAVING AGAINST ITS CRITICS

It wasn't long after Böhm-Bawerk's *Positive Theory of Capital* was published that socialist critics took aim at his thesis. In the 1900–1901 *Annals* of the American Academy of Political and Social Science, L.G. Bostedo and Eugen Böhm-Bawerk exchanged arguments about the role of savings. Bostedo took a pre-Keynesian "effective demand" position, arguing that final consumer demand is an "absolutely indispensable condition" for production, and that Böhm-Bawerk's case of an increase in the saving rate is "not only unnatural but impossible." Saving more only "decreases the general purchasing power, and therefore the demand for goods will throw capital out of use and curtail its production" (Ebeling 1991: 395–96, 399). The result would be depression. A better solution, argued Bostedo, would be to increase—not decrease—the demand for final consumption as a way to encourage capital production.

In response, Böhm-Bawerk took strong exception to Bostedo's anti-saving mentality. "If every attempt to curtail consumption must actually result in an immediate and proportionate curtailment of production, then indeed no addition to the accumulated wealth of society could ever result from saving" (Ebeling 1991: 405).

Böhm-Bawerk's argument in defense of saving is reminiscent of Bastiat's judgment that a good economist must view the effect of a policy on all sectors, not just one. He stated, "The truth is that a curtailment of consumption involves, not a curtailment of production generally, but only, through the action of the law of supply and demand, a curtailment in certain branches. If in consequence of saving, a smaller quantity of costly food, wine and lace is bought and consumed, less of these things will *subsequently*—and I wish to emphasize the word—be produced. There will not, however, be a smaller production of goods generally, because the lessened output of goods for immediate consumption may and will be offset by an increased production of 'intermediate' or capital goods" (Ebeling 1991: 405–6).

This exchange would not be the last in the debate over the role of saving in the economy. Keynes and Samuelson would raise the issue again in the twentieth century. Yet clearly the Austrians established themselves in the corner that favored saving, even a high rate of saving, as a key element in economic growth.

SUMMARY: MENGER, BÖHM-BAWERK, AND THE AUSTRIANS REVITALIZED THE CLASSICAL MODEL OF GROWTH

In sum, the Austrians arrived just in time to rescue the classical model of Adam Smith and David Ricardo from the devastating criticisms of Marx and the socialists. Through their theories of final demand, subjective value, marginal utility, and capital theory, the Austrians gave new intellectual life to capitalism as an ideal system.

In chapter 8, we shall see how the Austrian influence joined forces with the British school to create a "neoclassical" orthodoxy that would gain strength as we entered the twentieth century.

REFERENCES

Black, R.D. Collison, A.W. Coats, and Cranford D.W. Goodwin, eds. 1973. *The Marginal Revolution in Economics*. Durham, NC: Duke University Press.

Böhm-Bawerk, Eugen. 1959a [1884]. *Capital and Interest*. South Holland, IL: Libertarian Press.

————. 1959b. *The Positive Theory of Capital*. South Holland, IL: Libertarian Press.

————. 1962. *Shorter Classics of Eugen von Böhm-Bawerk*. South Holland, IL: Libertarian Press.

————. 1984 [1898]. *Karl Marx and the Close of His System*. Philadelphia: Orion Editions.

Bonar, James. 1888. "The Austrian Economists and Their View of Value." *Quarterly Journal of Economics* 3 (October), 1–31.

Cameron, Rondo. 1997. *A Concise Economic History of the World*. New York: Oxford University Press

Ebeling, Richard, ed. 1991. *Austrian Economics: A Reader*. Hillsdale, MI: Hillsdale College Press.

Ekelund, Robert B., and Robert E. Hébert. 2000. *Secret Origins of Modern Microeconomics*. Chicago: University of Chicago Press.

Garrison, Roger B. 1985. "Wests's 'Cantillon and Adam Smith': A Comment." *Journal of Libertarian Studies* 7: 2 (Fall), 287–94.

Hayek, Friedrich A. 1976. "Introduction: Carl Menger." In Carl Menger, *Principles of Economics*. New York: New York University Press.

Hennings, Klaus H. 1997. *The Austrian Theory of Value and Capital*. Cheltenham, UK: Edward Elgar.

Hülsmann, Jörg Guido. 2007. *Mises: Last Knight of Liberalism*. Auburn, AL: Mises Institute.

Jevons, William Stanley. 1965 [1871]. *The Theory of Political Economy*, 5th ed. New York: Augustus M. Kelley.

Menger, Anton. 1962 [1899]. *The Right to the Whole Produce of Labour*. New York: Augustus M. Kelley.

Menger, Carl. 1976 [1871]. *Principles of Economics,* trans. James Dingwall and Bert F. Hoselitz. New York: New York University Press.

Rosen, Sherwin. 1997. "Austrian and Neoclassical Economics: Any Gains from Trade?" *Journal of Economic Perspectives* 11 (Fall), 139–52.

Rothbard, Murray N. 1995. *Economic Thought Before Adam Smith*. Hants, UK: Edward Elgar.

Samuelson, Paul A. 1967. "Irving Fisher and the Theory of Capital." In *Ten Economic Studies in the Tradition of Irving Fisher*, ed. W. Fellner et al. New York: John Wiley.

Schumpeter, Joseph A. 1951. *Ten Great Economists from Marx to Keynes*. New York: Oxford University Press.

Seager, H.R. 1893. "Economics at Berlin and Vienna." *Journal of Political Economy* 1: 2 (March), 236–62.

Skousen, Mark, ed. 1992. *Dissent on Keynes*. New York: Praeger.

Smith, Adam. 1978. *Lectures on Jurisprudence*. New York: Oxford University Press.

Streissler, Erich W. 1990. "The Influence of German Economics on the Work of Menger and Marshall." In *Carl Menger and His Legacy in Economics*, ed. Bruce J. Caldwell. Durham, NC: Duke University Press.

————. 1994. "Menger's Treatment of Economics in the Rudolf Lectures." In *Carl Menger's Lectures to Crown Prince Rudolf of Austria*. Hants, UK: Edward Elgar.

Walras, Léon. 1954. *Elements of Pure Economics*. Homewood, IL: Richard D. Irwin.

Wieser, Friedrich von. 1893. *Natural Value*. London: Macmillan.

————. 1927 [1914]. *Social Economics*. New York: Greenberg.

Wicksell, Knut. 1958. *Selected Papers on Economic Theory*. London: Allen and Unwin.

Wicksteed, Philip H. 1933. *The Common Sense of Political Economy*, rev. ed. London: Routledge and Kegan Paul.

8

MARSHALLING THE TROOPS: SCIENTIFIC ECONOMICS COMES OF AGE

The success of the marginal revolution is intimately associated with the professionalization of economics in the last quarter of the nineteenth century.

—Mark Blaug (Black et al. 1973: 14)

The discovery of the principles of marginal analysis and subjective utility provided strong intellectual ammunition against the Marxists and socialists. After the last quarter of the nineteenth century, the discipline of political economy was never the same. It was rapidly becoming a grown-up science, with its own box of tools, systematic laws, and quantitative analysis. Economists hoped that political economy, once the domain of theology, philosophy, and law, could become a new science that would match the logic and precision of mathematics and the physical sciences. It was time to unburden the world of what Carlyle had caustically labeled the "dismal science," and replace it with a more formal objective discipline.

FROM POLITICAL ECONOMY TO ECONOMICS

The principal economist to carry out this revolutionary shift was **Alfred Marshall (1842–1924)**, a famed Cambridge professor. Marshall made a singular change that reflected this transformation. By calling his textbook *Principles of Economics*, he altered the name of the discipline from "political economy" to "economics," sending a signal that economics was as much a formal science as physics, mathematics, or other precise bodies of

♪ **Music selection for this chapter: Peter I. Tchaikovsky, Symphony No. 6, *Pathétique*, third movement, "Allegro Molto Vivace"**

knowledge (see the box below). Moreover, it acknowledged that the economy is governed by natural law rather than by political policy. His pathbreaking 1890 textbook introduced graphs of supply and demand, mathematical formulas, quantitative measurements of "elasticity" of demand, and other terms borrowed from physics, engineering, and biology. It wasn't long before many terms adopted from the physical sciences became standard fare—equilibrium and disequilibrium, statics and dynamics, velocity of money and inflation, and frictional unemployment. Ultimately, Marshall felt that "The Mecca of the economist lies in economic biology rather than in economic dynamics" (Marshall 1920: xx). Later in life, Marshall was to regret this attempt to scientize economics, suggesting that we are still greatly ignorant of economic behavior, but the die was cast (Schumpeter 1951: 109).[1] Economics would soon become a social science second to none in rigor and professional status.

Appropriately, Marshall's *Principles* went on to dominate the profession for the next forty years, going through eight editions.

WHAT?! YOU'RE MAJORING IN PLUTOLOGY?

Economics was originally called "political economy," not as an ideological dogma but to distinguish it from "household economy." It meant the economics of society or polity.

During the late nineteenth century, there was a strong move to discard the unwieldy name "political economy" in favor of something more up to date and scientifically precise. Authors suggested several choices, such as "plutology," "ergonomy," "chrematistics," "catallactics," and "ophelimity." Marshall and other professors preferred economics. Why?

W. Stanley Jevons summarized the reason: "I cannot help thinking that it would be well to discard, as quickly as possible, the old troublesome double-worded name of our Science. . . . But why do we need anything better than Economics? This term, besides being more familiar and closely related to the old term, is perfectly analogous to *Mathematics*, *Ethics*, *Aesthetics*, and the names of various other branches of knowledge, and it has moreover the authority of usage from the time of Aristotle. . . . It is thus to be hoped that *Economics* will become the recognized name of a science, which nearly a century ago was known to the French Economists as *la science economique*" (Jevons 1965 [1871]: xiv–xv).

So what did Jevons call his book? *The Theory of Political Economy!* Actually, the first edition came out in 1871, when "political economy" was still in vogue. He wrote the above comments in the second edition, which came out in 1879, and he added, "Though employing the new name [economics] in the text, it was obviously undesirable to alter the title-page of the book" (Jevons 1965: xv).

---

1. In his 1970 Nobel lecture, Paul Samuelson complained, "There is nothing more pathetic than to have an economist or a retired engineer try to force analogies between the concepts of physics and the concepts of economics" (1970: 8). Marshall said nearly the same thing: "But of course economics cannot be compared with the exact physical sciences: for it deals with the ever changing and subtle forces of human nature" (1920: 14). Yet the comparison continues to this day.

ECONOMIC SCIENCE BECOMES A SEPARATE DISCIPLINE

The period surrounding Marshall's textbook was a time of new beginnings in economic science. Official associations were established—the American Economic Association in 1885 and the British Economic Association in 1890 (renamed the Royal Economic Society in 1902). Journals were established—the *Quarterly Journal of Economics* at Harvard in 1887, the *Economic Journal* at Cambridge in 1891, and the *Journal of Political Economy* at Chicago in 1892 (*Le journal des économistes* in France had been publishing since December 1841). In 1894, Macmillan published the prestigious three-volume *Palgrave's Dictionary of Political Economy*, in which economist Henry Sidgwick noted that the term "economics" had "recently come more and more into use as a preferable alternative for political economy, so far as it is the name of a science" (1926: 678). By the turn of the century, major universities had finally established their own departments of economics, separate from law, mathematics, and political science, and had begun granting degrees in their own field. This was one of Marshall's most cherished ambitions. In 1895, the London School of Economics (LSE) was established, devoted almost entirely to economic studies (see the box on page 200).

In sum, Adam Smith had talked about his "Newtonian" method in his study of the wealth of nations, but not for another century did economics truly become established as a science and a separate discipline.

THE INFLUENCE OF JEVONS

Alfred Marshall was at the forefront of the movement to establish economics as a science, but his story cannot be told without first recounting the tremendous influence of his older British colleague, **William Stanley Jevons (1835–82)**.

Jevons, as we noted in chapter 7, was one of the founders of the marginalist revolution. Although Marshall was wont to give him credit, Jevons was noted for his mathematical and quantitative studies, and he pioneered the technique of index numbers.

Photograph 8.1
William Stanley Jevons (1835–82)
"I protest against deference for any man, whether John Stuart Mill, or Adam Smith, or Aristotle."
Courtesy of Mark Blaug.

A CHILD PRODIGY WITH A SENSE OF DESTINY

Though he lived only a short forty-six years, Jevons had a colorful and brilliant career, culminating in the marginalist revolution. Born in Liverpool in 1835, son of an engi-

THE BIZARRE ORIGINS OF THE FAMED LONDON SCHOOL OF ECONOMICS: FABIAN SOCIALISTS' DREAM BACKFIRES!

They were so convinced that unprejudiced study of economics
must lead to socialism.
—F.A. Hayek (1994: 81)

The London School of Economics, established in 1895, is considered one of the most prestigious colleges in the world. Many famous people have been associated with the LSE, including the playwright George Bernard Shaw, socialist Harold Laski, Nobel Prize–winning economist Friedrich A. Hayek, and rock-and-roll singer Mick Jagger (as a student).

LSE was created by prominent members of the Fabian Society, all socialists, including Sidney and Beatrice Webb and Bernard Shaw, the most gifted dramatist of the age. The Fabian Society was established in the mid-1880s to convince bourgeois intellectuals of the virtues of socialism. It was named after Quintus Fabius Maximus, a Roman general who avoided defeat by refusing to fight Hannibal head-on. The Fabian socialists rejected the revolutionary methods of the Marxists; rather, they sought to achieve the same ends by infiltrating and indoctrinating the political parties and institutions of the West. This indirect gradualist approach proved extremely successful in twentieth-century Britain, which experienced high levels of nationalization and welfarism. In fact, Sidney Webb established the British Labour Party in 1906.

The pen and ink rendering is from a photographic reproduction. Artist, William Discount.

Figure 8.1
The Fabian Window
Source: Dobbs (1964). Courtesy of the Veritas Foundation.

THE FABIAN WINDOW: A WOLF IN SHEEP'S CLOTHING!

George Bernard Shaw commissioned a stained-glass window, known as the Fabian Window, representing the Fabian Society's goals. As shown in Figure 8.1, in the reproduction, the two figures wielding hammers are G.B. Shaw and Sidney Webb. Operating the bellows is E.R. Pease, secretary of the Fabian Society. Thumbing his nose (lower left corner) is H.G. Wells, who left the Fabians and denounced them as "the new Machiavellians" (Dobbs 1964).

But the most notorious highlight of the Fabian Window is the picture located between Shaw and Webb, a political wolf in sheep's clothing!

SETBACK FOR THE FABIANS

However, their strategy was not as successful at LSE. At the time they established the LSE, the youthful Webbs and other Fabians were disillusioned with the economic liberalism of Adam Smith. Using an inheritance of £20,000, the Webbs founded the London School of Economics and Political Science in 1895, but were determined to make it an independent institution devoted to an impartial and scientific study of social issues. Sidney Webb was convinced that "the facts would speak for themselves"—in favor of collectivism (Dahrendorf 1995: 7). Consequently, the Webbs made no effort to insist upon doctrinal purity. In fact, the first LSE director, W.A.S. Hewins, was not a Fabian, let alone a socialist, and later became a Conservative member of Parliament! And the first economist to teach at LSE, Edwin Cannan, was a devotee of hard money and laissez faire who edited the definitive "Cannan edition" of *The Wealth of Nations* in 1904. By the early 1930s, the LSE economics chairman was Lionel Robbins and the most influential lecturer on campus was Friedrich Hayek. During the 1930s, the LSE was considered the primary rival of John Maynard Keynes and the Cambridge school. Moreover, Sidney and Beatrice Webb eventually fell into disrepute when they returned from a trip glorying the Soviet Union and Stalin for inaugurating a "new civilization."

This is not to say that the LSE did not have its share of socialists. Harold Laski and Sir William Beveridge taught at the LSE during the 1930s and, since Hayek left in the late 1940s, the LSE has not attached itself to any particular school of thought.

neer and iron merchant, the young Stanley entered University College in London at the age of sixteen to study chemistry and botany. As a heady teenager, Jevons had a strong sense of direction. He told his sister he had a special "mission" to perform in life, that his insight was "deeper than that of most men or writers" (Black et al. 1973: 18). Later he wrote, "I protest against deference for any man, whether John Stuart Mill, or Adam Smith, or Aristotle" (Jevons 1965 [1870]: 261). Jevons's parents were Unitarian, which may explain his nonconformist attitude. Curiously, he also was a lifelong music lover, and was fascinated by the "experimental" music of Wagner. "Jevons's early conviction about his own genius and originality almost exactly parallels Wagner's" (Ekelund and Hébert 1990: 354).

Stanley was forced to interrupt his studies after his father's business collapsed. He accepted a post as assayer at the Australian Mint in Sydney. He spent five years in Australia (1853–58), writing articles on meteorology and railway pricing. After returning to England, he earned a B.A. at University College in 1860 and an M.A. in 1862.

It was in the early 1860s that he first expressed his embryonic marginal utility theory, publishing his findings in an 1862 article when he was only twenty-seven.[2] By 1870, he felt the time was ripe for a full-scale bolt from the classical theory of value, and frantically wrote his pathbreaking work, *The Theory of Political Economy*. It was published by Macmillan in 1871.

Jevons taught at Owens College (now the University of Manchester). As a consequence of the fame he achieved for writing *The Coal Question* (1865) and *The Theory of Political Economy* (1871), he was appointed chair of political economy at University College in London in 1876.

JEVONS'S LIFE IS CUT SHORT

Jevons resigned from his position at University College in 1880 due to ill health. Two years later, at the age of forty-six, he drowned while swimming. It was a sudden end to a brilliant career, and he did not live long enough to see his fundamental utility theory revolutionize the economics profession.

JEVONS'S GOAL: TO OVERTHROW MILL AND RICARDO

Jevons's most important contribution was his mathematical and graphical demonstration of the principle of marginal utility. His purpose was consciously revolutionary: to overthrow "the noxious influence of authority" of David Ricardo and John Stuart Mill. After all, it was Mill who smugly wrote in his *Principles*, "happily, there is nothing in the laws of value which remains for the present or any future writer to clear up; the theory of the subject is complete" (Black et al. 1973: 181). Jevons's response: "Our English Economists have been living in a fool's paradise" (Jevons 1965: xiv). His aim was to cast free "from the Wage-Fund Theory, the Cost of Production doctrine of Value, the Natural Rate of Wages, and other misleading or false Ricardian doctrines" (Jevons 1965: xlv–xlvi).

Jevons's approach was distinct from Menger's, even though they reached similar conclusions about how value is determined at the margin. In fact, Jevons died in 1882 without realizing that Menger had written the *Grundsätze*! (Remember, it took twenty years—until the 1890s—before a consensus developed regarding the three economists who discovered the marginality principle. In fact, the term "marginal" was not commonly used until well into the twentieth century.)

2. He wrote his brother on June 1, 1860, "In the last few months I have fortunately struck out what I have no doubt is *the true Theory of Economy*, so thorough-going and consistent, that I cannot now read other books on the subject without indignation" (Wicksteed 1933: 1).

With a heavy background in mathematics and chemistry, Jevons applied many of the principles of the natural sciences to the social sciences and economics. Throughout his works, he constantly referred to empirical data, detailed formulas as well as deductive logic. He felt deeply that both theory and practice were necessary (Black et al. 1973: 104–5). For example, in his *Theory of Political Economy*, he wrote, "The keystone of the whole Theory of Exchange and of the principal problems of economics, lies in this proposition—*The ratio of exchange of any two commodities will be the reciprocal of the ratio of the final degrees of utility of the quantities of commodity available for consumption after the exchange is completed*" (Jevons 1965: 139). Jevons's economics appeared to be like Boyle's Law in chemistry. His goal was to reveal the "mechanics" of utility and value economics using mathematics.

Jevons's Central Doctrine

What were Jevons's contributions to economics?

First, Jevons challenged the orthodox classical model that cost determines value. He came to the same conclusion as Menger, though independently: "Repeated reflection and inquiry have led me to the somewhat novel opinion, that *value depends entirely upon utility*" (Jevons 1965: 2).

The Ricardian doctrine that value is determined by labor or costs of production "cannot stand for a moment." Jevons noted that labor (or capital) once spent has no influence on the future value of an article; bygones are forever bygones (pages 157, 159).

Jevons's Marginal Utility Borrowed from Bentham

Jevons began his treatise by talking of "a Calculus of Pleasure and Pain," a reference to Jeremy Bentham's utilitarianism. What determines value or price? Utility, not labor or cost. But how much utility?

Using water, he illustrated marginal analysis: "All that we can say, then, is that water up to a certain quantity is indispensable; that further quantities will have various degrees of utility; but that beyond a certain point, the utility appears to cease" (page 53).

Graphically, Jevons illustrated declining marginal utility (see Figure 8.2). As Jevons's diagram indicates, the supply of water satisfies a consumer's most urgent wants first, followed by his second most urgent needs. As more water is available, he can satisfy his least urgent needs. Thus with an increasing supply, total utility increases, but marginal utility declines. Jevons did not use the term "marginal" in any part of his work. Instead, he used the term "final degree of utility." It was Philip Wicksteed who would later popularize the word "marginal."

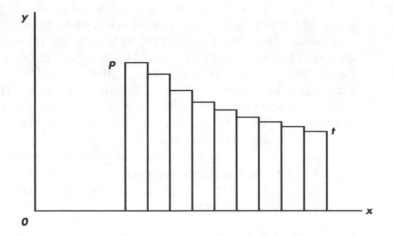

Figure 8.2
Jevons's Demonstration of the Law of Diminishing Marginal Utility
Source: Jevons (1965: 53).

Jevons also developed a theory of consumer behavior, arguing that individuals will tend to buy and use various goods and services so that their marginal utility is the same for each product, that is, where $MU_x = MU_y$, where x and y represent different goods. Later economists generalized Jevons's equimarginal principle to show that individuals allocate their income so that each product's marginal utility is equalized according to the price of the product. That is,

$$\frac{MU_x}{P_x} = \frac{MU_y}{P_y} = \frac{MU_z}{P_z}$$

MARSHALL BUILDS ON JEVONS'S INCOMPLETE WORK

Jevons's work was incomplete. He dissected the "mazy and preposterous" assumptions of the Ricardian school, and outlined the basic concepts of marginal utility. However, he never developed the downward-sloping demand curve, nor a complete supply-and-demand diagram. That work remained for Marshall to accomplish. Keynes summed it up well: "In truth, Jevons's *Theory of Political Economy* is a brilliant but hasty, inaccurate, and incomplete brochure, as far removed as possible from the painstaking, complete, ultra-conscientious methods of Marshall. It brings out unforgettably the notions of final utility and of the balance between the disutility of labour and the utility of the product. But it lives merely in the tenuous world of bright ideas when we compare it with the great working machine evolved by the patient, persistent toil and scientific genius of Marshall" (Keynes 1963: 155).

JEVONS PREDICTS FIRST ENERGY CRISIS

Gloomy official prophecies of the past have regularly been proven false.
—Julian Simon (1996: 165)

Prior to his discovery of marginal utility, Stanley Jevons was known for another book, *The Coal Question* (1865). Steeped in Malthusian language, this book predicted that coal, the essential resource of British industry, could not keep up with Britain's burgeoning population and would soon be exhausted, while the United States, which had an almost inexhaustible supply, would replace Great Britain as the world's industrial leader.

Jevons was right about the United States, but overly pessimistic about Britain's future. "It will appear that there is no reasonable prospect of any relief from a future want of the main agent of industry," Jevons warned. "We cannot long continue our present rate of progress. The first check for our growing prosperity, however, must render our population excessive" (Jevons 1865: xiv, xvi).

Yet Britain never ran out of coal, the population continued to grow, and the coal energy crisis never developed. Why? In part, because of the discovery of oil. Moreover, coal production increased. Capitalists searched out new coal deposits, entrepreneurs found better ways to unearth coal, transportation engineers developed cheaper ways to move coal, and inventors discovered more efficient ways to use coal. Today, Britain has higher coal reserves than it did in 1865, when Jevons wrote his book.

JEVONS THE ASTROLOGER!

Stanley Jevons normally had high marks for his statistical work, but his astrological "sunspot" theory of the business cycle is an exception. In the mid- to late 1870s, he wrote several papers insisting that the configuration of the stars and planets was the principal cause of commercial crises. "If the planets govern the sun, and the sun governs the vintages and harvest, and thus the prices of food and raw materials and the state of the money market, it follows that the configuration of the planets may prove to be the remote cause of the greatest commercial disasters" (Ecklund and Hébert 1990: 367).

Jevons propounded a "sunspot" theory of the business cycle in *Nature* and other scientific journals, arguing that the intensity of sunspots every ten to eleven years not only caused an agricultural crisis but a financial and economic crisis as well. Economists have long since abandoned this simplistic explanation and, in fact, Jevons later incorporated other explanations for the business cycle.

What did Marshall accomplish? Unlike Jevons, Marshall founded his own school, the so-called British or Cambridge school, with student prodigies such as A.C. Pigou and John Maynard Keynes. He was a synthesizer, combining the classical economics of cost (supply) and the marginalist economics of utility (demand). He often compared supply and demand to the combination of the blades of scissors—each is necessary to determine price. He took supply and demand far beyond a written expression: He developed the graphics for supply and demand, the mathematics of elasticity, and new concepts such as consumer's surplus. His formulas now serve as the foundation of any course in microeconomics.

MYSTERIOUS CIRCUMSTANCES SURROUND MARSHALL'S BIRTH

What kind of man was this towering figure who dominated economic thinking for generations?

After Marshall's death, John Maynard Keynes wrote a memoir of his mentor. Referring to this memoir in an exhaustive biography of Marshall, Peter Groenewegen commented: "His opening sentence lists date of birth, wrong place of birth, parents' names and wrong description of father's occupation" (Groenewegen 1995: 19). Why was Keynes, normally proficient in details, so wrong about Marshall's vital statistics?

The error was not Keynes's fault. Marshall was, in fact, deeply distressed by the circumstances surrounding his birth, and hid certain salient facts from Keynes and his biographers. He was a Victorian snob who was embarrassed by his upbringing. On his mother's side, he was descended from vagrant farmers and paupers, and on his father's side, from bankrupt businessmen and butchers. He listed his birthplace in 1842 as London, when in fact, it was Bermondsey, a dreary slum southeast of London known as the leather district, where pungent odors of the tanning process were emitted, "reeking with evil smells" of garden manure, glue making, and dog excrement. (The borough was destroyed in World War II.) Marshall outgrew his desperate beginnings, though he never shed his concerns for social welfare. In fact, he decided to study economics after a vacation during which he visited the poor districts of several cities.

To avoid his shameful origins, Marshall "took positive steps . . . by destroying family material from his private papers [shades of Adam Smith!], and by disguising the actual situation of his family life in such a way that no lies had to be told. Examples are his own descriptions of birthplace as Surrey or London rather than Bermondsey; and omitting his parents in autobiographical entries for reference works" (Groenewegen 1995: 40).

MARSHALL REBELS AGAINST HIS FATHER

Alfred Marshall's tyrannical father, William, was a Bank of England cashier who wrote a tract entitled *Man's Rights and Woman's Duties*. He pressured young Alfred to study Hebrew and the classics in preparation for the ministry, and to stay away from chess and mathematics.

Alfred rejected his father's demands and went on to study mathematics at Cambridge University, where he fell under the influence of Kant, Hegel, Darwin, and Spencer. Along the way, he lost his religious faith, although he was always sympathetic to Christian values and morals. (Regarding the influence of Darwin and social Darwinism on economics, see the box on page 215.)

After graduation, he stayed on as a fellow at St. John's, which required celibacy of its professors. He was forced to resign when he married his pupil, Mary Paley, who joined him in the field of economics and collaborated with him on a book, *The Economics of Industry* (1879).

He left Cambridge to teach at Bristol and Oxford, but returned in 1885 to become professor of political economy at Cambridge at the age of forty-three. He would never leave, heading up the economics department until he was replaced by his former student, A.C. Pigou, in 1908. The don of the British school went on to write several tomes, the most famous being his *Principles* textbook.

Photograph 8.2
Alfred Marshall (1842–1924)
"A tendency to be precise, pedantic and hypercritical."
Courtesy of Marshall Library, Cambridge University.

MARSHALL: A "PREPOSTEROUS, ODD AND IDIOSYNCRATIC INDIVIDUAL"

Marshall was a quirky fellow, especially in his old age. He disliked having photographs taken of him. "My face is poor, my photo is ugly," he wrote Harvard professor and friend Frank Taussig. He wrote Richard T. Ely in 1901 that "photographing is a nuisance." Marshall was considered vain by his portrait artist. He told the artist that his "ponderous left hand" was so large that it should be left out of the portrait (it was) (Groenewegen 1995: 768n, 628–29).

He frequently exhibited a meanness of spirit and had a hard time maintaining strong friendships. He unjustifiably refused to give credit to Jevons, Menger, and Walras for discovering marginal analysis, maintaining all along that he invented marginal utility himself under the influence of lesser-known predecessors (Dupuit, Cournot, and von Thünen). He was in fact annoyed when Jevons came out with his 1871 *Theory of Political Economy*, ahead of Marshall's own work (Keynes 1963: 153). Marshall also disliked the reformist Henry George (see next chapter) and the great Austrian Eugen Böhm-Bawerk, expressing deep hostility toward Böhm-Bawerk's theory of interest and capital. At a meeting in the Austrian Alps in 1909, a debate between Marshall and Böhm-Bawerk over interest-rate theory became so heated that their wives separated the two. At dinner, the two couples reunited and exchanged toasts, but "not a word was said about the rate of interest" (Groenewegen 1995: 477).

Marshall's voice would "rise to a very high pitch, almost squeak, followed usually by prolonged laughter" (Groenewegen 1995: 771).

DID MARSHALL HAVE A MADONNA COMPLEX?

If I had to live my life over again I should have devoted it to psychology.
—Alfred Marshall (Keynes 1963: 176)

Psychologists are at it again; this time it's about Alfred Marshall. He was heavily influenced by his mother; his sister; his aunt; and his wife, Mary Paley—all women in his life. Did he suffer from a "madonna complex," a reverence for women?

Biographer Peter Groenewegen suggests the Cambridge don possibly suffered from a form of Jungian introversion, "extreme caution in all attitudes, activities and affective dispositions" and a "tendency to be precise, pedantic and hypercritical," a pattern associated with sexual inadequacies. An observer noted that Marshall was "an ascetic man, all mind and no body," and Keynes thought he was "sterile." He had a childless marriage; his wife was a working middle-class woman. They had a dog and a cat as pets (Groenewegen 1995: 260–61).

MARSHALL—A DARWINIAN MISOGYNIST?

The chief distinction in the intellectual powers of the two sexes is shown by man's attaining to a higher eminence, in whatever he takes up, than can woman.
—Charles Darwin (1906: 858)

Marshall advanced economics in many ways, but his attitude toward women was controversial, to say the least. Before the late 1870s, he maintained progressive views on women's education and their role in society, but he had an abrupt change of heart right after his mother's death in 1878.

In 1880, while at University College in Bristol, he opposed the granting of B.A. degrees to women. After returning to Cambridge, he objected to the appointment of a woman as lecturer on the grounds that "public lecturing to largely male audiences was unsuitable for a woman and would damage her character" (Groenewegen 1995: 502). Nor should women students be eligible for scholarships. Marshall preferred all-women colleges, and his *Principles* textbook made the case for women's staying at home to care for children and for married women's avoiding working in factories (Marshall 1920: 69). Later in life he showed increasing hostility in what Groenewegen described as "the cult of the modern woman, who wanted the right to a job, economic independence, smoking in public, the vote and even degrees" (1995: 524). Marshall's views were considered extreme and opposed by nearly all his personal friends, but he felt justified in his beliefs by his understanding of evolutionists Darwin and Spencer (Groenewegen 1995: 500, 524).

Beatrice Webb, cofounder of the Fabian Society and the London School of Economics with her husband, Sidney Webb, had several run-ins with Alfred Marshall on women's issues. She wrote in her diary about a talk with him:

> It opened with chaff about men and women; he holding that woman was a subordinate being, and that, if she ceased to be subordinate, there would be no object for a man to marry. That marriage was a sacrifice of masculine freedom, and would only be tolerated by male creatures so long as it meant that devotion, body and soul, of the female to the male. Hence the woman

must not develop her faculties in a way unpleasant to the man: that strength, courage, independence were not attractive in women; that rivalry in men's pursuits was positively unpleasant. . . . If you compete with us we shan't marry you, he summed up with a laugh. (Groenewegen 1995: 517)

Marshall's Wife's Reaction

How did Mary Paley react to this growing anti-feminist prejudice by her husband? She was devoted to Alfred and his work, but given her strong views favoring women's rights, substantial friction broke out between them. Yet she invariably suppressed her objections in her husband's cause as the leader of a major school of thought. She coauthored his first book, served as proofreader for his many *Principles* editions, was the first woman lecturer at Cambridge (no objection from Alfred?), and wrote a memoir of their marriage. Comments Mark Blaug, "[She] might have had an outstanding career. However, on marriage to Marshall she submerged her career to his" (1999: 741).

Joan Robinson wrote "the more I learn about economics, the more I admire Marshall's intellect and the less I like his character" (1953: 14).

But Marshall also had a good side: He was conscientious about fulfilling his responsibilities. He was loyal to his friends, and his students found him inspirational. He was frequently generous and occasionally open-minded.

Marshall Suffers a Lonely Death

For most of his adult life, Marshall was virtually a shut-in, suffering from gallstones, high blood pressure, and nervous tension. In the end he died (of heart failure) a lonely invalid in 1924, within two weeks of his eighty-second birthday. Still, followers such as Keynes gave him high marks: "As a scientist he was, within his own field, the greatest in the world for a hundred years" (Keynes 1963: 140).

The Cambridge Don's Legacy in Economic Science

Marshall's primary contribution was advancing Smith's model into a quantitative science. Adam Smith provided the fundamental philosophy of economic growth ("universal prosperity" and the "system of natural liberty"), but Alfred Marshall created the engine to advance the Smith system.

What is this engine? The principles of supply and demand, the determination of price, the costs of production, and equilibrium in the short and long run. All these tools are found in today's microeconomics, the theory of individual consumers and producers. It is the toolbox economists employ today to analyze and illustrate a theory of consumer and firm behavior. Marshall developed this approach in a geometric and mathematical way, although he always relegated his graphs and equations to appendixes. He was perfectly justified in transforming "political economy" into the science of "economics."

MARSHALL'S PATRON SAINT: THE WORKING MAN

Like Smith, Marshall was intensely concerned about the progress of all mankind, not just the rich. In *Principles*, he defined economics as "a study of mankind in the ordinary business of life," particularly emphasizing "the use of the material requisites of wellbeing" (Marshall 1920: 1). He wanted to answer the question, "Are the opportunities of real life to be confined to the few?" (Keynes 1963: 138–39).

Illustration 8.1
Marshall's Patron Saint
"Portrait of a Working Man."
Reprinted by permission of Marshall Library, Cambridge University.

Marshall's favorite subject was the working man, and in the early 1870s he bought a small oil painting, "Portrait of a Working Man," for a few shillings and hung it in his college dorm. Today the painting, which shows a working man with a gaunt and wistful expression, is preserved in the Marshall Library at Cambridge University (see Illustration 8.1).

MARSHALL INTRODUCES A DIAGRAM THAT LINKS CLASSICAL AND MARGINALIST SCHOOLS

Principles is primarily a microeconomics textbook, the study of individual markets and industries, as opposed to the whole economy (macroeconomics). It deals with supply and demand and the "ordinary business" of a firm in creating material progress by producing goods and services.

Marshall was the first to popularize supply and demand diagrams. According to Marshall, both supply and demand are necessary to determine price and output of a product, like the two blades of a scissors. "We might as reasonably dispute whether it is the upper or the under blade of a pair of scissors that cuts a piece of paper, as whether the value is governed by utility or cost of production" (Marshall 1920: 348). The supply and demand diagram reproduced in Figure 8.3 first appeared in the 1890 edition of *Principles*.

In determining an equilibrium price, Marshall required a set of assumptions, or *ceteris paribus* conditions. He assumed that income remains the

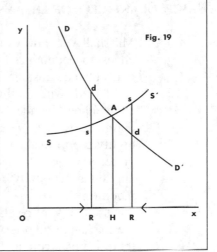

To represent the equilibrium of demand and supply geometrically we may draw the demand and supply curves together as in Fig. 19. If then *OR* represents the rate at which production is being actually carried on, and *Rd* the demand price is greater than *Rs* the supply price, the production is exceptionally profitable, and will be increased. *R*, the amount-index, as we may call it, will move to the right. On the other hand, if *Rd* is less than *Rs*, *R* will move to the left. If *Rd* is equal to *Rs*, that is, if *R* is vertically under a point of intersection of the curves, demand and supply are in equilibrium

This may be taken as the typical diagram for stable equilibrium for a commodity that obeys the law of diminishing return. But if we had made *SS′* a horizontal straight line, we should have represented the case of "constant return," in which the supply price is the same for all amounts of the commodity. And if we had made *SS′* inclined negatively, but less steeply that *DD′* (the necessity for this condition will appear more fully later on), we should have got a case of stable equilibrium for a commodity which obeys the law of increasing return. In either case the above reasoning remains unchanged without the alteration of a word or a letter; but the last case introduces difficulties which we have arranged to postpone.

Figure 8.3
Supply and Demand in Marshall's Principles of Economics
Source: Marshall (1920: 346).

same, that prices of substitutes and competitive products are fixed, and that expectations and foreign trade remain unchanged. Given these assumptions, we have a "partial" equilibrium in the short term.

In combining supply and demand, Marshall intended to draw from both the classical model of Smith and Ricardo and the new marginalist revolution. From the marginalist revolution, he created the demand curve, which reflected marginal utilities of buyers. From the classical school, he developed the supply schedule, which depended on the costs of production.

MARSHALL TRIES TO SALVAGE RICARDIAN ECONOMICS

Marshall developed short-run and long-run conditions for equilibrium. According to the Cambridge economist, demand and supply conditions could change radically and cause prices to change accordingly in the short run. But in the long run, concluded Marshall, prices are determined by their costs of production. Marshall and his followers insisted that costs were something real and absolute, a concept independent of utility. In this sense, Marshall defected from the Austrians, who demonstrated that value must ultimately be determined by utility or demand, and that costs are really nothing but forgone alternatives. In essence, he attempted to integrate marginal utility analysis into a Ricardian framework by making cost, not utility, the ultimate determination of value. Thus, he attempted to salvage Ricardian economics and its labor theory of value. Marshall was a revisionist, not a revolutionary. He came not to destroy but to fulfill classical economics.

MARSHALL INVENTS AN ENDLESSLY FASCINATING CONCEPT: PRICE ELASTICITY OF DEMAND

Marshall was always attempting to apply mathematics and the hard sciences to economics. Two most prominent examples are the elasticity concept and consumer's surplus.

In 1881, while sitting on the roof of a hotel in Palermo, Italy, Marshall came upon the idea of elasticity and, his wife reported, "was highly delighted with it" (Keynes 1963: 187n). Elasticity is an ingenious and highly useful mathematical construct that quantifies buyers' sensitivity to price, a subject producers are obviously interested in. It has also been applied successfully to the impact of taxation on prices, output, and incomes.

Essentially, price elasticity of demand shows you how sensitive buyers are to changes in price. An important question for producers is: If we raise the price of a commodity, will our revenues go up or down? Similarly, if we lower the price, will revenues rise or fall?

The equation for price elasticity of demand is:

$$e = \frac{\% \, \Delta \, Q}{\% \, \Delta \, P}$$

where P equals the price of the commodity, Q is the quantity bought, and e is elasticity.

An elasticity of 1 is "unitary"—a slight increase or decrease in the price has virtually no impact on the total revenues. Elasticity more than 1 means the commodity is relatively "elastic," meaning that an increase of the price decreases total revenues, and a decrease in price increases total revenues. On the other hand, elasticity less than 1 means that a commodity is "inelastic," signifying that an increase in the price increases revenues. Clearly, many producers would prefer commodities with low elasticities of demand, suggesting that they would benefit from rising prices. Yet new competitors might prefer markets whose demand is elastic, knowing that undercutting the market leaders will increase sales and attract new customers.

TAX ELASTICITY A MAJOR ISSUE IN SUPPLY-SIDE ECONOMICS

Legislators are also interested in knowing the "incidence" of a tax increase or decrease on production and government revenues. For example, will a cut in the capital gains tax rate from 28 percent to 20 percent increase or decrease revenues? Or, what will the impact be on the sales of automobiles if the federal government imposes a 10 percent luxury tax on cars selling for more than $30,000? Measuring the marginal impact of taxation on production and revenues is extremely useful.

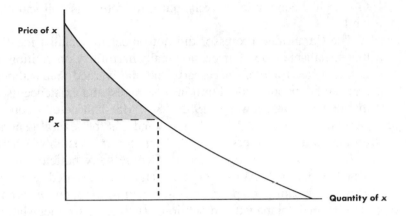

Figure 8.4
Marshall's Consumer's Surplus Concept

CONSUMER'S SURPLUS—A MEASURE OF ECONOMIC WELL-BEING?

Marshall also originated the concept of consumer's surplus, a way of measuring consumer satisfaction. In the diagram above, the shaded triangle represents consumer's surplus (see Figure 8.4).

As we can see, the market fixes a single price, *P*, for commodity *X*. However, note that many consumers are willing to pay a higher price than *P*. Have you ever gone into a store expecting to pay a certain amount for a product, only to discover it on sale at half the price? You have earned a consumer's surplus. For example, suppose the price of a 30-inch color television set is $500. That is the equilibrium price. Yet there are many customers willing to pay $600 or even $900 if necessary, to have a big color TV set. Not all people are willing to buy higher-priced TV sets—but some are—maybe even you yourself would be willing. When these willing buyers enter the TV showroom, they discover that they only have to pay $500, although they are willing to pay $900. These buyers have a consumer surplus of $400.

Marshall's concept of consumer's surplus reflects to some degree the level of satisfaction of consumers in the marketplace. A general lowering of prices reflects increased consumer satisfaction. More consumers are able to buy goods and services and fulfill their needs. Marshall's (and Smith's) desire for "universal opulence"—social benefits for the poor as well as the rich—is reflected in an expanding consumer's surplus.

MARSHALL OPPOSES POLITICAL REVOLUTION

Marshall's attitude about government policy can best be reflected in a statement he made in the preface to the fourth edition: "Economic evolution is gradual" (1920: xix). Not only did this remark mirror his approach to marginal economic analysis, but it reflected his political philosophy as well.

The Cambridge professor did not object to socialist idealism, but felt that socialism is too often economically harmful. Competition, private capital, and free trade are necessary, and "he warned that without capitalists and capital, people would turn into 'savages' and existence itself would be threatened" (Groenewegen 1995: 584). Marshall noted frequently that the capitalist system had raised living standards for several generations, even for agricultural workers. In short, Adam Smith's vision was being fulfilled.

In a lecture referring to Henry George's tax policies (see chapter 9), Marshall outlined less extreme alternatives. He favored slowing population growth, educating the poor, and encouraging cooperative communities. He also favored "managed competition," such as factory legislation and regulating business practices in manufacturing. He stressed the role of self-help, cooperation, and education for the working classes. Later, he supported redistribution schemes such as progressive taxation and the taxation of capital. It would be good "if the rich were somewhat less rich, and the poor were somewhat less poor" (Pigou 1925: 366).

Marshall favored the eight-hour workday and profit sharing, but grew fearful of trade unions. "I want these people to be beaten at all costs," he wrote. "The complete destruction of Unionism would be as heavy a price as it is possible to conceive: but I think not too high a price" (Pigou 1925: 400–401). He thought the trade union movement would reduce Britain's ability to compete worldwide.

But he was opposed to all forms of revolution. Marshall might be considered a social reformer, but never a capital S socialist.

CONCLUSION: MARSHALL TAKES TWO STEPS FORWARD, ONE STEP BACK

Alfred Marshall and his dominant textbook made great strides in incorporating the marginal utility revolution and in moving economics forward into the twentieth century. He developed many useful diagrams and mathematical techniques to apply the principles of economics in everyday consumer and commercial affairs. His scientific approach debunked the dismal views of Marx and the socialists, and thus helped to regenerate the benefits of Adam Smith's system of natural liberty and economic progress. His dominant Cambridge school attempted to preserve some forms of an antiquated classical model—such as a Ricardian labor-value theory in long-run costs and tax redistribution policies—but economics was clearly moving in the right direction.

LAISSEZ-FAIRE CAPITALISM: DOG-EAT-DOG SURVIVAL OF THE FITTEST IN A CHAOTIC JUNGLE!

Millionaires are the product of natural selection.
—William Graham Sumner (1963: 157)

The evolutionary ideas of **Charles Darwin (1809–82)** had an immense impact on science, religion, and philosophy; economics was no exception. Alfred Marshall, like most intellectuals of the nineteenth century, was deeply affected by Charles Darwin's *Origin of Species* (1859) and *The Descent of Man* (1871). Marshall himself believed that economics should best imitate biology, and stressed that marginal or small changes in economic behavior affected prices and output: "Economic evolution is gradual" (1920: xix).

But Darwinism inspired more than an economic calculus. It also caused market advocates to justify laissez-faire policies and market critics to label capitalism a ruthless, chaotic, dog-eat-dog world.

LAISSEZ FAIRE AND "SURVIVAL OF THE FITTEST"

The most influential social Darwinists were **Herbert Spencer (1820–1903)**, English philosopher and critic, and **William Graham Sumner (1840–1910)**, Episcopal clergyman and economics professor at Yale University. Both were indefatigable defenders of the capitalist system.

Herbert Spencer started writing about his single grand principle of evolution years before Darwin. He invented the term "survival of the fittest" in 1852, at the age of thirty-two. As a young man, he worked as a railroad construction engineer, which taught him the value of free private competition and the virtues of economic struggle for existence. Like Darwin, Spencer was affected by the writings of Robert Malthus, which asserted that a growing population puts pressure on resources. Unlike Malthus, Spencer saw this "survival" situation as beneficial and the very motor of progress. "It forces men into the social state . . . and mutually dependent relationships" (Oldroyd 1983: 207).

Spencer applied the biological principle of differentiation in plants and animals to the business world. As business expands, it becomes more differentiated, opening new branches and new products.

Yet Spencer's view of the economy as a "social organism" also painted a dreary picture of capitalism. He claimed, for example, that business was like a jungle, inherently chaotic, selfish, and rapacious, wrought with fraudulent and unscrupulous practices. In

Photograph 8.3
Herbert Spencer (1820–1903)
"The poverty of the incapable, the starvation of the idle . . . are the degrees of a large, farseeing benevolence."
Courtesy of Hulton-Getty Archives.

(continued)

his article "The Morals of Trade," Spencer forcefully revealed the "innumerable" forms of "illicit trade" in British commerce. He described various bribes, thefts, false trademarks, and tricks of the trade. Even the few honest people in business are "obliged" to cheat, he said. "It is a startling assertion, but it is none the less a true one, that those who resist these corruptions, often do it at the risk of bankruptcy" (Spencer 1865: 124).

SPENCER'S INDEPENDENT HERITAGE

Herbert Spencer was born in 1820 in Derby, England, to a family of dissenting clergymen who opposed church-state ties. Spencer inherited their antistate individualism and science-based rationalism. Like John Stuart Mill, he was home schooled in the natural sciences, classics, languages, and history, and then went to work as a railroad engineer. But he suffered from ill health and became a partial invalid. Turning to a literary career, he wrote for a radical dissenting journal, the *Nonconformist*, and for the *Economist*, the premier organ for free trade and laissez faire in Britain. He never married, although he had an emotional relationship with the eminent female novelist George Eliot.

LAISSEZ FAIRE AND EUGENICS

According to Spencer, laissez faire was the only appropriate policy in keeping with evolutionary principles. Society should not interfere with natural laws. The weakest members ought to go to the wall, which Spencer said would improve society by weeding out the less intelligent and less industrious. Although not advocated by Spencer, such thinking led directly to the eugenics movement, which, in its most extreme manifestation in Nazi Germany, called for compulsory sterilization and selective breeding to improve the quality of the population. Some critics contend that the abortion movement is the latest form of eugenics.

Spencer was an arch-individualist, favoring free trade and the abolition of government welfare. He vehemently attacked Henry George and land nationalizers. In his classic libertarian document, *Man Versus the State*, he declared, "The process *must* be undergone, and the sufferings *must* be endured. No power on earth, no cunningly-devised laws of statesmen, no world-rectifying schemes of the humane, no communist panaceas, no reforms that men ever did broach or ever will broach, can diminish them one jot" (1981 [1884]: 108).

Spencer became financially secure and world famous in the late nineteenth century, but he was neither happy nor in good health. He was deeply pessimistic during the drift toward socialism and communism. He died in 1903. Only recently has Spencerian sociology staged a comeback through evolutionary economics.

SUMNER'S INFLUENCE IN THE UNITED STATES

Social Darwinism got its widest support in the United States. As Alexis de Tocqueville reported in his *Democracy in America*, Americans had been ingrained with the inalienable right to personal liberty, the Jeffersonian conviction that "government that governs least governs best," and their enthusiasm for Adam Smith's doctrine of enlightened self-interest (1988: 525–26, 539).

(continued)

Leading the charge was Yale professor William Graham Sumner. Following Spencer's lead, Sumner saw competition as a "law of nature" and unfettered capitalism as inherently consistent with the laws of evolution. During the time that the "robber barons" John D. Rockefeller, Andrew Carnegie, and J.P. Morgan were under attack for their "cutthroat" competition, Sumner proclaimed, "Millionaires are the product of natural selection" (1963: 157). Business tycoons expressed approval. In *The Gospel of Wealth*, published in 1890, Carnegie wrote that individualism, private property, the "laws" of accumulated wealth and competition, were the "highest result of human experience" (Carnegie 1962: 16–17). And Rockefeller said, "The growth of a large business is merely a survival of the fittest . . . a law of nature and a law of God" (Hofstadter 1955: 45).

Sumner believed that competitive capitalism was a great advance. He opposed all forms of inheritance or estate taxes, arguing that inherited wealth preserved favorable characteristics from one generation to another.

SOCIAL DARWINISM GIVES CAPITALISM A BAD NAME

It is clear that the social Darwinism envisioned by Spencer and Sumner did little to change the already entrenched invective against economics, the "dismal" or "vulgar" science. Social reformers like Richard T. Ely and Francis A. Walker found economic Darwinism repellent, and sought less harsh socialistic alternatives.

CRITICISMS OF SOCIAL DARWINISM

There are problems in applying Darwinism to economics. The economy is not merely a Hobbesian jungle, as Upton Sinclair called it in one of his novels, but a system of spontaneous order and potential progress. Our economic system is characterized not just by competition, but by cooperation and the harmony of interests. It is not the survival of the fittest, but the survival and improvement of both weak and strong, poor and rich. Through the division of labor, even the weakest of human beings can find useful and productive work. Society witnesses big and small businesses competing, rich and poor working side by side. While there may be an inevitable boom and bust in the global economy, the market also witnesses a gradual improvement in the standard of living. Market participants are not just beasts rapaciously taking advantage of each other, but advanced human beings using a higher conscience and morality to live in harmony and mutual benefit with their fellow beings and nature. Finally, individuals in society can help the less fortunate through incentives, education, and training. The situation is far from hopeless. In sum, mankind can escape the jungle through the sound principles of thrift, industry, technology, charity, and integrity.

DARWINIAN ECONOMICS FALLS INTO DISREPUTE

Darwinian economics, under the dominance of Herbert Spencer and William Graham Sumner, reached its zenith between 1890 and 1914 but, by the end of the 1920s, had fallen out of favor. The ideological abuse of Darwinism had taken its toll as a result of World War I. Eugenics, sexism, and laissez-faire policies were viewed with suspicion if not outright disdain. Even among scientists, genetics was increasingly

(continued)

seen as playing a more dominant role than natural selection, as a driving force behind evolution.

Meanwhile, economist A.C. Pigou—Marshall's heir at Cambridge—turned his back on biological metaphors in economics. He preferred mechanics over biology, using terms such as mechanical equilibrium. During the thirties, the economy was viewed as a machine that could be manipulated, with government technocrats at the steering wheel. During World War II, the economy became a war machine, running full speed at full employment.

In microeconomic theory, a mechanistic model of imperfect competition was developed by Edward H. Chamberlin and Joan Robinson in the 1930s. Since then, this theory of imperfect competition has dominated the profession, despite serious dissension from Joseph Schumpeter, Israel Kirzner, and Murray N. Rothbard.

EVOLUTIONARY ECONOMICS MAKES A COMEBACK

Since the end of World War II, evolutionary economics has staged a comeback, although it has yet to derail the Chamberlin-Robinson model of competition. The first efforts came from Armen Alchian, Milton Friedman, and other market economists who saw evolution as a profit maximizer: "Natural selection," inherent in the competitive process, leads to the survival of the most profitable firms (see, for example, Alchian 1950).

The Austrian economist Friedrich Hayek also began writing about the market process in evolutionary terms, particularly his concept of "spontaneous order." Millions of individuals independently pursue their own self-interest in the production of multiple goods and services. There is no overall plan. No single person knows every aspect of the production process in creating a product, yet the product is made anyway. Richard Dawkins, writing on evolution, uses a simular concept, which he calls the "blind watchmaker." The watchmaker is blind, but the watch is made anyway.

In 1982, American economists Richard Nelson and Sidney Winter published *An Evolutionary Theory of Economic Change,* deemed "the most extensive and rigorous application of the evolutionary metaphor from biology in economics to date" (Hodgson 1999: 166). The book continues to be cited most frequently in management and business publications, but there is growing interest in economics in finding alternative models to today's standard imperfect competition model. Since 1991, the *Journal of Evolutionary Economics* has published papers on the subject. Yet, today's neoclassical model is not likely to be replaced until an alternative model can be developed that is both theoretically rigorous and empirically testable. As Robert Solow once confessed, "I know the wheel is crooked, but it's the only game in town" (Hodgson 1999: 81).

THE MATHEMATICAL ECONOMISTS FORMALIZE ADAM SMITH'S MODEL

Alfred Marshall wasn't the only figure to professionalize economics. Three other economists in Europe made significant advances: Léon Walras from France, Vilfredo Pareto from Italy, and Francis Edgeworth from Ireland. Their vital contributions were twofold: they introduced sophisticated mathematical methods to economics, and they attempted to mathematically validate Adam Smith's principal thesis, that the invisible hand of competition automatically transforms self-interest into the common good.

THE FIRST FUNDAMENTAL THEOREM OF WELFARE ECONOMICS

The idea that laissez faire leads to the common good has become known as the first fundamental theorem in a branch of economics today called "welfare economics." In welfare economics, "welfare" refers to the general well-being or the common good of the nation, not to people on welfare or government assistance. Welfare economics deals with issues of efficiency, justice, economic waste, and the political process in the economy. Walras, Pareto, and Edgeworth were the first economists to use advanced mathematical formulas and graphic devices to prove certain hypotheses in welfare economics. Thus, for the first time, Adam Smith's invisible-hand doctrine could be clothed in mathematical garb.

Since the late 1930s, when welfare economics was popularized by John Hicks, Kenneth Arrow, Paul Samuelson, and Ronald Coase (all would become Nobel Prize winners), the techniques of welfare economics have been extended to the issues of monopoly and various government policies. In most cases, the welfare economists have demonstrated that government-imposed monopolies and subsidies lead to inefficiency and waste.

Let's look more closely at the lives and ideas of three econometric wizards—Walras, Pareto, and Edgeworth—who founded the branch of welfare economics.

WALRAS: THE GREATEST PURELY THEORETICAL ECONOMIST?

Léon Walras (1834–1910), a longtime French economist at the University of Lausanne, was known initially as one of the founders of the marginalist revolution, but today he is better known for developing the first "general equilibrium" model. These two achievements, accomplished with mathematical precision, are considered so monumental that Joseph Schumpeter ranked Walras "the greatest of all economists" in terms of pure theoretical contributions (1954: 827). *The New Palgrave* concurs: "Walras has been surpassed by no one" (Walker 1987: 862).

Why would Schumpeter make such a strong endorsement when Walras's general-equilibrium model has been criticized for its static and sterile formulism, a style entirely antithetical to Schumpeter's dynamic entrepreneurial approach? The answer is clear: Walras provided theoretical proof that Adam Smith's invisible-hand system of competition maximizes social welfare. As Schumpeter wrote, "a state of pure competitive equilibrium all round guarantees a maximum of satisfaction for all parties concerned" (1954: 985).

In his original 1873 paper, "Principe d'une théorie mathematique de l'échange," Walras explained that his purpose was to weigh the merits of laissez faire, on grounds of efficiency and justice. Using a two-party, two-commodity barter system, he was able to show that a "freely competitive" market would maximize the social utility of the two parties through a series of exchanges. In *Elements of Pure Economics* (1874, 1877), Walras extended his analysis to multiparty, multicommodity exchange under the assumptions of free competition, perfect mobility of the factors of production, and price flexibility. Using these limiting assumptions, he built a system of simultaneous equations representing the economy, and then, noting that the number of equations equaled the number of unknowns, he concluded that the free-market system would necessarily reach a general-equilibrium (GE) solution, where supply equals demand for all commodities.

Photograph 8.4
Léon Walras (1834–1910)
Describes Two Periods in His
Life: "One during which I was a
madman, and one during
which everyone made my
discoveries before me."
Courtesy of Centre Walras-Pareto.

Contrary to popular belief, Walras did not limit his analysis to static equilibrium conditions. He continued his work with a quasi-realistic view of the competitive system under disequilibrium. By simulating a market auctioneering process he called *tâtonnement* (French for "groping"), Walras showed that prices change according to supply and demand, and "groped" toward equilibrium. Thus, he was able to demonstrate that, without central direction, a trial-and-error market system would still achieve maximum social satisfaction of wants.

Walras lived an unconventional life. Christened Marie Esprit Léon in 1834 in Normandy, France, he had several short careers: He was a journalist, a railroad clerk, a bank director, and even a romance novelist. He formed a common-law marriage with a woman who had a son by a previous liaison, but eventually they married. They had twin daughters in 1863, but one died, and after a long illness, his wife also expired. Five years later, in 1879, he married a second wife, who lived until 1900.

His father, himself an amateur economist, pushed Walras into studying economic issues, and he finally settled down in 1870 (at the age of thirty-six) to become a professor of political economy at the University of Lausanne in Switzerland. He remained there for twenty years, writing and researching. He published his two-volume *Elements of Pure Economics* in 1874 and 1877, adding much new material in successive editions. He referred to his work as having "pleasures and joys like those that religion provide to the faithful" (Henderson 1993: 848). He retired in 1902 and died in 1910.

Walras was very much in the French tradition of Turgot, Montesquieu, and Say in developing a macro model. He learned much from reading

Cournot and Dupuit while developing his own version of diminishing marginal utility, but for his general equilibrium model, Say is clearly his "true predecessor" (Schumpeter 1954: 828).

Walras, who called himself a "scientific socialist," was always worried that the economy was not competitive enough, and advocated government intervention to ensure a more competitive environment. Land and natural monopolies should be nationalized, he argued, and leased to private users as a way to raise revenues. He believed taxes were unjust and confiscatory, and should be abolished.

Walras was a tireless promoter of his theories, but did not see much success during his lifetime. He constantly complained of plagiarism and lack of recognition by Marshall, Jevons, and other English economists. His *Elements* was not translated into English until 1954. There had been two periods in his life, he complained: "one during which I was a madman, and one during which everyone made my discoveries before me." A few years before his death, he bemoaned, "I know that success of this sort does not become clearly apparent until after the death of the author" (Walker 1987: 862).

TODAY'S GREATEST THREAT IS— THE WALRASIAN GENERAL EQUILIBRIUM MODEL!

Here is a theory with absolutely no empirical content. Having "proved" the existence, uniqueness and local stability of multi-market general equilibrium, what have we learned about the economy? Absolutely nothing.

—Mark Blaug (1997: 22)

One of the fundamentals of formal economic theory is the Walrasian general-equilibrium model, named after Walras. (John Hicks and Kenneth Arrow shared the Nobel Prize in 1972, and Gerald Debreu won the Nobel in 1983, each for advancing GE theory.)

But GE theory has come under increasing criticism for its unreal view of the economic world. Its chief defect is that it focuses on the end result of competition rather than the process itself, how competition works. Historian Mark Blaug has written a blistering attack on the Walrasian GE model, condemning it as an "almost total failure" and an "utterly sterile innovation." He compared it to "a geographical map of the towns in a country without a map of the roads between towns." Such static modeling has led to central planners' thinking that they could calculate prices and make socialism work. Blaug concludes, "In short, after a century or more of endless refinements of the central core of GE theory, an exercise which has absorbed some of the best brains in twentieth-century economics, the theory is unable to shed any light on how market equilibrium is actually attained" (1997: 76).

What to do about this perversity? Blaug urges the abandonment of the perfect competition model, general equilibrium, and welfare economics, to be replaced by a neo-Austrian model of market processes as taught by Mises, Hayek, and Kirzner (1997: 79–81). "I have come slowly and extremely reluctantly to the view that they [the Austrians] are right and that we have all been wrong. . . . Adam Smith's 'invisible hand' referred to the dynamic process of competition and not to the static, end-state conception of perfect competition that came into economics with Cournot" (page 189).

THE MAN BEHIND PARETO OPTIMALITY

Photograph 8.5
Vilfredo Pareto (1848–1923)
"The lone thinker of Celigny."
Courtesy of Centre Walras-Pareto.

In 1895 **Vilfredo Pareto (1848–1923)** acceded to Walras's chair at the University of Lausanne, where he extended Walras's analysis to the distribution of income. Given free labor competition, according to Pareto, wages would reach their maximum level and could not be raised effectively by labor unions.

Pareto is best known for the concept of Pareto Optimality. Like Walras, Pareto attempted to show that a perfectly competitive economy achieves an optimal level of economic justice, where the allocation of resources cannot be changed to make anyone better off without hurting someone else.

Born in 1848 in Paris of an Italian exile father and a French mother, Pareto attended school in Italy and graduated with an engineering degree from the University of Turin. He then spent more than twenty years working as an engineer and director of two Italian railway companies, from which he was forced to resign after failing to raise enough capital to modernize an ironworks plant. He also suffered huge losses speculating in the London iron market. In 1892, he embarked on a second career, as an economics professor, and he replaced Walras at the University of Lausanne.

In 1889, at the age of forty-one, he married Russian Countess Alessandrina, known as Dina. Ten years later, he inherited from an uncle a fortune valued at more than two million gold lire! Yet it was a year of pain, too. No sooner had Pareto become independently wealthy than Countess Dina left him for a young servant. Two years later Pareto met a twenty-two-year-old Frenchwoman, Jeanne Regis, and they lived together.

Pareto resigned his chair in 1911 and retired to his home on Lake Geneva, where he became known as the "lone thinker of Celigny." He died in 1923 (Busino 1987: 799–804).

PARETO'S UNPREDICTABLE VIEWS

Pareto was enigmatic when it came to his political views. Early in his career, he was a laissez-faire liberal. A founder of the Adam Smith Society, he fought passionately in favor of free trade and against state subsidies to industry. Social legislation, according to Pareto, was a sure way to squander wealth and retard economic growth. Only increased production could help the working classes. Throughout his life, he was a pacificist and an active critic of the Italian government, and frequently denounced protectionism and militarism, which he considered the two greatest enemies of liberty.

Later in life, as he switched from economics to sociology, he seemed to sour on democratic liberalism. No one knows why—perhaps it was a result of his failures as a businessman, speculator, and husband, or of his inherited fortune.

PARETO'S ELITE THEORY: LIONS VERSUS FOXES

In any case, he warmed up to socialism. According to Pareto, socialism mobilizes more passion and is therefore more politically effective than libertarianism. The Italian economist went so far as to declare that a planned socialist economy could produce the same results as a market economy, clearly contradicting his earlier support for the invisible-hand doctrine.

In his crowning work, *The Mind and Society* (1916), he invented the term "elite" to describe the ruling few. According to Pareto's elitist theory, society goes through a cycle of "lion" and "fox" rulers. A nation is established by lions who obtain power through violence, but then settles down to be run by bureaucratic foxes. Eventually, society's identity and moral strength deteriorate, requiring the rise of another lion to seize power and reestablish society's sense of direction. Pareto's sociology has been accused of being protofascist. In 1923, near the end of Pareto's life, Mussolini's government appointed him a member of the Italian senate, but he declined to join.

EDGEWORTH—ANYTHING BUT INDIFFERENT!

Francis Y. Edgeworth (1845–1926), an Irish-born professor at Oxford and longtime first editor of the *Economic Journal*, represents the third of the econometric triumverate. Like Marshall, he was a toolmaker. Marshall created supply and demand curves, consumer's surplus, and elasticity; Edgeworth developed indifference curves, utility functions, and the fundamentals for the Edgeworth box, a way of expressing various trading relationships between two individuals or countries. (It is named after Edgeworth, but was actually drawn first by Pareto!)

Francis Y. Edgeworth was born in Ireland in 1845, the son of a British father and a Spanish mother. His birthplace was Edgeworthtown, established by his ancestors during Queen Elizabeth's reign. His forebears were notorious for having many wives. His great-great-grandfather married three times, and his grandfather, Richard, married four times and had twenty-two children. Francis Y. married . . . no one! He was a bachelor all his life. Edgeworth blamed it on the law of averages.

Edgeworth had a photographic memory and could repeat numerous passages from Milton, Pope, Virgil, and Homer in his old age. He knew Greek,

Photograph 8.6
Francis Ysidro Edgeworth
(1845–1926)
**"Shall I answer briefly,
or at length?"**
Courtesy of Mark Blaug.

Latin, German, Italian, and Spanish, having the advantage of Irish, Spanish, and French ancestors. Preparing to graduate from Oxford in 1869, it was said, he responded to an obscure question in finals, "Shall I answer briefly, or at length?" and then spoke for half an hour.

In 1891 he became the Drummond Professor of Political Economy at Oxford, and at the same time first editor of the *Economic Journal*, a position he held for the next thirty-five years, until his death in 1926. His biggest contribution came with the publication of *Mathematical Psychics* in 1881. Tall, well-dressed, with a long nose and a well-trimmed, pointed beard, Edgeworth was known as an absent-minded professor and a diffident lecturer. One student described his lectures: "[After] many hours . . . he at last made the supply curve intersect the demand curve. . . . One knew it was a great moment. He wagged his beard and muttered inaudible things into it. He seemed to be in a kind of ectasy" (Harrod 1951: 373). Edgeworth liked to use long, Latinate words. "Was it very caliginous in the Metropolis?" he once asked T.E. Lawrence at All Souls' Gate. Lawrence replied, "Somewhat caliginous but not altogether inspissated" (Newman 1987: 86).

Adam Smith made up for his bachelorhood with books and friends; Edgeworth had few possessions—"scarcely any furniture or crockery, not even books (he preferred a public library near at hand), no proper notepaper of his own or stationery or stamps" (Keynes 1963: 237).

Edgeworth was so brilliant that it was said, "Walras devotes more than 150 pages to outlining the general system of exchange equilibrium on the consumer's market; Wicksell performs the task in about 20 pages and Edgeworth does it in a footnote!" (Gardlund 1996 [1958]: 195–96).

THE DRAWBACKS TO WELFARE ECONOMICS

The work of Walras, Pareto, and Edgeworth initially upheld Adam Smith's vision of a beneficial capitalism, but its unrealistic assumptions made it difficult to sustain a free-market defense. Both Walras and Pareto, after years of laying the foundation of welfare economics, found themselves moving away from the Smithian vision.

The problem with Pareto Optimality is that it ignores the omnipresent trade-offs in economic life. Seldom is one policy undertaken that improves people's lives without injuring others. Opening trade, eliminating subsidies, and deregulating industries may help some groups and hurt others. Eliminating tariffs between the United States and Mexico will create many new jobs—but it will also destroy many traditional jobs. This is an inevitable feature of the mixed economy. The net effect is undoubtedly beneficial, but the transition may not fit Pareto Optimality.

THE EUROPEAN MODEL IS CARRIED ACROSS THE ATLANTIC

Marshall's neoclassical principles—enhanced by the mathematical wizardry of Edgeworth, Pareto, and Walras—spread across the sea to American institutions, which were developing their own economic views. The U.S. economists, such as John Bates Clark and Frank Fetter, made notable additions and improvements to the house that Marshall built. It was also challenged by a new "institutional" school of skeptics, led by iconoclast Thorstein Veblen. American economics is the subject of chapter 9.

REFERENCES

Alchian, Armen. 1950. "Uncertainty, Evolution, and Economic Theory." *Journal of Political Economy* 58: 2 (June), 211–22.

Black, R.D. Collison, A.W. Coats, and Cranford D.W. Goodwin, eds. 1973. *The Marginal Revolution in Economics*. Durham, NC: Duke University Press.

Blaug, Mark. 1997. *Not Only an Economist*. Cheltenham, UK: Edward Elgar.

———. 1999. *Who's Who in Economics*, 3d ed. Cheltenham, UK: Edward Elgar.

Busino, G. 1987. "Vilfredo Pareto." In *The New Palgrave: A Dictionary of Economics,* vol. 3, 799–804. London: Macmillan.

Carnegie, Andrew. 1962. *The Gospel of Wealth: And Other Timely Essays by Andrew Carnegie*, ed. E.E. Kirkland. Cambridge, MA: Belknap.

Dahrendorf, Ralf. 1995. *LSE, A History of the London School of Economics and Political Science, 1895–1995*. Oxford: Oxford University Press.

Darwin, Charles. 1906. *The Descent of Man*, 2d ed. London: John Murray.

Dawkins, Richard. 1986. *The Blind Watchmaker*. New York: Norton.

Dobbs, Zygmund. 1964. *The Great Deceit*. New York: Veritas Foundation.

Ekelund, Robert B., Jr., and Robert F. Hébert. 1990. *A History of Economic Theory and Method*, 3d ed. New York: McGraw-Hill.

Gardlund, Torsten. 1996 [1958]. *The Life of Knut Wicksell*. Cheltenham, UK: Edward Elgar.

Groenewegen, Peter. 1995. *A Soaring Eagle: Alfred Marshall, 1842–1924*. Cheltenham, UK: Edward Elgar.

Harrod, Roy F. 1951. *The Life of John Maynard Keynes*. London: Macmillan.

Hayek, F.A. 1994. *Hayek on Hayek*. Chicago: University of Chicago Press.

Henderson, David R., ed. 1993. *The Fortune Encyclopedia of Economics*. New York: Warner.

Hodgson, Geoffrey M. 1999. *Economics and Evolution*. Ann Arbor: University of Michigan Press.

Hofstader, Richard. 1955. *Social Darwinism in American Thought*. Boston: Beacon.

Jevons, William Stanley. 1865. *The Coal Question*. London: Macmillan.

———. 1965 [1871]. *The Theory of Political Economy,* 5th ed. New York: Augustus M. Kelley.

Keynes, John Maynard. 1963. *Essays in Biography*. New York: W.W. Norton.

Marshall, Alfred. 1920. *Principles of Economics,* 8th ed. London: Macmillan.

Marshall, Alfred, and M.P. Marshall. 1879. *The Economics of Industry.* London: Macmillan.

Newman, Peter. 1987. "Francis Ysidro Edgeworth." In *The New Palgrave: A Dictionary of Economics,* vol. 2, 84–98. London: Macmillan.

Oldroyd, D.R. 1983. *Darwinian Impacts,* 2d ed. Milton Keynes, UK: Open University Press.

Pareto, Vilfredo. 1983 [1916]. *The Mind and Society.* Providence, RI: AMS Press.

Pigou, A.C., ed. 1925. *Memorials to Alfred Marshall.* London: Macmillan.

Robinson, Joan. 1953. *On Re-Reading Marx.* Cambridge: Student Bookshop Ltd.

Samuelson, Paul A. 1970. *Collected Scientific Papers of Paul A. Samuelson,* vol. 2. Cambridge, MA: MIT Press.

Schumpeter, Joseph A. 1951. *Ten Great Economists: From Marx to Keynes.* New York: Oxford University Press.

———. 1954. *History of Economic Analysis.* New York: Oxford University Press.

Sidgewick, Henry. 1926. "Economics." In *Palgrave's Dictionary of Political Economy,* vol. 4, 677–79. London: Macmillan.

Simon, Julian L. 1996. *The Ultimate Resource 2.* Princeton: Princeton University Press.

Spencer, Herbert. 1865. *Essays: Moral, Political and Aesthetic.* New York: D. Appleton.

———. 1981 [1884]. *The Man Versus the State.* Indianapolis, IN: Liberty Classics.

Sumner, William Graham. 1963. *Social Darwinism: Selected Essays by William Graham Sumner,* ed. S. Persons. Engelwood Cliffs, NJ: Prentice-Hall.

Tocqueville, Alexis de. 1988. *Democracy in America.* New York: Harper Perennial.

Walras, Léon. 1954 [1874, 1877]. *Elements of Pure Economics.* Homewood, IL: Richard D. Irwin.

Walker, Donald A. 1987. "Léon Walras." In *The New Palgrave: A Dictionary in Economics,* vol. 4, 853–63. London: Macmillan.

Wicksteed, Philip H. 1933. *The Common Sense of Political Economy,* rev. ed. London: Routledge and Kegan Paul.

9

GO WEST, YOUNG MAN:
AMERICANS SOLVE THE
DISTRIBUTION PROBLEM
IN ECONOMICS

The broad treatment of economics in the United States [is]
a shining example of the necessary future development
in economics.

—British economist C.F. Bastable, 1894
(Dorfman 1949)

The European schools of economics—followers of Menger, Jevons, and Walras—had made a major breakthrough with the discovery of the marginality principle in economics. The Europeans used this principle to account for the value of goods and services in a capitalist system: The price of *X* is determined by how much consumers value the additional units of the supply of *X*. Thus, marginal supply and demand formed the basis of production decisions by firms and consumption decisions by consumers.

But what about the "distribution" problem? What determines rents, wages, profits, and interest income? Does the marginality principle apply to income earned by landlords, workers, and capitalists?

Capitalism has always been hailed as a powerful producer of goods and services, an unsurpassed engine of economic growth, but has been heavily criticized (by Marx as well as Mill) for its disturbing inequality of wealth and income. Is this criticism valid?

It fell upon the shoulders of American economists, especially John Bates Clark, to address these fundamental issues of income distribution. As the

♪ **Music selection for this chapter: Antonin Dvorak, Symphony No. 9,** *The New World*

United States became the largest economic powerhouse in the world at the turn of the twentieth century, so also did the American economics profession begin to gain prominence. In this chapter, we will discuss the American reaction to the marginalist revolution in Europe and the contributions made by U.S. economists in advancing scientific economics, especially in the areas of wage, rent, and capital theory.

The most prominent scholars at the turn of the twentieth century were John Bates Clark at Columbia University, Frank A. Fetter at Cornell and Princeton, Richard T. Ely at the University of Wisconsin, and Thorstein Veblen, who established the institutionalist school of economics.

It would be fair to say that the American economists were more remodelers than architects of a new building. As Alexis de Tocqueville wrote in the 1830s, "Americans have no school of philosophy peculiar to themselves" (1988 [1848]: 429). Nevertheless, using the marginality principle developed in Europe, they were able to solve a mystery that had remained unsolved for years—the so-called distribution problem in economics.

HENRY GEORGE ADDRESSES THE "LAND QUESTION"

First, let's discuss the debate over land. Rents and the role of landlords were controversial issues in the United States in the late 1800s. Marx himself had written, "Nothing seems more natural than to start with rent, with landed property, since it is bound up with land, the source of all production and all existence, and with the first form of production in all more or less settled communities, viz., agriculture" (Marx 1911: 302).

The classical position on land was the old Ricardian theory of rent. According to Ricardo, land being a fixed, nonreproducible resource, rent is a "free gift of nature," and therefore could be taxed or even expropriated by the state with no effect on the marginal cost of producing crops or goods. John Stuart Mill, relying on the view of his father James Mill, wrote that all "future increments of unearned rent" could be taxed away without harm.

In the United States, land prices often skyrocketed, creating a despised group of landlords who seemed to benefit from "unearned" gains. Henry George, a San Francisco newspaper reporter and social critic, took advantage of surging land prices to write a powerful anti-landlord book and create a worldwide following called the Single Tax Movement. George's movement would rival all other political or religious organizations of the nineteenth century.

GEORGE'S COLORFUL PAST

Who was this fellow who could engender such mighty allegiance? **Henry George (1839–97)** was born in Philadelphia—"poor, unheralded, unknown"—and died in New York City—"accorded the greatest funeral

Photograph 9.1
Henry George (1839–1897)
"Among the world's social philosophers is this great American thinker" (Andelsen 1992: 1).
Courtesy of Robert Schalkenbach Foundation.

which New York City had ever witnessed" (Andelson 1992: 1). As a young man, he was a sailor and prospector, and upon moving to San Francisco, became a newspaper reporter, editor, and publisher. In 1861 he eloped with Annie Fox, an eighteen-year-old Australian orphan, with whom he had four children. While in California in 1879, he wrote his magnum opus, *Progress and Poverty*. Mainstream publishers rejected the manuscript, so he had 500 copies self-published. In his polemical book, George pinpointed a single deficiency in the capitalist system, which, if corrected, could solve poverty and all the world's economic problems. What was this defect? Not capital and capitalists, as the Marxists proclaimed. Rather, it was monopoly of land. The landlords were the source of all evil.

To quote a famous passage from *Progress and Poverty*: "We have traced the unequal distribution of wealth which is the curse and menace of modern civilization to the institution of private property in land. We have seen that so long as this institution exists no increase in productive power can permanently benefit the masses; but, on the contrary, must tend still further to depress their condition" (1942 [1879]: 328).

GEORGE'S SINGLE SOLUTION: A LAND VALUE TAX

George's answer to the problem was simple: "We must make land common property" (1942: 328). How? Not by expropriation or land reform, as the socialists desired. Rather, by a tax on unimproved land value! The government would impose a tax equal to the value of the unimproved land, or ground rent. Every owner of property would be charged a monthly rental tax based on the value of the ground rent. There would be no tax on improvements or buildings, which George admitted would distort and retard production. To be effective, the land tax must be solely a tax on "pure economic rent."

What would be the effect of such a land tax? To quote one admirer: "This would, of course, eliminate all speculative profit in land-holding, depress land prices, and in effect bring back the frontier by making cheap land readily available to everyone. This would raise the margin of production, increase real wages, and stimulate building and productivity. At the same time, all other taxes would be abolished" (Andelson 1992: 3–4). George envisioned that the land tax would be so significant that all other taxes—income, sales, capital gains, estate, and import duties—could be eliminated, with the possible exception of licenses and stamp duties.

George called his simple solution a uniting of Adam Smith's laissez-faire economics and the noble dreams of the socialists (George 1942: xvii). It would, he said, alleviate poverty and unemployment, as well as the boom-bust business cycle.

GEORGE CAMPAIGNS AROUND THE WORLD

Henry George was so convinced he had a solution to the world's problems that he began a twenty-year campaign around the world, traveling to New York, Ireland, and Australia. In every visit, he blamed local economic problems on the landlords, not on overpopulation, free trade, or capitalism. Needless to say, George's message was well received, especially in places where land prices had risen dramatically and citizens were looking for a scapegoat.

George became a folk hero and was endorsed by many prominent citizens. He ran for mayor of New York City in 1886 and came in second (his supporters cried fraud). He ran a second campaign in 1897 but died of a stroke just five days before the election.

SUPPORTERS FROM WINSTON CHURCHILL TO SUN YAT-SEN

Over the years, Georgists have found popular support for their leader's philosophy from a wide range of politicians and idealists, including Winston Churchill ("This evil process [land monopoly] strikes at every form of industrial activity"), Leo Tolstoy ("Henry George's great idea . . . is so undeniably convincing, and, above all, so simple") and Dr. Sun Yat-sen in China ("The teachings of Henry George will be the basis of our program of reform") (Andelson 1992: 2). John Dewey, the famed American educator, idolized, "It would require less than the fingers of the two hands to enumerate those who, from Plato down, rank with Henry George among the world's social philosophers" (George 1942: vii), and some social historians claim that his anti-landlord news inspired the popular board game "Monopoly."

Yet today, Henry George is not listed in *The 100 Most Influential People in the World*, nor is his *Progress and Poverty* listed in *The 100 Most Influential Books Ever Written*. What happened? He died, and most of his theories died with him as too extreme.

CRITICS OF THE SINGLE TAX

Georgists blamed it on a conspiracy of the power elite (see the box on page 233). More reasoned minds would blame it on George's extreme policy recommendation of a single tax on land and abolishing all other forms of taxation.

American economists were prominent in arguing against Henry George's single-tax plan, especially John Bates Clark, Frank A. Fetter, Edwin Seligman, and Francis A. Walker (first president of the American Economic Association and president of MIT).

The principal critic of Henry George was John Bates Clark, the first American economist to gain an international reputation. In 1899, while teaching at Columbia University, Clark wrote a vital work, *The Distribution of Income*, which extended the marginality principle to land, labor, and capital. Clark began his critique by rejecting the Ricardian view that land is fixed. "The idea that land is fixed in amount," he wrote, "is really based on an error which one encounters in economic discussions with wearisome frequency" (1965 [1899]: 338). While the amount of land existing on earth does indeed remain constant, the supply of land *available for sale* varies with the price, as any other commodity. And land prices, like wages and capital goods, are determined by their marginal productivity—"at the margin"— allocated according to its most "productive" use (1965: 346–48).

Clark severely criticized George, arguing that if land is taxed, it would drive capital out of land into housing, thus misallocating capital in favor of housing. Edwin Seligman, Clark's colleague at Columbia and a renowned tax expert, also contended that a land tax would penalize farmland in favor of city land.

The British economist Alfred Marshall also became involved in the Georgist land controversy. He argued that George's single tax on land would cause grave social upheaval and risk civil war. In 1884, Marshall encountered Henry George at a meeting at Oxford. In a question-and-answer period,

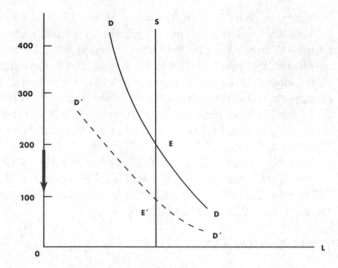

Tax on Fixed Land Is Shifted Back to Landowners, with Government Skimming Off Pure Economic Rent.
A tax on fixed land leaves prices paid by users unchanged at *E* but reduces rent retained by landowners to *E'*.
What can the landowners do but accept a lower return? This provides the rationale for Henry George's single-tax
movement, which aimed to capture for society the increased land values that result from urbanization.

Figure 9.1
Samuelson's Defense of Henry George's Land Tax
Source: Samuelson and Nordhaus (1998: 250). Reprinted by permission of McGraw-Hill.

Marshall doggedly attacked George for his "untrained" economics, his failure
to emphasize thrift and industry in *Progress and Poverty*, and his socialistic
views on rent. Marshall repeated the same question about rent again and
again, and George continually failed to answer it, much to the dismay and
delight of the Oxford student audience (Groenewegen 1995: 583–86).

But not all economists have opposed George's single tax plan. In fact,
Paul Samuelson, the most influential Keynesian economist of the twentieth
century, has repeatedly praised George and his single tax plan in his popular *Economics* textbook. "A tax on pure economic rent will lead to no
distortions or inefficiencies," he concludes (Samuelson and Nordhaus
1998: 250). Figure 9.1 reproduces a graph showing the alleged efficiency
of a pure rent on land.

Even free-market economists, including Milton Friedman, have supported the Georgist position. In an interview, Friedman once declared,
"The least bad tax is the property tax on the unimproved value of land, the
Henry George argument of many, many years ago" (1978: 14). Georgists
argue that a ground land tax is beneficial because unlike other taxes, land
taxes impose no excess burden on the economy, and thus stimulate more
rapid economic growth. Fred Foldvary (Santa Clara University) contends
that a land tax would reduce urban sprawl, dampen business cycles, and
curtail tax evasion (2005: 124–25).

Other economists disagree. American economist Murray Rothbard, for example, warned that Georgist taxes on ground rent would sharply curtail unused ("speculative") land, resulting in overcrowding and overuse. According to Rothbard, Georgists fail to understand the market's role in the allocation of scarce resources and the benefits of unused land. Imposing huge taxes on unimproved land would cause overcrowding in city centers, encouraging investors to eliminate empty lots and build higher skyscrapers in order to minimize land rents (Rothbard 1970: 91–100).

In essence, the American critics, from John Bates Clark to Murray Rothbard, have argued that the marginality principle does indeed apply to land. The total amount of land is fixed, but prices of *sellable* land are determined by the marginal number of buyers and sellers, which is not fixed. Rent and land prices help investors to allocate a scarce resource (land) to its most valued use in society. Rent controls and confiscatory land taxes can only create distortions in land use.

By George, It's a Conspiracy!

To stop Henry George the fortune hunters hired professors to corrupt economics and halt democratic dialogue. The use of that corrupted economics continues to this day.
— Mason Gaffney (1994: Cover)

"Henry George had to be stopped!" So began Fred Harrison, director of the Centre for Incentive Taxation, in his coauthored conspiratorial history, *The Corruption of Economics* (1994). Harrison, along with his coauthor, Mason Gaffney, economics professor at the University of California at Riverside, made the unbelievable claim that the world's "power elites" schemed to silence this popular social reformer of the nineteenth century. How? By buying off economics professors to speak out against George! Meanwhile, the establishment allowed Henry George's chief competitor— Karl Marx—to spread his doctrines throughout the world. The so-called conspiracy against George is labeled "one of the most heinous episodes in the history of the development of scientific knowledge" (Gaffney and Harrison 1994: 7).

According to Gaffney and Harrison, if it hadn't been for this conspiracy, Henry George would be a household name and a national hero instead of an obscure maverick in the history of economics.

Despite this grand secret combination, Georgists claim that Henry George's *Progress and Poverty* is the most influential economics book ever written, having been translated into twenty-five languages, and having outsold all books except the Bible! (Never mind that, like the Bible, *Progress and Poverty* is often given away or sold below cost.)

Conspiracy theories have abounded throughout history, advocated by tight-knit political or religious groups filled with true believers. Followers of Henry George fit this category in economics.

GEORGE IGNITES THE SOCIALISTS

Interestingly, George's greatest impact was contrary to his desires: Many of his listeners were so convinced of his rhetoric that they turned to socialism and Marxism! The great British playwright George Bernard Shaw said he started down the road to socialism after listening to George. Sydney Webb, leader of the Fabian Society, noted, "Little as Mr. Henry George intended it, there can be no doubt that it was the enormous circulation of *Progress and Poverty* which gave the touch that caused all seething influence to crystallize into a popular Socialist movement."

Bernard Shaw added, "Numbers of young men, pupils of Mill, Spencer, Comte, Darwin, roused by Mr. Henry George's *Progress and Poverty*, left aside evolution and free thought, took to insurrectionary economics [and] studied Karl Marx" (Hill 1997: 65). But Karl Marx, hearing of George's tax program, thought it was "capitalism's last ditch."

Photograph 9.2
John Bates Clark (1847–1938)
"Free competition tends to give to labor what labor creates."
Courtesy of Brown Brothers.

CLARK'S PRODUCTIVITY THEORY COUNTERS MARXIST DOCTRINE OF LABOR EXPLOITATION

Clark's application of the marginality principle to land was only the beginning. The second important outgrowth of the marginalist revolution in the United States was John Bates Clark's theory of marginal productivity of labor. This controversial theory countered the prevailing Malthus/Ricardo/Marxist view that wages could not rise permanently above the subsistence level and that capitalists received an unfair share of labor's product.

John Bates Clark (1847–1938) was the first American economist to gain international fame as an original theorist, and his principal claim to fame was his contribution to wage theory, which he called "the law of competitive distribution." Born in Providence, Rhode Island, in 1847, he came from a family of strict Puritans, and studied ethics, philosophy, and economics at Amherst College. He was fascinated by economics, but because there was no school of graduate studies in the field in the United States, he spent the next two years in Europe. There, he was exposed to the German historical school under the instruction of Karl Knies. While abroad, he met an American colleague, Richard T. Ely, who formed the American Economic Association (AEA) (see the box on page 238). Recall that the German historical school focused entirely on empirical work and denied the benefits of theory (see chapter 7). So what did Clark do when he returned to the United States? He wrote almost entirely on theory! Until Clark, almost all work in economics in the United States involved empirical studies and social reforms.

Most of his career was spent on the faculty of political science at Columbia University, from 1896 until 1923 (when his chair went to his son, John Maurice Clark). There he wrote his most famous work, *The Distribution of Wealth* (first published in 1899), which included his marginal productivity theories of land, labor, and capital. Over his lifetime, he gradually shifted ground, starting as a social reformer and becoming a conservative defender of the capitalist system. He spent the last years of his life writing on the preservation of peace, becoming the first director of the Carnegie Endowment for International Peace. He died in 1938, a year before war broke out again in Europe.

CLARK SOLVES THE "DISTRIBUTION" PROBLEM IN LABOR ECONOMICS

Clark's shift toward conservatism was undoubtedly influenced by his theoretical work on labor economics, specifically, his marginal productivity thesis. He developed this thesis when he was seeking to resolve a troublesome problem in economics: How does one allocate, among two or more cooperating inputs, the total product which they jointly produce? This joint-input problem had long been viewed as unsolvable, like deciding whether the father or mother was responsible for the baby. Indeed, Sir William Petty called labor the father of production and land the mother. Marx resolved the riddle by proclaiming that labor deserved the entire product, but this proved naive and unsatisfactory to the rest of the profession.

Building on the marginality concept of the Austrian economists, Clark

---

WHO DESERVES THE JOHN BATES CLARK MEDAL?

John Bates Clark was in more ways than one the grand old man of economics.
—Joseph Dorfman (1949: 205)

The John Bates Clark Medal is one of the most sought-after awards in economics, but to win it, an economist has to start publishing early. It's given only once every two years to the brightest, most prolific, American economist under the age of forty.

The first award was presented in 1947, the one-hundredth anniversary of the birth of John Bates Clark. The winner was Paul A. Samuelson, the *wunderkind* professor at MIT and leader of the new Keynesian school in the United States. Other distinguished recipients include Milton Friedman, James Tobin, Kenneth Arrow, Robert Solow, Gary Becker, Martin Feldstein, Joseph Stiglitz, Paul Krugman, Lawrence Summers, and Steve Levitt. Many others have also received the Nobel Prize in economics.

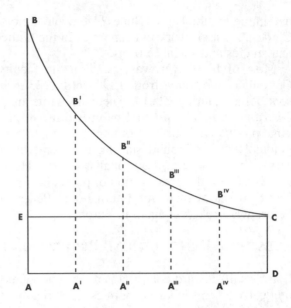

The average wage level (*DC*) is determined by the marginal product (*AB*).
The firm keeps adding workers until the marginal product equals the wage.

Figure 9.2
Clark's Marginal Theory of Wages
Source: Clark (1965: 198).

pioneered the concept that each input contributed its marginal product. Essentially, he argued that under competitive conditions, each factor of production—land, labor, and capital—is paid according to the "value added" to the total revenue of the product, or its marginal product. Clark called his theory of competitive distribution a "natural law" that was "just" (Clark 1965: v). "In other words, free competition tends to give to labor what labor creates, to capitalists what capital creates, and to entrepreneurs what the coordinating function creates" (1965: 3).

Figure 9.2 reproduces Clark's diagram showing how wages are equal to the marginal product of the last worker added to the labor force. Thus, if workers become more productive and add greater value to the company's long-term profitability, their wages will tend to rise. If wages rise in one industry, competition will force other employers to raise their wages, and thus "wages tend to equal the product of marginal labor," or what the last worker is paid (Clark 1965: 106).

MISES'S BUTLER: MARGINAL PRODUCTIVITY RAISES ALL WAGES

Austrian economist Ludwig von Mises carried Clark's productivity theory further by demonstrating that increased labor productivity benefits marginal workers. Real wages have not only risen for those with higher productivity, but also those whose productivity has remained the same. Mises used the example of a butler to make his point.

> A butler waits at the table of the British prime minister in the same way in which once butlers served Pitt and Palmerston. In agriculture some kinds of work are still performed with the same tools in the same way in which they were performed centuries ago. Yet the wage rates earned by all such workers are today much higher than they were in the past. They are higher because they are determined by the marginal productivity of labor. The employer of a butler withholds this man from employment in a factory and must therefore pay the equivalent of the increase in output which the additional employment of one man in a factory would bring about. It is not any merit on the part of the butler that causes this rise in his wages, but the fact that the increase in capital invested surpasses the increase in the number of hands. (Mises 1972: 88–89)

Clark's and Mises's marginal productivity theory undercut the socialist/Marxist exploitation argument in two ways. First, Clark's marginal productivity theory proved that, under competition, most workers are likely to be paid what they contribute to society. And second, workers who show no productivity gains could also benefit from the marginal productivity of workers in general.

CLARK DEFENDS THE STATUS QUO

Clark used his marginal productivity theory to justify the wage rates in the United States and criticized labor unions for trying to raise rates above this "natural law." For example, although he supported the Knights of Labor, Clark advocated compulsory arbitration to end long labor disputes, believing that striking workers should be paid wages prevailing in comparable labor markets elsewhere (Dewey 1987: 430). On the other hand, Clark opposed the power of monopolies and big business that attempted to exploit workers by forcing wages below labor's marginal product. A competitive environment in both labor and industry was essential to a legitimate wage and social justice. In fact, in 1914, Clark wrote a book on the subject entitled, *Social Justice Without Socialism.*

Clark's prescriptive economics was heavily criticized by fellow economists who made the allegation that "neoclassical economics was essentially an apologetic for the existing economic order" (Stigler 1941: 297). Thorstein Veblen, in particular, used Clark as a foil in his diatribes against the prevailing economic system (see chapter 10). Yet Clark's application of the marginality principle to labor had its impact. Even Marxists felt compelled to alter their extreme view of exploitation based on the labor theory of value. No longer could they demand that workers be paid "the whole produce of their labor." Now employees were exploited only if they received wages less than the value of the marginal physical product of labor (Sweezy 1942: 6).

A CHRISTIAN SOCIALIST ESTABLISHES THE AEA: FREE-MARKET ECONOMISTS REFUSE TO JOIN!

We regard the State as an agency whose positive assistance is one of the indispensable conditions of human progress.
—AEA Statement of Principles (1885)

I did have to fight and the fight at times was bitter.
—Richard T. Ely (1936: 145)

Photograph 9.3
Richard Theodore Ely
(1854–1943)
"This short, pink-cheeked, boyish-faced man influenced two generations of economists."
Courtesy of Mark Blaug.

What?! The American Economic Association, the world's largest and most prestigious organization of professional economists, a creation of socialist reformers?

Indeed, the architect of the AEA in 1885 was Richard T. Ely, a radical professor at Johns Hopkins University who was an outspoken critic of laissez-faire classical economics and a passionate promoter of organized labor. Ely's prospectus boldly declared, "the doctrine of laissez faire is unsafe in politics and unsound in morals" (Dorfman 1949: 206). His socialist sympathies created such strong dissension in the economics profession that many economists, especially followers of social Darwinist William Graham Sumner at Yale and Harvard, refused to join the AEA. Ely dropped the partisan language from the AEA statement of principles and eventually had to resign as first secretary of the AEA in 1892 to resolve the internal strife. Francis A. Walker, president of MIT and a former Civil War general, also resigned as first president of the AEA for the same reasons. (However, Sumner never did join.)

Richard T. Ely (1854–1943) led a fascinating life. Born in upstate New York, he graduated from Columbia College, and, like John Bates Clark, went to Germany to study under Karl Knies of the German historical school, where he became a socialist radical and labor supporter. Upon returning to the United States, he joined together with several like-minded reformers to establish the AEA. Initially, the AEA was not simply a professional association, but imitated the German Union for Social Policy by advocating state activism and Christian socialism. Twenty of the first fifty to join the AEA were former or practicing ministers. But protests from free-market economists forced Ely to resign, and from that time forward the AEA acquired its position of academic neutrality. Membership rapidly increased and today is over 25,000.

In 1892, Ely became a professor at the University of Wisconsin, where he grew increasingly conservative. Nevertheless, he was denounced for preaching in favor of

(continued)

labor strikes and socialism, and harboring a union agitator from outside the state. University officials ordered an investigation to determine if he were unfit to hold his post. During the inquiry, he denied the charges as "base and cruel calumnies." "I have maintained," he said, "that even could socialism be organized and put in operation it would stop progress and overthrow our civilization" (Dorfman 1949: 257). Weeks later, the university exonerated him in defense of academic freedom.

Ely came back to the AEA to serve as its president from 1900 to 1902. He became one of the founders of the progressive movement in Wisconsin, and became increasingly active in religious reform organizations. He also concentrated on labor and land economics at the economics department at the University of Wisconsin, themes that are still popular there. He died in 1943, a few years after writing his autobiography, *Ground Under Our Feet* (1938). Each year at the annual AEA meeting the feature lecture is delivered in Ely's name.

"THE GRAND OLD MAN OF ECONOMICS"

Economic historian Leonard J. Arrington recorded this description of an older, gentler Ely at the AEA meetings in Philadelphia in 1939:

> It was my great fortune to meet there that grand old man of economics, then in his eighty-fifth year, Richard T. Ely. He had founded the American Economic Association in 1885. . . . [A]rriving early at that session [were] Ely, his young second wife, and two children, the youngest of whom was only five years old. I took advantage of the opportunity and sat next to him and felt it a gift of heaven that I could talk with this short, pink cheeked, boyish-faced man, who had influenced two generations of economists and economic policy. Economics, he had written, should serve as an ethical guide to marketplace economies. People, not mechanical "laws of the market," should be the focus of the discipline. . . .
>
> When Ely learned I was from an Idaho farm, he talked about irrigation and the West. Guessing that I was a Mormon . . . he reminded me that he had written a complimentary essay on the Mormons that was published in *Harper's Monthly Magazine* in 1903—the first published treatment of Mormonism by an economist. . . . Ely firmly believed that religion was and should continue to be a major force in economic development. (Arrington 1998: 26)

VESTIGES OF SOCIALISM AT THE AEA?

The AEA's membership program still contains elements of Ely's influence. The AEA engages in a form of income equalization via price discrimination in membership dues. Members with annual incomes of $50,000 or less pay annual membership dues of $64 a year. For those who earn between $50,000 and $66,000, annual dues are $77. Those who earn more than $66,000 pay $90 a year. Students pay only $32 a year.

It might be interesting to see how many economists "cheat" by claiming a lower income category to save money on subscriptions to AEA publications. Would the *American Economic Review* dare publish such information?

AUSTRIAN CAPITAL THEORY COMES TO AMERICA

So far we have discussed land and labor in American economic thought. What about capital, the third factor of production, and the critical role of interest rates in the capital markets? Both John Bates Clark and Frank A. Fetter addressed the importance of capital and interest, primarily in relation to the breakthrough work of the Austrians.

In chapter 7, we discussed the contributions of the Austrians. Basically, Menger and Böhm-Bawerk rejected the simple two-sector classical model, which divided all goods into either consumer goods or capital goods. Rather, they envisioned consumer and capital goods as an *array* of goods—of the first order (consumer goods), second order (wholesale goods), third order (manufacturing goods), and fourth order (raw commodities). In essence, the Austrians stressed that all consumer and capital goods go through a series of stages of production, from unfinished, unusable products to finished, usable consumer and capital goods.

Here's how the Austrians viewed economic growth and the role of capital and interest rates: If society is to progress materially, individuals must work together to improve the production process of these goods and services—by saving and investing more in "roundabout" processes, by advancing technology, by workers becoming more knowledgeable and more productive. This is where interest rates come into play. If people saved and invested more, interest rates could be reduced, which would stimulate more investment and technology, the key to economic progress. But the savings and capital investment must be genuine—not created through artificial means by the state. This was the Austrian message, and Menger, Böhm-Bawerk, and Wieser were the messengers.

CLARK AND FETTER ARGUE OVER CAPITAL AND INTEREST

Clark saw things differently. In a series of debates in economics journals at the turn of the century, Clark argued with Böhm-Bawerk, saying that investment capital is a "permanent fund," like a big reservoir, where "the water that at this moment flows into one end of the pond causes an overflow from the other end" (Clark 1965 [1899]: 313).

Clark believed that interest rates were related to the size of the capital stock. "Make the social fund larger, and you make the rate of interest smaller," he declared (Clark 1895: 277).

Frank A. Fetter (1863–1949), economics professor at Cornell and Princeton, disagreed. If interest rates varied according to the size of the investment capital fund, as Clark contended, countries such as the United States would always have lower interest rates than Switzerland or Singapore. Obviously, there must be other factors influencing the rate of interest. For Fetter, that other factor was *time preference*. Fetter was the

premier defender of the Austrian theory of
capital and interest rates in the United States.

Fetter was born in rural Indiana in 1863.
He went to the state university, but family
financial problems forced him to temporarily
drop out of college, and he went into business operating a large bookstore in his native
town of Peru, Indiana.

After business hours Fetter read voraciously, and was deeply moved by Henry
George's *Progress and Poverty*. The book
caused him to make economics his life work.
After obtaining a B.A. from the University
of Indiana and an M.A. from Cornell
University, Fetter, like Clark and Ely, traveled to Europe and received a Ph.D. in
Germany in 1894. But he took more of a
liking to the Austrian than to the German his-

Photograph 9.4
Frank A. Fetter (1863–1949)
The Austrian American.
Courtesy of Mark Blaug.

torians, and became the leading exponent in the United States of
"Austrian" economics, and even received the Carl Menger Medal in 1927.
He taught successively at Indiana, Stanford, Cornell, and finally Princeton
(from 1911 to 1930), and was named president of the American Economic
Association in 1912. He died in 1949 at the age of eighty-six.

FETTER'S PIONEERING CONTRIBUTION:
TIME-PREFERENCE THEORY OF INTEREST

Fetter developed a "psychological" approach to explaining the trend in
interest rates. He called it "time preference." Time preference means that
individuals prefer present goods over future goods. Technically, he defined
time preference as an "index of the ratio inherent in the equilibrium of psychological forces, desires for present and future incomes" (Dorfman 1949:
363). Fetter was not always a clear writer. To understand what he meant,
look at it this way: If you could receive a gift of $10,000 now or $10,000
next year, which would you choose? Obviously, you'd take $10,000 now.
But what if you were offered either $10,000 now or $20,000 a year from
now? Clearly, there's a trade-off. Your decision depends on your time preference—how much do you value taking the money now versus receiving
twice that amount a year later?

In order to compensate an individual's time preference, lenders pay
savers a premium, or an annual rate of interest. There are of course many
interest rates, depending on the degree of risk and maturity of loan.
(Menger emphasized this point.) But Fetter argued that the market rate of
interest on loans is a reflection of a general time preference in the
economy—how much the public is willing to save at what interest rate.

Why do interest rates rise during war? Fetter argued because there is a sharp increase in the rate of time preference in the demand for present goods immediately usable for war purposes. Why do interest rates rise in times of inflation? Because people raise their time preference, increasing their purchase of goods now rather than waiting until later when prices are expected to be much higher. In the same way, interest rates tend to rise during a boom and fall during a recession due to expected changes in price levels. Why are interest rates lower in country A than in country B? Fetter argued that country A has a lower time preference and a greater propensity to save; country B saves less and must suffer higher interest rates to attract investment capital.

Fetter did not agree with everything the Austrians preached. For example, he disagreed with Böhm-Bawerk, who argued that interest rates were also influenced by the productivity of capital. Fetter's theory of interest laid exclusive emphasis on time preference, and he stated that "present goods are, as a rule, worth more than future goods" (Fetter 1977: 173). Yet Böhm-Bawerk's argument should not be dismissed entirely. It is quite probable that productivity and economic growth do have an indirect effect on interest rates. In developing countries intent on high capital-intensive growth, interest rates are often very high in order to attract much-needed domestic and foreign investment. Then, as nations become more developed and reach a high standard of living, interest rates often decline. Why? Because nations with higher income and living standards tend to have higher rates of saving, and a steady increase in the supply of savings causes interest rates to fall (assuming the demand for capital remains constant). Even Fetter admitted, according to Murray Rothbard, that "as the economy

---

AMERICANS MAKE ANOTHER PIONEERING BREAKTHROUGH: THE WORLD'S NUMBER 1 ECONOMIC RESEARCH CENTER

What we customarily called our "social sciences" must be made both more social and more scientific.
—Wesley C. Mitchell (1953: 11)

Today the National Bureau of Economic Research (NBER), under the able direction of Harvard's Martin Feldstein, publishes the best empirical research coming from more than 500 university professors. NBER sounds like a government agency, but isn't—it's a "private, nonprofit, nonpartisan research organization" founded in New York by the American business community in January 1920. (Today it's located in Cambridge, Massachusetts.) The research institute struggled financially in the 1920s and 1930s, but with the help of the Rockefeller Foundation, business groups, and government grants, has managed to survive and prosper during the postwar era.

(continued)

NBER FOUNDED IN A FRAY BETWEEN A SOCIALIST AND A CONSERVATIVE BUSINESSMAN

The idea behind an objective research organization came out of a heated argument between Nahum I. Stone, a radical socialist who had translated Marx's *Critique of Political Economy*, and Malcolm Rorty, a conservative engineer working for AT&T. Stone advocated a minimum wage law, Rorty opposed it. During the debate, the question arose regarding the distribution of income between workers and landlords. Stone and Rorty could agree on only one thing: the desperate need for an unbiased research organization to settle questions of fact. Stone suggested a research group representing every school of economics from extreme conservative to extreme radical and from various organized interests in society, including labor unions, agriculture, and business. Following World War I, Rorty went out and put together a group that eventually became the National Bureau of Economic Research.

NBER'S FIRST DIRECTOR: A GENTLEMAN, SCHOLAR, AND ATHLETE

NBER's first director fit the bill perfectly. He was Columbia professor **Wesley C. Mitchell (1874–1948)**, the economist everyone respected and liked, from Thorstein Veblen on one extreme to Milton Friedman on the other. Compared to the bizarre nature of most characters in this book, Mitchell looks like a saint. He was a Christian man who loved poetry and science; he was happily married to another college professor, and they had four delightful children and many grandchildren; he enjoyed sports all his life; and he was a master handyman and cabinet maker. He had a heart murmur. In the late 1890s, his doctor at the University of Chicago (where he got his B.A. and Ph.D. degrees) told him he would live only a year, but Mitchell turned out to have a wonderfully healthy life until he died in 1948 (of a heart attack). He was a social reformer in defense of many causes, including women's suffrage, racial equality, education, and assisting refugees. For a while he taught carpentry to a class of youngsters.

Photograph 9.5
Wesley Clair Mitchell
(1874–1948)
The man with no theory.
Courtesy of National Bureau of
Economic Research.

Arthur Burns, who took his place as director of NBER, wrote of his idyllic lifestyle: "Mitchell's life was serene, unhurried, well balanced. He found time for relaxation as well as work, read the classics extensively without neglecting detective stories, freely exercised his skill at golf and cabinet-making, loved gay repartee at the dinner table, and always had an apt remark or verse to enliven conversation" (Burns 1952: 51).

(continued)

MITCHELL GOES BY FOUR NAMES!

Digging deeper, we discover Mitchell had a few strange idiosyncrasies. He used tobacco (smoked a pipe) with gusto because Irving Fisher banned it. He entertained Veblen because he offended so many conservatives. A rigid time keeper, Mitchell kept a daily diary from 1905 to 1948, "So that I can see each day if I have wasted my time and not do it again!" (Burns 1952: 74). He had three nicknames: His mother called him Bonnie, his wife called him Robin, his friends called him Clair, and he signed his name professionally Wesley C. Mitchell.

Some mild critics said the initial "C." stood for "compromise." A famous economist (not identified) commented, "Mitchell saw a grain of truth in all things erroneous." Mitchell humorously replied, "There's a grain of truth in *that!*" (Burns 1952: 81). The moderate Mitchell was tolerant to a fault and hated divisiveness in academia and research. Joseph Dorfman, a colleague at Columbia, said Mitchell never spoke unkind words about another worker. At NBER, his vision was that intelligent men of all philosophies, whether socialists or anarchists, could "work harmoniously" on objective data so that reason could triumph over passion (Burns 1952: 31).

A TENACIOUS INVESTIGATOR

Mitchell wrote an exhaustive work entitled *Business Cycles* (1913), which formed the basis of his scrupulously conducted scientific research at NBER. According to Milton Friedman, Mitchell's "great genius" was his ability to tie together an enormous mass of data in an "orderly, lucid, and meaningful account" (Burns 1952: 243).

Mitchell gathered around him some remarkable researchers, including Simon Kuznets, Arthur F. Burns, Geoffrey Moore, and Milton Friedman, and insisted on the highest standards of meticulous research. My favorite of these researchers is Frederick C. Mills, who pioneered an "Austrian" time-structural model of the economy (see chapter 12 on Mises for more details). Prior to Mills's work, the NBER focused almost entirely on general price indices with little or no discussion of changes in price margins between raw commodities, producers' goods, and wholesale and retail markets. Mills gathered and analyzed separate price indices at each stage of production and then demonstrated that relative price changes between these stages were critically important in a business cycle. He noted that prices were more volatile in stages further away from the final consumer or retail stage, thus significantly altering the relative profit margins and production decisions between stages during a recession or recovery. *Prices in Recession and Recovery* (1936) applied this pioneering approach during the boom-bust phase of the U.S. economy between 1920 and 1936 (Skousen 1990: 58–60).

THE MAN WITH NO THEORY

If Mitchell could be faulted, it was for his lack of theory. In his lifelong work on business cycles, he made every effort to hide his beliefs and warned repeatedly that NBER work was to be devoid of personal biases. He was suspicious of deductive reasoning, and firmly believed that all theories needed to be tested, "checked out and corrected by inductive investigation" (Mitchell 1953: 11). Theories cannot be ignored, of course, but NBER, the ultimate "fact-finding" agency, was determined to test their validity.

For his statistical work the AEA presented Mitchell with the first Francis A. Walker Award in 1947. He died ten months later.

advances and more present goods are produced, the preference for present goods is lowered, and the interest rate therefore may be expected to fall" (Fetter 1977: 16). Thus, economic growth and productivity influence *indirectly* the degree of time preference and interest rates.

SUMMARY: ECONOMICS PROGRESSES WITH THE ECONOMY

The work of Marshall and his American counterparts went a long way toward formalizing the new science of neoclassical economics. The American economists, especially John Bates Clark and Frank A. Fetter, extended the marginalist revolution to the factors of production and the issue of income distribution.

With the "neoclassical" structure close to completion, critics from the halls of academia came forth to gauge the meaning of the new capitalist model. Analysis would come from both sides of the Atlantic Ocean, first from a heretical economist in the United States named Thorstein Veblen, and then from a German economist named Max Weber. Both would become famous in the new field known as sociology and would help establish a whole new school in economics known as the institutional school. They are the subject of chapter 10.

REFERENCES

Andelson, Robert V. 1992. "Henry George and the Reconstruction of Capitalism." *Economic Education Bulletin* 22: 9 (September), 1–4. Great Barrington, MA: American Institute for Economic Research.

Arrington, Leonard J. 1998, *Adventures of a Church Historian.* Urbana: University of Illinois Press.

Burns, Arthur F., ed. 1952. *Wesley Clair Mitchell: The Economic Scientist.* New York: National Bureau of Economic Research.

Clark, John Bates. 1895. "The Origin of Interest." *Quarterly Journal of Economics* 9 (April), 257–78.

———. 1914. *Social Justice Without Socialism.* Boston: Houghton Mifflin.

———. 1965 [1899]. *The Distribution of Wealth.* New York: Augustus M. Kelley.

Dewey, Donald. 1987. "John Bates Clark." In *The New Palgrave: A Dictionary of Economics*, vol. 1, 428–31, London: Macmillan.

Dorfman, Joseph. 1949. *The Economic Mind in American Civilization, 1865–1918,* vol. 3. New York: Viking Press.

Ely, Richard T. 1936. "The Founding and Early History of the American Economic Association." *American Economic Review* 26 (March), 141–50.

———. 1938. *Ground Under Our Feet: An Autobiography.* New York: Macmillan.

Fetter, Frank A. 1977. *Capital, Interest, and Rent,* ed. Murray N. Rothbard. Kansas City: Sheed, Andrews and McMeel.

Foldvary, Fred. 2005. "Geo-Rent: A Plea to Public Economists." *Econ Journal Watch* 2: 1 (April), 106–32.

Friedman, Milton. 1978. "An Interview with Milton Friedman." *Human Events* 38 [46] (November 18).

Gaffney, Mason and Fred Harrison, 1994. *The Corruption of Economics.* London: Shepheard-Walwyn.

George, Henry. 1942 [1879]. *Progress and Poverty*. New York: Robert Schalkenbach Foundation.

Groenewegen, Peter. 1995. *A Soaring Eagle: Alfred Marshall, 1842–1924*. Cheltenham, UK: Edward Elgar.

Hill, Malcolm. 1997. *The Man Who Said NO! The Life of Henry George*. London: Othila.

Marx, Karl. 1911. *A Contribution to the Critique of Political Economy*. Chicago: Charles Kerr.

Mills, Frederick C. 1936. *Prices in Recession and Recovery*. New York: National Bureau of Economic Research.

Mises, Ludwig von. 1972. *The Anti-Capitalist Mentality*. Spring Hill, PA: Libertarian Press.

Mitchell, Lucy Sprague. 1953. *Two Lives: The Story of Wesley Clair Mitchell and Myself*. New York: Simon & Schuster.

Mitchell, Wesley C. 1913. *Business Cycles*. Berkeley: University of California Press.

Rothbard, Murray N. 1970. *Power and Market: Government and the Economy*. Menlo Park, CA: Institute for Humane Studies.

Samuelson, Paul A., and William D. Nordhaus. 1998. *Economics*, 16th ed. New York: McGraw-Hill.

Skousen, Mark. 1990. *The Structure of Production*. New York: New York University Press.

Stigler, George. 1941. *Production and Distribution Theories*. New York: Macmillan.

Sweezy, Paul M. 1942. *The Theory of Capitalist Development*. New York: Modern Reader.

Tocqueville, Alexis de. 1988 [1848]. *Democracy in America*. New York: Harper Perennial.

10

THE CONSPICUOUS VEBLEN VERSUS THE PROTESTING WEBER: TWO CRITICS DEBATE THE MEANING OF CAPITALISM

Thorstein Veblen is the most creative mind American social thought has produced.

—Max Lerner (Diggins 1999: 214)

There has been the work of one man whom I have greatly admired. If I were to start out again, I would build upon his ideas. I am referring, of course, to Max Weber.

—Frank Knight (Swedberg 1998: 205)

By the turn of the twentieth century, a whole new model of the economy had been fashioned, thanks to the marginalist revolution in Europe and the United States. Adam Smith and the classical economists had provided the foundation, but it took another generation of economists to finish the job. It was now time to stand back and take a look at this brand-new model of modern capitalism.

Critics such as Thomas Carlyle and Karl Marx had taken potshots at the house that Adam Smith built, but that was before the marginalist revolution. It was time to take a second look, and it fell upon the shoulders of two social economists—today they are known as sociologists—to examine in detail the meaning of the new structure. They are the American Thorstein Veblen and the German Max Weber.

♪ **Music selection for this chapter: Claude Debussy, "Dialogue of the Wind and the Sea," from *La Mer***

THORSTEIN VEBLEN: VOICE OF DISSENT

First, let's discuss Veblen. The principal faultfinder and censor of the new theoretical capitalism was **Thorstein Bunde Veblen (1857–1929)**. Having taught at ten institutions, including Chicago and Stanford, he had little use for the rational-abstract-deductive approach of the neoclassical model. In fact, he never developed a formal model. Instead, he studied the institutional framework of the capitalist system, and how it evolved and impinged on people's lives and culture. In doing so, he established the American school of institutional economics, which has survived over the years through Wesley Mitchell, John R. Commons, and John Kenneth Galbraith. In many ways, Veblen was more a sociologist than an economist. He was, above all, a critic of the capitalist system rather than a creator of a new theory.

THE LIFE OF VEBLEN, THE OSCAR WILDE OF ECONOMICS

Veblen's bizarre life is in many ways more interesting than the books he wrote. No other economist comes close to him in terms of wacky, abnormal behavior. He was managing editor of the prestigious *Journal of Political Economy* at Chicago, yet was the only man who was permitted to lecture on socialism at the University of Chicago. He had a Ph.D. in philosophy from Yale, yet often dressed like a tramp, wearing corduroys and a coonskin cap. He taught at Stanford University, yet was dismissed for having an

Photograph 10.1
Thorstein Veblen (1857–1929)
"Tall, muscular and darkly handsome" and "a disturber of the intellectual peace."
Courtesy of Brown Brothers.

affair. He was considered a brilliant eccentric, a sloppy dresser, and a notorious womanizer.

Veblen attended, taught, and lectured at more higher institutions than any other economist:

1. Carleton College (a religious institution in Northfield, Minnesota)
2. Monona Academy (Monona, Wisconsin)
3. Johns Hopkins University (Baltimore, Maryland)
4. Yale College (New Haven, Connecticut)
5. Cornell College (Ithaca, New York)
6. University of Chicago (Chicago, Illinois)
7. Harvard College (Cambridge, Massachusetts) (lectures only)
8. Stanford University (Stanford, California)
9. University of Missouri (Columbia, Missouri)
10. New School for Social Research (New York, New York)

The sixth child of first-generation Norwegian immigrants, Thorstein Veblen grew up on a farm in Wisconsin speaking only Norwegian. When he was seven, his family moved to Minnesota. He attended Carleton College in Northfield, Minnesota, where he studied under John Bates Clark. Clark considered Thorstein an acute student, despite Veblen's reputation as a "disturber of the intellectual peace" who wrote papers about cannibals and drunkards, and violated the strict rules of student behavior (Jorgensen 1999: 20–22). Clark's lifelong admiration of Veblen is even more ironic given that Veblen reserved his most scathing attacks for neoclassical economics, a discipline that Clark helped establish.

Women would not let Veblen alone, especially after he became famous as the author of *The Theory of the Leisure Class* (1994 [1899]). This attraction is rather surprising given that Veblen was a misfit who never made his bed, seldom brushed his teeth, and was a heavy smoker. Somehow they found him brilliant, dangerous, and shocking. He was described as "tall, muscular and darkly handsome" (Jorgensen 1999: 4). He, in turn, loved women, and was considered one of the foremost "pro-feminists" of the nineteenth century. He was married twice, first to Ellen Rolfe while attending Carleton, and second to "Babe" Bevans, who was twenty years his junior. He also had a reputation as a sexual swashbuckler, having many affairs with students and professors' wives. It is one reason he never stayed long in one institution; he was fired from Chicago and Stanford for his sexual escapades.

After Carleton, he spent a term at Johns Hopkins University, and then transferred to Yale, where he obtained a Ph.D. in philosophy. But in the new arena of marginalism, the new doctor of philosophy found himself marginal to the world, unable to find a job from 1884 to 1891. One reason was his skepticism about religion in an era when most institutions were church affiliated. Another factor was his health; he came down with malaria. During this time, he lived off his family and then off his wife's family. His brother commented, "He read and loafed, and the next day he loafed and read" (Heilbroner 1992: 214).

Veblen's professional break came when he accepted a fellowship at Cornell University and befriended J. Laurence Laughlin. When Laughlin landed the job of chairman at John D. Rockefeller's newly established University of Chicago, Laughlin insisted on bringing Veblen along.

Veblen was never happy living in one place for long, however, and Chicago was no exception. For him, the windy city was too big, too unruly, too ugly. He considered himself smarter than the department chairman, who earned $7,500 a year. Veblen earned only $1,500.

VEBLEN GIVES ONLY CS!

Veblen taught a course on socialism, but his methods of teaching were eccentric. Aspirants to Phi Beta Kappa were discouraged, for he refused to give a grade higher than a C. A student described him as "an exceedingly queer fish. He never gave us an examination and at the end of the course he would say that with our permission he would register 'C' grade for each of us to conform to the necessary ritual of university life. . . . Very commonly with his cheek in his hand, or in some such position, he talked in a low, placid monotone, in itself a most uninteresting delivery and manner of conducting the class" (Dorfman 1934: 248–49). Another student at Chicago described Veblen as a dark character, shabbily dressed, appearing as if he hadn't slept the night before and speaking with mordant sarcasm: "A sardonic smile twisted his lips, blue devils leaped into his eyes" (Jorgensen 1999: 7).

VEBLEN'S *THEORY OF THE LEISURE CLASS*

While at Chicago, at the age of forty-two, Veblen wrote his bestseller, *The Theory of the Leisure Class.* First published in 1899, it was meant to be a social satire of the leisure classes of *fin-de-siècle* America. Using no notes or research, he had to put up a guarantee with the publisher against any loss. He once said that his ideas came from his father, whom he regarded as a deep thinker, even though the elder Veblen signed his name X (Jorgensen 1999: 9–10).

REACTION TO *LEISURE*

Reaction to *Leisure* was mixed. Many economists did not take it seriously, denouncing Veblen for sloppy scholarship, ill intentions, and unsupported evidence. His writing style was obtuse. One Chicago contemporary said, "I congratulated him and asked if he had thought of having it translated into English." But another reviewer said, "like some wine, [it] is strange, if not distasteful, to the beginner, but once familiar, it is heady, bitter and delightful" (Jorgensen 1999: 73–74).

MENCKEN'S VERBOSE CRITIQUE OF THE VERBOSE VEBLEN!

*To say what might have been said on a postage stamp he took
more than a page in his book.*

—H.L. Mencken (1982: 271)

H.L. Mencken, the *Baltimore Sun*'s famed social critic, did not think much of the "preposterous" Veblen. In 1919, he became distressed by the proliferation of Veblen books, Veblen pamphlets, Veblen clubs, and even Veblen girls. Mencken reviewed *The Theory of the Leisure Class*, complaining of Veblen's "incomprehensible syllogisms, . . . the learned gentleman's long, tortuous and . . . intolerably flapdoodlish phrases" (1982: 265–66). Mencken painted Veblen with his own brush, using the same outlandish verbosity to demonstrate Veblen's excesses.

Veblen wrote: "If we are getting restless under the taxonomy of a monocotyledonous wage doctrine and a cryptogamic theory of interest, with involute, loculicidal, tomentous, and moniliform variants, what is the cytoplasm, centrosome, or karyokinetic process to which we may turn, and in which we may find surcease from the metaphysics of normality and controlling principles?" (Dorfman 1934: 103).

Mencken responded: "It one tunneled under his great moraines and stalagmites of words, dug down into his vast kitchen-midden of discordant and raucous polysyllables, blew up the hard, thick shell of his almost theological manner, what one found in his discourse was chiefly a mass of platitudes—the self-evident made horrifying, the obvious in terms of the staggering" (1982: 269).

Still kicking, Mencken called Veblen's *Higher Learning in America* "clumsy, affected, opaque, bombastic, windy, empty." Furthermore, it was "loose, flabby, cocksure and preposterous thinking" (1982: 272).

Mencken reported that Veblen was "greatly upset" by his attacks, which "made him despair of the Republic" (1982: 265).

MARITAL TROUBLES AT STANFORD

In 1906, Thorstein Veblen and his wife Ellen moved to California and he began to teach at Stanford University, but trouble began almost immediately when the wild, avant-garde "Babe" Bevans, a married woman who had become his mistress, moved next door to do graduate work at the University of California at Berkeley. Ellen was not amused when Babe sent daily letters arguing that a loveless marriage was no marriage at all and demanding that Ellen give up Thorstein (Jorgensen 1999: 114–15).

Meanwhile, Veblen taught a course on socialism, similar to the one he taught at Chicago. One student wrote, "The first time I saw him ambling along the Quad with a slouch hat pulled down over his brow, with coat and trousers 'hanging'; with untrimmed hair and moustache creating a general unkempt appearance, I thought he was a tramp" (Dorfman 1934: 274). Despite his bohemian lifestyle, his classes were described as "dry" and "over the head" of most students.

The issue of Veblen's affair with Babe came to a head in late 1909 after Ellen sent letters and much evidence of her husband's clandestine activities to David Starr Jordan, the president of Stanford. Veblen was fired.

If Ellen's intention was to regain Veblen's affections, it was a pyrrhic victory. Thorstein immediately left California to live with Babe in a remote mountainous region of Northern Idaho. Appropriately, the place was called "Nowhere." Arriving at Christmastime, he almost died of pneumonia, but was nursed back to health by his devoted Babe.

Colleagues at Stanford and other colleges around the country rallied around Veblen to get him appointed a professorship at the University of Missouri. Stanford's Allyn Young called Veblen "the most gifted man whom I have ever known," and Harvard's Frank Taussig joined the chorus by stating, "Veblen came as near to being a genius as any economist we have" (Jorgensen 1999: 134). In early 1911, he began teaching in Columbia, Missouri, but his condition was poor. Students reported he was skinny and emaciated, his skin wrinkled, but faculty and students alike regarded the author of *Theory of the Leisure Class* with awe. One colleague, admitting Veblen was not a good teacher, nevertheless reported: "I recall that I was once looking through the window of the heavy oak door to his classroom. Not a word was audible to me. You could not even see his lips move. The students sat like mummy figures out of the sleeping palace. But every few minutes all would be shaking in restrained laughter" (Jorgensen 1999: 137).

A year later, Veblen divorced Ellen and in 1914 he finally married Babe; he was fifty-seven and she was thirty-seven. But Babe said she felt like a "worn-out woman," having gone through a previous marriage with two children. She would have no more.

VEBLEN'S INCREDIBLE POWERS OF PROPHECY

Veblen's theories may have been suspect, but not his ability to look into the future. In 1911, he told a colleague at the University of Missouri (Jorgensen 1999: 149):

- A world war might break out soon in Europe.
- A Russian Revolution was "imminent" and would result in the loss of more blood than the French Revolution.
- If peace failed after the first world war, there might be a second world war in which Japan would team up with Germany and they would become war-mongering aggressors against the West.

Veblen wrote and published articles and books about some of his predictions. These publications include *Imperial Germany and the Industrial Revolution* (1915) and *An Inquiry into the Nature of Peace and the Terms of Its Perpetuation* (1917).

HERETIC IN NEW YORK CITY

In 1918, after a brief stint with the Food Administration in Washington, D.C., Veblen moved to New York to become an editor of the *Dial*, an avante-garde political magazine located in Greenwich Village, known at the time as a center for "century-old ideas for a better life. . . . Socialism, Communism, Syndicalism, Anarchism, Ibsenism, Nietzschianism, Shavianism, New Republicanism, Progressivism, Liberalism . . . Feminism, Vegetarianism, free-lovism, nudism" (Jorgensen 1999: 157).

Apparently the atmosphere brought out the radicalism in Veblen. In an essay entitled "Bolshevism Is a Menace—to Whom?" he wrote favorably about the Soviet experiment with communism, arguing that abolishing private gain in Russia would heighten efficiency. "The Bolshevik is the common man who has faced the question: What do I stand to lose? and has come away with the answer: Nothing" (Dorfman 1934: 421).

This version was not edited. Veblen refused to let *Dial* editors change a single word, including punctuation marks, in any of his writings. The editors asked Veblen to limit his articles to a thousand words, and he laughed; "it took him that much space to get started" (Dorfman 1934: 411–12). Not surprisingly, Veblen exasperated his editors.

VEBLEN SUPPORTERS ATTEMPT A "PALACE REVOLT" BY NOMINATING THEIR LEADER AS AEA PRESIDENT!

In 1924, Wesley Mitchell, founder of the prestigious National Bureau of Economic Research (NBER), and Paul H. Douglas, a Veblen enthusiast who later became a U.S. senator, tried to push through Thorstein Veblen's nomination as president of the American Economic Association (AEA). At first, they tried to make Veblen an "honorary" president, but the nominating committee failed to act. Then Mitchell, president of AEA at the time, appointed a new nominating committee consisting largely of Veblen's friends. After considerable in-fighting, in which Veblen was accused of being a sociologist instead of an economist, he was offered the job on condition that he join the AEA and that he give an acceptance speech. Veblen, an inveterate nonjoiner who dreaded public functions, turned down the post, saying, "It gave me great pleasure to refuse him. They didn't offer it to me when I needed it." His decision could also have been due to poor health. He was sixty-seven and would die five years later, in 1929 (Dorfman 1934: 491–92).

Veblen was famous for his extremely shy and taciturn personality. Colleagues, students, and visitors were put off by his apparent inability to carry on a conversation. He would be invited to dinner, and never say a word the entire evening. Once he attended a lecture by Jack London on socialism. Afterward, he was asked to make a comment, but said he had nothing to say. Upton Sinclair, an admirer, declared upon meeting him that "he was one of the most silent men I ever met. I do not think I ever met a man who would sit in a company and listen so long without ever speaking" (Dorfman 1934: 273, 423–24).

But, oh, how he could write! He wrote hundreds of articles and numerous books. A collection of essays from the *Dial* was compiled into *The Engineers and the Price System* (1921), a book that became all the rage after he died and the Great Depression ensued. (Albert Einstein was so convinced that he converted to socialism!) In one essay, Veblen wrote agreeably about the need for a "soviet of technicians," engineers who would seize control of national industry and abolish private rights. Essentially, the essay concluded that the nation would benefit by the overthrow of capitalism, to be replaced by a Soviet-style group of engineers (Dorfman 1934: 512–13).

Veblen became one of the founders of the experimental New School for Social Research in New York City, along with Charles Beard and Wesley Mitchell. Veblen taught there for several years (his topic: socialism!) but, according to one colleague who met with him for lunch, "Veblen's face throughout wore an expression of deep gloom, almost of despair. Nothing aroused him, or stirred more than a flicker of interest" (Jorgensen 1999: 164). He tired of teaching and in 1926 moved back to California.

His heart gave out in the summer of 1929, when he was seventy-two. Guido Marx, his colleague at Stanford and the New School for Social Research, described him in his later years: "If ever there lived a man at whose heart there was a snake constantly gnawing, Veblen was that man" (Jorgensen 1999: 182). But another biographer, Rick Tilman, commented upon his life: "Thorstein Veblen . . . was arguably the most original and penetrating economist and social critic that the United States has produced" (1992: ix).

WHERE IS VEBLEN'S TOMBSTONE?

Thorstein Veblen didn't have a cemetery plot because he was cremated. After he died of a heart attack on August 3, 1929, a penciled note was found in his bedroom. "It is also my wish, in case of death, to be cremated . . . as expeditiously and inexpensively as may be, without ritual or ceremony of any kind: that my ashes be thrown loose into the sea or in some sizeable stream running to the sea, that no tombstone, slab, epitaph, effigy, tablet, inscription or monument of any name or nature, be set in my memory . . . that no obituary, memorial, portrait or biography of me, nor any letters written to or by me be printed or published, or in any way reproduced, copied or circulated" (Dorfman 1934: 504).

Except for the cremating, none of his wishes were granted.

VEBLEN'S DARWINIAN VIEW OF THE WORLD

What was Thorstein Veblen's message to the world? Let's begin with his best known work, *The Theory of the Leisure Class*. Like many economists, Veblen was greatly influenced by Darwinian evolution. He saw industrial capitalism as a form of early "barbaric" evolution, like the ape. Imitating Proudhon's famous statement, "Property is theft," Veblen stated that private property was nothing more than "booty held as trophies of the successful raid" (Veblen 1994 [1899]: 27). Capitalists' pursuit of wealth, leisure, and the acquisition of goods in competition with their neighbors are part of the "predatory instinct" (page 29). A life of leisure has "much in common with the trophies of exploit" (page 44). Gambling and risk-taking reflect a "barbarian temperament" (pages 276, 295–96). Women are, like slaves, treated as property, to be dominated by the prowess of the owner (page 53). Patriotism and war are badges of "predatory, not of productive, employment" (page 40). According to Veblen, patriotism, which had its roots in early barbarism, was one of the strongest forces promoting war.

VEBLEN'S ATTACK ON SPORTS AND RELIGION

Even sports and religion are part of the animalistic spirit and support the barbarian's urge to dominate. "The addiction to sports in a peculiar . . . degree marks an arrested development of man's moral nature," he declared (Veblen 1994: 256). College sports were a "rival to the classics," he said (page 397). Religious ceremonies and shrines, temples, churches, and sacraments serve "no immediate material end." They are "items of conspicuous waste," declared Veblen, and are "a curtailment of the community's economic efficiency . . . [and] a lowering of the vitality of the community" (page 307). Veblen was highly critical of everything connected with the leisure class. Even the wearing of a cap and gown at graduation ceremonies was labeled "a notable element of conspicuous consumption" (page 372).

REPLACE CAPITALISM WITH WHAT?

Progress meant that primitive capitalism needed to be advanced toward a higher social level. War must be rejected (Veblen was a pacificist). Capitalism must be replaced by a form of workers' socialism and technocracy, a "soviet of technicians" (see the box on Taylorism on page 256). But he rejected Marxism as a philosophy. In a series of lectures in 1906 at Harvard, Veblen criticized Marxist doctrines for failing the evolutionary test. According to Veblen, many nations have collapsed without any class struggle. "The doctrine that progressive misery must effect a socialistic revolution [is] dubious," he declared. "The facts are not bearing . . . out [Marx's theories] on certain critical points" (Jorgensen 1999: 90).

TAYLOR'S "SCIENTIFIC MANAGEMENT": VEBLEN'S EMBODIMENT OF TECHNOLOGY?

In the past the man was first; in the future the system will be first.
— Frederick W. Taylor (Kanigel 1997: 438)

Frederick Taylor has probably had a greater effect on the private and public lives of the men and women of the twentieth century than any other single individual.
— Jeremy Rifkin (Kanigel 1997: 8)

Thorstein Veblen lauded industry and physical labor, but despised business and finance as "wasteful." Ideally, Veblen endorsed a "soviet of technicians," a society where engineers ran the world in pursuit of productivity, not profit. He had no use for men of finance.

Frederick Winslow Taylor (1856–1915), the father of business efficiency, was equally convinced that the solution to all social ills lay in "scientific management." Taylor's goal was to maximize worker efficiency through standardized factories, work schedules, and stopwatches. Known as "Speedy Taylor," he wrote his theories down, and they would eventually be published as *The Principles of Scientific Management* (1947). His theme: Regularity and order would lead to prosperity and efficiency. Out of Taylorism came Henry Ford's assembly line, Edwards Deming's quality techniques, and Peter Drucker's time management.

Taylorism was universally felt, especially in wartime. After all, was it not Taylor's efficiency methods that tripled U.S. output in World War II, made the trains run on time in Mussolini's Italy, and encouraged German precision engineering? Did not Lenin come under Taylor's spell in announcing the infamous Five Year Plans, adding, "We must introduce in Russia the study and teaching of the new Taylor System and its systematic trial and adaptation" (Kanigel 1997: 18)?

Photograph 10.2
Frederick Winslow Taylor
(1856–1915)
"How could they write whole libraries about some Kant and take only slight notice of Taylor, of this prophet who saw ten centuries ahead?"
(Kanigel 1997: 15)?
Courtesy of Frederick Winslow Taylor Collection, Stevens Institute of Technology.

ORGANIZED LABOR REBELS

But to organized labor, Taylorism was nothing more than a way to extract more sweat from labor. It turned workers into impersonal slaves and workaholics. His cruel system was driving men too hard too fast. "Scientific management was degrading. . . . In

(continued)

standing over you with a stopwatch, peering at you, measuring you, rating you, it treated you like a side of beef. You weren't supposed to think. Whatever workmanly pride you might once have possessed must be sacrificed on the altar of efficiency" (Kanigel 1997: 534).

Of course, Taylor saw it differently. He saw himself as the Great Harmonizer, achieving at once higher wages, higher profits, and lower prices. He envisioned Adam Smith's dream of universal opulence. One day, he wrote, "the luxuries of one generation [will become] the necessities of the next [and] the working people of our country will live as well and have the same luxuries, the same opportunities for leisure, for culture, and for education, as are now possessed by the average business man" (Kanigel 1997: 506–7). His revolution would bring about a thousand years of industrial peace.

Would Veblen endorse Taylorism as the best form of scientific engineering? I doubt it.

VEBLEN VERSUS MARX: DIFFERENT VERSIONS OF CLASS STRUGGLE

Veblen envisioned a different kind of class conflict than Marx. Rather than dividing the world into capitalists and proletariats, the haves and the have-nots, Veblen emphasized the alliance of the technicians and engineers, and the opposing businessmen, lawyers, clergymen, military, and gentlemen of leisure. He saw conflict between industry and business, between the blue-collar manual laborers and the white-collar workers, and between the leisure class and the working class.

The most famous chapter in *Theory of the Leisure Class* is chapter 4 on the "conspicuous consumption" of the wealthy class, which he describes cynically in great detail. "High-bred manners and ways of living are items of conformity to the norm of conspicuous leisure and conspicuous consumption," he wrote (1994 [1899]: 75). Veblen condemned the wealthy for purposely engaging in "wasteful" spending and ostentatious behavior, withdrawn from the industrial process. The rich achieve fame through the "expenditure of superfluities." He added, "In order to be reputable it must be wasteful" (96–100, 334). Moreover, "the leisure class is more favourable to a warlike attitude and animus than the industrial classes" (271). (Query: But who gets into barroom brawls?)

VEBLEN REJECTS ADAM SMITH

In highlighting the excesses of the "vulgar" class, Veblen expressed severe hostility to business culture, which he characterized as "waste, futility, and ferocity" (1994: 351). In his introduction to Veblen's book, Robert Lekachman wrote that Veblen had dismissed the commercial society as "a profoundly anti-evolutionary barrier to the full fruition of man's life-giving instinct of workmanship" (page x). Clearly, Veblen is gloomily antithetical to everything Adam Smith expressed about the benevolence of commercial society. Where Adam Smith saw order, harmony, benevolence, and rational self-interest, Veblen saw chaos, struggle, and greed. "Veblen was able to contradict flatly almost every premise and assumption upon which the ideology of capitalism rested" (Diggins 1999: 13).

Veblen ignored the benefits of wealth creation—the expansion of capital, the investment in new technology, the funding of higher education, and the philanthropic generosity of the business community. Rather, he lumped them all together in a disdainful "leisure class." Veblen saw absolutely no improvement in the standard of living of the common man during his lifetime (Dorfman 1934: 414). He cited approvingly the view first expressed by John Stuart Mill, who wrote in his *Principles of Political Economy* textbook, "Hitherto it is questionable if all the mechanical inventions yet made have lightened the day's toil of any human being" (Mill 1891 [1848]: 516). This same quote is found in Karl Marx's *Capital* (1976 [1860]: 492).

We can forgive Mill and Marx for making such uninformed statements in the mid-nineteenth century, but for Veblen it demonstrates astonishing ignorance of consumer statistics. By 1918, when Veblen made this statement, millions of American consumers were beginning to enjoy refrigeration, electricity, the telephone, running water, indoor toilets, and automobiles. No wonder Veblen left this life in a depressed state—his gloomy view of capitalism transpired during the Roaring Twenties, when American consumers were making tremendous advances.

IN DEFENSE OF THE RICH

Veblen's main failure was his inability to look beyond the frivolous tastes of the leisure class. More importantly, the existence of a growing wealthy class provides numerous benefits to the entire economy:

1. Wealthy people are the first to finance expensive new consumer products. They are the only ones who can afford to pay for automobiles, televisions, personal computers, cellphones, and other technological breakthroughs when they are first introduced as high-priced prototypes. The profits from the wealthy are used to expand operations and cut prices so that eventually everyone can afford them. As Andrew Carnegie stated, "Capitalism is about turning luxuries into necessities."
2. The wealthy class is the main source for investment capital. The rich provide the capital base for investing in new technologies, improved production processes, and job creation. Without the wealthy, there would be little or no surplus wealth for an expanding economy.
3. People in the higher income class use much of their surplus wealth to finance higher education, libraries, churches, galleries, and charitable organizations.

4. Today the wealthy pay most of the federal income taxes. For example, the top 1 percent of U.S. income earners pay 34 percent of federal income taxes.

Update
John Kenneth Galbraith: A Bourgeois Veblen

Veblen was a genius, the most penetrating, original, and uninhibited— indeed the greatest—source of social thought of [his] time.
—J.K. Galbraith (Diggins 1999: 217)

The closest thing to a modern-day Veblen is John Kenneth Galbraith (1908–2006). Both men came from hard-working immigrant families. Both wrote eloquently about the cultivated wastefulness of affluence, Veblen in *Theory of the Leisure Class*, Galbraith in *The Affluent Society* (1958). Both questioned the free-market premise of a "consumer sovereignty." Both favored a technocracy running the country—Veblen a "soviet of technicians," Galbraith a "technostructure" for a "new industrial state." And both came up with clever phrases to describe the capitalist society—Veblen with his "conspicuous consumption," and Galbraith with his "conventional wisdom" and "countervailing power."

Photograph 10.3
John Kenneth Galbraith and His Wife in India
"One of the most gifted writers . . . the most quotable critic of society."
Courtesy of Harvard University Archives.

(continued)

But the comparisons end there. Galbraith was a former ambassador to India under President John F. Kennedy and a much better writer. He was also extremely tall—six feet, eight inches—making him the world's tallest economist. Born in 1908 in Ontario, Canada, the son of Scotch Canadian immigrants, he earned a doctorate in agricultural economics at the University of California, Berkeley, in 1934. He spent his college years, during the Great Depression, reading Veblen and Marx. Upon traveling to Cambridge, England, he encountered Keynes's *General Theory*, which he accepted immediately. During World War II, he was appointed Deputy Director of the Office of Price Administration in 1941. Because of his experience in wartime, Galbraith supported wage-price controls as a remedy for controlling inflation. Following the war, he began a lifelong career at Harvard University, interrupted only by his diplomatic mission to India in 1961–63. In 1972, he served as president of the American Economic Association. Throughout his career, he was active in politics and a lifelong member of the Democratic Party.[1]

Galbraith was a prolific writer, and many of his works are still in print. One of his most enduring books is *The Great Crash, 1929,* which blames the stock market crash and subsequent financial crisis primarily on "bad" distribution of income, "bad" corporate structure, and a "bad" banking system. Unfortunately, it doesn't blame enough of the crisis on the major cause—"bad" monetary policy by the Federal Reserve (Galbraith 1955: 173–93).

Galbraith is best known for his trilogy on American economics: *American Capitalism* (1952), *The Affluent Society* (1958), and *The New Industrial State* (1967). All emphasize the need for a large and ubiquitous state. *American Capitalism* made the case for big government as a necessary "countervailing power" against big business and big labor. (But with a gradual decline in union power and the ever-expanding role of entrepreneurial growth businesses around the globe, does not his thesis now suggest a diminished, rather than increasing, role for government?)

THE AFFLUENT SOCIETY AND THE PROBLEM OF "SOCIAL IMBALANCE"

Galbraith's biggest claim to fame is his book *The Affluent Society* (1958), which became a bestseller and is still in print. Like Veblen's *Theory of the Leisure Class, The Affluent Society* is a social commentary on wealth and inequality in America. With great enthusiasm and poetic prose, Galbraith accurately described the disparity between the public and private sectors. His theme is that "public services have failed to keep abreast of private consumption" (1958: 257). While the private sector produces cars, clothes, and cruise ships abundantly, the public sector hurts for quality education, good roads, and clean air. Galbraith's solution to this egregious "social imbalance" seems obvious: transfer funds (via taxes) from the affluent private sector to the starved public sector.

Critics have asked a more basic question: Why is the public sector always underfinanced and underperforming relative to the private sector? This question is even more perplexing given that government has grown faster than private enterprise during the past hundred years. The source of public indulgence lies in the funda-

(continued)

1. For a full-length, friendly biography, see Parker (2006).

mental flaw of government programs—their lack of competition and market incentives. The solution, then, is not to transfer more private wealth to the public sector but to apply private-sector principles to the public sector, such as privatizing government programs and imposing user fees on public services. Unfortunately, privatization and other market solutions are absent from Galbraith's agenda, even in his fortieth-anniversary edition.

GALBRAITH CHANGES HIS MIND ABOUT INEQUALITY

Galbraith, Veblen, and other institutional economists have always worried about the issue of income inequality. In this regard, Galbraith makes an interesting confession in *The Affluent Society:*

> Over the centuries those who have been blessed with wealth have developed many remarkably ingenious and persuasive justifications of their good fortune. The instinct of the liberal is to look at these explanations with a rather unyielding eye. Yet in this case the facts are inescapable. *It is the increase in output in recent years, not the redistribution of income, which has brought the greatest material increase, the well-being of the average man.* And, however suspiciously, the liberal has come to accept the fact. (1958: 96–97; italics added)

THE NEW INDUSTRIAL STATE

The final volume of Galbraith's trilogy, *The New Industrial State* (1967), has created the most controversy, and many critics argue that it led to his downfall as a credible economist. He made three basic hypotheses:

1. Big business has become bigger and more concentrated. Many important markets are dominated by only a few giant firms.
2. Major corporations are run by skilled engineer-managers, creating a "technostructure" unbeholden to shareholders; they seek to maximize power, not necessarily profits.
3. The technostructure of big business seeks to reduce risk by controlling its markets through planning; prices and output are no longer determined by supply and demand, despite the "conventional wisdom."

Recent empirical work has disputed all three hypotheses of Galbraith. There is no evidence that industry has become more concentrated; in fact, globalization has increased the number of competitors in major industries, such as automobiles. Big business has not been immune to the forces of competition or shareholder dissatisfaction. Since *The New Industrial State* was published in 1967, shareholder demands for increased performance have led to major restructuring of big corporations, including downsizing and leveraged buyouts. Finally, big firms influence but do not control their customers through advertising (what Galbraith calls the "dependence effect"). As William Breit and Roger L. Ransom note, "If it [the large firm] can control demand, it need not incur the enormous costs of developing new products; it need only convince buyers to continue to purchase existing models" (1971: 184).

MAX WEBER: A SPIRITED DEFENSE OF "RATIONAL" CAPITALISM

Fortunately, Thorstein Veblen was not the only social commentator on capitalism at the turn of the century. His chief antagonist came from across the Atlantic—the German sociologist and economist **Max Weber (1864–1920)**, author of the famous book *The Protestant Ethic and the Spirit of Capitalism* (1930 [1904–5]). Weber's views on capitalism were more in the spirit of Adam Smith than of Veblen. As John Patrick Diggins states, "No two social theorists could be more intellectually and temperamentally opposed than Thorstein Veblen and Max Weber" (1999: 111).

Both Veblen and Weber were obsessed with the meaning of contemporary industrial society—the issues of power, management, and surplus wealth. Both published their bestselling works near the turn of the twentieth century. Both were highly critical of the Marxist interpretation of history.

Yet Weber came to far different conclusions than Veblen or Marx. He rejected both Veblen's description of modern capitalism as a form of barbaric evolution and Marx's theory of exploitation and surplus value. Rather, the development of modern society ("the heroic age of capitalism") came about because of strenuous moral discipline and joyless devotion to hard work, leading to long-term investments and advanced corporate management. Where did this powerful source of Western economic development come from? Unlike Veblen and Marx, Weber saw this source as coming from religion, specifically from the Protestant Reformation and its doctrines of frugality and a moral duty to work, and its concept of the "calling."

RELIGION PLAYS A MAJOR ROLE IN WEBER'S LIFE

Although Weber was an economist by profession, he had a permanent interest in religion. He was born in 1864 in Erfurt, Germany, to a pious mother and a secular father. His mother, who came from a wealthy Huguenot background, was intensely religious. In contrast, his father was nonreligious, a magistrate who would later become a deputy in the German parliament, the Reichstag, which required the family to move to Berlin in 1869. Max resented the way his secular authoritarian father treated his puritanical mother, who detested frivolity and devoted herself to her religious duties and helping the poor.

Max was a precocious child, secretly reading Goethe's collected works in forty volumes while in school. In preparation for his confirmation, he taught himself Hebrew and read the Old Testament in the original. He liked to give his parents gifts of historical essays. At age fifteen, he presented them with an essay entitled "Observations on the Ethnic Character, Development, and History of the Indo-European Nations."

In 1882, Weber attended several German universities and studied law under Karl Knies, one of the founders of the historical school (see chapter 7). He took only one course in economics, but by 1893, at the age of twenty-nine, he became a professor of economics and finance (officially, *National-ökonomie und Finanzwissenschaft*) at the University of Freiburg. He demonstrated he was a quick study by writing a popular educational pamphlet for workers, called "The Stock Exchange." His teaching skills were so well received that in 1896 he was appointed to replace his old teacher Karl Knies at the University of Heidelberg.

Photograph 10.4
Max Weber (1864–1920)
"Anyone who has once been thunderstruck by contact with him can never see the world in the same light again."
Courtesy of Richard Swedberg.

WEBER SUFFERS A NERVOUS BREAKDOWN—FOR SIX YEARS!

By 1897, Weber was the picture of success. Only in his early thirties, he held a highly respected university position, and had published several important works. He had married a distant cousin, Marianne Schnitger, four years earlier.

But Max was overworked and exhausted. Then he had a terrible quarrel with his overbearing father, who was living with Max and Marianne. In June 1897, Weber for the first time defied his father's authoritarian spirit and ordered him out of the house. He never saw his father alive again; the old man died seven weeks later. Guilt-ridden, Max lapsed into a melancholic depression that lasted six years. Unable to teach, give public lectures, or carry out any scholarly work, he could hardly talk, concentrate, or read. He suffered from chronic back pain, insomnia, nervous ailments, and periodic visitations of "demons." He took morphine and a variety of pills, and made trips abroad. He searched in vain for a solution. Seeing him slouched on a sofa, semiconscious, and staring out the window for hours, his wife Marianne referred to him as "an eagle with broken wings." He was so tormented by his illness that he was unable to take on teaching responsibilities for another fifteen years, until 1918.

A TRIP TO AMERICA REVIVES WEBER

In 1903, Weber and his wife took a trip to the United States. This trip was Weber's turning point. He toured the country and even gave a public address. Enthralled by his visit to America, Weber returned invigorated and ready to write his most famous work, *The Protestant Ethic and the Spirit of Capitalism*. Originally published as two essays in 1904 and 1905, the book was revised in 1920 and translated into English in 1930. This work, along with several other unfinished projects in world religions and economics, catapulted Weber into the front ranks of the founders of modern sociology.

THE CHARISMATIC MAX WEBER

Except during his prolonged illness, Weber made a deep, riveting impression on everyone he met. With his heavy outward demeanor, he was a serious scholar of intense passion and dogma. Students recalled his dignified and stately appearance, and one colleague declared, "Anyone who has once been thunderstruck by contact with him can never see the world in the same light again" (Wrong 1970: 69). Weber himself was never much of an egotist, however. He had no interest in writing bestselling books or exploiting the lecture circuit. In a German society that emphasized hero worship and ceremony, he never received an honorary degree.

A SECRET LIFE?

Weber worked hard, but never denied himself the pleasures of life. Oddly enough, he showed an intense interest in religion but never attended church regularly. He had a rousing social life, sometimes all-nighters drinking with friends, ending with a swim in a local river. Sometimes his lust for life got him into trouble, including two long-term extramarital affairs. One was with Else Jaffé, his first female student at the University of Heidelberg, and the other was with Mina Tobler, a Swiss pianist. Before World War I, he became involved in a libertarian free-love group called Ascona, and after the war, he spent as much time with Else and Mina as with his wife Marianne, in what might be described as an informal life of polygamy. Both Else and Marianne were at Max's deathbed in 1920, and afterward they were lifelong friends (Diggins 1996: 43–44, 163–64).

A national liberal, Weber was intensely patriotic, supporting a strong German state. He took an active part in politics, especially during World War I. At the age of fifty, he tried to enlist. Turned away, he volunteered to work in a German hospital. After the war, he was a participant in the German delegation to Versailles. In 1918, he accepted a position in economics at the University of Vienna, where he befriended Ludwig von Mises. But his heart was in Germany, and a year later he was appointed a professor at the University of Munich. He was so popular in Vienna and Munich that the lecture halls were never large enough. Teaching and writing at full capacity, he caught pneumonia and died in the early summer of 1920, having lived only fifty-six years.

WEBER AND SCHUMPETER FIGHT IT OUT IN A VIENNA COFFEEHOUSE

This is intolerable!

—Max Weber

Max Weber and Joseph Schumpeter were opposites in personality. Weber was a dogmatic, restless, hard-driving Huguenot with deeply held convictions, who took nothing lightly. Schumpeter, the gifted *wunderkind* of Viennese economics, was light-hearted, reasonable to a fault, and a virtuoso at playing any political game (see chapter 16).

Weber spent 1918 teaching at the University of Vienna. Near the end of the term, he met Schumpeter at the Cafe Landmann, opposite the university. Felix Somary, a university student who later became a prominent Swiss banker, reported the incident. They talked about the Russian Revolution that had occurred a year earlier. Schumpeter expressed satisfaction that socialism was no longer just a theory but could be tested in the real world. Weber responded heatedly that communism in Russia was a crime and would lead to unheard-of misery and a terrible catastrophe.

"That may well be," said Schumpeter, "but it would be a good laboratory [in which] to test our theories."

"A laboratory heaped with human corpses!" Weber rejoined.

"Every anatomy classroom is the same thing," Schumpeter shot back.

The discussion turned into a raging debate. Weber became more vehement and raised his voice as Schumpeter became more sarcastic and lowered his. All around, customers stopped reading their newspapers and playing cards and listened eagerly as the two exchanged verbal insults. Finally, Weber sprang to his feet and rushed out into the Ringstrasse, crying "This is intolerable!" A friend rushed out with Weber's hat, trying to calm him. Schumpeter, who remained behind, only smiled and said, "How can someone carry on like that in a coffee house!" (Somary 1986: 120–21).

WEBER'S GREAT ACHIEVEMENT

Weber's *Protestant Ethic and the Spirit of Capitalism* is a profound work offering a unique contribution to institutional economics. As noted earlier, intellectuals of the nineteenth and early twentieth centuries disapproved of formal religion. The German philosopher Friedrich Nietzsche viewed faith as a crutch for the morally crippled. Freud saw religion as a delusion and an irrational mental disorder, a neurosis. The materialist Marx argued that economic forces shaped religion, but Weber took the opposite point of view. He praised Christianity as a "social bond of world-encompassing brotherhood" (Diggins 1996: 95). He disapproved of Marx, contending instead that capitalism had its origins in religious ideals rather than historical materialism. In particular, the Protestant reformation transformed Western civilization and brought about the rise of capitalism, "the most fateful force in our modern life" (Weber 1930: 17).

According to Weber, it was not unbridled avarice and the unfettered pursuit of gain that brought about the age of capitalism. Such an impulse has existed in all societies of the past. That "greed" is the driving force behind capitalism is a "naive idea" that "should be taught in the kindergarten of cultural history." Echoing Montesquieu and Adam Smith, Weber exclaimed, "Unlimited greed for gain is not in the least identical with capitalism, and is still less its spirit. Capitalism *may* even be identical with the restraint, or at least a rational tempering, of this irrational impulse" (Weber 1930: 17).

So what did cause the historical development of modern capitalism, especially in the West? Weber's basic thesis is that religion, which had a firm grip on people's minds for centuries, kept capitalism back until the Protestant reformation of the seventeenth century. Until then, the making of money was looked down upon by almost all religions, including Christianity. Medieval Catholicism, under the influence of St. Paul, St. Augustine, and St. Thomas Aquinas, stressed the monastic order and vows of poverty. Their motto was, "Let the ungodly run after gain" (Weber 1930: 83).

All that changed, according to Weber, with the Lutheran doctrine of the "calling," the Calvinist and Puritan doctrine of labor to promote the glory of God ("You may labor to be rich to God, though not for the flesh and sin"), and the Methodist admonition against idleness. Only among the Protestants could the devout Christian hear John Wesley's sermon on wealth: "Earn all you can, save all you can, give all you can" (Weber 1930: 175–76).

Weber had to overcome the Protestant appearance of a gloomy, fatalistic outlook on mankind. After all, didn't ascetic Calvinism preach predestination, that no one but God knew who the elect were? But Weber discovered that Calvinism, despite its emphasis of faith over works, had in fact encouraged worldly gain as a means of easing earthly pain.

What did Protestant theology lead to? The calling to the business world ("God blesseth his Trade") meant constant self-control, honesty, and hard work. Begging and slothfulness were forbidden. "To wish to be poor was, it was often argued, the same as wishing to be unhealthy" (Weber 1930: 163).

Protestantism not only promoted industry; it also stressed a critical element in economic growth, the virtue of thrift. Wesley preached, "Earn all you can, *save all you can*, give all you can." Wesley did not say, "spend all you can." As Weber explained, Christianity proclaimed self-denial and abstinence while warning against materialism and pride. Protestant preachers disapproved of "conspicuous consumption," and so capitalists and workers saved and saved and saved. As John Maynard Keynes commented, "Herein lay, in fact, the main justification of the Capitalist System. If the rich had spent their new wealth on their own enjoyments, the world would long ago have found such a regime intolerable. But like bees they saved and accumulated, not less to the advantage of the whole community because they themselves held narrower ends in prospect" (Keynes 1920: 19). The laboring classes were enjoined to save also. "The duty of 'saving' became nine tenths of virtue and the growth of the cake the object of true religion. . . . Individuals would be exhorted not so much to abstain as to defer, and to cultivate the pleasures of security and anticipation" (page 20).

WEBER LOOKS TO AMERICA'S FRANKLIN TO DEMONSTRATE HIS THESIS

Weber's crucial journey to the United States in 1903 may have sparked an idea in his fertile mind. He focused on America as the historical embodiment of the "Protestant ethic," in particular the life and writings of Benjamin Franklin. (It should also be noted that Weber's mother, Helene, and aunt, Ida, both devout women, were greatly influenced by the American Transcendentalist theologians William Channing and Theodore Parker.)

Weber saw in this American founding father the epitome of the Protestant ethic. Weber felt that Franklin's Quaker-founded Pennsylvania was imbued with the "capitalist spirit," and witnessed in Franklin's ethical philosophy the doctrine of the calling, "which his strict Calvinist father had drummed into him again and again in his youth" (Weber 1930: 53). His book cites quotation after quotation from Franklin, such as "Remember, time is money" and "Money can beget money, and its off-spring can beget more." According to Weber, Franklin's virtues of punctuality, industry, and frugality reflected the "spirit of modern capitalism," that is, "the earning of more and more money, combined with the strict avoidance of all spontaneous enjoyment of life" (Weber 1930: 48–56). Weber contrasted Franklin with Jacob Fugger, merchant banker of Germany, who supposedly lacked civil conscience and was interested solely in making money.

CRITICS OF WEBER'S THESIS

Of course, Weber's thesis wasn't entirely new. After all, had not Montesquieu already remarked, "Capital is protestant" (Dorfman 1949: 345)? England, the greatest Protestant country, was also the most advanced industrial nation and made the largest investment in machinery and capital goods. Meanwhile, Catholic France, by revoking the Edict of Nantes, drove out large groups of artisans and thereby retarded its economic development for centuries.

Other historians have disagreed with Weber. The cause of capitalism's rise in the West is far less cut and dried. After all, capitalism first flourished in the Middle Ages in the Italian city-states, which were Catholic. Indeed, found in a 1523 Florentine account is the first pro-capitalist statement, "In the name of God and of profit" (Rothbard 1995: 142). Antwerp in the middle of the sixteenth century was a flourishing financial and commercial center—and it was Catholic. The Spanish scholastics, mainly Jesuits and Dominicans in the mid-sixteenth and the seventeenth centuries, advocated capitalism and free markets.

Critics also point to Weber's oddly chosen examples—Benjamin Franklin and Jacob Fugger. Granted, Franklin promoted the old-fashioned virtues of frugality and asceticism in *Poor Richard's Almanac*, but Weber completely ignored Franklin's lust for life and his pleasure-seeking passions throughout his long career as a businessman, statesman, and ambassador. Indeed, Franklin was no great lover of toil and preferred to multiply the comforts of American life. Meanwhile, Weber's attack on Jacob Fugger is ill-founded. Fugger, a practicing Catholic from southern Germany, worked all his life and refused to retire, announcing that "he would make money as long as he could." If anyone represents Weber's ideal type, it is Jacob Fugger (Rothbard 1995: 142).

CONCLUSIONS

Despite these criticisms, Weber's thesis went a long way toward dispelling the negative cultural notions of modern capitalism and religious faith as expressed by Veblen. Weber stressed spiritual rather than material factors in the development of capitalism. While Veblen the anthropologist viewed modern capitalism as an example of barbarian exploitation, Weber the sociologist saw capitalist ethics and moral discipline as a decisive break from the predatory behavior of men. While Veblen depicted the capitalist as a predator and status-seeker, Weber emphasized individual conscience and Christian exhortations against idleness and wastefulness.

According to John Patrick Diggins, historian at the City University of New York who has written biographies on both Veblen and Weber, Weber has recently eclipsed Veblen in scholarly influence (1999: 112).

ECONOMICS SHOULD BE "VALUE FREE"

The Protestant-ethic thesis was not the only contribution Weber made in economics. In the debate over methodology between the German historical school and the Austrian school of economics, Weber sided with the Austrians. He firmly believed that if economics was ever going to succeed as a pure formal science, it must be a value-free, objective social science. He had personally witnessed in Germany the efforts of Gustav von Schmoller, arch enemy of Carl Menger, as he played favorites in establishing chairs in various university departments.

Throughout the centuries, economic theory has been tainted by historical events and political biases. But economics has gradually risen above these prejudices to become an impartial scientific discipline. How? First, by constantly reexamining the logic of its premises and, second, by repeatedly testing its theories with empirical studies. Weber used historical evidence to support his Protestant-ethic thesis. His evidence may have been incomplete and suspect, but it was the beginning of empirical testing. Most advances in economics during the twentieth century have been due to empirical studies confirming or denying the various new theories proposed by economists, forcing the profession to constantly reevaluate its theories and tools.

WEBER'S FINAL WARNING: BEWARE THE IRON CAGE OF LIBERTY

Despite his repeated criticisms of socialism and central planning, Weber was not as optimistic about the market economy as was Adam Smith. His vision of modern capitalism was ultimately a tragic one. He worried that the bureaucrats and the leisure class would overtake the entrepreneur class, destroying the vitality of capitalism. (Schumpeter expressed similar concerns a generation later.)

Weber also warned modern society about the "iron cage" of liberty. He recognized that modern capitalism brought enormous wealth and prosperity to the masses, but it also had its darker side—an iron cage of impersonal, regimented bureaucracy in the corporate world, devoid of spiritual values and happiness, that could create and destroy jobs and people's lives at will. He occasionally wrote of the brutality of "adventurers' capitalism" (Swedberg 1998: 121, 190). Science and technology, Veblen's sources of strength, could not fill the void. For Weber, the modern condition was an unhappy one, from which there was no escape (Gamble 1996: 178).

There is an element of truth to Weber's iron cage. The modern capitalist society is often criticized as too impersonal and lacking community values. In the traditional economy, people knew and worked with their neighbors. Today, under an impersonal capitalism, people can live anonymously without interacting with their neighbors. Yet as the capitalist economy advances worldwide, it provides new opportunities, new surplus wealth, and friendships among business associates and voluntary organizations.

ONE FINAL MISSING KEY IN THE NEOCLASSICAL MODEL

The neoclassical model of modern economics, having been remodeled and scrutinized many times over, was now facing one more challenge as it entered the twentieth century. There was one missing element in the capitalist model: the critical role of money. The money question is the central unanswered issue of twentieth century macroeconomics, and, as we shall see, the failure to find an answer to this vital question almost destroyed the system of natural liberty that Adam Smith created. Let us begin the next chapter with the economist who spent his entire career searching for the missing link in macroeconomics.

REFERENCES

Breit, William, and Roger L. Ransom. 1971. *The Academic Scribblers.* New York: Holt Rinehart Winston.

Diggins, John Patrick. 1996. *Max Weber: Politics and the Spirit of Tragedy.* New York: Basic Books.

———. 1999. *Thorstein Veblen, Theorist of the Leisure Class.* Princeton: Princeton University Press.

Dorfman, Joseph. 1934. *Thorstein Veblen and His America.* Clifton, NJ: Augustus M. Kelley.

———. 1949. *The Economic Mind in American Civilization 1865–1918,* vol. 3. New York: Viking.

Galbraith, John Kenneth. 1952. *American Capitalism.* Boston: Houghton Mifflin.

———. 1955. *The Great Crash, 1929.* Boston: Houghton Mifflin.

———. 1958. *The Affluent Society.* Boston: Houghton Mifflin.

———. 1967. *The New Industrial State.* Boston: Houghton Mifflin.

Gamble, Andrew. 1996. *Hayek: The Iron Cage of Liberty.* Cambridge, UK: Polity Press.

Heilbroner, Robert L. 1992. *The Worldly Philosophers,* 6th ed. New York: Simon & Schuster.

Jorgensen, Elizabeth, and Henry Jorgensen. 1999. *Thorstein Veblen: Victorian Firebrand.* Armonk, NY: M.E. Sharpe.

Kanigel, Robert. 1997. *The One Best Way: Frederick Winslow Taylor and the Enigma of Efficiency.* New York: Viking Penguin.

Keynes, John Maynard. 1920. *Economic Consequences of the Peace.* New York: Harcourt, Brace and Howe.

———. 1936. *The General Theory of Employment, Interest and Money.* London: Macmilllan.

Marx, Karl. 1976 [1860]. *Capital,* vol. 1. New York: Penguin.

Mencken, H.L. 1982. *A Mencken Chrestomathy.* New York: Random House.

Mill, John Stuart. 1891 [1848]. *Principles of Political Economy.* New York: D. Appleton.

Parker, Richard. 2006. *John Kenneth Galbraith: His Life, His Politics, His Economics.* New York: Farrar, Straus and Giroux.

Rothbard, Murray N. 1995. *Economic Thought Before Adam Smith.* Hants, UK: Edward Elgar.

Somary, Felix. 1986. *The Raven of Zurich: The Memoirs of Felix Somary.* New York: St. Martin's Press.

Swedberg, Richard. 1998. *Max Weber and the Idea of Economic Sociology.* Princeton: Princeton University Press.

Taylor, Frederick W. 1947. *The Principles of Scientific Management.* New York: Harper and Brothers.

Tilman, Rick. 1992. *Thorstein Veblen and His Critics, 1891–1963.* Princeton: Princeton University Press.

Veblen, Thorstein. 1926. *The Engineers and the Price System.* New York: Viking.

———. 1965 (1916). *The Higher Learning in America.* New York: Augustus M. Kelley.

———. 1994 [1899]. *The Theory of the Leisure Class.* New York: Penguin.

Weber, Max. 1930 [1904–5]. *The Protestant Ethic and the Spirit of Capitalism.* New York: HarperCollins.

Wrong, Dennis H. 1970. *Max Weber.* Englewood Cliffs, NJ: Prentice-Hall.

11

THE FISHER KING TRIES TO
CATCH THE MISSING LINK
IN MACROECONOMICS

Irving Fisher is the greatest economist America has produced.
—James Tobin (1987: 369)

*Gosh, he's supposed to know all the answers, and look how
he got burned!*

—A New Yorker's comment on Irving Fisher
after the 1929 crash (I.N. Fisher 1956: 263)

As we entered the twentieth century, there was one final hurdle to over-come—understanding the vital role of money and credit in the economy.

So far, economic theorists had developed a pretty good understanding of *microeconomics*, that is, how individual prices and quantities of goods are determined. Every day, in the classrooms of academia, instructors cried out, "Supply and demand, supply and demand!" More specifically, prices and output are grounded in the actions of individual consumers and producers. According to the marginalist revolution, price is determined by the quantity available and the intensity of consumer demands for that good, based on its marginal utility to consumers.

♪ **Music selection for this chapter: Franz Schubert, Symphony No. 8, *The Unfinished Symphony***

Economists had also developed a fairly sophisticated understanding of *macroeconomics*, that is, how the economy works as a whole. Most endorsed the classical model of economic liberalism and the positive role of saving and capital investment in maximizing the wealth of nations.

J.-B. Say's law of markets was almost universally accepted as the classical macroeconomic model: increased capital, technology, and productivity lead to rapidly rising living standards. Say's law also explained the occasional economic recession: firms were sometimes misled into producing goods that consumers failed to buy, resulting in a financial crisis and an economic slump.

THE MISSING LINK BETWEEN MICRO AND MACRO

But there was one piece missing from the economist's tool box—the mystery of money. Comprehending the role of money and credit, the lifeblood of the economy, was the unresolved link between micro and macro.

The idea of a money commodity as a medium of exchange is one of the greatest inventions of mankind. Unlike other commodities, money is never consumed. It serves as a medium of exchange to buy other goods, and as a store of value, to be used to buy things in the future. Economists in Europe and the United States looked upon money as entirely distinct from other commodities, and did not think to subject money to the new theory of marginal analysis. Money and the "price level" were increasingly being analyzed totally apart from the rest of the market economy.

THE ORIGIN OF MONEY

What was the origin of money? Gustav Schmoller and other members of the German historical school viewed money as a separate category from the rest of economic analysis. Currencies such as the German mark and the British pound were neither goods nor services, but mere inventions of the state to help facilitate trade, create wealth, and finance public works. However, Carl Menger, Schmoller's nemesis, disputed this thesis. "The origin of money," declared Menger, is "entirely natural and thus displays legislative influence in the rarest instances. Money is not an invention of the state. It is not the product of a legislative act" (Menger 1976: 262). He showed that in the natural marketplace, money began as specific commodities, especially gold and silver, that are durable, indestructible, recognizable, and stable—characteristics favorable as a medium of exchange.

Other economists noted that national currencies, such as the pound sterling, the French franc, and the U.S. dollar, were nothing more than specific weights of gold or silver. For example, in medieval England the "pound sterling" was legally defined as a pound weight of sterling silver.[1] Eventually every major industrial nation adopted either a gold or a silver standard, which established currency rates between nations. But originally all currencies were nothing more than different weights of gold or silver.

There was another major issue. Could an international gold standard provide the stability under which economic liberalism could flourish? It appeared that the historical gold standard was far from perfect. From time to time, there appeared a general "inflation" of *all* prices (also known as a loss of purchasing power) and, at other times, there seemed to be "shortages of money" and depressions. What was the cause of this boom-bust business cycle?

Many observers blamed the business cycle on the gold standard, an essential ingredient in Adam Smith's model of capitalism. The gold rushes of California, Australia, and South Africa created considerable inflations from time to time. These inflationary boom times were followed by sudden collapses, layoffs, bankruptcies, and a slide in trade. Economists called it "the trade cycle," or more broadly, the "business cycle." The business cycle appeared to be something outside the supply and demand of individual products. A search for the cause of the boom-bust trade cycle was one of the burning issues of the nineteenth century, and it continued into the twentieth century.

Finally, there was the question of banking. Fractional reserves and unregulated "wildcat" banking exacerbated the boom-bust cycle. Some economists demanded that banks be required to maintain 100 percent specie reserves to back their deposits, or even outlaw paper money entirely. Others insisted on the need for a central bank to regulate private banks and the issuance of credit. Thus, issues of banking and credit were paramount in the minds of economists and legislators.

FISHER: FOUNDER OF THE MONETARIST SCHOOL

The financial and economic crises of the nineteenth century raised serious questions about the role of money and credit: What is the ideal monetary standard? What constituted a sound money banking system? Was Adam Smith's system of natural liberty inherently unstable?

Many economists sought to unravel the mysteries of money and banking, but no one spent more time searching for the answer than **Irving Fisher (1867–1947)**, the eminent Yale professor and modern founder of the "monetarist" school. From James Tobin to Milton Friedman, top economists have hailed Fisher as the forefather of monetary macroeconomics and one of the greatest theorists in their field. Mark Blaug called him "one of the greatest and certainly one of the most colourful American economists who ever lived" (Blaug 1986: 77). His entire career, both

1. For a fascinating account of the origins of money and national currencies, see Murray N. Rothbard, *What Has the Government Done to Our Money?* (1990).

professional and personal, was devoted to the issue of money. Money was in his blood and in his mind. He invented the famed Quantity Theory of Money, and he would be accused all his life of believing that "only money matters." Through today's monetarists, led by Milton Friedman and the Chicago school, Fisher's theoretical work lives on.

Photograph 11.1
Irving Fisher (1867–1947)
"He wrote the greatest
doctoral dissertation in
economics ever written."
Courtesy of Brown Brothers.

THE AMBITIOUS IRVING FISHER

Irving Fisher, born in upstate New York in 1867, always knew he would be "a great man" (Tobin 1987: 371). Son of a Congregationalist minister, Irving carried a spirit of New England puritanism and evangelism throughout his life. He attended Yale College, his father's alma mater, and was graduated first in his class in 1889. He was also elected a member of the secretive Order of Skull and Bones.

At Yale, Fisher developed a lifelong love of mathematics. Under the influence of his favorite professor, William Graham Sumner, he became a pioneer in mathematical economics. His Ph.D. dissertation, "Mathematical Investigations in the Theory of Value and Price," established the marginalist and utility equilibrium functions in neoclassical economics. Paul Samuelson described it as "the greatest doctoral dissertation in economics ever written" (Allen 1993: 11). Fisher later (1930) became the first president of the Econometric Society.

Fisher taught mathematics at Yale. In 1893, at the age of twenty-six, he married Margie Hazard, with whom he had two daughters and a son. The couple had a lifelong, devoted relationship.

His professional interest was monetary economics. In 1895, Fisher presented his first paper before the newly formed American Economic Association meetings. Its title was "The Relation of Change in the Volume of Currency to Prosperity." Money would be a lifelong interest for Fisher.

A DEADLY DISEASE SUDDENLY STRIKES

In 1898, at age thirty-one, Irving Fisher was at the beginning of a promising career. Healthy, strong, newly married, and just promoted to full professor in the political science department at Yale, the young professor was enjoying the good life.

Then he received the tragic news. Fisher was diagnosed with tuberculosis (TB), which in those days was a death sentence. Few recovered from the dreaded disease. His own father had died of TB fourteen years earlier. Fisher's doctor was so shaken by the diagnosis that he couldn't face Fisher directly; instead he told his patient's wife.

FISHER BECOMES A CRUSADER FOR HEALTH CAUSES

Fisher was determined to beat the "incurable" TB. The only known cure was lots of fresh air and healthy living—if one acted early. He secluded himself in New York; spent a year in Colorado Springs; and finally moved to Santa Barbara, California.

In Colorado, he met an individual he would never forget—Roger W. Babson. The New Englander had much in common with Fisher. Both suffered from TB, and both were fascinated by economics and the stock market. They created inventions to treat TB, and both crusaded for healthy outdoor living. Both went on to write extensively on monetary and financial topics. Yet they ended up on opposite sides during the great bull market on Wall Street during the 1920s— Fisher was the eternal optimist, and Babson the permanent bear. (See the box on Roger Babson on page 279.)

AN ODD FELLOW

Fisher was eccentric. Firm and self-righteous, prim and straight-laced, he was self-disciplined in every way. He survived TB, which changed his entire outlook on life. His life-and-death struggle caused him to campaign for outdoor living, fresh air, diet and nutrition, exercise, antismoking, and Prohibition. He was humorless and seldom smiled (but see Photograph 11.3 on page 278, taken during the Roaring Twenties). Standing nearly five feet, nine inches tall and weighing around 150 pounds, he became the picture of health, exercising regularly with weights and riding a bicycle to work. He was always a stylishly dressed professor, wearing a mustache, and later in life, a short, trimmed beard.

He normally arose at seven A.M., jogged around the neighborhood, and had a breakfast of fruit, toast, and acidophilus milk. He did not smoke, or drink alcohol, coffee, or tea. He refused to eat chocolate or use pepper. He followed a strict diet, emphasizing bananas and peanut butter, and seldom ate meat. Sometimes when he was away on trips, he would enter the hotel kitchen and instruct the chef on the precise food he wanted and how to prepare it (Allen 1993: 147–48).

He was an activist, extolling the virtues of world peace, the League of Nations, 100 percent deposit reserve banking, antismoking leagues, and eugenics. He firmly believed in racial purity and opposed interracial marriage. He attended church services throughout his life, although religion was never one of his causes.

Fisher was devoted to his wife Margie, and treated her as his intellectual equal. When traveling, he never let a day pass without writing, telephoning, or telegraphing her. His letters to her, which always started with "Dearest Love," were full of declarations of love and occasional poetry.[2]

Yet the Yale professor was considered by many to be vain and self-righteous, even domineering at times. He believed that a man's place was in the workplace and a woman's place in the kitchen and bedroom, although later in life he supported the Equal Rights Amendment on economic grounds. He thought traditional society undervalued women's abilities.

Tragedies in his personal life, such as his TB, frequently influenced his career. During the spring of 1918, his oldest daughter became engaged to an enlisted man who was about to sail to France. Fisher urged her to marry before her fiancé left and, under the social pressure, she suddenly had a nervous breakdown. Months passed and she still failed to recover. She died of pleurisy in the hospital, only weeks before Fisher delivered his presidential address for the American Economic Association. Fisher hated war, and after the death of his daughter, he intensified his fight for world peace and the League of Nations.

FISHER WRITES OVER THIRTY BOOKS

Fisher was a prodigious writer. In economics, he wrote about capital and interest, a new monetary standard, the business cycle, index numbers, and the dollar. In each he explored the critical role of money. Monetary economics was his favorite topic, and price stability was his determined policy goal.

FISHER INVENTS THE ROLODEX AND BECOMES A MILLIONAIRE

Irving Fisher was also a gadgeteer, always searching for a way to become rich. He tinkered with various small inventions in school, but his biggest breakthrough came in 1910, when he invented an index card system. Digging through index file cards was always a cumbersome task, so Fisher came up with a solution: cut a notch at the bottom of the index card and attach it to a metal strip through the notch. The Rolodex was born.

Today millions use the Rolodex, especially the circular variety. Fisher received his first patent on the Rolodex in December 1912, but he was unable to find a company to manufacture and market the device. He

2. Irving wrote the following to his wife upon the twenty-fifth anniversary of their engagement: "I seem to feel a new sweet tenderness of love which I wish I could express or picture to you in some way. These serene skies, the hushed air, the stately grandeur of California and a subtle subconscious special association of California with you because, in particular, you were here the winter we were engaged, fills my soul to the brim. What a complex thing love is! It seems so simple yet it has as many sides as a diamond or colors as a rainbow or mansions as our Father's house . . . you are for me the wonder of wonders. Your soul and mine possess each other's keys and I have a mystic feeling, which seems especially intense since I have been here, that you have led and are leading me into a wonderland of soul experience" (Allen 1993: 152–53).

formed his own company, the Index Visible Company, and starting selling his invention in 1913.

A dozen years later, his company started making a profit. In 1925, it was purchased by another company, which later merged with Remington Rand. Fisher's sudden millionaire status allowed him to buy a large Lincoln automobile and hire a chauffeur to drive it. The university professor was now a financial tycoon and market forecaster.

IRVING FISHER BECOMES AN ADVISOR TO IL DUCE!

Madmen in authority, who hear voices in the air, are distilling their frenzy from some academic scribbler of a few years back.
— John Maynard Keynes (1973 [1936]: 383)

Irving Fisher was above all a crusader who would stop at nothing to achieve his political objectives. When he heard that the Italian dictator Benito Mussolini was interested in monetary affairs, he wrote Mussolini a letter, hoping to gain his support for a world monetary conference. Il Duce responded favorably, and Fisher headed for Europe in 1927. After delivering a series of lectures in Geneva, he and a friend took a train to Rome.

After waiting hours, they were finally ushered into the presence of Il Duce. Fisher exclaimed, "You are one of the few great men in the world who are interested in the subject of inflation and deflation, unstable money and stabilization." He presented the Italian leader with a copy of *The Money Illusion* (1928) and a letter he hoped Il Duce would sign, supporting an international monetary conference. Mussolini avoided signing by asking Fisher about Italy's economic conditions. Fisher replied that it was a grave mistake to deflate the monetary system in order to go back on the gold standard. Fisher left with high hopes.

Mussolini never signed the letter, nor was there any personal response from the Italian president until June 1931, when Mussolini informed Fisher through an ambassador that he had read *The Money Illusion* and was deeply interested. Encouraged, Fisher wrote back, but never heard from Mussolini again. Apparently, the Italian dictator had other more pressing needs on his mind during the 1930s (Allen 1993: 196–97, 238).

Photograph 11.2
Benito Mussolini
Entertained Irving Fisher and his monetary proposals.
Courtesy of Hulton-Getty Archives.

THE ORACLE OF WALL STREET

Fisher's millionaire status made him the "oracle of Wall Street" during the 1920s. He was quoted frequently in the New York newspapers about the outlook for the stock market and the economy. Joining Columbia professor Wesley C. Mitchell, he became a principal advocate of the "New Era" optimism of the Roaring Twenties, one of the upbeat apostles of a new and better world. Fisher saw the booming stock market as a reflection of the New Era of permanent prosperity in America, and felt that the newly established central bank, the Federal Reserve, would avert any future depression or monetary crisis (Skousen 1993: 249–56).

Photograph 11.3
A Rich and Happy Irving Fisher in 1927—Before the Stock Market Crash
Courtesy of Culver Pictures.

In addition to holding his Rand shares, he invested heavily in small-growth stocks, hoping to multiply his wealth. He even bought on margin and his stock holdings were estimated to be worth $10 million at the height of the bull market.

FISHER, THE BULL, VERSUS BABSON, THE BEAR

In the fall of 1929, Fisher publicly feuded with his longtime friend Roger Babson, about the direction the market was headed. Babson was a notorious doomsdayer who had warned as early as 1926 that Wall Street was engulfed in a classic bubble and would suffer a crash. When the bearish Babson alerted investors again in September 1929 that a crash was "imminent," the bullish Fisher told the New York papers, "There may be a recession in stock prices, but not anything in the nature of a crash."

For nearly two months, Fisher appeared to have the upper hand over Babson. Although stock prices wavered during this time, no crash occurred. On Monday, October 16, 1929, less than two weeks before the crash, Fisher made the soon-to-be-immortal prediction that "stock prices have reached what looks like a permanently high plateau" (Skousen 1993: 252–53).

Meanwhile, the Dow Jones Industrial Average had hit a peak of 381 on September 3, 1929. It would be decades before it reached that pinnacle again. By the end of the year, the Dow would drop as low as 200, losing nearly half its value. The crash in late October was only the beginning of a long, tortuous decline in share values.

But Fisher was not deterred. By mid-December 1929, he had written a book, *The Stock Market Crash—And After*, a bold, unrepentant attempt to

ROGER BABSON, THE "GLOOMY GUS OF WALL STREET"

*Perhaps the foremost lesson which I have learned is that emotions
rule the world, rather than statistics, information, or anything else.*
—Roger W. Babson

Roger W. Babson (1875–1967), financial guru and business economist, lived a life surprisingly similar to Irving Fisher's. Like Fisher, Babson was a New Englander fascinated with business statistics, the stock market, health issues, and righteous causes. Both were inventors, defenders of prohibition, and health nuts.

Like Fisher, Babson was deeply affected by his bout with tuberculosis. In addition to his religious causes, Babson became a believer in sunshine and fresh air. He kept his windows open all year long at his offices in Boston, even during the winter (see Photograph 11.4). He created special gloves for his secretary to wear so that she could continue typing in the freezing temperatures. After World War I, he and his wife bought a home in Florida near Lake Wales, where they spent their winters. The community is now known as Babson Park, home of Webber College, a business school for women. He had previously founded Babson College, a business school in Massachusetts.

CRAZY ABOUT NEWTON

A graduate of MIT, Babson became fascinated with Sir Isaac Newton's third law of physics: "For every action there is an equal and opposite reaction." He was so enthralled with Newton that he reerected Newton's London parlor, with the same walls, doors, and shutters, in the Babson Institute Library in Babson Park, Massachusetts. Like Adam Smith, Babson tried to apply Newton's laws to economics and finance. His "Babsoncharts" showed how output, commodity prices, and stock indices move above and below the Babson trendline. In many ways, Babson was a forerunner of technical analysis. He was the chartist of the 1920s.

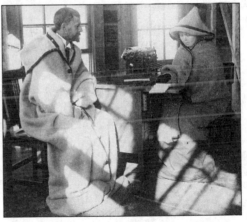

Photograph 11.4
**Roger Babson Dictating to His Secretary: Babson
Believed in Fresh Air—Even in the Dead of Winter!**
Courtesy of Babson College.

Based on his reading of the Babsoncharts, Babson became bearish on the stock market as early as September 1926. At the time, the Dow Jones Industrial Average was around 160, and it would move another 200 points higher before topping out. Babson admitted that this was his biggest mistake: "Although I gave a very pessimistic address immediately preceding the collapse in September 1929, yet I had been giving similar warnings for

(continued)

about eighteen months. Although a study of newspaper files shows that the Babson Organization was given almost exclusive credit for forecasting the great depression of 1929–35, yet it should be emphasized that we thought the break would come before it did. In the same way we thought the upward turn would come before it did in 1932" (Babson 1950: 267).

In 1940, Babson became the Prohibition Party candidate for president. He wrote numerous books, including his autobiography, the title of which—*Actions and Reactions*—is based on Newtonian physics.

Babson was also known for his wise statements:

1. "Most men already have far more knowledge than they use. They need the inheritance and development of character which will cause them properly to apply this knowledge."
2. "Unfortunately, I am not like a doctor, who is able to have his mistakes buried under four feet of earth."
3. "The successful man is not so superior in ability as in action."
4. "We should read more books written twenty, forty, or eighty years ago, and fewer modern books" (Babson 1950).

Regarding the last quote, perhaps he had his own books in mind. All are currently out of print.

reestablish optimism in the nation. He stubbornly rationalized, "I had stated my opinion in September, preceding the panic, that the market had reached its peak, as proved to be the case. I also expressed the view that the recession would not be in the nature of a serious crash, in which I was mistaken. I also predicted that the new plateau of stock prices would survive any recession. This has proven true." He went on to say, "For the immediate future, at least, the outlook is bright" (Fisher 1930: vii).

FISHER FACES BANKRUPTCY

Unfortunately, Fisher couldn't have been more wrong. Despite his faith in President Herbert Hoover's program to stem the tide, the Dow industrials fell an additional 200 points before bottoming out in 1932 at around 40 points. The average stock fell over 90 percent during the 1929–32 debacle. Fisher's own portfolio was practically wiped out by the extended Wall Street bear market. Biographer Robert Loring Allen comments, "He had great difficulty in accepting the idea that he had been wrong about the crash and the depression" (Allen 1993: 220).

To end the depression in the early thirties, Fisher advocated reflation, devaluation, and abandoning the gold standard. Hoover did none of these things, and conditions worsened. Banks collapsed and one out of every four Americans was without a job. Welcoming Franklin D. Roosevelt's bank holiday in 1933, Fisher felt the bottom had been reached and he could finally stave off bankruptcy. He favored expansion of the money supply, not public works programs, as the solution to the depression. He became an informal advisor to Roosevelt, writing him 100 letters from 1933 to 1944 (Roosevelt wrote 20 letters in response). Fisher opposed the National Industrial Recovery Act, the Agricultural Adjustment Act, and other FDR interventions in the production process. He also opposed the income and capital gains taxes, which he regarded as counterproductive. Roosevelt adopted Fisher's idea of government insurance on bank deposits, but rejected his other monetary proposals.

During the 1930s, Fisher, in his sixties, taught only one class a year at Yale, and spent the rest of the time as an economic reformer and crusader. The market recovered, but Fisher's personal financial condition did not. He never recuperated from the crash and was constantly forced to juggle heavy debts, failing assets, and terrible battles with the federal tax authorities over his previous earnings. His wife's wealthy sister rescued him from bankruptcy, lending him $100,000 at one point. January 1931 was a low point; he caught pneumonia and at the same time received a letter from the IRS demanding $61,234 in back taxes. It took him years to work off his debt to the government.

FISHER DIES A BROKEN MAN

In 1935, Fisher faced compulsory retirement at Yale. He was unable to make mortgage payments on his home, so Yale agreed to buy the home and then rent it back to the Fishers on a life-tenancy agreement. By 1939, he owed his sister-in-law over $750,000, which he never fully repaid. In 1940, his beloved wife Margie died, and he spent months traveling and living out of a suitcase. He searched for ways to make back his millions, falling prey to nutty schemes that never materialized. He invented a collapsible three-legged chair that he tried to sell to Sears Roebuck, which turned him down. Finally, in 1947, he lost his battle with cancer and died. Allen notes, "His efforts made him into the country's most well-known and unsuccessful monetary reformer whose poor judgment cost him his fortune, his businesses, and his home. . . . For the most part . . . he failed at what he hoped to accomplish as a businessman, investor, policy advisor, politician, publicist, eugenicist, health enthusiast, and do-gooder" (1993: 269–70, 297–98).

FISHER'S MONETARY MODEL: WHAT WENT WRONG?

Although his fortune undoubtedly blinded him to the approaching storm, Irving Fisher's failure to anticipate the greatest financial collapse in the twentieth century was not due simply to his vested interests in the market. Instead, it was principally due to his incomplete monetary vision of the economy.

His overwhelming deficiency was his excessively "macro" approach to monetary theory. He refused to look at the inner workings of the monetary economy. When it came to money, Fisher ignored the theory of individual behavior and microeconomics. Instead, he viewed money through large, aggregate glasses. He watched the broad economic trends, such as how fast money and credit were growing in the economy, but paid no attention to which individuals and institutions got the money first. He monitored what was happening to the general price level and pioneered the making of price indices, but ignored how individual prices were doing in specific sectors of the economy. He measured the industrial output of the nation, but failed to concentrate on the ups and downs of individual industries and markets. Fisher had the propensity to aggregate and the reluctance to disaggregate. In short, he failed to recognize the serious structural imbalances in the economy and the banking system.

FISHER TREATS CAPITAL AS A FUND

Fisher's work was excessively macro from the very beginning. His first books on capital and interest, published in 1906–7, treated capital as a large conglomerate fund that could be easily manipulated and moved around as interest rates rise and fall and the economic structure changes. "Capital is a fund and income a flow," he wrote (Fisher 1906: 52). Thus, according to Fisher, capital was fluid enough that the economy could adjust quickly to any kind of capital dislocation and economic crisis. He took the same view as John Bates Clark (and later Frank Knight): that capital was a homogeneous fund that could be shifted around efficiently to its most productive use without much dislocation. It was like a reservoir where the water would quickly seek the appropriate equilibrium.

This view was in sharp contrast to the views of Eugen Böhm-Bawerk and the Austrians, who argued that capital was largely heterogeneous and highly illiquid. The Austrians argued that capital in the form of money and investment funds is homogeneous and highly liquid, but that capital invested in buildings, equipment, and machinery is heterogeneous and illiquid. Austrians recognized a huge distinction between capital investment and capital *goods*.

The nature of capital was a major debate issue at the turn of the twentieth century because economists wanted to know how quickly the economy could adjust and recover from a depression. If capital were homogeneous and highly liquid, then the adjustment process should not take long and the economy could soon be back on its feet. But if capital were heterogeneous and not easily transferable to other uses, then the adjustment process could take much longer and it might take years for a nation to recover from a depression.

Fisher took the optimistic view—capital heterogeneity and liquidity were not significant problems and were unlikely to cause a major depression. It would turn out to be his Achilles' heel.

FISHER'S MAJOR CONTRIBUTION: THE QUANTITY THEORY OF MONEY

Irving Fisher's most famous contribution appeared in his next book, *The Purchasing Power of Money* (1922 [1911]). It was this book that catapulted Fisher to the top of the profession. Published by Macmillan in 1911, it was translated over the years into Japanese, German, Russian, and French, and parts of it were republished in anthologies on money and banking. In this book, Fisher introduced to the world a mathematical formula for his monetary model, the quantity theory of money.

The main theme of the quantity theory of money is that inflation (the general rise in prices) is caused primarily by the expansion of money and credit, and that there is a direct correlation between changes in the general price level and changes in the money supply. If the money supply doubled, prices would double, more or less.

Many economists held to this monetary theory prior to Fisher, including David Hume and John Stuart Mill. In 1752, Hume warned his countrymen, "But . . . augmentation [in the quantity of money] has no other effect than to heighten the price of labour and commodities" (Friedman 1987: 3). In 1844, Mill concluded, "The issues of a *Government* money, even when not permanent, will raise prices" (Friedman 1987: 10).

FISHER CREATES A MATHEMATICAL FORMULA

Fisher went further. He developed a mathematical equation to represent his theory. He started with an "equation of exchange" between money and goods formulated by Simon Newcomb in 1885:

$$M \times V = P \times Q$$

where

M = quantity of money in circulation
V = velocity of money, or the annual turnover of money
P = general price level
Q = quantity of goods produced during the year

The equation of exchange is really nothing more than an accounting identity. The right-hand side of the equation represents the transfer of money, the left-hand side represents the transfer of goods. The value of goods must be equal to the money transferred in any exchange. Similarly, the total amount of money in circulation multiplied by the average number of times the money changes hands in a year must equal the dollar amount of goods and services produced and sold during the year. If the money supply amounts to $200 billion in a nation, and this $200 billion circulates from one person to another an average of five times a year, total spending in the economy equals $1 trillion. Therefore, if you add up all the goods and services produced and sold during the year, the value of the total output purchased by consumers (or sold by producers) should equal $1 trillion. Hence, by definition, $M \times V$ must be equal to $P \times Q$.

The equation of exchange is not a theory. It is true by definition, in essence, a tautology.

However, Fisher turned the equation of exchange into a theory. He assumed that both V (velocity) and Q (output) remained relatively stable and therefore changes in the price level must be directly related to changes in the money supply. As Fisher stated, "The level of prices varies in direct proportion with the quantity of money in circulation, provided that the velocity of money and the volume of trade which it is obliged to perform are not changed" (1963 [1922]: 14).

He called this the *quantity theory of money*.

FISHER'S MODEL LEADS HIM ASTRAY

Fisher firmly believed in the long-term neutrality of money; that is, an increase in the money supply would result in a proportional increase in prices without causing any long-term ill effects. While he did refer to "mal-adjustments" and "overinvestments" (terms used by the Austrians) that might occur in specific lines of production, Fisher regarded them as points of short-term disequilibrium, caused mostly by institutional factors (contracts, customs, and legal restrictions) which would eventually work themselves out (Fisher 1963: 184–85).

Thus, in the mid-1920s, he suggested that the business cycle no longer existed in the economic system. This naive conviction led to his undoing. He favored the gradual expansion of credit by the Federal Reserve and, as long as prices remained relatively stable, he felt there should be no problem. Fisher, a New Era economist, had a great deal of faith in America's new central bank and expected the Federal Reserve to intervene if a crisis arose.

PRICE STABILITY DECEIVED FISHER IN THE 1920S

According to Fisher, the key variable to monitor in the equation was P, the general price level. If prices were relatively stable, there could be no major crisis or depression. Low price inflation would mean low interest rates and stable profits.

Price stabilization was Fisher's principal monetary goal in the 1920s. He became a leading advocate of the "stable money" movement, having organized the Stable Money League in 1920–21. Other leading members of the stabilization assocation were economists Alvin Hansen, Arthur C. Pigou, Ralph G. Hawtrey, Knut Wicksell, Gustav Cassel, and John Maynard Keynes.

Fisher felt that the international gold standard could not achieve price stability on its own. It needed the help of the Federal Reserve, which was established in 1913 in order to create liquidity and credit when necessary and to stabilize the economy and prevent depressions or crises. According to Fisher, if wholesale and consumer prices remained relatively stable, everything would be fine. But if prices began to sag, threatening deflation, the Fed should intervene and expand credit.

In fact, wholesale and consumer prices in the United States were remarkably stable, and declined only slightly during the 1920s. Thus the New Era monetarists thought everything was fine as the 1929 crash approached. In fact, Milton Friedman, a modern-day monetarist, referred to the 1920s as "The High Tide of the Reserve System," stating, "The twenties were, in the main, a period of high prosperity and stable economic growth" (Friedman 1963: 296).

CRITICISM OF THE QUANTITY THEORY

A fundamental flaw in Fisher's approach was his overemphasis on long-run macroeconomic equilibrium. In Fisher's world, the primary effect of

---

WAS THE STOCK MARKET OVERVALUED IN 1929?

Had high employment and economic growth continued, prices in the stock market could have been maintained.
—Anna J. Schwartz (1987: 130)

What?! Wall Street wasn't a speculative orgy in 1929? Was Irving Fisher justified in saying on October 21, 1929, the eve of the crash, "even in the present high market, the prices of stocks have not yet caught up with their real values" (Skousen 1993: 253)? Indeed, so argue the modern financial monetarists Anna J. Schwartz and Gerald Sirkin. Schwartz boldly defended Fisher: "Application of the theory of stock values as affected by expectations of growth of earnings now suggests, as Irving Fisher believed, that market overvaluation of stocks was not general" (Schwartz 1987: 130). Curiously, she published her article the year the stock market crashed again (1987)!

She cited the work of Gerald Sirkin, professor of economics at City University of New York. Based on seemingly reasonable price-earnings ratios for most blue-chip stocks in 1929, Sirkin concluded that overall stock prices in 1929 "hardly presented a picture of 'speculative orgy'" (Sirkin 1975: 223–31).

IVORY-TOWER ACADEMIA RUN AMOK

This is a classic example of smug ivory-tower thinking. Price-earnings ratios often mask a speculative bubble because both prices and earnings tend to rise in a bull market. A better test would be to compare the total return of stocks versus GDP or industrial output. For example, from 1926 to 1929, industrial production advanced only 8.1 percent and commodity prices fell 4.7 percent, while common stock prices rose 93 percent! According to the Standard Statistics Common Stock Average, a well-diversified holding of United States stocks would have more than tripled in value from 1924 to 1929. I'd call that a speculative orgy.

monetary inflation was a general rise in prices, not structural imbalances and the business cycle. Earlier we noted that, in the late 1920s, Fisher even went so far as to deny the existence of the boom-bust business cycle. This was a fatal error. John Maynard Keynes was especially critical of this fanciful perspective of the monetarists, calling it a "misleading guide to current affairs." He wrote, "Economists set themselves too easy, too useless a task if in tempestuous seasons they can only tell us that when the storm is long past the ocean is flat again"[3] (Keynes 1971: 65).

Unfortunately, Fisher and his followers, by focusing solely on aggregate statistics, underestimated the structural imbalances in the 1920s economy. By emphasizing long-run equilibrium and price stabilization in the United States, Fisher and other New Era economists failed to consider the following vulnerable aspects of the American economy:

1. **Interest rate policy of the Federal Reserve.** The Fed engaged in an "easy money" policy throughout most of the 1920s, reducing the discount rate from 7 percent in 1921 to 3.5 percent into early 1928. Benjamin Anderson said that "excessive cheap money and unlimited bank credit available for capital uses and speculation" caused an artificial boom between 1922 and 1928 (Skousen 1993: 263). This easy-money policy was followed by a deliberate increase in interest rates in 1928–29, which broke the artificial boom and burst the bubble on Wall Street. By October 1929, the Fed's discount rate had been pushed up to 6 percent, and the call rate on stock margin loans reached 15–20 percent. Such high rates should have rung alarm bells for any seasoned speculator, but not for Fisher, who was blinded by his quantity theory and New Era enthusiasm.

2. **Structural imbalances in the economy.** Contrary to Fisher's model, inflation is not uniform in its effects on the economy. An easy-credit policy will affect various sectors of the market differently, especially the capital-goods markets. During the 1920s, there was no commodity or consumer price inflation, but there was a manufacturing production boom, and an asset inflation in real estate and the stock market. Economists referred to this situation as an "overinvestment" or "malinvestment" boom, where housing, capital-intensive businesses, and stocks advance at an unsustainable growth rate. In particular, the real estate booms in Florida and Manhattan reflected this imbalance. When interest rates shot up in 1929, the overinvestment boom came to an abrupt end.

---

3. It was in this context, a critique of the monetarists' quantity theory of money, that Keynes first made his most famous statement, "In the long run, we are all dead." See the box on this subject in chapter 13, p. 352.

3. **The international gold standard.** Fisher and his followers also underestimated the power of the international gold standard. If the world economy had abandoned gold in favor of a fiat money standard (Fisher's ideal system), the inflationary boom probably could have lasted much longer. But under a gold standard, the hands of central banks are sometimes tied. The central bankers could not continue to expand the domestic money supply without causing a negative reaction overseas. For example, domestic inflationary pressure may result in gold flowing out of the country, forcing the Federal Reserve to raise interest rates, curtail credit, and bring on a recession. Losing gold was a legitimate fear of Federal Reserve officials during the 1929–32 crisis.

UPDATE
WERE THE 1929 CRASH AND THE GREAT DEPRESSION PREDICTABLE?

The collapse from 1929 to 1933 was neither foreseeable nor inevitable.
— Milton Friedman (1963: 247)

In the September 1988 issue of the *American Economic Review*, three top econometricians from Harvard and Yale attempted to go back into history and see if they could forecast the 1929 crash and the Great Depression using modern time-series analysis. They used the very same data available to Irving Fisher at Yale and to the Harvard Economic Service, both of whom failed to anticipate the crash and subsequent depression.

Their conclusion? The 1929–33 debacle was "unforecastable." Their econometric model, like Fisher's, failed to anticipate the greatest economic crisis of the twentieth century. Were they humbled by this conclusion? No! Rather than blame Fisher and the Harvard Economic Service for losing, they claimed they both "tied." The three concluded that facing an imminent worldwide disaster, Yale and Harvard "would be justified in appearing optimistic about the economy on the eve of and in the months following the Crash" (Dominguez et al. 1988: 605). Some comfort to the thousands of investors who followed their advice!

Curiously, the three economists from Harvard and Yale ignored the warnings of several Fisher contemporaries who forecast these events, including the "sound money" economists Benjamin M. Anderson, chief economist at Chase Manhattan Bank, and H. Parker Willis, professor of banking at Columbia University and editor of the *Journal of Commerce*. Both economists were highly critical of Fisher and his quantity theory of money. The 1988 article also ignored the prescience of the Austrians Ludwig von Mises and Friedrich Hayek (see chapter 12), the Swiss banker Felix Somary, and New Englander E.C. Harwood, economics writer for *The Annalist* (Skousen 1993: 262–83).

SUMMARY: THE NEED FOR A NEW MONETARY THEORY

The failure of the monetarist Irving Fisher to forecast the greatest monetary disaster in world history forced economists to search for a new theory of macroeconomics. Before we examine the new theories that developed during the 1930s, we must take a look at Fisher's chief rival, a monetary theory that had developed on the European continent—the work of the Austrians Ludwig von Mises and Friedrich Hayek. Mises and Hayek, drawing upon the profound monetary theories of Knut Wicksell and other contemporaries, were able to anticipate the 1929–32 crisis and provide a more complete solution to the monetary missing link. Mises, Hayek, and Wicksell are the subjects of chapter 12—in the high drama of economics.

REFERENCES

Allen, Robert Loring. 1993. *Irving Fisher: A Biography.* Cambridge, MA: Blackwell.

Babson, Roger W. 1950. *Actions and Reactions: An Autobiography*, 2d ed. New York: Harper and Brothers.

Blaug, Mark. 1986. *Great Economists Before Keynes.* Atlantic Highlands, NJ: Humanities Press International.

Dominguez, Kathryn M., Ray C. Fair, and Matthew D. Shapiro. 1988. "Forecasting the Depression: Harvard Versus Yale." *American Economic Review* 78: 3 (September), 595–612.

Fisher, Irving. 1906. *The Nature of Capital and Interest.* New York: Macmillan.

———. 1928. *The Money Illusion.* New York: Adelphi.

———. 1930. *The Stock Market Crash—And After.* New York: Macmillan.

———. 1963 [1922]. *The Purchasing Power of Money,* 2d ed. New York: Augustus M. Kelley.

Fisher, Irving N. 1956. *My Father Irving Fisher.* New York: Comet Press.

Friedman, Milton. 1987. "Quantity Theory of Money." In *The New Palgrave: A Dictionary of Economics,* vol. 4, 3–20. London: Macmillan.

Friedman, Milton, and Anna J. Schwartz. 1963. *A Monetary History of the United States, 1867–1960.* Princeton: Princeton University Press.

Keynes, John Maynard. 1971. *Activities 1906–1914: India and Cambridge. The Collected Works of John Maynard Keynes,* vol. 15. London: Macmillan.

———. 1973 [1936]. *The General Theory of Employment, Interest and Money.* London: Macmillan.

Menger, Carl. 1976. *Principles of Economics.* New York: New York University Press.

Rothbard, Murray N. 1990. *What Has the Government Done to Our Money?* 4th ed. Auburn, AL: Ludwig von Mises Institute.

Schwartz, Anna J. 1987. "Understanding 1929–1933." In *Money in Historical Perspective,* 110–51. Chicago: University of Chicago Press.

Sirkin, Gerald. 1975. "The Stock Market of 1929 Revisited: A Note." *Business History Review* 49: 2 (Summer), 223–31.

Skousen, Mark. 1993. "Who Predicted the 1929 Crash?" In *The Meaning of Ludwig von Mises,* ed. Jeffrey M. Herbener, 247–83. Norwell, MA: Kluwer Academic Publishers.

Tobin, James. 1987. "Irving Fisher." In *The New Palgrave: A Dictionary of Economics,* vol. 2, 369–76. London: Macmillan.

12

THE MISSING MISES: MISES (AND WICKSELL) MAKE A MAJOR BREAKTHROUGH

At last, economics was whole, an integrated body of analysis grounded on individual action; there would have to be no split between money and relative prices, between micro and macro.

—Murray N. Rothbard (1980: 245)

Mises and Hayek articulated and vastly enriched the principles of Adam Smith at a crucial time in this century.

—Vernon L. Smith (1999: 208)

The failure of the eminent Yale economist Irving Fisher to forecast the terrible events of 1929–32 was a telling sign of the times. Monetary economics—the role of money, credit and banking—was not going to be an easy subject to figure out. Fisher's own solution, his mathematical quantity theory of money, proved painfully inadequate in explaining or predicting the ups and downs of prices, trade, and industrial activity. Imagine telling his colleagues that the business cycle was a thing of the past only months before the greatest economic collapse in history.

Fisher's old nemesis, Roger Babson, did a better job of forecasting monetary and business conditions, but even his Babsoncharts caused him to forecast prematurely, sometimes by years.

♪ **Music selection for this chapter: Ludwig van Beethoven, Symphony No. 5**

John Maynard Keynes, the famed British economist who successfully predicted the negative impact of the World War I Peace Accords and the British depression caused by an overvalued pound, had absolutely no luck in prognosticating the events of 1929–32. He tried to develop a "credit cycling" forecasting model, but gave up in the late 1920s on any form of market timing (Keynes 1983: 100). Keynes joined the other established economists, such as Irving Fisher, Ralph Hawtrey, and Wesley C. Mitchell, in their New Era optimism about America in the 1920s and shared their notion that no depression was possible as long as commodity prices were stable and the central banks were in control. (Keynes's pre-1929 views are discussed in chapter 13.)

THE AUSTRIANS TO THE RESCUE—AGAIN

However, there was a school of economics that did forecast a market collapse and worldwide depression, a forecast based on a sophisticated monetary theory. This school came from the up-and-coming generation of Austrian economists, headed by Ludwig von Mises and Friedrich A. Hayek. Because of their record of achievement and theoretical insights, Mises and Hayek are regarded as the founders of the "neo-Austrian school" of the twentieth century.

Of the two founders, Mises was the originator of the basic Austrian theory of money and the business cycle, although, as we shall see, Hayek made considerable advances that caused him to win the Nobel Prize in Economics in 1974.

Mises's revolutionary macro model drew also upon the earlier path-breaking works of the Scottish philosopher David Hume; the British financier David Ricardo; the Swedish economist Knut Wicksell; and Mises's teacher, Eugen Böhm-Bawerk. They made critical contributions, but it was Mises who put it all together into an integrated monetary theory.

Mises argued, contrary to Irving Fisher, that monetary inflation is inherently unstable and creates structural imbalances in the economy that cannot last. To use Mises's word, money is "nonneutral." According to Mises and his followers, the decision by central banks to inflate and reduce interest rates in the 1920s inevitably created an artificial boom. However, under the international gold standard, such an inflationary boom could only be short lived. The bust was inevitable—and could be severe.

When the dire predictions of Mises and Hayek came true in 1929–32, the economics profession paid considerable attention. Economists from all over the world flocked to Vienna to attend the famous Mises seminar. Mises's works were translated into English, while Hayek, his younger colleague, was invited to teach at the prestigious London School of Economics. Decades later, in 1974, Hayek won a Nobel Prize for his path-breaking work in the 1930s, and this in turn aroused a new interest in the Austrian vision of economics.

Let us begin our story with this man who generated a new approach to monetary theory, Ludwig von Mises.

THE STORY OF MISES: WILL OF IRON, MIND LIKE STEEL

The life of **Ludwig von Mises (1881–1973)** began in the city of Lemberg, which at the time was part of the Austro-Hungarian Empire. Located 350 miles east of Vienna, Lemberg is today named Lviv and is part of Ukraine. Lu (as he was fondly called) was the oldest of three sons in a prestigious Jewish family; his father was a construction engineer on whom was conferred the honorary title "von" for special work on the Austrian railroads (see the box on "von" below). His mother's uncle was a deputy of the Liberal Party in the Austrian parliament.

OH, TO BE DUBBED A "VON"

by Herr Dr. Professor Extraordinaire Mark von Skousen

Europeans are famous for conferring accolades and titles of nobility upon citizens, making them lords, baronesses, chevaliers, and dukes. In Austria, "archduke" was a title used by members of the royal family of Habsburg until the end of World War I. Like Prussian Germany, the Austro-Hungarian Empire emphasized hero worship, ceremony, and honorary degrees.

"Von" was one title in the Austrian Empire. It was conferred upon servants of government and occasionally upon professionals or businessmen for special merits. It was rather like "Sir," in Great Britain, but it was inherited by all male and by unmarried female descendants. Thus, Ludwig von Mises inherited the title from his father, who received the honorary title "von" for his work on Austrian railroads. Other Austrian economists who carried the title include Böhm-Bawerk, Wieser, and Hayek. Menger himself dropped "von" in early childhood. Hayek dropped it after becoming a naturalized British citizen.

After the Austro-Hungarian Empire was disbanded in 1918, the "von" title was abolished and most bearers ceased to use it in their names. However, it was still generally applied by other persons. According to Hayek, these names ought to be inserted in an alphabetical list according to the initial letter of the surname proper (e.g., Mises, not von Mises), unlike the Dutch surnames beginning with "Van."

Now that the Great War is over, I guess I'll have to go back to my original humble title at Columbia University and Rollins College: *adjunct* professor of economics.

Lu entered the University of Vienna at the turn of the twentieth century, where he read Menger's *Grundsätze* and attended the famous Böhm-Bawerk seminar. Under their influence, Mises rejected the prevalent socialism of the times. In 1906, at the age of twenty-five, he received a doctorate in laws and was ready to make a contribution to the world.

MISES DISCOVERS THE MISSING LINK AT AGE THIRTY-ONE

With his Ph.D. in hand, Mises soon became chief economist at the Vienna Chamber of Commerce, but his real goal was to obtain a professorship at Vienna University. In 1912, he finished his breakthrough book, *Theorie des Geldes und der Umlaufsmittel*, later translated as *The Theory of Money and Credit*, which offered a sophisticated monetary model that challenged Irving Fisher's quantity theory of money. *Money and Credit* forged the missing link between micro- and macroeconomics. It was a tour de force. His work was sufficiently recognized that Mises was offered a post at the university, but as a *privatdozent*, unpaid and part time. After the war, when it was time to appoint full-time replacements for Böhm-Bawerk and Wieser, the university rejected Mises and choose two others. He remained a *privatdozent*.

Photograph 12.1
Ludwig von Mises (1881–1973)
"He suffered from a
hopeless pessimism."
Courtesy of
Ludwig von Mises Institute.

DISCRIMINATION ON THREE COUNTS

Mises failed to be appointed for three reasons:

1. He was Jewish in a country that was increasingly anti-Semitic.

2. He was an uncompromising advocate of laissez-faire liberalism in an age of national socialism.

3. He was personally dogmatic and intransigent. As Mises himself admitted, "Occasionally I was reproached because I made my point too bluntly and intransigently, and I was told that I could have achieved more if I had shown more willingness to compromise. . . . I felt the criticism was unjustified" (L. Mises 1978: 74).

Mises continued his work at the government-run Vienna Chamber of Commerce, where he became an informal advisor to the government. Two stories are worth retelling.

MISES AND RED VIENNA

Following World War I, several Eastern European countries were tempted to follow the Bolshevik Revolution in Russia. Austria was still suffering from the Allied food blockade during the winter of 1918–19. Additionally, "Austro-Marxist" radicals, led by Otto Bauer, had taken control of "Red

Vienna" and planned to take the entire country into the Bolshevik camp. Mises, who had befriended Bauer before the war in Böhm-Bawerk's seminar, spent day and night trying to convince Bauer and his Marxist wife that a communist regime would mean greater blockades by the Allies and a complete discrediting of their cause. Finally, Mises convinced Bauer to back off his revolutionary scheme, and Austria was saved from destruction. Mises later claimed credit for single-handedly preventing a Bolshevik takeover of Austria (Rothbard 1988: 31), but Otto Bauer later became embittered by the affair. Reviled as a traitor by his radical comrades, Bauer hated Mises and tried to get him removed from his university post. They never spoke to each other again (Hülsmann 2007: 332–35).

MISES'S VERSION OF "HOW TO STOP INFLATION"

The second story occurred in the early 1920s. Suffering from the excessive burdens of the Peace Accords, Austria, like Germany, resorted to hyperinflation. Friedrich Hayek recalled that his salary went from 5,000 kronen a month in October 1921, to 15,000 kronen in November, and to 1 million kronen by July 1922. In Germany, inflation was even worse. Mises expected at any time to be named finance minister to resolve the inflationary crisis, but he was never called.

Finally, at the height of the hyperinflation, a League of Nations commission was sent to Vienna. Along with worried Austrian government officials, they paid a visit to Mises to seek his advice on how to end the terrible inflation. He replied bluntly, "Meet me at twelve o'clock midnight at this building and I'll tell you." The officials shook their head quizzically, but finally agreed. Meeting him at the specified location at midnight, they asked anxiously, "Professor Mises, how can we stop this inflation?" He replied, "Hear that noise? Turn it off!" The building turned out to be the government printing office, which was running round the clock printing new banknotes. Turning off the noise was precisely what the Austrian government did, and the inflation ended (Hayek 1994: 70).

LIVING IN THE TWENTIES

The Roaring Twenties was a busy time for Mises. He wrote a book on socialism that would later be acclaimed as a classic. He also carried on Böhm-Bawerk's tradition of the private seminar between 1920 and 1934. The private seminar was an informal discussion forum on major economic and political issues, held every other Friday evening at his office at the Chamber of Commerce. Afterward, the group would go out to dinner at their favorite coffeehouse and stay until one o'clock in the morning. The seminar was attended by invitation only and participants considered it a great honor to be invited.

Mises himself was a very private man. A confirmed bachelor for many decades, he lived with his mother. He did not marry until he was nearly

MISESIAN RIVALRY: RICHARD VERSUS LUDWIG

Richard was brilliant; everyone understands economics.
—Mrs. Richard von Mises, comparing the two brothers

[Richard] was a positivist from his first day until his last.
—Ludwig von Mises, speaking of the death of his brother

Ludwig von Mises always feared he would be outdone by his younger brother, Richard. Ludwig received his doctorate in laws at the University of Vienna at age twenty-five, but Richard earned his doctorate in a much tougher subject, mathematics, a year later at age twenty-four. Ludwig developed brilliant new theories in economics, but was unable to obtain a full-time, paid academic position. Richard was immediately appointed a mathematics professor at the University of Strassburg. In 1913, Richard learned to fly an airplane and taught one of the first university courses on aerodynamics. Both brothers fought for Austria in the Great War, but Ludwig was an artillery officer at the front, while Richard was chief engineer in charge of developing military aircraft and helped develop an original wing design. Richard was considered one of the great pioneers in aircraft design.

After the war, the rivalry continued to favor Richard. Ludwig became the chief economist at the Vienna Chamber of Commerce, and he was an informal advisor to the government. Finally he was appointed an instructor at the University of Vienna—as an unpaid *privatdozen*. Meanwhile, Richard returned to teaching mathematics at the prestigious University of Berlin, where he wrote books on statistics (a subject Keynes also wrote about) and aerodynamics.

Photograph 12.2   **Photograph 12.3**
Richard von Mises   Ludwig von Mises

Richard Versus Ludwig
A lifelong rivalry in the Mises family.
Courtesy of Harvard University Archives and the Mises Institute.

(continued)

In 1933, the Nazis tried to enlist Richard as an aircraft engineer, but he refused and left Germany to accept a post at the University of Istanbul. Ludwig, also facing Nazi repression, left his beloved Vienna in 1934 and accepted a one-year professorship at the University of Geneva. Finally, a paid academic post for Ludwig!

This post was not to last. Swiss officials, under political pressure, made Ludwig feel unwelcome. Nearly sixty, depressed, and impoverished, Ludwig emigrated with his wife to the United States, arriving in New York City in August 1940.

Who was there to greet him? Younger brother Richard, who in 1939—nearly two years earlier—had joined the staff at Harvard University! By 1944, Richard became the Gordon McKay Professor of Aerodynamics and Applied Mathematics, a position he held until his death in 1954.

Meanwhile, the frustrated Ludwig was never able to find another full-time paid position. He ended his career as a permanent *visiting* professor at New York University. His salary was subsidized by friends.

Ludwig and Richard occasionally got together but were never close. For one thing, they violently disagreed on philosophy. Richard was a member of the Vienna Circle, a group of philosophers. Included in the group were Ludwig Wittgenstein and Karl Popper, who favored logical positivism, the use of empirical evidence to test one's theories. Mises rejected positivism in favor of pure deductive reasoning. Murray Rothbard, who studied under Mises in New York, once asked Ludwig what he thought of his brother's book, *Positivism*, which had been published by Harvard College in 1951. "Mises drew himself up into an uncharacteristically stern pose, eyes flashing: 'I disagreed with that book,' he stated in no uncertain terms, 'from the first sentence until the last.' It was not a tone that invited further inquiry" (Rothbard 1988: 79).

Today, a generation later, the older brother may finally have the upper hand. Only one of Richard's books, *The Theory of Flight*, is still in print, while Ludwig's books on economics and philosophy are being published and read around the world. There's even a public foundation established in his name, the Ludwig von Mises Institute, located near Auburn University in Alabama.

fifty-seven years old. It was in 1938, while he was living in Geneva, Switzerland, that he married an actress, Margit Sereny-Herzfeld, a widow with two children (Hülsmann 2007: 517–21, 730–33).

PREDICTING THE 1929–32 ECONOMIC CRISIS: "THAT WILL BE A BIG SMASH!"

During the 1920s, Mises and Hayek established the Austrian Institute of Economic Research, which monitored and forecast economic conditions in Europe. As early as 1924, Mises was convinced that an economic crisis was coming. Based on his path-breaking book *Theorie des Geldes*, Mises realized that the easy-credit policies of the central banks would lead to disaster under an international gold standard.

One of his students, Fritz Machlup, recalled Mises's "gift of prophecy": "As his assistant in the university seminar which met every Wednesday afternoon, I usually accompanied him home. On these walks we would pass through a passage of the Kreditanstalt in Vienna [one of the largest banks in Europe]. From 1924, every Wednesday afternoon as we walked through the passage for pedestrians he said: 'That will be a big smash.' Mind you, this was from 1924 onwards; yet in 1931, when the crash finally came, I still held some shares of the Kreditanstalt, which of course had become completely worthless" (Machlup 1974: 12).

In the summer of 1929, Mises was offered a high position at the Kreditanstalt Bank. His future wife, Margit, was ecstatic, but Lu surprised her when he decided against it. "Why not?" she asked. His response shocked her: "A great crash is coming, and I don't want my name in any way connected with it." He preferred to write and teach. "If you want a rich man," he said, "don't marry me. I am not interested in earning money. I am *writing* about money, but will never have much of my own"[1] (M. Mises 1984: 23–24).

After Wall Street collapsed several months later, world trade suffered and in May 1931, Kreditanstalt went bankrupt. This, more than any other event, extended the depression throughout Europe.

After the depression was in full swing, Mises commented on his prediction in an introduction to the English translation of *Money and Credit* (written in June 1934):

> From 1926 to 1929 the attention of the world was chiefly focused upon the question of American prosperity. As in all previous booms brought out about by expansion of credit, it was then believed that the prosperity would last forever, and the warnings of the economists were disregarded. The turn of the tide in 1929 and the subsequent severe economic crisis were not a surprise for [Austrian] economists; they had foreseen them, even if they had not been able to predict the exact date of their occurrence.[2] (L. Mises 1971 [1934]: 14–15)

HAYEK ALSO PREDICTS THE CRASH

Mises's colleague, Friedrich A. Hayek, also forecast an economic crisis, specifically in the United States. His timing appeared to be more precise than Mises's. As director of the Austrian Institute of Economic Research, Hayek forecast trouble in early 1929. Referring to his prediction in an interview in 1975, Hayek stated:

1. Mises's statement is not unlike Karl Marx's mother's complaint about her son: "If only Karl had made capital instead of writing about it!" (Padover 1978: 344).

2. Mises's predictive powers were not always prescient, however. In September 1931, Ursula Hicks (wife of John Hicks) was attending Mises's seminar in Vienna when England suddenly announced it was going off the gold standard. Mises predicted the British pound would become worthless within a week, which never happened. Thereafter, Mises always expressed deep skepticism about the ability of economists to forecast. (*Source:* Private interview with John Hicks, July 1988, at his home near Oxford, England; cf. Hülsmann 2007: 641.)

I was one of the only ones to predict what was going to happen. In early 1929, when I made this forecast, I was living in Europe which was then going through a period of depression. I said that there [would be] no hope of a recovery in Europe until interest rates fell, and interest rates would not fall until the American boom collapses, which I said was likely to happen within the next few months.[3] (Hayek 1975)

Who Is Hayek?

Hayek's name will always be linked with Ludwig von Mises as cofounder of the neo-Austrian school. Hayek advanced the Misesian theory of the business cycle, was a major critic of socialist central planning, and made important contributions to political theory. In 1974, a year after Mises died, Hayek was granted the Nobel Prize in economics, which many regard as a delayed tribute to Mises. (The prize cannot be awarded posthumously.)

Hayek and Mises, though close collaborators, differed in appearance, background, and personality. Hayek was tall, Mises was short. Hayek was Christian, Mises was Jewish. Hayek was outgoing and upbeat, Mises was reserved and lugubrious. Yet they managed to maintain their friendship.

Friedrich A. Hayek (1899–1992), born in Vienna, was seventeen years Mises's junior. Throughout his life, he was surrounded by natural scientists. His grandfather was a zoologist, his father an M.D. and a professor of botany, his brothers teachers of botany and chemistry, his daughter a biologist and his son a bacteriologist. For a single generation, Hayek switched to the social sciences.

Hayek grew to be over six feet tall, striking, and intelligent. He was going to major in the physical sciences, but the devastation of the Great War, where he served as an artillery officer, changed his interest to law and politics. He rapidly earned *two* doctorates at the University of Vienna, in law in 1921 and political science in 1923.

In 1923, he spent a year in New York and, impressed with the statistical work of Wesley C. Mitchell and the National Bureau of Economic Research (NBER), returned to his native land to convince Mises to set up the Austrian Institute of Economic Research. Hayek was tempted by Fabian socialism, but upon reading Mises's 1922 book *Socialism*, he changed his mind. "To none of us young men who read the book when it appeared," he recalled, "was the world ever the same again" (Hayek 1992: 133). Thereafter, Hayek became Mises's protégé and colleague. He read the other Austrians. "I found Menger's *Grundsätze* such a fascinating book, so satisfying," he wrote (1994: 48).

---

3. In the preface to the first edition of *Prices and Production*, Lionel Robbins wrote that the Austrian Institute of Economic Research, of which Hayek was director, had predicted the American deflation in the "spring of 1929" (Hayek 1931: xii). However, I have been unable to find a record of Hayek's forecast in any of the monthly publications of the institute.

THE AUSTRIAN SCHOOL ACHIEVES WORLDWIDE ACCLAIM

The ability of Mises and Hayek to forecast the depression catapulted the Austrian school back into the limelight in the early 1930s. Many young economists in Britain and the United States, searching for an explanation for the 1929–32 collapse, were readily attracted to the Austrian version. Lionel Robbins, chairman of the economics department at the London School of Economics, heard about Mises and Hayek and traveled to Vienna to attend Mises's famous seminar. Afterward, he invited Hayek to deliver a series of lectures on the Austrian theory of the business cycle at the LSE with the specific purpose "to fight Keynes" (Hayek 1994: 77). The lectures were delivered in May 1931, and published soon afterward as *Prices and Production* (1931). This slim book extended Austrian principles into a full-fledged macroeconomic model.

HAYEK'S TRIANGLES

In *Prices and Production*, Hayek created a unique diagram known as "Hayek's triangle" to represent the time structure of the economy. Figure 12.1 reproduces his first diagram.

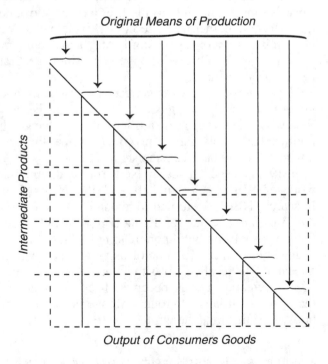

Figure 12.1
Hayek's Triangle—A Time-Structural Model of the Economy
Source: Hayek (1935: 39).

The triangle starts at the top with the earliest stage of production—natural resources—and continues downward toward the production of manufactured goods until it reaches the final stage, retail consumption. Note that the triangle enlarges with time as each stage adds value to goods and services being produced. The area of the triangle represents total spending in the economy for all goods and services during the year.

According to Hayek, the structure of the triangle changes with interest rates. An increase in the saving rate could lengthen the triangle, resulting in lower costs and higher output in the long run, and a new macro equilibrium. On the other hand, an artificial increase in the money supply would send false signals to producers and consumers, creating an inflationary boom that would

Photograph 12.4
Frederich von Hayek (1899–1992)
Moved to London
"to fight Keynes."
Courtesy of Hulton-Getty Archives.

inevitably turn into a bust. The triangle would initially grow, but eventually shrink.

HAYEK'S BOOK TAKES ENGLAND BY STORM

Hayek and his explanation of the slump initially took England by storm. Nobel laureate John Hicks noted, "When the definitive history of economic analysis during the nineteen-thirties comes to be written, a leading character in the drama (it was quite a drama) will be Professor Hayek" (Hicks 1967: 203). Joseph Schumpeter claimed that the 160-page book "met with a sweeping success that [had] never been equaled by any strictly theoretical book" (Schumpeter 1954: 1120).

Hayek gave a logical explanation for why the 1929–32 debacle had occurred, especially in America: using his famous triangles, Hayek showed that the slump was an inevitable result of an unsustainable boom in the 1920s. Robbins was so enthusiastic that he had Hayek appointed Tooke Professor of Economic Science at the London School of Economics (LSE), a position he held for eighteen years. "Good wine needs no bush, and Dr. Hayek provides a vintage over which all true economists will linger long," Robbins wrote in the preface to Hayek's *Prices and Production* (Hayek 1931: xi).

Robbins spearheaded a revival of Austrian economics in England, including the translation of Mises's *Money and Credit* and other Austrian works. Robbins himself wrote a full-length work, *The Great Depression* (1934), outlining the causes and cures of the depression. According to Robbins, the depression was not caused by capitalism, but by the "negation" of capitalism. "It was due to monetary mismanagement and State intervention operating in a *milieu* in which the essential strength of capitalism had already been sapped by war and by policy" (Robbins 1934: 194).[4] The LSE, previously known as a hotbed of socialist thinking, was now being dominated by free-market thinkers.

HAYEK ATTACKS KEYNES

Inevitably, Hayek met up with John Maynard Keynes. Although they were friends most of the time, they were professional adversaries. Hayek attacked Keynes's two-volume *Treatise on Money* (1930–31) for lacking a theory of capital and, in return, Keynes denounced Hayek's *Prices and Production* as unintelligible and "a thick bank of fog" (Skousen 1990: 47–51). The "Young Turks" at the LSE were enthusiastic about Hayek's monetary theory, but the "Cambridge Circus" surrounding Keynes was unmistakably hostile.

KEYNES WINS THE BATTLE

Hayek and Keynes represented opposite sides during the 1930s. Keynes favored "money management" by the state; Hayek believed in a noninterventionist policy by government. Keynes advocated inflation and deficit spending; Hayek favored a neutral money policy and a reliance on market flexibility in prices and wages. Keynes said hoarding and increased savings were bad during a depression; Hayek debunked the "paradox of saving" and defended the traditional value of thrift. The gulf between them was wide.

In the pages of the London *Times*, Hayek and Keynes debated the role of government. A letter to the editor on October 17, 1932, signed by Keynes, A.C. Pigou, and other economists, opposed thrift during a slump. It was followed by a letter on October 19, signed by Hayek, Robbins, and others, criticizing government spending.

Eventually, as the depression wore on, the "do-nothing" policies of Hayek and the Austrians lost out to the activist approach of Keynes and the Keynesians. Mises and Hayek may have explained the cause of the depression, but their cure appeared unworkable and dismal. Suddenly, all eyes shifted to Cambridge and Keynes's new book, *The General Theory of Employment, Interest and Money* (1936).

Hayek never did write a critique of *The General Theory*, an action he eventually regretted. When Keynes's *General Theory* was published in 1936, Hayek thought it was just "another tract of the times" that would have no permanent effect. He was dead wrong.

4. Robbins's depression book was also quite prophetic about the dangers of wars and the Nazis, "men to whom the kindly virtues of peace are contemptible and for whom the destruction of life is a better thing than its preservation" (Robbins 1934: 196). This was written in 1934.

In sum, the fortunes of the Austrian school suffered a dramatic reversal and it would be years before Hayek would recover. Mises himself never recovered from this intellectual defeat. The young Turks of the LSE—John Hicks, Abba Lerner, Nicholas Kaldor, and Kenneth Boulding—all switched to become disciples of Keynes. Paul Sweezy, the Harvard transplant, switched to Keynes and then to Marx. Even Hayek's closest friend, Lionel Robbins, abandoned ship. In his autobiography, Robbins called his siding with Hayek in the 1930s the "greatest mistake of my professional career . . . it will always be a matter of deep regret to me that, although I was acting in good faith and with a strong sense of social obligation, I should have so opposed policies which might have mitigated the economic distress of those days" (Robbins 1971: 154–5).

Hayek was so depressed by these turns of events that by the early 1940s he stopped writing about economics and turned to political theory. During World War II, he was forced to move to Cambridge and found himself "supporting Keynes in his struggle against wartime inflation, and at that time wished nothing less than to weaken his [Keynes's] authority" (Hayek 1983: 47).

MEANWHILE, BACK IN VIENNA, THE NAZIS ARE COMING

In Austria during the 1930s, Mises's primary worry shifted from economics to politics. According to Fritz Machlup, Mises predicted as early as 1927 that the end of freedom in Central Europe was coming, and urged Machlup and other free-market economists to leave Europe. By 1938, said Machlup, "most of us had acted upon the master's advice and had taken the first chance we got to leave our native country in good time" (Machlup 1974: 13). Fritz Machlup went to Buffalo, Oskar Morgenstern to Princeton, Gottfried Haberler to Harvard, and Paul Rosenstein-Rodan to MIT. Joseph Schumpeter had already been at Harvard since 1932.

In the fall of 1934, with the Nazis' influence expanding rapidly, Mises decided to leave his beloved Austria to accept a position at the Graduate Institute of International Studies in Geneva, Switzerland. The Nazi Party viewed Mises, a laissez-faire Jew, as an enemy of the state. In 1938, on the night the Nazis stormed Vienna, they rushed into Mises's apartment; confiscated his library, writings, and personal documents; packed it all into thirty-eight cases; and drove away. For the rest of his life, Mises thought the Nazis had destroyed his valuable papers, but in the 1990s, twenty years after Mises's death, Richard Ebeling of Hillsdale College discovered the long-lost library among KGB files in Moscow. Apparently the Russians had confiscated Mises's property from the Nazis after World War II and transported them to Moscow. (Mises's personal library is now located at Hillsdale College in Michigan.)

FROM FREEDOM TO TYRANNY ALMOST OVERNIGHT

Margit Mises described what it was like when Hitler marched into Vienna on March 14, 1938: "That night he [Hitler] made his first speech over the radio. His voice still rings in my ears. I shall never forget it. It was rough, throaty, and vulgar, but it had an almost unbearable strength combined with a hypnotic power of persuasion. As much as his voice frightened me, I listened to the very end" (M. Mises 1984: 29).

Finally, Margit (who was Ludwig's fiancée at the time) and her daughter escaped and made their way to Switzerland, where they were met by a teary-eyed Lu. During their entire marriage of thirty-five years, Margit saw her husband cry only this once. "He wept—unrestrained and unabashed" (M. Mises 1984: 31).

Margit recounted the previous days in Nazi-controlled Austria. "The terror of the past few weeks still lingered in my mind. Though nothing really happened to us, I had been constantly conscious of the danger around us. Our freedom was at stake; I could not do what I wanted to do. There were spies everywhere, spies who watched you, misinterpreted the simplest of your actions, and reported you. Household employees who had grown old with families they lived with, suddenly became enemies. Children were taught to observe their parents and report on them. The Germans had organized everything so thoroughly beforehand that it took only a few days for freedom to turn into tyranny" (M. Mises 1984: 31).

EXILED IN THE NEW WORLD

After six years of teaching in Geneva, Mises and his family were forced to flee to the United States. Friends such as Henry Hazlitt, economics writer for the *New York Times*, and John Van Sickle of the Rockefeller Foundation helped Mises get settled in New York City, but Mises suffered for years from a "hopeless pessimism." His writings, now in English, were full of despair, especially with Keynesianism and national socialism spreading throughout the Western world. "He was the most depressing person I ever saw," Peter Drucker once remarked. Drucker, who knew Mises in his youth in Vienna, would occasionally encounter Mises on the New York University (NYU) campus, and always found him glum and disinterested.

While his Austrian colleagues and even his brother (see box on page 294) were able to obtain prestigious positions in academia, Mises himself was forced to accept grants and part-time posts. He became a permanent "visiting professor" at New York University, his salary subsidized by the William Volker Fund. However, his part-time status was not entirely involuntary. He was offered a position at the University of California at Los Angeles (UCLA), but stubbornly refused to leave New York.

Mises was deeply antagonistic toward other academic economists in the postwar era. He engaged in polemics and exchanged *ad hominem* attacks with his enemies. The Keynesians dismissed their free-market critics as "reactionary," "narrow-minded fanatics," and "old-fashioned." Mises responded by calling the interventionists "anti-economists," "pseudo-progressives," and "ignorant zealots." There was a lot of bad blood.

Once asked to speak before a major ivy league university (probably Harvard), Mises turned down the invitation as a "waste of time." "One hour of sound economics against several years of indoctrination of errors!" exclaimed Mises. "Now, exploding any one of them [economic errors] requires much more time than that assigned to me in your program" (L. Mises 1980: 166). By accepting the invitation, Mises perhaps could have influenced a few students to study alternatives to Keynesianism and socialism—a foot in the door—but he never took the chance. By contrast, Marxists such as Paul Sweezy never missed a chance to promote Marxism.

"YOU'RE ALL A BUNCH OF SOCIALISTS!"

Friends of Mises gave differing reports on Mises's personality. Murray Rothbard, who attended Mises's private seminar in New York, described him as gentle and sweet, with hundreds of enthusiastic admirers, including one who composed songs in honor of Mises's seminar. "As a scholar, as an economist, and as a person," wrote Rothbard, "Ludwig von Mises was a joy and an inspiration, an exemplar for us all" (Rothbard 1988: 71–74).

Those who disagreed with Mises's ideas saw a harsher side of intolerance. He was known to hold a grudge for years, refusing to speak to someone who had offended him. He often showed little patience with his colleagues who favored moderate forms of government intervention. The most infamous story is told of a 1953 meeting of the Mont Pelerin Society, a group of political and economic libertarian thinkers organized by Hayek (see the box on page 304). Milton Friedman, who chaired a session on income distribution, wrote, "I particularly recall a discussion of this issue, in the middle of which Ludwig von Mises stood up, announced to the assembly 'You're all a bunch of socialists,' and stomped out of the room." Friedman added that the group "contained not a single person who, by even the loosest standards, could be called a socialist" (1998: 161).

At another Mont Pelerin Meeting, Fritz Machlup, one of his favorite students and a Johns Hopkins professor, gave a talk in which he questioned the gold standard and came out in favor of flexible exchange rates. Mises was so incensed that he refused to speak to Machlup for three years. Eventually, with the help of friends, they were reconciled (Friedman 1995: 37).

Even Margit Mises disagreed with the adjective "gentle" when applied to her husband: "He was gentle with me because he loved me. But actually he was not gentle. He had a will of iron and a mind like a steel blade. He could be unbelievably stubborn" (1984: 144).

HAYEK CREATES THE FIRST INTERNATIONAL FREE-MARKET ASSOCIATION

We must raise and train an army of fighters for freedom.

—F.A. Hayek

Before the Adam Smith Institute, the Heritage Foundation, the Cato Institute, and other influential free-market organizations came along, there was the Mont Pelerin Society, established in 1947. Only the Foundation for Economic Education (FEE), organized by Leonard Read in 1946, is older.

In an effort to reverse the tide of totalitarianism and socialism, Hayek wrote *The Road to Serfdom* in 1944, and with the help of an admirer, organized an international forum of like-minded scholars in Mont Pèlerin, Switzerland, above Lake Geneva, in the spring of 1947. Thirty-nine individuals came from ten countries, including Ludwig von Mises, Karl Popper, and Milton Friedman. Hayek dedicated the meeting to the spirit of Adam Smith: "Modern economic liberalism, as I see it, is the legitimate off-spring of the union between two first cousins: Adam Smith's penetrating and essentially sound scientific analysis of the economic world of his day, and Adam Smith's inborn love of freedom, constructive effort and wealth" (Cockett 1994: 111).

Hayek originally wanted to call the group the Acton-Tocqueville Society, but Frank Knight objected, "You can't call a liberal movement after two Catholics!" So they finally settled on a nonpolitical name, the Mont Pelerin Society.

The meeting was so successful that it has been going strong ever since, and today has become an exclusive club that is almost impossible to join. Candidates have to be nominated by two members, attend two previous meetings by invitation, and even then, if you're an American economist, your chances of membership are slim. Founders of the Mont Pelerin Society have always maintained that it is an international organization that should not be dominated by Americans.

The Mont Pelerin Society is not a think tank or a political pressure group. Meetings are private, speeches are not recorded, and papers are seldom published. Annual meetings are held around the globe (recently in Japan, France, and Chile) and members and guests come from all continents. Milton Friedman commented, "The Mont Pelerin Society has veritably been a spiritual fountain of youth, to which we could all repair once a year or so to renew our spirits and faith among a growing company of fellow believers" (Ebenstein 1996: 138).

MISES'S MAGNUM OPUS: *HUMAN ACTION*

Mises, deprived of a full-time university position, spent much of his time writing books and articles in his New York apartment. His wife described him as sitting for hours in front of his old typewriter, smoking cigarettes, and refusing to take off his jacket even in the hottest of summers with no air conditioning (M. Mises 1984: 143–44).

GARY NORTH'S FAT-BOOK THEORY

Another damned, thick, square book! Always scribble, scribble, scribble!
Eh! Mr. Gibbon?
—William Henry, Duke of Gloucester, upon receiving volume 2 of
Edward Gibbon's *Decline and Fall of the Roman Empire* (1781)

Economic historian Gary North has a "fat-book" theory: Producing a revolution requires a fat book. According to North, all great economists have written massive tomes. He cites Adam Smith's *Wealth of Nations* (2 volumes, 1,097 pages), Karl Marx's *Capital* (3 volumes, 2,846 pages), Joseph A. Schumpeter's *History of Economic Analysis* (1,260 pages), and Murray N. Rothbard's *Man, Economy and State* (2 volumes, 987 pages). Not surprisingly, North himself has written several weighty works of wisdom. His *Tools of Dominion* (1,287 pages) is actually the third volume in a serial commentary on the book of Exodus. It is self-published. "I have no illusions about its becoming a bestseller," North admits (1990: 2).

North would surely be disappointed in John Maynard Keynes's *General Theory*, which runs only 486 pages, but would be delighted with Mises's *Human Action* (a treatise of 907 pages), and Milton Friedman's *Monetary History of the United States* (860 pages).

But ultimately, we must reject North's labor theory of value. After all, how can he explain the influence of such small works as *The Communist Manifesto* (a mere 62 pages), or the Four Gospels of the Bible (only 177 pages)?

Mises's most important work from the postwar era is *Human Action*, first published by Yale University Press in 1949. *Human Action* is to Austrians what *Das Capital* is to Marxists, a full-scale economics treatise. And, like *Das Capital*, Mises's tome, running over 900 pages, is twice the size of any previous work (see the box above, "Gary North's Fat Book Theory"). "What's *Human Action* about?" you may ask. Its admirers respond, "Everything!" Rothbard described it as "Mises's greatest achievement and one of the finest products of the human mind in our century" (Rothbard 1988: 64).

Human Action is not easy reading, especially in the early chapters on methodology. With chapters such as "The Formal and Aprioristic Character of Praxeology," *Human Action* has been relegated to graduate courses in economics. But the faithful keep reading it. It went through three revisions during Mises's life, and has been translated into five languages. Amazingly, it was an alternate selection of the Book-of-the-Month Club when it came out in 1949, probably due to favorable reviews by *Newsweek* ("it should be the leading text") and the *Wall Street Journal* ("it ought to be on the bookshelf of every thinking man") (L. Mises 1966: dustjacket).

Mises, however, was never too far from tragedy, and the second edition of *Human Action* is a bizarre example of an academic scandal. In 1963, Yale University Press agreed to print the second revised edition of *Human Action*. When it appeared a year later, it was clear someone at Yale was trying to sabotage the book. It was a typographical nightmare. On page 322, four lines were omitted. Page 468 was missing altogether. Page 469 was printed twice. On page after page, some paragraphs were printed in a light type, others in a dark boldface type. Whole pages of boldface are found opposite whole pages of lighter type. Yale printed an errata sheet, but did little else to compensate Mises for this hatchet job by an unknown assailant. Mises was deeply disturbed by this event, unable to sleep for months. Finally, he obtained a new contract from a friendly publisher, Henry Regnery, and the third revised edition was issued in 1966.

MISES'S FINAL YEARS

Like Carl Menger, Mises felt no vindication in his old age. In his eighties, he continued to lecture at the Foundation for Economic Education in Irvington-on-Hudson, New York (the oldest free-market think tank, founded in 1946 by Leonard Read), and went on speaking tours to Mexico and Argentina. Yet he felt little hope of a return to free-market principles in academia or politics. In 1969, the American Economic Association honored Mises as a distinguished fellow, but he found this honor little consolation. When he was ninety, he became ill, and two years later, in 1973, he died in New York City.

SUMMARY: THE MISSING MISES

Mises was a profound thinker and his books, particularly *The Theory of Money and Credit*, *Socialism*, and *Human Action*, went further than the works of any other economist toward establishing a fully integrated model of the economy. He solved many of the remaining puzzles in economics, especially with regard to money. Yet his obstinate refusal to integrate himself into the modern economics community after World War II set back the case for his Austrian theories for an entire generation. The Austrian model—its theory of capital and business cycle—was expunged from the textbooks and the journals. Mises became the missing Mises.

HAYEK AND THE REBIRTH OF AUSTRIAN ECONOMICS

Could Hayek, Mises's protégé, restore Austrian economics? Not for a long time. Hayek also fell into a depressed state after World War II. Like his mentor, he continued to write furiously, but not about economics. Unhappy with the Keynesian takeover of the economics profession, he turned to political and philosophical issues.

In 1944, near the end of World War II and while he was still at Cambridge, Hayek finished writing *The Road to Serfdom*, a book that would prove to be a highly influential bestseller. It warned the West about the dangers of socialism and fascism, and concluded that "only capitalism makes democracy possible" (Hayek 1976 [1944]: 69–70). Hayek's outlook on politics was deeply cynical. He quoted Lord Acton, "Power tends to corrupt, and absolute power corrupts absolutely." Chapter 10 was titled "Why the Worst Get on Top." No doubt Hayek was thinking of Hitler, Stalin, and Mussolini, and perhaps even of Roosevelt. In the 1976 preface to the book, his pessimism persisted: "And both the influence of socialist ideas and the naive trust in the good intentions of the holders of totalitarian power have markedly increased since I wrote this book" (1976 [1944]: xxi).

Hayek was surprised by the success of *The Road to Serfdom*. A first edition sold out within a few days in Britain. Even Keynes extolled its virtues. "It is a grand book. . . . Morally and philosophically I find myself in agree-

---

HAYEK EMBROILED IN A PERSONAL SCANDAL

I'm sure that was wrong, and yet I have done it. It was just an inner need to do it.
—F.A. Hayek (Ebenstein 1996: 157)

In the early 1920s, a youthful Fritz Hayek fell in love with his cousin, Helene Bitterlich. But she married someone else, and Fritz was obliged to seek another. A secretary in his office caught his fancy, a woman who not only looked like his first love but had an almost identical name, Helen (though she was called Hella). It seemed a perfect match. Hayek married Helen von Fritsch in the summer of 1926 and they had two children, a daughter born in Austria and a son born in England. Nevertheless, for the next twenty-five years, the Hayeks suffered from an unhappy marriage. Hayek said Hella was a good wife, but they constantly fought.

At the end of the war, Hayek returned to Vienna and encountered his cousin, Helene, who announced happily that she was no longer married. They immediately fell in love, and Hayek determined to divorce his wife. Back in England, an upset Hella refused, and the ensuing divorce proceedings were so bitter that Fritz's friend, Lionel Robbins, and the rest of the economics department at LSE would not speak to him. They firmly believed that Hayek had mistreated his wife. But Hayek was resolute in his decision. He moved out, left England (even though he had become a naturalized British citizen), and headed for Arkansas, which was known for its permissive divorce laws. He spent part of a year at the University of Arkansas, and when his divorce came through in 1950, he moved on to the University of Chicago (Ebenstein 1996: 156–57; Hayek 1994: 22–23).

It was another ten years before Hayek became reconciled with his old friend Lionel Robbins, with whom he had had a falling out about the marriage scandal. Even then, few spoke kindly of his new wife, Helene, who often refused to let old friends and colleagues contact Hayek in his later years. "She was impossible!" Hayek's son, Lawrence, once declared at a Mont Pelerin Society meeting.

ment with virtually the whole of it; and not only in agreement with it, but in a deeply moved agreement." His only quarrel was in the area of planning; he thought the state should engage in more planning, not less (Keynes 1980: 385–87).

The University of Chicago, Hayek's American publisher, arranged for a book tour in the United States in the spring of 1945. Henry Hazlitt gave *The Road to Serfdom* a rave review as the lead feature in the Sunday *New York Times Book Review*, and *Reader's Digest* published a condensed version. Hayek arrived in New York harbor to find himself a cause célèbre. The academic book became a huge bestseller and Hayek enjoyed a whirlwind tour of lectures and interviews.

HAYEK AT CHICAGO AND AT FREIBERG

Hayek's classic became his ticket to success. However, in the late 1940s, he became embroiled in a personal scandal that would alter everything. In 1950, Hayek divorced his wife and married his childhood sweetheart (see the box on page 307). He left England and moved to the United States, hoping to teach at the University of Chicago, which had published his influential book. But for the first time Hayek encountered the same troubles Mises had—finding a post at a major university. Chicago finally hired Hayek, but as a professor in the Committee on Social Thought—not economics. Hayek's salary, like Mises's, had to be subsidized by the Volker Fund. Still, he was glad to be in Chicago, among his friends Milton Friedman, George Stigler, and Aaron Director.

In Chicago, he wrote *The Constitution of Liberty* (1960), which has gradually gained popularity over the years. Milton Friedman felt that the book couldn't have been written had Hayek not come to Chicago: "*The Constitution of Liberty* is Hayek's descent into the Chicago school. It's the only one of his works that makes extensive reference to absolute experience" (Ebenstein 1996: 193).

Longing to return to Europe, Hayek applied for and obtained a post at the University of Freiberg, the third oldest university in Germany, at the age of sixty-three. He continued to write books about law and political philosophy, spending his summers in the Austrian Alps.

SURPRISE! HAYEK WINS THE NOBEL PRIZE

Hayek was in his sunset years in the 1970s. Physically, he felt weak and was often ill. He suffered from deafness in his left ear (humorously noting that Karl Marx was deaf in his right). His lifelong friend Mises died in 1973. A year later, Hayek received a telephone call from Sweden that would transform his career—and his physical condition. He had just won the Nobel Prize in economics for his work in monetary theory and the business cycle. Although he had to share the award with socialist Gunnar

Myrdal (and neither man was happy about sharing the award), he felt a sense of vindication for his economic work in the 1930s. Moreover, the award renewed his spirits and he improved physically. He lectured widely and even returned to writing on economic issues—socialism, inflation, and monetary reform—especially his last great book, *The Fatal Conceit: The Errors of Socialism*, published in 1988. In the early 1990s, he started losing his memory, and finally passed away in Germany in 1992.

MISES'S FIRST CONTRIBUTION: THE NATURE OF MONEY

Now let us look at the writings of Mises and Hayek. Mises's—and later Hayek's—first major contribution was an explanation of the nature of money. We noted in chapter 11 that Irving Fisher had unsuccessfully attempted to unravel the mysteries of money. Now it was Mises's turn to try.

The first and primary goal Mises tried to achieve was to integrate money into the economic system. As noted earlier, the classical and neoclassical economists treated money as a separate box, not subject to the same analysis as the rest of the system. Irving Fisher's equation of exchange, not marginal utility or price theory, formed the basis of monetary analysis. Economists like Fisher spoke in aggregate terms—price level, money supply, velocity of circulation, and national output. Moreover, national currencies, such as the dollar, the franc, the pound, and the mark, were viewed as units of account that were arbitrarily defined by government edict. As the German historical school declared, money is the creation of the state. Thus, microeconomics (the theory of supply and demand for individual consumers and firms) was split from macroeconomics (the theory of money and aggregate economic activity). Mises took up the task of connecting the two.

THE REGRESSION THEOREM

The Theory of Money and Credit links micro to macro by first showing that money was originally a commodity with several unique characteristics. Mises noted that, under the international gold standard, all major currencies were defined as specific weights of gold. For example, when Mises was writing in 1912, the British pound was defined as approximately 1/4 ounce of gold, and the dollar as 1/20 ounce of gold. Thus, the exchange rate was fixed at £1 equal to $5.

However, the weights and exchange rates of currencies were not arbitrarily determined by various governments. The original values of the national currencies were convenient measures of precious metals, principally silver. For example, the earliest British pound was literally a pound of silver (thus the name, pound sterling). The American dollar came from the Spanish dollar, which was called a thaler, originally a privately minted silver coin. Over time, through depreciation and political corruption, the national currencies took on values almost entirely separate from their original values.

If one could travel back to a time before national banks were created, the first banknotes would be found to be nothing more than warehouse receipts redeemable in gold or silver held by scriveners and goldsmiths. Banknotes were claims on gold and silver on deposit. Going back even further, money originated out of barter as a useful commodity, usually gold, silver, or copper.

Mises called his approach the regression theorem. The regression theorem helps answer an all-important puzzler in economics: How can today's paper currencies command values completely unrelated to their cost? A $20 bill costs only 4 cents to produce, yet it commands $20 worth of goods and services. In the business world, prices and costs are related, at least over the long run. But why not money? The answer is Mises's regression theorem. Government can set an arbitrary value to its currency because it used to be backed by a valued commodity like gold or silver. Without its historical claim, government fiat money could not command the value it does today.

APPLYING THE MARGINALITY PRINCIPLE OF MONEY

Second, Mises applied marginal utility theory to the supply and demand for money itself. It was a brilliant move. Specifically, Mises showed that money was no different from any other commodity when it came to marginal value. In microeconomics, the price of any good is determined by the quantity available and the marginal utility of that good. The same principle applies to money, only in the case of money, the "price" is determined by the general purchasing power of the money unit. The willingness to hold money (or what economists call "cash balances") is determined by the marginal demand for cash balances. The interaction between the quantity of money available and the demand for it determines the price of the dollar. Thus, an increase in the supply of dollars will lead to a fall in the dollar's value or price.

NO SOCIAL BENEFIT TO MONETARY INFLATION

While an increase in the money supply reduces its value, or its purchasing power, Mises noted a unique characteristic of money—unlike all other commodities, an increase in the supply of money offers no social benefit. (Gold as a useful consumer or producer good does confer additional value, but as money it does not.) As Mises stated, "The increase of money cannot be regarded as an increase in the income or wealth of society"—it does not increase the "quantity of goods that are at the disposal of the community" (1971 [1934]: 138–39). Those who receive the new money benefit at the expense of those who don't get the money. Monetary inflation may redistribute national income, or create an inflationary boom, but its net effect is zero over the long term.

Mises's insight confirms the much misunderstood and reviled statement by John Stuart Mill about money: "There cannot . . . be intrinsically a more insignificant thing, in the economy of society, than money; except in the character of a contrivance for sparing time and labour" (Mill 1884 [1848]: 293).

THE DEFICIENCIES OF THE QUANTITY THEORY OF MONEY

The relationship between price and the supply of money is of course a crude form of Fisher's quantity theory of money. If you increase the money supply, the price of money will fall. But by how much?

Recall Fisher's quantity theory, stated below in mathematical form:

$$M \times V = P \times Q$$

where

M = money supply
V = velocity or annual average turnover of money
P = the general price level
Q = the annual quantity of goods and services produced

Fisher assumed that V and Q were relatively constant, and therefore M and P would vary directly and proportionally. His quantity theory offered one valuable positive feature: It showed that inflation or a general rise in prices was not due to labor union power, monopoly capitalism, or foreign trade, but was caused primarily by monetary policy, that is, the inflating of the money supply. Mises agreed with this basic premise.

But Fisher's formula could not help him understand or anticipate the business cycle. The reason: instead of focusing on M, the money supply, Fisher concentrated almost entirely on P—the prices of commodities and consumer goods—as an indication of economic stability. As long as prices were stable, he thought, everything would be fine and an economic collapse would be impossible. Fisher spent most of his time constructing price indices as his key indicators.

In *The Theory of Money and Credit*, Mises recognized that Fisher was focusing on the wrong part of the equation. According to Mises, P is not a leading indicator of business fluctuations. Mises was critical of Fisher's price-index stabilization scheme as a replacement for the international gold standard. Fisher's proposal "could not in any way ameliorate the social consequences of variations in the value of money," he wrote (L. Mises 1971: 402). Business activity could boom without a rise in commodity or consumer prices and, equally, the economy could collapse before general price deflation set in. Mises also criticized Fisher's attempts to establish price indices, warning that an objective, unbiased price index was impossible to construct.

MISES FINDS THE MONETARY KEY

According to Mises, what Fisher should have concentrated on was M: the money supply and the government's monetary policy in the equation of exchange. That was the missing link and the key to an understanding of monetary economics.

According to Mises's new theory, M was the independent variable that created havoc in the economy, and its impact was not simply to raise prices, as Fisher theorized, but to create structural imbalances in the economy. In Mises's terms, money was "nonneutral." It affects all the other variables in Fisher's equation of exchange—velocity (V), prices (P) and the quantity of goods and services (Q). Mises scolded Fisher for assuming V and Q were constant, and that P would move proportionally up or down with M. The relationship between money and prices is scarcely proportional. An increase in the money supply will indeed tend to lower the value of money, but it is impossible to say by how much. For instance, national output might increase so sharply that prices might not go up. If national output is high enough, prices may even decline slightly, as they did in the 1920s. In general, the price level depends on what happens to the marginal utility of money and the demand of the public for cash balances. To focus solely on prices as a leading indicator can be highly misleading, Mises said.

THE AUSTRIAN THEORY OF THE BUSINESS CYCLE

Finally, Mises applied his monetary theory to the business cycle, which turned out to be his most fruitful exercise. In developing his thesis, he borrowed from previous economists the following valuable ideas:

1. The natural interest rate hypothesis of Knut Wicksell, Swedish economist.

2. The capital theory of Eugen Böhm-Bawerk, Mises's Austrian mentor.

3. The Hume-Ricardo specie-flow mechanism, named after Scottish philosopher David Hume and British economist David Ricardo.

It's important to see how each of these ideas influenced Mises, so let's review each one.

WICKSELL'S NATURAL INTEREST RATE HYPOTHESIS

In his most important contribution to macroeconomics and business-cycle theory, *Interest and Prices* (1898), Knut Wicksell made the clear distinc-

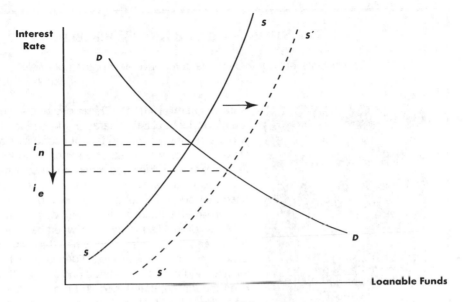

Figure 12.2
Conditions Under Which the Government Pushes
the Market Rate Below the Natural Rate of Interest

tion between the "natural" rate of interest and the "market" rate of interest.
A discrepancy between the two formed the basis of his cycle theory.
Wicksell defined the *natural* rate of interest as the interest rate that equal-
izes the supply and demand for saving, that is, the social rate of time
preference. For example, if the Swiss have a higher saving rate than the
Swedish, the natural rate of interest would tend to be lower in Switzerland
than in Sweden.

On the other hand, Wicksell defined the *market* rate of interest as the
rate of interest banks charge for loans to individual customers and businesses. In a stable economy, Wicksell noted, the natural rate (time
preference) is normally the same as the market rate (loan market). If the
two part ways, however, trouble brews.

For example, suppose the government promotes an easy-money policy
and artificially reduces the market rate below the natural rate. Figure 12.2
demonstrates the effect of this policy.

According to Wicksell's natural interest rate hypothesis, if the market
rate is less than the natural rate, a "cumulative process" of price inflation
occurs. However, the inflationary boom cannot last. The economy gets
overheated, forcing interest rates to rise above the natural rate. Eventually,
high real interest rates choke off the boom, resulting in a depression.
Wicksell's policy prescription was simple and direct: government should
maintain a cycle-neutral policy whereby the market rate is always equal to
the natural rate. It should avoid artificial easy-money inflation.

THE STRANGE LIFE OF KNUT WICKSELL

No finer intellect and higher character have ever graced our field.

—Joseph Schumpeter

Photograph 12.5
Knut Wicksell (1851–1926)
Jailed for blasphemy!
Courtesy of Mark Blaug.

Knut Wicksell (1851–1926) was one of the most profound yet iconoclastic characters in economics. He wrote scholarly works and taught economics at Lund University, yet was a stubborn nonconformist and free thinker who defended feminism, socialism, abortion, and blasphemy. He even spent two months in prison for speaking out against the Virgin Mary.

Born in Stockholm in 1851, Knut was the youngest of six children. His mother died when he was almost seven and his father died when he was fifteen. Lonely, he came under the influence of a Lutheran minister and piously meditated and studied the Bible. Even though he abandoned and mocked formal religion later in life, Wicksell knew the church hymnbook by heart, as well as the Psalter, the Sermon on the Mount, and many other passages in the Bible.

Wicksell was a brilliant student who earned his bachelor's degree in mathematics and physics in only two years at Uppsala University. His life changed when he entered upon his graduate studies. He lost his religious faith and soon became an outspoken critic of Christianity and a feverish radical. Traveling abroad, he encountered many new ideas and came under the influence of English writer George Drysdale's tome, *The Elements of Social Science*, with its frank subtitle, *Physical, Sexual, and Natural Religion; An Explanation of the True Causes and Cure of the Three Primary Evils of Society—Poverty, Prostitution, and Celibacy.* Wicksell was deeply affected by this book, which was highly neo-Malthusian in tone. Thereafter, he became an advocate of birth control, including abortion, as a means of reducing crowding, poverty, and prostitution.

A COMMON-LAW MARRIAGE

Desperately searching for female companionship when he was in his twenties, the shy Swede became depressed by two failed love affairs, first with a girl he had never met and then with the wife of his closest friend. In 1888, Wicksell met the love of his life, Anna Bugge, a Norwegian high school teacher eleven years his junior. He proposed a common-law marriage, from which they had two sons. "My enthusiasm for work has grown considerably since I married," he wrote a friend (Gardlund 1996 [1958]: 124). Anna later became Sweden's first female diplomat and a leader in the suffrage and peace movements.

Because of his radical views, he was not able to obtain a teaching post until he was fifty years old. He barely survived on grants, inheritances, and a teacher's income.

(continued)

From 1901 until 1916, Wicksell taught economics at Lund University. His personal approach was as radical as his ideas; he lectured in rustic work clothes and wore a fisherman's cap. He frequently came to his lectures with a market basket of produce, meats, and fruits. His unconventional attire was influenced by Mill's *On Liberty*, which defended unorthodox behavior.

AN AUSTRIAN FELLOW TRAVELER

Wicksell was a prolific writer of books, articles, and tracts, many of which are only now being translated into English. He was profoundly inspired by the work of the Austrian Eugen Böhm-Bawerk and his *Positive Theory of Capital*, which he said "was a revelation to me. . . . All of a sudden I saw, as if before my eyes, the roof being erected on a scholarly edifice." He counted himself a staunch defender of the Austrian concepts of marginal utility, derived demand, roundabout methods of production, and capital theory, although he rejected some aspects of the Austrian business-cycle theory (Wicksell 1997: 26–38).

WICKSELL GOES TO PRISON FOR RELIGIOUS BLASPHEMY

In November 1908, Wicksell was incensed by the sentencing of an anarchist who publicly attacked religion. Regarding this case as an infringement of freedom of speech, Wicksell addressed a large Stockholm audience on the subject, in a speech entitled "The Throne, the Altar, the Sword, and the Bag of Money," satirizing the story of the Virgin Mary. Wicksell was arrested, tried, and convicted of religious blasphemy and sentenced to two months in prison. He used the time to write a tract on overpopulation, arguing that Sweden's optimum population should be 3 million instead of 5 million inhabitants, and that Europe should reduce its population by a quarter. Clearly, Wicksell failed to acknowledge that medical and agricultural technological advances have defused the population bomb (see chapter 3 on Malthus).

DEATH AT AGE SEVENTY-FOUR

Throughout his life, Wicksell rejected all academic and legal formalities, including official marriage and baptism ceremonies and accepting honorary degrees. He must have been turning over in his grave when his wife arranged an elaborate funeral following his death in 1926 (due to a stomach disorder followed by pneumonia).

APPLYING BÖHM-BAWERK'S CAPITAL THEORY

Second, Mises applied Böhm-Bawerk's theory of "roundaboutness" and the structure of capital. A government-induced inflationary boom would inevitably cause the roundabout production process to lengthen, especially in the capital-goods industries, a process that could not be reversed easily during a slump. Moreover, once new funds were invested in machinery, tools, equipment, and buildings, capital would became heterogeneous, and it would not be easy to sell off assets, equipment, and inventories during a slowdown. In short, when the boom turned into a bust, it would take time—sometimes years—for the economy to recover.[5]

THE GOLD STANDARD: A STRICT TASKMASTER

Finally, Mises saw the international gold standard as a disciplinarian that would cut short any inflationary boom in short order. Borrowing from the Hume-Ricardo specie-flow mechanism, Mises outlined the series of events whereby an inflationary boom would quickly come to an end under gold:

1. Under inflation, domestic incomes and prices rise.

2. Citizens buy more imports than exports, causing a trade deficit.

3. The balance of payments deficit causes gold to flow out.

4. The domestic money supply declines, causing a deflationary collapse.

In sum, Mises and Hayek developed a logical explanation for a financial crisis and economic collapse to follow an inflationary expansion, even if prices did not rise.

WHY DIDN'T THE AUSTRIAN MODEL CATCH ON?

If the Austrian theory of monetary economics and the business cycle had all the answers, why didn't it catch on? After all, Mises's *Money and Credit* was published in 1912. Why didn't Fisher, Keynes, and other contemporary economists pick up on these penetrating monetary insights as 1929 approached?

One answer is that Mises's theories were largely ignored by the profession until it was too late. His 1912 book was not translated into English until after the Great Depression started. Keynes reviewed *Theorie des Geldes* in the prestigious Cambridge *Economic Journal* in 1914, but dismissed Mises's work as neither "constructive" nor "original" (1914: 417–19). Only years later did Keynes admit that he was not well versed in reading German, confessing that "new ideas are apt to be veiled from me by the difficulties of the language" (1930, I: 199, n. 2). Hayek responded, "The world might have been saved much suffering if Lord Keynes's German had been a little better" (M. Mises 1984: 219).

The same could be said about Knut Wicksell and his cogent "natural" rate of interest hypothesis. Wicksell's cycle theories were virtually unknown outside Sweden until the Austrians introduced his vital analysis

---

5. Hayek used his triangles to demonstrate the expansion and contraction of the economy under a fiat-money inflation. See Hayek (1935: 32–68). For a more modern update of the impact of monetary inflation, see Skousen (1990: 282–331).

THERE'S METHOD TO MISES'S MADNESS!

In the 1920s, Mises made important contributions to monetary economics, business cycle theory and of course socialist economics, but his later writings on the foundations of economic science are so cranky and idiosyncratic that we can only wonder that they have been taken seriously by anyone.

—Mark Blaug (1980: 93)

Mises's books contain no charts, no tables, and no graphs. They contain no mathematical formulas or econometric models, no empirical studies, no quantitative proofs of any economic theory, not even supply and demand schedules, which Mises described as "two hypothetical curves" (L. Mises 1966: 333).

"Cranky" and "idiosyncratic" indeed. Mises claimed in *Human Action* that the only pure economic science is radical apriorism—using solely deductive reason without the help of experience. He built his entire system on logic and self-evident assumptions, similar to geometry. Mises rejected all forms of inductive aposteriorism, or the use of empirical studies or history to prove a theory. Mises solemnly declared, "Its particular theorems are not open to any verification or falsification on the grounds of experience" (1966 [1949]: 862). Further, he claimed, "History cannot teach us any general rule, principle, or law. . . . History speaks only to those people who know how to interpret it on the grounds of correct theories" (1966: 41).

Mises rejected econometrics and mathematics in economics. "The mathematical method must be rejected not only on account of its barrenness. It is an entirely vicious method, starting from false assumptions and leading to fallacious inferences. . . . There is no such thing as quantitative economics" (1966: 350–51).

METHODOLOGICAL DUALISM

Finally, Mises separated the social from the physical sciences, dubbing the social sciences *praxeology*, defined as the study of human action. (Mises invented other terms, such as "catallactics," signifying the theory of exchange. Introduction of new terminology is always a sign of a new school of thought. Marx and Keynes also invented terms.)

Mises was a dualist who divided nature into two components:

1. Human beings, who think, adopt values, make choices, and learn from the past (the social sciences).
2. Animals and things (organic and inorganic matter), who are mechanical and predictable (the physical sciences).

As Mises indicated, "Reason and experience show us two separate realms. . . . No bridge connects—as far as we can see today—these two spheres" (1966: 18). Mises and Hayek were critical of attempts by economists to imitate the physical sciences with terms such as "elasticity," "velocity," and "frictional unemployment." Hayek called such attempts "scientism."

(continued)

EVEN MISES'S DISCIPLES QUESTION HIS EXTREME APPROACH

Even his most devoted students didn't go along with Mises on every aspect of his radical methodology. Hayek used graphs (known as Hayek's triangles) to demonstrate the Austrian macroeconomic model, and Rothbard collected and interpreted a wide range of historical data to support the Austrian explanation of the Great Depression. Mises's adamant refusal to use empirical studies to make the case for a free market is one reason the Austrian school has floundered and been left behind in an era when empirical work and quantitative studies have advanced the cause of economics. The Chicago school of free-market economics, in particular, has achieved widespread approval by the profession because of its skill in statistics and quantitative studies. (Examples of these studies are shown in the updates in chapters 1 and 3 of this book.)

SOME SUPPORT FOR MISES

Yet there is method to Mises's madness. It is not always possible to test economic laws in a controlled experiment as can be done in physics or chemistry. In theory, economists must establish *ceteris paribus* ("all things being equal") conditions, making assumptions that may not exist in real life. Forecasting models based on formulas and equations rely upon the past, and these calculations may vary in the future because people are not machines or lemmings; they can alter their attitudes and behavior in unpredictable ways.[6]

Case study: In 1962, economic advisors to President John F. Kennedy supported the theories of John Maynard Keynes, who argued that running a deliberate deficit could stimulate an economic recovery. Congress acted on their advice, cut taxes, and ran a deficit in 1962–63. The result? Sure enough, national output rose sharply.

However, other economists disagreed with the Keynesian advisors. Followers of the monetarist (or Chicago) school, led by Milton Friedman, argued that the test was not valid and did not validate Keynesian theory. Friedman pointed out that during this same period in 1962–63, the Federal Reserve's monetary policy was also active, and the rapid growth of the money supply was actually responsible for the economic recovery. At the same time, the supply-siders took another approach. They contended that the tax cut itself stimulated productivity by putting more funds in the hands of individual consumers and private investors, which in turn caused the recovery.

Who was right, the Keynesians, the monetarists, or the supply-siders? The empirical evidence was inconclusive because all three variables—taxes, deficits, and the money supply—were changing concurrently.

(continued)

---

6. However, a whole new area of research called "experimental economics" has developed under the leadership of Vernon L. Smith. See his *Papers in Experimental Economics* (1991), and see "Experimental Methods in Economics" in *The New Palgrave*. Interestingly, many of the conclusions of experimental economics are more in sync with the Austrians' (especially Hayek's) concept of market processes than with the Chamberlin-Robinson theory of imperfect competition.

Causality Versus Uncertainty

Mises pointed to two principles in economic behavior that often work against each other, making it difficult if not impossible to make accurate forecasts. The first principle is causality—for every cause there is an effect. As Mises states, "Human action is purposeful behavior" (1966: 11). Yet, at the same time, there is the principle of uncertainty. People have multiple reasons for acting and they sometimes change their minds. It is simply impossible to know what everyone is doing and why. Say wrote about this a century earlier (see chapter 2). The complexity of knowledge often makes us ignorant and incapable of knowing the future—of stock prices, new products, changing consumer demand, and government policies. An astronomer can know the exact time the sun will come up in the morning, but can anyone predict precisely when a student will get out of bed in the morning? Thus, sophisticated computer models that make forecasts about interest rates, inflation, and movement of the financial markets are almost always off the mark. The high degree of ignorance in the economy is one reason Mises and Hayek dismissed the possibility of socialist central planning. Hayek, in particular, has written extensively on "the unavoidable imperfection of man's knowledge" and the "unintended consequences" of man's actions (1984: 211–80).

This is not to say that individuals can never predict anything with any certainty. Some economists, such as Ludwig M. Lachmann and George Shackle (known as fellow travelers of the Austrian school), have argued that uncertainty is so pervasive that no one can predict anything. Others, especially extreme technical analysts in the financial market, believe they have the tools to accurately forecast the future of stock and commodity prices. In Hayek's mind, the truth lies somewhere between "complete knowledge" and "complete ignorance" of the future. Sometimes cause-and-effect is so strong that the future is fairly easy to predict; at other times, uncertainty is so great that an accurate forecast is nearly impossible.

Mises generally sided more with uncertainty. Regarding his anticipation of the 1929–32 economic crisis, he wrote that, even though he had foreseen these events, he could not predict "the exact date of their occurrence" (1971 [1934]: 15). Elsewhere he wrote, "There are no rules according to which the duration of the boom or the following depression can be computed" (1966: 870–71).

However, it is the role of the entrepreneur qua businessman or financial advisor—a key figure in Austrian economics—to try to predict future events. But he must be a loner, a contrarian, to do so (Skousen 1993: 279–80).

to England. (Under Robbins's and Hayek's encouragement, Wicksell's *Lectures* were translated into English in 1934–35.)

Thus, the Mises-Wicksell monetary views got their day in the sun only after the worst economic collapse in history had occurred. Mises, Hayek, and Wicksell had filled the gaps in neoclassical economics, and had helped complete the restructuring of the building that Adam Smith had begun. The economics profession was close to achieving a unified body of theory without the need for "schools." But the Mises-Wicksell theories received a good hearing for only a few brief years in the 1930s. Part of the problem was their solution to the depression, which was regarded largely as consisting of "do-nothing" policy recommendations. Hayek and Mises advocated lower wage rates and prices, lower taxes, and less government interference in commerce and trade, but they adamantly counseled against reinflation and deficit spending. "It would only mean that the seed would already be sown for new disturbances and new crises," Hayek insisted. The only solution was "to leave it to time to effect a permanent cure"—in other words, wait it out and let the market take its natural course (Hayek 1935: 98–99). Such a prescription might have worked during a garden-variety recession, but apparently wasn't enough to counter a full-scale deflationary collapse.

With the Austrians offering few explanations and no cure for the seemingly never-ending depression, economists eventually looked elsewhere for a solution. The Austrians could explain the cause of the depression, but failed to offer a workable cure. Who could come to the rescue and save capitalism? An economist who stepped forward to offer a new theory of macroeconomics and a vigorous policy for curing the depression is the subject of chapter 13.

REFERENCES

Böhm-Bawerk, Eugen. 1959. *The Positive Theory of Capital.* South Holland, IL: Libertarian Press.

Blaug, Mark. 1980. *The Methodology of Economics.* Cambridge: Cambridge University Press.

Cockett, Richard. 1994. *Thinking the Unthinkable: Think-Tanks and the Economic Counter-Revolution, 1931–1983.* New York: HarperCollins.

Ebenstein, Alan. 1996. "Hayek, Philosopher of Liberty." Manuscript.

Friedman, Milton. 1995. "Interview." *Reason* (June), 32–38.

Friedman, Milton, and Rose D. Friedman.1998. *Two Lucky People.* Chicago: University of Chicago Press.

Gardlund, Torsten. 1996 [1958]. *The Life of Knut Wicksell.* Cheltenham, UK: Edward Elgar.

Hayek, Friedrich A. 1931. *Prices and Production.* London: George Routledge and Sons.

———. 1935. *Prices and Production,* 2d ed. London: George Routledge and Sons.

———. 1960. *The Constitution of Liberty.* Chicago: University of Chicago Press.

———. 1975. Interview. *Gold and Silver Newsletter* (June). Newport Beach, CA: Monex International.

———. 1988. *The Fatal Conceit.* Chicago: University of Chicago Press.

———. 1976 [1944]. *The Road to Serfdom.* Chicago: University of Chicago Press.

———. 1983. "The Keynes Centenary: The Austrian Critique." *Economist* (11 June), 45–48.

———. 1984. *The Essence of Hayek,* ed. Chiaki Nishiyama and Kurt R. Leube. Stanford: Hoover Institution Press.

———. 1992. *The Fortunes of Liberalism. The Collected Works of F.A. Hayek,* vol. 4. Chicago: University of Chicago Press.

———. 1994. *Hayek on Hayek.* Chicago: University of Chicago Press.

Hicks, John. 1967. "The Hayek Story." In *Critical Essays in Monetary Economics,* 203–15. London: Oxford University Press.

Hülsmann, Jörg Guido. 2007. *Mises: Last Knight of Liberalism.* Auburn, AL: Mises Institute.

Keynes, John Maynard. 1914. "Review of *Theorie des Geldes und der Umlaufsmittel* (1912)." *Economic Journal* 24: 417–19.

———. 1930–31. *A Treatise on Money,* 2 vols. London: Macmillan.

———. 1936. *The General Theory of Employment, Interest and Money.* London: Macmillan.

———. 1980. *The Collected Writings of John Maynard Keynes, Activities 1940–46,* vol. 27. London: Macmillan.

———. 1983. "Keynes as an Investor." In *The Collected Writings of John Maynard Keynes,* vol. 30, ed. Donald Moggridge, 1–113. London: Macmillan.

Laidler, David. 1999. *Fabricating the Keynesian Revolution.* Cambridge: Cambridge University Press.

Machlup, Fritz. 1974. "Tribute to Mises." *Mont Pélérin Society Proceedings* (September 13).

Mill, John Stuart. 1884 [1848]. *Principles of Political Economy,* abridged and ed. by J. Lawrence Laughlin. New York: D. Appleton.

———. 1989. *On Liberty and Other Writings.* Cambridge: Cambridge University Press.

Mises, Ludwig von. 1966 [1949]. *Human Action: A Treatise on Economics,* 3d ed. Chicago: Regnery.

———. 1971 [1934]. *The Theory of Money and Credit,* 2d ed. New York: Foundation for Economic Education.

———. 1978. *Notes and Recollections.* Spring Hill, PA: Libertarian Press.

———. 1980. *Planning for Freedom,* 4th ed. Spring Hill, PA: Libertarian Press.

Mises, Ludwig von. 1981 [1936]. *Socialism.* Indianapolis, IN: Liberty Classics.

Mises, Margit von. 1984. *My Years with Ludwig von Mises,* 2d ed. Cedar Falls, IA: Center for Futures Education.

Mises, Richard von. 1951. *Positivism.* Cambridge, MA: Harvard College.

———. 1959 [1945]. *Theory of Flight.* Toronto: Dover.

North, Gary. 1990. *Tools of Dominion.* Tyler, TX: Institute of Christian Economics.

Padover, Saul K. 1978. *Karl Marx: An Intimate Biography.* New York: McGraw-Hill.

Robbins, Lionel. 1934. *The Great Depression.* London: Macmillan.

———. 1971. *Autobiography of an Economist.* London: Macmillan.

Rothbard, Murray N. 1980. "The Essential von Mises." In Ludwig von Mises, *Planning for Freedom,* 4th ed., 234–70. Spring Hill, PA: Libertarian Press.

———. 1988. *Ludwig von Mises: Scholar, Creator, Hero.* Auburn, AL: Ludwig von Mises Institute.

Schumpeter, Joseph A. 1954. *History of Economic Analysis.* New York: Oxford University Press.

Skousen, Mark. 1990. *The Structure of Production.* New York: New York University Press.

———. 1993. "Who Predicted the 1929 Crash?" In *The Meaning of Ludwig von Mises,* ed. Jeffrey M. Herberner, 247–83. Auburn, AL: Ludwig von Mises Institute.

Smith, Vernon L. 1987. "Experimental Methods in Economics." In *The New Palgrave: A Dictionary in Economics,* vol. 2, 241–49. London: Macmillan.

———. 1991. *Papers in Experimental Economics.* Cambridge: Cambridge University Press.

———. 1999. "Reflections on *Human Action* After 50 Years." *Cato Journal* 19: 2 (Fall), 195–210.

Wicksell, Knut. 1936 [1898]. *Interest and Prices.* London: Macmillan.

———. 1997. *Selected Essays in Economics,* ed. Bo Sandelin. London: Routledge.

13

THE KEYNES MUTINY: CAPITALISM FACES ITS GREATEST CHALLENGE

A thousand years hence 1920–1970 will, I expect, be the time for historians. It drives me wild to think of it. I believe it will make my poor Principles, *with a lot of poor comrades, into waste paper.*[1]

—Alfred Marshall (1915)

Keynes was no socialist—he came to save capitalism, not to bury it. . . . There has been nothing like Keynes's achievement in the annals of social sciences.

—Paul Krugman (2007)

The capitalist system of natural liberty—founded by Adam Smith, revised by the marginalist revolution, and refined by Marshall and the Austrians—was under siege. The classical virtues of thrift, balanced budgets, low taxes, the gold standard, and Say's law were under attack as never before. The house that Adam Smith built was threatening to collapse.

The Great Depression of the 1930s was the most traumatic economic event of the twentieth century. It was especially shocking given the great

---

1. This prophetic statement was made in a letter from Alfred Marshall to a Cambridge University colleague, Professor C.R. Fay, dated February 23, 1915. He made no reference to Keynes as the instigator of this revolution, but Marshall did have a favorable opinion of his student. See Pigou (1925): 489–90.

♪ **Music selection for this chapter: Aram Khachaturian, "Sabre Dance," from the ballet** *Gayne*

advances achieved in Western living standards during the New Era twenties. Those living standards would be strained during 1929–33, the brunt of the depression. In the United States, industrial output fell by over 30 percent. Nearly half the commercial banks failed. The unemployment rate soared to over 25 percent. Stock prices lost 88 percent of their value. Europe and the rest of the world faced similar turmoil.

The Austrians Mises and Hayek, along with the sound-money economists in the United States, had anticipated trouble, but felt helpless in the face of a slump that just wouldn't go away. A nascent recovery under Roosevelt's New Deal began in the mid-1930s, but didn't last. U.S. unemployment remained in double-digit levels for a full decade and did not disappear until World War II. Europe didn't fare much better; only Hitler's militant Germany was fully employed as war approached. In the free world, fear of losing one's job, fear of hunger, and fear of war loomed ominously.

The length and severity of the Great Depression caused most of the Anglo-American economics profession to question classical laissez-faire economics and the ability of a free-market capitalist system to correct itself. The assault was on two levels—the competitive nature of capitalism (micro) and the stability of the general economy (macro).

WAS THE CLASSICAL MODEL OF COMPETITION IMPERFECT?

On the micro level, two economists simultaneously wrote books that independently challenged the classical model of competition. In 1933, Harvard University Press released *The Theory of Monopolistic Competition* by **Edward H. Chamberlin (1899–1967)** and Cambridge University Press published *Economics of Imperfect Competition* by **Joan Robinson**

Photograph 13.1
Joan Robinson (1903–83)

Photograph 13.2
Edward Chamberlin (1899–1967)

"Competitive capitalism is imperfect."
Courtesy of Mark Blaug.

(1903–83). Both economists introduced the idea that there are various levels of competition in the marketplace, from "pure competition" to "pure monopoly," and that most market conditions were "imperfect" and involved degrees of monopoly power. The Chamberlin-Robinson theory of imperfect competition captured the imagination of the profession and has been an integral feature of microeconomics ever since. It has strong policy implications: Laissez faire is defective and cannot ensure competitive conditions in capitalism; the government must intervene through controls and antitrust actions to curtail the natural monopolistic tendencies of business.

THE RADICAL THREAT TO CAPITALISM

But this threat was minor compared to the radical noncapitalist alternatives being proposed in macroeconomics. Marxism was all the rage on campuses and among intellectuals during the 1930s. Paul Sweezy, a Harvard-trained economist, had gone to the London School of Economics (LSE) in the early 1930s, only to return a full-fledged Marxist, ready to teach radical ideas at his alma mater. Sidney and Beatrice Webb returned from the Soviet Union brimming with optimism, firm in their belief that Stalin had inaugurated a "new civilization" of full employment and economic superiority. Was full-scale socialism the only alternative to an unstable capitalist system?

WHO WOULD SAVE CAPITALISM?

More sober intellectuals sought an alternative to wholesale socialism, nationalization, and central planning. Fortunately, there was a powerful voice urging a middle ground, a way to preserve economic liberty without destroying the foundations of Western civilization.

It was the voice of John Maynard Keynes, leader of the new Cambridge school. In his revolutionary 1936 book, *The General Theory of Employment, Interest and Money*, Keynes preached that capitalism is inherently unstable and has no natural tendency toward full employment. Yet, at the same time, he rejected the need to nationalize the economy, impose price-wage controls, and interfere with the microfoundations of supply and demand. All that was needed was for government to take control of a wayward capitalist steering wheel and get the car back on the road to prosperity. How? Not by slashing prices and wages—the classical approach—but by deliberately running federal deficits and by spending money on public works that would expand demand and restore confidence. Once the economy got back on track and reached full employment, the government would no longer need to run deficits, and the classical model would function properly. As Keynes himself wrote, "But beyond this no obvious case is made out for a system of State Socialism which would embrace most of the economic life of the community" (1973a [1936]: 378). His message was really quite simple, yet revolutionary: "Mass unemployment had a single cause, inadequate demand, and an easy solution, expansionary fiscal policy" (Krugman 2007).

Keynes's model of aggregate demand management changed the dismal science to the optimists' club: man could be the master of his economic destiny after all. Keynes's claim that government could expand or contract aggregate demand as conditions required seemed to eliminate the cycle inherent in capitalism without eliminating capitalism itself. Meanwhile, a laissez-faire policy of economic freedom could be pursued on a microeconomic level. In short, Keynes's middle-of-the-road policies were viewed not as a threat to free enterprise, but as its savior. In fact, it brought its chief rival theory, Marxism, to a total halt in advanced countries (Galbraith 1975 [1965]: 132).

"LIKE A FLASH OF LIGHT ON A DARK NIGHT"

The Keynesian revolution took place almost overnight, especially among the youngest and the brightest, who switched allegiance from the Austrians to Keynes. John Kenneth Galbraith wrote of the times, "Here was a remedy for the despair. . . . It did not overthrow the system but saved it. To the non-revolutionary, it seemed too good to be true. To the occasional revolutionary, it was. The old economics was still taught by day. But in the evening, and almost every evening from 1936 on, almost everyone discussed Keynes" (1975: 136). Milton Friedman, who later became a vociferous opponent of Keynesian theory, said, "By contrast with this dismal picture [the Austrian laissez-faire prescription], the news seeping out of Cambridge (England) about Keynes's interpretation of the depression and of the right policy to cure it must have come like a flash of light on a dark night. It offered a far less hopeless diagnosis of the disease. More importantly, it offered a more immediate, less painful, and more effective cure in the form of budget deficits. It is easy to see how a young, vigorous, and generous mind would have been attracted to it" (1974: 163).

The Keynesian model of aggregate demand management swept the profession even faster than the marginalist revolution, especially after World War II seemed to vindicate the benefits of deficit spending and massive government spending. It wasn't long before college professors, under the tutelage of Alvin Hansen, Paul Samuelson, Lawrence Klein, and other Keynesian disciples, began teaching students about the consumption function, the multiplier, the marginal propensity to consume, the paradox of thrift, aggregate demand, and $C + I + G$. It was a strange, new, exciting doctrine.

THE DARK SIDE OF KEYNES

Keynes may have offered a plausible cure for the depression, but his theories also created a postwar environment favorable toward ubiquitous state interventionism, the welfare state, and boundless faith in big government. His theories encouraged excess consumption, debt financing, and progressive taxation over saving, balanced budgets, and low taxes. Critics saw Keynesian economics as a direct assault on traditional economic values and the most serious threat to the principles of economic freedom since Marxism. To them, Keynes's *General Theory* "constitutes the most subtle and mischievous assault on orthodox capitalism and free enterprise that has appeared in the English language" (Hazlitt 1977: 345; cf. Hutt 1979: 12) As Paul Krugman notes, "If your doctrine says that free markets, left to their own devices, produce the best of all possible worlds, and that government intervention in the economy always makes things worse, Keynes is your enemy" (2007).

Despite occasional pronouncements that Keynes is dead, Keynesian thinking is still so pervasive in academia, the halls of Parliament, and Wall Street, that *Time* magazine aptly voted Keynes the most influential economist of the twentieth century. Biographer Charles Hession writes, "More books and articles have been written about him than any other economist, with the possible exception of Karl Marx" (1984: xiv). Appropriately, *The New Palgrave* gives Keynes its longest biography—twenty pages, as compared to fifteen for Marx. And the latest biographer, Robert Skidelsky, places Keynes on a pedestal: "Keynes was a magical figure, and it is fitting that he should have left a magical work. There has never been an economist like him" (1992: 537).

Photograph 13.3
John Maynard Keynes (1883–1946)
"A leaping mind with riotous eyes."
Courtesy of Hulton-Getty Archives.

KEYNES BORN AMID BRITAIN'S RULING ELITE

What kind of man was Keynes, who could engender such devotion and such hostility?

John Maynard Keynes (1883–1946) was an intellectual elitist from his earliest childhood. Once, when asked how to pronounce his name, he replied, "*Keynes*, as in *brains*." Born in 1883 (the year Marx died) in the center of Britain's most cerebral environment, he was the son of John Neville Keynes, an economics professor at Cambridge University and a friend of Alfred Marshall. Neville would actually outlive his son, Maynard, by three years, dying in 1949 at age ninety-seven. His mother, Florence Ada Keynes, also distinguished herself as Cambridge's first woman mayor.

Keynes was always close to his mother, while his father was distant. His father wrote in his diary in 1891, when Maynard was only eight years old, "The only person he would like to be is his mother; at any rate, he would desire to resemble her in everything" (Hession 1984: 11).

Keynes went to Eton, the exclusive school, and then attended, as expected, Cambridge University, where he obtained a degree in mathematics in 1905. Keynes would later write a controversial book on probability theory.

KEYNES BECOMES AN "APOSTLE"

His friends considered him precocious, clever, and sometimes rude. His most distinguishing features were his "riotous eyes" and "leaping mind" (Skidelsky 1992: xxxi). Keynes viewed himself as "physically repulsive." Nevertheless, he was selected as one of only a dozen members of the Apostles, an exclusive secret society at Cambridge (not unlike the Skull and Bones at Yale). Membership is for life. Other noteworthy members have included the poet Alfred Lord Tennyson, philosopher/mathematician Bertrand Russell, philosophers G.E. Moore and Alfred North Whitehead, and biographer Lytton Strachey. The Apostles were a close-knit group, meeting every Saturday night to discuss papers.

At the turn of the twentieth century, the Apostles, under the influence of G.E. Moore, developed a deep contempt for Victorian morality and bourgeois values. They even propounded the subversive idea that homosexuality was morally superior. Keynes was a practicing homosexual during his early adult life, although he apparently abandoned it upon marrying Lydia Lopokova in 1925 at the age of forty-four (see the box on page 329).

After graduation, Keynes entered the British Civil Service, spending two years in the India office (although never visiting India). In 1909 he became a teaching fellow at Cambridge, and from 1911 to 1944 he served as the general editor of Cambridge's *Economic Journal*. He was not trained in economics, having taken only a single course from Alfred Marshall, but quickly acquired the skills to teach it.

THE TRUTH ABOUT KEYNES'S HOMOSEXUALITY

[It] is too late to change. I remain, and will always remain, an immoralist.
—John Maynard Keynes (Hession 1984: 46)

In Keynes's official biography, economist Roy Harrod wrote about his friend, "In regard to his faults, I am not conscious of any suppression [of facts]. Criticisms have been made by the malicious or ill-informed which have no foundation in fact" (Harrod 1951: viii). In fact, there was suppression. Harrod carefully covered up Keynes's sexual behavior, which he felt would reflect badly on Keynes's reputation.

In today's tell-all school of biography (and this book is no exception), Harrod's biography is out of date. More recent histories by Robert Skidelsky (2003), D.E. Moggridge (1992), and Charles Hession (1984) spare few details of Keynes's sexual adventures. Moggridge even goes so far as to print Keynes's sexual engagement diary in an appendix (1992: 838–39).

Keynes's sexual proclivities may have been influenced by his family life (overprotective mother, weak father); the Eton school, an all-male institution where Greek philosophy taught that platonic love between men is spiritually higher than the carnal love between man and woman; and the collegiate ideas of G.E. Moore, who preached a disregard for morals and universal rules of conduct. Keynes firmly believed in living the "good life," without concern for right or wrong.

WAS KEYNES A MISOGYNIST?

Keynes's predilection for men may have affected his attitudes toward women. Like Marshall, he disliked the presence of female students in his classes. In 1909, while teaching at Cambridge, he wrote, "I think I shall have to give up teaching females after this year. The nervous irritation caused by two hours' contact with them is *intense*. I seem to hate every movement of their minds. The minds of the men, even when they are stupid and ugly, never appear to me so repellent" (Moggridge 1992: 183–84).

Historians Elizabeth and Harry Johnson even went so far as to suggest that Keynes's misogynistic attitude extended to his theories about saving and investing. The Johnsons noted that Keynes and his followers often referred to savings as female and investment as male. Female saving was usually seen in a negative light and male investment in a positive way. "The maleness of investment is attested to by among other things the frequent references by Joan Robinson and other Cambridge writers to 'the animal spirits' of entrepreneurs; the femaleness of savings is evident in the passive role assigned to savings in the analysis of the determination of employment equilibrium" (Johnson and Johnson 1978: 121). Keynes himself wrote in his *Treatise on Money*, "Thus, thrift may be the handmaid and nurse of enterprise. But equally she may not" (1930, 2: 132).

However, Keynes was sometimes ambiguous about the sexual identity of saving. In the same *Treatise*, Keynes commented on the lack of economic progress in Europe in the 1920s. "Ten years have elapsed since the end of the war. Savings have been on an unexampled scale. But a proportion of them has been wasted, spilt on the ground" (1930, 2: 185). This is an allusion to the biblical story of Onan, who spilled his seed on the ground (Genesis 38: 8–9).

THE SHOCKING NEWS IN 1925

Keynes shocked his homosexual friends in Bloomsbury when he announced his engagement and subsequent marriage to Lydia Lopokova, a Russian ballerina, in 1925. Based on private letters between Maynard and Lydia, their marriage was far from platonic. "Sexual relations certainly developed," biographer Robert Skidelsky writes (1992: 110–11).

Photograph 13.4
The Shocking News
Lydia Lopokova Marries Maynard Keynes!
Courtesy of Dr. Milo Keynes.

KEYNES'S DUAL NATURE: A KEY TO HIS CREATIVE GENIUS?

Biographer Charles Hession erected a novel theory that Keynes's revolutionary ideas and creative genius were the result of his androgynous background, which combined "the masculine truth of reason and the feminine truth of imagination" (Hession 1984: 107, 17–18). Skidelsky agrees, "Even his sexual ambivalence played its part in sharpening his vision" (1992: 537). But why should intuition and creativity be solely feminine and reason and logic solely masculine?

Keynes Writes a Bestseller

In 1919, following World War I, Keynes served as a senior Treasury official in the British delegation to the Versailles Peace Conference. Distressed by the proceedings, he resigned and wrote *The Economic Consequences of the Peace* (1920). It became a bestseller and propelled Keynes into fame and fortune.

Writing in trenchant prose, Keynes condemned the Allies for imposing impractical and unrealistic reparations on the Germans. The defeated nations were required to pay the complete Allied costs of the war, including pay, pensions, and death benefits of troops—up to $5 billion "whether in gold, commodities, ships, securities or otherwise," before May 1, 1921. "The existence of the great war debts is a menace to financial stability everywhere," warned Keynes (1920: 279). A pessimistic Keynes predicted negative consequences in Europe. He implied that Germany would have no recourse but to inflate her way out. In a famous passage, Keynes noted, "Lenin was certainly right. There is no subtler, no surer means of overturning the existing basis of society than to debauch the currency. The process engages all the hidden forces of economic law on the side of destruction, and does it in a manner which not one man in a million is able to diagnose" (1920: 236).[2]

Keynes Makes Another Brilliant Prediction in 1925

Keynes followed this success with another insightful analysis in 1925 when Britain, under Chancellor of the Exchequer Winston Churchill, returned to the gold standard at the overvalued prewar fixed exchange rate of $4.86. Keynes campaigned against this deflationary measure. In his booklet *The Economic Consequences of Mr. Churchill*, the Cambridge professor warned that deflation would force Britain to reduce real wages and retard economic growth (Keynes 1963 [1931]: 244–70). Once again, Keynes proved prescient; Britain suffered from an economic malaise that only worsened as the Great Depression approached.

Unfortunately, Keynes's gift of prophecy disappeared in the late 1920s. In his 1923 *Tract on Monetary Reform* (which Milton Friedman rates as Keynes's greatest work), he joined the monetarist Irving Fisher in rejecting the gold standard and hailed the stabilizing influence of the U.S. dollar between 1923 and 1928 as a "triumph" of the Federal Reserve.

---

2. In a misguided review called *The Carthaginian Peace or the Economic Consequences of Mr. Keynes*, French economist Etienne de Mantoux later blamed Keynes for starting World War II. According to Mantoux, Keynes vastly underestimated Germany's capacity to pay the war reparations and convinced the world that the Versailles Peace Accords had crushed Germany and that therefore somehow the Nazi danger was minor. It's hard to imagine a more wrong-headed interpretation of Keynes's book. See Mantoux (1952).

"WE WILL NOT HAVE ANY MORE CRASHES IN OUR TIME"

Like Fisher, Keynes was a New Era advocate who was bullish on stocks and commodities in the 1920s. In 1926, he met with Swiss banker Felix Somary, anxious to buy stocks. When Somary expressed pessimism about the future of the stock market, Keynes declared firmly, "We will not have any more crashes in our time" (Somary 1986 [1960]: 146–47). Somary had been trained in Austrian economics at the University of Vienna and knew that the New Era boom was unsustainable. But Keynes, like Irving Fisher, ignored the Austrians and pinned his hopes on the Federal Reserve and price stabilization.

In late 1928, Keynes wrote two papers disputing that a "dangerous inflation" was developing on Wall Street, concluding that there was "nothing which can be called inflation yet in sight." Referring to both real estate and stock values in the United States, Keynes added, "I conclude that it would be premature today to assert the existence of over-investment. . . . I should be inclined, therefore, to predict that stocks would not slump severely (i.e., below the recent low level) unless the market was discounting a business depression." Such would not be probable since the Federal Reserve Board would "do all in its power to *avoid* a business depression" (Keynes 1973b: 52–59; Hession 1984: 238–39).

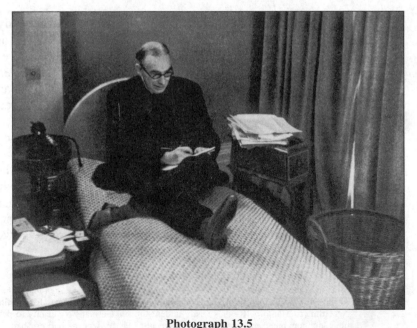

Photograph 13.5
John Maynard Keynes in Bed!
Courtesy of Hulton-Getty Archives. Photograph taken in March 1940, at his home in Bloomsbury.

MAKING MONEY FROM HIS BEDROOM

Keynes should not have been so confident. By the late 1920s, he had developed a reputation for financial wizardry trading currencies, commodities, and stocks. He was chairman of the National Mutual Life Insurance Company and bursar of King's College in Cambridge. His personal account included a heavy commitment to commodities and stocks. He held long positions in futures contracts in rubber, corn, cotton, and tin, as well as several British automobile stocks.

Indeed, he was known for making trading decisions while still in bed. Reports Hession, "Some of this financial decision-making was carried out while he was still in bed in the morning; reports would come to him by phone from his brokers, and he would read the newspapers and make his decisions" (1984: 175).

KEYNES IS WIPED OUT BY THE CRASH

Tragically, Keynes misread the times and failed to anticipate the crash. His portfolio was almost wiped out: He lost three-quarters of his net worth, primarily due to commodity losses (Moggridge 1983: 15–17; Skidelsky 1992: 338–43). In his *Treatise on Money*, published in 1930–31, he admitted that he had been misled by stable price indices in the 1920s, and that a "profit inflation" had developed (1930: 190–98).

However, Keynes, a stubborn investor, held onto his stocks and added substantially to his portfolio starting in 1932. Although he was incapable of getting out at the top, he had an uncanny ability to acquire stocks at the bottom of the market (Skousen 1992: 161–69). He bought securities that were clearly out of favor, such as utilities and gold stocks, and was so sure of his strategy that he bought heavily on margin. In 1944, he wrote a fellow money manager, "My central principle of investment is to go contrary to general opinion, on the ground that, if everyone is agreed about its merits, the investment is inevitably too dear and therefore unattractive" (Moggridge 1983: 111).

KEYNES STILL MANAGES TO DIE SPECTACULARLY RICH

Keynes was so spectacularly successful in choosing stocks that his net worth reached £411,000 by the time he died in 1946. Given that his portfolio was worth only £16,315 in 1920, that's a 13 percent compounded annual return, far superior to what most professional money managers achieve and an amazing feat during an era when there was little or no inflation and, in fact, much deflation. And this extraordinary return was achieved despite fantastic setbacks in 1929–32 and 1937–38. Only David Ricardo had a superior record as a financial economist.

KEYNES, THE PALM READER

Hands! Hands! Hands! Nothing else is worth looking at.
—J.M. Keynes (Skidelsky 1992: 286)

One of Keynes's eccentricities was his obsession with people's hands. The Cambridge don made a lifelong study of the size and shape of hands, which he regarded as a primary clue to character. He was so enamored of chirognomy—the reading of personality by the appearance of the hands—that he had casts made of his and his wife's hands, and even talked of making a collection of those of his friends (Harrod 1951: 20).

His younger brother, Geoffrey, opined that Keynes's strange fixation may have been caused by a traumatic bicycle accident at the age of nine, which resulted in a permanent deformity in one of his fingers (M. Keynes 1975: 29–30).

Keynes first commented about the hands of Sir George Darwin, brother of Charles Darwin, in a letter to his father in 1899: "His hands certainly looked as if they might be descended from an ape" (Harrod 1951: 19).

Whenever Keynes met a colleague, politician, or stranger, he focused immediately on the hands, often making a snap judgment about the person's character. Upon meeting President Woodrow Wilson at the Treaty of Versailles, he noted that his hands, "though capable and fairly strong, were wanting in sensitiveness and finesse" (Keynes 1920: 40). At the same conference, Keynes expressed disappointment that French president Georges Clemenceau wore gloves (pages 20–21).

No wonder Keynes did not take well to Adam Smith's doctrine of the invisible hand!

STARING AT ROOSEVELT'S HANDS

Upon meeting President Franklin D. Roosevelt the first time in 1934, Keynes was so preoccupied with examining FDR's hands that he faltered, "hardly knowing what I was saying about silver and balanced budgets and public works." Roosevelt reportedly was unimpressed with Keynes, and Keynes was disappointed as well. FDR's hand analysis: "Firm and fairly strong, but not clever or with finesse, shortish round nails like those at the end of a business-man's fingers" (Harrod 1951: 20). Keynes determined that Roosevelt's hands reminded him of Sir Edward Grey's.

In 1936, Keynes sat at dinner next to the British playwright W.H. Auden and paid close attention to his fingers. Auden, wrote Keynes, was "altogether delightful, but but but—his finger nails are eaten to the bones with dirt and wet, one of the worst cases ever, like a preparatory schoolboy." Auden's fingernails suggested "something unsatisfactory in his work" (Skidelsky 1992: 628).

Okay, okay, I'll get a manicure!

A REVOLUTIONARY BOOK APPEARS

Keynes's failure to predict the crash and the Great Depression deeply influenced his thinking. He was bitterly resentful of the speculators who drove prices down to ridiculously low levels and nearly put him into the poorhouse. He had long before rejected laissez faire as a general organizing principle in society, but the 1929–32 crisis only strengthened his rejection of conventional classical economics. On BBC radio addresses, he lashed out at hoarders, speculators, and gold bugs, while urging deficit spending, inflation, and abandonment of the gold standard as solutions to the slump. He criticized Friedrich Hayek and the London School of Economics for believing that the economy was self-adjusting and for urging wage reductions and balanced budgets as solutions to the depression.

All the while, at his home in Cambridge, Keynes was working on a book creating a new model of economics, with the help of Richard Kahn, Joan Robinson, and the Cambridge Circus that developed around him. On New Year's Day, 1935, Keynes wrote playwright George Bernard Shaw, "I believe myself to be writing a book on economic theory, which will largely revolutionise—not, I suppose, at once but in the course of the next ten years—the way the world thinks about economic problems" (Skidelsky 2003: 518). It was an arrogant prognostication, but one that proved to be right.

As already mentioned, *The General Theory of Employment, Interest and Money* first appeared in 1936.[3] Like other economists, Keynes identified with the great scientists of the past. Adam Smith and Roger Babson compared their analytical systems to those of Sir Isaac Newton, and Keynes emulated Albert Einstein. Keynes's book title mimicks Einstein's general theory of relativity. His book, he said, creates a "general" theory of economic behavior while relegating the classical model to a "special" case and treating classical economists as "Euclidean geometers in a non-Euclidean world" (Skidelsky 1992: 487).

Like Marx, Keynes had high hopes that his magnum opus would be read by students and the general public and convinced Macmillan to price the 400-page treatise at only 5 shillings. But this was wishful thinking. *The General Theory* turned out to be Keynes's only unreadable book, full of technical jargon and incomprehensible language (see the box on page 336). Even Paul Samuelson, a dutiful Keynesian, declared, "It is a badly written book, poorly organized; any layman who, beguiled by the author's previous reputation, bought the book was cheated of his five shillings. It is not well suited for classroom use. It is arrogant, bad-tempered, polemical, and not overly generous in its acknowledgements. It abounds in mares' nests or

---

3. Some Keynesians, such as Charles Hession and John Kenneth Galbraith, emphatically insist that the correct title is *The General Theory of Employment Interest and Money*, without the comma. True, no commas were used on the cover of the the original, but in the preface, Keynes added a comma after "employment." Another case of Keynesian ambiguity, or should I say trivial pursuit?

PROFESSOR KEYNES'S PROPENSITY TO CONFUSE

*It is astonishing what foolish things one can temporarily believe
if one thinks too long alone, particularly in economics.*
—J.M. Keynes (1973a [1936]: Preface)

Ricardo and Marx had their book of headaches, and so did Keynes. The following simple questions will demonstrate a few of the difficulties found in *The General Theory*:

Q: Please, Professor Keynes, what do you mean by "involuntary unemployment"?

A: My definition is . . . as follows: Men are involuntarily unemployed if, in the event of a small rise in the price of wage-goods relative to the money-wage, both the aggregate supply of labour willing to work for the current money-wage and the aggregate demand for it at that wage would be greater than the existing volume of employment (page 15).

Q: Humm . . . sounds very enlightening, Professor Keynes. Now tell us, please, what governs private investment in a market economy?

A: Our conclusions can be stated in the most general form . . . as follows: No further increase in the rate of investment is possible when the greatest amongst the own-rates of own-interest of all available assets is equal to the greatest amongst the marginal efficiencies of all assets, measured in terms of the asset whose own-rate of own-interest is greatest (page 236).

Q: Yes, I see. . . . One last question, Professor Keynes. Doesn't monetary expansion trigger an artificial boom?

A: [A]t this point we are in deep water. The wild duck has dived down to the bottom—as deep as she can get—and bitten fast hold of the weed and tangle and all the rubbish that is down there, and it would need an extraordinarily clever dog to dive down and fish her up again (page 183).

Q: Thanks, Professor Keynes. And congratulations on winning the Nobel Prize in Literature.

Source: Thanks to Roger Garrison, economics professor at Auburn University, for providing this bit of satire.

confusions. . . . Flashes of insight and intuition intersperse tedious algebra. An awkward definition suddenly gives way to an unforgettable cadenza. When finally mastered, its analysis is found to be obvious and at the same time new. In short, it is a work of genius" (Samuelson 1947 [1946]: 148–89).

The General Theory is still in print but only because of the elucidating work of his disciples, especially Alvin Hansen of Harvard and Paul Samuelson of MIT, who deciphered Keynes's convoluted jargon, translated it into plain English, and transformed the profession.

KEYNES AT WAR

Keynes was fifty-two—his friends might say he was now working with a full deck—when he completed *The General Theory*, his final major work. He was at the height of his powers. Keynes was never a bookish scholar and recluse like his Cambridge colleagues Arthur Pigou or Dennis Robertson. He was a man of worldly affairs who loved the limelight and the social life, enjoyed the company of writers and artists, and was a devotee of cards, roulette, and speculations on Lombard Street and Wall Street. His magnetic personality attracted the highest leaders of government, who sought his counsel. He was a master of the written word and an entertaining speaker who regularly appeared on BBC radio.

After suffering a heart attack in 1937, Keynes had to slow down. He and his wife became active in promoting the arts and establishing the Arts Theatre in Cambridge. In 1940, when the war with Germany broke out, Keynes returned to the Treasury as an advisor and wrote an influential booklet, *How to Pay for the War*. He recommended restrictions on consumption and investment, and a forced savings program as a way to reduce demand and inflation.

In May 1942, Keynes's name was submitted to the king, nominating him to become Baron Keynes of Tilton, and in July he took his seat in the House of Lords. On his sixtieth birthday, Keynes was made High Steward of Cambridge, an honorary post. He reveled in the adulation and his elite status.

Near the end of the war, Keynes and his wife traveled to the United States to help negotiate a new international financial agreement. Keynes was one of the architects of the Bretton Woods agreement, which established a fixed exchange rate system based on gold and the dollar and created the International Monetary Fund (IMF) and the World Bank. Two years later, he died of a heart attack at the age of sixty-two.

KEYNES UNSYMPATHETIC TO ADAM SMITH

Let us now turn to Keynes's approach to economics. It should be noted at the outset that although Keynes has been lauded as the savior of capitalism, his model and policy recommendations were in fact both a direct repudia-

KEYNES'S WHIPPING BOY BECOMES A SOVIET SPY!?

World War I was a shock to him, and he was never the same afterwards.
—C.R. Fay

Keynes used classical economist **Arthur C. Pigou (1877–1959)** as his favorite scapegoat in *The General Theory* (1973a: 7 passim). To the shy, even reclusive, professor, the attack seemed unfair, and he lashed back in a harsh review in *Economica* (Pigou 1936). Yet in his old age Pigou managed to forgive Keynes, and even became an admirer.

In 1908, at the youthful age of thirty-one, Pigou succeeded Alfred Marshall as professor of political economy at Cambridge, and he never left. In his early years, he was known as a vibrant orator, a first-rate teacher, and a prolific writer on labor and welfare issues. But then came the Great War in 1914. The son of a decorated British officer, he nevertheless became a conscientious objector during the war. Like many pacifists, he spent his vacations with an ambulance unit run by the Quakers. The bitterness of war deeply affected him, and he began withdrawing into the life of a recluse. A confirmed bachelor, Pigou spent his spare time mountain climbing in the Alps or quietly entertaining male companions at his home on Lake Buttermere.

How shy was Pigou? He would dictate letters through a half-opened door to his secretary in another room. The next day she would return the typescript, using the college mail (Graaff 1987: 877)!

FROM FREE TRADER TO COMMUNIST SYMPATHIZER

Photograph 13.6
Arthur C. Pigou (1877–1959)
Cambridge don, a Soviet spy?
Courtesy of Cambridge University.

It's difficult to say at what point Pigou shifted views and became an underground supporter of revolutionary causes. Outwardly he had built a reputation as a staunch free trader and winner of the Adam Smith Prize, yet he pioneered welfare economics, which embodied strong sympathy toward distributive justice and interests of the poor. He favored redistribution schemes (graduated income taxes and high death taxes), and during the depression he joined Keynes in advocating deficit spending and public works projects. Later, he advocated nationalizing all "monopolistic" industries such as coal and railways. Convinced that socialism was more efficient than capitalism, Pigou publicly declared his sympathy toward socialism, approving a gradual democratic nonviolent takeover of the means of production in *Socialism Versus Capitalism* (Pigou 1937: 138–39).

Yet there is considerable evidence that he had been an underground agent for revolutionary causes much earlier in his career. According to British agent Richard Deacon (a pseudonym), in 1905 Pigou attended a

(continued)

clandestine meeting of the Russian Social Democrats in London and decided to become a secret agent, committed to developing a British spy network and arranging payments for arms shipments to Russia. He even kept a diary that year written entirely in code (Deacon 1989: 44–45).

If Pigou was indeed a spy, he kept his spy activities in Britain a closely guarded secret, completely separate from his professional responsibilities at Cambridge. He held strong anti-fascist and anti-Nazi views, but frequently praised the achievements of the Soviet Union, who were allies during World War II. Meanwhile, he allegedly met with the Soviet Secret Service to provide strategic information concerning the location of airfields and squadrons in the Cambridge area. He also helped recruit young men to join the ring of Soviet spies in Britain. He would invite them on hiking trips or to his lakefront home.

At one point, Pigou approached Friedrich Hayek, who had transferred from London to Cambridge during the war. Hayek, like Pigou, was an avid mountain climber whom Pigou invited to stay at his lakefront home and go hiking. According to Hayek, Pigou was interested in the names of people who could cross frontiers. But Pigou suddenly dropped Hayek, who was singularly unsympathetic to Pigou's cause (Hayek 1994: 136–37).

Pigou's alleged spying activities for the Soviet Union became known by British Intelligence only after his death, and were not raised publicly until the late 1980s. His reputation has never suffered among the economics profession. "The quality of all his books is outstanding," wrote Mark Blaug, "but he has only slowly won a place as an economist of first distinction" (1999: 893).

---

tion of and assault on Adam Smith's laissez-faire system. Keynes as much as admitted this when he said, "It is *not* true that individuals possess a prescriptive 'natural liberty' in their economic activities. . . . Nor is it true that self-interest generally *is* enlightened. . . . Experience does *not* show that individuals, when they make up a social unit, are always less clear-sighted than when they act separately" (Keynes 1963 [1931]: 312). This speech, appropriately titled "The End of Laissez-Faire," was given in 1926, a full decade before *The General Theory* was written. It was a clear attack on Adam Smith's system of natural liberty.

In the early 1930s, Keynes became increasingly disillusioned with capitalism, both morally and aesthetically. The ideas of Sigmund Freud were fashionable at the time, and Keynes adopted the Freudian thesis that money making was a neurosis, "a somewhat disgusting morbidity, one of the semi-criminal, semi-pathological propensities which one hands over with a shudder to specialists in mental disease" (1963: 369). Later, in 1933, he indicted the capitalist system: "The decadent international but individualistic capitalism, in the hands of which we found ourselves after the war, is not a success. It is not intelligent, it is not beautiful, it is not just, it is not virtuous—and it doesn't deliver the goods. In short, we dislike it and are beginning to despise it. But when we wonder what to put in its place, we are perplexed" (Hession 1984: 258). This is a far cry from Adam Smith!

KEYNES, THE HERETIC, TURNS CLASSICAL ECONOMICS UPSIDE DOWN

The General Theory did not aim to rebuild the classical model; it aimed to replace it with elaborate unconventional concepts and a new *Weltanschauung*. Until the 1930s, the economics profession had largely sanctioned the basic premises of the classical model of Adam Smith—the virtues of thrift, balanced budgets, free trade, low taxes, the gold standard, and Say's law. But Keynes turned the classical model upside down.

Instead of Smith's classical system being considered the general or universal model, Keynes relegated it to a "special case," applicable only in times of full employment. His own general theory of "aggregate effective demand" would apply during times of underemployed labor and resources, which, under Keynesianism, could exist indefinitely. Under such circumstances, Keynes offered the following principles:

1. An increase in savings can contract income and reduce economic growth. Consumption is more important than production in encouraging investment, thus reversing Say's law: "Demand creates its own supply" (1973a: 18–21, 111).

2. The federal government's budget should be kept deliberately in a state of imbalance during a recession. Fiscal and monetary policy should be highly expansionary until prosperity is restored, and interest rates should be kept permanently low (1973a: 128–31, 322).

3. Government should abandon its laissez-faire policy and intervene in the marketplace whenever necessary. According to Keynes, in desperate times it may be necessary to return to mercantilist policies, including protectionist measures (1973a: 333–71).

4. The gold standard is defective because its inelasticity renders it incapable of responding to the expanding needs of business. A managed fiat money is preferable (1973a: 235–56; 1971: 140). Keynes held a deep-seated hatred of the gold standard and was largely successful in dethroning gold as a worldwide monetary numeraire.

Keynes was, in fact, a social millennialist who ultimately envisioned a world evolving to the point of infinite accumulation of capital. His utopian vision is best expressed in his essay, "Economic Possibilities for Our Grandchildren" (1963: 358–73). By progressively expanding credit to promote full employment, Keynes believed that the universal economic problem of scarcity would finally be overcome. Interest rates would fall to zero, and mankind would reenter the Garden of Eden. In Keynes's mind, the gold standard severely limited credit expansion and preserved the status quo of scarcity. Thus, gold's inelasticity—which the classical economists considered its primary virtue—stood in the way of Keynes's paradise and must be abandoned in favor of fiat-money inflation (1963: 360–73). The Bretton Woods agreement was the first step toward removing gold from the world's monetary system. Undoubtedly Keynes would be pleased to see gold playing such a moribund role in international monetary affairs in the twenty-first century.

In short, Keynes's goal was not to save Adam Smith's house, as his adherents contended, but to build another house entirely—the house that Keynes built. It was his belief that economists would live and work most of the time in Keynes's house, while using Smith's house occasionally, perhaps as a vacation home.

IS CAPITALISM INHERENTLY UNSTABLE?

Keynes rejected the classical notion that the capitalist system is self-adjusting over the long run. *The General Theory* was written specifically to create a model based on the view that the market system is inherently and inescapably flawed. Capitalism is unstable and therefore can be stuck indefinitely at varying degrees of "unemployed equilibrium," depending on the level of uncertainty in a fragile financial system. Keynes wanted to show that the economy remains "in a chronic condition of sub-normal activity for a considerable period without any marked tendency either toward recovery or toward complete collapse" (1973a: 249, 30). Paul Samuelson correctly understood the meaning of Keynes: "With respect to the level of total purchasing power and employment, Keynes denies that there is an *invisible hand* channeling the self-centered action of each individual to the social optimum" (Samuelson 1947: 151).

Keynes explained what he meant by "unemployment equilibrium," but used no diagram to illustrate it. In a masterful article, "Mr. Keynes and the Classics," British economist John Hicks developed a graphic framework (known as the *IS-LM* diagram) to demonstrate Keynes's version of full-employment equilibrium (the special classical theory) versus unemployment equilibrium (the general theory) (Hicks 1937). Today's textbooks use a similar diagram (see Figure 13.1, page 344) to demonstrate aggregate supply (*AS*) and aggregate demand (*AD*).

In Figure 13.1, we see how the economy is stable at less than full employment. According to Keynes's model, the classical model only applies when the economy reaches full employment (Q_f), while the Keynesian general theory applies at any point along the *AS* curve where it intersects with the *AD* curve.

WHO'S TO BLAME? IRRATIONAL INVESTORS!

Keynes blamed the instability of capitalism on the bad behavior of investors. *The General Theory* creates a macroeconomic model based essentially on a financial instability hypothesis. As Keynesian economist Hyman P. Minsky declares, "The essential aspect of Keynes's *General Theory* is a deep analysis of how financial forces—which we can charac-

"RADICAL SUBJECTIVISM" LEADS TO THE NEW SCHOOL OF IGNORANCE!

The social object of skilled investment should be to defeat the
dark forces of time and ignorance which envelop our future.
—John Maynard Keynes (1973a: 155)

Keynes talked so much about the inherent uncertainty of business psychology that the British G.L.S. Shackle and the German Ludwig M. Lachmann argued that economics is like a kaleidoscope, where the outcome changes in an unpredictable way with every turn of the economic scene. Thus, the economics of Keynes was a general theory of uncertainty and ignorance (Shackle 1974; Lachmann 1977).

Keynes himself gave credence to this "radical subjectivism" in macroeconomics. In commenting about his approach toward *The General Theory*, he stated, "The fact that our knowledge of the future is fluctuating, vague and uncertain, renders wealth a peculiarly unsuitable subject for the methods of classical economic theory. . . . There is no scientific basis on which to form any calculable probability whatsoever. We simply do not know" (1973b: 114).

THE AGE OF HUBRIS

By the 1960s, Keynesian economists had forgotten these humbling comments by their master and were convinced that they had discovered how to fine-tune the economy through Keynesian tools. But then came the chaotic seventies, which left many economists in a stupor, forcing a frank admission that their theories and policies had failed them. As Hayek stated when he received the Nobel Prize in 1974, "We have indeed at the moment little cause for pride: As a profession we have made a mess of things" (Hayek 1984: 266).

THE AGE OF IGNORANCE

Since then, a new school has developed which I have dubbed the "Ignorance School of Economics." It often consists of very bright economists who reflect a strange new malaise, an eerie complacency about the burning economic issues of the day. Examples of this new nihilism:

- Herbert Stein, former chairman of the Council of Economic Advisors, wrote "I am more and more impressed by my ignorance. . . . I don't know whether increasing the budget deficit stimulates or depresses the national income. I don't know whether it is M2 or M1 that controls the level of spending. I don't know how much a 10 percent increase in the top rate of individual income tax will raise the revenues. . . . I do not know how to pick winning stocks" (1993).

- Charles R. Bean, economist at the London School of Economics, wrote a forty-seven-page article on European unemployment in the *Journal of Economic Literature* and concluded, "This huge rise in high unemployment is a major puzzle" (1994: 573).

- Robert J. Barro, Harvard professor and proponent of the new classical school, wrote regarding the 1991–92 recession: "The questions I am asked most often these days are: Why is the economic recovery weaker than expected? How will the

(continued)

economy do over the next year? What should government do to help? As a first approximation, the right answers to questions like these are: 'I don't know,' 'I don't know,' and 'nothing'" (1991).

- Paul Krugman, neo-Keynesian professor at Princeton University, proclaimed in a book entitled *Peddling Prosperity* that economists don't understand the business cycle, and "don't know how to make a poor country rich, or bring back the magic of economic growth when it seems to have gone away." Furthermore, "Nobody really knows why the U.S. economy could generate 3 percent annual productivity growth before 1973 and only 1 percent afterward; nobody really knows why Japan surged from defeat to global economic power after World War II, while Britain slid slowly into third-rate status" (Krugman 1994: 9, 24). And Krugman earned the John Bates Clark Medal and won the Nobel Memorial Prize in economic sciences in 2008!

AGE OF IGNORANCE OR ENLIGHTENMENT?

To be sure, there is always a level of uncertainty and ignorance in the marketplace, but to plead excessive ignorance is not a virtue, either. St. Paul warned Timothy about intellectuals who are "ever learning, and never able to come to the knowledge of the truth" (2 Timothy 3: 7).

A CERTAIN RESPONSE TO AN UNCERTAIN TRUMPET

The standard-bearers of sound economics could provide answers to the queries of Stein, Bean, Barro, and Krugman. Does the deficit stimulate or retard economic growth? Transfers from the *productive* private sector to the *unproductive* public sector inevitably depress economic growth in the long run. Does the money supply control the level of spending? Adam Smith and Ludwig von Mises tell us that purchasing power is not determined by the money supply but by productivity and output. Do marginal tax rate increases raise revenues? Not always—sometimes marginal tax cuts increase revenues! Can't pick winning stocks? Perhaps sitting down with financial entrepreneurs Peter Lynch, Warren Buffett, John Templeton, and other analysts might help Mr. Stein.

What is the cause of stubbornly high unemployment in Europe? The evidence is growing: excessively high payroll taxes, and restrictive labor rules (mandatory paid vacations, limited workweek, inability to fire workers, and so on). If European governments would liberalize their labor markets, unemployment rates would fall to U.S. levels.

What should the government do to create a permanent recovery? Not raise taxes, as Bush did in 1991. It would be better to cut taxes and business regulations.

Why do poor nations become rich? The common denominators of the economic miracle of southeast Asia are a strong, stable, and lean government, low taxes, high levels of saving and investment, open markets, and minimal concern with income distribution. Could these reasons help explain Asia's postwar success story? Pro-growth government, high saving rates, low taxes on investment, emphasis on training, and quality improvements. Or why Britain stagnated? High taxes, price and exchange controls, excessively powerful labor unions, bureaucracy, and welfarism.

In short, this isn't the age of ignorance. It's the age of enlightenment.

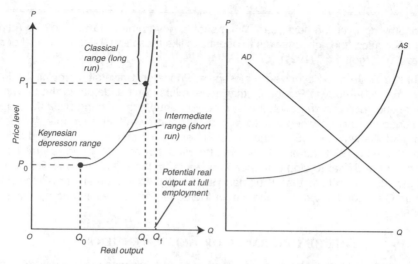

Figure 13.1 An Illustration of Keynes's Theory of Unemployed Equilibrium: General and Classical Models

Source: Byrns and Stone (1987: 311). Reprinted by permission of Scott, Foresman and Co.

terize as Wall Street—interact with production and consumption to determine output, employment, and prices" (1986: 100). Allan H. Meltzer at Carnegie Mellon University offers a similar interpretation, that Keynes's theory of employment and output was not so much related to rigid wages as to expectations and uncertainty in the investment and capital markets[4] (Meltzer 1988).

Numerous passages in *The General Theory* support this view. Keynes complained of the irrational short-term "animal spirits" of speculators who dump stocks in favor of liquidity during such crises. Such "waves of irrational psychology" could do much damage to long-term expectations, he said. "Of the maxims of orthodox finance none, surely, is more anti-social than the fetish of liquidity, the doctrine that it is a positive virtue on the part of investment institutions to concentrate resources upon the holding of 'liquid' securities" (1973a: 155). According to Keynes, the stock market is not simply an efficient way to raise capital and advance living standards, but can be likened to a casino or game of chance. "For it is, so to speak, a game of Snap, of Old Maid, of Musical Chairs—a pastime in which he is victor who says *Snap* neither too soon nor too late, who passes the Old Maid to his neighbor before the game is over, who secures a chair for himself when the music stops" (1973a: 155–56).

Keynes was speaking from experience. He reasoned that the 1929–32 crisis destroyed his portfolio without any rational economic cause—the

4. See also my version of this thesis in "Keynes as a Speculator: A Critique of Keynesian Investment Theory," in Skousen (1992: 161–69).

panic was due to Wall Street's irrational demand for cash, what he termed "liquidity preference" and a "fetish of liquidity" (1973a: 155).

THE CULPRIT: UNINVESTED SAVINGS

If Keynes were Sherlock Holmes, the economist-investigator would point an accusing finger at Miss Thrifty in his murder mystery, "The Case of the Missing Savings." In Keynes's model, the key factor in causing an indefinite slump is the delinking of savings and investment. If savings failed to be invested, total spending in the economy would fall to a point below full employment. If savings were hoarded or left in excessive reserves in the banks, as was the case in the 1930s, the fetish for liquidity would make national investment and output fall.

In *The General Theory*, Keynes argued that as income and wealth accumulate under capitalism, the threat grows that savings won't be invested. He introduced a "psychological law" that the "marginal propensity to save" increases with income (1973a: 31, 97). That is, as individuals earn more income and become wealthier, they tend to save a greater percentage. Thus, there is a strong tendency for savings to rise disproportionately as national income increases. But wouldn't a growing capitalist economy always be under pressure to invest those increased savings? Keynes responded, "Maybe, maybe not." If savings aren't invested, the boom will turn into a bust.

Actually, this criticism of uninvested savings is an old saw with Keynes. He acknowledged the necessity of thrift and self-denial during the nineteenth century in a delightful passage of *The Economic Consequences of the Peace* (1920: 18–22)—stating that thrift "made possible those vast accumulations of fixed wealth and of capital improvement which distinguished that age from all others" (1920: 19). But in *A Treatise on Money* (1930), the Cambridge economist raised the likely possibility that saving and investment could grow apart, creating a business cycle. In a modern society, saving and investing are done by two separate groups. Saving is a "negative act of refraining from spending," while investment is a "positive act of starting or maintaining some process of production" (1930: 155). The interest rate is not an "automatic mechanism" that brings the two together—they can "get out of gear" (1963: 393) and savings can be "abortive." If investment exceeds savings, a boom occurs; if saving exceeds investment, a slump happens.

During the depression of the 1930s, Keynes lashed out at frugal savers and hoarders. The conventional wisdom in bad times has always been to cut costs, get out of debt, build a strong cash position, and wait for a recovery. Keynes was opposed to this "old-fashioned" approach, and he was joined by other economists, including British Treasury official Ralph Hawtrey and Harvard's Frank Taussig, in encouraging consumers to spend. In a radio broadcast in January 1931, Keynes asserted that thriftiness could cause a "vicious circle" of poverty, that if "you save five shillings, you put a man out of work for a day." He encouraged British housewives to go on a buying spree and government to go on a building binge. He urged, "Why not pull down the whole of South London from Westminster to Greenwich, and make a good job of it. . . . Would that employ men? Why, of course it would!" (1963: 151–54).

Keynes's bias against thrift reached its zenith in *The General Theory*, where he referred to traditional views on savings as "absurd." He boldly wrote, "The more virtuous we are, the more determined by thrift, the more obstinately orthodox in our national and personal finance, the more our incomes will fall" (1973a: 111, 211). Keynes praised the heterodox notions of underworld figures and monetary cranks, such as Bernard de Mandeville, J.A. Hobson, and Silvio Gessell, who held underconsumptionist views (1973a: 333–71). He was undoubtedly influenced by the popularity of Major Douglas of the social credit movement and underconsumptionists Foster and Catchings during the 1920s (see the box on page 347).

KEYNES FOCUSES ON SPENDING AS THE KEY INGREDIENT

In Keynes's mind, saving is an unreliable form of spending. It is only "effective" if savings are invested by business. Thus, saving that is hoarded under a mattress or piled up in a bank vault is a drain on the economy.

Only "effective demand"—a powerful new term introduced in chapter 3 of *The General Theory*—counts. What consumers and businesses spend determines national output. Keynes defined effective demand as aggregate output (Y), which is the sum of consumption (C) and investment (I). Hence,

$$Y = C + I$$

Today we call Y, or aggregate "effective demand," gross domestic product (GDP). GDP is defined as the value of the final output of goods and services during the year. Simon Kuznets, a Keynesian statistician, developed national income accounting in the early 1940s as a way to measure Keynes's aggregate effective demand (it was called gross national product or GNP). (For more on Kuznets, see the box on page 377.)

Keynes effectively demonstrated that if savings aren't invested by business, GDP does not reach its potential; recession or depression indicates a lack of effective demand.

DEMAND CREATES ITS OWN SUPPLY!

What was Keynes's solution to recession? Increase effective demand! By stimulating demand through additional spending, more goods would have to be produced and the economy would recover. In this sense, Keynes turned Say's law upside down. Demand creates supply, not the other way around (see the box on page 348, "What Does Keynes Say About Say?").

To increase Y (national output), the choices are limited in a recession. During a downturn, the business community might be afraid to risk their capital on I (investment). Equally, consumers might be unwilling to increase consumption (C) due to the uncertainty of their incomes. Both investors and consumers are more likely to pull in their horns when left to their own devices.

UNDERCONSUMPTIONISTS OFFER $5,000 REWARD TO DISPROVE THEIR THEORY!

Keynes wasn't the first to question the virtue of thrift. Over the years, a small group of radical thinkers, known generally as underconsumptionists, have dissented from the traditional endorsement of thrift. They include Simonde de Sismondi, Karl Rodbertus, J.A. Hobson, and Karl Marx. Keynes expressed sympathy toward the "heretical" views of Major C.H. Douglas, an engineer who began the social credit movement in Canada in the 1920s and wrote several books championing "economic democracy" (1973a: 370–71). Believing that saving created a permanent deficiency in a nation's purchasing power, Major Douglas advocated strict below-market price controls so that consumers could afford to buy the products they produced.

William T. Foster, past president of Reed College, and Waddill Catchings, an iron manufacturer and partner in the investment firm of Goldman Sachs, proposed a different scheme. Foster and Catchings wrote a series of books on a similar antisaving theme. "[E]very dollar which is *saved and invested*, instead of *spent*, causes one dollar of deficiency in consumer buying unless that deficiency is made up in some way" (Foster and Catchings 1927: 48). What way? Foster and Catchings advocated that the government issue new money credits to consumers to make up for consumer buying deficiency.

To generate interest in their theory and proposal, in 1927 they offered a prize of $5,000 to anyone who could refute them. They published the top essays a few months later, but the best critique was written by the Austrian economist Friedrich A. Hayek in 1929. His essay, "The 'Paradox' of Saving," was translated and published in *Economica* in May 1931.

According to Hayek, the Foster-and-Catchings dilemma depended on a single erroneous assumption. They assumed a "single-stage" model, so that investment depends entirely and immediately on consumer demand. Under such a restrictive assumption, "there would be no inducement . . . to save money . . . [or] . . . to invest their savings," noted Hayek (1939 [1929]: 224, 247). Using a capital-using, time-oriented period of production, Hayek demonstrated that increased savings lengthens the capitalistic process, increases productivity, and thereby enlarges profits, wages, and income sufficiently for consumers to buy the final product.

Foster and Catchings rejected all arguments and never paid the prize money.

Adding G to the Equation

There is only one way out, wrote Keynes. Get government to start spending. Keynes added G (government) to the national income equation, so that

$$Y = C + I + G$$

Keynes saw government (G) as an independent agent capable of stimulating the economy through the printing presses and public works. An expansionary government policy could raise "effective demand" if resources were underutilized, without hurting consumption or investment. In fact, during a recession, a rise in G would encourage both C and I and thereby boost Y.

Digging Holes in the Ground:
Keynes Endorses an Activist Fiscal Policy

Keynes overturned the classical solution to a slump, which had been to "tighten one's belt" by cutting prices, wages, and wasteful spending while waiting out the slump. Instead, during a recession, he recommended delib-

---

What Does Keynes Say About Say?

The old orthodoxy, against which the Keynesian revolution was raised, was based on Say's Law—there cannot be a deficiency of demand.
                                                    —Joan Robinson (1976: 121)

In 1936 John Maynard Keynes created a straw man in *The General Theory of Employment, Interest and Money* and generated a revolution in economics. The straw man was J.-B. Say and his famous law of markets. Steven Kates calls *The General Theory* "a book-length attempt to refute Say's Law." But to do this, Keynes gravely distorted Say's law and classical economics in general. As Kates discloses in his remarkable book, *Say's Law and the Keynesian Revolution*, "Keynes was wrong in his interpretation of Say's Law and, more importantly, he was wrong about its economic implications" (Kates 1998: 212).

How Keynes Got It Wrong

In the introduction to the French edition of *The General Theory*, published in 1939, Keynes focused on Say's law as the central issue of macroeconomics. "I believe that economics everywhere up to recent times has been dominated . . . by the doctrines associated with the name of J.-B. Say. It is true that his 'law of markets' has long been abandoned by most economists; but they have not extricated themselves from his basic assumptions and particularly from his fallacy that demand is created by supply. . . . Yet a theory so based is clearly incompetent to tackle the problems of unemployment and of the trade cycle" (1973a: xxxv).

(continued)

Unfortunately, Keynes failed to understand Say's law. He incorrectly paraphrased Say's law as "supply creates its own demand" (1973a: 25), a distortion of the original meaning. In effect, Keynes altered Say's law to mean that everything produced is automatically bought. Hence, according to Keynes, Say's law cannot explain the business cycle. Keynes falsely concluded, "Say's law . . . is equivalent to the proposition that there is no obstacle to full employment" (1973a: 26).

Interestingly, Keynes never quoted Say directly, and some historians have thus surmised that Keynes never read Say's actual *Treatise*, relying instead on Ricardo's and Marshall's comments on Say's law of markets. (For a detailed discussion of Say's law, including direct quotes from Say's *Treatise*, see chapter 2 of this book.)

Keynes went on to say that the classical model under Say's law "assumes full employment" (1973a: 15, 191). Other Keynesians have continued to make this point, but nothing could be further from the truth. Conditions of unemployment do not prohibit production and sales from taking place that form the basis of new income and new demand.

Say actually used his own law to explain recessions. As such, Say's law specifically formed the basis of a classical theory of the business cycle and unemployment. As Kates states, "The classical position was that involuntary unemployment was not only possible, but occurred often, and with serious consequences for the unemployed" (Kates 1998: 18).

Say's law concludes that recessions are not caused by failure of the level of demand (Keynes's thesis), but by failure in the *structure* of supply and demand. According to Say's law, an economic slump occurs when producers miscalculate what consumers wish to buy, thus causing unsold goods to pile up, production to be cut back, workers to be laid off, income to fall, and finally, consumer spending to drop. As Kates elucidates, "Classical theory explained recessions by showing how errors in production might arise during cyclical upturns which would cause some goods to remain unsold at cost-covering prices" (1998: 19). The classical model was a "highly-sophisticated theory of recession and unemployment" that was "obliterated" with one fell swoop by the illustrious Keynes (Kates 1998: 20, 18).

In his broad-based book, Kates highlights other classical economists, including David Ricardo, James Mill, Robert Torrens, Henry Clay, Frederick Lavington, and Wilhelm Röpke, who extended this classical model of Say's law. Many classical economists focused on how monetary inflation exacerbated the business cycle.

KEYNES'S NEMESIS

On one point Keynes was right: Say's law is Keynes's nemesis. It specifically refutes Keynes's basic thesis that a deficit in aggregate demand causes a recession and that artificially stimulating consumer spending through government deficits is a cure for depression. To quote Kates, "Say clearly understood that economies can and do enter prolonged periods of economic depression. But what he was at pains to argue was that increased levels of unproductive consumption are not a remedy for a depressed level of economic activity, and contribute nothing to the wealth creation process. Consumption, whether productive or unproductive, uses up resources, while only productive consumption is capable of leaving something of an equivalent or even higher value in its place" (1998: 34).

erate deficit spending by the federal government to jump-start the economy. He endorsed an even more radical approach during a deep depression like that of the 1930s: Government spending could be totally wasteful and it would still help. "Pyramid-building, earthquakes, even wars may serve to increase wealth," he proclaimed (1973a: 129). Of course, "It would, indeed, be more sensible to build houses and the like," but productive building wasn't essential. According to Keynes, spending is spending, no matter what the objective, and it has the same beneficial effect—increasing aggregate demand.

KEYNES FAVORS PUBLIC WORKS OVER MONETARY INFLATION

Keynes felt that tinkering with fiscal policy (changes in spending and taxes) was more effective than monetary policy (changes in the money supply and interest rates). He had lost faith in monetary policy and the Federal Reserve in the 1930s, when interest rates were so low that reducing them wouldn't have made much difference. Inducing the Federal Reserve to expand the money supply wouldn't be very effective either, because banks refused to lend excess reserves anyway. Keynes called this a "liquidity trap." The new money would just pile up unspent and uninvested because of "liquidity preference," the desire to hold cash during a severe depression (1973a: 207).

HOW THE MULTIPLIER GENERATES FULL EMPLOYMENT

Public works would serve several benefits. First, public works promote positive spending, putting people to work and money into business's pockets. Moreover, they have a multiplier effect, based on the nation's marginal propensity to consume.

The multiplier, a concept introduced by Richard Kahn, was a powerful new tool in the Keynesian tool box, demonstrating that a "small increment of investment will lead to full employment" (Keynes 1973a: 118). Suppose in a recession that the government hires construction workers and suppliers to construct a new federal building costing $100 million. These previously unemployed workers are now getting paid. In the first round of spending, $100 million is added to the economy.

Now suppose that the public's marginal propensity to consume is 90 percent, that is, these workers spend 90 cents of every new dollar earned. (Another way of saying it: their marginal propensity to save is 10 percent.) In the second round of spending, $90 million is added to the economy.

Then there is a third round. After the workers spend their new money, that $90 million becomes the revenues of other businesses—shopping malls, gas stations, supermarkets, car dealerships, and movie theaters. These businesses may in turn hire new workers to handle the new demand, paying them more wages, too, and these workers also spend 90 percent of that income. They receive an additional $81 million (90 percent of $90 million) of spending power. Ultimately, the public investment has a multiplier effect that generates round after round of gradually declining spending. By the time the new spending has run its course, the aggregate spending has increased tenfold. Keynes's formula for the multiplier k is

$$k = \frac{1}{1 - MPC}$$

where MPC = marginal propensity to consume.

Since $MPC = .90$ in the example above, $k = 10$. As Keynes stated, "the multiplier k is 10; and the total employment caused by . . . increased public works will be ten times the primary employment provided by the public works themselves, assuming no reduction of investment in other directions" (1973a: 116–17).

KEYNES MAKES A MISCHIEVOUS ASSUMPTION

Note that in the Keynesian model, only consumption spending generates additional income and employment in the economy. Keynes assumes that saving is sterile, that it aborts into cash hoarding or excess bank reserves. Thus, the Keynesian model as originally proposed is considered a "depression" model. As we shall see in the next chapter, this was a crucial mistake that led to much mischief and misunderstanding in economics in the postwar era.

KEYNES OFFERS A DRASTIC MEASURE TO STABILIZE CAPITALISM

The Cambridge leader was not satisfied with temporary measures such as public works and deficit spending to reestablish full employment. Once maximum output was reached, he reasoned, there is no reason to believe it will stay there. Investment is unpredictable and ephemeral, Keynes said. Long-term expectations, a stable business climate, and savings equal to investment could never be guaranteed as long as irrational "animal spirits" operated in a laissez-faire financial marketplace. What was Keynes's solution? He favored a gradual but comprehensive "socialisation of investment" as the "only means of securing an approximation to full employment" (1973a: 378). This was by no means "state socialism," but it could mean government ownership of the entire capital markets. Keynes also sanctioned a small "transfer tax" on all securities sales as a way to dampen speculative fever.[5]

A TURNING POINT IN TWENTIETH-CENTURY ECONOMICS

Two factors created the right atmosphere for the Keynesian revolution to sweep the economics profession. First, the depth and length of the Great

---

5. Nobel laureate James Tobin has entertained a similar measure, known as the Tobin tax on stock and foreign exchange transactions, a legal step that would surely reduce liquidity and enlarge the bid-ask spreads on stocks and foreign exchange.

WHAT DID KEYNES REALLY MEAN, "IN THE LONG RUN WE ARE ALL DEAD"?

I even consider it as the only correct declaration of the neo-British Cambridge school.
—Ludwig von Mises (1980: 7)

Keynes is famous for his cavalier statement, "In the long run we are all dead." Many economists consider his remark an affront to Frédéric Bastiat's classical view ("What Is Seen and What Is Not Seen"—see chapter 2) that economists must take into account the long-run and not just the short-run effects of government policies. For example, deficit spending may stimulate certain sectors of the economy in the short run, but what will be the impact in the long run? Tariffs may save some manufacturing jobs, but what impact will it have on consumers? As Henry Hazlitt declares, "The art of economics consists in looking not merely at the immediate but at the longer effects of any act or policy; it consists in tracing the consequences of that policy not merely for one group but for all groups" (1979 [1946]: 17). And Ludwig von Mises, another critic, concludes, "we have outlived the short-run and are suffering from the long-run consequences of [Keynesian] policies" (1980: 7).

Keynes may have indeed used his dictum to support short-term policies like deficit spending, but he also used it in other contexts.

KEYNES ATTACKS MONETARISM

The first time Keynes made the famous remark quoted above, he used it to deride Irving Fisher's extreme monetarism, which claimed that monetary inflation has no ill effects in the long run but only raises prices (see chapter 11). Keynes retorted, "Now 'in the long run' this is probably true . . . but this *long run* is a misleading guide to current affairs. *In the long run* we are all dead. Economists set themselves too easy, too useless a task if in tempestuous seasons they can only tell us that when the storm is long past the ocean is flat again" (1971: 65). No doubt Hazlitt and Mises would find much in agreement with this statement.

BRITAIN FIRST!

Keynes also used his famous phrase in the context of British foreign policy and wartime. In 1937, when Churchill advocated rearmament and warned against appeasing Hitler, Keynes seemed to support short-term peace initiatives: "It is our duty to prolong peace, hour by hour, day by day, for as long as we can. . . . I have said in another context that it is a disadvantage of 'the long run' that in the long run we are all dead. But I could have said equally well that it is a great advantage of 'the short run' that in the short run we are still alive. Life and history are made up of short runs. If we are at peace in the short run, that is something. The best we can do is put off disaster" (Moggridge 1992: 611). Was Keynes advocating peace at any price?

After Pearl Harbor was attacked in December 1941, Keynes reacted in dismay to the British Foreign Office argument that free trade with America would be beneficial to Britain "in the long run." Keynes blustered, "The theory that 'to get our way in the long run' we must always yield in the short reminds me of the bombshell I threw into economic theory by the reminder that 'in the long run we are all dead'. If there was no one left to appease, the F.O. [Foreign Office] would feel out of a job altogether" (Moggridge 1992: 666).

This was Keynes the mercantilist in true form.

Depression seemed to justify the Keynesian-Marxian view that market capitalism was inherently unstable and that the market could be stuck at unemployed equilibrium indefinitely.

Economic historians have noted that the only countries that appeared to make headway in eliminating unemployment in the 1930s were totalitarian regimes in Germany, Italy, and the Soviet Union. Curiously, Keynes himself acknowledged, in the German edition of *The General Theory*, that his theory "is much more easily adapted to the conditions of a totalitarian state, than is the theory of the production and distribution of a given output produced under conditions of free competition and a large measure of laissez-faire" (1973a: xxvi).

Second, World War II came along right after the publication of *The General Theory*, giving strong empirical evidence of Keynes's policy prescription. Government spending and deficit financing increased dramatically during World War II, unemployment disappeared, and economic output soared. War was "good" for the economy, just as Keynes suggested (1973a: 129). As historian Robert M. Collins wrote, "World War II set the stage for the triumph of Keynesianism by providing striking evidence of the effectiveness of government expenditures on a huge scale" (1981: 12). The following quote from a popular textbook repeated what other textbooks were saying in the postwar period: "Once the massive, war-geared expenditure of the 1940s began, income responded sharply and unemployment evaporated. Government expenditures on goods and services, which had been running at under 15 percent of GNP during the 1930s, jumped to 46 percent by 1944, while unemployment reached the incredible low of 1.2 percent of the civilian labor force" (Lipsey, Steiner, and Purvis 1987: 573).

Keynes died in 1946, right after the war. It would be left to his disciples to lead the charge and create a "new economics." Fortunately for Keynes, a young *wunderkind* was ready to fill his shoes. His name was Paul Samuelson, and he would write a textbook that would dominate the profession for more than an entire generation. Chapter 14 tells his story.

REFERENCES

Barro, Robert J. 1991. "Don't Fool with Money, Cut Taxes." *Wall Street Journal* (November 21), A14.

Bean, Charles R. 1994. "European Unemployment: A Survey." *Journal of Economic Literature* 32: 2 (June), 573–619.

Blaug, Mark. 1999. *Who's Who in Economics*, 3d ed. Cheltenham, UK: Edward Elgar.

Byrns, Ralph T. and Gerald W. Stone. 1989. *Economics*, 4th ed. Glenville, IL: Scott, Foresman.

Chamberlin, Edward H. 1933. *The Theory of Monopolistic Competition*. Cambridge, MA: Harvard University Press.

Collins, Robert M. 1981. *The Business Response to Keynes, 1929–1964*. New York: Columbia University Press.

Deacon, Richard. 1989. *Superspy.* Armonk, NY: Futura.

Foster, William T., and Waddill Catchings. 1927. *Business Without a Buyer*. Boston: Houghton Mifflin.

Friedman, Milton. 1974. "Comment on the Critics." In *Milton Friedman's Monetary Framework,* ed. Robert J. Gordon, 132–37. Chicago: University of Chicago Press.

Galbraith, John Kenneth. 1975 [1965]. "How Keynes Came to America." In *Essays on John Maynard Keynes*, ed. Milo Keynes, 132–41. Cambridge: Cambridge University Press.

Graaff, J. de V. 1987. "Arthur Cecil Pigou." In *The New Palgrave: A Dictionary of Economics*, vol. 3, 876–78. London: Macmillan.

Harrod, Roy. 1951. *The Life of John Maynard Keynes*. New York: Harcourt, Brace.

Hayek, Friedrich A. 1939 [1929]. "The 'Paradox' of Thrift." In *Profits, Interest and Investment*, 199–263. London: George Routledge and Sons.

———. 1984. *The Essence of Hayek*, ed. Chiaki Nishiyama and Kurt R. Leube. Stanford, CA: Hoover Institution.

———. 1994. *Hayek on Hayek*. Chicago: University of Chicago Press.

Hazlitt, Henry. 1977 [1960]. *The Critics of Keynesian Economics*, 2d ed. New York: Arlington House.

———. 1979 [1946]. *Economics in One Lesson,* 3d ed. New York: Arlington House.

Hession, Charles H. 1984. *John Maynard Keynes*. New York: Macmillan.

Hicks, J.R. 1937. "Mr. Keynes and the 'Classics': A Suggested Interpretation." *Econometrica* 5: 2 (April), 147–59.

Hutt, W.H. 1979. *The Keynesian Episode: A Reassessment.* Indianapolis, IN: Liberty Press.

Johnson, Elizabeth S., and Harry G. Johnson. 1978. *The Shadow of Keynes*. Oxford: Basil Blackwell.

Kates, Steven. 1998. *Say's Law and the Keynesian Revolution*. Cheltenham, UK: Edward Elgar.

Keynes, John Maynard. 1920. *The Economic Consequences of the Peace*. New York: Harcourt, Brace.

———. 1923. *A Tract on Monetary Reform*. London: Macmillan.

———. 1930. *A Treatise on Money,* 2 vols. London: Macmillan.

———. 1940. *How to Pay for the War*. London: Macmillan.

———. 1963 [1931]. *Essays in Persuasion*. New York: Norton.

———. 1971. *Activities, 1906–1914: The Collected Writings of John Maynard Keynes,* vol. 15. London: Macmillan.

———. 1973a [1936]. *The General Theory of Employment, Interest and Money*. In *The Collected Writings of John Maynard Keynes*, vol. 7. London: Macmillan.

———. 1973b. *The General Theory and After, Part I, Preparation*. In *The Collected Writings of John Maynard Keynes*, vol. 13. London: Macmillan.

Keynes, Milo, ed. 1975. *Essays on John Maynard Keynes*. Cambridge: Cambridge University Press.

Krugman, Paul. 1994. *Peddling Prosperity*. New York: W.W. Norton.

———. 2007. "Introduction" to John Maynard Keynes, *The General Theory of Employment, Interest and Money*. New York: Palgrave Macmillan.

Lachmann, Ludwig M. 1977. *Capital, Expectations, and the Market Process*. Kansas City, MO: Sheed, Andrews and McMeel.

Lipsey, Richard G., Peter O. Steiner, and Douglas D. Purvis. 1987. *Economics,* 8th ed. New York: Harper and Row.

Mantoux, Etienne de. 1952. *The Carthagian Peace*. Pittsburgh, PA: University of Pittsburgh Press.

Meltzer, Allan H. 1988. *Keynes's Monetary Theory: A Different Interpretation*. Cambridge: Cambridge University Press.

Minsky, Hyman P. 1986. *Stabilizing an Unstable Economy*. New Haven, CT: Yale University Press.

Mises, Ludwig von. 1980 [1952]. *Planning for Freedom,* 4th ed. Spring Hill, PA: Libertarian Press.

Moggridge, D.E. 1983. "Keynes as an Investor." In *The Collected Works of John Maynard*

Keynes, vol. 12, 1–113. London: Macmillan.

———. 1992. *Maynard Keynes, An Economist's Biography.* London: Routledge.

Pigou, Arthur C. 1936. "Mr. J.M. Keynes' General Theory of Employment, Interest and Money." *Economica* 3 (May), 115–32.

———. 1937. *Socialism Versus Capitalism.* London: Macmillan.

Pigou, Arthur C., ed. 1925. *Memorials of Alfred Marshall.* London: Macmillan.

Robinson, Joan. 1933. *Economics of Imperfect Competition.* London: Macmillan.

———. 1976. *Collected Economic Papers*, 5 vols. Oxford: Basil Blackwell.

Samuelson, Paul A. 1947 [1946]. "Lord Keynes and the General Theory." In *The New Economics,* ed. Seymour Harris. New York: Alfred A. Knopf. Originally appeared in *Econometrica* (July 1946).

Shackle, G.L.S. 1974. *Keynesian Kaleidics.* Edinburgh: Edinburgh University Press.

Skidelsky, Robert. 1992. *John Maynard Keynes: The Economist as Saviour, 1920–1937.* London: Macmillan.

———. 2003. *John Maynard Keynes: Economist, Philosopher, Statesman.* New York: Penguin Books.

Skousen, Mark, ed. 1992. *Dissent on Keynes: A Critical Appraisal of Keynesian Economics.* New York: Praeger.

Somary, Felix. 1986 [1960]. *The Raven of Zurich.* London: C. Hurst.

Stein, Herbert. 1993. "The Age of Ignorance." *Wall Street Journal* (June 11), A10.

14

PAUL RAISES THE KEYNESIAN CROSS: SAMUELSON AND MODERN ECONOMICS

I don't care who writes a nation's laws—or crafts its advanced treaties—if I can write its economics textbooks.

—Paul A. Samuelson (1990: ix)

The year was 1948, one of those watershed years that occasionally crops up in economics. Remember 1776, 1848, and 1871?

In early 1948, the Austrian émigré Ludwig von Mises, secluded in his New York apartment, was typing a short article, "Stones into Bread, the Keynesian Miracle," for a conservative publication, *Plain Talk*. "What is going on today in the United States," he declared solemnly, "is the final failure of Keynesianism. There is no doubt that the American public is moving away from the Keynesian notions and slogans. Their prestige is dwindling" (Mises 1980: 62).

Perhaps it was wishful thinking, but Mises couldn't have misread the times more egregiously in 1948. It was that very year that the new economics of John Maynard Keynes was being hailed by Keynes's rapidly growing number of disciples as the wave of the future and the savior of capitalism. Literally hundreds of articles and dozens of books had been published about Keynes and the new Keynesian model since Keynes wrote *The General Theory of Employment, Interest and Money*.

♪ Music selection for this chapter: Johannes Brahms, Hungarian Dance No. 5

THE OTHER CAMBRIDGE

The year 1948 was also when Seymour E. Harris, chairman of the economics department at Harvard, produced an edited volume, *Saving American Capitalism*. This was a sequel to his 1947 edited work, *The New Economics*. Both bestsellers were filled with laudatory articles by prominent economists preaching the new economics of Keynes.

Darwin had one bulldog to propagate his revolutionary theory, but Keynes had three in America—Seymour Harris, Alvin Hansen, and Paul A. Samuelson. They all came from the "other Cambridge"—Cambridge, Massachusetts. Both Harris and Hansen were conservative Harvard teachers who had converted to Keynesianism and devoted their energies to convincing students and colleagues of the efficacy of this strange new doctrine.

The American advancement of Keynesian economics represented a subtle but clear shift from Europe to the New World. Before the war, Cambridge and London had shaped the economic world. After the war, the magnets for the best and the brightest graduate students were Boston, Chicago, and Berkeley. Students came from all over the world to do their work in America, and not just in economics.

THE YEAR OF THE TEXTBOOK

Finally, 1948 was the year in which an exciting new breakthrough textbook came forth from Harvard's neighboring university, the Massachusetts Institute of Technology (MIT). Written by the "brash whippersnapper go-getter" Paul Samuelson (his own words!), *Economics* was destined to become *the* most successful textbook ever published in any field. Eighteen editions have sold more than four million copies and have been translated into over forty languages. No other textbook, including those of Jean-Baptiste Say, John Stuart Mill, and Alfred Marshall, can compare. Samuelson's *Economics* survived a half-century of dramatic changes in the world economy and the economics profession: peace and war, boom and bust, inflation and deflation, Republicans and Democrats, and an array of new economic theories.

Samuelson's textbook was popular not so much because it was well written, but because it elucidated and simplified the basics of Keynesian macroeconomics through the deft use of simple algebra and clear graphs. It took the profession by storm, selling hundreds of thousands of copies every year. Samuelson updated the textbook every three years or so, a practice that every textbook publisher now imitates. *Economics* sold over 440,000 copies at the height of its popularity in 1964. Even a conservative institution such as Brigham Young University, my alma mater, used the Samuelson textbook.

THE ACME OF PROFESSIONAL SUCCESS

Samuelson is known for more than just pop-
ularizing Keynesian economics. He is
considered the father of modern macroeconomic theorizing. He has made innumerable
contributions to pure mathematical economics, for which he has been honored and
blamed; honored for making economics a
pure logical science and blamed for carrying
the Ricardian vice and Walrasian equilibrium
analysis to an extreme, devoid of any empirical work. (See chapters 4 and 8.)

For his popular and scientific works, the
academic community has awarded Samuelson
virtually every honor it confers, including the
first John Bates Clark Medal for the brightest
economist under forty, the first Nobel Memorial
Prize in economic sciences for an American, in
1970, and, beyond economics, the Albert
Einstein Medal in 1971. There's even an annual

Photograph 14.1
Paul Anthony Samuelson
(1915–)
"The young, brash wunderkind."
Courtesy of Paul A. Samuelson.

award named after him, the Paul A. Samuelson Award, given to published works
in finance. His articles have appeared in all the major (and many minor) journals.
He was elected president of the American Economic Association (AEA), has
received innumerable honorary degrees from other universities, and has been the
subject of many *Festschrifts*, gatherings at which scholars honor a fellow colleague with essays about his work (see, for example, Szenberg et al. 2006).

WHO INVENTED THE TERM "MACROECONOMICS"?

For those who had lived through the 1929–35 Great Depression,
the best of the existing texts were almost comical in their macroeconomics.
That word had not yet been invented.
—Paul A. Samuelson (1997: 157)

Did Paul Samuelson invent the word "macroeconomics"? The term does not appear
in the first edition of his *Economics*. Samuelson believes that the distinction between
"micro" and "macro" goes back to econometricians Ragnar Frisch and Jan Tinbergen,
the first Nobel Prize winners in economics. Frisch created the word "econometrics,"
while the word "macroeconomics" can be traced back to Erik Lindahl in 1939
(Samuelson 1997: 157).

Yet the distinction between "micro" and "macro" goes back even further, into the
late nineteenth century. The Austrian economist Eugen Böhm-Bawerk wrote this sentence in January 1891: "One cannot eschew studying the microcosm if one wants to
understand properly the macrocosm of a developed country" (Böhm-Bawerk 1962:
117). The Austrians do it again!

"THE YOUNG, BRASH *WUNDERKIND*"

Paul A. Samuelson was born in Gary, Indiana, in 1915 to Jewish parents, and moved to Chicago, where he received his B.A. degree in 1935—at the tender age of twenty—from the University of Chicago. Chicago in the 1930s, as it is today, was the citadel of laissez-faire economic thought. In those days, it was run by Frank Knight, Jacob Viner, and Henry Simons, among others. Paul's first class in economics was taught by Aaron Director, who was perhaps the most libertarian among the faculty, and who later became Milton Friedman's brother-in-law. Both Friedman and George Stigler were graduate students at the time. Director's laissez-faire philosophy failed to take in the youthful reformist Samuelson, who enjoyed being an intellectual heretic in a conservative institution and who was influenced by a father known as a "moderate socialist." Moreover, during the depression, most of the leaders of the Chicago school advocated deficit spending and other government activist policies as temporary measures (see chapter 15 on the sometimes not so laissez-faire tradition at Chicago). Samuelson did inherit one concept from Chicago that he carried with him until he encountered Keynes—monetarism. He later called himself a "jackass" for having been taken in (Samuelson 1968: 1).

Samuelson immediately went to Harvard, where he witnessed an amazing transition. His teacher, Alvin Hansen, a long-standing classical economist, converted to Keynesianism (see the box on page 362). Suddenly Keynes and his *General Theory* became all the rage, and Samuelson quickly abandoned his monetarism for Keynesianism. Samuelson found it an exciting time to be an economist: "To have been born as an economist before 1936 was a boon—yes. But not to have been born too long before!" (Harris 1947: 145). He applied the following familiar lines from William Wordsworth's *The Prelude* (which have already been quoted, in chapter 3):

> Bliss was it in that dawn to be alive,
> But to be young was very heaven!

It was also a time to be in love, and in 1938 Paul married a Radcliffe *summa cum laude*, Marion Crawford, also an economist. The couple had two daughters and four sons, including economist Robert J. Samuelson. Marion Samuelson died in 1978, and Paul Samuelson was married again in 1981 to Risha Eckaus.

Samuelson completed his dissertation in 1941, and it won the David A. Wells Award that year. In 1947 it was published as *Foundations of Economic Analysis* (1972 [1947]). In this work Samuelson broke with Alfred Marshall by contending that mathematics, not literary expression, should be the primary exposition of economics.

But after graduation he discovered that heaven was not so sweet. He declared his preference to teach at Harvard, but his youthful exuberance, arrogant personality, and Jewish background all worked against him. His cocky attitude had long irritated his chairman, Harold Hitchings Burbank, and the department offered him only an instructorship. Determined to stay in Cambridge, he accepted a position at the relatively unheralded department of economics at the Massachusetts Institute of Technology.

It was a mistake Harvard soon regretted. By 1947, Samuelson had been awarded the first John Bates Clark Medal for being the brightest young economist, his school had granted him a full professorship, and MIT had been ranked as one of the best economics departments in the country. And Samuelson was only thirty-two! A year later he would drop the bomb that would be the envy of every economics department: the first edition of *Economics*, Samuelson's new testament of macroeconomics. Harvard professor Otto Eckstein remarked, "Harvard lost the most outstanding economist of the generation" (Sobel 1980: 101).

HOW SAMUELSON CAME TO WRITE HIS FAMOUS TEXTBOOK: "A SINGULAR OPPORTUNITY"

During the war, Samuelson worked at the MIT Radiation Lab developing computer techniques to track airplanes. In the early postwar period, Harvard students studied economics from outdated textbooks that said nothing about the war and little about the new economics of Keynes. "Students at Harvard and MIT often had that glassy-eyed look," commented Samuelson. His department head asked him to write a new text. Three years later, after he toiled through nights and summers ("my tennis suffered"), *Economics* was born.

ATTACKED FROM BOTH SIDES

The first edition, published by McGraw-Hill, sold over 120,000 copies through 1950 and just kept selling. But it soon came under attack from the business community, on the one hand, who complained of its socialistic tendencies, and the Marxists, on the other hand, who complained of its capitalistic tendencies. William F. Buckley, Jr.'s *God and Man at Yale* (1951) protested that Samuelson's textbook was antibusiness and progovernment. An organization called the Veritas Foundation published *Keynes at Harvard* and identified Keynesianism with Fabian socialism, Marxism, and fascism. Marxists took umbrage when Samuelson noted that Marx's predictions about the capitalist system were "dead wrong." A massive two-volume critique, *Anti-Samuelson* (1977), was published to counter Samuelson and introduce Marxism to students. Samuelson was pleased to hear that in Stalin's day *Economics* was kept on a special reserve shelf in the library, along with books on sex, forbidden to all but specially licensed

ALVIN HANSEN SWITCHES SIDES TO BECOME THE "AMERICAN KEYNES"

Alvin Hansen did more than any other economist to bring the Keynesian Revolution to America.

—Mark Blaug (1985: 79)

Photograph 14.2
Alvin H. Hansen (1887–1975)
The "American Keynes"
predicted stagnation.
Courtesy of
Harvard University Archives.

Paul Samuelson's mentor, Harvard professor **Alvin H. Hansen (1887–1975)**, was Keynes's prophet in America. Most older economists at first rejected Keynes's heretical ideas, including Hansen, who was at the University of Minnesota. Only Marriner Eccles, the exceptional Utah banker who became head of the Federal Reserve, and Lauchlin Currie, an economic aid to Roosevelt, were prominent Keynesian advocates.

Then, in the fall of 1937, Hansen transferred to Harvard and suddenly—at the age of fifty—recognized the revolutionary nature of Keynes. He would become an outspoken exponent—the "American Keynes." His fiscal policy seminar attracted many enthusiastic students, including Samuelson, and convinced many colleagues, including Seymour Harris. Keynes had to be translated into plain English and easy-to-understand graphs and math, and Hansen was the principal interpreter, from *Fiscal Policy and Business Cycles* (1941) to *A Guide to Keynes* (1953). Hansen also campaigned for the Employment Act of 1946.

"STAGNATION THESIS" DISCREDITS HANSEN AND ALMOST DESTROYS SAMUELSON'S REPUTATION

However, Hansen fell into a trap. Logically he extended Keynes's unemployment equilibrium theory into a "secular stagnation thesis." In his presidential address before the AEA in 1937, Hansen boldly announced that the United States was stuck in a "mature economy" rut from which it couldn't escape, due to its lack of technological innovations, American frontier, and population growth rate. His stagnation thesis was vigorously attacked by George Terborgh in his book, *The Bogey of Economic Maturity* (1945) and then soundly disproved with a vibrant recovery after World War II. The stigma of this unfulfilled prediction haunted him throughout his life.

Paul Samuelson, under the Hansen stagnation spell, almost suffered the same fate. In 1943, he wrote an article warning that unless the government acted vigorously after the end of the war, "there would be ushered in the greatest period of unemployment and industrial dislocation which any economy has ever faced." In a two-part article published in *The New Republic* in the autumn of 1944, Samuelson predicted a replay of the 1930s depression (Sobel 1980: 101–02).

Although he, along with most Keynesians, was proved inaccurate about the postwar period, Samuelson gradually began expressing strong optimism about the U.S. economy in his textbook. "Our mixed economy—wars aside—has a great future before it" (1964: 809).

readers. "Actually," responded Samuelson, "when your cheek is smacked from the Right, the pain may be assuaged in part by a slap from the Left" (1998: xxvi). Meanwhile, Samuelson offered a seemingly balanced brand of economics that found mainstream support. While he favored heavy involvement in "stabilizing" the economy as a whole, he appeared relatively laissez-faire in the micro sphere, supporting free trade, competition, and free markets in agriculture.

THE HIGH TIDE OF SAMUELSON'S *ECONOMICS*

The success of Keynesian economics and Samuelson's textbook reached its zenith in the early 1960s. The MIT professor became president of the AEA in 1961, the year John F. Kennedy was inaugurated as president. Samuelson, along with Walter Heller and other top Keynesians, was a close advisor to Kennedy and helped steer through Congress the Kennedy tax cut of 1962, a Keynesian program designed to stimulate economic growth through deliberate deficit financing. It appeared to work, as the economy flourished through the mid-1960s. By that time, Samuelson's textbook reigned atop the profession, selling more than a quarter of a million copies a year. When the Nobel Memorial Prize in economic sciences was established in 1969 by the Bank of Sweden, the first prize—after the required nod toward Scandinavian economists—went to Paul A. Samuelson.

Samuelson's textbook has been on the decline since the early 1970s, and today it no longer tops the list in popularity and has been surpassed by more free-market textbooks. From 1985 until its last edition (2004), *Economics* has been coauthored by Yale professor William D. Nordhaus, and Samuelson's hair has turned from blond to brown to gray in his sunset years. Yet "his memory dazzles even when it fails," wrote an admirer (Elzinga 1992: 878).

THE WORLD'S MOST CONCEITED ECONOMIST?

Paul Samuelson was never known for a false sense of modesty. After winning the Nobel Prize, he unabashedly compared himself to Sir Isaac Newton and to the great German mathematician Gauss (Samuelson 1977: 881–96). He has admitted to making mistakes, such as his "gross error" in predicting a postwar depression in 1944, and his claim that the Soviet Union would likely surpass the United States in economic performance. Yet he has also boasted, "I have regretted almost no chapter, article, note, or footnote my quill has penned" (Breit and Spencer 1986: 69). He certainly is a clever, hard-hitting writer, perhaps the most entertaining economist to read. His critique of Marx is a classic, for example (Samuelson 1967b).

Yet, despite his "natural vanity," he has always been approachable. Speaking personally, after having publicly criticized Samuelson, sometimes harshly, I was surprised that he responded respectfully to all my letters to him. (Milton Friedman is another opinionated economist who always responded to my letters; unfortunately, I can't say the same about Berkeley's Barry Eichengreen.)

SAMUELSON'S GOAL: TO RAISE THE KEYNESIAN CROSS ATOP A NEW HOUSE OF ECONOMICS

What was Paul Samuelson trying to achieve? There is no real Samuelson school of economics; he considered himself "the last generalist in economics." (But what about Kenneth Boulding?) The MIT professor's intention was, first and foremost, to introduce Keynesianism to the classroom: the multiplier, the propensity to consume, the paradox of thrift, countercyclical fiscal policy, national income accounting, and $C + I + G$ were all new topics introduced in the first edition of *Economics* in 1948. Only John Maynard Keynes was honored with a biographical sketch in early editions, and only Keynes, not Adam Smith or Karl Marx, was labeled "a many-sided genius" (Samuelson 1948: 253).

The "Keynesian cross" income-expenditure diagram, invented by Samuelson and reproduced below, was printed on the cover of the first three editions.

The Keynesian cross incorporates all the elements of the new "general" theory. In the diagram below, note that saving (*S*) increases with national income (*NI*). As people earn more, they save more. However, investment (*I*) is autonomous and independent of saving. It is set at a fixed amount because, according to Keynes's theory, investment is fickle and varies with the "animal spirits" and expectations of investors and businessmen. So the investment schedule is set at any level, unrelated to income. Equilibrium

HOW SAVING AND INVESTMENT
DETERMINE INCOME

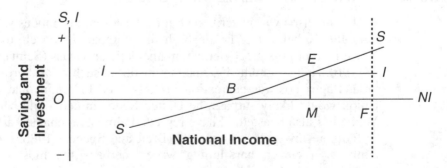

Figure 14.1
The Keynesian Cross of National Income Determination:
How Saving and Investment Determine Income
Source: Samuelson (1948: 259). Reprinted by permission of McGraw-Hill.

MATHEMATICAL RIGOR—MORTIS![1] HOW ECONOMIC THEORY BECAME FORMALIZED, MATHEMATIZED, STERILIZED!

*It has sometimes been suggested that our most advanced students
know everything except common sense.*
—Paul A. Samuelson (1960: 1652–53)

*Mathematical economic theory has recently become
more and more abstract, transparent and sterile.*
—Michio Morishima (1976: viii)

Paul Samuelson is often regarded as the founder of modern mathematical economics after he wrote *Foundations of Economic Analysis* in the 1940s. Since then, formalistic model building and the testing of these models (known as econometrics) have been an integral part of the scientific age of economics, but not without controversy.

The Old Guard response to Samuelson's avant-garde theories can best be summarized by Chicago's Frank Knight. At an AEA executive meeting in the 1950s, he bluntly told the group, "If there is anything I can't stand it's a Keynesian and a believer in monopolistic competition."

"What about believers in the use of mathematics in economic analysis, Frank?" asked a colleague.

"Can't stand it either," he replied firmly (Samuelson 1977: 886-87).

Math entered the economic arena with the marginalist revolution in the 1870s, with Stanley Jevons and Léon Walras (but not Carl Menger) using formal equations. Stanley Jevons, in the preface to his textbook, contended that "all economic writers must be mathematical so far as they are scientific at all" (1965 [1879]: xxi). Alfred Marshall, who did more than anyone to turn economics into a scientific discipline, used mathematics and graphics repeatedly.

"BURN THE MATHEMATICS"

However, Marshall was worried that mathematical economics could become a Ricardian vice; he hid his formulas and diagrams in his textbook's appendixes. In a letter to a friend, he warned that good mathematical theory might not be good economics. He came up with five rules:

(1) Use mathematics as a shorthand language, rather than as an engine of inquiry. (2) Keep to them till you have done. (3) Translate into English. (4) Then illustrate by examples that are important in real life. (5) Burn the mathematics. (6) If you can't succeed in 4, burn 3. This last I did often. . . . I think you should do all you can to prevent people from using Mathematics in cases in which the English language is as short as the Mathematical. (Groenewegen 1995: 413)

Such reproachful comments remind one of Ludwig von Mises's extreme views on the subject: "The mathematical method must be rejected not only on account of its barrenness. It is an entirely vicious method, starting from false assumptions and leading to fallacious inferences" (Mises 1966: 350).

(continued)

---

1. With thanks to Robert Heilbroner, who was the first to use this tantalizing phrase.

SAMUELSON GOES ON THE OFFENSIVE

Paul Samuelson took umbrage at Marshall's agnosticism and Mises's atheism. In the spirit of Occam's Razor, Samuelson's purely mathematical *Foundations of Economic Analysis* "exactly reversed" Marshall's dictum (Samuelson 1972 [1947]: 6). He preferred mathematical formulas to the traditional literary style.

Paul Samuelson in the United States and John Hicks in England led the way by converting the geometry of the 1930s to the multivariate calculus of the 1950s and 1960s. In the 1940s, John von Neumann added game theory. By 1964, Samuelson proclaimed victory: "Economics has become mathematical and technical as never before" (Samuelson 1972: xii). Indeed, by the early 1980s, a full 96 percent of all papers published in the *American Economic Review* were primarily mathematical in nature. Nearly 38 percent made no reference to historical facts at all (McCloskey 1998 [1985]: 139–40). Milton Friedman once described the emphasis on mathematical economics this way: "At Chicago, economics was a serious subject to be used in discussing real problems. . . . For Harvard, economics was an intellectual discipline on par with mathematics" (Ebenstein 2007: 131).

A GROWING BACKLASH

For a while, the mathematical victory was so complete that almost every school of economics, including Marxists, took up analytical geometry, differential equations, and least-squares regressions. "Theorems, lemmas, and mathematics are in. English is out," reported Arjo Klamer and David Colander (1990: 4).

But the results were often unsatisfactory. For example, in the 1960s, the Cambridge school of Joan Robinson and Piero Sraffa challenged the Austrian theory of capital in what became known as the Cambridge "reswitching" debate.[2] Using sophisticated mathematical formulas, these radical economists attempted to refute the standard neoclassical growth model that a higher saving rate leads to lower interest rates and more productive, roundabout production (see chapter 7). At one point, even Paul Samuelson and Robert Solow (members of the other Cambridge) were convinced by a purely theoretical proof. But the critics could never come up with any empirical evidence to make their case and eventually the controversy became obsolete. In 1987, Robert Solow, in his Nobel Prize acceptance speech, declared that the "reswitching" debate was a "waste of time" (1988: 307–17).

Surveys by Klamer and Colander showed that graduate students in economics are depressed by academia's Ricardian vice, the growing gulf between high theory and reality. "Why did we have this gut feeling that much of what went on there was a waste?" (Klamer and Colander 1990: xiv). Robert Kuttner remarks, "Departments of economics are graduating a generation of *idiots savants*, brilliant at esoteric mathematics yet innocent of actual economic life" (1985: 74). Even the testing of models, known as econometrics, has come under fire. "Let's Take the Con Out of Econometrics" is a well-known article on the misuse of mathematics and statistics in economics (Leamer 1983). A high R-squared does not prove that one variable causes another. In his colorful fable, "Life Among the Econ," Axel Leijonhufvud (University of California–Los Angeles) poked fun at the "Math-Econ" priestly caste as a "heartless" group that leads to a "blind alley" (1981: 350, 355).

Many economists have demanded a return to reality, and more recent editions of the *American Economic Review (AER)* and other journals have been more down to earth. Recognizing the growing complaints that the *AER* and other professional pub-

(continued)

---

2. For my summary of this debate, see Skousen (1990: 117–20).

lications were becoming increasingly unreadable—and therefore unread—the AEA began publishing the *Journal of Economic Perspectives (JEP)* in the mid-1980s. The *JEP*, from which math is largely absent, is now considered the most widely read economics journal in the world. As David Colander recently concluded, "The commitment to theorems and proofs has declined and there is a much stronger empirical branch of economics" (2007:15).

(M) is set at the point where $S = I$, which you will note falls short of full-employment income (F). Thus, the Keynesian cross reflects underemployment equilibrium.

The model represents Samuelson's (and Keynes's) view that capitalism is inherently unstable and can be stuck indefinitely at less than full employment (M). No "automatic mechanism" guarantees full employment in the capitalist economy (Samuelson and Nordhaus 1985: 139). Samuelson compared capitalism to a car without a steering wheel; it frequently runs off the road and crashes. "The private economy is not unlike a machine without an effective steering wheel or governor," he wrote. "Compensatory fiscal policy tries to introduce such a governor or thermostatic control device" (Samuelson 1948: 412).

How the Multiplier Works Magic

How does compensatory fiscal policy work? There are two ways for the economy to grow and reach full employment under Keynesian theory: Shift investment schedule I upward, or shift saving schedule S to the right.

First, let's look at investment. Schedule I can be shifted upward by restoring business confidence, primarily through increased government spending or tax cuts. Either technique has a multiplier effect—either a $100 billion spending program or a tax cut can create $400 billion in new income.

But Samuelson noted that under the Keynesian system, government spending has a higher multiplier than a tax cut. Why? Because 100 percent of a federal program is spent, while only a portion of a tax cut is spent—some of it is saved. Samuelson called his discovery the "balanced budget multiplier." Thus, a new federal spending program is preferred over a tax cut by Keynesians because the expenditure side is considered a more potent weapon against recession than a tax cut.

The Paradox of Thrift Denies Adam Smith

The second way out of a recession is to increase the public's propensity to consume, which would shift saving schedule S to the right.

Note that in the Keynesian model, if the public decides to save more during an economic downturn, it only makes matters worse. Consumers buy less, producers lay off workers, and households end up saving less. An

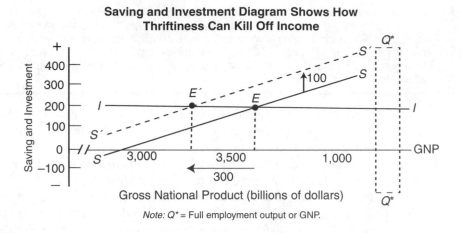

**Saving and Investment Diagram Shows How
Thriftiness Can Kill Off Income**

Note: Q* = Full employment output or GNP.

Figure 14.2
Samuelson's "Paradox of Thrift"
Source: Samuelson and Nordhaus (1989: 184). Reprinted by permission of McGraw-Hill.

increased supply of savings cannot lower interest rates and encourage investment under the crude Keynesian model because interest rates are assumed to be constant. In the above diagram, more savings means that the saving schedule *S* shifts backward to the left, and has no effect on raising the *I* schedule.

Samuelson called this phenomenon the "paradox of thrift"—an increase in desired thrift results in less total savings! "Under conditions of unemployment, the *attempt to save* may result in *less*, not more, saving," he declared (Samuelson 1948: 271). Keynes, of course, said practically the same thing, only more eloquently: "The more virtuous we are, the more determinedly thrifty, the more obstinately orthodox in our national and personal finance, the more our incomes will have to fall" (Keynes 1973: 111). See Figure 14.2.

Samuelson delighted in this attack on the orthodoxy of Adam Smith and Benjamin Franklin. Smith found thrift a universal virtue, writing that "What is prudence in the conduct of every private family, can scarce be folly in that of a great kingdom" (1965 [1776]: 424). Franklin counseled every child, "A penny saved is a penny earned." But Samuelson labeled this thinking a "fallacy of composition." "What is good for each person separately need not be good for all," he countered. Moreover, Franklin's "old virtues [of thrift] may be modern sins" (1948: 270). As one modern-day textbook put it, "While savings may pave the road to riches for an individual, if the nation as a whole decides to save more, the result could

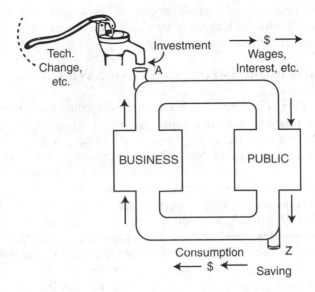

Technological change, population growth, and other dynamic factors keep the investment pump handle going.
Income rises and falls with changes in investment, its equilibrium level, at any time,
being realized only when intended saving at Z matches intended investment at A.

Figure 14.3
Saving Leaks Out of the System While the Hydraulic Investment Press Pumps Up the Economy
Source: Samuelson (1948: 264). Reprinted by permission of McGraw-Hill.

be a recession and poverty for all" (Baumol and Blinder 1988: 192).

The Keynesians readily endorsed savings as a virtue during periods of full employment, but Samuelson was convinced it seldom happened. "But full employment and inflationary conditions have occurred only occasionally in our recent history," he wrote. "Much of the time there is some wastage of resources, some unemployment, some insufficiency of demand, investment, and purchasing power" (1948: 271). This paragraph remained virtually the same throughout the first eleven editions.[3]

SAVING AS LEAKAGE

Echoing Keynes, Samuelson declared war on uninvested saving, which could "leak" out of the system and "become a social vice" (1948: 253). He produced a diagram (see Figure 14.3) separating saving from investment. The diagram shows saving leaking out of the system, unconnected to the

---

3. Amazingly, Samuelson recently protested being labeled an "antisaving Keynesian." After noting that Martin Feldstein publicly complained that economists at Harvard also attacked savings in his college days, Samuelson said he regularly appeared before Congress to urge more saving and investment and less consumption. My response: Then why didn't he say so in his textbook?

investment hydraulic handle above. (This diagram led observers to call the model "hydraulic Keynesianism," with the emphasis on priming the pump through government spending.)

IS CONSUMPTION MORE IMPORTANT THAN SAVING?

The Keynesian model leads to the odd conclusion that consumption is more productive than saving. As noted above in the Keynesian cross model, an increase in the "propensity to consume" (a lower saving rate) leads to full employment. Keynes applauded "all sorts of policies for increasing the propensity to consume," including confiscatory inheritance taxes and the redistribution of wealth in favor of lower-income groups, who consumed a higher percentage of their income than the wealthy (1973 [1936]: 325). Canadian economist Lorie Tarshis, the first to write a Keynesian textbook, warned that a high rate of saving is "one of the main sources of our difficulty," and one of the goals of the federal government should be "reducing incentives to thrift" (Tarshis 1947: 521–12). Keynesian economist Hyman Minsky confirmed this unorthodox approach when he said, "The policy emphasis should shift from the encouragement of growth through investment to the achievement of full employment through consumption production" (Minsky 1982: 113). Of course, all of this Keynesian theory goes counter to traditional classical growth theory that a high level of saving is a key ingredient to economic growth.

IS KEYNESIANISM POLITICALLY NEUTRAL?

Samuelson contended that the Keynesian "theory of income determination" is politically "neutral." For example, "it can be used as well to defend private enterprise as to limit it, as well as to attack as to defend government fiscal interventions" (1948: 253). But the evidence disputes this claim.

For instance, the balanced-budget multiplier (which Samuelson considers one of his proudest "scientific discoveries") favors government spending programs over tax cuts as a countercyclical policy. According to Samuelson, progressive taxation (imposing higher tax rates on the wealthy) has a "favorable" redistributionist effect on the economy: "To the extent that dollars are taken from frugal wealthy people rather than from poor ready spenders, progressive taxes tend to keep purchasing power and jobs at a high level" (1948: 174).

Samuelson also endorsed Social Security taxes, farm aid, unemployment compensation, and the rest of the welfare state as "built-in stabilizers" in the economy. The index of Samuelson's textbook consistently lists "market failures" (including imperfect competition, externalities, inequalities of wealth, monopoly power, and public goods) but not "government failures." His bias is overwhelmingly evident.

THE STRANGE CASE OF THE LIGHTHOUSE

*Government provides certain indispensible public services without which
community life would be unthinkable and which by their nature
cannot appropriately be left to private enterprise.*
—Paul Samuelson (1964: 159)

In his chapter entitled "The Economic Role of Government," Samuelson used the lighthouse as an example of an ideal public good that private enterprise could not provide. "Its beam helps everyone in sight. A businessman could not build it for a profit, since he cannot claim a price for each user" (1964: 159).

Really? In a classic article, Chicago economist Ronald H. Coase revealed that numerous lighthouses in England were built and owned by private individuals and companies prior to the nineteenth century, who earned profits by imposing tolls on ships docking at nearby ports. The Trinity House was a prime example of a privately owned operation granted a charter in 1514 to operate lighthouses and charge ships a fee for their use (Coase 1988 [1974]).

TOP ECONOMISTS IGNORE HISTORY

Coase noted that Samuelson was not the only economist who simply assumed that lighthouses were public services provided by government without checking the facts. Even prominent British economists John Stuart Mill, Henry Sidgwick, and Arthur C. Pigou were apparently unaware of the history of private lighthouses in their own country. "The lighthouse is simply plucked out of the air to serve as an illustration," Coase concluded.

Samuelson went on to recommend that lighthouses be financed out of general revenues. According to Coase, such a financing system has never been tried in Britain; "the service [at Trinity House] continued to be financed by tolls levied on ships" (1988: 213).

What's even more amazing, Coase wrote his trail-blazing (and well publicized) article in 1974, but Samuelson continued to use the lighthouse as an ideal public good only the government could supply. After I publicly chided Samuelson for his failure to acknowledge Coase's revelation (Skousen 1997: 145), Samuelson finally admitted the existence of private lighthouses "in an earlier age," in a footnote in the sixteenth edition of his textbook, but then insisted that private lighthouses still encountered a "free rider" problem (1998: 36).

APOLOGIST FOR THE NATIONAL DEBT

In early editions, Samuelson denied that the national debt is a burden. The first edition favors the "we owe it to ourselves" argument: "The interest on an internal debt is paid by Americans to Americans; there is no direct loss of goods and services" (1948: 427). In the seventh edition (1967a), after raising the specter of "crowding out" of private investment, Samuelson went on to say: "On the other hand, incurring debt when there is no other feasible way to move the $C + I + G$ equilibrium intersection up toward full employment actually represents a negative burden on the intermediate future to the degree that it induces more current capital formation than would otherwise take place" (1967a: 346). At the end of an appendix on the national debt, Samuelson compared federal debt financing to private debt financing, such as AT&T's "never-ending" growth in debt (1967a: 358). By implication, he suggested that government debt could also grow continually, rather than necessarily being balanced over the business cycle.[4]

In sum, Keynesian economics as presented by Samuelson became an apology for big-government capitalism in the postwar period. "A laissez-faire economy cannot guarantee that there will be exactly the required amount of investment to insure full employment" (1967a: 197–78). Only a powerful state can.

CRITICS BEGIN A LONG BATTLE AGAINST KEYNESIAN ECONOMICS

Samuelson claimed in his first edition that the Keynesian system was "increasingly accepted by economists of all schools of thought" (1948: 253). Certainly, judging from the popularity of Samuelson's textbook, he was right. In the 1950s and 1960s, scholars in the major departments spent their entire careers doing empirical studies on the consumption function, the multiplier, national income statistics, and other Keynesian aggregates. Keynesian macroeconomics also became popular among journalists, because it was easy to understand (increasing consumer spending is "good for the economy"), and among politicians, because deficit spending bought votes. Robert Solow, Samuelson's colleague at MIT and a Nobel laureate, summarized the new orthodoxy when he proclaimed, with considerable pride, that "short-term macroeconomic theory is pretty well in hand. . . . All that is left is the trivial job of filling in the empty boxes" (1965: 146).

---

4. A popular work coinciding with Samuelson's support of deficit spending was *A Primer on Government Spending*, by Robert L. Heilbroner and Peter L. Bernstein. It states, "Recent experience indicates that the economy grows faster when the government runs a deficit and slower when revenues exceed outlays" (1963: 119).

THE PIGOU EFFECT: THE FIRST ASSAULT

But over time critics have chipped away at the Keynesian structure. The first objection was the "liquidity trap" doctrine, Keynes's fear that the economy could be trapped indefinitely in a deep depression where interest rates are so low and "liquidity preference" so high that reducing interest rates further would have no effect (1973: 207). The man who first countered the liquidity-trap doctrine was Arthur C. Pigou, ironically the straw man Keynes vilified in *The General Theory*. In a series of articles in the 1940s, Pigou said that Keynes overlooked a beneficial side-effect of a deflation in prices and wages: Deflation increases the real value of cash, Treasury securities, cash-value insurance policies, and other liquid assets of individuals and business firms. The increased value of these liquid assets raises aggregate demand and provides the funds to generate new buying power and hire new workers when the economy bottoms out (Pigou 1943, 1947). This positive real wealth effect, or what Israeli economist Don Patinkin later named the "real balance effect" in his influential *Money, Interest and Prices* (1956), did much to undermine the Keynesian doctrine of a liquidity trap and unemployed equilibrium.

The Pigou "wealth" or "real balance" effect can also be extended to the issue of wage cuts during a downturn. Keynes rejected the classical argument that wage cuts are necessary to adjust the economy to new equilibrium conditions, from which a solid recovery could occur. Arguing against the conventional view that persistent unemployment is caused by excessive wage rates, Keynes claimed that wage cuts would simply depress demand further and do nothing to reduce unemployment. But Keynes and his followers confused wage rates with total payroll. Facing a recession and widespread unemployment, business leaders recognize that a reduction in wage *rates* can actually boost net employment and total payroll. Cutting wages allows firms to hire more workers at the bottom of a slump. When the economy bottoms out, well-managed companies begin hiring more workers at low wages, so that even though the wage rate remains low, the total payroll increases, and thus puts the economy back on the road to recovery (Hazlitt 1959: 267–69; Rothbard 1983 [1963]: 46–48).

GROWTH DATA CONTRADICT ANTITHRIFT DOCTRINE

Economic historians had serious doubts almost immediately about the Keynesian antipathy toward saving, which has always been considered a key ingredient to long-term economic growth. They point especially to European and Asian countries, such as Germany, Switzerland, Japan, and Southeast Asia, whose growth rates have benefited tremendously from high rates of saving during the postwar period. Nobel laureate Franco Modigliani, as well as top textbook writer Campbell McConnell, both

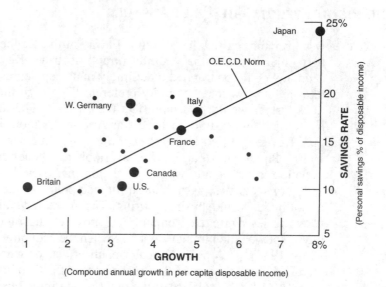

Figure 14.4
Saving and Growth Go Hand in Hand:
Growth Rates and Saving Rates in Select Countries
Source: Modigliani (1986: 303). Reprinted by permission of the Nobel Foundation.

Keynesians, have recognized the direct relationship between saving rates
and economic growth. For example, the graph in Figure 14.4 was included
in Franco Modigliani's Nobel Prize paper in 1986.

Historically, the evidence is overwhelming: higher saving rates lead to
higher growth rates, just the opposite of the standard Keynesian prediction.
As one recent Keynesian textbook declared after teaching students about
the paradox of thrift: "The fact that governments do not discourage saving
suggests that the paradox of thrift generally is not a real-world problem"
(Boyes and Melvin 1999: 265).

But then why teach the paradox of thrift at all? Not only is it historically unproved, but it is fundamentally flawed. The problem is that
Keynesians treat savings as if it disappears from the economy, that it is
simply hoarded or left languishing in bank vaults uninvested. In reality,
saving is simply another form of spending, not on current consumption,
but on future consumption. The Keynesians stress only the negative side
of saving, the sacrifice of current consumption, while ignoring the positive side, the investment in productive enterprise. As noted in chapter 7,
the Austrian economist Eugen Böhm-Bawerk stressed the positive side of
saving: "For an economically advanced nation does not engage in
hoarding, but invests its savings. It buys securities, it deposits its money
at interest in savings banks or commercial banks, puts it out on loan, etc."
(1959: 113).

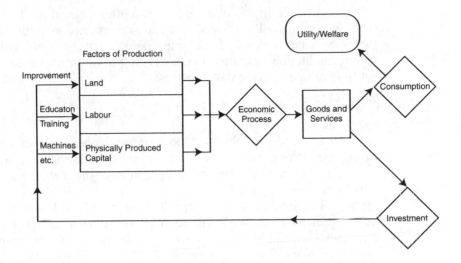

Figure 14.5
How Saving Is Invested into the Economic System
Source: Ekins and Max-Neef (1992: 148). Reprinted by permission of Routledge.

SAVING HAS A MULTIPLIER, TOO!

Saving is in fact a better form of spending because it offers a potentially infinite payoff in future productivity (thus Franklin's refrain, "A penny saved is a penny earned"). If the public saves more generally, the pool of savings enlarges, interest rates decline, old equipment is replaced, and more research and development, new technology, and new production processes evolve. The future benefits are incalculable. Meanwhile, funds spent on pure consumer goods are used up within a certain period, or depreciated over time.

The Keynesian multiplier k is higher as the public consumes more. But proponents assume that the savings remain uninvested, a false assumption under normal conditions. In truth, both components of income—consumption and savings—are spent. Thus, the multiplier k is infinite! The saving component also has a multiplier effect in the economy as it is invested in the intermediate production stages. Moreover, the savings k is theoretically more productive than the consumption k because it is not used up as fast.

Going back to Samuelson's hydraulic model (Figure 14.3), saving does not leak out of the system, but goes back into the system to improve the factors of production (land, labor, and capital) through new technology, education, and training. Figure 14.5 demonstrates how saving, consumption, and the economy really operate.

The diagram in Figure 14.5 is what Samuelson should have published over the years in his textbook instead of the hydraulic model. Here in this chart, the ultimate purpose of economic activity is to provide increasing utility. Note how in this diagram, consumption is used up. It is consumption—not saving—that "leaks" out and is consumed as utility. Saving, on the other hand, is invested back into the economic process over and over again, facilitating new investment and improving our standard of living (utility/welfare). An amazing contrast.

Solow's Growth Model

MIT professor Robert Solow, who won the Nobel Prize in 1987, recognized the strong historical connection between saving and capital formation in promoting economic growth. In the 1950s and 1960s, he developed what is now known as the Solow growth model (Solow 2000 [1969]). The Solow model attempts to determine the relative importance of varying determinants of growth, such as natural resources, population, capital formation, and technical progress. He came to two conclusions, based on empirical work with input-output models.

First, he concludes that increased saving has a positive impact on economic growth, but saving is subject to the law of diminishing returns. In other words, increased savings encourages economic growth in the initial stages, but eventually its impact diminishes. Figure 14.6 illustrates the diminishing returns of saving.

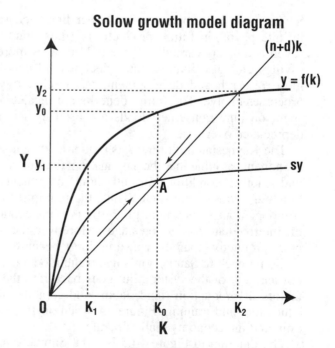

Solow growth model diagram

Figure 14.6
Increased Saving Has Diminishing Returns on National Output

GDP INVENTED BY A RUSSIAN KEYNESIAN!

The inventor of the familiar Gross Domestic Product (GDP) and Gross National Product (GNP) was Russian economist and Harvard professor **Simon Kuznets (1901–85)**. Kuznets was born in Russia and worked briefly as a statistician for the Bolsheviks before emigrating to the United States in 1922, where he received advanced degrees, including a Ph.D., from Columbia University. His mentor Wesley Mitchell asked him to join the National Bureau of Economic Research (NBER) (see chapter 9), where he pioneered the basic data on national income and product statistics for the United States and other nations. Before Kuznets, GDP never existed.

Photograph 14.3
Simon Kuznets (1901–85)
Putting empirical flesh on the Keynesian skeleton
Courtesy of Mark Blaug.

When Keynes published *The General Theory* in 1936, Kuznets put empirical flesh on the Keynesian skeleton by creating a new statistic called gross national product (GNP) to represent the familiar C + I + G formula for total final spending in the economy. GNP (now GDP) adds together all purchases of goods and services by consumers, business, and government during the calendar year. With its emphasis on *final* spending (what Keynes called "effective demand"), GDP is essentially a Keynesian statistic. It leaves out all intermediate production.

DOES G BELONG IN GDP?

But there was a problem. The most controversial part of national income and product statistics was the addition of G—government. Should government spending be included in national output? Kuznets seriously entertained the idea of leaving G out entirely from GDP statistics because of the potential distortion of government spending, especially during war. With G left in, GDP grew rapidly during World War II and collapsed (down 17 percent!) in 1946. It gave the impression that war was good for the economy, and ending war caused a depression instead of a recovery.

Clearly something was wrong. In his 1945 NBER publication, *National Product in Wartime*, Kuznets created a separate national product statistic with C + I only. G was left out, and it showed real private sector spending declining slightly during World War II and rising sharply in 1946—a more accurate view of the effects of war and recovery (Higgs 1992: 44–50).

But ultimately Kuznets believed in a "peacetime concept" of GDP, in which most government spending represents a flow of goods to consumers or toward capital formation. So he decided to leave G in the formula for national product and we have lived with a growing G ever since. In 1971, Kuznets won the Nobel Prize for his pioneering statistical work on national income.

Second, Solow calculated that about four-fifths of the growth in U.S. output per worker was attributable to technical progress. Technology seems to be more important to economic advancement than public saving, labor, or natural resources.

A CRITICAL FLAW IN THE KEYNESIAN MODEL

The central problem with the Keynesian model is that it fails to comprehend the true nature of the production-consumption process. The Keynesian system assumes that the only thing that matters is *current* demand for final consumer goods—the higher the consumer demand the better. Despite talk that Keynes is dead, this Keynesian preoccupation with consumer demand is almost universally accepted in the establishment media today. For example, Wall Street monitors retail sales figures to determine the direction of the economy and the markets. They seem to be disappointed if consumers don't spend enough. They act as if they want the Christmas season to last all year!

Yet is consumer spending the cause or the effect of prosperity? If everyone went on a buying spree at the local department store or grocery store, would investment in new products and technology expand? Certainly, investment in consumer goods would expand, but increased expenditures for consumer goods would do little or nothing to construct a bridge, build a hospital, pay for a research program to cure cancer, or provide funds for a new invention or a new production process.

According to business-cycle analysts, retail sales and other measures of current consumer spending are lagging indicators of economic activity. Almost all of the components of the U.S. Commerce Department's Index of Leading Economic Indicators are production and investment oriented, for example, contracts and orders for plant equipment, changes in manufacturing and trade inventories, changes in raw material prices, and the stock market, which represents long-term capital investment (Skousen 2007: 307–12).

Typically in a business cycle, consumption starts declining after the recession has already started; similarly, consumer spending picks up after the economy begins its recovery stage.

This myth of a consumer-driven economy persists in part because of a misunderstanding of national income accounting. The media frequently reports that consumer spending accounts for 70 percent of GDP. Recall from chapter 13 that $GDP = C + I + G$, and typically in the United States (figures do not add up to 100 percent because net exports are negative):

C = 70 percent
I = 17 percent
G = 18 percent

Therefore, the media concludes that, since consumption accounts for approximately 70 percent of GDP, the economy must be consumer-driven.

Not so. GDP is defined as the value of all *final* goods and services produced in a year. It ignores all intermediate production in the economy at the wholesale, manufacturing, and natural-resource stages. If one measures spending at all levels of production, the results are surprisingly different.

I have created a national income statistic called gross domestic expenditures (GDE), which measures gross sales at all stages of production.[5] Using this new, broader definition of total spending in the economy, it becomes apparent that consumption represents only about one-third of economic activity, and business spending (investment plus goods-in-process spending) accounts for more than half of the economy. Thus, business investment is far more important than consumer spending in the United States (and in most other nations).

The Keynesian macroeconomic model suffers from the defect of oversimplification—it assumes only two stages, consumption and investment, and it assumes that investment is a direct function of current consumption only. If current consumption increases, so will investment, and vice versa.

HOW THE ECONOMY REALLY WORKS

William Foster and Waddill Catchings committed this same error (see chapter 13, page 347). As Hayek pointed out in his critique of the Foster-Catchings debate, investment is actually multistaged and changes form and structure when interest rates rise or fall. Investment is not simply a function of current demand, but of future demand; both long-term and short-term interest rates influence investment and capital formation (Hayek 1939). For example, suppose the public decides to save more of their income for a better future. Spending for cars, clothing, entertainment, and other forms of current consumption may level off or even fall. But this temporary slowdown in consumption does not cause a broad-based recession. Instead, the increased savings leads to lower interest rates, which encourage businesses, especially in capital-goods industries and research and development, to expand operations. Lower interest rates means lower costs. Businesses can now afford to upgrade computers and office equipment, construct new plants and buildings, and expand inventories. Lower interest rates can even reverse the slowdown in car sales by offering cheaper financing to prospective car buyers. Contrary to the dire predictions of the Keynesians, an increase in the propensity to save pays for itself. It does not lead to a "recession and poverty for all" (Baumol and Blinder 1988: 192). Only the structure of production and consumption changes, not the total amount of economic activity.

5. See Skousen, *The Structure of Production* (2007 [1990]: 185–92), for details of this new statistic. Recently, the U.S. Department of Commerce has developed a new statistic called "Gross Output" that approaches my GDE. See Table 8, "Gross Output by Industry, 2001–06," www.bea.gov/industry (January 29, 2008).

AN EXAMPLE: BUILDING A BRIDGE

A hypothetical example may be useful in reinforcing the benefits of increased savings. Suppose St. Paul and Minneapolis are separated by a river and that the only transportation between the two cities is by barge. Travel between the twin cities is expensive and time-consuming. Finally, the city fathers call a meeting and decide to build a bridge. Everyone agrees to cut back on current spending and put their savings to work to build the bridge. In the short run, retail sales, employment, and profits in local department stores decline. Yet new workers and new investment funds are assigned to the building of the bridge. In the aggregate, there is no reduction in output and employment. Moreover, once the bridge is completed, the twin cities benefit immensely from lower travel costs and increased competition between St. Paul and Minneapolis. In the end, the twin cities' sacrifice has been transformed into a higher standard of living.

SAY'S LAW REDUX: PRODUCTION IS MORE IMPORTANT THAN CONSUMPTION

In essence, the Keynesian demand-driven view of the economy fails to recognize another force that is even stronger than current demand—the demand for *future* consumption. Spending money on current consumer goods and services will do nothing to change the quality and variety of goods and services of the future. Such change requires new savings and investment.

Thus, we return to the truism of Say's law: Supply (production) is more important than demand (consumption). Consumption is the effect, not the cause, of prosperity. Production, saving, and capital formation are the true cause.

Let us return to Samuelson's model of income determination, the Keynesian cross he invented to represent unemployment equilibrium (see Figure 14.1 on page 364). We see now that saving and investment do not involve two separate schedules at all. Except in extreme circumstances, savings are invested. As income increases, savings and investment both increase together. Thus, there is no intersection of S and I at a single point and therefore no determination of macro equilibrium. The Keynesian cross crumbles under its own weight.

THE INFLATIONARY SEVENTIES: KEYNESIAN ECONOMICS ON THE DEFENSIVE

Often experience is a far greater teacher than high theory. While the theoretical battle over Keynesian economics ensued during the postwar era, no event raised more doubts about the Keynesian-Samuelson model than the inflationary crises of the 1970s, when oil and commodity prices skyrocketed while industrial nations roiled in recession. Under standard Keynesian analysis of aggregate demand, inflationary recession was not supposed to happen.

Keynesians relied heavily on the Phillips curve, a concept that was popularized in the 1960s and was based upon empirical studies on wage rates and unemployment conducted in Great Britain by economist A.W. Phillips (1958). Many economists were convinced that there was a trade-off between inflation and unemployment. Reproducing an idealized Phillips trade-off curve (see Figure 14.7), Samuelson described the "dilemma for macro policy"—if society desires lower unemployment, it must be willing to accept higher inflation; if society wished to reduce the high cost of living, it must be willing to accept higher unemployment. Between these two tough choices, Keynesians considered unemployment a more serious evil than inflation (Samuelson 1970: 810–12).

But in the 1970s and 1980s, the idealized Phillips trade-off fell apart—Western nations found that higher inflation didn't reduce unemployment, but made it worse.

The emergence of an inflationary recession and the collapse of the Phillips curve caused economists to question for the first time their textbook models. In their search for alternative explanations, a sudden renaissance of new economic theories arose—from Marxism to Austrian economics.

KEYNESIAN ECONOMICS MAKES A COMEBACK: THE CREATION OF AGGREGATE SUPPLY AND DEMAND

Yet Keynesian economics was able to make a surprising recovery with the discovery of a new tool that could explain the crises of the 1970s: aggregate supply and demand, or *AS-AD*. When Bill Nordhaus signed up as coauthor of the twelfth edition (1985), Samuelson's *Economics* added the new *AS-AD* diagrams. Samuelson and other Keynesians used *AS-AD* to explain the inflationary recession of the 1970s (see Figure 14.8).

As Samuelson stated, "Supply shocks produce higher prices, followed by a decline in output and an increase in unemployment. Supply shocks thus lead to a deterioration of all the major goals of macroeconomic policy" (1998: 385).

Alan Blinder, a leading Keynesian, also used *AS-AD* to explain the contortions in the traditional Phillips curve. According to Blinder, prior to the 1970s, fluctuations in aggregate demand had dominated the data. In the 1970s, however, aggregate supply dominated, and the result was stagflation. "That inflation and unemployment rose together following the OPEC shocks in 1973–74 and in 1979–80 in no ways contradicts a Phillips-curve trade-off" (1987: 42).

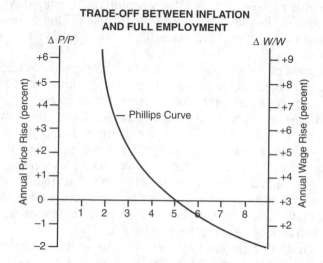

Figure 14.7
The Phillips Curve: Trade-Off Between Inflation and Full Employment
Source: Samuelson (1970: 810). Reprinted by permission of McGraw-Hill.

Thus, Keynesian economics recovered from the 1970s crises and *AS-AD* diagrams filled the pages of modern textbooks. In the words of G.K. Shaw, modern Keynesian theory "not only resisted the challenge but also underwent a fundamental metamorphosis, emerging ever more convincing and ever more resilient" (1988: 5). The remaining Keynesian precepts achieved a certain kind of "permanent revolution."

POST-KEYNESIAN ECONOMICS TODAY

What's left of modern Keynesian theory? Was Keynesianism a "permanent" revolution, as G.K. Shaw says, or an unfortunate interlude, as Leland Yeager calls it, a temporary "diversion" from the neoclassical model? Keynes and his disciples still hold fast to a central belief that the system of Adam Smith is inherently precarious, especially under a laissez-faire global financial system, and required government intervention (constantly adjusting fiscal and monetary policy) to maintain a high level of "aggregate effective demand" and full employment without much inflation. Paul Krugman (2007) identifies four Keynesian ideas that permeate today's economics:

1. Economies often suffer from a lack of aggregate demand, which leads to involuntary unemployment.
2. The market response to shortfalls in demand operates slowly and painfully.

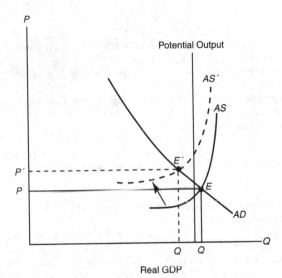

Sharply higher oil, commodity, or labor costs increase the costs of doing business. This leads to stagflation—stagnation combined with inflation. In the AS-AD framework, the higher costs shift the AS curve up from AS to AS', and the equilibrium shifts from E to E'. Output declines from Q to Q', while prices rise. The economy thus suffers a double whammy—lower output and higher prices.

Figure 14.8
Effects of Supply Shocks—Aggregate Supply Shifts Backward, Raising Prices and Cutting Output, Characteristics of an Inflationary Recession
Source: Samuelson (1998: 385). Reprinted by permission of McGraw-Hill.

3. Government policies can make up for this shortfall in demand, reducing unemployment.

4. Monetary policy may not always be sufficient to stimulate private sector spending; government spending must at times step into the breach.

Keynesianism still permeates our economic way of thinking, such as when the media warns that falling consumer confidence poses a threat to the economy, or when politicians promise that their tax cuts will create jobs by putting spending money in people's pockets, or when they warn consumers that saving their tax cut won't stimulate the economy.

A DAVID APPEARS ON THE SCENE TO CHALLENGE THE KEYNESIAN GOLIATH

Economists cannot destroy a theory without having another, stronger theory to take its place. Just such a new model of economics was quietly being created in the postwar period—a model which would challenge the very foundations of the Keynesian-Samuelson instability hypothesis. Milton Friedman, the economist who created this new model, is the subject of chapter 15.

REFERENCES

Baumol, William J., and Alan S. Blinder. 1988. *Economics: Principles and Policy*, 4th ed. New York: Harcourt Brace Jovanovich.

Blaug, Mark. 1985. *Great Economists Since Keynes*. Cambridge: Cambridge University Press.

Blinder, Alan S. 1987. *Hard Heads, Soft Hearts*. Reading, MA: Addison-Wesley.

Böhm-Bawerk, Eugen. 1959. *The Positive Theory of Capital*. South Holland, IL: Libertarian Press.

———. 1962. "The Austrian Economists." In *Shorter Classics of Böhm-Bawerk*. South Holland, IL: Libertarian Press. Originally appeared in *Annals of the American Academy of Political and Social Sciences* (January 1891).

Boyes, William, and Michael Melvin. 1999. *Macroeconomics*, 4th ed. Boston: Houghton Mifflin.

Breit, William, and Roger W. Spencer, eds. 1986. *Lives of the Laureates*. Cambridge, MA: MIT Press.

Buckley, William F. 1951. *God and Man at Yale*. Chicago: Regnery.

Coase, Ronald H. 1988 [1974]. "The Lighthouse in Economics." In *The Firm, the Market, and the Law*, 187–213. Chicago: University of Chicago Press.

Colander, David. 2007. *The Making of an Economist, Redux*. Princeton: Princeton University Press.

Dobbs, Zygmund. 1962. *Keynes at Harvard*. New York: Probe.

Ebenstein, Lanny. 2007. *Milton Friedman, A Biography*. New York: Palgrave Macmillan.

Ekins, Paul, and Manfred Max-Neef. 1992. *Real-Life Economics: Understanding Wealth Creation*. London: Routledge.

Elzinga, Kenneth G. 1992. "The Eleven Principles of Economics." *Southern Economic Journal* 58: 4 (April): 861–79.

Groenewegen, Peter. 1995. *A Soaring Eagle: Alfred Marshall, 1842–1924*. Cheltenham, UK: Edward Elgar.

Hansen, Alvin. 1941. *Fiscal Policy and Business Cycles*. New York: Norton.

———. 1953. *A Guide to Keynes*. New York: McGraw-Hill.

Harris, Seymour E., ed. 1947. *The New Economics: Keynes' Influence on Theory and Public Policy*. New York: Alfred A. Knopf.

———. 1948. *Saving American Capitalism*. New York: Alfred A. Knopf.

Hayek, Friedrich. 1939. "The 'Paradox' of Thrift." In *Profits, Interest and Investment*, 199–263. London: Routledge.

Hazlitt, Henry. 1959. *The Failure of the "New Economics."* Princeton, NJ: D. Van Nostrand.

Heilbroner, Robert, and Peter L. Bernstein. 1963. *A Primer on Government Spending*. New York: Random House.

Higgs, Robert. 1992. "Wartime Prosperity? A Reassessment of the U.S. Economy in the 1940s." *Journal of Economic History* 52: 1 (March): 41–60.

Jevons, William Stanley. 1965 [1879]. *The Theory of Political Economy*, 5th ed. New York: Augustus M. Kelley.

Keynes, John Maynard. 1973 [1936]. *The General Theory of Employment, Interest and Money*. London: Macmillan.

Klamer, Ajo, and David Colander. 1990. *The Making of an Economist*. Boulder, CO: Westview.

Krugman, Paul. 2007. "Introduction" to John Maynard Keynes, *The General Theory of Employment, Interest and Money*. New York: Palgrave Macmillan.

Kuttner, Robert. 1985. "The Poverty of Economics." *Atlantic Monthly* (February): 74–84.

Leamer, Edward. 1983. "Let's Take the Con Out of Economics." *American Economic Review* 73: 1 (March): 31–43.

Leijonhufvud, Axel. 1981. *Information and Coordination*. New York: Oxford University Press.

Linder, Marc. 1977. *Anti-Samuelson*. 2 vols. New York: Urizen.

McCloskey, Deirdre. 1998 [1985]. *The Rhetoric of Economics,* 2d ed. Madison: University of Wisconsin Press.

Minsky, Hyman P. 1982. *Can "It" Happen Again? Essays on Instability and Finance.* Armonk, NY: M.E. Sharpe.

Mises, Ludwig von. 1966. *Human Action,* 3d ed. Chicago: Regnery.

———. 1980. *Planning for Freedom*, 4th ed. Spring Hill, PA: Libertarian Press.

Modigliani, Franco. 1986. "Life Cycle, Individual Thrift, and the Wealth of Nations." *American Economic Review* 76: 3 (June): 297–313.

Morishima, Michio. 1976. *The Economic Theory of Modern Society*. Cambridge: Cambridge University Press.

Patinkin, Don. 1956. *Money, Interest and Price*. New York: Harper and Row.

Pigou, Arthur C. 1943. "The Classical Stationary State." *Economic Journal* 53 (December): 343–51.

———. 1947. "Economic Progress in a Stable Environment." *Economica* 14 (August): 180–88.

Phillips, A.W. 1958. "The Relationship Between Unemployment and the Rate of Change in Money Wage Rates in the United Kingdom, 1861–1957." *Economica* 25 (November), 283–99.

Rothbard, Murray N. 1983 [1963]. *America's Great Depression,* 4th ed. New York: Richardson and Snyder.

Samuelson, Paul A. 1948. *Economics,* 1st ed. New York: McGraw-Hill.

———. 1960. "American Economics." In *Postwar Economic Trends in the U.S.,* ed. Ralph E. Freeman. New York: Harper.

———. 1964. *Economics*, 6th ed. New York: McGraw-Hill.

———. 1967a. *Economics,* 7th ed. New York: McGraw-Hill.

———. 1967b. "Marxian Economics as Economics." *American Economic Review* (May).

———. 1968. "What Classical and Neoclassical Monetary Theory Really Was." *Canadian Journal of Economics* 1 (February), 1–15

———. 1970. *Economics,* 8th ed. New York: McGraw-Hill.

———. 1972 [1947]. *Foundations of Economic Analysis*. New York: Atheneum.

———. 1977. *The Collected Scientific Papers of Paul A. Samuelson,* vol. 4. Cambridge, MA: MIT Press.

———. 1990. "Foreword." In *The Principles of Economics Course*, ed. Phillips Saunders and William B. Walstad. New York: McGraw-Hill.

———. 1997. "Credo of a Lucky Textbook Author." *Journal of Economic Perspectives* 11: 2 (Spring): 153–60.

Samuelson, Paul A., and William D. Nordhaus. 1985. *Economics,* 12th ed. New York: McGraw-Hill.

———. 1989. *Economics,* 13th ed. New York: McGraw-Hill.

———. 1998. *Economics,* 16th ed. New York: Irwin-McGraw-Hill.

Shaw, G.K. 1988. *Keynesian Economics: The Permanent Revolution*. Hants, UK: Edward Elgar.

Skousen, Mark. 2007 [1990]. *The Structure of Production*. New York: New York University Press.

———. 1997. "The Perseverance of Paul Samuelson's *Economics*." *Journal of Economic Perspectives* 11: 2 (Spring): 137–52.

Smith, Adam. 1965 [1776]. *The Wealth of Nations*. New York: Modern Library.

Sobel, Robert. 1980. *The Worldly Economists*. New York: Free Press.

Solow, Robert M. 1965. "Economic Growth and Residential Housing." In *Readings in Financial Institutions*, ed. M.D. Ketchum and L.T. Kendall, 142–64. Boston: Houghton Mifflin.

————. 1988. "Growth Theory and After." *American Economic Review* 78: 3 (June), 307–17.

————. 2000 [1969]. *Economic Growth: An Exposition.* New York: Oxford University Press.

Szenberg, Michael, Lall Ramrattan, and Aron A. Gottesman, ed. 2006. *Samuelsonian Economics and the Twenty-First Century.* New York: Oxford University Press.

Tarshis, Lorie. 1947. *The Elements of Economics.* Boston: Houghton Mifflin.

Terborgh, George. 1945. *The Bogey of Economic Maturity.* Chicago: Machinery and Allied Products Institute.

15

MILTON'S PARADISE:
FRIEDMAN LEADS A MONETARY
COUNTERREVOLUTION

*The weakest and least satisfactory part of current economic
theory seems to me to be in the field of monetary dynamics.*

—Milton Friedman (1953: 42)

*To keep the fish that they carried on long journeys lively and
fresh, sea captains used to introduce an eel into the barrel. In the
economics profession, Milton Friedman is that eel.*

—Paul Samuelson (Sobel 1980: 144)

At the end of the twentieth century, the editors of *Time* magazine gathered to choose the Economist of the Century. Ultimately, they selected John Maynard Keynes, but they came very close to naming Milton Friedman, the diminutive founder of the Chicago monetarist school. In fact, Norman Pearlstine, the editor in chief, voted for Friedman because of his unique ability to "articulate the importance of free markets and the dangers of undue government intervention" (1998: 73). A short man stands tall.

Milton Friedman (1912–2006) was one of the most famous economists of the twentieth century and received numerous honors, including a Nobel Prize in 1976. But it wasn't always that way. In the 1950s and 1960s, when he launched his scholastic career at the University of Chicago, his theories were frequently dismissed as "extreme" and "antediluvian."

> ♪ **Music selection for this chapter: Peter Ilyich Tchaikovsky, "1812 Overture"**

Larry Wimmer, an economics professor at Brigham Young University, tells the story of the time Friedman debated a top Keynesian economist at Cambridge University around 1970. Nicholas Kaldor, a local favorite, was treated with the utmost respect and deference. But when the guest Milton Friedman approached the podium, he was greeted with laughter and a derisive murmur among the students. In those days, monetarism—the view that money matters—was still viewed as extremist and old-fashioned in the citadel of Keynes. As Samuelson wrote in an early edition of his textbook, "Today few economists regard federal reserve monetary policy as a panacea for controlling the business cycle" (Samuelson 1955: 316). But Friedman had the last laugh. His counterattack was so formidable and remorseless that the crowd of students came away with grudging respect for the stubborn Chicago economist. As Mark Blaug notes, "All those who have ever seen him in the flesh will testify, he is the greatest stand-up debater in the economics profession" (1985: 62).

DEFENDER OF THE FAITH

If anyone could take on the Keynesians and restore classical economics, it was Milton Friedman. His fierce, combative style and ideological roots were ideally suited for the task. In many ways, Adam Smith was his mentor. "The invisible hand has been more potent for progress than the visible hand for retrogression," Friedman wrote in his bestseller, *Capitalism and Freedom* (1982 [1962]: 200). It was entirely appropriate that Friedman won the Nobel Prize in economics exactly 200 years after the Declaration of Independence was signed and *The Wealth of Nations* was published. He almost single-handedly brought economics back from the brink of a complete Keynesian victory.

"ON THE CRITICAL SIDE THERE IS A GREAT DEARTH"

Except for Friedman, the free-market response to Keynesian theory was almost completely ineffectual. Ludwig von Mises, the dean of the Austrian school, wrote little about Keynes; his magnum opus, *Human Action* (1966), makes only a handful of references. Friedrich Hayek, the leading anti-Keynesian of the 1930s, made the strategic error of ignoring *The General Theory* when it came out in 1936, a decision he later deeply regretted. After the war, he lost interest in economics and went on to write about political philosophy. He returned to the subject only in 1979 with his booklet, *A Tiger by the Tail: The Keynesian Legacy of Inflation*.

William H. Hutt, a bright economist who taught at the University of Cape Town, devoted considerable time to dissecting Keynes. His first major work, *The Theory of Idle Resources,* is a profound analysis of unemployment. His basic theme is that unemployment is "always and solely due to a defect in the administration of the pricing mechanism," not to a deficiency in purchasing power, as Keynes alleged (Hutt 1977 [1939]: 20). During the late 1930s, Hutt spent much time figuring out *The General Theory*, but the war cut short his publishing plans. He tied up his voluminous typescripts and placed them in a cupboard, only to publish them thirty years later under the title *Keynesianism: Retrospect and Prospect* (1963). However, his book is often unclear and rambling. He introduced new terminology that rivals Keynesian terminology in complexity and potential for misinterpretation, with phrases such as "real damping effect," "pseudo-idleness," "savings hump," "cushioning effect," "supposed decumulation," "elasticity of release of capability," and "maximum price fixation." Keynes would have been impressed! Needless to say, Hutt's book was not well received. He confessed, "I must frankly admit to a failure in communication in my 1963 *Keynesianism.* My argument failed to get across, on some points, even to my friends" (Hutt 1979: 16–17).

A JOURNALIST TAKES ON KEYNES

In the late 1950s, journalist Henry Hazlitt (author of *Economics in One Lesson*—see chapter 2) was dismayed by the failure of free-market economists to displace Keynes in the classroom. "The Keynesian literature has perhaps grown to hundreds of books and thousands of articles. There are books wholly devoted to expounding the *General Theory* in simpler and more intelligible terms. But on the critical side there is a great dearth. The non-Keynesians and anti-Keynesians have contented themselves either with short articles, a few parenthetic pages, or a curt dismissal on the theory that his work will crumble from its own contradictions and will soon be forgotten" (Hazlitt 1973 [1959]: 4).

Hazlitt, a business and literary journalist with no formal training in economics, took on the task, writing a lengthy, chapter-by-chapter, page-by-page critique of *The General Theory*. Hazlitt's *Failure of the "New Economics"* (1973 [1959]) was reviewed favorably in the press when it was first published, but was dismissed in the academic journals. Abba P. Lerner called the work a "most depressing book" and likened Hazlitt to an intelligent student who writes clearly and interestingly, yet misses every question on the exam and therefore gets an F (Lerner 1960: 234).

Hazlitt made a penetrating, scholarly, and intelligent dissection of every page of *The General Theory*, but he got bogged down in Keynes's esoteric terminology. In order to understand the lucid Hazlitt, you had to read the oblique Keynes. Hazlitt used a popular title, which sold plenty of copies, but his book gathered dust on the shelves of conservatives and business people while being largely ignored by the economics profession. Ultimately, Hazlitt gave up the task of dealing with all the errors of Keynesianism as "hopeless"[1] (Hazlitt 1973: 8).

1. For further details, see my article, "This Trumpet Gives an Uncertain Sound: The Free-Market Response to Keynesian Economics," in Skousen (1992: 9–34).

ROTHBARD'S ATTEMPTED COUP

Following Hazlitt, libertarian economist **Murray N. Rothbard (1926–95)** took up the task of defeating Keynesianism in the early 1960s. In many ways, Rothbard was perfectly suited to the task. Like Friedman, he was born of Jewish immigrants from Eastern Europe and was raised in New York City. In school he excelled in mathematics (his middle name is Newton), and in 1956 he earned his Ph.D. in monetary economics from Friedman's alma mater, Columbia University, under the able direction of historian Joseph Dorfman and teacher Arthur F. Burns. Like Friedman, Rothbard was short, headstrong, and bright. They even suffered from the same physical ailment—a weak heart (Rothbard died of a massive heart attack in 1995; Friedman had two heart bypass surgeries). And both belonged to the Mont Pelerin Society.

Photograph 15.1
Murray N. Rothbard (1926–95)
The N stands for Newton.
Courtesy of the Mises Institute.

But there the similarity ends. Instead of joining a major university, Rothbard accepted a position with the conservative William Volker Fund, and then taught for twenty years at the little-known Brooklyn Polytechnic Institute of New York, an engineering school. He attended Mises's private seminar in New York, but refused to join the American Economic Association or write for the academic journals, choosing instead to write books. His books were published out of Princeton, New Jersey, not by Princeton University Press but by the subsidized Van Nostrand and Co. In other words, he made the costly mistake of staying outside the discipline.

Despite these drawbacks, Rothbard's books offer a lucid and penetrating critique of Keynesian economics. *Man, Economy and State* (1962) is a massive treatise on free-market economics, written logically and persuasively. Rothbard recognized early in his career that "it is a mistake to dismiss [Keynesianism] brusquely, as many conservative economists have done . . . failure to deal with its fallacies in detail and in depth has left the field of ideas open for Keynesianism to conquer" (1960: 150).

Rothbard devoted substantial sections of his magnum opus to a free-market counterattack on Keynesianism, including a critique of the accelerator principle, the multiplier, liquidity preference, the consumption function, and deficit financing. Regarding the national debt, Rothbard wisely reprimanded political conservatives who "greatly exaggerated the dangers of the public debt and have raised persistent alarms about imminent 'bankruptcy,'" noting that government, unlike private citizens, has the ability to "obtain money by coercion" via taxation or the printing presses.

At the same time, he lambasted the Keynesian slogan, "we owe it to our-selves," noting shrewdly that the "we" and the "ourselves" are not necessarily the same people. "For we might just as well say that taxes are unimportant for the same reason" (Rothbard 1962: 882). Lenders (investors in treasury bonds) tend to be wealthy and retired, while tax-payers tend to be middle-class wage earners. Thus, Rothbard contended that deficit spending could cause an unnatural redistribution of wealth from the poor and middle classes to the rich.

Rothbard continued his critique in his 1963 book, *America's Great Depression* (1983 [1963]). In addition to his assault on the liquidity trap, wage rigidity, the acceleration principle, the stagnation thesis, and other Keynesian theories, Rothbard used quantitative research to support an "Austrian" explanation of the 1929–32 crisis and argued that the Federal Reserve's easy-money policies caused an artificial unsustainable boom in the Roaring Twenties. In the second edition, written in 1971, he gave an astute "Austrian" explanation of stagflation, arguing that consumer price inflation is "a general and universal tendency in recessions." That is, "the prices of consumer goods always tend to rise, relative to the prices of pro-ducer goods, during recessions," only this time, in the early 1970s, government inflationary policies were so strong that consumer prices rose "absolutely and visibly as well" (Rothbard 1983: xxv–xxvi).

Unfortunately, Rothbard's bold analysis fell on deaf ears outside his lib-ertarian audience. From 1984 until his death in 1995, he taught economics at the University of Nevada at Las Vegas. Proclaiming himself an "anarcho-capitalist," he became embroiled in Libertarian Party politics. For fifteen years, he worked piecemeal on his history of economic thought book, completing only two volumes, through Marx (see Preface for more details). Rothbard's history has numerous insights, but is marred by his failure to recognize the majesty of Adam Smith's work, which he labeled "deeply flawed" and "confused" (Rothbard 1995: 436–37).

Friedman's Brilliant Strategy

Milton Friedman's story was far more auspicious. He was in a key position to develop a successful campaign to counter Keynes and restore the funda-mental principles of classical economics. He received a Ph.D. in economics from Columbia University; won the highly prestigious John Bates Clark Medal two years after Paul Samuelson won it; and taught economics at one of the top institutions in the country, the University of Chicago. In other words, he had impeccable credentials in technical economics and was at the right place to pursue his goals. His focus on monetary policy and the quan-tity theory of money was particularly attractive in an age of inflation.

Moreover, Friedman ingeniously exploited an academic formula that would in time revolutionize and advance the economics profession beyond Keynes to new heights in prestige and honors. How did he do it? Friedman himself calls it "luck" in his autobiography, but luck is often the opportunity one makes for oneself. Here is his improbable story.

FRIEDMAN'S PROLETARIAN ORIGINS

Milton Friedman was born in 1912 in Brooklyn, the only son and the youngest of four children of Eastern European Jewish immigrants who worked in sweatshops upon arriving in New York. Despite tough conditions and the Great Depression, America was still the land of opportunity for the Friedmans. Milton accepted a scholarship from Rutgers University, where he excelled in mathematics and economics, while working as a waiter in a local restaurant and as a salesman in a department store.

Photograph 15.2
Milton Friedman (1912–2006)
"He is the greatest stand-up debater in the economics profession."
Courtesy of Milton Friedman.

"MY KIND OF TOWN, CHICAGO IS"

In 1932, at the depths of the depression, Friedman won another scholarship, this one to study economics at the University of Chicago. There he met George Stigler, who became his lifelong colleague and friend. He later wrote, "He was a delightful office companion, a stimulating conversationalist, a highly constructive critic, and, like myself, lived, breathed, and slept economics" (Friedman and Friedman 1998: 149).

Friedman also met his future wife, Rose Director, at Chicago. In his first quarter, he took price theory from a gifted historian, Jacob Viner, who taught him the logic of economic theory.[2] Because the students were seated alphabetically, he sat next to Rose. She was the sister of Aaron Director, probably the most libertarian member of the Chicago faculty. In 1938, Milton and Rose married. They were partners and coauthors until his death and had two children, David (also an economist) and Janet (a lawyer).

Milton also encountered Paul Samuelson at Chicago. It's interesting that two economists can be educated at the same institution at approximately the same time, yet one goes on to be a Keynesian and the other a free-market monetarist. Curiously, Samuelson started out as a monetarist and became a Keynesian, while Friedman entertained Keynesian thinking (see

2. Paul Samuelson notes that Professor Viner was "celebrated for [his] ferocious manhandling of students, in which he not only reduced women to tears but on his good days drove returned paratroopers into hysteria and paralysis" (Samuelson 1977: 887). In his graduate seminar, Viner would call out the name of a student chosen from a deck of index cards, and would subject the student to tough questions. If a student failed to answer three questions, he or she was dropped from the class. "Three strikes and you were out, with no appeal possible to any higher court," reported Samuelson (Shils 1991: 543). Viner typically flunked one-third of the class.

WHAT? CHICAGO SCHOOL KEYNESIANS BEFORE KEYNES?

*Keynes had nothing to offer those of us who had sat
at the feet of Simons, Mints, Knight, and Viner.*
—Milton Friedman (Gordon 1974: 163)

Why weren't Friedman, Stigler, and most other students at Chicago attracted to Keynes? Because stars such as Frank H. Knight, Henry Simons, and Jacob Viner had advocated large and continuous deficit spending throughout the early 1930s to combat mass unemployment and deflation. They were Keynesians before Keynes.

Photograph 15.3	Photograph 15.4	Photograph 15.5
Frank H. Knight	Henry Calvert Simons	Jacob Viner
(1885–1972)	(1899–1946)	(1892–1970)

The Original Chicago School of Economics
Courtesy of University of Chicago Archives.

Frank Knight (1885–1972), the dean of the Chicago school until 1955, opposed letting the economy adjust downward in a deflationary spiral. In a 1932 letter to Congress, a dozen Chicago economists, including Knight, warned of "tremendous losses, in wastage of productivity capacity, and in acute suffering." They encouraged Congress to favor "fiscal inflation" during the depression, especially deficit spending financed by new money (Davis 1968: 477).

Jacob Viner (1892–1970) supported a Keynesian-style countercyclical fiscal policy, operating surpluses in boom times and deficits in bad times. During prosperous times, the traditional principles of finance were to tax heavily, spend lightly, and redeem the debt. But, according to Viner, such policies are unwise during a depression. Government should do the opposite: tax lightly, spend heavily, and borrow more (Davis 1968: 477–78).

HENRY SIMONS: THIS IS LAISSEZ FAIRE?

Henry Simons (1899–1946) is a prime example of the Chicago school during the 1930s. He emphasized the need to restore business confidence during the depression and advocated deficit spending and tax cuts as the primary tool for promoting recovery. Milton Friedman himself comments, "There is great similarity between the views expressed by Simons and by Keynes—as to the causes of the Great Depression, the impotence of monetary policy, and the need to rely extensively on fiscal policy" (Davis 1968: 476).

(continued)

Simons also worried about excessive "natural" monopolies under capitalism and favored nationalization of railroads, utilities, and all other "uncompetitive" industries in a book ironically called *Economic Policy for a Free Society* (1948).

It should be emphasized that outside of depression, and antitrust measures, Chicago economists were strong free-market advocates, favoring free trade, stable money, and no controls on wages or prices. Simons emphasized a government policy of "rules over authority," a tradition Friedman built upon.

comments on pages 406–7) and then became a monetarist! Milton and Paul were lifelong friends, despite their severe differences in economics and political outlook.

Friedman earned a master's degree from Chicago in 1933, but faced with empty pockets during the depression and with the help of Arthur Burns, he gained another scholarship to study at Columbia University in New York.[3] It was there he worked for the National Bureau of Economic Research (NBER) and, under the direction of Wesley C. Mitchell and Simon Kuznets, learned the value of high-quality empirical research. (For more on the NBER, see the box on page 243.) One of his research reports was on professional incomes, where he discovered a large gap between the incomes of physicians and dentists. He was convinced by the data that the difference was due to monopolistic practices in the medical profession. This was the first case in which Friedman learned that scientific, objective empirical work could lead to powerful policy conclusions.

In 1940–41, Friedman was invited to be a visiting professor at the University of Wisconsin, but his visit was cut short due to anti-Semitism and campus politics. Madison was populated mostly by German immigrants, and the Friedmans were anti-Nazi and pro-British. The economics department was also heavily influenced by doctrinaire followers of Keynes and Veblen. However, Walter Heller, a Keynesian chairman of the Council of Economic Advisors during the Kennedy administration, defended Friedman and demanded he stay on the faculty. Friedman always maintained friendship with Keynesian economists like Heller and Samuelson, but he soon resigned and moved back to New York (Ebensein 2007: 41–42).

FRIEDMAN MAKES THE WORST MISTAKE OF HIS CAREER

World War II interrupted Friedman's Ph.D. program. He went to work for the Treasury Department in Washington, D.C., and, in 1941–42, contributed to a government scheme that eventually caused the growth of big

---

3. Imagine, Mr. Veblen, where this great economist would be if it weren't for wealthy donors who fund college scholarships!

government in the United States—income tax withholding! As a result, ordinary workers who had previously been exempt from federal income taxes started paying large chunks of their regular paychecks to the IRS. Interestingly, IRS officials opposed the "temporary" wartime measure as burdensome, but Friedman and others pressed their case. Years later Friedman confessed, "It never occurred to me at the time that I was helping to develop the machinery that would make possible a government that I would come to criticize severely as too large, too intrusive, too destructive of freedom" (Friedman and Friedman 1998: 123).

Would he do it over again? "I have no apologies for it," he said in a *Reason* interview in 1995, "but I really wish we hadn't found it necessary and I wish there were some other way of abolishing withholding now" (Friedman 1995: 33). It was World War II, and his patriotic duty was calling. Besides, Germany and Britain were already withholding at source, and no doubt the United States would have adopted this efficient tax collection technique sooner or later. Yet the governments of Germany and Great Britan did not require annual tax returns to adjust the final payment; Friedman and Co. insisted on an annual tax adjustment, with additional payments or refunds required.

Friedman Runs Afoul on Both Sides

The tax withholding case was only the beginning of trouble for the bright star. After the war, Friedman spent a year at the University of Minnesota, where he collaborated with George Stigler to write "Roofs or Ceilings?"—a pamphlet arguing that postwar rent controls were counter-productive and should be removed. It was published in 1946 by the Foundation for Economic Education, a free-market think tank created by Leonard Read. Highly controversial at the time, it was attacked on both sides of the political spectrum. The novelist Ayn Rand labeled the pamphlet "collectivist propaganda" and "the most pernicious thing ever issued by an avowedly conservative organization" because the two economists favored lifting rent controls on practical, humanitarian grounds, not in defense of "the inalienable right of landlords and property owners" (Rand 1995: 326). Friedman later commented, "She really did have an imagination!" (1998: 621).

Similarly, a Keynesian economist assailed Friedman and Stigler in the *American Economic Review*, but for entirely different reasons: "Removal of rent controls now would not solve the housing problem, but it could easily contribute to a worsening inequality" (Bangs 1947: 482–83).

Friedman Becomes a Monetarist Upon Returning to Chicago

Finally, in 1946, after earning his Ph.D. from Columbia, Friedman returned to teaching full-time at the University of Chicago, where he stayed until his official retirement in 1977. Following Frank Knight's retirement in 1955,

TOP ECONOMISTS' HANDWRITING ANALYZED— SECRET PERSONALITIES REVEALED!

In every man's writings, the character of the writer must lie recorded.

—Thomas Carlyle

First there was Karl Marx, the phrenologist; then came Stanley Jevons, the astrologer, who was followed by Maynard Keynes, the palm reader. Now we have Milton Friedman, the handwriting analyst!

That's right. Friedman claimed in his autobiography that he could analyze a person's character through his handwriting, a hobby he picked up while he was a student at Columbia in 1933–34. "I have been an amateur graphologist ever since," he stated.

During 1953–54, Friedman spent a year at Cambridge University on a Fulbright fellowship. One day, Peter Bauer (later Lord Bauer) showed Friedman a letter from Richard Kahn, Keynes's famous student who invented the multiplier, and Friedman immediately noted Kahn's distinctive handwriting, which had separate lines sloping very sharply downward. "Kahn," Friedman announced to Bauer, "is certainly an extreme pessimist."

The next day Friedman had lunch with Kahn and in the course of the discussion, Kahn remarked, "The big difference is that Keynes was an inveterate optimist and I am an inveterate pessimist." Touché! At a sherry party later, Kahn showed Keynes's handwriting to Friedman, and sure enough, Keynes's lines sloped sharply upward, a clear "tipoff to optimism."

Joan Robinson asked Friedman to analyze another handwriting specimen. Friedman responded, "This is obviously the writing of a foreigner, so it's difficult for me to analyze. But I would say it is written by someone who had considerable artistic but not much intellectual talent." It turned out to be the handwriting of Lydia Lopokova, the world-famous Russian ballerina whom Keynes had married. "That was surely my greatest triumph of the year at Cambridge!" (Friedman and Friedman 1998: 245).

FOUR ECONOMISTS ANALYZED

Can handwriting give us clues to personality? I decided to test Friedman's hypothesis by commissioning a "certified" graphologist to analyze the handwritten notes of four economists—Adam Smith, Karl Marx, John Maynard Keynes, and Milton Friedman. (The signatures of these four are shown in Figure 15.1.)

According to the specialist, Adam Smith's handwriting shows him to be "optimistic and ambitious" (true), but a "very sensual person" (very doubtful). Marx was found to be either "extremely optimistic" and "very sociable" or "impatient" and "moody," characteristics that could apply to most people. Keynes's writing style shows a "dominant and occasionally aggressive personality" (true), but one who would hate to have his handwriting analyzed (doubtful). And Friedman's notes indicate an "optimistic and persistent" individual with a "temper" (true), but one who "can be evasive in his communications" (anything but!). In short, I have serious doubts about the reliability of graphology, which appears to be more of an art than a real science.

(continued)

But then again the graphologist said my handwriting demonstrated a "good teacher and lecturer," an "original" thinker, and a person "sensitive to the feeling of others." Hey, maybe Friedman is onto something.

Notably, in an age of typewriters and personal computers, Friedman wrote all his articles and books by hand until he was in his eighties. His papers could keep graphologists busy for decades. Write on, Mr. Friedman!

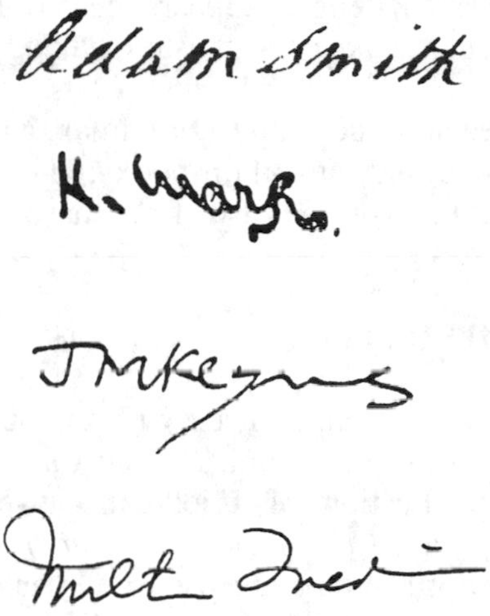

Figure 15.1
Four Famous Economists' Signatures: Can You Tell Which One Is the Pessimist?

Friedman continued the Chicago tradition and even strengthened it with an upgraded version of Irving Fisher's quantity theory of money, which he applied to monetary policy. He wrote on numerous topics related to monetary economics, culminating in the research and writing of his most famous empirical study, *A Monetary History of the United States, 1867–1960*, which was published by the prestigious National Bureau of Economic Research and coauthored by Anna J. Schwartz (1963). Essentially, his monumental study demonstrated the unrelenting power of money and monetary policy in the ups and downs of the U.S. economy, including the Great Depression and the postwar era, when mainstream economists believed that "money didn't matter." Even Yale's James Tobin, a friendly critic, recognized its greatness: "This is one of those rare books that leaves their mark on all future research on the subject" (1965: 485). As we shall see, it was Friedman's *Monetary History* that paved his way to the commanding heights of the economics profession and the political world, although it would take years to climb the mountain.

FACING A HOSTILE ENVIRONMENT

The Keynesian revolution had become so entrenched in academia by the 1950s and 1960s that free-market economists had a hard time being heard on campus. We have already mentioned in chapter 12 ("The Missing Mises") the extreme difficulty Mises, Hayek, and the Austrian school faced in obtaining positions in academia; Friedman and the Chicago school experienced a similar challenge. Appearances by Friedman before academic audiences were not unlike creationists speaking out against Darwinian evolution in a science class. Proponents of laissez faire were simply shouted down or laughed at. According to Friedman, a university as well respected as Duke refused to carry any of his books. The economics department there did not consider his work worthy of purchase.

FRIEDMAN WRITES A BESTSELLER

The long road back began in 1962 with the publication of a slim work, a defense of laissez-faire economics called *Capitalism and Freedom* (1982a [1962]). The publication of Friedman's two most significant works, *Monetary History* and *Capitalism and Freedom*, coincided with the twenty-fifth anniversary of Milton and Rose Friedman's marriage.

Capitalism and Freedom, Friedman's first attempt to introduce the principles of the free market to the general public, was written after a series of lectures he gave at Wabash College. At the time, Friedman was still relatively unknown outside the profession and the book was never reviewed by any of the major press. Yet it has sold more than half a million copies and remains in print. In addition to being an eloquent defense of free markets and condemnation of excessive government power, *Capitalism and Freedom* introduced some of the policy recommendations Friedman is famous for—flexible exchange rates, school vouchers, and the negative income tax. A decade later, even Samuelson recommended it as a "rigorously logical, careful, often persuasive elucidation of an important point of view" (Samuelson 1973: 848).

In the late 1960s, Friedman was invited to debate strident Keynesian Leon Keyserling at the University of Wisconsin. Near the end of the debate, Keyserling read the list of fourteen items Friedman highlighted as "unjustified" government activities in *Capitalism and Freedom*. Keyserling made fun of the points as he read them, hoping to win the debate. He clearly gained favor with the students as he went through Friedman's castigation of social security, rent controls, agricultural supports, and national parks. But when he came to point 11, he ran into unexpected trouble. Point 11 called for the elimination of military conscription during peacetime. Friedman's opposition to the draft brought ardent applause and won him the debate (Friedman 1982: ix).

Combative with Colleagues and Tough on Students

Debate became a common quality of Friedman's style. A short man, little more than five feet tall, with a thin, nasal voice, he was always considered blunt and intense in his opinions, and could anger easily. "Diplomacy was not my strong suit," he admitted (Friedman and Friedman 1998: 51). As an example, in 1971 he met with President Richard Nixon, who complained about troubles the country was having with wage-price controls. "Don't blame George Schulz for this monstrosity," Nixon said. Friedman quickly responded, "I don't blame George. I blame you, Mr. President" (1998: 386–87).

Students at Chicago trembled before his nimble mind and snap judgments. He was quick to point out errors in a colleague's work, even if the person was his superior. He was often surprised when they felt insulted. Like his old teacher, Jacob Viner, Friedman had little patience with students who couldn't keep up in class (Ebenstein 2007: 85–95). One story is told of a student who was having difficulty with a concept at the beginning of the school year. Friedman told him to work on the problem over the weekend. If he couldn't figure it out by Monday morning, what do you think Friedman recommended? Was it (a) hire a tutor, (b) come see him in his office, or (c) transfer to another course? His answer was c! Thomas Sowell said Friedman was a tough grader—he got one of only two B's in his price-theory class. He gave no A's (Sowell 2000: 126).

On the other hand, once students had demonstrated their ability, Professor Friedman was known for spending countless hours helping them complete their dissertations at Chicago. As Gary Becker writes, "Friedman exerted a profound influence on students and on other faculty not only through this course, but also from his comments on their research, especially on dissertations" (Shils 1991: 143).

"They Call Me Mr. Friedman!"

Chicago professors hate it when students address them as "Doctor." Since everyone has an advanced graduate degree, they consider it pretentious. Instead, the faculty members have a longstanding tradition of calling each other by the ordinary salutation "Mister." "Mr. Friedman" is preferable even to "Professor Friedman." And Mr. Friedman (like any other Chicago economist) would never be caught dead publishing a book with the designation "Dr. Milton Friedman, Ph.D." on the jacket. Such titles are considered gauche. No doubt German academics, who are famous for designations such as Herr Professor Extraordinaire Doktor, would be alarmed by this undignified greeting.

FRIEDMAN FINALLY MAKES AN IMPACT

Friedman's efforts finally started paying off in the late 1960s. In 1967, he was elected president of the AEA; more and more economists were recognizing the vital role of money and monetary policy in the economy and his genuine scholarship in technical economics. A year later, Friedman squared off against Walter E. Heller, former chairman of President Kennedy's Council of Economic Advisors and architect of the famed 1964 tax cut, in a famous debate published as *Monetary vs. Fiscal Policy.* Heller began by admitting, "The issue is *not* whether money matters—we all grant that— but whether *only* money matters, as some Friedmanites . . . would put it" (Friedman and Heller 1969: 16). Heller used the examples of the 1964 tax cut and the Vietnam War budget to demonstrate "the potency of fiscal policy—both good and bad" (page 31). In response, the "towering iconoclast" Friedman denied that he ever favored a view that only money mattered, calling such an extreme position "absurd," but then went on to note how often changes in fiscal policy "can be accompanied by a change in monetary policy" (pages 47, 52). For example, the 1964 tax cut and the buildup of the Vietnam War in the late 1960s were both accompanied by a liberal monetary policy (see the box on page 401).

Photograph 15.6
Milton Friedman ("Mr. Macro") and George Stigler ("Mr. Micro") of the Chicago School
The long and short of it!
Courtesy of Economics Department, University of Chicago.

Paul Samuelson's textbook is a good measure of the profession's evolving views on Friedman and monetary policy. The third edition indicates, "Today few economists regard federal reserve monetary policy as a panacea for controlling the business cycle" (1955: 316). By the time the

"Only Money Matters"!

That is an absurd position, of course, and one that I have never held.
—Milton Friedman

In the 1968 debate with Walter Heller, Friedman denied the criticism leveled at him that "only money matters" (Friedman and Heller 1969: 47). Yet, in the same debate, he claimed that fiscal policy, "the state of the budget by itself has no significant effect on the course of nominal income, on inflation, on deflation, or on cyclical fluctuations" (page 51). Monetary policy, on the other hand, had a tremendous effect.

No Supply Sider?

On another occasion, Friedman was asked about "supply-side" economics and the impact of tax cuts on the economy. "I am not a supply-side economist," he declared. "I am not a monetarist economist. I am an economist." Then he added, "I have never believed that fiscal policy, *given monetary policy*, is an important influence on the ups and downs of the economy" (Friedman 1982b: 53–54).

Rx for Japan: Print More Money!

But then Friedman published a column in the December 17, 1997, issue of the *Wall Street Journal* on the solutions to Japan's weak economy in the 1990s. The entire piece stressed the "inept" monetary policies of the Bank of Japan and the need for Japan to accelerate its money supply, almost as the sole solution. Friedman made no mention of free-market alternatives: cutting taxes, deregulating the banking system, or promoting free trade and immigration. Once again, readers were left with the impression that Friedman, despite his protests, thinks that only money matters.

---

ninth edition was written, in the midst of double-digit inflation, Samuelson opined that "both fiscal and monetary policies matter much" (1973: 329). In 1998, in the sixteenth edition, Samuelson (and his coauthor William Nordhaus) virtually switched sides and gave in to the monetarists: "Fiscal policy is no longer a major tool of stabilization policy in the United States. Over the foreseeable future, stabilization policy will be performed by the Federal Reserve monetary policy" (1998: 655). This statement continues the same in current editions.

A Bicentennial Nobel Marred by Demonstrations

In 1976, Friedman matched Paul Samuelson's prize-winning abilities with a Nobel Prize of his own, fittingly awarded on the 200th anniversary of America's Declaration of Independence. In fact, all seven Nobel laureates that year were Americans. Quite an American affair was held at Stockholm that December.

Friedman's presence at the Nobel award ceremonies was not without controversy. His selection, which had to be approved by Sweden's Royal Academy, was preceded by a heated debate over his involvement with Chile and its controversial dictator, General Augusto Pinochet. During the Nobel ceremonies in Stockholm, demonstrators protested Friedman's presence. He was regarded as the intellectual architect and unofficial advisor to the team of Chilean free-market economists known as the "Chicago Boys."

CHILE AND THE CHICAGO BOYS

Chile had gone through a wretched economic crisis in the early 1970s. Salvador Allende was the first democratically elected Marxist, but his socialistic policies of nationalization, high wages, and price controls created such an economic disaster that the military under General Augusto Pinochet staged a coup d'état in September 1973, and Allende committed

---

THE NOBEL PRIZE: NOBLE OR IGNOBLE?

Prizes shall be awarded to those persons who during the previous year have rendered the greatest services to mankind.
—Alfred Nobel's will (Fant 1993: 329)

Economists are lucky fellows. Among social scientists, they are the only ones who have been able to convince the Swedish Academy to add a new Nobel category since Alfred Nobel made his will in 1895. There's no Nobel Prize in sociology, business, psychology, linguistics, mathematics, or education. But since 1969, the Central Bank of Sweden has funded the Nobel Prize in economic science. Gunnar Myrdal, the Swedish economist, was able to convince the academy that economics, more than any other social science, had achieved such a high level of scientific inquiry that it deserved special honors (although he later recanted and wished he had refused the prize because, he now argued, economics could not match the precision and value of the physical sciences).

Photograph 15.7
Alfred Nobel (1833–96)

Ponder these facts:

- Friedrich Hayek recovered from bad health upon receiving the prize and lived another eighteen years; John F. Nash, who suffered from paranoid schizophrenia and lived in poverty, regained his old elegant self; but William Vickery died three days after winning his Nobel.

- Marxists have won numerous Nobels in literature, none in economics.   *(continued)*

- In 1989, Chicago's Robert Lucas Jr. agreed in a divorce settlement to give his ex-wife half the Nobel winnings if he won the prize within five years. A few weeks before the agreement expired, he won the Nobel Prize—and lived up to his contract. "A deal is a deal," he said.

- Gunnar Myrdal, the only Swede to win the prize, was distraught because he had to share it with free-market economist Friedrich Hayek.

- More professors at the University of Chicago have won Nobel prizes than at any other institution—over half of the prizes in the 1990s.

- The prize money has gradually increased from $77,000 to $1.6 million, but the fund has been poorly managed and has underperformed the U.S. and European indexes for years. If it had been invested in the S&P 500 index since 1969, the prize today would be worth over $4 million. (Franco Modigliani, the 1985 winner, appears to be the smartest investor—he put most of his winnings into stock index funds.)

- The Tax Reform Act of 1986 eliminated the tax-free status of the Nobel Prize. The first to be taxed was MIT's Robert M. Solow, who ended up with only half the monetary award.

- The most embarrassed Nobel laureates: financial economists Robert C. Merton and Myron S. Scholes, winners in 1997, for their involvement in Long Term Capital Management, a hedge fund that used their option strategies and lost $4 billion before it was bailed out.

- Only one black economist, Princeton's W. Arthur Lewis, has won the Nobel; only one Asian, Harvard's Amartya Sen, has won; no women have won the award, although Cambridge's Joan Robinson was in the running in the 1970s for her seminal work on "imperfect competition," but her ardent defense of Communist China and North Korea embarrassed supporters and critics alike.

- One economist has won the Nobel Peace Prize—Muhammad Yunus, founder of the Grameen Bank and the microcredit revolution, won it in 2006.

SWEDES REWARD MOSTLY FREE-MARKET ECONOMISTS

There's no better indicator of the renaissance of free-market economics than the list of winners of the Nobel Memorial Prize in Economic Science, one of the most prestigious awards in the world. Since 1969, when Sweden added the sixth Nobel category, the vast majority of awards have gone to free-market economists. Keynesians who have won include Paul Samuelson, James Tobin, Robert Solow, Joseph Stiglitz, and Paul Krugman, but since 1974, when Friedrich Hayek shared the prize with socialist Gunnar Myrdal, the scales have tipped noticeably toward free-market advocates.

Moreover, most of the winners have taught at or attended the University of Chicago. During the 1990s, the majority of Nobels went to this one school, including Ronald Coase, Gary Becker, Robert Fogel, and Robert Lucas.

Why? First, Chicago economists combined powerful theory and sophisticated empirical work to advance economic science into new arenas, such as finance, discrimination, welfare, and economic history. Second, the five-man committee chosen

(continued)

by the Bank of Sweden that awards the prize each year has gradually shifted ideology from socialism to capitalism. Marxists and Keynesians feel cheated. In the November 12, 1990, issue of *BusinessWeek*, Robert Kuttner bemoaned the fact that several prominent Keynesians were ignored by the Nobel committee during their lifetimes, including Joan Robinson, Nicholas Kaldor, and Sir Roy Harrod. But free-market economists can make the same argument. Certainly Ludwig von Mises deserved the prize but never received it.

NOTABLE MISSES

The Nobel committees in other disciplines have often missed people who were famous in their fields and who certainly qualified for "rendering the greatest service to mankind." Mark Twain and Leo Tolstoy never received Nobel honors in literature. Bell Labs labeled "electricity" the number one engineering feat of the twentieth century, yet Thomas Edison never won the Nobel Prize for his invention of the electric light bulb. Other scientists who were overlooked: Orville and Wilbur Wright for the airplane; Henry Ford for mass production; George Washington Carver for agricultural techniques; Filo Farnsworth, Vladimir Zworykin, and Isaac Shoenberg for television; Robert Watson-Watts for radar; Frank Whittle and Hans Pabst von Ohain for the jet engine; Chester Clarson for xenography; Howard Aiken, John P. Eckert, Jr., and John W. Mauchly for the digital computer; Jonas Salk for the polio vaccine; and Ted Hoff for the microprocessor. The greatest irony is the failure to award Edward Teller, father of the atomic bomb. After all, Alfred Nobel himself developed a lesser explosive— dynamite.

Previous Nobel laureates and other top economics professors from seventy-five institutions worldwide nominate candidates. A five-man committee makes the selection after extensive reviews and debate. Finally, the Swedish members of the academy (260 persons) vote by secret ballot in October, and award the prize with an early morning surprise call to the winner. The award is presented and the Nobel lecture is delivered in Stockholm in December.

suicide. When the global inflationary recession made things worse in Chile, General Pinochet called in the Chicago Boys for help. These were Chilean economists who had been trained at the University of Chicago under a longstanding scholarship program. They recommended drastic cuts in government spending, denationalization, tax reform, and strict control of the money supply. (Later, during the copper crisis of 1982, they would recommend the first highly successful privatization of their social security program.)

The coup was disputed from the beginning because the military junta intervened in a democratically elected government and, following the coup, summarily imprisoned and tortured many Allende and Marxist supporters. In addition to the human rights issues, critics labeled the Chicago Boys' economic policies "draconian" and "anti-progressive."

Nevertheless, Chile recovered and achieved an economic miracle of high economic growth, low inflation, and a booming export market. During the past twenty years, Chile has become the new model for Latin

America. And since 1990, it has returned to democratic rule. In many ways, Friedman has been vindicated in his positive role in Chile's amazing success story.

FRIEDMAN GOES ON THE OFFENSIVE: THE *FREE TO CHOOSE* VIDEO

Friedman enjoyed writing for the general public in his *Newsweek* column, which he wrote from 1966 to 1984, but his crowning achievement came in January 1980, with the broadcast of a television miniseries on the Public Broadcasting System (PBS) called *Free to Choose*, which aimed at spreading free-market ideas to the general public. Three years in the making at a cost of over $2.5 million, the ten-part series "launched us on the most exciting venture of our lives" (Friedman and Friedman 1998: 471).

The biggest hurdle was convincing PBS to broadcast the program; PBS program directors considered Friedman a "fascist extremist." But since they had previously aired John Kenneth Galbraith's biased *Age of Uncertainty*, they felt compelled to broadcast Friedman's *Free to Choose*.

The format was alluring. Each program began with a public lecture by Friedman, followed by lively debates between advocates and dissenters. Topics included "Who Protects the Consumer?" "Who Protects the Worker?" and "How to Cure Inflation." The programs had an international flavor, with filming and commentary in the United States, Europe, and Asia. Hong Kong was represented as a showcase of the benefits of free markets under the most adverse circumstances.

The response was overwhelming. Over three million Americans viewed *Free to Choose*, an extremely large audience for PBS. The book of the same name eventually sold over a million copies (Friedman and Friedman 1980).

FROM CHICAGO TO CALIFORNIA

Friedman retired from the University of Chicago in 1977, and accepted a position at the Hoover Institution at Stanford University in California. He used the proceeds from the Nobel Prize ($180,000 tax-free in 1976) to buy a beautiful apartment on Russian Hill overlooking San Francisco. But retirement was not in Friedman's vocabulary. He and his wife were actively involved in the Mont Pelerin Society and various public causes, including tax limitation. Friedman acted as an informal advisor to President Ronald Reagan, as he had previously done with President Richard Nixon and presidential candidate Barry Goldwater. In the late 1990s, they established the Milton and Rose D. Friedman Foundation to promote the use of school vouchers as a means of improving public education, especially among disadvantaged families. "Schooling is one of the technically most backward of our major industries," Friedman stated (1998: 349). After two open-heart surgeries in the 1980s, Friedman slowed down a bit, but remained active in writing, advising leaders, lecturing, and traveling. He was always a prodigious letter writer. More important, he did more than any other economist to reverse the Keynesian tide and reestablish the virtues of neoclassical economics. In 1988 he received the Presidential Medal of Freedom and in 2002 a Lifetime Achievement Award. He died in November 2006 at the age of ninety-four. In 2008, the University of Chicago announced the establishment of the Milton Friedman Institute to pursue path-breaking research in economics.

HOW FRIEDMAN SUCCEEDED WHERE OTHER FREE-MARKET ECONOMISTS FAILED

How did Friedman almost single-handedly change the intellectual climate back from the Keynesian model to the classical model of Adam Smith?

First, as indicated earlier, Friedman acquired impeccable credentials within the economics profession. With a Ph.D. from Columbia, a full professorship at Chicago, and the coveted John Bates Clark Medal, he was ready to take on the Keynesian world.

Second, Friedman focused in his early career on scholarly technical work; only after establishing his academic credentials did he start writing for the general public. Thus, he patiently gained the respect of his professional colleagues first and then spoke out in the public arena.

Third, he developed sophisticated empirical evidence for his theories. Theory, even brilliant sophisticated logic, would not be enough to dislodge the Keynesian system, as the neo-Austrians found out. One needed reliable data, quantitative analysis, and sophisticated mathematical skills to test and support one's thesis. He learned this lesson well from Simon Kuznets, Wesley Mitchell, and other stars at the National Bureau of Economic Research.

FRIEDMAN USES A CONTROVERSIAL STRATEGY

The fourth and most surprising way in which Friedman attacked the Keynesian model was by using the same Keynesian language and theoretical apparatus to undermine Keynesianism and offer a countermodel known as monetarism. Many free-market economists have misunderstood this controversial tactic by Friedman, but it was a brilliant and effective move.

FRIEDMAN'S KEYNESIAN PAST

One of the most remarkable revelations made by Friedman's 1998 autobiography was his temporary flirtation with Keynesian economics in the early 1940s. During his stint with the Treasury Department, Friedman was asked to give testimony on ways to fight inflation during World War II. His reply, couched in Keynesian ideology, mentioned several options: cut government spending, raise taxes, and impose price controls. Nowhere did he mention monetary policy or controlling the money supply, policies for which Friedman is now famous. "I had completely forgotten how thoroughly Keynesian I then was," he commented (1998: 113).

During the 1930s, Friedman had "strong New Deal leanings" and favored Keynesian-style deficit spending as a way out of the depression (Ebenstein 2007: 39). Friedman's mentor was not Keynes, but his teachers at the University of Chicago (see the box on page 393).

In an article published in 1986, Friedman glorified Keynes as a "brilliant scholar" and "one of the great economists of all time." He described *The General Theory* as a "great book," although he considered Keynes's *Tract on Monetary Reform* as his best work. Moreover, he declared, "I believe that Keynes's theory is the right kind of theory in its simplicity, its concentration on a few key magnitudes, its potential fruitfulness" (Friedman 1986: 52).

"WE ARE ALL KEYNESIANS NOW"

Quotations such as the above have led some critics, such as economists Roger Garrison and Robert J. Gordon, to classify Friedman as a Keynesian monetarist, that is, one who favors monetary policy instead of fiscal policy as a way to stimulate the economy.

These quotations are misleading. The reality is that Friedman, while developing his skills in the Keynesian toolbox, never bought the Keynesian mindset. As Friedman wrote me in a letter, "I was never a Keynesian in the sense of being persuaded of the virtues of government intervention as opposed to free markets." He was entirely "hostile" to the Keynesian notion that the Great Depression was a market phenomenon (Gordon 1974, 48–49).

Reviewing the background on another controversial quote should put the matter to rest. On December 31, 1965, *Time* magazine put John Maynard Keynes on the cover and quoted Friedman as saying, "We are all Keynesians now." Later, Friedman said he was quoted out of context. "In one sense, we are all Keynesians now; in another, no one is a Keynesian any longer. We all use the Keynesian language and apparatus; none of us any longer accepts the initial Keynesian conclusions" (1968: 15).

This is the crux of the issue. In essence, Friedman, a scholar who was intimately familiar with the Keynesian system, used the language and apparatus of Keynes to prove him wrong. As he stated following his laudatory comments about Keynes in 1986, "I have been led to reject it [Keynesian economics] . . . because I believe that it has been contradicted by experience" (1986: 48).

FIRST ATTACK: THE PERMANENT INCOME HYPOTHESIS

In the early 1950s, Friedman joined other professional economists in developing quantitative studies to elucidate Keynesian concepts such as the investment multiplier and the consumption function. One of Friedman's first contributions, the permanent-income hypothesis, was along these lines. His 1957 book, *A Theory of the Consumption Function*, which Friedman regards as his best technical work, is a classic example of Friedman's use of Keynesian terminology to discredit Keynes. Crucial to the Keynesian case for increased government spending to bring about full employment is the consumption function—the notion that there is a stable relationship between household consumption spending and household current income. According to the Keynesian model, government spending would increase household incomes through a leveraged multiplier effect.

However, using a massive study of consumption data in the United States, Friedman demonstrated that households adjust their expenditures only according to long-term or permanent income changes, and pay little attention to transitory patterns. Therefore, the Keynesian consumption function was fundamentally flawed and any leveraging of government expenditure through the multiplier was much smaller than expected. Friedman's diligent and comprehensive work set a new high standard for empirical studies, and research by Franco Modigliani, James Tobin, and other Keynesian scholars confirmed this "life-cycle" theory of consumption. Further studies also confirmed Friedman's conclusion that the multiplier is closer to 1 than to the textbook version of 6 or 7.

Friedman's permanent-income theory of consumption also helped counter the Keynesian case for progressive income and death taxes as well as Alvin Hansen's "secular stagnation" thesis (see chapter 14). Keynes contended that the marginal propensity to consume fell as income rose and, therefore, as a nation became wealthier, new investment opportunities had to expand more rapidly to handle the faster growing savings rate. Keynesians called this the "savings gap." Keynes's conjecture was a major component of Hansen's secular stagnation thesis, which suggested that unless the government ran huge deficits, the United States would be condemned to stagnation. Keynes also recommended that high taxes be imposed on wealthy individuals to encourage a high-consumption society and avoid stagnation.

However, Friedman's permanent-income thesis showed that higher incomes would not necessarily lead to higher saving rates, and confirmed Simon Kuznets's studies at NBER, which show that since 1899 the percentage of income saved has remained steady despite a substantial rise in real income. Thus, high taxes on wealthy individuals would not necessarily increase the propensity to consume, as Keynes had supposed.

It should be pointed out, of course, that even if Keynes's hypothesis were true—that the savings rate rises with income—it would not be a bad thing. Rather, higher savings would induce more capital investments and technological breakthroughs. There is no limit to entrepreneurial ability and technological advances or the capacity for sound investment.

FRIEDMAN STRIKES AT THE HEART OF THE KEYNESIAN MODEL

Yet Friedman's critique of the consumption function was just preliminary window dressing compared to a much more vital issue. The core assumption behind Keynesian economics is the deep-seated suspicion that free-enterprise capitalism is inherently unstable and could be stuck at less than full employment indefinitely unless government intervenes to increase "effective demand" and restore its vitality. As James Tobin put it, the "invisible" hand of Adam Smith requires the "visible" hand of Keynes (Breit and Spencer 1986: 118). Did not the Great Depression prove this thesis, that a free-market economy was not self-regulating and thus had to be controlled?

FRIEDMAN FOCUSES ON MONEY AND INFLATION

Friedman addressed this critical issue in an indirect manner—by engaging in a massive study of money and monetary policy in the United States since the Civil War. He engaged the help of a disciplined researcher at NBER, Anna J. Schwartz, who became his coauthor.[4] Together they spent years gathering a wide variety of statistics on money, credit, interest rates, and the policies of federal monetary authorities. It culminated in a monumental fat book—*A Monetary History of the United States, 1867–1960*, published jointly by the NBER and Princeton University Press (1963). Its professional approach could not be ignored.

Friedman had a twofold mission in researching and writing *Monetary History*. First, he wanted to dispel the prevailing Keynesian wisdom that "money doesn't matter," that somehow an aggressive expansion of the money supply during a recession or depression would not be effective, like "pushing on a string." Friedman and Schwartz showed time and time again that monetary policy was indeed effective in both expansions and contractions. Friedman's work on monetary economics became increasingly important and applicable as inflation heated up in the 1960s and 1970s. Friedman's most famous line is "Inflation is always and everywhere a monetary phenomenon" (Friedman 1968: 105).

FRIEDMAN DISCOVERS THE REAL CAUSE OF THE GREAT DEPRESSION

That money mattered was an important proof, but the research by Friedman and Schwartz revealed a much deeper purpose. One startling

---

4. Friedman took great offense once when I referred to Anna J. Schwartz as Friedman's "researcher" rather than "coauthor." He wrote, "If you really want to know something about how *Monetary History* was written, you are welcome to examine the extensive material in the Hoover Archives" (private correspondence, Sept. 6, 1994). Interestingly, in the December 1994 issue of *American Economic Review*, Anna Schwartz was honored as a Distinguished Fellow and a one-page summary of her career used the words "research," "statistics," and "data" eleven times!

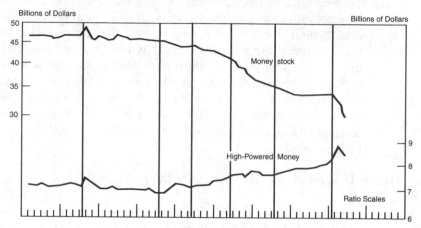

THE GREAT CONTRACTION
The Stock of Money and Its Proximate Determinants, Monthly,
1929–March 1933

Figure 15.2
The Dramatic Decline in the Money Stock, 1929–33
"The stock of money fell by over a third."
(Friedman and Schwartz 1963: 333). Reprinted by permission of Princeton University Press.

sentence in their entire 860-page book changed forever how economists and historians would view the cause of the most cataclysmic economic event of the twentieth century:

> *From the cyclical peak in August 1929 to the cyclical trough in March 1933, the stock of money fell by over a third.* (Friedman and Schwartz 1963: 299)

For thirty years, an entire generation of economists did not really know the extent of the damage the Federal Reserve had imposed on the United States economy from 1929 to 1933. They had been under the impression that the Federal Reserve had done everything humanly possible to keep the depression from worsening, but like "pushing on a string," were impotent in the face of overwhelming deflationary forces. According to the official apologia of the Federal Reserve System, it had done its best, but was powerless to stop the collapse.

Friedman radically altered this conventional view. "The Great Contraction," as Friedman and Schwartz called it, "is in fact a tragic testimonial to the importance of monetary forces" (Friedman and Schwartz 1963: 300). On another occasion, Friedman explained, "Far from being testimony to the irrelevance of monetary factors in preventing depression, the early 1930s are a tragic testimony to their importance in producing depression" (1968: 78–79). The government had acted "ineptly" in turning a garden-variety recession into the worst depression of the century.

One of the reasons for this ignorance about monetary policy is that the government did not publish money supply figures until Friedman and Schwartz developed the concepts of M1 and M2 in their book (1963). Friedman commented, "If the Federal Reserve System in 1929 to 1933 had been publishing statistics on the quantity of money, I don't believe that the Great Depression could have taken the course it did" (Friedman and Heller 1969: 80). See Figure 15.2 for the money supply figures during the 1929–32 crash. It speaks volumes.

Thus, Friedman concluded, "The fact is that the Great Depression, like most other periods of severe unemployment, was produced by government mismanagement rather than by any inherent instability of the private economy" (1982 [1962]: 38). Furthermore, he wrote: "Far from the depression being a failure of the free-enterprise system, it was a tragic failure of government" (1998: 233). From this time forward, thanks to the profound work of Friedman and Schwartz, the textbooks would gradually replace "market failure" with "government failure" in their sections on the Great Depression.

FRIEDMAN RAISES DOUBTS ABOUT THE MULTIPLIER

The Chicago economist continued his attack on Keynesianism in his 1962 book *Capitalism and Freedom*, where he questioned the effectiveness and stability of Keynesian countercyclical finance. He debunked the concept of the multiplier, calling it "spurious." "The simple Keynesian analysis

---

DID THE GOLD STANDARD CAUSE THE GREAT DEPRESSION?

Far from being synonymous with stability, the gold standard itself was the principal threat to financial stability and economic prosperity between the wars.
—Barry Eichengreen (1992: 4)

Friedman dispelled the widely held belief that the international gold standard was responsible for the depression. Critics of the gold standard pointed out that in a crucial time period, 1931–32, the Federal Reserve raised the discount rate for fear of a run on its gold deposits. If only the United States had not been shackled by a gold standard, they argued, the Federal Reserve could have avoided the reckless credit squeeze that pushed the country into depression and a banking crisis.

However, Friedman and Schwartz pointed out that the U.S. gold stock *rose* during the first two years of the contraction. But the Fed reacted ineptly. "We did not permit the inflow of gold to expand the U.S. money stock. We not only sterilized it, we went much further. Our money stock moved perversely, going down as the gold stock went up" (Friedman and Schwartz 1963: 360–61).

In short, even under the defective gold exchange standard, there may have been room to avoid a devastating worldwide depression and monetary crisis.

implicitly assumes that borrowing the money does not have any effects on other spending" (Friedman 1982 [1962]: 82). Inflation and crowding out of private investment are two possible effects of Keynesian deficit spending. Friedman also noted that the federal budget is the "most unstable component of national income in the postwar period." The Keynesian balance wheel is usually "unbalanced," and it has "continuously fostered an expansion in the range of government activities at the federal level and prevented a reduction in the burden of federal taxes" (pages 76–77).

FRIEDMAN ALSO RAISES DOUBTS ABOUT THE PHILLIPS CURVE

In his AEA presidential address, published in 1968, Friedman introduced the "natural rate of unemployment" concept to counter the Phillips curve. As noted in chapter 14, Keynesians quickly incorporated the Phillips curve to justify a liberal fiscal policy; to them, inflation could be tolerated if it meant lower unemployment. A "little inflation" could do no harm and considerable good.

Friedman objected, arguing that "there is always a temporary trade-off between inflation and unemployment; there is no permanent trade-off." Accordingly, any effort to push unemployment below the "natural rate of unemployment" must lead to an accelerating inflation. Moreover, "the only way in which you ever get a reduction in unemployment is through *unanticipated* inflation," which is unlikely. Friedman concluded that any acceleration of inflation would eventually bring about higher, not lower, unemployment. Thus, efforts to reduce unemployment by expansionary government policies could only backfire in the long run as the public anticipated its effect (Friedman 1969: 95–110).

By the late 1970s, Friedman was proved right. The Phillips curve became unrecognizable as inflation and unemployment started rising together, opposite to what had happened in Britain in the 1950s. In a famous statement, British prime minister James Callaghan confessed in 1977, "We used to think you could spend your way out of a recession. . . . I tell you, in all candor, that that option no longer exists; and that insofar as it ever did exist, it only worked by injecting bigger doses of inflation into the economy followed by higher levels of unemployment at the next step. That is the history of the past twenty years" (Skousen 1992: 12). In his Nobel lecture, Friedman warned that the Phillips curve had become positively inclined, with unemployment and inflation rising simultaneously.

Out of this Phillips curve controversy arose a whole new "rational expectations" school, led by Robert Lucas, Jr., who won the Nobel Prize in 1995. Rational expectations undermine the theory that policymakers can fool the public into false expectations about inflation. Accordingly, government policies are frequently ineffective in achieving their goals.

FRIEDMAN SEARCHES FOR AN IDEAL MONETARY STANDARD

Friedman came to the conclusion that once the monetary system is stabilized, Adam Smith's system of natural liberty can flourish. Contrary to Keynes's belief, Friedman faithfully maintained that the neoclassical model represents the "general" theory, and only a monetary disturbance by the government can derail a free-market economy. In short, according to Friedman, the business cycle is government—not market—induced, and monetary stability is an essential prerequisite for economic stability.

As Friedman recognized this principle in the early 1950s, he began writing about the ideal monetary standard. In his research, he was greatly influenced by Irving Fisher, his quantity theory of money, and his solution to the business cycle—a 100 percent reserve banking system. Henry Simons had picked up on Fisher's idea and promoted it at the University of Chicago.

But Friedman realized that Fisher (and Simons) had made a mistake in applying his quantity theory of money. Recall Fisher's equation of exchange, from chapter 11:

$$M \times V = P \times Q$$

where M = the quantity of money, V = velocity of circulation, P = price level, and Q = real output of goods and services.

As we emphasized in chapter 11, Fisher made the fatal error of focusing too much on the price level (P) and price stabilization in his forecasting model. Thus, he failed to anticipate the 1929–32 crisis. At Chicago, Simons made the same mistake. He established a price-index rule as the ideal monetary goal.

A "SUDDEN FLASH"

Friedman rightly changed the emphasis to monetary policy. M, the quantity of money, was more important than P. His "fresh and very different opinion" from Fisher and Simons, his monetary mentors, came like a "sudden flash," he reported. "A rule in terms of the quantity of money seems to me far superior, for both the short and the long-term, than a rule in terms of price-level stabilization" (Friedman 1969: 84). Mises had come to the same conclusion in 1912, when he wrote *The Theory of Money and Credit* (see chapter 12).

RULES VERSUS AUTHORITY

One principle Friedman learned from Simons was that strict monetary rules are preferable to discretionary decision making by government authorities. "Any system which gives so much power and so much discretion to a few men that mistakes—excusable or not—can have such

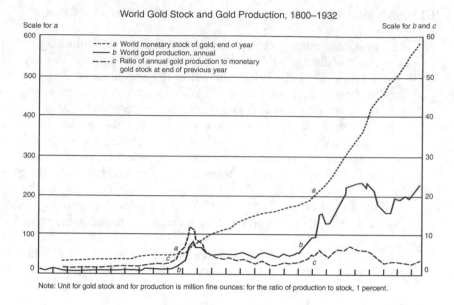

Figure 15.3
The Gradual Increase in Monetary Metal Under a Gold Standard, 1800–1932
Note that line a, representing the world gold stock, never declines.
Source: Tucker (1934: 12).

far-reaching effects is a bad system," he wrote (Friedman 1982: 50).

Friedman studied two monetary systems that offered rules instead of authorities: a gold standard and a fiat monetary rule standard.

FRIEDMAN CONTEMPLATES THE GOLD STANDARD

Could not a genuine gold standard provide the stable monetary framework Friedman desired? Since Adam Smith's time, gold and silver had been favored as the foundation of a sound monetary system. A full-fledged commodity standard, in which banknotes were backed 100 percent by gold or silver, was endorsed by such diverse individuals as Thomas Jefferson, David Ricardo, Francis A. Walker (first president of the AEA), and, more recently, Murray N. Rothbard.[5]

Gold offers a number of attractions. Because gold is so durable, the total amount of above-ground gold reserves tends to rise steadily (1–3 percent a year), thus providing a relatively stable monetary target (see Figure 15.3). The only exception is during gold rushes, but such inflations have been short lived. Neither severe deflation nor inflation is therefore likely under

5. For a complete history and theoretical development of the gold standard, see Skousen, *Economics of a Pure Gold Standard* (1996).

a pure gold standard. Gold provides a strict discipline on government finances and prohibits inflationary abuses. "A full-fledged gold standard in which all money consisted of gold or warehouse receipts for gold except perhaps for a fixed fiduciary issue would have the great merits of complete automaticity and freedom from governmental control," wrote Friedman in *A Program for Monetary Stability* (1959: 119).

A 100 percent gold standard would also have avoided the "inherently unstable" nature of today's fractional-reserve banking system. Friedman agreed with his teacher Henry Simons, who stated, "There is likely to be extreme economic instability under any financial system where *the same funds* are made to serve as *investment funds for industry and trade* and as *the liquid cash reserves of individuals*" (Simons 1948: 55, emphasis added).

Historically, Friedman wrote favorably about the classical gold standard which lasted until 1914, the outbreak of World War I: "The blind, unde-signed, and quasi-automatic working of the gold standard turned out to produce a greater measure of predictability and regularity—perhaps because its discipline was impersonal and inescapable—than did deliberate and conscious control exercised within institutional arrangements intended to promote stability" (Friedman and Schwartz 1963: 10).

FRIEDMAN ULTIMATELY REJECTS THE GOLD STANDARD

Like Irving Fisher and Henry Simons, Friedman ultimately abandoned gold as a monetary numeraire. He objected on two grounds, its high resource cost and its impractical implementation. Friedman expressed almost universal concerns when he noted the high level of resources—per-haps as much as 4 percent of annual GDP—required to produce a monetary metal. Economists from Adam Smith to Paul Samuelson worried about "squandering" valuable land, labor, and capital to produce the "barbarous relic" (Keynes's term) when paper money could "involve a negligible use of real resources to produce the medium of exchange" (Friedman 1960: 5–7).

Paul Samuelson went further by declaring, in a famous passage in the eighth edition of his textbook, "How absurd to waste resources digging gold out of the bowels of the earth, only to inter it back again in the vaults of Fort Knox, Kentucky!" (Samuelson 1970: 700).

The high-cost-of-resources argument was accepted as orthodoxy until Auburn economist Roger W. Garrison challenged it. In an insightful article, Garrison noted that with or without the gold standard, the resource costs of gold production are "unavoidable." Even after the world went off the gold standard in 1971, "gold continues to be mined, refined, cast or minted, stored, and guarded; the resource costs continue to be incurred." Moreover, he reasoned, more resources may be applied if government inflates the money supply irresponsibly, causing investors to hoard an inordinate number of coins and bullion (Rockwell 1985: 70).

METHODOLOGICAL MADNESS, PART II

> *To be important, therefore, a hypothesis must be*
> *descriptively false in its assumptions.*
> —Milton Friedman (1953: 14)

Chapter 12 describes Ludwig von Mises's "cranky" methodology, wherein he dismissed the use of history, mathematics, graphs, or any other technique outside pure deductive reasoning.

Mises's unorthodox philosophy is outlined in his 1949 book *Human Action*. Four years later, Milton Friedman came out with an article entitled "The Methodology of Positive Economics" that has become equally controversial (1953: 3–43). Adding to the fire of controversy is the fact that Friedman has refused to comment on his article or respond to critics; he said something about wanting to "do economics" rather than "writing about how economics should be done" (Friedman and Friedman 1998: 215).

Basically, Friedman argued that an economic model should be judged solely on its predictive power, "the only relevant test," not the realism of its assumptions. But he went even further, declaring that "in general, the more significant a theory, the more unrealistic the assumptions." A theory with "realistic" assumptions will undoubtedly be "useless," Friedman insisted. The assumptions can even be "false" if the theory "yields sufficiently accurate predictions" (1953: 14–15). Finally, Friedman borrowed Karl Popper's falsification theorem which holds that you can never demonstrate that anything is materially true, only that a theory can be proved false through empirical observation.

Friedman used this approach to analyze Keynes's model. He found beauty in Keynes's simplistic assumptions, but ultimately rejected the model "because I believe that it has been contradicted by the experience" (1986: 48).

WHAT ABOUT FRIEDMAN'S OWN PREDICTIONS?

The Chicago economist had to reexamine his own monetary theories as a result of predictions gone awry, such as his forecasts of higher inflation in the 1980s.

False and misleading assumptions can lead to trouble in economics. For example, computer-generated econometric models have been developed to forecast stock, bond, and option trends based entirely on historical patterns. These financial models, known as technical analysis, often ignore fundamentals and focus strictly on "what works," that is, what has worked in the past. Typically, these models worked for a while, sometimes for several years, but then collapsed when the underlining fundamentals "unexpectedly" took over. This is in essence what happened to Long Term Capital Management, which, as mentioned previously, lost $4 billion in 1998. In sum, one must be suspicious of any heuristic theory that ignores fundamental economic behavior.

Although Friedman later accepted Garrison's deft observation, he has rejected the gold standard on practical grounds. For one thing, Friedman determined that gold production can seldom keep up with economic growth and would therefore be somewhat deflationary.

INTRODUCING THE MONETARIST RULE

Friedman decided that a better approach would be to adopt a strict fiat money standard, a monetary system based on irredeemable paper money that would include a 100 percent reserve requirement on demand deposits (checking accounts) at banks, and then to adopt a legislative rule which would require the money supply to increase at a steady rate approximately equal to a nation's economic growth rate. Friedman suggests a monetary target of between 3–5 percent. The monetary rule would be so simple to implement that a computer could replace the Federal Reserve.

Of course, one of the major problems facing the monetarist rule is to determine what constitutes the "money supply." Should it be a narrowly defined money supply such as M1 (currency and checking accounts) or a broader M2 (M1 plus money market deposits), or something even broader? Generally, Friedman favored a broader, M2 type of definition.

Although Friedman's influence has been widespread, no nation has yet adopted his 100 percent bank reserve policy or monetary rule. Political and economic leaders are fearful of a laissez-faire policy in this vital area. They do not like the idea of having their hands tied to a blind computer when a monetary or financial crisis hits.

Nevertheless, it is worth noting that the major central banks in the G7 countries have gradually reduced the level and volatility of their monetary policies over the years. In the 1970s, M2 used to grow at double-digit rates; by the late 1990s M2 was growing at single-digit rates. Perhaps as a result of increasing pressure from the financial markets, monetary leaders are quietly following Friedman's monetary rule after all. Federal Reserve chairman Ben Bernanke said, "Friedman's monetary framework has been so influential that, in its broad outlines, it has nearly become identical with modern monetary theory and practice" (Ebenstein 2007: 238). It should be noted, however, that in the final years, Friedman expressed surprise at and approval of the "activist" policies of the Federal Reserve to regulate the business cycle, expressing tentative approval of "inflation targeting"—seeking stable aggregate prices—as a long-term monetary goal instead of his traditional targeting of the money supply (Ebenstein 2007: 232).

The world has yet to adopt an ideal monetary standard as envisioned by Friedman and the anti-inflation monetarists and therefore is still vulnerable to potential financial or economic instability. This is one area where reality has not lived up to the rhetoric and undoubtedly will threaten global markets in the future. It could be the global economy's Achilles' heel.

FRIEDMAN TRANSFORMS THE INTELLECTUAL CLIMATE

Let us review this tour de force of the postwar era, this man who disengaged one of the most powerful engines in intellectual history. Friedman brilliantly dismantled the "house that Keynes built" and led economists back to the foundations of Adam Smith. Friedman ultimately achieved his goal of reestablishing the rationale behind Adam Smith's system of natural liberty. Shorn of government mismanagement, capitalism is not inherently unstable or irrational after all. As Friedman himself declared after he wrote *A Monetary History*, "It is now widely agreed that the Keynesian proposition is erroneous on the level of pure theory. . . . [T]here always exists in principle a position of full employment equilibrium in a free market economy" (Friedman and Meiselman 1963: 167).

Friedman's monetarist counterrevolution has been so effective that Axel Leijonhufvud recently admitted, "Many prominent economists at present consider Keynes's work so deeply flawed, riddled with error, even, that it need no longer be studied. . . . For the younger generation of macroeconomists nowadays, *not* understanding Keynes seems a necessary, if not sufficient, condition for professional advancement" (1999: 16, 30). Indeed, the current opinion is that pure Keynesian macroeconomics, rather than a "permanent" revolution, was an unfortunate interlude, or as Leland Yeager put it, a temporary "diversion" from the neoclassical model (Yeager 1973).

Milton Friedman's counterrevolution would not be complete, however, without the help of another revolutionary development in the late 1980s and early 1990s—the tearing down of the Berlin Wall and the collapse of the Soviet-style system of socialist central planning. These events and their impact on the intellectual climate are the subject of chapter 16.

REFERENCES

Bangs, Robert. 1947. "Review of 'Roofs or Ceilings?' " *American Economic Review* 57: 2 (June), 482–83.

Blaug, Mark. 1985. *Great Economists Since Keynes.* Cambridge: Cambridge University Press.

Breit, William, and Roger W. Spencer, eds. 1986. *Lives of the Laureates: Seven Nobel Economists.* Cambridge, MA: MIT Press.

Davis, J. Ronnie. 1968. "Chicago Economists, Deficit Budgets, and the Early 1930's." *American Economic Review* 58 (June), 476–82.

Eichengreen, Barry. 1992. *Golden Fetters: The Gold Standard and the Great Depression.* New York: Oxford University Press.

Ebenstein, Lanny. 2007. *Milton Friedman.* New York: Palgrave Macmillan.

Fant, Kenne. 1993. *Alfred Nobel: A Biography.* New York: Arcade.

Friedman, Milton. 1953. *Essays in Positive Economics.* Chicago: University of Chicago Press.

———. 1957. *A Theory of the Consumption Function.* Princeton: Princeton University Press.

———. 1960. *A Program for Monetary Stability.* New York: Fordham University Press.

————. 1968. *Dollars and Deficits.* New York: Prentice-Hall.

————. 1969. *The Optimum Quantity of Money and Other Essays.* London: Macmillan.

————. 1982a [1962]. *Capitalism and Freedom.* Chicago: University of Chicago Press.

————. 1982b. "Supply-Side Policies: Where Do We Go from Here?" In *Supply-Side Economics in the 1980s,* 53–63. Atlanta: Federal Reserve Bank of Atlanta.

————. 1986. "Keynes's Political Legacy." In *Keynes's General Theory: Fifty Years On,* ed. John Burton. London: Institute of Economic Affairs.

————. 1995. "Best of Both Worlds," Interview by Brian Doherty. *Reason* (June), 32–38.

Friedman, Milton, and David Meiselman. 1963. "The Relative Stability of Monetary Velocity and the Investment Multiplier in the United States, 1897–1958." In Commission on Money and Credit, *Stabilization Policies,* 165–268. Englewood Cliffs, NJ: Prentice-Hall.

Friedman, Milton, and George J. Stigler. 1946. "Roofs or Ceilings? The Current Housing Problem." New York: Foundation for Economic Education.

Friedman, Milton, and Walter W. Heller. 1969. *Monetary vs. Fiscal Policy.* New York: W.W. Norton.

Friedman, Milton, and Rose Friedman. 1980. *Free to Choose.* New York: Harcourt Brace Jovanovich.

————. 1998. *Two Lucky People: A Memoir.* Chicago: University of Chicago Press.

Friedman, Milton, and Anna J. Schwartz. 1963. *A Monetary History of the United States, 1867–1960.* Princeton: Princeton University Press and NBER.

Gordon, Robert J. 1974. *Milton Friedman's Monetary Framework.* Chicago: University of Chicago Press.

Hazlitt, Henry. 1973 [1959]. *The Failure of the "New Economics."* New York: Arlington House.

Hayek, Friedrich. 1979. *A Tiger by the Tail: The Keynesian Legacy of Inflation.* Washington, DC: Cato Institute.

Hutt, William H. 1977 [1939]. *The Theory of Idle Resources,* 2d ed. Indianapolis, IN: Liberty.

————. 1963. *Keynesianism—Retrospect and Prospect.* Chicago: Regnery.

————. 1979. *The Keynesian Episode: A Reassessment.* Indianapolis, IN: Liberty.

Lerner, Abba P. 1960. "Review of Hazlitt's *Failure of the 'New Economics.'*" *Review of Economics and Statistics* 42, 234–35.

Leijonhufvud, Axel. 1999. "Mr. Keynes and the Moderns." In *The Impact of Keynes on Economics in the 20th Century,* ed. Luigi L. Pasinetti and Betram Schefold. Cheltenham, UK: Edward Elgar.

Mises, Ludwig von. 1966. *Human Action,* 3d ed. Chicago: Regnery.

Pearlstine, Norman. 1998. "Big Wheels Turning." *Time* (December 7), 70–73.

Rand, Ayn. 1995. *Letters of Ayn Rand,* ed. Michael S. Berliner. New York: Dutton.

Rockwell, Llewellyn J., Jr., ed. 1985. *The Gold Standard: An Austrian Perspective.* Lexington, MA: Lexington.

Rothbard, Murray N. 1960. "Review of Hazlitt's *Critics of Keynesian Economics.*" *National Review* (December 3), 150–51.

————. 1962. *Man, Economy and State.* Princeton, NJ: Van Nostrand.

————. 1983 [1963]. *America's Great Depression,* 4th ed. New York: Richardson and Snyder.

————. 1995. *Economic Thought Before Adam Smith.* Hants, UK: Edward Elgar.

Samuelson, Paul A. 1955. *Economics,* 3d ed. New York: McGraw-Hill.

————. 1970. *Economics,* 8th ed. New York: McGraw-Hill.

————. 1973. *Economics,* 9th ed. New York: McGraw-Hill.

————. 1977. *The Collected Scientific Papers of Paul A. Samuelson,* vol. 4. Cambridge, MA: MIT Press.

Samuelson, Paul A., and William Nordhaus. 1998. *Economics,* 16th ed. New York: McGraw-Hill.

Shils, Edward, ed. 1991. *Remembering the University of Chicago*. Chicago: University of Chicago Press.

Simons, Henry C. 1948. *Economic Policy for a Free Society*. Chicago: University of Chicago Press.

Skousen, Mark 1996. *Economics of a Pure Gold Standard*, 3d ed. New York: Foundation for Economic Education.

Skousen, Mark, ed. 1992. *Dissent on Keynes*. New York: Praeger.

Sobel, Robert. 1980. *The Worldly Economists*. New York: Free Press.

Sowell, Thomas. 2000. *A Personal Odyssey*. New York: Free Press.

Tobin, James. 1965. "The Monetary Interpretation of History: A Review Article." *American Economic Review* 55 (June), 466–85.

Tucker, Refus. 1934. "Gold and the General Price Level." *Review of Economic Statistics* 16 (January 15), 8–16; (February 15), 25–27.

Yeager, Leland. 1973. "The Keynesian Diversion." *Western Economic Journal* 11 (June), 150–63.

16

THE CREATIVE DESTRUCTION OF SOCIALISM: THE DARK VISION OF JOSEPH SCHUMPETER

Can capitalism survive? No. I do not think it can. . . .
Can socialism work? Of course it can.

—Joseph Schumpeter (1950: 61, 167)

Was Schumpeter right? No, I do not think he was.

—Robert Heilbroner (1981: 456)

The Herculean efforts of Milton Friedman, Friedrich Hayek, and other libertarian economists are not the only reason neoclassical economics has made a stupendous comeback. The other major reason is the collapse of Soviet communism and the socialist central planning model in the early 1990s. Since then, globalization has opened the floodgates to freer economic policies, especially within developing countries. Nations that for decades engaged in systematic policies of nationalization, protectionism, import substitution, foreign exchange controls, and corporate cronyism have opened their borders to foreign investment, denationalization and privatization, deregulation, and other market policies. Even the World Bank, once a severe critic of the capitalist model, has shifted dramatically in favor of market solutions to underdevelopment problems.

♪ **Music selection for this chapter: Ludwig van Beethoven, Symphony No. 7**

The Century-Old Debate over Socialist Central Planning

But it wasn't always that way. In fact, during most of the twentieth century, heavy-handed central planning was considered more efficient and more productive than laissez-faire capitalism.

Ludwig von Mises was the first to question this collectivist zeitgeist with a critique of socialism on purely economic grounds in a 1920 article, "Economic Calculation in the Socialist Commonwealth." He wrote on this subject in response to socialists' hailing the creation of a real-world communist state in Russia following the 1917 revolution, and Italian Enrico Barone's 1908 mathematical formulation of socialist production (Hayek 1935: 245–90). Despite Barone's formal model, Mises demonstrated that a central authority operating within a full-blown socialist state without private property, exchange, and competition could not rationally calculate prices and costs, and therefore could not build an efficient, productive economy. He used the example of building a railroad. "Should it be built at all, and if so, which out of a number of conceivable roads should be built? In a competitive and monetary economy, this question would be answered by monetary calculation." But under a socialist regime? "There is only groping in the dark. Socialism is the abolition of rational economy," he concluded (Mises 1990 [1920]: 24, 26). Mises predicted shortages, lack of innovation and incentives, malinvestment, and underinvestment under pure socialism in the Soviet Union or wherever it was tried.

At the depths of the 1930s Great Depression, when intellectuals were especially attracted to central planning, Friedrich Hayek had Mises's essay translated into English and published along with several other articles in a volume entitled *Collectivist Economic Planning* (Hayek 1935). In later articles and books, Hayek contended that competitive prices provide critical information necessary for a well-run coordinated economy between producers and consumers. Vital information is inherently local in nature, Hayek noted, and if channeled through a central planning board, actions determined by the state will distort the signals necessary to run an economy efficiently. For a central authority to "assume all the knowledge . . . is . . . to disregard everything that is important and significant in the real world" (Hayek 1984: 223). In sum, decision making must be decentralized.

"Market Socialism" Wins the Day

The socialists counterattacked with an argument of their own, known as "market socialism." Oskar Lange, a Polish socialist, and Fred M. Taylor, president of the American Economic Association (AEA), contended that central planning boards could determine prices through "trial and error." A price could be set to determine the supply and demand of each product. If shortages occurred, the price could be raised; if surpluses abounded, the

Photograph 16.1
Oskar Lange (1904–65)
"Market" socialist:
"Set prices randomly."
Courtesy of Mark Blaug.

price could be lowered. Lange even suggested that the central planning board could "randomly" set prices and the resulting shortages or surpluses would determine the board's response (Lange and Taylor 1938: 70).

Surprisingly, most economists convinced themselves that this "trial-and-error" approach, as used by the market socialists, could work. As Jan Drewnowski wrote, "Mises, as everybody agrees now, was wrong in his main contention that economic calculation under socialism is theoretically impossible" (Lavoie 1985: 4). Even Joseph Schumpeter, one of Mises's most illustrious classmates, rejected Mises's thesis. He wrote, "Can socialism work? Of course it can," adding, "The capitalist order tends to destroy itself and centralist socialism is . . . a likely heir apparent" (Schumpeter 1950: 167).

THE ALLEGED SOVIET ECONOMIC MIRACLE

Another major factor in converting intellectuals to socialism was the apparent economic success story of the Soviet Union. Journalists returned from tours of Russia exclaiming, "I have been to the future, and it works" (Malia 1999: 340). In 1936, Sidney and Beatrice Webb came back with glowing reports of a "new civilization" and the "re-making of man," a vibrant nation with full employment, good working conditions, free education, free medical services, child care and maternity benefits, and the widespread availability of museums, theaters, and concert halls. Even John Maynard Keynes, who despised Marxism, found the Webbs' report "impressive." Convinced that Soviet leaders had shed Marxism, Keynes expressed optimism about his own country in a British Broadcasting Corporation (BBC) address in 1936: "It leaves me with a strong desire and hope that we in this country may discover how to combine an unlimited readiness to experiment with changes in political and economic methods and institutions, while preserving traditionalism and a sort of careful conservatism" (1982: 333–34).

Indeed, after World War II, European and Latin American countries began experimenting with socialism on a gigantic scale, nationalizing industry after industry, raising taxes, imposing wage-price controls, inflating the money supply, creating national welfare programs, and engaging in all kinds of collectivist mischief.

Economists were convinced by data from the Central Intelligence Agency (CIA) that Soviet-style socialist central planning had produced high levels of economic growth, even faster than that experienced by market economies in the West. Paul Samuelson was one who became convinced of Soviet economic superiority. By the fifth edition, Samuelson's *Economics* began including a graph indicating that the gap between the United States and the USSR was narrowing and possibly even disappearing (1961: 830). In the twelfth edition, the graph was replaced with a table declaring that, between 1928 and 1983, the Soviet Union had grown at a remarkable 4.9 percent annual growth rate, higher than that of the United States, the United Kingdom, or even Germany and Japan (1985: 776). Ironically, in the thirteenth edition, published right before the Berlin Wall was torn down, Samuelson and Nordhaus confidently declared, "The Soviet economy is proof that, contrary to what many skeptics had earlier believed [a reference to Mises and Hayek], a socialist command economy can function and even thrive" (1989: 837).

Samuelson was not alone in this optimism about Soviet socialism. In their popular textbook, Richard G. Lipsey and Peter O. Steiner boldly claimed, in 1987, "The Soviet citizens' standard of living is so much higher than it was even a decade ago, and is rising so rapidly, that it probably seems comfortable to them" (see Skousen 1997: 148). Robert Heilbroner and Lester Thurow made similar statements: "Can economic command significantly impress and accelerate the growth process? The remarkable performance of the Soviet Union suggests that it can. In 1920 Russia was but a minor figure in the economic councils of the world. Today it is a country whose economic achievements bear comparison with those of the United States" (1984: 629).

FREEDOM COMES AT A COST?

Even conservative economist Henry C. Wallich, a Yale economist and former member of the Federal Reserve Board, was so convinced by CIA statistics that he wrote a whole book arguing that freedom leads to lower economic growth, greater income inequality, and less competition. In *The Cost of Freedom*, he concluded, "The ultimate value of a free economy is not production, but freedom, and freedom comes not as a profit, but at a cost" (1960: 146).

SCHUMPETER: *ENFANT TERRIBLE* OF THE AUSTRIAN SCHOOL

There is no better example of the confusing nature of the capitalist-socialist debate in the first half of the twentieth century than Joseph Schumpeter, the eminent Harvard economist and *enfant terrible* of the Austrian school.

Today, Schumpeter is highly regarded for his introduction of a dynamic-process theory of competition, the central role of the entrepreneur, and his rejection of static "perfect competition" modeling (1950: 81–86). In a 1986 article, "Modern Prophets: Schumpeter or Keynes?" management guru Peter F. Drucker preferred Schumpeter, predicting that of "these two greatest economists of this century . . . it is Schumpeter who will shape the thinking . . . on economic theory and economic policy for the rest of this century, if not for the next thirty or fifty years" (Drucker 1986: 104). And Galbraith ranked Schumpeter "the most sophisticated conservative of this century" (Swedberg 1991: 150).

Notwithstanding these accolades, Schumpeter was the most bizarre character in economics history, even more colorful than Veblen or Marx. Beyond his eccentric personality, Schumpeter's economics were even more unpredictable. He defended socialist economics, predicted the demise of capitalism, and named Léon Walras, the father of the static general equilibrium model, the "greatest of all economists" (Schumpeter 1954: 827).

Let us review his strange story.

An Enigmatic Life

Photograph 16.2
Joseph A. Schumpeter (1883–1950)
"Light-hearted, snobbish,
and a virtuoso at playing
any political game."
Courtesy of
Harvard University Archives.

Joseph A. Schumpeter (1883–1950), born in Moravia in the Austro-Hungarian empire, had much in common with his chief lifelong rival, John Maynard Keynes. Both were born in 1883, the year Karl Marx died. A mystic might suggest that Marx was reincarnated as two powerful and creative figures--Keynes and Schumpeter.

As was true of Keynes, the most important person in Schumpeter's life was his mother. His father died when he was only four, and his stepfather was a stern aristocrat who moved the family to Vienna, where he graduated from gymnasium (high school) and entered the University of Vienna Law School in 1901. His interests gravitated toward economics, and he studied under Friedrich Wieser and Eugen Böhm-Bawerk. After graduation in 1906, he wrote his first book, *Theory of Economic Development* (1934 [1912]), which was published in the same year as Mises's *Theory of Money and Credit* (1912). The whole work is Austrian in tone, emphasizing the dynamic role of the entrepreneur in economic progress. But Schumpeter was an *enfant terrible* of the Austrian school, always eclectic and willing to alter his political opinions to suit his political and financial ambitions. Schumpeter was arrogant and snobbish, yet he left no definitive school.

SCHUMPETER FLIRTS WITH SOCIALISM

After World War I and the rise of Soviet communism, Austria was controlled by socialists. (Recall the story of Red Vienna in chapter 12.) Schumpeter flirted with Marxism, proclaiming Marx "a great genius," and in 1919 convinced the minister of foreign affairs to have him appointed finance minister, thus following in the footsteps of his teacher, Eugen Böhm-Bawerk. Immediately upon his appointment, Schumpeter began living an extravagant lifestyle, renting a castle and acquiring a stable of riding horses. Asked about his high living, he responded with disdain, "*Krone ist Krone*," meaning "a crown is a crown." Ordinary Austrians, who were suffering starvation and poverty, were not amused (Swedberg 1991: 63).

SCHUMPETER'S OUTRAGEOUS BEHAVIOR

Not surprisingly, Schumpeter lasted only a year as a public official. Then, with "former finance minister" on his résumé, he arranged to become chairman of the board of a new bank. Earning a huge salary with sizable overdraft privileges, Schumpeter resumed his former extravagant lifestyle, including an outlandish love life. When told to be more discreet, he "rented a pair-drawn open *Fiaker* [carriage] and rode up and down Kartnerstrasse—a main boulevard in the inner city—at midday with an attractive blond prostitute on one knee and a brunette on the other" (Swedberg 1991: 68).

In 1924, a severe economic crisis hit Austria, the bank was forced to restructure, and Schumpeter found himself suddenly facing a mountain of debts and back taxes without a job. A year later, however, his luck changed when he was offered the chair of public finance at the University of Bonn.

A STRANGE SERIES OF MARRIAGES—AND DEATHS!

Schumpeter's love life was bizarre, to say the least. In 1906, while visiting London, he suddenly married a British woman twelve years his senior. He abandoned her when he returned to the continent to teach at Bonn and never officially divorced her. After a series of extramarital affairs, Schumpeter, then thirty-two, set his heart on a twelve-year-old (!) named Annie Reisinger. He made arrangements for her to receive an education and to marry him when she came of age. In November 1925, the twenty-two-year-old Annie and the forty-two-year-old Joseph were married in a Lutheran church (even though he was Catholic).

But the soap opera was never ending for Schumpeter. A year into the marriage, the first woman in his life—his mother—died. At the same time, Annie was experiencing a difficult pregnancy, which was aggravated by his first wife's threats to sue Schumpeter for bigamy. In August 1926, a month after his mother died, Annie suddenly died in childbirth.

Schumpeter was so affected by these tragic events that for years he would not change anything in Annie's bedroom, and did not even remove her clothes from the room. Every morning he placed a rose on Annie's grave. Perversely, he began a daily ritual of meticulously copying passages from Annie's diary, imitating her handwriting and faulty punctuation. When he had copied the whole diary, he started over. Influenced subconsciously by his Catholic upbringing, he started praying to both his deceased wife and his mother. "Whenever he was about to do something difficult, he asked for their support; and when something had gone well, he thanked them profusely" (Swedberg 1991: 74–75). Schumpeter sometimes wrote "Hasen sei Dank" (the Hasen be thanked). (Hasen, literally a rabbit, denotes a person who is deeply loved.)

A CALL FROM HARVARD

Given Schumpeter's odd personal behavior, one wonders how Schumpeter managed to achieve such high acclaim in the economics profession. Apparently, he was highly respected for his earlier work on economic development. In 1932, Frank Taussig, the grand old man of economics at Harvard, offered him a position at Harvard University. Desiring a radical change in his life, Schumpeter left Germany, never to return to Europe. He left behind twenty-eight trunks of belongings, including his papers and manuscripts. He didn't even take a copy of his first book.

Schumpeter moved into Taussig's home and stayed there for five years. Taussig became the father Schumpeter never had. To avoid thinking about his past family tragedies, Schumpeter worked ruthlessly all the time— nights, days, even weekends—and graded himself in his private diary. He suffered depression and various illnesses.

In 1935, Schumpeter paid off all his debts and took over Taussig's popular graduate course in economics when Taussig retired at age seventy-five. Taussig's teaching method was Socratic: After introducing a problem, he would patiently guide students toward a solution without providing the answer. Schumpeter's style of teaching was more international—he broadened the scope beyond the British economists and introduced students to a variety of continental and American theorists. Though Schumpeter, with his thick Viennese accent, was sometimes difficult to understand, he impressed Paul Samuelson:

> After, and not before, the students had assembled for the class hour, in would walk Schumpeter, remove hat, gloves, and topcoat with sweeping gestures, and begin the day's business. Clothes were important to him: he wore a variety of well-tailored tweeds with carefully matched shirt, tie, hose, and handkerchief. (Harris 1951: 50–51)

Known informally by the students as "Schumpy," Schumpeter was friendly, especially with graduate students, who could meet with him regularly at the local coffee shop. Like Mises, he was an easy grader. The joke was that he gave A's to only three categories of students: all the Jesuits, all the women, and all the rest (Swedberg 1991: 114).

ANTI-KEYNES

When Harvard became the center of Keynesian economics, the jealous Schumpeter was appalled by Keynes's success. He wrote an extremely negative review of Keynes's *General Theory,* and when Keynes died in 1946, Schumpeter's memorial in the *American Economic Review* was filled with acid comments (Schumpeter 1946). "We all like a sparkling error better than a trivial truth," he wrote in his diary. Schumpeter, like Mises and Hayek, always maintained that the depression must run its course and not be interfered with through deficit spending or reinflation.

Perhaps Schumpeter's hostility was founded on professional jealousy. Keynes upstaged Schumpeter, whose own massive study, *Business Cycles* (1939), had been given a poor review by Simon Kuznets. Schumpeter always had a high opinion of himself, but recognition for his two classics, *Capitalism, Socialism and Democracy* (1950 [1942]) and *History of Economic Analysis* (1954) would not be established until long after his death.[1]

ANTI-ROOSEVELT

During the war years, Schumpeter seemed to become more eccentric, more imbalanced, and more isolated. He continued to direct monologues to his deceased wife and mother. His diary was full of references to death and included occasional outbursts against "niggers, Jews and subnormals." One statement declared: "Just as the nigger dance is the dance of today, so is Keynesian economics the economics of today." At a cocktail party in 1944, when Roosevelt was running for his fourth term as president, a woman approached Schumpeter and asked whether he would vote for Roosevelt. Schumpeter replied acidly, "My dear lady, if Hitler runs for President and Stalin for Vice President, I shall be happy to vote for that ticket against Roosevelt" (Swedberg 1991: 141). He thought that Hitler would win the war.

His reactionary behavior remained unsubdued by another marriage, this one to Elizabeth Boody in 1937. His new wife herself was accused of being violently anti-Roosevelt and pro-Japanese, but she would be instrumental in completing his "never-ending" history of economics.

SCHUMPETER WRITES AN INTERNATIONAL BESTSELLER

During his isolated, depressed state in the 1940s, Schumpeter published his most famous work, *Capitalism, Socialism and Democracy* (1942), which

---

1. Schumpeter was heard to say that he had three goals in life—to become the world's greatest lover, the world's greatest horseman, and the world's greatest economist. He noted wryly that he had achieved only two out of the three.

he revised twice in his lifetime. The book went on to become an international bestseller and has been translated into sixteen languages, including Persian, Korean, and Hindi. It goes far beyond economics into political science and sociology, and has had widespread application to other social science disciplines.

THE DYNAMICS OF "CREATIVE DESTRUCTION"

Capitalism, Socialism, and Democracy, a 431-page book, is tortuous reading as a whole, yet it is sprinkled with genuine gems and powerful paragraphs. Schumpeter wrote eloquently about the dynamics of market capitalism and how the disruptive forces of technology undermined equilibrium conditions. Sometimes his phrasing, such as "creative destruction," sounds like a Marxist interpretation of history. Borrowing from his Viennese teacher Friedrich von Wieser, he saw the entrepreneur as the central catalyst in what Schumpeter called the "creative destruction" of the market system. Capitalism "never can be stationary." The industrial process "incessantly revolutionizes the economic structure *from within*, incessantly destroying the old one, incessantly creating a new one" (Schumpeter 1950: 82–83).

Schumpeter was not alarmed by the growth of big firms such as Ford, Standard Oil, or International Business Machines, corporations that monopolized an industry. In fact, he welcomed it. Monopolistic firms in their embryonic growth stages are highly innovative and require enormous risk capital, Schumpeter observed. They also attract strong competition, so that a generation later, new upstarts replace the old monopolies. Schumpeter would not be surprised to see Microsoft overtake IBM, or Toyota surge ahead of Ford. He rejected out of hand the Chamberlin-Robinson "perfect competition" model as any kind of ideal. In Schumpeter's mind, competition is a process, not a state—a process constantly reinventing itself, not a point of static equilibrium. He concluded, "Now a theoretical construction which neglects this essential element of the case . . . is like *Hamlet* without the Danish prince" (1950: 86).

SCHUMPETER TURNS PREMATURELY PESSIMISTIC

Like Mises and Weber, Schumpeter was deeply fatalistic about the future of capitalism and socialism. In *Capitalism, Socialism, and Democracy*, he had written the section, "Can Capitalism Survive?" in 1935 during the depths of the depression, but his gloomy outlook on capitalism was not due to capitalism's failures (he rejected outright Hansen's "secular stagnation" theory of vanishing investment opportunities) but to its successes (Schumpeter 1950: 61–163). He believed that an advancing capitalist system would inevitably undermine itself as bureaucratic managers replaced innovative entrepreneurs, and prosperity would create an attitude of anticapitalist hostility in bourgeois society.

Moreover, Schumpeter bought the idea that "there is a strong case for believing in its [socialism's] economic efficiency" over capitalism. Rejecting Mises's rationale that socialism could not efficiently allocate resources, Schumpeter argued that a well-run socialist democracy could eliminate business cycles, unemployment, and inflation. He might not like it, but it was inevitable. He played the role of the devil's advocate so well in *Capitalism, Socialism and Democracy* that some accused him of being a socialist. But he denied it.

"I do not advocate socialism," Schumpeter declared in the last week of December 1949, before the annual AEA meeting. He was delivering his presidential address on "The March into Socialism," which would turn out to be his final speech. Nevertheless, "the capitalist order tends to destroy itself and the centralist socialism is . . . a likely heir apparent." Modern society desired "security, equality, and regulation"—economic engineering, not entrepreneurship (Schumpeter 1950: 416–18).

No doubt Schumpeter rightly recognized powerful forces of a benefit-corrupted society that would increasingly favor the stability of a welfare state, but he also grossly underestimated the entrepreneurial spirit in the postwar era. Today, global capitalism is more vibrant than ever before, and socialism is often on the defensive.

SCHUMPETER MAKES ONE FINAL CONTRIBUTION

Schumpeter's last work was published after his untimely death in 1950 at the age of sixty-seven. For nearly a decade, he had been working on his heavy tome, *History of Economic Analysis*. He fretted constantly over the "blasted History," a never-ending project which he never completed. After his death, his widow, Elizabeth, found various parts of the manuscript scattered around his home and office. With the help of Wassily Leontief, Paul Sweezy, and other friends, she painstakingly worked at editing and typing the manuscript for several years. Eventually, she had to sell the house to complete the work. It was so exhausting that Elizabeth died before the book could be published. Finally, it was published by Oxford University Press in 1954, a mammoth 1,260 pages. Today it is considered the definitive history of economic thought.

THE END OF THE DEBATE: "MISES WAS RIGHT!"

The collapse of the Soviet Union and Eastern bloc communism virtually ended the century-old debate over comparative economic systems. Schumpeter turned out to have been prematurely pessimistic about the future of capitalism and wildly optimistic about the capabilities of socialism.

One of Schumpeter's students at Harvard, Robert Heilbroner, became a socialist and toyed with Marxism in his early years. He would later write

The Worldly Philosophers (1999 [1953]), the most popular history of economics ever written. Under the influence of Schumpeter and Adolph Lowe, among others, Heilbroner joined the rest of the profession and concluded that Mises was wrong and that socialism could work. He maintained that position for decades, as noted earlier.

In the late 1980s, shortly before the collapse of the Berlin Wall and the fall of the Soviet Union, Heilbroner began to reconsider his views. In a stunning article in the *New Yorker* entitled "The Triumph of Capitalism," Heilbroner wrote that the longstanding debate between capitalism and socialism was over and capitalism had won. He went on to say, "The Soviet Union, China, and Eastern Europe have given us the clearest possible proof that capitalism organizes the material affairs of humankind more satisfactorily than socialism: that however inequitably or irresponsibly the marketplace may distribute goods, it does so better than the queues of a planned economy; however mindless the culture of commercialism, it is more attractive than state moralism; and however deceptive the ideology of a business civilization, it is more believable than that of a socialist one" (Heilbroner 1989: 98).

In a follow-up article after the demise of the Eastern bloc, he was even more explicit: "Socialism has been a great tragedy this century. . . . There is no doubt that the collapse marks its end as a model of economic clarity." Furthermore, the debate between Lange and Mises had to be reexamined in light of contemporary events. "It turns out, of course, that Mises was right," declared Heilbroner (1990: 91–92). These articles did not endear Heilbroner to his socialist colleagues, as evidenced by the reaction in *Dissent* and other socialist publications, but Heilbroner's change of heart signaled a paradigm shift.

NEW EMPIRICAL WORK CONFIRMS MISES'S THESIS

The fall of the Soviet Union brought about a major revision of economic history under communism. Based on research coming out of the previously secret KGB files in Moscow, historians confirmed Mises's negative views about socialist central planning. In her work about Soviet Russia in the 1930s entitled *Everyday Stalinism*, Sheila Fitzpatrick countered the old conventional view held by Sidney and Beatrice Webb and George Bernard Shaw, that the Soviet system during the 1930s was a glorious "new civilization." On the contrary, Fitzpatrick wrote, "With the abolition of the market, shortages of food, clothing, and all kinds of consumer goods became endemic. As peasants fled the collective villages, major cities were soon in the grip of an acute housing crisis, with families jammed for decades in tiny single rooms in communal apartments. . . . It was a world of privation, overcrowding, endless queues, and broken families, in which the regime's promises of future socialist abundance rang hollow. . . . Government bureaucracy often turned everyday life into a nightmare" (Fitzpatrick 1999: cover).

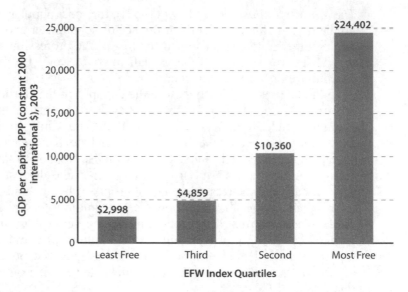

Figure 16.1
Positive Correlation Between Economic Freedom and Per Capita Income, 2005
Source: Gwartney and Lawson (2007). Reprinted by permission of the Fraser Institute.

NATIONS GROW FASTER UNDER ECONOMIC FREEDOM

In addition, recent studies comparing the economic growth of nations and their degree of freedom have confirmed Mises's thesis. According to the work of James Gwartney (Florida State) and his colleagues, countries with the greatest level of economic liberty enjoy the highest standard of living. The economic freedom graph, shown in Figure 1.2 on page 25, reflects these findings (reproduced above, Figure 16.1).

And so ends a critical chapter in the history of economics. Mises, long dead, was finally vindicated. The words of the physicist Max Planck apply here: "Science progresses funeral by funeral."

As we enter the twenty-first century, the winds of change are everywhere. As Francis Fukuyama declared in *Time* magazine, "If socialism signifies a political and economic system in which the government controls a large part of the economy and redistributes wealth to produce social equality, then I think it is safe to say the likelihood of its making a comeback anytime in the next generation is close to zero" (2000: 111).

THE WINDS OF CHANGE IN DEVELOPMENT ECONOMICS

The shift from pro-government activism to pro-market solutions would also be seen in development economics, but not until the late twentieth century. Following World War II, economists focused on the fate of poor nations in Asia, Africa, and Latin America, dubbed the Third World, or officially the less developed countries (LDCs). Generally, they experienced

low literacy rates, high unemployment, rapid population growth, and agri-
cultural-based economies. Many suffered from high rates of inflation,
shortages, black markets, and capital flight. How could poor nations participate in Adam Smith's goal of universal opulence?

After the 1930s had discredited capitalism and the postwar Marshall
Plan demonstrated the efficacy of government aid, the new orthodoxy
became state-driven growth. International development organizations,
such as the World Bank and the Alliance for Progress, were established to
assist LDCs.

In 1960, MIT's W.W. (Walt Whitman) Rostow wrote his "noncommu-
nist manifesto," *The Stages of Economic Growth*, which quickly became
the standard bearer for Third World planning. Rostow felt that the precon-
dition to the "takeoff" stage of sustained economic growth was a
centralized nation-state.

The Keynesian approach to development is embodied in the Harrod-
Domar model of economic growth, named after Roy Harrod and Evsey
Domar (Eltis 1987). The Harrod-Domar model contends that economic
growth is purely a function of the national capital-output ratio, so that the
growth of fixed capital generates increased profits and economic growth.
The Harrod-Domar model emphasizes almost exclusively the need to
expand the capital stock and technology as the keys to growth—either
through an increase in domestic saving, foreign aid, private investment,
government spending, or monetary inflation. Efficiency, incentives, and
trade are neglected. Their model virtually ignores the role of entrepreneurs
using capital and new ideas to create wealth. Since LDCs suffer from a
"vicious cycle of poverty" and cannot internally generate growth, Rostow
and other development economists emphasized the necessity of the state to
break the vicious cycle through massive investment projects.

P.T. BAUER: THE VOICE OF DISSENT

One ardent critic of the development orthodoxy was P.T. Bauer of the
London School of Economics (LSE). In the postwar period, Peter Bauer
waged a lonely battle against foreign aid, comprehensive central planning,
and nationalization. He noted that industrial nations such as Britain refuted
the "vicious cycle of poverty" thesis, adding, "Throughout history innumerable individuals, families, groups, societies, and countries—both in the
West and the Third World—have moved from poverty to prosperity
without external donations" (Dorn 1998: 27). He denied that advanced capitalist countries had progressed at the expense of poor ones and argued that
foreign investment is a key ingredient to development of the Third World.
State planning is not a benevolent program of growth, according to Bauer,
but a concentration of power in the hands of a political elite that would
inevitably lead to corruption and abuse.

In one of his classic articles, he wrote about an Asian country which, at the end of World War II, was poverty stricken. It had hardly any natural resources and was forced to import all its oil and raw materials, and even most of its water. It faced massive immigration and eventually became the most densely populated country in the world. Its trading partners were thousands of miles away. "You would think that this country must be doomed, unless it received large external donations," commented Bauer. Yet, the tiny colony of Hong Kong has flourished due to its laissez-faire government, and today it is the second most prosperous country in the Pacific Basin (Bauer 1981: 185–90).

Since the collapse of the Soviet central planning model, Rostow's thesis has been largely discredited and Bauer's less orthodox views have triumphed. Even Rostow recently admitted, "There are, evidently, serious and correct insights in the Bauer position" (1990: 386). Recently the World Bank has moved toward Bauer's side. In a 1993 study of the Four Tigers and the East Asian economic miracle, it concluded, "The rapid growth in each country was primarily due to the application of a set of common, market-friendly economic policies, leading to both higher accumulation and better allocation of resources" (World Bank 1993: vi). The bank's 1996 development report, *From Plan to Market*, clearly falls on the side of the market. Joseph Stiglitz, then chief economist of the World Bank, noted, "Most [economists] conclude that [foreign] aid crowds out national saving" (Schmidt-Hebbel and Serven, 1999: 17–18).

CRITIC OF FOREIGN AID

Most of the World Bank's $500 billion in loans, grants, and aid since inception has gone to governments, often bypassing the individual poor. Lord Peter Bauer has not been the only critic of this policy. One of the most prominent proponents of private-enterprise solutions to Third World poverty has been Muhammad Yunus, former professor at the Chittagong University in Bangladesh, the world's poorest country. In 1983, Yunus established the Grameen Bank to provide much-needed microcredit to needy entrepreneurs. Today hundreds of private micro-lending organizations are bringing people out of poverty. For his work, Yunus and the Grameen Bank were awarded the Nobel Peace Prize in 2006.

In his *Banker to the Poor*, Yunus decried the World Bank: "We at the Grameen Bank have never wanted or accepted World Bank funding because we do not like the way the bank conducts business." Nor did he much like foreign aid: "Most rich nations use their foreign aid budgets mainly to employ their own people and to sell their own goods, with poverty reduction as an afterthought. . . . Aid-funding projects create massive bureaucracies, which quickly become corrupt and inefficient, incurring huge losses. . . . Aid money still goes to expand government spending, often acting against the interests of the market economy. . . . Foreign aid becomes a kind of charity for the powerful while the poor get poorer" (1999: 145–56).

Yunus's statements are all the more amazing given that he grew up under the influence of Marxist economics. But after earning a Ph.D. in economics at Vanderbilt University, he saw firsthand "how the market [in the United States] liberates the individual." "I do believe in the power of the global free-market economy and in using capitalist tools. . . . I also believe that providing unemployment benefits is not the best way to address poverty." Believing that "all human beings are potential entrepreneurs," Yunus is convinced that poverty can be eradicated by loaning poor people the capital they need to engage in profitable businesses, not by giving them a government handout or engaging in population control (1999: 203–5).

His former Marxist colleagues call it a capitalist conspiracy. "What you are really doing," a communist professor told Yunus, "is giving little bits of opium to the poor people. . . . Their revolutionary zeal cools down. Therefore, Grameen is the enemy of the [communist] revolution" (Yunus 1999: 203–5).

THE STORY OF PRIVATIZATION

With the collapse of Eastern bloc communism, the paramount question became how to dismantle the socialist state and reestablish capitalism. The watchwords became denationalization, privatization, and deregulation.

Privatization had already got its impetus a decade earlier under Prime Minister Margaret Thatcher in Britain. But it was Austrian-born management guru Peter F. Drucker who wrote about "reprivatization" in a chapter aptly called "The Sickness of Government," in *The Age of Discontinuity* (Drucker 1969: 234). Robert Poole, Jr., founder of the Reason Foundation, shortened the term to "privatization."

What did Drucker have in mind about privatization? He wrote in 1969 that government had proved it could do only two things well—wage war and inflate the currency (he failed to mention its ability to tax). Otherwise, government was a dismal failure. When it came to running businesses, providing services to the public, paying out a living pension for retirees, or supplying decent welfare to the poor and the needy, government was a "fiasco." In short, Drucker concluded, "Modern government has become ungovernable" (Drucker 1969: 220).

To help solve society's growing problems, Drucker advocated turning to business and private enterprise, because of their natural advantage in managing change, innovating, and responding to consumer needs. Most importantly, he said, business is the only institution that takes risks and can abandon what doesn't work and move on to what does. Government, on the other hand, is conservative and therefore has a hard time abandoning services that cost too much or aren't getting results. In other words, government has no business running businesses.

One of Drucker's main messages is that private business—not government—should be the "representative social institution" in providing economic stability, social justice, and improving living standards. In particular, he stated that big business—the large multinational corporation—is best suited to assume social responsibilities such as providing job security, training and educational opportunities, generous medical and pension plans, and other social benefits. Drucker called this new social-industrial order the only "free non-revolutionary way" (1969: 236–40).

Drucker was prescient in his call for business to take the lead in building a free industrial society. Private companies have proved better at providing social services and running businesses than government. Private pension systems, health care insurance, charities, and corporate benefit plans are, more often than not, more generous than government welfare programs.

Drucker sensed the signs of the times when he advocated that society rely more on private enterprise and less on government to provide for society's economic and social needs. As the Israeli economist Shlomo Maital states, "The health and the wealth of a large number of individual businesses—small, medium and large—determine the economic health and wealth of a nation. When they succeed, managers create wealth, income, and jobs for large numbers of people. . . . It is *businesses* that create wealth, not countries or governments. It is businesses that decide how well or how poorly off we are" (Maital 1994: 6).

PRIVATIZATION: FROM DREAM TO REALITY

When Peter Drucker first wrote about privatization in 1969, it was only a dream. Then, under Prime Minister Margaret Thatcher, Britain began selling off national industries, starting with British Petroleum in 1979. The real trailblazer came in 1984 with the sale of British Telecom (BT). Millions of British citizens were encouraged to buy shares at low prices, and public support for privatization rose dramatically when stock prices skyrocketed as BT went public. Moreover, telephone service improved significantly. Prior to privatization, the British telephone system was antiquated. It took months to get a new telephone, and many out-of-service public phones went unrepaired for months. That all changed quickly after BT went public on the London Stock Exchange.[2]

Photograph 16.3
Peter F. Drucker,
Inventor of Privatization
Capital is the future!
Courtesy of Peter F. Drucker.

2. For a more detailed review of the success of privatization in Britain, see Madsen Pirie, *Blueprint for a Revolution*, published (appropriately) by the Adam Smith Institute (1992). The Adam Smith Institute, run by Madsen Pirie and Eamonn Butler, has been at the forefront of privatization efforts throughout the world.

Since then, support for privatization widened considerably as workers and customers became shareholders, government revenues increased, and companies became more profitable. Since Britain's successful program, privatization has become a full-blown global industry. According to the magazine *Privatisation International*, an estimated 100,000 medium- and large-sized firms have been divested around the world, generating proceeds of more than $1 trillion. Everything under the sun has been sold off by the state: oil companies, utilities, telephone companies, banks, post offices, hotels, restaurants, airports, railroads, mines, garbage collection, prisons, fire departments, taxi services, farms, supermarkets, churches, even movie theaters. Almost every country on every continent, including India, Russia, China, Vietnam, Mexico, and Peru, has privatized some or most state-owned businesses.

PRIVATIZING SOCIAL SECURITY

Drucker talked about the natural advantages of private enterprise over public services. Soon, free-market economists were applying this principle to social security, nationalized medicine, and public schooling, where government had traditionally played a heavy role.

Privatization of social security has already advanced significantly outside the United States. Latin American countries have followed the Chilean model, which was greatly influenced by Milton Friedman and the Chicago school. In the early 1980s, Chile switched from a state-run, pay-as-you-go pension system to a privatized individual retirement program for workers.

The Chilean privatized pension system, the world's first, proved a huge success in deepening the nation's capital market, boosting its savings rate, and stimulating economic growth (an average 5.4 percent since 1982). Today, 93 percent of Chile's labor force is enrolled in twenty separate private pension plans, some of which can be invested abroad. Government pension experts from around the world have traveled to Chile to see how the private sector has built a better social retirement program than the government. Today thirty-one countries enjoy some form of private retirement accounts, according to José Piñera, director of the International Center for Pension Reform.

Private social security systems have been tried in other Latin American and European countries, but efforts to create such a system in the United States have been stymied, perhaps because the American government has not yet faced the imminent bankruptcy of its social security system, as Chile did in 1982. As Drucker notes, government is not good at radical surgery or at abandoning poorly run programs.

THE BLOSSOMING OF FREE-MARKET ECONOMICS

The breakthrough scholarly work of Milton Friedman, Friedrich Hayek, and other free-market economists, as well as the demise of the socialist model, brought about a flowering of new market-friendly schools and new agendas throughout the world. These include the supply-siders, public-choice theorists, the new classical economists, behavioral analysts, and even advocates of modern portfolio theory. They have breathed new life into the economics of the invisible hand. Chapter 17 tells their remarkable story.

REFERENCES

Bauer, P.T. 1981. *Equality, the Third World and Economic Delusion.* Cambridge, MA: Harvard University Press.

Dorn, James A., Steve H. Hanke, and Alan A. Walters, eds. 1998. *The Revolution in Development Economics.* Washington, DC: Cato Institute.

Drucker, Peter F. 1969. *The Age of Discontinuity.* New York: Harper and Row.

———. 1986. *The Frontiers of Management.* New York: Harper and Row.

Eltis, Walter, 1987. "Harrod-Domar Growth Model." In *The New Palgrave: A Dictionary of Economics,* vol. 4, 602–4. London: Macmillan.

Fitzpatrick, Sheila. 1999. *Everyday Stalinism.* New York: Oxford University Press.

Gwartney, James, and Robert Lawson. 2007. *Economic Freedom Around the World.* Vancouver, BC: Fraser Institute.

Harris, Seymour E., ed. 1951. *Schumpeter, Social Scientist.* Cambridge, MA: Harvard University Press.

Hayek, Friedrich A., ed. 1935. *Collectivist Economic Planning.* London: George Routledge and Sons.

———. 1984. *The Essence of Hayek,* ed. Chiaki Nishiyama and Kurt R. Leube. Stanford: Hoover Institution Press.

Heilbroner, Robert L. 1981. "Was Schumpeter Right?" In *Schumpeter After Forty Years,* ed. Arnold Heertje. New York: Praeger.

———. 1989. "The Triumph of Capitalism." *New Yorker* (January 23), 98–109.

———. 1990. "Reflections After Communism." *New Yorker* (September 10), 91–100.

———. 1999 [1953]. *The Worldly Philosophers,* 7th ed. New York: Simon & Schuster.

Heilbroner, Robert L., and Lester C. Thurow. 1984. *The Economic Problem,* 7th ed. Englewood Cliffs, NJ: Prentice-Hall.

Keynes, John Maynard. 1982. *The Collected Writings of John Maynard Keynes: Social, Political, and Literary Writings,* vol. 27. London: Macmillan.

Lange, Oskar, and Fred M. Taylor. 1938. *On the Economic Theory of Socialism.* Minneapolis: University of Minnesota Press.

Lavoie, Don. 1985. *Rivalry and Central Planning: The Socialist Calculation Debate Reconsidered.* Cambridge: Cambridge University Press.

Malia, Martin. 1999. *Russia Under Western Eyes.* Cambridge, MA: Harvard University Press.

Maital, Shlomo. 1994. *Executive Economics.* New York: Free Press.

Mises, Ludwig von. 1990 [1920]. *Economic Calculation in the Socialist Commonwealth.* Auburn: Ludwig von Mises Institute.

Rostow, W.W. 1990. *Theorists of Economic Growth from David Hume to the Present.* New York: Oxford University Press.

Samuelson, Paul A. 1961. *Economics,* 5th ed. New York: McGraw-Hill.

———. 1985. *Economics,* 12th ed. New York: McGraw-Hill.

Samuelson, Paul A., and William Nordhaus. 1989. *Economics,* 13th ed. New York: McGraw-Hill.

Schmidt-Hebbel, Klaus, and Luis Serven, eds. 1999. *The Economics of Saving and Growth.* New York: Cambridge University Press.

Schumpeter, Joseph A. 1934 [1912]. *The Theory of Economic Development.* Cambridge, MA: Harvard University Press.

———. 1939. *Business Cycles,* 2 vols. New York: McGraw-Hill.

———. 1946. "John Maynard Keynes, 1883–1946." *American Economic Review* 36: 4 (September), 495–518.

———. 1950 [1943]. *Capitalism, Socialism and Democracy.* New York: Harper and Row.

———. 1954. *History of Economic Analysis.* New York: Oxford University Press.

Skousen, Mark. 1997. "The Perseverance of Paul Samuelson's *Economics*." *Journal of Economic Perspectives* 11: 2 (Spring), 137–52.
Swedberg, Richard. 1991. *Schumpeter: A Biography*. Princeton: Princeton University Press.
Wallich, Henry C. 1960. *The Cost of Freedom*. New York: Collier.
World Bank. 1993. *The East Asian Miracle*. New York: World Bank.
Yunus, Muhammad. 1999. *Banker to the Poor*. New York: Public Affairs.

17

Dr. Smith Goes to Washington: The Near Triumph of Market Economics

To judge from the climate of opinion, we have won the war of ideas. Everyone—left or right—talks about the virtues of markets, private property, competition, and limited government.

—Milton Friedman (1998: 582)

In the postwar years, Keynes's theories of government management of the economy appeared unassailable. But half a century later, it [is] Keynes who has been toppled and Hayek, the fierce advocate of free markets, who is preeminent.

—Daniel Yergin and Joseph Stanislaw[1] (1998: 14–15)

Ever since Milton Friedman took his first class in economics from Jacob Viner at the University of Chicago, he has been impressed with the "coherent, logical whole" of sound economic theory. "That course was unquestionably the greatest intellectual experience of my life," he said (Breit and Spencer 1982: 83).

Friedman's longtime hope has been the integration of economics into one coherent, logical whole, a body of simple universal principles that "can

1. *The Commanding Heights* by Daniel Yergin and Joseph Stanislaw is the best available history of the battle between government and the marketplace in the twentieth century, with separate chapters on individual countries.

♪ Music selection for this chapter: Modest Mussorgsky, "The Great Gate at Kiev" from *Pictures at an Exhibition*

be written on one page"[2] (Breit and Spencer 1982: 91). He has always hated the fragmentation and bickering between schools of economics, which has occurred ever since Marx detached himself from the "classical" school of Smith and Ricardo. In 1974, when vacationing at his summer home in Vermont, Friedman spoke informally at a nearby conference about Austrian economics. He bluntly told the audience, "There is no Austrian economics—only good economics and bad economics"[3] (Dolan 1976: 4). His point was that any useful concepts coming out of Austrian economics (he specifically made reference to Hayek's contributions) should be incorporated into the body of mainstream economic theory. In 1982, he made the same point at a conference on supply-side economics. "I am not a supply-side economist. I am not a monetarist economist. I am an economist"[4] (Friedman 1982: 53).

By the end of a long, productive career, Milton Friedman was beginning to witness a widespread consensus in economics, a body of beliefs that he himself helped formalize. Granted, there are wars still being fought and theories under dispute, but the fundamental concepts have finally been worked out.

THE NEOCLASSICAL MODEL IS REESTABLISHED

First and foremost, a growing number of economists recognize that the neoclassical model is the keystone of economic analysis. In microeconomics, this means incorporating the principles of supply and demand, and profit and loss, which, under broad-based competition, leads to an efficient allocation of resources and a self-regulating economy. Under competition, man's natural tendency toward self-assertion leads to social well-being. It suggests that the behavior of "economic man" is rational and thus capable of statistical analysis and even scientific predictability within certain limitations.

In macroeconomics, it means teaching the classical model of thrift, a stable monetary policy, fiscal responsibility, free trade, widespread economic and political freedom, and a consistent rule of law for the justice system.

2. In response to Friedman's challenge, I have attempted to write the fundamental principles of economics on one printed page. See "Economics in One Page" at www.mskousen.com.

3. British economist Lionel Robbins wrote the same thing a generation earlier: "It has been well said that there are only two kinds of Economics—good Economics and bad Economics. All other classifications are misleading." See his introduction to Friedrich Hayek's *Monetary Theory and the Trade Cycle* (1975 [1933]: 6).

4. As a counterpoint, schools of economics do offer the benefit of highlighting areas that the standard neoclassical model might miss. For example, the Austrian school emphasizes competition as a process through a capital-using economy; Marxism stresses the role of labor in the social structure of capitalism; supply-side economics focuses on taxes and incentives; and monetarism on the role of money in society. By narrowing their focus, schools of thought have contributed to the whole body of sound economics.

SO HERE'S TO YOU, MRS. ROBINSON:
IS THERE A FEMINIST ECONOMICS?

Joan Robinson was an extremely controversial, and remarkable, economist with whom I got along well personally, though we were worlds apart in our views.
—Milton Friedman (1998: 245)

Photograph 17.1
Joan V. Robinson (1903–83)
The V stands for Violet—
"Indefatigable, tough-minded,
inspiring, nonconformist."
Courtesy of Mark Blaug.

Of the two hundred economists highlighted in Mark Blaug's *Great Economists*, Cambridge professor Joan Robinson is identified as "the only woman ever to have achieved outstanding eminence in economic theory" (1985: 207). Specifically, Blaug referred to her *Economics of Imperfect Competition* (1933), which, along with Edward Chamberlin's book, *The Theory of Monopolistic Competition* (1933), formed the foundation of modern neoclassical micro theory of the firm. For this achievement, many economists, including Milton Friedman, felt she deserved the Nobel Prize, but alas, in 1975, the Year of the Woman, she was passed over because of her extreme political views. Although she was not a pure Marxist, she constantly defended the communist regimes in China, North Korea, and Cuba, airing views that proved embarrassing to friends and foes alike.

Joan Robinson (1903–83) was born in Surrey, England, attended Cambridge University, and married economist E.A.G. Robinson (later Professor Sir Austin Robinson) in 1926. But she clearly outshone her husband. As a prominent member of the "Cambridge Circus" in the 1930s, she advanced the cause of Keynesian economics. Unlike most economists, who gradually returned to classical economics after World War II, Joan Robinson became more and more unorthodox. In the mid-1950s, she, along with Piero Sraffa and others, launched the "Cambridge controversies," a wholesale attack on standard neoclassical economics. She felt she had found a fatal flaw in economic theory, and particularly in the marginal productivity theory of labor and capital. As the economics profession largely rejected her seditious "post-Keynesian" view, she became even more radical and hostile in her old age, writing numerous books and articles on socialism, Marxism, and other "economic heresies." (Her *Collected Papers* fill five volumes.) After suffering a stroke in 1983, she died six months later in a Cambridge hospital.

FEMINIST ECONOMICS

Many economists have noted the dominance of men in the profession of economics. In a world where the majority of college students are now women, economics con-

(continued)

tinues to experience a fairly low percentage of female students majoring in that subject. In Mark Blaug's *Great Economists*, only three out of the two hundred economists listed are female. Dorothy Lamden Thomson blames this low percentage on the emphasis on advanced mathematics in economics, which many woman find unappealing (Thomson 1973: 135–36). Deirdre N. McCloskey, whose name used to be Donald, goes even further to claim that today's formalistic mathematical modeling is fundamentally masculine in nature. "The boys' games seem to me now to be even sillier than I had thought," she declared after a sex-change operation. According to McCloskey, it's time for the economists to get out of their "sandbox" of "prudence" and add "courage, temperance, justice, and love." She also comments, "If you ever read Adam Smith's other book, *The Theory of Moral Sentiments*, you will find an articulation of the five virtues that puts Prudence of *The Wealth of Nations* in its proper context" (McCloskey 1998: 191–92).

To counter the male-dominant trend in economics, several women economists established the International Association of Feminist Economics in the mid-1990s and began publishing *Feminist Economics*, an academic journal focusing on women's issues in economics. I noticed that Anna J. Schwartz, coauthor with Milton Friedman of the famed *Monetary History of the United States*, was not listed among the many contributors. I asked Schwartz if there's such a thing as feminist economics. Her reply: "I am not affiliated with a group that professes that the content of economics is different for issues that concern women than for issues that concern men" (private correspondence, June 7, 2000).

Granted, institutions such as the financial, religious, and judicial systems play a significant role in both microeconomic decision making and macroeconomic policy making. But the role of institutions is a two-way street. Institutions are positive if they enhance the above principles; institutions are negative if they retard and distort economic growth and liberty.

All these basic principles were established over 200 years ago in Adam Smith's *Wealth of Nations* (1965 [1776]).

A SHOCKING COUNTERREVOLUTION AT HARVARD

This shift back to market principles and the classical model is best illustrated by the recent works of Harvard's Gregory Mankiw. With his textbook, *Macroeconomics*, written in the early 1990s, Mankiw surprised the profession by beginning with the classical model and ending with the short-term Keynesian model, the reverse of the standard Samuelson pedagogy. It was a brilliant, revolutionary—or rather counterrevolutionary—move, a reflection of a changing fundamental philosophy. In the preface, Mankiw justifies his new approach, stating that "in the aftermath of the Keynesian revolution, too many economists forgot that classical economics provides the right answers to many fundamental questions" (Mankiw 1994: Preface).

This statement is all the more amazing given that Mankiw considers himself a neo-Keynesian and named his dog Keynes!

Dubbing the classical model "the real economy in the long run," Mankiw pinpoints the effects of an increase in government spending—that rather than act as a multiplier, it "crowds out" private capital. "The increase in government purchases must be met by an equal decrease in [private] investment. . . . Government borrowing reduces national saving" (Mankiw 1994: 62).

In previous textbooks, Samuelson and his colleagues emphasized the cyclical nature of capitalism and how the economy could be stabilized. By contrast, in *Macroeconomics*, Mankiw discusses economic growth up front. Using the Solow growth model, Mankiw takes a strong pro-saving approach. Accordingly, "the saving rate is a key determinant of the steady-state capital stock. If the saving rate is high, the economy will have a large capital stock and a high level of output. If the saving rate is low, the economy will have a small capital stock and a low level of output" (1994: 62). What is the effect of higher savings? "An increase in the rate of saving raises growth until the economy reaches the new steady state," although the law of diminishing returns suggests that "it will not maintain a high rate of growth forever" (1994: 62). Far from accepting the paradox of thrift, Mankiw writes favorably about those nations with high rates of saving and investment, and even includes a case study on the miracles of Japanese and German postwar growth (examples virtually ignored in Samuelson's textbook). Mankiw therefore supports policies aimed at increasing the rates of saving and capital formation in the United States, including the possibility of altering Social Security from a pay-as-you-go system to a fully funded plan, though he does not discuss outright privatization (1994: 103–34).

Unemployment is another issue Mankiw approaches in a non-Keynesian way. What causes unemployment? Relying on Friedman's "natural" rate of unemployment hypothesis, Mankiw suggests that unemployment insurance and similar labor legislation reduce incentives for the unemployed to find jobs. He provides evidence that unionizing labor and adopting minimum-wage laws actually increase the unemployment rate. Finally, he offers a case study on Henry Ford's famous $5 workday as an example of higher productivity and increasing wages.

He approvingly quotes Milton Friedman on monetary theory: "Inflation is always and everywhere a monetary phenomenon." Mankiw uses numerous examples, including hyperinflation in interwar Germany, to confirm the social costs of inflation (1994: 161–69).[5]

THE IMPACT OF RATIONAL EXPECTATIONS AND SUPPLY-SIDE ECONOMICS

Mankiw and other textbook writers have been heavily influenced by the "rational expectations" school of John Muth, Thomas Sargent, and Robert

---

5. The most famous work on the effects of monetary hyperinflation is by Phillip D. Cagan (Columbia University), who studied seven hyperinflations and their effect on money, prices, and output (Cagan 1956). Runaway inflation continues to haunt the global economy. In the 1990s, countries such as Yugoslavia and Argentina destroyed the value of their currencies. And in 2008, Zimbabwe broke all records by issuing a 10 billion Zimbabwean dollar bill.

Lucas, Jr. (who won the Nobel Prize in 1995). Most economists recognize now that federal fiscal and monetary policies are frequently anticipated in the economy, thus making activist policies less effective, or perhaps even perverse. For example, in the past, deficit spending or an "easy money" policy might stimulate economic activity, but when individuals anticipate these policies, the economy might falter as private investment is crowded out or interest rates rise. The theory of rational expectations has been effectively applied in many areas, including government policy and the financial markets (Sargent 1987).

In the second half of his textbook, Mankiw introduces the standard tools of Keynesian macroeconomics as the economy in the "short run"—aggregate supply and demand, the multiplier and accelerator, and the income-expenditure model. But they appear almost as an afterthought, irrelevant most of the time in today's dynamic, full-employment economy.

If there is a shortcoming to Mankiw's textbook, it would be his analysis of the effect of tax cuts on the economy. In Mankiw's model, a tax cut has the same effect as deficit spending—by raising consumption, a tax cut "crowds out investment and raises the interest rate" (1994: 64). He reports that the Reagan tax cuts enlarged the deficit, thereby raising interest rates and lowering national savings. Yet he ignores the fact that tax revenues rose during every year of the Reagan administration, as the supply-siders predicted. The supply-side school of economics, led by Robert Mundell, Paul Craig Roberts, Martin Anderson, and Arthur B. Laffer, has been highly critical of Keynesian demand-side policies. The school gained popularity in the 1980s during the Reagan administration by advocating tax cuts, deregulation, and free trade, rather than deficit spending and easy money. According to the supply-siders, the government should encourage production and supply rather than consumption and demand.

Furthermore, they disagree with Keynesian economists who claim that government spending stimulates the economy more effectively than tax cuts. Highly progressive taxes are a strong disincentive to work, to invest, and to save, they claim. As Paul Craig Roberts states:

> Supply-side economics brought a new perspective to fiscal policy. Instead of stressing the effect on spending, supply-siders showed that tax rates directly affect the supply of goods and services. Lower tax rates mean better incentives to work, to save, to take risks, and to invest. As people respond to the higher after-tax rewards, or greater profitability, incomes rise and the tax base grows, thus feeding back some of the lost revenues to the Treasury. The saving rate also grows, providing more financing for government and private borrowing. (1984: 25)

TAX RATES AND THE LAFFER CURVE

Supply-siders refer to the Laffer curve to support their contention that cutting marginal tax rates can stimulate economic growth and actually

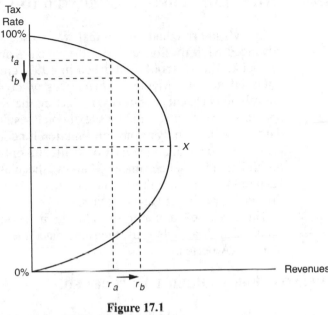

Figure 17.1
Laffer Curve
A tax cut can increase tax revenues.

increase tax revenues. The Laffer curve (see Figure 17.1) shows a theoretical relationship between the tax level and tax revenues. It was invented by Arthur B. Laffer, a former economics professor at University of Chicago and University of Southern California, who allegedly drew the famous curve on a napkin at a Washington, D.C., restaurant in the late 1970s, to prove his point that tax cuts could, under certain circumstances, increase tax revenues.

According to the Laffer curve, an increase in tax rates will generate more revenues to the government as long as the rates aren't too high. But once the tax rate exceeds X, further increases in tax rates will actually shrink revenues because higher tax rates discourage work effort and encourage tax avoidance and even illegal evasion. In Figure 17.1, if tax rates have reached a prohibitive range, a tax cut (t_a to t_b) could increase revenues (from r_a to r_b). Supply-siders point to capital gains tax cuts in 1978 and 1996 in the United States, where tax cuts increased revenues to the U.S. Treasury from capital gains.

Most Keynesian textbook writers are wary of the supply-side arguments, but perhaps the granting of the Nobel Prize to Columbia professor Robert Mundell (a well-known supply-sider) in 1999 will help reverse the discrimination against supply-side economics and the Laffer curve in most textbooks.

KEYNES'S "GENERAL" THEORY RELEGATED TO A "SPECIAL" CASE

Mankiw's intermediate macro text was so successful that in 1992 he was advanced $1.1 million to write the "next Samuelson"—an introductory textbook. The textbook, published in 1997, created a sensation. Like his intermediate text, Mankiw's *Principles of Economics* is devoted almost entirely to classical economics, relegating the Keynesian model to the end chapters. Amazingly, Mankiw's textbook doesn't mention most of the standard Keynesian analysis: no consumption function, no Keynesian cross, no propensity to save, no paradox of thrift, and only one brief reference to the multiplier. In essence, under Mankiw, the classical model becomes the "general" theory and the Keynesian model becomes the "special" case— the very opposite of Keynes's thesis.

Thus, we see a major sea change in economics, and from where? Cambridge, Massachusetts, the same place the Keynesian revolution originated in America.

SAMUELSON: FISCAL POLICY DETHRONED!

Even Paul Samuelson has been convinced to change his focus in recent editions of his famed textbook, perhaps in part due to the influence of his coauthor, Bill Nordhaus. Samuelson may have also changed his mind due to the growing evidence that full employment is the norm, not the exception, so that even under the Keynesian model, classical economics should prevail.

Samuelson's fiftieth-anniversary edition (1998) is telling. While he wasn't willing to put the classical model first, his attitudes within the text have changed dramatically. Examples: He replaced the old antisaving "paradox of thrift" with a major section bemoaning the low saving rate in the United States, blaming it in part on Social Security and high taxes (1998: 422–24). Deficit spending, a perennial policy recommendation in earlier editions, has become anathema. According to the new Samuelson, "a large public debt is likely to reduce long-run economic growth" (page 652). But the biggest shock is Samuelson's abandonment of fiscal policy as a macroeconomic stabilizer. His sixteenth edition highlights this statement in color: "Fiscal policy is no longer a major tool of stabilization policy in the United States. Over the foreseeable future, stabilization policy will be primarily handled by Federal Reserve monetary policy" (page 655), a statement that he continues to use in the latest edition.

In short, Milton Friedman, Friedrich Hayek, and the free-market proponents may have lost the debate early on, but they seem to have won the war. "The growing orientation toward the market," concluded Samuelson, "has accompanied widespread desire for smaller government, less regulation, and lower taxes" (1998: 735). Samuelson expressed dismay at this outcome, ending his fiftieth-anniversary work on a sour note by calling the new global economy "ruthless" and characterized by "growing" inequality and a "harsh" competitive environment. But the deed—the triumph of the market and classical economics—appears irreversible. Friedman and Hayek, representing two schools of free-market economics (Chicago and Vienna), have combined forces for a one-two punch that has reversed the tide of ideas (Yergin and Stanislaw 1998: 98).

GROWTH OF MARKET-FRIENDLY TEXTBOOKS

While the Keynesian textbooks have become less and less Keynesian, textbooks with a strong free-market bias have become more prevalent. Popular market-oriented textbooks include Paul Heyne's *Economic Way of Thinking* (11th ed., 2006), which does not even include aggregate supply and demand (*AS/AD*) diagrams; Roger LeRoy Miller's *Economics Today* (14th ed., 2007), which has always been in the forefront of applying free-market micro principles to real-world cases; and James Gwartney and Richard Stroup's *Economics: Public and Private Choice* (12th ed., 2008), which stresses public choice economics and privatization.

The seventh edition of *Principles of Economics* (2000) by Roy J. Ruffin and Paul N. Gregory (both at the University of Houston) offered a whole new approach. The authors focused on four major historical events ("Defining Moments in Economics") throughout the text: first, the industrial revolution and Adam Smith; second, the rise and fall of socialism, with discussions about Karl Marx, Ludwig von Mises, and Friedrich Hayek; third, the Great Depression, with contributions by Keynes and Friedman; and fourth, globalization and David Ricardo. They also spent space on privatization, public choice, the gold standard, and economic success stories in Europe and Asia. Previous editions made no mention of Mises and Hayek.

REPLACING THE KEYNESIAN *AS/AD* MODEL

Much progress has been made in improving the teaching of economics, but one overwhelming issue remains—what should replace the faulty Keynesian "aggregate supply and demand" model currently in use? As noted above, many economists have relegated the *AS/AD* model to the back of the textbooks, discussing it solely as a "short-term" explanation of the business cycle. Even then, more economists recognize its shortcomings. David Colander (Middlebury College), who considers himself a neo-Keynesian, warned, "The *AS/AD* model . . . is seriously flawed . . . a model of the worst type—a model that obscures, rather than clarifies" (1995: 169).

To understand some of the problems associated with the *AS/AD* model, we reproduce it in Figure 17.2.

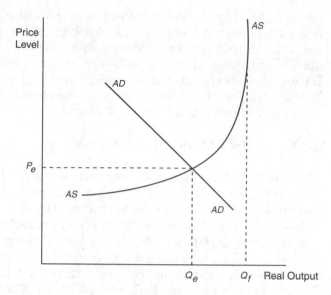

Figure 17.2
Aggregate Supply (AS) and Demand (AD) at Less Than Full Employment

One flaw in the *AS/AD* diagram is that it justifies the Keynesian thesis that the free market cannot guarantee full employment—that the economy can be at equilibrium at less than full employment. But how can the economy be at general equilibrium when the labor market is in disequilibrium? Clearly, the *AS/AD* model is self-contradictory, a position most Keynesians now admit.

Second, the diagram supports the Keynesian policy prescription that increased government spending can stimulate economic activity and push the *AD* curve forward until full employment is achieved, where the *AS* curve is vertical. The *AS/AD* model also attempts to explain inflationary recessions caused by "supply shocks," resulting in rising prices and unemployment at the same time.

Yet the model does a poor job of explaining what happens to the economy under full employment (where the *AS* curve is vertical). The model suggests that further deficit spending or inflating the money supply will drive prices up without affecting real output. Yet numerous studies of countries suffering from inflation demonstrate that inflation does not simply drive prices up, but causes economic distortions and a decline in real output.

THE WICKSELL "NATURAL INTEREST RATE" MODEL

In short, more and more economists are calling for the Keynesian *AS/AD* model to be scrapped. But what should take its place? One powerful, over-

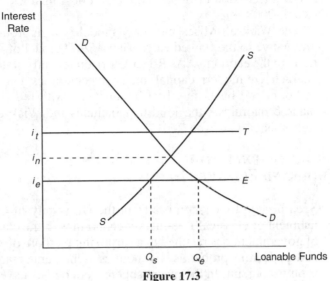

Figure 17.3
Wicksell's Natural Interest Rate Model

looked tool is Wicksell's "natural interest rate" model, reproduced in Figure 17.3.

We discussed this monetary macro model in chapter 12. The Wicksell model focuses on the role of time and interest rates in the economy, a topic of prime interest in today's global economy. Alfred Marshall was correct when he wrote, "The element of time . . . is the centre of the chief difficulty of almost every economic problem" (Marshall 1920: vii).

The Wicksell model illustrates general equilibrium in the credit markets where the supply of savings equals the demand for credit based on the public's time preference for money at the natural rate of interest (i_n). It does a good job of describing macro disequilibrium and how a business cycle occurs when government fiscal and monetary policies shift the supply (SS) or demand (DD) curve away from the "natural" rate of interest. For example, the Wicksell model—in conjunction with the Austrian (Mises-Hayek) intertemporal model of the economy—shows the effect of an "easy money" policy. As line E demonstrates, an easy-money policy temporarily reduces the market rate of interest below the natural rate, so that government credit ($Q_e - Q_s$) makes up for the shortfall in private savings (Q_s). The result is an artificial boom in capital-asset industries, such as the stock market (illustrated by the boom in technology stocks in the late 1990s) and real estate (illustrated by the mortgage boom of 2000–2005).

The Wicksell-Mises model also illustrates a "tight money" condition, line T, where market interest rates rise above the natural rate. Here we see how savings exceeds investment, a Keynesian-type condition that brings about a recession or depression, and a bust in stocks (2000–2003) or real estate (2007–8).

The Wicksell-Mises monetary model is a rigorous and more accurate alternative to the flawed Keynesian *AS/AD* model of "short-term" fluctuations in the economy.[6] As Roger Garrison recently stated, "the troubles that characterize modern capital-intensive economics, particularly the episodes of boom and bust, may best be analyzed with the aid of a capital-based macroeconomics," the kind that includes the Wicksell-Mises disequilibrium model (Garrison 2001: 8).

From Dismal Science to Imperial Science: May a Thousand Flowers Bloom

Spearheaded by economists from the University of Chicago, the reestablishment of classical free-market economics in the classroom and the halls of government has resulted in a surprising plethora of applications to social and economic problems. Economics is no longer an ivory-tower philosophical pursuit. In the macro sphere, economists have sent clear signals to governments—that inflation and deficit spending have an adverse effect on the economy; high taxes and excessive regulation discourage the work ethic; and protectionism hurts consumers. Market principles also show that government does have a positive, albeit limited, role—providing a fair justice system, enforcing property rights, establishing a sound infrastructure of roads, bridges, water and sewage systems, and power plants. Limited sound government can encourage a vibrant business climate.

The principles of microeconomics have expanded far beyond the traditional range of economic issues. Using powerful new theoretical and statistical tools, economists have had an impact on politics, history, law, crime, race relations, medicine, sports, religion, finance, and environmentalism. They have helped create auctions for governments (multibillion-dollar mobile telecommunications licenses, Treasury securities) and private companies (selling on eBay, taking Google public). They have even changed the way Treasury bills are auctioned. Economics has been used with such widespread applications in other fields that it's hard to keep up with the results.[7] Kenneth E. Boulding (1919–93), longtime professor at the University of Colorado and former AEA president, always believed that economics should be eclectic and should be shared with other disciplines. Now his dream is being fulfilled.

---

6. For elaborations of the Wicksell-Mises monetary model, see Skousen, *Economic Logic* (2008), chapter 25, "Expansion and Contraction: Economics of the Business Cycle"; and Skousen, *The Structure of Production* (2007 [1990]).

7. See Skousen, *EconoPower: How a New Generation of Economists Is Transforming the World* (2008). The best survey of theoretical and applied economics today for the general reader is *The Concise Encyclopedia of Economics*, ed. David R. Henderson (2008, available online). It includes contributions by 141 economists, representing most schools of thought.

In this chapter, we highlight just a few examples of the new economic imperialism.

GARY BECKER: EXPANDING ECONOMICS BEYOND THE TRADITIONAL

Gary Becker of the University of Chicago has been instrumental in applying the principles of supply and demand to the human behavioral sciences, such as racial discrimination, crime, and marriage. In fact, he called his book for the general public, *The Economics of Life* (1997). Many of his case studies involve the application of commonsense market principles, such as "behavior responds to incentives." For example, Becker has applied the incentive principle to show that increasing the cost of crime through stiffer jail sentences, quicker trials, and higher conviction rates effectively reduces the number of criminals who rob, steal, or rape. "According to the economic approach, criminals, like everyone else, respond to incentives" (1997: 143). Becker has coaxed more out of the demand curve than anyone else in the profession.

As a result of the work of Becker, Steven Levitt, and other Chicago economists, a whole new discipline has developed in economics and the law. What are the financial consequences of gun control, drug laws, landlord restrictions, comparable worth rules, and environmental regulations? Again, the University of Chicago has been at the forefront of the process of analyzing the economic effects of civil and criminal law, with major contributions by Judge Richard Posner and law professor Richard Epstein, among others.

For his path-breaking work in nontraditional areas, Becker won the Nobel Prize in 1992, but the road to acceptance was hard. He noted that at first, "This work was not well received by most economists," and the attacks from his critics were "sometimes very nasty" (Becker 1997: 3). The results of his work have affected public policy, but only in a delayed and roundabout way.

ACADEMIA GOES TO WALL STREET—AND MAIN STREET

One of the most rewarding areas in which ivory-tower economics has become an applied science is in personal finance. A new area of study, known as behavioral economics, has made significant advances in how to improve people's ability to earn, save, invest, retire, budget, and get out of debt. Behavioral economists contend that investors, consumers, and businesspeople do not always act according to the "rational economic man" standard of the textbooks but, instead, suffer from overconfidence, overreaction, fear, greed, herding instincts, and other "animal spirits," to use John Maynard Keynes's term. Consider the titles of recent books by behavioral economists on the subject: *Irrational Exuberance* (2000, 2005), by Robert Shiller (Yale), who correctly warned investors that the bull market on Wall

---

THE PROLIFERATION OF FREE-MARKET THINK TANKS

I think there are too damn many think tanks now.
—Milton Friedman (1995: 37)

In 1948, when Samuelson's first edition of *Economics* appeared, only one free-market think tank existed—the Foundation for Economic Education in Irvington, New York, founded by Leonard Read. Meanwhile, there were plenty of progovernment institutions, such as the Brookings Institution, the RAND corporation, and the Committee for Economic Development.

One of the reasons Friedrich Hayek established the Mont Pelerin Society was to spread the concepts of economic liberty and to restore the principles of classical economics. Then along came a British chicken farmer, **Sir Anthony Fisher (1915–88)**, who established the Institute of Economic Affairs in London. Fisher was so enamored with the idea of setting up free-market foundations that he created an organization for the very purpose of creating more institutes around the world: the Atlas Economic Research Foundation, based in Fairfax, Virginia. Gradually, his vision has succeeded. Today there are hundreds of free-market think tanks throughout the world, and many institutions previously considered antimarket, such as the Brookings Institution and the World Bank, have become market friendly. Atlas lists 500 organizations, including such big names as Heritage, Cato, and the American Enterprise Institute, but also lists dozens of free-market think tanks in Europe, Latin America, and Asia. Many of them are profoundly underfunded and exist on shoestring budgets.

There has also been a proliferation of state think tanks, such as the Mackinac Center in Michigan, the James Madison Institute in Florida, the Goldwater Institute in Arizona, and the Cascade Policy Institute in Oregon. These state organizations have been largely successful and have attracted contributions by specializing in local issues.

Street in 2000 and in U.S. real estate in 2006 was not sustainable; and *Why Smart People Make Big Money Mistakes* (1999), by Gary Belsky and Thomas Gilovich.

The behavioral economists had their first success with the passage of the 2006 Pension Protection Act, which encourages companies to sign up employees for 401(k) plans automatically and, according to studies, could double the saving rate of workers. The law was based on the work of Brigitte Madrian (Harvard) and Richard Thaler (Chicago). According to Madrian and Thaler, new institutional measures borrowed from the principles of psychology can be introduced to minimize error and misjudgment.

Economists have been involved in Wall Street for more than fifty years. The popularity of stock index funds and modern portfolio theory comes from academic scholarship beginning in the 1950s. Harry Markowitz, who was then a graduate student at the University of Chicago and a protégé of Milton Friedman, wrote an article on portfolio theory for the March 1952 issue of

The Journal of Finance. This was the first attempt to actually quantify risk in stock and portfolio selection. Prior to his approach, investors were certainly aware of the wide risk of various stocks and investments, but did not measure that risk in any scientific way. Markowitz and other finance professors developed highly mathematical ways to measure risk, including the concepts of standard deviation and beta coefficients.

Out of this modern portfolio theory came several recommendations: (1) investors can increase returns and reduce risk by diversifying their portfolios; (2) high returns are associated with high risks, so that those who invest in growth stocks must expect greater volatility; and (3) beating the market averages is extremely difficult over the long term, and therefore, most investors should invest in broad-based stock index funds.

The third concept is known as the "efficient market" or "random walk" theory, which created an uproar when it was first proposed in the late 1950s. Burton Malkiel (Princeton University) expounded this strange new doctrine in his popular book, *A Random Walk Down Wall Street:* "It means that short-run changes in stock prices cannot be predicted. Investment advisory services, earnings predictions, and complicated chart patterns are useless. . . . Taken to its logical extreme, it means that a blindfolded monkey throwing darts at a newspaper's financial pages could select a portfolio that would do just as well as one carefully selected by the experts" (1990: 24). Malkiel's bestseller is now in its ninth edition.

These ivory-tower theories were initially greeted with scorn by Wall Street. However, over the years, studies have supported the academic theories. Few money managers and mutual funds have consistently beaten the Standard & Poors 500 Stock Index. As a result, index funds are now the largest type of mutual fund sold on Wall Street today—and for his pioneering work, Harry Markowitz (along with Merton Miller and William Sharpe) won the 1990 Nobel Prize in economics.[8]

The latest advances in stock market analysis have come from Jeremy Siegel (Wharton School), who has attempted to improve modern portfolio theory and discover anomalies in efficient markets. He is most famous for his best-selling work, *Stocks for the Long Run* (2008 [1998]). In his latest edition, the fourth, he reveals a number of discoveries, including what he calls the "growth trap," in which investors make the mistake of consistently paying too much for technology stocks. He also demonstrates that investors can do better than the averages with less risk by buying a well-diversified portfolio of dividend-paying stocks. He has joined forces with fund manager Michael Steinhardt to create the Wisdom Tree group of dividend-linked stock market funds as an alternative to the standard market-capitalized indexes, such as the S&P 500.

---

8. For an excellent history of modern finance theory, see Peter L. Bernstein's *Capital Ideas Evolving* (2007).

A CONTROVERSIAL BOOK ON AMERICAN SLAVERY

Another Chicago economist, Robert W. Fogel, joined forces with Stanley Engerman to apply statistical analysis (known as "cliometrics") to the issue of American slavery. *Time on the Cross* (1974) contested the view that slavery was an inefficient and unprofitable mode of production and would have disappeared on its own without the Civil War. With painstaking research,[9] Fogel and Engerman insisted that slavery was so efficient that only war could have brought about its demise. Fogel was accused of being a racist, even though he married a black woman, but finally felt some vindication upon winning the Nobel Prize in 1993, which he shared with historian Douglass C. North.

ECONOMIC HISTORIAN RESOLVES THE MYSTERIES OF THE GREAT DEPRESSION

Another example of revisionist history is a new interpretation of the Great Depression by economic historian Robert Higgs of Seattle University. Essentially, there were three transition periods in this critical event: the Great Contraction (1929–32), the Great Duration (1933–39), and the Great Escape (1940–46). What caused the Great Depression? Why did it last so long? Did World War II really restore prosperity?

As we learned in chapter 15, Milton Friedman was instrumental in answering the first question, the cause of the Great Contraction. It was not free enterprise, but the government-controlled Federal Reserve that pushed the economy over the edge in 1929–32.

What produced the decade-long stagnation of the world economy that in turn caused a paradigm shift from classical economics to Keynesianism? Higgs provided an answer that economists had only vaguely considered. In an in-depth study of the 1930s, Higgs focused on the lack of private investment during this period. Most economists recognize that investment is the key to recovery in a slump. Higgs showed how New Deal initiatives greatly hampered private investment time and time again, destroying much-needed investor and business confidence. These programs included the National Recovery Act, prolabor legislation, government regulation, and tax increases (Higgs 2006: 3–29).

In another path-breaking analysis, Higgs attacked the orthodox view that World War II saved us from the depression and restored the economy to full employment. The war gave only the appearance of recovery because everyone was employed. In reality, however, private consumption and investment declined while Americans fought and died for their country. A

---

9. During the summers of 1970 and 1971, I served as one of many researchers on the Fogel-Engerman slavery project, compiling statistics about the age, sex, and occupation of slaves from county estate records.

return to genuine prosperity—the true Great Escape—did not happen until after the war ended, when most of the wartime controls were abolished and most of the resources used in the military were returned to civilian production. Only *after* the war did private investment, business confidence, and consumer spending return to the fore (Higgs 2006: 61–80).

Ignoring the government (*G*) in GDP figures leads to a better understanding of what occurred during World War II. Consumption (*C*) and investment (*I*) slowed and even declined slightly during 1940–45, then rose sharply after the war in 1946–48.

Not everyone has accepted these relatively new findings, but a growing consensus contends that "government failure" has to take much of the responsibility for the troublesome 1930–45 period of the American economy.

PUBLIC FINANCE AND PUBLIC CHOICE: FROM "MARKET FAILURE" TO "GOVERNMENT FAILURE"

During the 1950s and 1960s, *Public Finance in Theory and Practice* (1958) by Harvard professor Richard Musgrave was a popular and virtually unchallenged textbook. Musgrave saw the need for a three-pronged government policy: (1) allocation—to provide public goods that the private sector couldn't; (2) distribution—to redistribute wealth and institute social justice; and (3) stabilization—to stabilize an inherently vacillating capitalist economy.

In a 1998 debate, Musgrave defended social insurance, progressive taxation, and the growth of the public sector as the "price we pay for

Photograph 17.2
Richard A. Musgrave (1910–2007)

Photograph 17.3
James M. Buchanan (1919–   )

The Old School of Public Finance Versus the New School of Public Choice
Courtesy of Mark Blaug and James Buchanan.

civilization" (Buchanan and Musgrave 1999: 75). Addressing today's worries about an overbloated government, Musgrave wrote, "Is the state of our civilization really that bad? . . . There is much that should go on the credit side of the ledger. The taming of unbridled capitalism and the injection of social responsibility that began with the New Deal. . . . Socializing the capitalist system . . . was needed for its own survival and for building a good society" (1999: 228). He also mentioned the "enormous gains" by blacks and women in the twentieth century.

Musgrave debated James Buchanan, a professor at George Mason University and one of the founders of the public-choice school. Buchanan blamed Democratic politics for a "bloated" public sector, "with governments faced with open-ended entitlement claims," resulting in "moral depravity" (Buchanan and Musgrave 1999: 222). He argued in favor of constraining government through constitutional rules and limitations. He succinctly described the difference between the two: "Musgrave trusts politicians; we distrust politicians" (1999: 88).

Who won the debate? Musgrave's views are still prevalent in Keynesian textbooks, but his books are seldom cited and are long out of print. On the other hand, James Buchanan won a Nobel Prize in 1986[10] and public-choice theory has been added to most curricula. Even Samuelson cites the public-choice work of James Buchanan and Gordon Tullock in his latest textbook.

What are the basics of public choice? In *Calculus of Consent* (1962), Buchanan and Tullock contended that politicians, like businesspeople, are motivated by self-interest. They set policies in order to be reelected, for example. But the incentives and discipline found in the marketplace are frequently missing from government. Voters have little incentive to control the excesses of legislators, who in turn are more responsive to powerful interest groups. As a result, government subsidizes the vested interests of commerce and other groups while it imposes costly, wasteful regulations and taxes on the general public.

Buchanan and other public-choice theorists have recommended a series of constitutional rules to alter the misguided public sector into acting more responsibly. These include: (1) imposing severe limitations on legislators' ability to raise taxes, such as requiring supermajorities (two-thirds vote); (2) protecting minority rights, such as the U.S. Constitution's Bill of Rights and state voting referendums; (3) returning legislative and regulatory power to local governments, to increase competition among government units.

---

10. It is a shame that Gordon Tullock was not honored along with Buchanan, since even Buchanan admitted that it was Tullock who was the "catalyst" behind public-choice theory. For one thing, Tullock invented "rent seeking," one of the most powerful concepts in public-choice theory (see the box in chapter 4 on page 111).

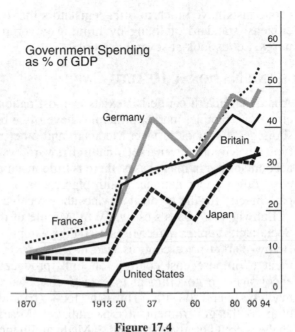

Figure 17.4
The Growth of Government in Five Industrial Nations
Source: Economist (April 6, 1996). Reprinted by permission.

UNFINISHED BUSINESS: CREEPING
SOCIALISM OR CRUMBLING SOCIALISM?

The application of market principles has indeed expanded in every direction in the recent past, but the triumph of free-market economics is far from complete. Many victories have been won on paper, but not in policy. Despite U.S. president Bill Clinton's observation, "The era of big government is over," the size of government in industrial nations has reached gigantic proportions (see Figure 17.4). As Milton Friedman commented at the fiftieth anniversary meeting of the Mont Pelerin Society (1997), "We have gained on the level of rhetoric, lost on the level of practice" (Friedman 1998: 583).

On the positive side, it appears that the sizes of governments have reached their upper bounds. In most countries, the private sector is now growing faster than the public sector, so that in percentage terms the state is beginning to shrink. One good example is China, where government spending as a proportion of the economy has fallen from 80 percent to 20 percent. But this new trend may not last if economic conditions reverse direction and the world suffers another slump or crisis.

Despite privatization, deregulation, and supply-side tax cuts, governments are still intrusive, revenue hungry, and bureaucratic. Free-market economists have much to offer legislators that can help them to improve citizens' standard of living by limiting government to its essential purposes. Let us look at several examples.

ECONOMICS AND NATIONAL HEALTH CARE

A national health care crisis exists in most nations. In nationalized medicine, for example, market principles have often been ignored, resulting in shortages and poor service. Medicare and other nationalized health plans typically violate the market's natural reward system and the principle of accountability. In many cases, there is little incentive to innovate or to keep costs down under national health plans, as most health care users do not pay directly for the medical services they receive.

Ludwig von Mises's essay, "Why Middle of the Road Policy Leads to Socialism," applies here. Mises used the example of price controls on milk. Below-market price controls lead to shortages, which forces the government to impose cost controls on milk producers; cost controls in turn encourage the government to extend cost controls to suppliers of farm machinery; and so forth. "This is no longer capitalism; it is all-round planning by the government, it is socialism" (Mises 1980 [1952]: 24). His analysis could easily be applied to Medicare in the United States, where an increasing share of the medical service industry is controlled by the federal government. In 2003 Congress added pharmaceutical drugs covered under Medicare. Meanwhile, market economists urge adoption of new measures for restoring market incentives to the medical system, such as Health Savings Accounts (HSAs) and large annual deductibles, which would encourage consumers to shop around and to minimize unnecessary visits to physicians' offices. Many businesses are now offering HSAs to their employees; although many public interest groups are lobbying for a "single-payer" national health plan in the United States.

THE ATTACK ON "OUT-OF-CONTROL" CAPITALISM

In this era of globalization and technological revolutions, laissez-faire capitalism is under constant attack. The bookstores are full of popular books with such titles as:

- *The Crisis of Global Capitalism: Open Society Endangered*, by George Soros

- *False Dawn: The Delusions of Global Capitalism*, by John Gray

- *The Case Against the Global Economy*, edited by Jerry Mander and Edward Goldsmith

- *The Overworked American*, by Juliet B. Schor

- *The End of Affluence*, by Jeffrey Madrick

- *The Confiscation of American Prosperity*, by Michael Perelman

Although most of these authors are not professional economists, they express anxiety over the uncertainties of free trade, technology, multinational corporations, the banking system, and the new world economy, and demand that a powerful state step forward to correct the imbalances of the new global environment.

Free-market economists, on the other hand, tend to be less alarmist and more upbeat about the dynamics of globalization. They believe that the short-term disruptions in jobs and businesses that occur during the process of globalization will result in better jobs and more profitable businesses in the long run—and a higher standard of living for everyone.

TODAY'S DEBATE: THE NEW CHALLENGE OF KEYNES AND MARX

It would inaccurate and highly misleading to suggest that Keynes, or even Marx, is dead. Quite the contrary. Keynesian and Marxist thinking still carry a strong voice today. If a country falls into a military conflict, a deep slump, or financial crisis, the Keynesian model immediately comes to the forefront: inject liquidity and maintain spending at all costs, even if it means significant deficit financing. The misleading Keynesian notion that consumer spending, rather than saving, capital formation, and technology, drives the economy, is still very much in vogue in the halls of government and in financial circles. Countries such as China and Japan are criticized for saving too much; Keynesians insist that they need to stimulate "domestic demand" if they hope to advance. Fear that a laissez-faire global financial world is subject to unexpected and debilitating crises (2008 being the latest example) is common among both Keynesians and Marxists. They also express deep concern that the entrepreneurs, speculators, and the wealthy class in general are benefiting more from the new global economy and the political process than the middle and lower classes. "Tax cuts help the rich more than the poor" is a common refrain. Critics of the market also constantly complain about growing inequality of income, wealth and opportunity, despite claims to the contrary by free-market economists. They are sharply critical of free-trade agreements and the potential loss of jobs to overseas producers in China, Mexico, and other developing countries.

The central role of government monetary policy is a global concern. Fiscal policy may have been dethroned as a stabilization tool, but central bank policy may fail to do its job in maintaining macroeconomic stability. Monetary authorities have been known to blunder, overshooting their interest-rate or inflation targets. The latest crisis (the credit crunch of 2008) may not be the last. Their response to every crisis, whether a currency crisis or economic downturn, seems to be to adopt an "easy money" policy by injecting liquidity into the system and cutting interest rates below the natural rate. The result has been increasing structural imbalances and asset bubbles in stocks, real estate, and other sectors. How far they can go with such unstable policies without creating a major global financial crisis remains to be seen. The price of gold is a valuable monitor of global economic instability, and it has been rising lately.

STIGLITZ'S CHALLENGE: IS MARKET IMPERFECTION PERVASIVE?

Joseph Stiglitz, Columbia professor and winner of the Nobel Prize in 2001 for his work on the economics of information, is a Keynesian who has taken a hardened stance against Adam Smith and the competitive equilibrium model. The invisible hand, according to Stiglitz, is either "simply not there, or at least that if is there, it is palsied" (2001:473). He declares that market imperfections and market failures are so pervasive and so serious that the market is always inefficient and requires government correction. Information imperfection exists in labor, products, money, trade, and capital markets. Serious unemployment could exist even without minimum wage laws or labor unions, he contends. During the Great Depression, "had there been more wage and price flexibility, matters might have been even worse," he states (2001: 477). According to Stiglitz, involuntary unemployment is still a problem. Gary Becker, Milton Friedman, and other Chicago school economists might claim that the competitive marketplace discourages discrimination, unemployment, and poverty, but Stiglitz's hometown of Gary, Indiana, "even in its heyday . . . was marred by poverty, periodic unemployment, and massive racial discrimination" (2001: 473).

Stiglitz makes the whole new paradigm shift back to a Keynesian model of imperfect information that "undermines" the foundations of competitive analysis, including the denial of the "law" of supply and demand, the law of the single price, and the efficient market hypothesis (2001: 485). Why? Because information in a decentralized market economy is "asymmetric"—"the fact that different people know different things" which in turn can lead to "thin or non-existent markets" (2001: 488–89). What Hayek views as positive, Stiglitz sees as negative.

EXPERIMENTAL ECONOMICS AND MONOPOLY POWER

Market economists counter Stiglitz by arguing that, while imperfect information may indeed be pervasive, the outcome of the imperfect competitive market system acts "as if" it is perfectly competitive. For example, experimental economics seems to confirm this "as if" approach.

Vernon L. Smith, Nobel laureate at Chapman University and founder of experimental economics, ran an experiment to test the Chamberlin-Robinson "imperfect competition" model. Recall from chapter 5 that this model suggested that a small number of sellers (or buyers) creates an imperfect form of competition, causing prices to rise and output to fall. The imperfect monopolistic model was therefore inefficient, and gave support to government antitrust actions to break up big businesses and force more competition into the industry.

However, Smith made an interesting observation. When he reduced the number of buyers and sellers to only a few in his experiments, the results were the same—the final price approached the same competitive price that was achieved with a large number of buyers and sellers. By implication, competition within an industry is not necessarily reduced when it is limited to only a few large companies (Smith 1987: 241–46).

Smith's observation confirmed the earlier work of George Stigler, Harry Johnson, and other members of the Chicago school, that competition is strong even among only a few large firms. Monopolistic firms tend to keep prices competitive because of the ever-present threat of entry by other large firms. The world is "as if" fully competitive (Bhagwati 1998: 411–12).

ECONOMISTS DEBATE ENVIRONMENTAL ISSUES

Free-market economists have responded cautiously to environmental issues: environmentalists, like Malthusians, are excessively pessimistic about the prospects of the planet. When Gary Becker was asked about this global crisis, he responded, "Yes, all this is a real problem. But it has certainly been exaggerated." Milton Friedman added, "Private industry tends to reduce pollution. . . . But without modern technology, pollution would be far worse. The pollution from horses was much worse than what you get from automobiles. . . . The air today is cleaner in most of the United States." And Albert O. Hirschman stated, "There's a tendency to blame capitalism for environmental damage, but now we find that in the socialist bloc the situation is much worse" (Ravaioli 1995: 9–12, 32).

Environmentalism has become a popular subject on college campuses and a major issue in the halls of Congress. How can nations grow and increase their standards of living without destroying the air, polluting the water, cluttering the environment, and causing global warming? The debate goes back to Robert Malthus and is related to historical and present-day concern over unlimited growth and limited resources. In this ecological debate, economists, while not alarmists, have made numerous contributions to minimize pollution and other environmental problems. To solve the "tragedy of the commons," for example (see chapter 3), free-market economists have emphasized the need to establish defensible resource rights in water, fishing, and forestland, so that owners can preserve these resources in a balanced way. In the case of air pollution, economists have also recommended pollution fees and marketable permits to pollute. Pollution fees are taxes on polluters that penalize them in proportion to the amount they discharge, a common practice in Europe. Marketable permits allow polluters to sell their permits to other firms, although the market in pollution permits has been controversial (Anderson and Leal 2001).

THE GLOBAL MONETARY SYSTEM: IS THERE A SOLUTION?

Perhaps the greatest threat to a healthy growing economy is an unstable world monetary system. The current system is a hodgepodge network of financial systems that grew out of the Bretton Woods agreement in 1944, which John Maynard Keynes helped create. Each nation has a separate banking system involving varying interest rates, currencies, money supplies, and banking regulations. Since they abandoned the gold standard in 1971, the world's central banks have had considerably more leeway in making monetary decisions, but the financial order is still based on a fragile fractional reserve banking system that depends on the public's faith in governments' ability to keep monetary matters orderly. In a global laissez-faire financial system, one crisis can lead to another very quickly. So far the various central banks have been able to coordinate their rescue efforts, but what happens if the situation somehow gets out of hand? It could bring the whole system down.

In 1954, Milton Friedman wrote a prophetic essay, "Why the American Economy Is Depression-Proof," based on a lecture he had delivered in Sweden. He argued that improved monetary policy and federal deposit insurance would protect against another deflationary collapse à la 1929–32 (1968: 72–96). So far, he has been proved right, but what about the future? The world may not have suffered another global 1930s-style depression, but we have experienced severe monetary or financial crises in Europe, Asia, and the United States from time to time, precipitating major interventionist measures by central banks to handle unexpected failures of banks, hedge funds, and other financial institutions. Such monetary catastrophes have created much economic hardship and generated considerable criticism of the capitalist system, even though government policy may be ultimately responsible.

THE FINANCIAL CRISIS OF 2008

The global financial crisis of 2008 raised the specter that another Great Depression is not impossible. The trouble began with falling U.S. real estate prices following a lengthy period where the federal government encouraged broad-based home ownership with loose financing, the development of a poorly regulated mortgage securities market, and a bubble in property prices. The Federal Reserve's decision under Alan Greenspan to lower interest rates to 1 percent in 2004, far below the natural rate of interest, exasperated the problem and created systematic risk and unsustainable asset bubbles. The mortgage securities market extended to commercial banks and large financial institutions throughout the world, and when the real estate bubble burst in 2007–8, investment banks, brokerage firms and mortgage institutions, including government-sponsored companies such as Fannie Mae and Freddie Mac, collapsed one after another, creating an unprecedented credit crunch, bank runs, and financial chaos.

Federal Reserve chairman Ben Bernanke and Treasury Secretary Henry Paulson considered the standard rescue measures (injecting liquidity and reducing interest rates) insufficient to solve the crisis, and turned to the U.S. government and congressional authority to bailout the troubled monetary system to the tune of $850 billion. It remains to be seen whether these extreme measures will be sufficient to patch up what most economists consider a fragile global monetary system, and create "moral hazard" threats in the future. The most recent financial crisis is surely not the last.

To reduce these risks of instability, Friedman himself argued in favor of 100 percent reserves on demand deposits, which would virtually eliminate bank runs when another monetary crisis occurs. But we do not have anything near 100 percent reserves.

One solution has been suggested by the "free banking" school, led by Lawrence White (University of Missouri) and George Selgin (University of Georgia). In books and articles, they have argued that a deregulated banking system, including nationwide branching, would ensure a stable monetary framework. Although gold is preferred as a bank reserve under their program, it is not essential. Their laissez-faire approach to banking is a bit intimidating: "There is no government control of the quantity of exchange media. There is no state-sponsored central bank. There are no legal barriers to the entry, branching, or exit of commercial banks. . . . There are no reserve requirements. . . . There are no government deposit guarantees" (Selgin and White 1994: 1718–19). We are not likely to see such a system anytime soon.

Certainly, flexible exchange rates, competitive currencies, and global branching, as advocated by Friedman and Hayek, have helped reduce the buildup of world monetary crises, and the financial markets have been an important and growing restraint against government fiscal and monetary mismanagement. Yet there is a growing concern that a stable monetary system has remained elusive and that a mammoth monetary crisis could derail the remarkable economic growth the world has experienced in recent times. Gold is no longer the monetary anchor it once was during the classical gold standard, but would a global financial panic encourage nations to return to the "barbarous relic"?

THE RETURN OF ADAM SMITH'S VISION

We have come a long way since Adam Smith proposed that the key to economic growth and prosperity lies in nations' granting citizens the maximum freedom possible to pursue their public and private interests under a tolerable system of justice. But Adam Smith's system of natural liberty has been challenged in every generation since his *Wealth of Nations* was published in 1776. As Milton Friedman has written, "Freedom is a rare and delicate plant" (1998: 605). Today is no exception.

Adam Smith's vision of economic liberty flourished initially across the English channel among J.-B. Say, Frédéric Bastiat, and the French *philosophes*, but it wasn't long before our hero came under attack in the least likely place—from his own British school. Robert Malthus and David Ricardo turned the optimistic world of Adam Smith upside down into the abyss of the iron law of subsistence wages. John Stuart Mill joined social reformers in seeking a utopian alternative to the so-called dismal science, and, when voluntary means were not forthcoming, along came the irrepressible Karl Marx, who plunged economics into a new dark age of alienation and class struggle.

Just as we were about to give up on our almost-dead protagonist, three good Samaritans revived the life of Adam Smith—Stanley Jevons, Carl Menger, and Léon Walras. The marginalist revolution restored the Smithian soul, and with the help of Alfred Marshall in Britain and J.B. Clark in America, among others, resurrected Smith and transformed him into a whole new classical man. Despite efforts by Thorstein Veblen and other institutionalists to denounce capitalism, the critics were effectively countered, especially by Max Weber. The neoclassical model stood tall, ready to make contributions to a new scientific age.

The golden age of neoclassical economics continued to face hurdles as Irving Fisher, Knut Wicksell, and Ludwig von Mises searched for the ideal monetary standard to house Adam Smith, but no consensus had been achieved by the time the 1929 stock market crash plunged the world into the worst depression of modern times. Once again, Smith faced an imminent demise. Marxists were in the wings waiting to take over when a new doctor, John Maynard Keynes, presented the world with a new medicine, with which he proposed to save Adam Smith and restore him as the father of capitalism. But Keynes turned out not to be a savior at all, but a mischief maker who gave the patient bad medicine. It would take the inventiveness of Milton Friedman, an intellectual descendant of Adam Smith, to correctly analyze the cause of the distress and restore the model underlining competitive capitalism.

WHAT COULD HAVE BEEN

No doubt the bold challenges made by Marx, Veblen, Keynes, and other critics of capitalism have had a positive effect—they have caused market economists to respond and improve the classical model that Adam Smith established. What doesn't kill makes the patient stronger. Today the neoclassical market framework is the preferred model, and its applications are ubiquitous.

Still, one cannot help but wonder how much economic progress could have been achieved under the following conditions:

- If Marxism-Leninism hadn't enslaved and impoverished a third of the world's population in the twentieth century;
- If Keynesians had recognized sooner that it was government ineptness, not private enterprise, that caused the Great Depression;
- If textbook writers such as Paul Samuelson had advanced sooner the positive principles of classical economics (rule of law, thrift, balanced budgets, limited government, sound money, free trade);
- If development economists had rejected the foolishness of nationalization, import substitution, government-to-government foreign aid, and central planning;
- If social reformers had applied the principles of sound economics to Social Security, health care, and poverty and welfare systems.
- If the federal government and the Federal Reserve had not encouraged reckless easy money and easy mortgages in the real estate market.

Economic thinkers and political leaders have been slow to change, and we have suffered the consequences of a leviathan government—slow growth, deep depressions, monetary crises, widespread poverty, conflict, and death for millions. Adam Smith was right: "There is a great deal of ruin in a nation" (Ross 1995: 327).

ADAM SMITH'S DREAM: SOLVING THE ECONOMIC PROBLEM

One cannot help but wonder what would have happened if economists and government leaders had consistently applied Adam Smith's system of natural liberty. Undoubtedly, we would have avoided the Great Depression, which was the worst economic calamity of the twentieth century, and we might even have avoided two world wars. There is no telling how high the economic growth rate could have been—even 10 percent a year?—and how many millions would have avoided starvation and poverty in communist-controlled lands and the Third World. In fact, perhaps we wouldn't even be talking about a "third world" because poverty-stricken areas would have been eradicated decades ago. Residents of the areas that we call the Third World would be enjoying much more wealth; would be doing more meaningful, fulfilling work; and would have bountiful leisure time in which to pursue nonmaterial goals.

In 1930, John Maynard Keynes wrote an optimistic essay, "Economic Possibilities for Our Grandchildren." After lambasting his disciples who predicted never-ending depression and permanent stagnation, Keynes foresaw a bright future. Through technological improvements and capital formation, mankind could solve its economic problem within the next hundred years, he said. Goods and services would become so abundant and cheap that leisure would be the greatest challenge. What productive things can be done in one's spare time? According to Keynes, capital could become so inexpensive that interest rates might fall to zero. Interest rates have not fallen to zero, but our standards of living have advanced remarkably, at least in most areas of the world. Keynes concluded, "It would not be foolish to contemplate the possibility of a far greater progress still" (Keynes 1963 [1930]: 365).

THE FUTURE IS BOUNDLESS

There is no telling how high the world's standard of living can reach through expanded trade, lower tariffs, deregulation, a simplified tax system, school choice, Social Security privatization, a fair system of justice, and a stable monetary system. As Adam Smith wrote, "Little else is required to carry a state to the highest degree of opulence from the lowest barbarism, but peace, easy taxes, and a tolerable administration of justice" (Danhert 1974: 218).

Yet bad policies, socialistic thinking, and class hatred die slowly. Unless free-market economists are vigilant, natural liberty and universal prosperity will be on the defensive once again.

The spirit of Adam Smith—with its twin doctrines of the invisible hand and natural liberty—has lived on through the centuries of progress and poverty. These doctrines have been given up for dead several times, but have always somehow recovered. The "house that Adam Smith built" is always under construction. Despite its occasional poor architecture and annoying hackings by unauthorized builders, its structure is highly promising and has a certain beauty about it. To quote from John Keat's "Ode on a Grecian Urn," a favorite of Milton Friedman's since childhood:

> *Beauty is truth, truth beauty—that is all*
> *Ye know on earth, and all ye need to know.*

REFERENCES

Anderson, Terry L., and Donald R. Leal. 2001 [1991]. *Free Market Environmentalism.* New York: Palgrave Macmillan.

Becker, Gary S., and Guity Nashat Becker. 1997. *The Economics of Life.* New York: McGraw-Hill.

Bernstein, Peter L. 2007. *Capital Ideas Evolving.* New York: Wiley & Sons.

Bhagwati, Jagdish. 1998. *A Stream of Windows.* Cambridge, MA: MIT Press.

Blaug, Mark. 1985. *Great Economists Since Keynes.* Cambridge, UK: Cambridge University Press.

Breit, William, and Roger W. Spencer. 1982. *Lives of the Laureates: Seven Nobel Economists.* Cambridge, MA: MIT Press.

Buchanan, James M., and Gordon Tullock. 1962. *The Calculus of Consent.* Ann Arbor: University of Michigan Press.

Buchanan, James M., and Richard A. Musgrave. 1999. *Public Choice and Public Finance: Two Contrasting Views of the State.* Cambridge, MA: MIT Press.

Cagan, Phillip D. 1956. "The Monetary Dynamics of Hyperinflation." In *Studies in the Quantity Theory of Money,* ed. Milton Friedman. Chicago: University of Chicago Press.

Chamberlin, Edward. 1933. *The Theory of Monopolistic Competition.* Cambridge, MA: Harvard University Press.

Clark, Colin G. 1940. *Conditions of Economic Progress.* London: Macmillan.

Colander, David. 1995. "The Stories We Tell: A Reconsideration of AS/AD Analysis." *Journal of Economic Perspectives* 9: 3 (Summer), 169–88.

Danhert, Clyde E., ed. 1974. *Adam Smith, Man of Letters and Economist.* New York: Exposition Press.

Dolan, Edwin G., ed. 1976. *The Foundations of Modern Austrian Economics.* Kansas City: Sheed and Ward.

Fogel, Robert William, and Stanley L. Engerman. 1974. *Time on the Cross.* Boston: Little, Brown.

Friedman, Milton. 1968. *Dollars and Deficits.* Englewood Cliffs, NJ: Prentice-Hall.

———. 1982. "Supply-Side Policies: Where Do We Go from Here?" In *Supply-Side Economics in the 1980s.* Atlanta: Federal Reserve Bank of Atlanta.

———. 1995. "Best of Both Worlds: Interview with Milton Friedman." *Reason* (June), 32–38.

Friedman, Milton, and Anna J. Schwartz. 1963. *A Monetary History of the United States, 1867–1960.* Princeton, NJ: Princeton University Press.

Friedman, Milton, and Rose Friedman. 1998. *Two Lucky People.* Chicago: University of Chicago Press.

Fukuyama, Francis. 2000. "Will Socialism Make a Comeback?" *Time* (May 22), 110–12.

Garrison, Roger W. 2001. *Time and Money.* London: Routledge.

Gwartney, James D., and Richard L. Stroup. 2005. *Economics: Public and Private Choice,* 11th ed. New York: Harcourt.

Hayek, Friedrich A. 1975 [1933]. *Monetary Theory and the Trade Cycle.* New York: Augustus M. Kelley.

———. 1984 [1974]. "The Pretence of Knowledge." In *The Essence of Hayek,* ed. Chiaki Nishiyama and Kurt R. Leube. Stanford, CA: Hoover Institution Press.

Henderson, David B., ed. 1993. *The Fortune Encyclopedia of Economics.* New York: Warner.

Heyne, Paul, Peter Boettke, and David Prychitko. 2006. *The Economic Way of Thinking,* 11th ed. Englewood Cliffs, NJ: Prentice-Hall.

Higgs, Robert. 2006. *Depression, War, and the Cold War.* New York: Oxford University Press.

Keynes, John Maynard. 1963 [1930]. *Essays in Persuasion.* New York: W.W. Norton.

Malkiel, Burton G. 1990. *A Random Walk Down Wall Street,* 5th ed. New York: W.W. Norton.

Mankiw, N. Gregory. 1994. *Macroeconomics,* 2d ed. New York: Worth.

———. 1997. *Principles of Economics.* New York: Dryden Press.

Markowitz, Harry. 1952. "Portfolio Selection." *Journal of Finance* 7: 1 (March), 77–91.

Marshall, Alfred. 1920. *Principles of Economics,* 8th ed. London: Macmillan.

McCloskey, Deirdre. 1998. *The Rhetoric of Economics,* 2d ed. Madison: University of Wisconsin Press.

Miller, Roger LeRoy. 2007. *Economics Today,* 14th ed. New York: Addison-Wesley.

Mises, Ludwig von. 1980 [1952]. *Planning for Freedom,* 4th ed. Spring Hill, PA: Libertarian Press.

Musgrave, Richard A. 1958. *Public Finance in Theory and Practice.* New York: Macmillan.

Ravaioli, Carla. 1995. *Economists and the Environment.* London: Zen.

Roberts, Paul Craig. 1984. *The Supply Side Revolution.* Cambridge, MA: Harvard University Press.

Robinson, Joan. 1933. *Economics of Imperfect Competition.* London: Macmillan.

———. 1951–79. *Collected Economic Papers.* 5 vols. Oxford: Basil Blackwell.

Ross, Ian Simpson. 1995. *The Life of Adam Smith*. Oxford: Clarendon.

Ruffin, Roy J., and Paul N. Gregory. 2000. *Principles of Economics*, 7th ed. New York: Addison-Wesley.

Samuelson, Paul A., and William D. Nordhaus. 1998. *Economics*, 16th ed. New York: Irwin McGraw-Hill.

Sargent, Thomas J. "Rational Expectations." In *The New Palgrave: A Dictionary in Economics*, vol. 4, 76–79. London: Macmillan.

Selgin, George, and Lawrence White. 1994. "How Would the Invisible Hand Handle Money?" *Journal of Economic Literature* 22 (December), 1718–49.

Shiller, Robert J. 2005 [2000]. *Irrational Exuberance*, 2d ed. Princeton: Princeton University Press.

Siegel, Jeremy. 2008 [1994]. *Stocks for the Long Run*, 4th ed. New York: McGraw-Hill.

Skousen, Mark. 1990. *The Structure of Production*. New York: New York University Press.

———. 2000. *Economic Logic*. Washington, DC: Capital.

———. 2007 [1990]. *The Structure of Production*. New York: New York University Press.

———. 2008 [2000]. *Economic Logic*, 2d ed. Washington, DC: Capital.

———. 2008. *EconoPower: How a New Generation of Economists Is Transforming the World*. New York: Wiley & Sons.

Smiley, Gene. 1994. *The American Economy in the 20th Century*. Cincinnati, OH: South-Western.

Smith, Adam. 1965 [1776]. *The Wealth of Nations*. New York: Modern Library.

Smith, Vernon L. 1987. "Experimental Methods in Economics." In *The New Palgrave: A Dictionary in Economics,* vol. 2, 241–49. London: Macmillan.

Stiglitz, Joseph E. 2001. "Information and the Change in the Paradigm in Economics." Speech delivered as the 2001 Nobel Prize Lecture, Oslo, Sweden, December 8.

Thomson, Dorothy Lamden. 1973. *Adam Smith's Daughters*. New York: Exposition Press.

Yergin, Daniel, and Joseph Stanislaw. 1998. *The Commanding Heights*. New York: Simon & Schuster.

INDEX

ABOUT THE AUTHOR

Mark Skousen (Ph.D., economics, George Washington University) is a professional economist, investment expert, university professor, and author of over 25 books. Currently he holds the Benjamin Franklin Chair of Management at Grantham University. He has taught economics and finance at Columbia Business School, Columbia University, Barnard College, Mercy College, and Rollins College. Since 1980, Skousen has been editor in chief of Forecasts & Strategies, an award-winning investment newsletter (www.markskousen.com). He is also editor of *The Worldly Philosophers*, a weekly e-letter (www.worldlyphilosophers.com). He is a former analyst for the Central Intelligence Agency (CIA), a columnist to Forbes magazine, and past president of the Foundation for Economic Education (FEE) in New York. He has written for the *Wall Street Journal, Forbes,* the *Christian Science Monitor,* and the *Journal of Economic Perspectives.* He has appeared on CNN, ABC News, Fox News, C-SPAN Book TV, and is a regular contributor to CNBC's Kudlow & Co. His economics books include *The Structure of Production* (New York University Press), *Dissent on Keynes* (Praeger Publishing), *The Big Three in Economics* (M.E. Sharpe), *Economic Logic* (Capital Press), and *EconoPower* (Wiley & Sons). In 2006, he compiled and edited *The Compleated Autobiography, by Benjamin Franklin* (Regnery). In honor of his work in economics, finance, and management, Grantham University renamed its business school the Mark Skousen School of Business.

Web sites: www.markskousen.com; www.mskousen.com; www.worldly-philosophers.com; www.freedomfest.com
E-mail address: editor@markskousen.com